Microsoft® Visual InterDev™

Glenn Fincher, John J. Kottler, et al.

UNLEASHED

Copyright © 1997 by Sams.net Publishing

FIRST EDITION

International Standard Book Number: 1-57521-285-4

Library of Congress Catalog Card Number: 96-72400

2000 99 98 97   4 3 2

Interpretation of the printing code: the rightmost double-digit number is the year of the book's printing; the rightmost single-digit, the number of the book's printing. For example, a printing code of 97-1 shows that the first printing of the book occurred in 1997.

Composed in AGaramond, Function, and MCPdigital by Macmillan Computer Publishing

Printed in the United States of America

Trademarks

President, Sams Publishing	*Richard K. Swadley*
Publishing Manager	*Mark Taber*
Acquisitions Manager	*Beverly M. Eppink*
Director of Editorial Services	*Cindy Morrow*
Director of Marketing	*Kelli S. Spencer*
Product Marketing Managers	*Wendy Gilbride*
	Kim Margolius
Assistant Product Marketing Manager	*Jennifer Pock*
Marketing Coordinator	*Linda Beckwith*

Acquisitions Editor
Randi Roger

Development Editor
Kelly Murdock

Software Development Specialist
Bob Correll

Production Editors
Keith Davenport
Kimberly K. Hannel

Copy Editors
Carolyn Linn
Beth Spencer

Technical Reviewer
Will Kelly

Editorial Coordinators
Mandie Rowell
Katie Wise

Technical Edit Coordinator
Lorraine E. Schaffer

Resource Coordinators
Deborah Frisby
Kimberly K. Hannel

Editorial Assistants
Carol Ackerman
Andi Richter
Rhonda Tinch-Mize

Cover Designer
Jason Grisham

Book Designer
Gary Adair

Copy Writer
David Reichwein

Production Team Supervisors
Brad Chinn
Charlotte Clapp

Production
Jena Brandt
Michael Dietsch
Paula Lowell
Tim Osborn

Dedications

Thanks to Penny and my family for their constant nurturing and support

—Jay Kottler

To Kathryn and Cassandra

—Jerry Ablan

To my Mom for loving me unconditionally and for teaching me to look at others in the same light, and to my Dad for being the silent push behind my undivided attention to the excitement of learning

—Susie Adams

To my father, mother, sisters, and brother… may life bring you joy and happiness, one after another

—Tarek El Abbadi

To my family

—Marc Gusmano

To my wife, Emily, and my daughters, Mabel and Katherine, for their love, support, and patience

—Hei Lam

I dedicate this work to my son, Justin Cuento Leavitt, who was born precisely one week before my first manuscript of this work was due (despite his due date three weeks later). While I hope it is not obvious by the content, I literally wrote a portion of this between his mom's contractions in the delivery room. Welcome to our family, Justin!

—Keith Leavitt

To Emily, Sarah, and Basia with all my love

—Michael Marsh

To my beautiful wife and children who have always been my inspiration for everything I do, and to my mother and father for always supporting me through everything I've done

—Rob Niemela

Overview

Contents

Part IV Programming with Visual InterDev

Acknowledgments

Glenn Fincher: I'd like to acknowledge the assistance and support that I receive from my wife, Jan. She is my constant companion, editor, audience, and sometimes critic. She is incredibly creative in anything she pursues, and I rely on her judgment in every area of our life together. She complements my weaknesses and encourages my strengths. Jan's attention to my needs and the needs of our children often is at her own expense, and she is tireless in her care for us. Juggling the needs of our household while I spend long hours writing is a task she accepts with great patience. I quite literally could not do it without her!

I'd like to also acknowledge my co-authors' knowledgeable additions to this book. Tight schedules and last-minute additions can be conflicting goals when writing about leading-edge technology, but the expertise exhibited here is unequaled. I congratulate each of you!

There are a vast number of people whose efforts are needed to produce a book of this scope. The team at Sams.net is an amazing group of dedicated individuals who have labored with us to produce this book. Special thanks are also extended to the editors who labored at sharpening and polishing our words.

Armando Flores: To my Lord, for allowing me to earn a living doing what I enjoy. To my wife, for her love and support. To my kids, thanks for the stolen "pajama party" time. To all who have made a difference in my career.

My thanks to Randi Roger and the Sams.net team for the opportunity to collaborate in this project.

Michael Marsh: First, I would like to thank Stellcom Technologies, where anything technical is possible. In particular, thank you Mark Fackler, CEO, for support way above and beyond.

No rookie plays well without a great coach. Thank you, Randi!

A big "thank you" to my mother, Isela Chavez, for years of support and love.

Finally, thank you, Barbara, for finding creative ways of keeping the little ones at bay and for getting the manuscripts off on time!

David Silverlight: The following people generously contributed to my chapter with their knowledge, opinions, and feedback, often in greater quantity than I required: Victor Lyons, Interim, Inc.; Leon RivKin, Powernet International, Inc.; Maricel Lam, Financial Data Planning; and Robert Grindell, Financial Data Planning.

About the Authors

LEAD AUTHORS

Glenn Fincher (fincher@usa.net) is a Senior Support Engineer for Intergraph Corporation. With some 16 years in the computer industry, he has continued to stay abreast of the latest advances in this quickly changing field. He served for two years as Webmaster for Intergraph Software Solutions (http://www.intergraph.com/) and continues to be active in developing company standards for the adoption of Internet technology. His current position at Intergraph is Technical Liaison to Microsoft, where he serves as Intergraph's primary development contact with Microsoft. Author of *Internet Explorer 3 Unleashed*, Glenn has also co-authored a number of works including *Special Edition: Using Windows 95*, *Killer Windows 95*, *Netscape Unleashed*, and *Web Site Administrator's Survival Guide*. Glenn makes his home in historic Mooresville, Alabama, with his wife, Jan, who stays equally busy home-schooling their three children, Ashley, Will, and Aimee. Glenn wrote Chapters 1–3 and 33, as well as the Introduction.

John J. Kottler (jkottler@aol.com) has been programming for 14 years and has spent the past six years developing applications for the Windows platform. In addition to Windows development, John has been programming multimedia and Internet applications for more than two years. His knowledge includes C/C++, Visual Basic, multimedia and digital video production, and Internet application development. He has published numerous magazine articles on writing original programs and instructing developers on programming techniques. John has been recently published in Sams.net's *Netscape Unleashed*, *Web Publishing Unleashed*, *Presenting ActiveX*, *Web Page Wizardry*, and *Java Unleashed*, and in Sams Publishing's *Programming Windows 95 Unleashed*. He was also a co-developer of the shareware application Virtual Monitors. A graduate of Rutgers University with a degree in computer science, he enjoys inline skating, cycling, and playing digital music in his spare time. John wrote Chapters 15–20.

CONTRIBUTING AUTHORS

Jerry Ablan (munster@mcs.net) has been involved in computers since 1982 and actually remembers life before the Internet. He has worked on and owned a variety of microcomputers. He has programmed in many languages, including several that are not cool (RPG II, for example). As for his real job, Jerry is the Manager of Internet/Intranet Software Development at the Chicago Board Options Exchange.

Jerry is the author of *Developing Intranet Applications with Java* from Sams.net Publishing and the co-author of *Web Site Administrator's Survival Guide* from Sams.net. He also was a contributing author to the following books: *Special Edition: Using Java* (Que); *Platinum Edition Using HTML v3.1, CGI, and Java* (Que); *Java Unleashed, Second Edition* (Sams.net); and *Intranets Unleashed* (Sams.net).

When not playing multiplayer games on the Internet with his friends, working, writing, or otherwise cavorting, Jerry and his brother Dan (dma@mcs.net) operate NetGeeks (http://www.netgeeks.com), an Internet presence consulting firm. Jerry wrote Chapter 39.

Susie Adams is a Senior Consultant at Financial Dynamics, a client/server and Internet solutions consulting firm in McLean, Virginia. She has over 11 years of application development experience and currently focuses her attention on the design and development of active-content Web applications. Susie wrote Chapter 13.

Craig Eddy (craig.eddy@cyberdude.com) currently resides in Richmond, Virginia, with his wife and two children. Craig holds a B.S. in Electrical Engineering from Virginia Tech. He is currently employed as Senior Developer and Webmaster for Pipestream Technologies, Inc., a leading developer of sales-force automation and customer information management software. Craig specializes in Visual Basic, SQL Server, Access, and Web development. He has been an author for *Access 95 Unleashed, Office 95 Unleashed, VBScript Unleashed, Access 97 Unleashed,* and *Teach Yourself Access 97 in 24 Hours,* as well as co-author of *Web Programming with Visual Basic.* Craig's interests outside the computer field include private business development and interactive marketing. Craig can often be found relaxing on North Carolina's Outer Banks. Craig wrote Chapters 21–25 and Appendix G.

Tarek El Abbadi is an Information Services consultant specializing in Internet and intranet technology at Unisys Corporation. A 1996 Electrical Engineering graduate of the University of Illinois at Champaign-Urbana, Tarek held positions at the National Center for Supercomputing Applications and the Beckman Institute for Advanced Science and Technology. Concurrent to these as well as taking a full course load, Tarek launched an Internet information services company with a partner to design, create, and enable an Internet presence for local merchants and businesses. His experiences in programming began on the popular Apple II+ and Apple IIe computers in Hong Kong at the age of 12. His passion for programming continued with increasingly advanced languages and systems through his residency in Egypt, Canada, and the United States. Tarek wrote Chapter 6.

Armando Flores (aflores@cgcg.com) is an Information Technology Architect for Coral Gables Consulting Group in South Florida, where he specializes in cross-platform systems integration, (mainframe, midrange, client/server, and Web). Armando brings the unique perspective of having worked for IBM and KPMG Peat Marwick as a Systems Engineer, Instructor, and Consultant. His current interests are design and implementation of Distributed Objects System. Armando is a Microsoft Certified Professional. Armando wrote Chapter 38.

Marc Gusmano is the President of the Bismarck Group, a client/server software development firm in Chicago, Illinois. Marc has been involved in systems integration and software development for 15 years, currently focusing on building Microsoft-centric intranet and extranet business solutions using Active Server Pages, Visual InterDev, Visual Basic, Visual C++, Microsoft Access, SQL Server, and the Active Client features of the Internet Explorer. Marc speaks at major conferences including The Internet and Java Advisor Workshop, Microsoft Developer

Days, Web Design and Development, and Microsoft TechEd, and is also a frequent contributor to the Chicago-based Microsoft Interactive Developer Group (MIDG). Marc has contributed to articles in publications such as *The Visual Basic Programmers Journal* and has written an article series on Visual InterDev and Active Server Pages for *Java and ActiveX Advisor Magazine*. Marc is also a Microsoft Certified Trainer focusing on Visual Basic, Visual C++, and Internet development technologies. Marc wrote Chapter 37.

Neil Jenkins (100265.1327@compuserve.com) is a full-time consultant specializing in client/server systems, local area networking, and wide area networking. Neil has worked extensively in the USA and Europe. He has designed, developed, project-managed, and implemented client/server systems and networks in Europe, Latin America, and North America. He is currently a freelance consultant working for clients on client/server, systems management, information systems strategy, research and development, local area networking, wide area networking, and PC support. Neil is the author of *Understanding Local Area Networks, Fifth Edition,* and *Client/Server Unleashed,* both by Sams Publishing. Neil wrote Chapter 40.

Scot Johnson (sjohnson@i3solutions.com) is a Managing Consultant at Automated Concepts, Inc., and focuses on architecting and implementing Web-enabling client/server applications. Scot has spoken on various Internet technologies at developer conferences and writes articles for various trade magazines. He is the author of *Special Edition: Using Active Server Pages* (Que). Scot wrote Chapter 36.

Kevin Jullion has been an Access and Visual Basic Developer for over three years. He has recently become very active as an Internet developer and in the integration of Access and SQL Server databases with the World Wide Web. Kevin is a Microsoft Certified Solutions Developer and is working toward becoming a Systems Engineer and Certified Trainer.

Kevin is the President of Aragon Technology Consulting, Inc., a consulting firm in South Florida that specializes in custom application development and intranet/Internet-enabling for small- to medium-sized businesses. Kevin wrote Chapter 12.

John Jung spends his days providing telephone support for other systems administrators. When he's not at his real job, he spends his time reading books, watching TV, and playing video games. He's also co-authored an HTML book and worked on about a dozen other books. John wrote Appendixes B and F.

Hei Lam (hei.lam@trw.com) is a senior software engineer for the Systems Integration Group of TRW Inc. in Los Angeles. He has been involved in software development for 16 years. He spends most of his time in PC software development, especially in the Microsoft Windows environment, client/server system development, and R&D projects.

His favorite software development tools are Visual Basic, Visual C++, and Visual InterDev. Hei holds a B.S. in Computer & Electronic from California State Polytechnic University, Pomona, and a M.S. in Software Engineering from National University. Hei wrote Chapter 4.

Keith Leavitt is currently Manager of Advanced IT Evaluation and Development at a large aerospace firm in Southern California, but has the higher honor of being the husband of Mrs. Rosemarie Cuento Leavitt and the father of two wonderful boys, Eric and Justin. Keith wrote Chapters 5 and 35.

Michael Marsh earned his B.A. in Aquatic Biology at the University of California at Santa Barbara in 1984. He quit graduate school in San Diego to become a professional programmer in 1987. He began programming in 1978, when his organic chemistry teacher let him fool around with an Apple II in the lab. At that point he was hooked. His professional interests include multimedia, particularly audio and music; image processing; Web-based client/server applications; database design and implementation; and software engineering processes. His non-professional interests include making music, making beer, and reading. Michael wrote Chapters 14 and 26–29.

Michael Morrison (mmorrison@thetribe.com, www.thetribe.com) is a writer, skateboarder, and amateur homebuilder living in Nashville, Tennessee, with his longtime love, Mahsheed. Michael is the author of *Presenting JavaBeans* and *Teach Yourself Internet Game Programming with Java in 21 Days,* as well as the lead author of *Java Unleashed.* Besides being a nerd professionally, Michael enjoys battering himself on skateboards and wielding power tools with his dad. Michael wrote Chapters 30–32 and Appendixes D and H.

Rob Niemela (robn@kirmac.com) is the Webmaster/Web Application Developer for Kirmac Information Technologies Inc. in British Columbia, Canada. Rob is responsible for developing client/server intranet enterprise systems. Rob was also the speaker at the annual Microsoft DevDays this year in Vancouver, B.C., for the Microsoft Visual InterDev presentation. Rob runs a consulting business on the side which, aside from Web-site development, specializes in developing Microsoft Windows applications geared toward maximizing Web development solutions for programmers and nonprogrammers. Aside from freelance programming work, full-time Web work, authoring contributions, public speaking, and raising three children, Rob can usually be found stranded somewhere trying to catch a few ZZZs in his unforgiving carb-eating mini-van. "HARAD ROAD FOREVER!" Rob wrote Chapter 8.

Dick Oliver is the tall, dark, handsome author of lots of great books and software, including *Web Page Wizardry, Netscape Unleashed, Create Your Own Web Page Graphics*, and *Tricks of the Graphics Gurus.* He is also the president of Cedar Software and the warped mind behind the Nonlinear Nonsense Netletter at http://netletter.com (and several other Web sites). When he isn't banging on a keyboard, he's usually snowboarding, sledding, skiing, or warming up by the wood stove in his cozy Northern Vermont home (where they celebrate a day of summer each year, too). He likes writing HTML, eating killer-spicy Indian food, and waltzing wildly around the office with his daughters—not necessarily in that order. He also thinks it's pretty cool that authors get to write their own "About the Author" sections. Dick wrote Appendix C.

David Silverlight (DavidS@IssConsult.com) is the president of Independent Software Solutions (http://www.issconsult.com), a company dedicated to the development of Web-based database applications, custom software, and the evolution of Internet commerce.

He also contributes to the software community as the President of the Southeast Florida Database Developers Group, a Miami-based user group for software developers. He has been an advanced Visual Basic developer for many years, most recently utilizing the newer technologies of Visual InterDev and FrontPage. His aim is to develop more commanding technologies for the Internet; he directs his focus particularly to bringing proficient database connectivity to Access and SQL Server.

David has presented at numerous developers' conferences and to user groups on topics ranging from advanced Java concepts in Visual J++ to innovative techniques using FrontPage. His most recent appearances were at Microsoft Developer Days 97 and at this year's NetCom. David wrote Chapter 34 and Appendix A.

L. Michael Van Hoozer is a Senior Manager for BSI Consulting and has over nine years of systems development experience. For the last six years, Mike has focused solely on client/server, and now Internet-related, technologies. Mike has strong ties to Microsoft; he has been very involved with the alpha and beta testing of products including Visual Basic and Visual InterDev. Mike has also implemented solutions for his clients based on these tools, using his strong application development and user interface design skills. Mike wrote Chapters 9–11.

Matt Watson (mwatson@bsihome.com) is a consulting manager for BSI Consulting, a Houston-based information technology consulting company. Previously, Matt worked as a consulting manager for Andersen Consulting and has over seven years of experience in information technology consulting. Matt has worked on a number of client/server engagements in a variety of industries. Recently, Matt has focused his attention on Internet technologies and electronic commerce, including co-authoring a white paper on electronic commerce in the energy industry. Matt holds a B.S. in computer science from Baylor University and lives in Houston with his wife, Chris, and their two children, Taylor and Travis. Matt wrote Chapter 7.

John West has been providing network solutions since 1989, using the best in client/server operating systems. As a Microsoft Certified Systems Engineer, Mr. West has installed network solutions for companies such as Entergy, Siemens Corporation, and Lockheed Martin. Mr. West is currently employed as a technical analyst with a Houston-based corporation, Paranet. Paranet is a premier provider of the integration, support, and management of distributed computing environments. John wrote Appendix E.

Tell Us What You Think!

As a reader, you are the most important critic and commentator of our books. We value your opinion and want to know what we're doing right, what we could do better, what areas you'd like to see us publish in, and any other words of wisdom you're willing to pass our way. You can help us make strong books that meet your needs and give you the computer guidance you require.

Do you have access to CompuServe or the World Wide Web? Then check out our CompuServe forum by typing **GO SAMS** at any prompt. If you prefer the World Wide Web, check out our site at http://www.mcp.com.

> **NOTE**
>
> If you have a technical question about this book, call the technical support line at 317-581-3833 or send e-mail to support@mcp.com.

As the team leader of the group that created this book, I welcome your comments. You can fax, e-mail, or write me directly to let me know what you did or didn't like about this book—as well as what we can do to make our books stronger. Here's the information:

FAX: 317-581-4669

E-mail: newtech_mgr@sams.mcp.com

Mail: Mark Taber
           Comments Department
           Sams.net Publishing
           201 W. 103rd Street
           Indianapolis, IN 46290

Introduction

by Glenn Fincher

> "Blackbird singing in the dead of night
> Take these broken wings and learn to fly...
> You were only waiting for this moment to arise."
> —Paul McCartney

These words from the haunting song "Blackbird" by Paul McCartney serve as a fitting introduction to a book about Microsoft's Visual InterDev. Like the blackbird in the song, Visual InterDev has come a long way from its "broken wings," and has indeed found its moment to arise. You see, Blackbird was the code name that Microsoft gave to Visual InterDev when it was first introduced back in early 1995. The tool was created to help companies developing content for the new Microsoft Network online service create compelling content. The goal of the tool was to allow these content providers to have state-of-the-art layout tools for the new service and to help them manage that content with a coherent user interface.

Another feature of Blackbird was an integrated development environment, which provided graphical assistance for the designer when creating the visual elements of his creation and also provided robust tools for accessing dynamic information such as databases. When it was first introduced with Windows 95 in August 1995, the Microsoft Network (MSN) had a large number of companies that provided unique information. In addition to features in categories such as entertainment, news, and travel planning, content was also introduced from sources as diverse as The Black Entertainment Network and companies such as Intergraph Corporation, a manufacturer of high-end computer-aided design (CAD) hardware and software. All the content on MSN was created with Blackbird—the precursor to Visual InterDev.

As MSN took off and the growth of the Web accelerated to a fever pitch, Microsoft announced that Blackbird was being re-crafted as an Internet authoring tool. The popularity of the Web forced Microsoft to admit that the open standards of the Internet were a more suitable environment for the future of MSN. Renamed Internet Studio, Blackbird was rebuilt from the ground up to craft compelling Internet content. No longer shackled to its proprietary "broken wings" of MSN content, but free to mine the depths of the Internet, Internet Studio—now Visual InterDev—has truly found its "moment to arise." As you use Visual InterDev and learn more about it from this book, you'll find it to be as powerful as you want it to be.

With Visual InterDev you can create a Web site as simple or as complicated as you desire. You can easily create simple Web pages and sites using the supplied FrontPage Web-authoring tool, or you can create full-blown Web-based applications—"Weblications"—that rival the best "traditional" standalone client/server applications available.

> **NOTE**
>
> For the most up-to-date information about Visual InterDev, look at
>
> `http://www.microsoft.com/vinderdev/`

What This Book Can Do for You

Internet development is the reason you bought Visual InterDev, and Internet Development *with* Visual InterDev is the subject of this book. Whether you are developing for the Internet, the intranet, or the "Extranet," Visual InterDev is up to the task. Visual InterDev makes it relatively easy to build innovative Web sites exploiting the latest Internet technologies, tools, and protocols while also giving you necessary access to any legacy data and/or systems you may have. Because Visual InterDev is built to support current Internet standards, you will immediately find it an indispensable part of your Web arsenal. Microsoft is known for its Rapid Application Development (RAD) tools, and Visual InterDev shows itself a worthy addition to these tools. As you use Visual InterDev and apply the information you gain from this book, you'll begin to wonder how you got by before Visual InterDev.

The *Visual* in Visual InterDev

If you are a seasoned user of Microsoft development tools, the Visual part of the product's title can mean nothing more than the integrated development environment that has been available in Visual C++, Visual J++, and recently in Visual Basic. Developer Studio (see Figure I.1) is now the main development environment for all the Microsoft developer tools. There's even an all-in-one collection of these tools under the name Visual Studio, with all the applications sharing the same Developer Studio visual environment. When you've used one of the tools in this suite, you will quickly get up to speed on another—the only difference being the subtleties of the language itself. Visual InterDev is somewhat different from each of the other tools; with Visual InterDev, you actually can string together any kind of application, script, or database to create new and dynamic applications or Web sites. This book introduces you to all the features of Visual InterDev and helps you exploit those features to create compelling Web applications. The Visual InterDev interface gives you ready access to every facet of designing your Web application. You'll see some more features of Developer Studio later in this introduction.

> **NOTE**
>
> In Visual InterDev parlance, *any* Web site can be thought of as a "Web application." Your site should present a unified context and purpose, whether it uses databases, multimedia, scripting, or embedded components—all these are the presentation of your Web "application."

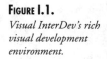

Figure I.1.

Visual InterDev's rich visual development environment.

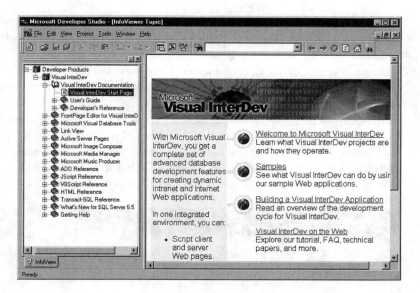

If you aren't sure what Visual InterDev will do for you, I suggest that you begin in Part I, "Client/ Server Solutions with Visual InterDev," for a good overview of Visual InterDev's design. If you need to understand the main features of Visual InterDev, go directly to Part II, "Getting Started with Visual InterDev," for a full description of all the conceptual pieces that comprise Visual InterDev. If you have just installed Visual InterDev and are itching to get started, you may want to jump right to Part III, "Visual InterDev Hands-On," for a step-by-step guide to using Visual InterDev. Or if you are a seasoned programmer or Webmaster and want to learn how to get more out of the tools that comprise Visual InterDev, you might be most interested in Part IV, "Programming with Visual InterDev."

If it's Web publishing you're interested in or you want to exploit one of the new technologies such as ActiveX or Java, you'll find it in these pages. If you are already using Visual InterDev and want become really proficient with it, you'll find just the kind of information you need to fully exploit this powerful tool.

Unleash the Power of the Your Web Site

In many ways, creating innovative content for the Web can be an intimidating task. To really create a compelling site, one that has people coming back for more, you need to add dynamic content to your repertoire. What is dynamic content? Pages that live with fresh information every time the user visits your site. Using Visual InterDev to design your site will give you access to the full features of Microsoft's Internet Information Server (IIS). Because Visual InterDev enables you to create Active Server Pages (ASP files), your site will benefit from the best framework for the creation of exciting dynamic Web sites.

When Microsoft introduced IIS 3.0 and ASP files, it unleashed a new paradigm for empowering your Web site. Unlike the Common Gateway Interface (CGI) files that you might be most familiar with, ASP files open up new possibilities such as the ability to run scripts, applications, or database queries, all on the server side of the connection. And with the built-in browser recognition of ASP, you will have the ability to tailor the output to the browser to best suit the capabilities of that browser. ASP enables you to bring together standard HTML, scripting, and components to give your Web application a richness that wasn't possible before. And Visual InterDev is the best way to fully exploit ASP. Even if you don't run IIS, Visual InterDev is still the best way to manage your site and to create your Web content. Visual InterDev's integrated tools are most clearly geared toward IIS and ASP, but its color-coded HTML editor and combined FrontPage WYSIWYG editor and site-management tools add greatly to any Web site.

> **NOTE**
>
> For the most up-to-date information about Internet Information Server, look at
>
> `http://www.microsoft.com/vinderdev/`

Publish—and Program—on the Web

With Visual InterDev, you'll have one of the best tools available for quickly getting your information published on the Web. With the integrated version of Microsoft FrontPage (see Figure I.2) and the Personal Web Server for Windows 95, you'll have the ability to immediately begin serving the data you create using Visual InterDev. You can prototype your site on Windows 95 and then use the integrated management tools to post that content to your "real" Web.

FIGURE I.2.

Visual InterDev includes an integrated version of FrontPage 97.

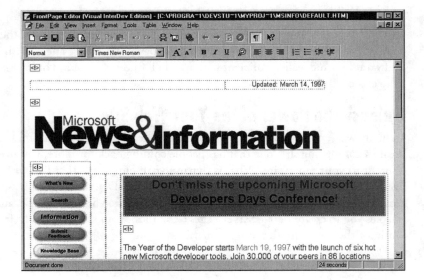

With the many other applications that are included with Visual InterDev, you will have all the tools in your arsenal to enhance your existing site or create a new site from scratch. Using Microsoft Image Composer (see Figure I.3) and GIF Animator (see Figure I.4), you will quickly learn to design Web graphics like the pros. Or if your site is one that will benefit from some hot tunes, Microsoft Music Producer (see Figure I.5) will quickly turn you into a composer! The integrated database tools will help you quickly access any ODBC-compliant database and easily design pages accessing all your data. If you are a Webmaster looking for ways to enhance your Web presence, you'll learn how to use the latest programming tools and technologies such as scripting, ActiveX, and Java to really make your Web site hot!

FIGURE I.3.

Microsoft Image Composer assists in the creation of innovative Web graphics.

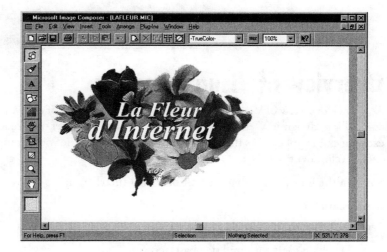

FIGURE I.4.

Microsoft GIF Animator easily creates animated images to enhance your pages.

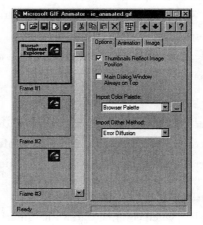

FIGURE I.5.

*Microsoft Music
Producer makes you
an original music
composer.*

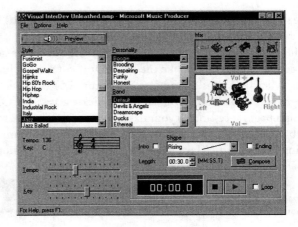

Overview of Visual InterDev

As a quick overview of Visual InterDev 1.0, let's look at some of the ways it can help you create compelling, dynamic Web sites. Visual InterDev has a rich set of core features as well as some exciting extra applications that work together to give you the widest range of tools in any Web site–development package.

Some of the innovations that are part of Visual InterDev are as follows:

Core Features

- Visual development environment
- Database tools for rapid database access
- Integrated Web site management and visualization tools
- Scripting support for VBScript and JavaScript
- Can use client/server components created with any language
- ODBC database support

Extra features

- Ability to create compelling graphic images with Microsoft Image Composer
- Ability to create GIF animations with Microsoft GIF Animator
- Ability to create original compositions with Microsoft Music Producer

Visual Development Environment

As mentioned earlier, when you first start Visual InterDev, you will find yourself in the Developer Studio environment. This environment is the same whether you are a Visual C++, Visual J++, or Visual Basic developer. If you use multiple Microsoft programming languages, this environment will soon fit you like an old shoe. Even if Visual InterDev is your only development tool, you will soon find that the integrated environment helps you become more productive. Unlike using Web tools from an assortment of vendors, Visual InterDev integrates all the tools you need in one complete package. Take a quick look at Figure I.6 for one view of Developer Studio. Note that in this view, the InfoView pane is open, showing the complete set of documentation integrated into Visual InterDev. You can easily select any of the sections to display the information.

FIGURE I.6.

The Developer Studio InfoView pane, showing a portion of the included documentation.

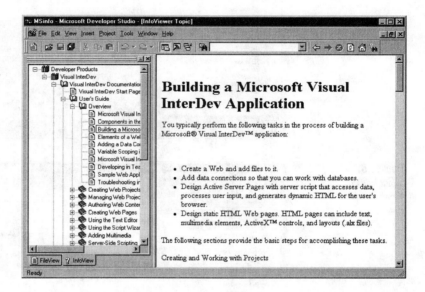

When you are working with a Web project, you will see an additional view added—the File View (see Figure I.7). Note that in this view, each file that comprises your Web site is displayed in a hierarchical fashion. When you are in this view, you can select individual files to edit in the integrated color-coded HTML editor, or manage your Web site using the Link View (see Figure I.8). Using the Link View enables you to graphically view the contents of your Web site in a coherent fashion, enabling you to easily see the structure of your site as well as any broken links that need repairing.

Each of these views adds to the overall richness of the Visual InterDev environment. You can easily switch from editing the source code for your Web site to checking a subtle point of design in the documentation or to previewing your current site in the browser, all within the Visual InterDev environment. (See Figure I.9 for the integrated browser preview.)

FIGURE 1.7.

Developer Studio File View with selected HTML file displayed in viewer window.

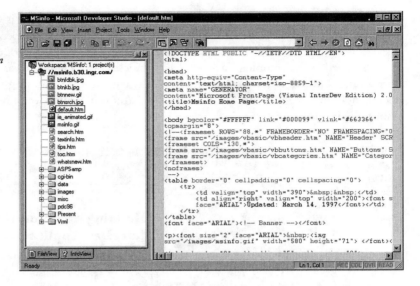

FIGURE 1.8.

The Link View graphically details your site.

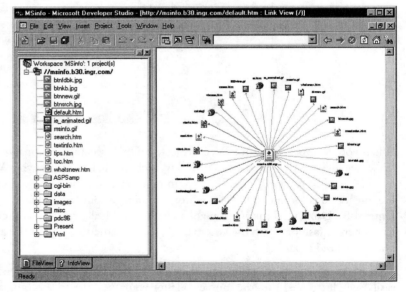

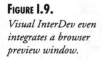

Figure I.9.

Visual InterDev even integrates a browser preview window.

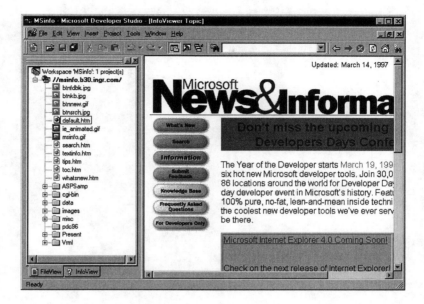

The *Visual InterDev Unleashed* CD-ROM

An exciting addition to this book is the included CD-ROM. On the CD-ROM, you'll find Microsoft Visual J++ 1.1 Trial Edition; Microsoft Visual Basic, Control Creation Edition; and Microsoft Internet Information Server. We've included all the sample code from the book, covering examples of ASP, HTML, VBScript, JavaScript, and Java. Most of this is in the form of reusable code to assist you in creating your own exciting Web sites or just to help you learn more about the latest technology of the Internet.

Accessing Examples from the Book

The integrated browser within Visual InterDev will let you view any of the HTML examples or even incorporate the examples in your own Web applications.

We've put together everything we could think of to make this the one resource you use daily alongside Visual InterDev as you design the next "Cool Site of the Day" or that killer intranet application. We're sure that you'll find all the information you need to really unleash Microsoft's Visual InterDev.

I

PART

Client/Server Solutions with Visual InterDev

Web Technologies and Traditional Web Programming

by Glenn Fincher

IN THIS CHAPTER

CHAPTER

1

In this chapter, I try to relate a short history of the Web and its traditional modes of programming. My intent is to set the stage for a thorough understanding of the innovations that Visual InterDev brings to the Web by detailing the current state of the Web. In Chapter 2, "Relational Databases and Client/Server Technology," I try to do the same for database and client/server technology.

A Brief History of Internet Time

With apologies to Stephen W. Hawking, exploring the evolution of Web technologies is somewhat analogous to the study of astrophysics. Because so many significant developments have occurred, a concrete timeline is virtually impossible; there are an abundance of knowledgeable pundits; and finally, everybody has their version about what is or was important to the story.

> **NOTE**
>
> If you are already familiar with the current state of the Web in regards to programming paradigms, you may want to skip to the next chapter. Of course, the same holds true if you are already familiar with relational databases and client/server technology; you may want to jump ahead to Chapter 3, "Microsoft's Vision and Visual InterDev." But if you are a newcomer to the Web world, this introduction to the Web may be just the sort of information you need to quickly get up to speed on this exciting medium.

The phrase *Internet Time* has been in use for about as long as the Web has been a phenomenon. It's meant to denote the relative fast pace of advancements that have occurred in Internet-related technologies in the short span of time that we have been surfing the Web. In as little as four years at this writing, the Web has become the whole of what most people know of the Internet. Most people would speak of the Web and the Internet as synonymous terms, even though they are only related by their shared technology. In fact, the Web would not be here at all if it were not for the Internet. To many people it may seem like the perfect "chicken and egg" story, but in this case, it is quite clear which came first. The Internet gave birth to the Web in an almost inevitable fashion. The Web in turn is giving birth to a whole range of new possibilities in global communication.

> **NOTE**
>
> Stephen Hawking's landmark book, *A Brief History of Time*, details current astrophysical theory, and actually covers considerably more real time in its scope than could a chapter on Web technologies, but the title was too hard to resist!

Internet Beginnings

With its beginnings in 1957 when the United States formed the Advanced Research Projects Agency, or ARPA, the Internet is actually older than most people think. Although it would be another 12 years before the ARPAnet was created, ARPA and the problems that it sought to solve were the breeding ground for the Internet. ARPA was originally created to lead the American advance into science and technology as an answer to the Russian Sputnik satellite, to lead the charge to make America a technological leader in the race to space. It was this climate that birthed the Internet.

Although ARPA was a military organization, its research needed the input of scientists across the nation. Military, academic, and even private industry began to work together on the research involved in building a satellite worthy of Earth orbit. Because of the need to apply many minds to the intricate details of space exploration, ARPA set up research centers across the country in several universities. It was these physically disconnected research centers that gave rise to the evident need for some sort of reliable communication technology. The Internet was, like most inventions, born of necessity.

The ARPAnet was commissioned in 1969 to solve the communication problems using some sort of networked computer architecture. Because of the usual security fears associated with a military endeavor, this network had some unusual design requirements. Bolt, Baranek, and Newman (BBN) won the contract to build the network. The network had to be designed in such a manner that if any of its individual links or segments were cut, the network as a whole could still function. This meant that each node on the network had to be able to originate and receive data, and also serve as a transmitter to pass on data not addressed to that node. This also meant that the data had to have enough "intelligence" so that each node could determine whether the information was meant for it or to be passed on. These *packets* of data, as they were called, contained the destination address, the sending address, and the actual data being communicated. Each packet of several pieces of data comprising a complete transmission could find its own way across the ARPAnet to its destination node, and if necessary, take separate routes entirely. Although this seems at first glance an awkward way to communicate, it really is an elegant design because it means that if there is a break in one section of the network, as long as another path exists to the destination node, the packets can find their way. This simple but ingenious method of encapsulating data in small, autonomous packets remains today as the way data is moved across the Internet.

> **NOTE**
>
> For a good overall view of the beginnings of the Internet, look at the timeline at BBN:
>
> `http://www.bbn.com/customer_connection/timeline.htm`
>
> (See Figure 1.1.)

FIGURE 1.1.

*One of the early
pioneers of the Internet,
BBN, keeps an updated
timeline of the Internet.*

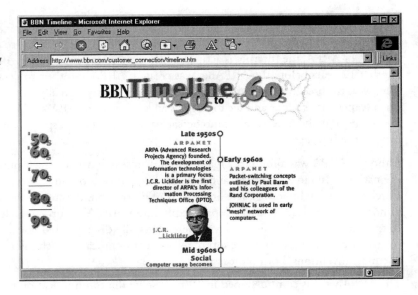

The 1970s saw a relative explosion of nodes connected to ARPAnet. New technologies such as e-mail, UUCP, and Usenet began their own revolutions. These all benefited from the current structure of the Internet, and were innovations that exposed more and more people to the party. The public got its first glimpse of the new network at the International Conference on Computer Communications in 1972, and it was an unqualified hit. 1973 was an equally important year as the first transatlantic connections were made to England and Norway. An important development in 1974 was the specification of a Transmission Control Protocol—the TCP in TCP/IP. Also in 1974, BBN opened the first commercial packet data network.

The Net came of age in the 1980s. Important developments such as the TCP/IP protocol, Domain Name Server (DNS), and the Network News Transfer Protocol (NNTP) provided the base infrastructure for the network of networks—the Internet. The founding of the NSFnet in 1986 opened the network and provided for the first time reasonably affordable access to the network for universities. By 1988 there were approximately 60,000 hosts connected via this worldwide network. And before the decade ended, this number blossomed to 100,000! The Internet really became a worldwide network of networks with countries like Japan, Australia, and the United Kingdom joining in 1989.

The Evolution of the Web

In 1991, Tim Berners-Lee created the World Wide Web. The Internet would never be the same. The problems that Berners-Lee was trying to solve were typical of an organization in a constant state of flux. Basically, these issues revolved around the smooth flow of information critical to the ongoing research community at CERN—the European Laboratory for Particle Physics, where Berners-Lee was employed. There was a high turnover rate at CERN due to the flux expected in a highly technical academic community. Two years was the typical length of stay at CERN, and with such a constant change of staff there was no good way to assure that necessary information was captured and passed on to new personnel. There was also the even more fundamental problem that all the information about a specific technology might not be readily available to everyone who needed it in the first place. There were in function "islands of information" that kept the whole of CERN from being visible to all members of its staff. The possibility existed that information was being lost or important efforts duplicated because of the lack of a uniform way to share information within CERN. Berners-Lee saw that the fundamental problem was that the information available within CERN was ordered in a strict hierarchical fashion that required a rigid set of rules to navigate. It was not easy to move from one body of information to another without navigating a difficult tree structure to get to related information. He envisioned a hypertext system whereby all the information available at CERN could be arranged in a single virtual document with hypertext links connecting all the data. A new hire could easily be pointed to the main document as the source for all information about CERN, and could easily navigate to items of interest from this central node. What has become familiar to many of us as an intranet was the result of Berners-Lee's invention. Berners-Lee proposed and then designed the first WWW server and client software to illustrate his concepts, and seemingly overnight the Internet became a household word. In two short years, the number of hosts jumped from 100,000 to 1 million.

NOTE

One of the best sources for more information on the evolution of the Web is available at the World Wide Web Consortium's (W3C) page at this address (see Figure 1.2):

`http://www.w3.org/pub/WWW/WWW/`

Another good source of early history is at CERN's page at this address (see Figure 1.3):

`http://www.cern.ch/CERN/WorldWideWeb/WWWandCERN.html`

And still another source from a slightly different angle from the PBS television series "Life on the Internet" is at this address (see Figure 1.4):

`http://www.pbs.org/internet/history/`

Other problems that Berners-Lee was attempting to solve in the quest for a complete information system were also typical of many corporations today. Users needed remote access to information using various dissimilar operating environments. The information itself was physically distributed across multiple locations and systems. Because TCP/IP had only been widely adopted at CERN in 1989 when it joined the newly formed Internet, there was still a lot of information floating around CERN via other protocols like XNS and even RS232 Serial Communications. Thus, TCP/IP's wide acceptance at CERN was critical to the evolution of the Web as well. Equally important to the success of the proposed project was the acceptance of a new paradigm of information access. Berners-Lee proposed a "browser" to access all the information in CERN's burgeoning enterprise. This browser had to answer all the problems that were identified, or at least the bulk of them, and must have an easily understood set of navigation tools or features. The birth of the Web browser and server was the result of Berners-Lee's innovative proposal to CERN.

FIGURE 1.2.

The W3C's WWW history page as it appeared in early 1997.

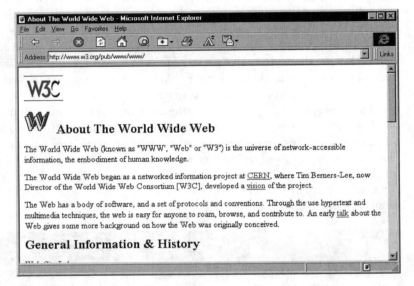

FIGURE 1.3.

CERN's WWW pages also contain a lot of interesting history about the origins of the Web.

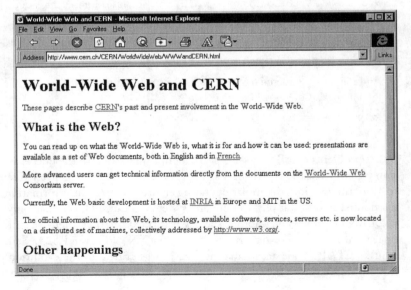

FIGURE 1.4.
The Public Broadcast-ing System is another interesting source of Internet history.

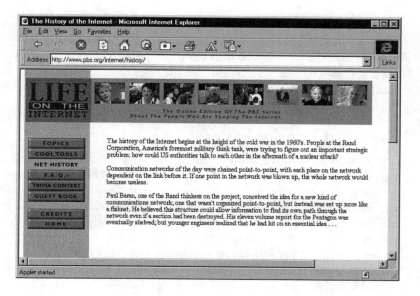

The main features of this new "web" of information were defined in the following key areas:

- HTTP Transfer Protocol
- Hypertext format
- Client and server
- Programming standards

These areas are still the main areas of definition of the Web, and will be used to elaborate on the nature of the Web for the remainder of our discussion. HTTP, HTML, and server and client software are the lingua franca of the Web. As we look at these pieces that comprise the Web, I will try to give enough detail so that the current state of the Web is clearly understood. You'll use these basic building blocks with Visual InterDev to create the weblications that will ultimately replace much of the proprietary applications that you create today.

Defining the Web

As mentioned earlier, when Berners-Lee began defining his new information web, the Internet was a relatively new phenomenon. It was, however, fairly mature in its scope and also in its base infrastructure. That infrastructure made it possible for Berners-Lee to concentrate on the problem at hand and let other folks worry about the lower-level problems. With TCP/IP as the underlying protocol, a number of other transfer mechanisms had been developed for different types of data. NNTP used a "store and forward" metaphor to allow a large body of information to be accessed almost simultaneously by a worldwide audience. File Transfer Protocol (FTP) was developed for the primary purpose of "getting" or "putting" files between remote machines. And of course, e-mail and the Simple Mail Transfer Protocol (SMTP) were created to transfer single messages from sender to recipient. This new hypertext web of information needed its own transfer mechanism, and the Hypertext Transfer Protocol, or HTTP, was created specifically to handle hypertext data. Let's look at HTTP briefly to see what makes it suited to its task.

Hypertext Transfer Protocol

This new media needed a new protocol to handle its specific type of information. As the FTP protocol was specific to moving single files one by one, HTTP needed to understand and facilitate a somewhat serendipitous information retrieval. Because Berners-Lee envisioned a single virtual document comprising all the connected documents of a web, and ultimately all the documents in the World Wide Web, so a user could potentially navigate all the existing documents via the hyperlinks, a frugal protocol was required. What do I mean by "frugal"? I mean that unlike FTP or SMTP, which require some sort of connection or even a login, HTTP needed to log in only when a specific bit of data was requested. HTTP was thus born as a connectionless protocol. In function, when a user clicks on a link on a page, HTTP requests a "get" of the data; then the HTTP server responds with that data or sends an error condition reporting why the data cannot be retrieved at this time. An HTTP client and server thus negotiate each individual request as a unique, unrelated transaction. When Berners-Lee first devised his Web, the only kind of data that was to be retrieved was text data. As the Web developed beyond its roots, people increasingly began to add other types of data like graphic images and sounds. These additions to a page, though, are retrieved individually with separate "get" requests from the server. Therefore, if you have created a Web page with some text, an image or two, and maybe a multimedia file, when a user retrieves the individual file, individual HTTP requests are made for each entity on the page. Originally, only one request would be made because the page would not contain additional items. But because of the way HTTP was designed, it was and is an open technology that can easily be adapted and added to as needed. Berners-Lee may not have foreseen the rich data that is common on the Web today, but he did have enough foresight to design an extensible system for the future.

Today, the state of HTTP is shepherded by the Wide World Web consortium, chaired by none other than Tim Berners-Lee. The W3C, as it's usually known, is the international standards body responsible for the ongoing development of the Web (see Figure 1.5). The members of the W3C are primarily representatives of commercial organizations who have agreed to be contributing members of the organization to help further the open adoption of Web standards. An open environment for development serves the dual purpose of leveling the playing field and helping to push quick adoption of innovation. It's in each participant's best interest to genuinely support the peer process so that they all can benefit from the technology.

FIGURE 1.5.

The World Wide Web Consortium's Web site is one of the best places to follow the ongoing development of the Web.

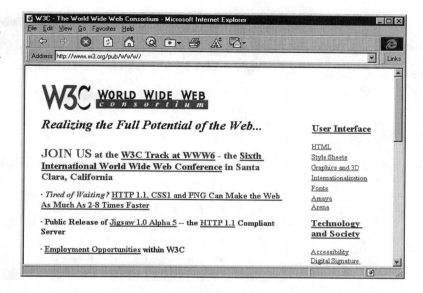

NOTE

HTTP is detailed on these W3C pages:

`http://www.w3.org/pub/WWW/Protocols/`

`http://www.w3.org/pub/WWW/Protocols/HTTP/HTTP2.html`

Another organization that contributes to the development of the Web is the Internet Engineering Task Force (IETF) (see Figure 1.6). The IETF differs from the W3C in that membership is open to any individual and that the primary focus is the underlying protocols of the Internet as a whole rather than only the Web. But the developments of the IETF are still of great importance especially as you attempt to understand the current and future state of the Internet and the Web.

NOTE

The IETF's site is at the following address:

`http://www.ietf.org/`

FIGURE 1.6.

The IETF Web site is another indispensable site for following the ongoing development of the Internet.

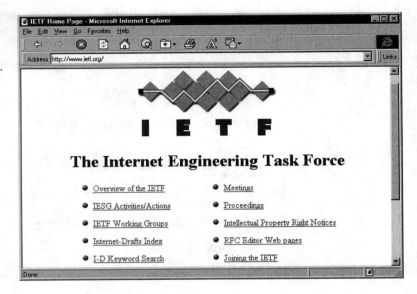

HTTP 1.0

HTTP 1.0 defined features such as its connectionless state, but also included other significant features such as a defined format for all requests. In a similar fashion, a standard set of responses for success or error conditions was defined. The specification details the format of any communication between the server and client and specifies exactly what they must support. For example, the now familiar format for the HTTP URL is specified in section 3.2.2 of RFC 1945 as follows:

> The http scheme is used to locate network resources via the HTTP protocol. This section defines the scheme-specific syntax and semantics for http URLs.

```
http_URL       = "http:" "//" host [ ":" port ] [ abs_path ]
host           = <A legal Internet host domain name
                 or IP address (in dotted-decimal form),
                 as defined by Section 2.1 of RFC 1123>
port           = *DIGIT
```

Although this is the familiar format to most Web users by now, the definition here is just a sample of what the RFC contains. Clients are expected to request information from servers using this format. Servers are given the set of responses they are expected to return.

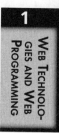

NOTE

Some of the original design issues are detailed by Berners-Lee at this address:

`http://www.w3.org/pub/WWW/Protocols/DesignIssues.html`

while the current HTTP 1.0 specification (see Figure 1.7) is detailed at this address:

`http://www.w3.org/pub/WWW/Protocols/rfc1945/rfc1945`

FIGURE 1.7.

The HTTP 1.0 specification is now detailed in Informational RFC 1945.

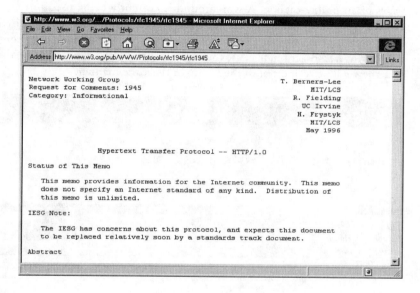

The original HTTP specification has been in place since Berners-Lee designed it. It has served the Web well, but now that the Web has grown, HTTP is going through its own transformation. The Web has evolved at such a meteoric rate that HTTP 1.0 simply can't support the continued growth. Some of the very strengths of the original design have now become impediments to growth, so the W3C and IETF have recently released the proposed HTTP 1.1 specification.

TIP

It's beyond the scope of this chapter to detail the complete HTTP specifications. Look at Appendix B, "HTTP 1.1 Specification" for the current specifications, or online at `http://www.w3.org/Protocols/` for the most up-to-date version.

HTTP 1.1

HTTP 1.1 adds some significant features that when implemented are sure to alleviate some of the problems inherent in the 1.0 specification. I mentioned that HTTP 1.0 was a connectionless protocol. This is both a feature and a problem. As a connectionless protocol, HTTP has no way to maintain states between connections. *States* in this context means identification information about the client that is necessary to maintain a single user identity as the site is traversed. For example, if a user connects to a commercial site to purchase a product or service, there's no way within the 1.0 specification to maintain information about the user between pages of an online catalog. A workaround is currently being used in the form of something called a *cookie*, but that isn't part of the 1.0 spec, and thus not really required of clients or servers to support. And although cookies are widely supported and used to maintain state information during a transaction, because they are not yet an official specification there is no guarantee that they will be supported in the future in the same manner.

NOTE

The proposed HTTP 1.1 specification is detailed at this address (see Figure 1.8):

`http://www.w3.org/pub/WWW/Protocols/rfc2068/rfc2068`

FIGURE 1.8.

The proposed HTTP 1.1 specification is detailed in proposal RFC 2068.

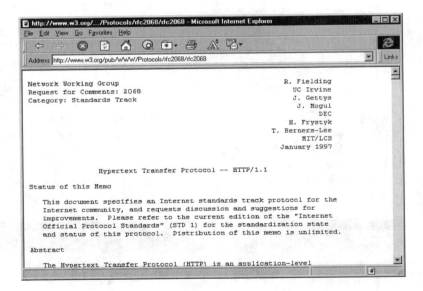

The design of HTTP brings another problem to the Web in the form of requiring an unnecessarily large number of connections to retrieve data from a complicated page. A typical HTML page today contains multiple objects in the form of multiple hyperlinks, images, sounds, applets, objects, scripts, and so on. In today's world, each of these entities on a page requires a separate connection between the server and the client. The way today's browsers handle this is to automatically attempt to open several connections simultaneously to get these multiple pieces of a Web page. This essentially compounds the problem by creating additional traffic. HTTP 1.1 proposes a "keep alive" extension known as *persistent connections* to the protocol so that once a connection is established, that single connection can be kept alive to fetch any and all related information in that single session. With the addition of pipelining as part of the specification, the primary goal of decreasing HTTP's load on the Internet will be realized as the client can make additional requests across that single, persistent connection.

> **NOTE**
>
> Bob Metcalfe, the creator of Ethernet, recently wrote a good article heralding the arrival of HTTP 1.1:
>
> `http://www.infoworld.com/cgi-bin/displayArchive.pl?/97/13/o04-13.42.htm`

A significant server-side change the 1.1 specification adds is the definition of *virtual* servers or hosts. This is the capability of one Web server to answer requests on multiple TCP/IP addresses or hostnames, even though the content physically resides on a single machine. Though it is widely in use with servers all over the globe, there is currently no hardware-neutral method defined to implement virtual hosts. Most Web servers support some form of virtual host, but each of them does so in a proprietary manner. Internet service providers currently must use the specific format of their present Web server software, and know that when or if they change this software that their current scheme won't work. This creates a situation in which server software is differentiated not on real merit, but on its implementation of a now-standard feature. HTTP 1.1 specifies the manner in which all 1.1-compliant servers support virtual hosts. This will result in the feature being implemented in a uniform manner.

Other significant developments that HTTP 1.1 brings to the Web are integrated support of proxy servers and facilities for cache improvements. *Proxy servers* are servers that fetch data for a client as if it *were* that client. In function, a proxy server acts in place of a client to retrieve requested information. Common in intranets, proxy servers provide a number of important features that ultimately serve to reduce the number of unique connections on the Web. For example, a company using a proxy server has all its users use the proxy to retrieve data. Data that is regularly retrieved by a large number of users will be retrieved by the proxy for the first client, and then when the next client requests the same data, the proxy doesn't have to retrieve it again. The data can be sent directly to the new client without requiring a new request from the source. HTTP 1.1 adds caching definitions to the protocol to assist in the identification of data held in the proxy's cache. Currently the main method that is used to find out whether cached data is "stale" is to maintain some sort of checksum or a "last modified" date for the data. Then, at the minimum, a request has to be made to the source to see if the data has changed since that last date, or the data is again retrieved. HTTP 1.1 promises a thorough treatment of caching to facilitate current practices like offline cache uses as well as defining the methods that a proxy uses to validate cached data. In many cases, 1.1 will result in no additional network traffic at all; in some cases, a significant reduction in current traffic patterns will occur.

> **TIP**
>
> See Appendix B for a detailed treatment of HTTP 1.1.

Hypertext Format Definition

In addition to defining the protocol that is used to transmit data across the Internet, the original Web standards included the format used for hypertext. This area of the Web has undergone the most innovation, and is in a virtual state of flux. Because it is the primary data format on the Web, HTML has been the subject of much debate and revisions since the 1.0 version. Like the other standards for the Web, the W3C "owns" the HTML standard and is responsible for defining its evolution. And because HTML is the way we express ourselves on the Web, its history and current state is of the utmost importance to anyone wanting to build Web sites or Web applications.

> **TIP**
>
> Although tools like Visual InterDev allow you to edit and create HTML documents without knowledge of HTML, it is still a requirement that you learn HTML. Without this knowledge, you won't recognize HTML formatting problems when they occur; with the knowledge, you will be able to hand code intricate elements that aren't yet supported by the tools.

HTML Beginnings

The Hypertext Markup Language (HTML) has gone through three major revisions in the same time that HTTP has stayed at 1.0! As a subset of SGML (Standard Generalized Markup Language—see Figure 1.9), HTML inherits much of the format of that page formatting language. SGML is a format that is popular in the print publishing business that allows any application to output its data in an open format that can be recognized by any other application or print program. SGML has a concept of a Document Type Definition, or DTD, that defines the parameters of a given document; and since its inception, HTML has had its own DTD. Thus an HTML document can be readily recognized and, probably more importantly, rendered in approximately the fashion expected by the creator of the document. SGML concerns itself more with document structure than with visual representation, but it is this structure that provides it with the visual accuracy. Accurate rendering is of great importance in the print field, and in a similar way, of significant importance on the Web.

NOTE

For a detailed introduction of SGML, see

`http://www.brainlink.com/~ben/sgml/`

FIGURE 1.9.

Benoît Marchal's "An Introduction to SGML" is a great place to start for more information on SGML.

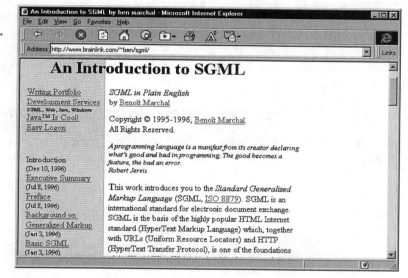

Berners-Lee's original HTML definition was not as much concerned with an exact rendering of a printed page, but with a common-denominator approach so that a document could be represented with reasonable accuracy across a wide range of hardware and software platforms with differing capabilities. The original data did not require much in the way of formatting, and the hardware/software environments that were being used were mostly text based, so exact control over visual elements were not required. The original standards gave an HTML author the ability to display simple text with formatting as needed, such as boldface type added to a chapter heading. Additionally, markup for items like bulleted or numbered lists was available. A couple items that were missing from the original specification were for common elements like inline graphics, tables, and the now popular *imagemap*—a graphic with defined coordinates that allow graphic navigation. There was no way to use so-called active components like Java applets or ActiveX components in a Web page. Many of the elements that we take for granted today were impossible in earlier versions of HTML, primarily because they were not needed at the beginning.

The evolution of HTML went from 1.0 to 2.0 largely as the result of vendor usage. When the Web became a commercial entity in the mid-1990s, companies like Netscape and the newcomer to the Internet, Microsoft, were using widely popular features that were not in the existing

1.0 specifications. Inline images using the IMG tag were supported by Navigator, Mosaic, and the first release of Internet Explorer, but they weren't strictly supported in the existing standards. The HTML 2.0 (see Figure 1.10) specification was written to codify the common usage of HTML at the time, and with its release in September 1995 quickly became the standard for browsers and Webmasters. But that was then and this is now! HTML 2.0 as a standard was quickly shown to be insufficient for the kinds of information that vendors and the burgeoning Web public wanted. HTML 3.0 was proposed as a new standard, but was never adopted as such by the standards bodies. It would ultimately never be adopted, and instead would be replaced by HTML 3.2, which we will look at briefly next. Remember that until HTML 3.2 was accepted as an official W3C recommendation for HTML in January 1997, HTML 2.0 was the existing standard, and the only standard that you could absolutely depend on being supported by all clients.

FIGURE 1.10.

HTTP 2.0 was finally codified in November 1995.

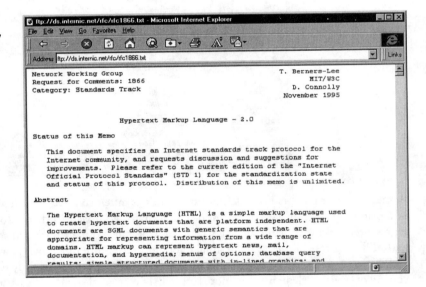

HTML 3.2 and Beyond

The current HTML standard is version 3.2 (see Figure 1.11). As I mentioned earlier, it became an official standard in January 1997. This version replaced the proposed but expired version 3.0 that had languished for several months. Although many vendors claimed to support HTML 3.0, in fact, everyone supported some subset of the proposed features while offering their own extensions or superset of the HTML 2.0 standard. Standardization by W3C of HTML 3.2

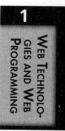

was an attempt to "put a stake in the ground" with the current accepted practices that all vendors were supporting. At the same time, it was decided that it was necessary to distance this standard from 3.0 in such a way that 3.2 would be the standard to which everyone wrote.

FIGURE 1.11.
HTTP 3.2 became a W3C recommendation in January 1997.

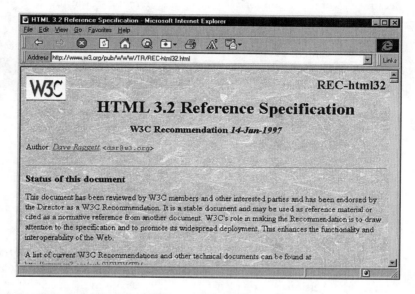

> **TIP**
>
> See Appendix C, "HTML 3.2 Reference," for a detailed treatment of HTML 3.2.

HTML 3.2 codified what had become one of the most used features on the Web—tables. Tables have become popular as both an obvious way to display tabular data as well as a convenient formatting technique used to lay out pages. It is the latter usage that was most needed in HTML as more companies opened *webzines*—Web versions of printed magazines. Without any real control of placement of elements on a Web page beyond simple justification like centering, right or left justified, and so on, tables offered a little more control over placement of key elements. Using tables, an HTML author can display graphics or text more precisely. This feature alone served to make HTML 3.2 a welcome standard. Also added to the standard were the needed definition of adding applets to HTML, as well as defining additions to the IMG tag for inline images. Another key feature that was added was the definition of so-called *client-side imagemaps,* which helped to reduce the amount of processing required to process coordinates within an image. Client-side imagemaps allow you to define coordinates to URL mapping within the current document, thus making a return to the server for processing unnecessary. Because part of the reason for 3.2 was to assist in reducing the already building congestion on the Web, implementation of this feature has greatly reduced the traffic associated with imagemaps.

> **NOTE**
>
> The HTML 2.0 specification is online at this address:
>
> `ftp://ds.internic.net/rfc/rfc1866.txt`
>
> The HTML 3.2 specification is available at this address:
>
> `http://www.w3.org/pub/WWW/TR/REC-html32.html`

Even though HTML 3.2 was meant to represent the state of the Web in January 1997, it actually left out some expected features that were already in common usage on the Web. Missing was a definition of the FRAME tag that lets you divide the browser window into clearly designated areas. Because they could not reach a consensus on the support of frames without jeopardizing the release of the standard, the W3C decided to leave it out of the spec while reserving it for another version. Another key feature that was not in the specification was a standard for adding scripting to HTML documents. Netscape had first introduced JavaScript scripting with Navigator 2.0, and Microsoft introduced support for this and added its own—Visual Basic Scripting. Both of these add a new level of programmability and interaction to HTML documents, but neither made it into the standard. Still another feature that was already implemented by Microsoft but not Netscape was style sheets. Style sheets add the capability to globally change the appearance of a document or sets of documents using a single file. Now called *Cascading Style Sheets,* or CSS, this definition will definitely make it into the next specification that is already being defined, and now is simply called Cougar (see Figure 1.12).

Cougar intends to pick up where HTML 3.2 left off by adding the features I've mentioned, as well as addressing a few additional elements that will serve to create a more interactive HTML experience. The specification will also address increased access to Web data for people with disabilities. Items such as how to navigate without a mouse or with alternate pointing devices such as those used by partially paralyzed persons will be addressed. As the Web becomes ubiquitous and finds itself in schools, libraries, and other public places, these kinds of considerations are a necessity.

FIGURE 1.12.

*Cougar is the next
version of HTML.*

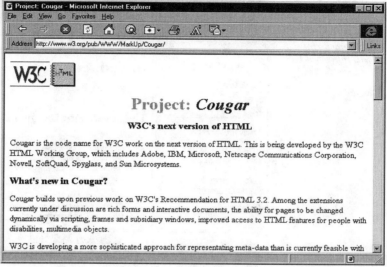

> **Project: *Cougar***
>
> **W3C's next version of HTML**
>
> Cougar is the code name for W3C work on the next version of HTML. This is being developed by the W3C
> HTML Working Group, which includes Adobe, IBM, Microsoft, Netscape Communications Corporation,
> Novell, SoftQuad, Spyglass, and Sun Microsystems.
>
> **What's new in Cougar?**
>
> Cougar builds upon previous work on W3C's Recommendation for HTML 3.2. Among the extensions
> currently under discussion are rich forms and interactive documents, the ability for pages to be changed
> dynamically via scripting, frames and subsidiary windows, improved access to HTML features for people with
> disabilities, multimedia objects.
>
> W3C is developing a more sophisticated approach for representing meta-data than is currently feasible with

NOTE

The next version of HTML is simply called Cougar:

`http://www.w3.org/pub/WWW/MarkUp/Cougar/`

One of the most significant features that will likely make it into Cougar is the definition of an
HTML object model. Programmers will be quite familiar with the idea of an object model as
a key feature needed to take HTML to the level of an application platform. Netscape introduced a limited HTML object model when it released JavaScript (see Figure 1.13) with Navigator 2.0. But because this model is a proprietary definition, there's no compelling reason for
others to support the specifics. Microsoft wisely supports the current definition so that it can
utilize both JavaScript and VBScript, but the object model simply doesn't go far enough.
Because both companies are working with the W3C, an object model will finally be standardized, but for now you have to be content with the existing JavaScript object model as it is implemented in Navigator and Internet Explorer. If adoption of Cougar moves quickly, Microsoft
and Netscape may support a common object model with the next versions of their browsers.
When a common object model is defined, it will serve to make the Web more dynamic. Any
element of a Web page would be accessible programmatically, making dynamic manipulation
of a Web document possible. In fact, Microsoft calls a significant new feature of its upcoming
Internet Explorer 4.0 browser *Dynamic HTML*. This feature includes a comprehensive object
model as its most important element, and may actually be very close to what the W3C eventually adopts.

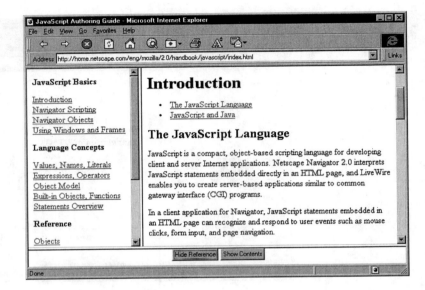

Clients and Servers

Because the Web was an attempt to bring information in a uniform manner to a wide range of people, the original standards included a definition of the software programs destined to deliver that information. Berners-Lee created the first Web server and browser at CERN, and the HTTP protocol standard defines the minimum set of features that these applications must support. To aid in the proliferation of the standards, Berners-Lee created a "reference" server and browser both to demonstrate and to test the standards. This tradition continued with each release of a new standard, and resulted in a widely accepted level of basic functionality in other client and server products. For example, the HTTP 1.1 specification defines the format of requests and responses between a client and server. It defines exactly how the client and server should identify themselves, as well as the exact format of the expected conversations that occur. This definition results in assurances that when a server reports it is an HTTP 1.1–capable server, the client is guaranteed that any HTTP 1.0 or 1.1 feature can be expected.

The current reference client and server applications from the W3C are Amaya (see Figure 1.14) and Jigsaw (see Figure 1.15). These applications serve as test beds for demonstrating the features of the current standards for HTML and HTTP, and are thus a good platform to test some of your own Web creations. Because they are freely available and not commercial products, they can be used to demonstrate concepts when you are designing a set of pages. Additionally, the current source code is also available, making it easier for programmers to see exactly how to code support for the standards involved.

FIGURE 1.14.

The Amaya browser from W3C is the reference Web client for HTTP 1.1 and HTML 3.2.

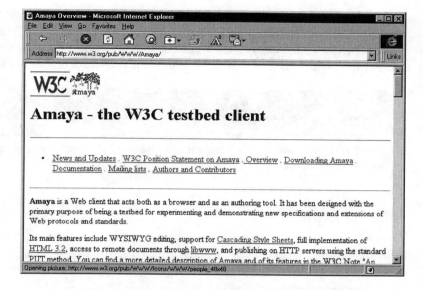

FIGURE 1.15.

The Jigsaw server from W3C is the reference Web server for HTTP 1.1 and HTML 3.2.

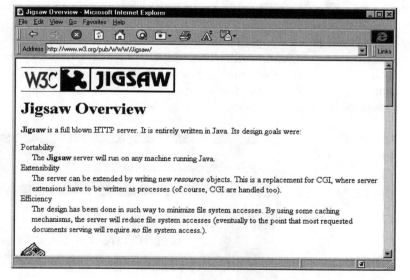

One of the key features of a standards definition for clients and servers is identification. The HTTP and HTML standards define the expected methods these applications use to communicate the versions of the standards they support. And because these transactions are intentionally designed to be backward compatible, an older browser will be able to connect to a newer server. Instead, this should result in the server sending in data with the appropriate level of compatibility. This provides for a guaranteed level playing field where users with older clients will still be able to expect a certain level of access to data even if it is served by a newer server. A browser like Internet Explorer can identify itself to the server by revealing its capabilities. Servers like IIS 3.0, and soon IIS 4.0, are able to further assist in this negotiation by offering browser recognition code to provide programmatic support of unique browser features.

> **NOTE**
>
> Though such features as browser recognition are commonly implemented in a Web server, if vendors strictly followed the standards, such recognition would be unnecessary. This is the much-hoped-for outcome of the standardization efforts of the W3C.

Internet Explorer

Although Amaya is available to demonstrate the features of the current Web standards, Microsoft's Internet Explorer 3.0 (see Figure 1.16) is really an excellent example as well. Microsoft has committed itself to following standards on the Web, and its support of HTML 3.2 is well demonstrated in its browser. Internet Explorer (IE) 3.01 is included with Visual InterDev, so you can use it with Visual InterDev right out of the box. IE 3.01 and the current version of Internet Explorer 3.02 also support both CSS and the Netscape JavaScript object model. The next version of Internet Explorer will support the final version of these standards, and if necessary, Microsoft will change the implementation to match the released standards. Designing for IE and recommending that your Web clients use IE will allow you the greatest range of support for the current standards. But, if you want to design for Navigator as well, or for another client, Visual InterDev is up to the challenge.

FIGURE 1.16.

The current and future versions of Internet Explorer are detailed at Microsoft's site.

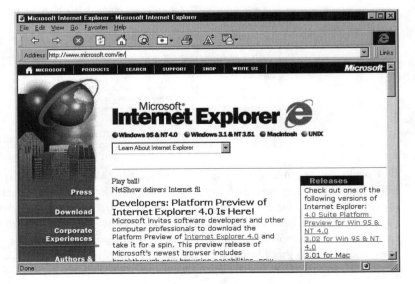

Internet Information Server

In the same way that IE represents the current "state of the art" in Web clients, Internet Information Server (IIS—see Figure 1.17) is representative of a full-featured Web server. IIS 3.0 is included with Visual InterDev, in case you don't already have it installed with your version of Windows NT Server. Visual InterDev also includes updated versions of the Personal Web Server for Windows 95 and Peer Web Services for Windows NT Workstation so that you can use your own system for creating and testing your Web applications. IIS doesn't currently support HTTP 1.1, but this support is expected in the next release of IIS. But the features that IIS does support are firmly rooted in HTTP 1.0 and other practices that have become standards by their common usage. In addition, IIS supports Active Server Pages (ASP) that are a key feature of Visual InterDev. With ASP you can create full-blown Web applications unlike anything you are able to create with any other Web server. And because Active Server Pages have built-in support for any client using its browser recognition, you can serve data to any client while still getting the full functionality of ASP.

> **NOTE**
>
> More information on Active Server Pages is available in Chapter 15, "Introduction to Active Programming." More information on IIS is available in Chapter 33, "Serving with Personal Web Server and Internet Information Server."

FIGURE 1.17.

The current version of Internet Information Server is detailed at Microsoft's site.

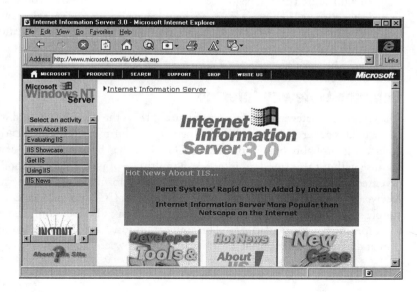

Programming Standards

Programming standards for the Web have probably changed as much as any other single aspect of the environment. As you've seen, the Web was originally designed to deliver static text. As more and more people joined the party, the need for more interactions became obvious. One of the first features needed was some format for getting input from a client to the server. The use of form input was an early creation, although it wasn't expanded to a practical state until NCSA released the Mosaic Web browser. With forms, a user is able to enter information such as an e-mail message, address or demographic data, or even preferences, which can then be processed by the server. Form elements were not codified until HTML 2.0, but have been an integral part of the standards since. The early creation of the Web included a definition of a gateway specification called the Common Gateway Interface (CGI). This gateway provided a standard manner in which external applications could provide interactive or dynamic information to a client. CGI provided a standard method to access databases, process form information, and even do rudimentary image animation using a CGI program.

Another common format for programming the Web that is fairly popular involves pre-processing information via *server-side includes*, or SSI. Whereas most CGI applications are the result of specific user interactions such as in database access, SSI provided the first means to create dynamic pages when the client first connected. A typical use of SSI would be to change the default page a server sends in answer to a request from a static document to a SSI file. This file could be dynamically created using a CGI program that used browser recognition to deliver a full-featured default page based on known features of the user's browser. I've already mentioned that current Web programming doesn't have access to state information, or indeed any real usable information to identify a specific user. The cookie specification is the only way currently to maintain state information about a specific user. Let's look at each of these in turn to see how they work.

Common Gateway Interface

The Common Gateway Interface (see Figure 1.18) is the current standard way that most interactive data is generated on the Web. Whether it's a form-handling application or live database access, it is probably being done using CGI. CGI has been a lifesaver of sorts for the Web, because without this standard interface, a multitude of proprietary methods would have been invented. CGI defines common methods to pass information to an external program and to receive information back from that same application. CGI applications can be implemented as simple scripts using popular scripting languages such as Perl, or compiled executables created for a specific hardware platform. The application just has to conform to the interface definition and provide its output in a format that the browser understands.

FIGURE 1.18.

The Common Gateway Interface is detailed at NCSA's Web page.

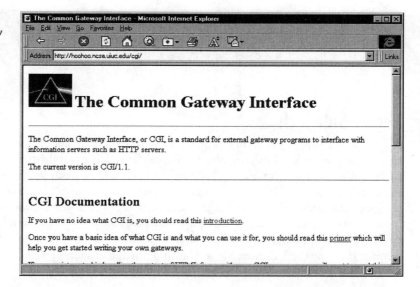

> **NOTE**
>
> The Web address for information on CGI is here:
>
> `http://hoohoo.ncsa.uiuc.edu/cgi/`

Because CGI applications run as external processes that are executed on the fly, their use can seriously affect the overall server performance. The use of CGI applications increases the system memory as well as other resources that are in use, affecting the overall performance of the system. If a popular site uses many CGI applications, it can literally bring the site to its knees as it tries to serve all the clients' requests while it is running multiple copies of the CGI application. This is the primary problem with CGI. This is also the reason most server vendors have created alternate forms of application support so that the interactivity that CGI offers can be implemented without the inherent drawbacks of CGI. The main thing you need to remember about CGI is to use it sparingly, and especially to avoid it for key features of your site. If your site demands interactivity, investigate the features of your server that provide alternate interfaces to CGI. For example, IIS has CGI support, but offers several alternate ways to provide dynamic interactivity using ISAPI, ASP, or IDC files. Each of these methods offers its own set of problems as well, but are all a better choice than CGI in many cases.

Server-Side Includes

Although not supported by the CERN server, server-side includes (see Figure 1.19) are another common method of providing some programmatic capability to the Web. Introduced by NCSA for their public-domain NCSA Web server, SSI quickly gained in popularity. Since the creation of SSI by NCSA, most other Web servers have supported at least some if not all of the methods introduced by NCSA. SSI became the common way to provide the beginnings of interactivity and identification. Using the SSI EXEC command is the standard way that many sites have implemented graphic page counters. Another common SSI command is FLASTMOD, which outputs the time the indicated file was last modified; it is a useful way to document recent revisions of a Web document.

FIGURE 1.19.

Server-side includes are detailed at NCSA's Web pages.

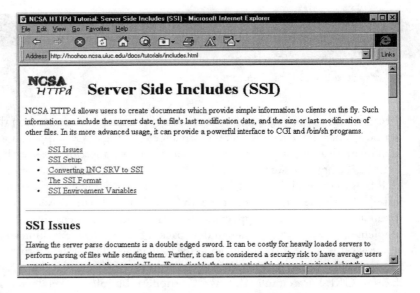

Probably the single most popular SSI command is the INCLUDE command, which can be used to create boilerplate text such as a standard header or footer. Using such a file can greatly decrease the amount of edits that are needed if a site changes these footers regularly. Using a statement like `<!--#INCLUDE file="boilerplate.htm" -->` would result in the contents of `boilerplate.htm` being inserted in the current document at the same point in the document. If a site wanted to periodically change this section of the site, only one file would have to be changed instead of many. But SSI does have its drawbacks. The INCLUDE example requires another visit to the server to pick up the contents of the included file. The EXEC command executes a script, batch file, or executable every time the SSI file is requested. Another problem with the EXEC command is that there is a potential security risk involved if malicious individuals use it to gain access to other executables using the EXEC format. Although popular, SSI still has the same problems that CGI exhibits, especially the server-performance issues.

> **TIP**
>
> Because of some of the inherent problems, IIS doesn't currently support the full set of common SSI commands. For compatibility with other servers, the next release of IIS is expected to support a full range of such commands.

Cookies

I mentioned cookies earlier, but they remain one of the only methods of keeping track of clients as they navigate a site or recording other information about the state of the clients' visits to your Web. Netscape introduced cookies with Navigator 2.0, and the feature was soon seen as a powerful advancement. A *cookie* is a small piece of information that a server sends to the client to store on the client's computer. This information can be used to track the user navigation around the Web site, or to store certain information about the user. A typical use is storing user preferences so that subsequent visits to the site will provide the user with customized appearance or default choices. A cookie can contain any amount of information, and a large number of sites are using them to maintain this kind of state information.

> **NOTE**
>
> The only real specification for cookies is at the following URL:
>
> `http://www.netscape.com/newsref/std/cookie_spec.html`
>
> A good online article about use of cookies is available at this address:
>
> `http://www.netscapeworld.com/nw-07-1996/nw-07-cookies.html`

An example of what could be done using cookies would be a sports site that allows a user to customize the default sports he sees when he visits the site. This information would be stored in the `cookie.txt` file on the client's machine. On subsequent visits, this information would be used to display only relevant sport choices or even to offer certain special ads or other commercial pitches based on those preferences. Look at Listing 1.1 for an example of a typical cookie file.

Listing 1.1. Typical contents of `cookie.txt` file.

```
# Netscape HTTP Cookie File
# http://www.netscape.com/newsref/std/cookie_spec.html
# This is a generated file!  Do not edit.
.netscape.com      TRUE   /   FALSE   946684799   NETSCAPE_ID
c98ffb1e,c68818dc
.infoseek.com      TRUE   /   FALSE   859574919   InfoseekUserId
D2679D5862DEA4FE=
cgi.netscape.com   FALSE  /   FALSE   946684799   NETSCAPE_VERIFY
c65ff94b,c6a6abcb
.adobe.com         TRUE   /   FALSE   946684799   INTERSE
123.123.123.1231212183113897
```

Note that in this example, the user has several cookies stored from each of several hosts. When the client connects to `infoseek.com`, the client will send the cookie for Infoseek along with the request. Then Infoseek can take appropriate action based on the content. The information may be an encoded user's name, preferences, or demographic details. An important thing to note in this transaction is that the server does not know anything about the other cookies that the client has stored. The client sends the contents of the cookie related to that specific host and nothing more. Also, when a server sends a cookie to the client using the `Set-Cookie` response header, it is up to the client to store that cookie, or with some recent browser like IE, to deny storing the cookie if the user has disabled this function.

If you want to program interactive dynamic Web sites using the traditional methods, you will be using a combination of server-side scripts, CGI programs, SSI directives, and cookies on your client's machine. There are other options, but they are usually proprietary formats that may or may not be available on other servers. Visual InterDev and IIS offer the best range of options, and you will find that the performance issues all but disappear as you change your existing CGI applications into dynamic ASP applications.

Summary

We've detailed a quick history of the Internet and the Web in this chapter. You've learned about the significant features of HTML and HTTP and the current way that Web programming is performed. In the next chapter we will be looking at relational databases and client/server technology. You'll learn the main features of client/server technology and the rudiments of relational databases, as well as some of the inherent problems with this technology when it is moved to the Web. In the last chapter of this part of the book, we will cover some of the vision and philosophy behind Microsoft's Visual InterDev.

Relational Databases and Client/Server Technology

by Glenn Fincher

CHAPTER 2

IN THIS CHAPTER

What makes a database *relational*? What does *client/server* really mean? Which one's the client? What does a server serve? What is a database, really? And what does any of this have to do with the Web? These are some of the questions that come to mind as I think about the real reason behind the creation of Visual InterDev. You see, Microsoft has an ulterior motive with Visual InterDev. It has a goal with this piece of software. And it's not just making money! The goal is all tied up in the concepts of databases, client/server, and the Web. The goal from Microsoft for Visual InterDev is the eventual realization of information at your fingertips (IAYF). With its native support of ODBC, ADO, and ultimately OLE DB, Visual InterDev comes closer to enabling a new level of access to data—wherever it exists.

IAYF requires immediacy of information. It requires data that is pertinent and persistent. If pertinent, it must also be personal. If persistent, it must be accurate and stay accurate. It's not just information that I want—it is *my* information. It's not necessarily my private information, but information that *I* want. If I drive to the ATM to take out money for pizza, I'm interested in pertinent (how much does my account hold), persistent (if I had $500 yesterday, I should have $500 today), and of course personal (my money, not Jay's). I am only interested in my account and whether the $20 I want is available at the moment. (I know, $20 isn't a lot of money, but remember, you just bought a $40 book!) When I put my card in the ATM, it knows who it thinks I am, and when I enter my PIN it knows who I really am. My request for $20 will be honored if somewhere in its electronic data it finds at least $20 next to my name. How does this example illustrate or hint at the meaning of IAYF? Any information I want or need for any activity could be as personal, immediate, and rewarding as that ATM transaction. IAYF applied to an ATM means that my money is available when I want it. IAYF applied to the Web means that whatever a Web site offers to its customers, the information needs to be available as soon as the customer wants it. Each of these instances imply a "database"—in this sense a collection of information with an implied order and access model.

In this chapter I introduce you to some basic database concepts as well as some of the underlying concepts defining client/server computing. One is inextricably tied to the other. Client/server computing was really designed as a means to facilitate database access. Databases have evolved because of client/server computing. Another area I want to look at in this chapter is how client/server computing and database access are being accomplished on the Web. What you'll see is that the Web has some definite shortcomings when it comes to providing true client/server computing. We'll look at a few of those shortcomings and problems and see how people are working around them. I'll cover the following in this chapter:

- Databases 101
- Relational databases
- Client/server computing
- Problems and solutions

Databases 101

I know what you're saying: "Do I *have* to learn about databases to build Web sites?" That's the first thing that I thought about when I contemplated writing this section of the book. The whole topic of databases has been, to some of us, a necessary evil. Sure, I'm glad that my employer has a database somewhere that knows how much I'm supposed to be paid for my work, and somehow that database generates a weekly paycheck, but what does that have to do with the Web? Consider my earlier example of using the ATM machine. I'm equally glad that my bank has a database somewhere that keeps track of the amount of money I have on hand at any given time. I'm also thankful the bank has an accurate database that not only knows how much money I have at a given time, but also knows my address so I can get monthly statements. So, databases are an important part of my life after all. Maybe there is a reason to learn a little bit more about databases after all. That's the intent of this introductory section. If you are past the level of a database novice, you may want to skip ahead to the middle of the chapter to the section on client/server computing, but if you are like I was until very recently, wade in and learn a little about this unknown world.

Databases drive much, if not most, of the computing that is being done today, no matter what kind of computing you are involved in. Obviously, the Web is full of examples of database usage. In fact, some would say that the Web *is* a database. You can certainly use database models to understand the structure of the Web. The Web is similar to a hierarchical database—a database whose members or records are arranged in a pyramid fashion. You can start at a site like Yahoo! or AltaVista and start navigating link by link from a single URL through layers upon layers of hyperlinks. The problem with this serendipitous traversal is that the database we call the Web is not coherently ordered or structured. There's no real way to categorize all the information on the Web without imposing a structure on the Web from outside. That's exactly what the sites we mentioned have done. Yahoo! and AltaVista have imposed a structure on the Web to enable searches of all this disparate data. And guess what? Yahoo! and AltaVista both keep all this data in a database.

What do you think of when you hear the word *database*? Your answer to this question will reveal a lot about your understanding of databases as a topic for discussion and, probably more important, whether you really need to follow this discussion further. Whether you are a database guru or database Luddite, I hope to raise your level of understanding of databases and their use on the Web at least a little bit! So... back to my question. What comes to mind when you see the word *database*? Do you immediately think of words like Access, SQL Server, Oracle, Informix, or DB2? If so, your concept of databases is tied to the engine that builds and manages data in databases. If your answer is instead the tool you use to retrieve or analyze data, then you're more of a tools person. Your database may just as easily be a spreadsheet or even a 3×5 card catalog! You think that the database is synonymous with the tool you use to access your information. Or you may think of the concept of a database as an ordering principle that enables you to understand the entire workings of the company you own or work for. You see, you tend to understand the concept of a database based on the component that you work with the most. Any of these answers are acceptable when we talk about databases, because databases are all those things. For our discussion, though, we'll briefly look at the database concept under these three heads: engines, tools, and models. Then we'll define the four common database models in use today, and then turn our attention to one of the most commonly used databases—the relational database. But first, let's define a few terms.

Common Terms

When you talk about databases, you continually encounter a few terms over and over again. These terms are used to describe the features that make a set of data a data*base*. Let's define some of those terms to start with. What makes a database? I mentioned 3×5 cards earlier as well as spreadsheets, and actually those are fairly good illustrations of some of the basic characteristics of databases. Let's look at the spreadsheet model first, both because it's one of the places that people store data most and because its idea of tables of information will be a good starting point for relating databases later in our discussion.

A spreadsheet is an excellent way to organize sets of related information. For example, if you wanted to catalog the books in your private collection, you could easily do so using a spreadsheet. You'd have to spend a little time up front to look at the information that you want to catalog about the books, and also how you want to order the information. The time spent in evaluating or modeling your data will affect not only the amount of information that you ultimately collate but also the structure of that data. So, a database is not just information, but structured data. You could simply record all the information about your books in a freeform manner, but until you apply some structure to the information, it won't be much more useful than simply perusing your shelves. So, we have a concept of structure in a database. In your spreadsheet, this could begin with the categories of information you decide to catalog. But it also includes the order in which you decide to store the information. So, your book catalog might look something like Table 2.1.

Table 2.1. A sample book catalog.

Title	Author	Publisher	Type
Debt of Honor	Clancy, Tom	Putnam	hardback
The Chamber	Grisham, John	Doubleday	paperback
The Road Ahead	Gates, Bill	Penguin	hardback
Executive Orders	Clancy, Tom	Putnam	hardback
Silicon Snake Oil	Stoll, Clifford	Anchor Books	paperback

If I only have five books I don't need a database, but if I have all of Tom Clancy's, John Grisham's, Tolkien's, Twain's, Stephen King's, and of course the entire Sams.net collection of computer books, this spreadsheet becomes more real. What you see in this example is that the data is ordered into rows and columns of related information, or *tables*. What database designers have discovered is that people easily understand data that is arranged in a tabular fashion. You'll also notice that I have structured the data using similar information about each book. You might also see that the same type of data occurs regularly—that is, the data has *regularity*. So, we have *structure* and *regularity* as database concepts. Also, look at the Author column of data. This column of information is additionally ordered. I've decided to structure the data in this column in *lastname, firstname* order. Thus, I've applied a *schema* to the information by defining how the information is to be stored in that column. Another example of a schema would be if I chose to store the price that I paid for the books in another column and specified that the information be formatted in dollars and cents. I would apply monetary formatting to that information that in itself adds to the value of my database, because I could then determine how much money I had invested in my collection, or easily find out my most expensive book. Each line or row of my data stands alone as an individual *record*, a complete set of related information about a single entity.

We could create the same database using 3×5 cards. Remember when you were in high school working on a research paper, and you had to use 3×5 cards to research your paper? My teacher had a standard format that we had to follow when we took notes for our paper. We had to place the name and author of the resource in the upper-left corner of the card, the date it was published in the upper right, and the page number(s) in the lower right. We then put the related point in our outline under the name of the resource on the left margin, and finally the information that we intended to use in our own words in the center of the card. We had to create such a card for every resource we used in our research. Why the stickler for such formatting? All this was because we were creating a *database*. The teacher or even another student in the class could pick up my deck of cards and quickly find the author, date, and page number to look up the information. Each card had a *regular* set of information on it, the information was *structured* physically on the page, and there was a *schema* to the content of each *field* on the cards. Each card stands alone as a single *record*.

What I've done here is defined the main features that make an otherwise unrelated set of data into a database. Admittedly, the database that your bank uses is almost infinitely more complex than either of these examples, but these basic terms are used over and over again when talking about databases.

Before we continue, I need to mention a couple of other terms that arise when we talk about databases. These have more to do with the purpose of the database as it relates to a time component. Ask yourself if the data in your database will have to be instantly available and up to date. Your immediate answer might be yes, but let me explain further. If I am the designer of a database for an emergency 911 service, I understand that a dispatcher will have to have an ability to immediately assign a unit to respond to a fire and know exactly where each and every unit close by is at a given time. If one unit is already responding to a call, another unit may need to be dispatched. This clearly fits the definition of a mission-critical application. And the type of data access that is required here is termed *transactional*. The database engine and even the data model must be capable of real-time transactions. And these database transactions must occur before the next call comes in, and another dispatcher in another physical location needs to know the status of that same unit. We add the concept of a *transaction* to our list of terms. A transaction is essentially a single *accomplished* operation on a set of data or record. Whether it's a query or posting new information to a record, a transaction is a completed action.

Another term that we use when we talk about databases is the term *analytic* database. An analytic database is one whose data model is optimized for analysis that is not by nature time critical. A corporate financial database may be structured in such a fashion. There is a regular need to analyze data, say for a quarterly financial statement, but the same type of data that is accumulated for these reports is not needed on a daily basis. So, an analytical view of a corporate database might use weekly accumulations of data as the smallest increment of data (even though the daily data is still available in a larger database) or even a larger increment like monthly accumulations. These databases are designed to be accurate to the time period given, but are optimized for analysis of key business metrics such as sales by region or product line. A transactional model would be overkill in this instance. An executive of the company wouldn't usually need an hourly or daily update of an existing product line, but the ability to look at accumulated sales over a period of months would be very useful.

Database Engine

The *database engine* is the application that is used to populate the database. When one uses Microsoft Access, the database that is created is of a specific type. The .MDB file that is native to Access is constructed in a specific fashion by the database engine that is part of Access. Note that the engine is different than all the tools that enable you to visually manipulate the data. The engine is only part of the database model that touches the raw data. It is responsible for the basic integrity of the data store or file. The database engine understands the business of opening or closing the file or files, as well as locating, changing, or adding information. The engine deals directly with the data in its most abstract form. If you look at the raw data that is actually stored in a database file, or even in an Excel spreadsheet, it wouldn't look much like your data at all. But it is important to think of this piece of the database as a separate component, because it will make the importance of client/server computing easier to understand later. Whether a transactional or analytic model is involved will also affect the design of this engine. The engine will have a different set of requirements with either of these. It may be useful for you to think about the engine as the proprietary application like SQL Server or Oracle, but it doesn't have to be proprietary in that sense. Let's look now at the tools and how they differ from the engine.

Database Tools

When the receptionist at the company where I work, Intergraph, gets a phone call for an employee she is unfamiliar with, she looks up the name in our corporate electronic phone book (see Figure 2.1). It's easy to think of this tool as the corporate phonebook database. It is the tool that we all use to look up fellow employees, but it isn't really the database. The tool has a query component to it, and it has a user interface—the buttons, text entry, and output fields. Even though this is a simple tool and the database it uses is simple as well, it illustrates the concept of the database tool. It is also interesting that this particular tool is designed to work with a local data store or, if desired, over the LAN to a central database. It is useful to note that in this case, the engine is built into the tool. The tool contains an engine that understands the raw data format. The tool itself doesn't know anything about accessing the data itself. The tool simply enables the user to ask a few simple questions that the engine uses to get the data the user wants to see. It's not surprising that we have taken this tool and placed it on our intranet for all users to use. I've replaced the user interface (UI) with the browser interface, but basically the same query tools are provided and the results are nearly identical, as shown in Figure 2.2.

FIGURE 2.1.

A corporate phonebook application—a database tool.

What's important to note with this example is that the data is what needed to be preserved when we converted this into a Web tool. The interface wasn't as important. In this instance, we even replaced the existing engine with a Perl script engine—again, the data being important, the tool or the engine being immaterial.

FIGURE 2.2.
*The same information
has been repackaged as
a Web-based tool.*

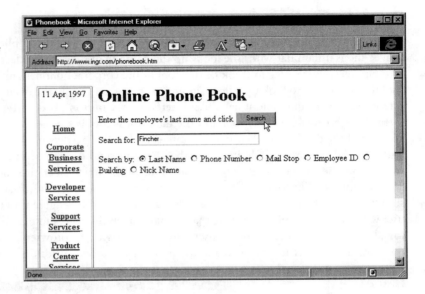

Database Model

What do I mean when I talk about modeling the data? The *database model* is in many ways the most important part of the creation of any database. The model is the definition of the raw structure, the schema—all aspects of the data that will eventually be stored in our database. The more time you spend defining the data model, the better the resulting database will be at storing the data, and equally important, enabling efficient access to the data. The data model concerns itself not only with categories of data, but also the way that data will be ordered in the database. For example, the phone book database I mentioned earlier contains current employee information such as phone number, employee number, e-mail address, and so on. Because this information is a corporate resource with information that is likely to be needed by many other departments, employee information will be an integral part of the overall corporate data model. It is important to think about these pieces of information that may have scope outside of the immediate need for the data. Data modeling will determine the scope of the database, as well as its principal design.

Database Technologies

Although I won't spend a lot of time on this topic, we need to briefly look at the types of databases that you might encounter as you attempt to create your Web application. One of the real benefits of Web technology is that it offers new and innovative methods to access your existing legacy data, no matter where that data currently resides. Although much data may already exist in popular relational databases, a wide range of data still exists in older hierarchical or so-called network databases. And an increasing body of data is being managed using object-oriented databases. Let's look at these briefly, but I will reserve a separate section for relational databases, the current most widely deployed type of database.

Hierarchical Databases

The oldest data model for database storage is probably the *hierarchical* database. Data arranged as a hierarchy is very common. The widely used organizational chart is an example of a hierarchy, as is the file system on your computer. A hierarchy is normally arranged from top down, from the complex to the simple. To retrieve data from a hierarchical database you navigate from the topmost member down through the underlying entities or categories until you locate the data you need. This traversal process is typical of a hierarchical database, and until the data gets more complex, or you have a need to query the data in a manner that wasn't originally envisioned, it works reasonably well. Another example of a hierarchical database could be data for a sales organization (see Figure 2.3).

A corporate sales organization could have a database ordered in the following fashion. In this illustration, think of this entire structure as a single database. As you can see, the structure proceeds from complex data to simple data. There is one U.S. Sales organization, with four regions, with many salespeople, with many more customer accounts, each ordering a larger set of products. If I want to discover the amount of sales that a single salesperson generated, I have to first search for that salesperson in each of the regional categories. When I've located the salesperson, it is fairly simple to get the sales numbers for that person. If instead I wanted to see how much of a single product was sold overall by all regions, I would have to navigate to the bottom of the tree for each region to extract that data. What makes this database model more complex is that it isn't geared to handle ad hoc queries. For example, if I wanted to find out how sales are going in the banking industry, I would have to navigate each tree separately to the Accounts category and interrogate each and every record separately for the needed information. Database programmers would try to build into the database application and engine the necessary queries that a user might need to make, but as the data gets more complex, the hierarchical model begins to get very unwieldy. What happens when the levels increase to 50 or more? Navigating down this tree becomes increasingly more complicated.

FIGURE 2.3.

A simple hierarchical database model.

2

RELATIONAL DATABASES AND TECHNOLOGY

Network Databases

Although it might seem at first glance that something called a *network* database would be ideal for the Web, the name has nothing to do with the network as a series of connected computers at all! The word *network* in this context has the connotation of a net laid across several hierarchical models in such a manner that data is now infinitely navigable. As Figure 2.4 shows, with just the addition of four lines across my database, I've greatly increased the general accessibility of data. I can now collect all the account data by navigating a single tree. Even if I changed this to four separate databases, the complexity could increase but the general access to data would only be complicated by the extra file manipulation. The data could still be navigated and interrogated faster than a hierarchical model alone. Note also that when you add a network model over a hierarchical model, the resulting navigation itself is more complex simply because there are more choices available to you. This increased complexity has been seen as the network model's curse as well as its advantage.

FIGURE 2.4.

A simple network database model.

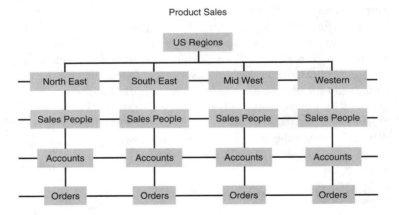

Relational Databases

As you might expect, the relational database model was created to fix all the problems inherent in both earlier models. Whether it has done that or simply created its own unique set of problems is for others to argue, but it can be said that relational databases are the most prevalent form of database model in use today. What may surprise you is the fact that relational databases have nothing to do with relationships. Its name derives from a mathematical concept where a relation is an unordered set of *n*-tuples. Now don't worry, you won't be tested on this. An *n*-tuples can be thought of as a record, and a relation can be thought of as a set of records or even a file. So, in relational database terms, each file is thought of as a *table*, containing records, which are rows composed of fields of data, called *columns*. Relational databases use this concept of a table because it is a fairly intuitively understandable construct. Don't, however, put too much stock in the term and attempt to read too much into it.

What you find out as you delve into this brave new relational world is that a relational database actually does buy you an ability to easily manage relationships after all. It is fairly simple to *join* tables to create new relationships, even when no relationship existed previously. This is one of the major differences between a relational model and the network model. Only predefined relationships exist or can exist with the network model. How does this model accomplish this magic? By using features such as the capability to create ad hoc relationships through constructs like the join, as well as by the use of one of the most powerful general additions to database technology—an integral *query language*. It is the query language that provides much of the power of this model. All early relational implementations were delivered with a query language, which soon evolved into the formally defined Structured Query Language or SQL (pronounced see-quel) that is ubiquitous. Today, the large majority of databases in use, whether large or small, are queried using SQL.

SQL

A standard query language brought database technology to a new level of usability. Without SQL, users had to learn to use whatever query interface the designer delivered with the database. There was no ability to do ad hoc queries. Users of other databases were tied to the specific implementation with no recourse at all to gaining access to the data outside of that implementation. SQL is thus a key component of taking legacy databases to the Web. Because data is not tied to a specific UI, engine, or query interface, you can easily devise a new Web-based UI and interpose a new engine and other interfaces to the data. And because SQL is standardized, you can depend on similar queries being supported by all database vendors in an identical fashion. If a database product supports SQL, you can build interchangeable solutions using appropriate pieces from the vendor whose product best meets your needs.

Since it was first adopted as a standard in 1986, SQL has gone through a few major revisions, and is now separately listed as a standard by ISO (see Figure 2.5), ANSI, and FIPS. The National Institute of Standards has maintained a SQL testing suite to qualify SQL implementations for some time. The ISO standard numbers concerning SQL are in Listing 2.1, and the ANSI standards are listed in Listing 2.2. The importance of the SQL standard cannot be overemphasized. It levels the playing field when it comes to database creation, access, and available tools. For example, Microsoft has several database products in its product line, all of which are SQL compatible. From the popular consumer database product Access to the fully scaleable, industrial-strength SQL Server. In between, Visual FoxPro offers a new level of Web automation that offers to bring a whole class of legacy data online. You'll learn much more about using Visual InterDev and SQL statements later in Chapter 12, "Database Management with the Visual Data Tools," and in Part V, "Creating Database Applications with Visual InterDev."

FIGURE 2.5.

The International Organization for Standardization is one body that has released standards for SQL.

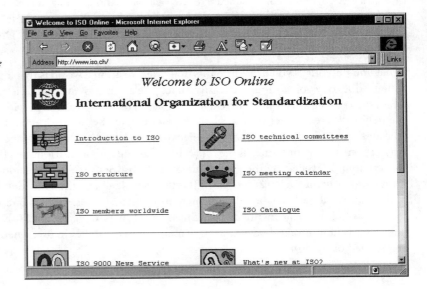

Listing 2.1. ISO standards for SQL.

```
ISO/IEC 9075:1992 Information technology -- Database languages -- SQL
ISO/IEC 9075-3:1995 Database languages -- SQL -- Part 3: Call-Level Interface (SQL/
➡CLI)
ISO/IEC 9075-4:1996 Database languages -- SQL -- Part 4: Persistent Stored Modules
➡(SQL/PSM)
```

Listing 2.2. ANSI standards for SQL.

```
ANSI X3.135-1992 : Information Systems - Database Language - SQL (includes ANSI
➡X3.168-1989)
ANSI/ISO/IEC 9075-3-1995 : Information Technology - Database Languages - SQL - Part
➡3: Call-Level
ANSI X3.168-1989 : Information Systems - Database Language - Embedded SQL (included
➡in ANSI X3.135)
ANSI/ISO/IEC 9579-2-1993 : Information Technology - Remote Database Access - Part
➡2: SQL Specialization
```

The SQL language enables you to create freeform queries using a fairly simple but rich set of reserved words or commands, and plain English statements. A typical SQL statement might be something like Listing 2.3, which demonstrates the compact power of SQL. This statement joins two tables (remember that in SQL parlance, a *table* is roughly synonymous to a *file*) and selects three fields using the value of US as a defining criteria. It results in locating all the orders made by U.S. companies with the date of the orders as well. To perform a similar query in either the hierarchical or network database would require the original programmer to build this capability directly into the database at creation time. Even if you are a database novice, this power is apparent.

Listing 2.3. A typical SQL statement.

```
SELECT Customer.company_name, Orders.order_id,
Orders.order_date;
FROM tastrade!customer INNER JOIN tastrade!orders ;
ON Customer.customer_id = Orders.customer_id;
WHERE Customer.country = "US"
```

SQL really enabled a new paradigm of database access because the database itself did not have to contain the detailed structure and query interface. Developers could build any manner of UI to access data as long as they used SQL to talk to the database. New and interesting combinations of data access could be built without knowing the internal structure of a database, and the capability to use new advances in user interface design could be easily exploited. SQL really ushered in the promise of client/server computing because it enabled the design of so-called lightweight clients without the underpinnings of a database engine and unique query language. We'll look at client/server computing next in our discussion, but before we leave the topic of SQL, I want to point out a couple interesting sites that you may want to visit if you want to learn more about SQL.

Inquiry.com

Inquiry.com (see Figures 2.6 and 2.7) was created for IT professionals to provide a one-stop source for product information, trade journal comparisons, and peer-to-peer as well as technical professional advice and comment. Because it contains information from all the vendors of a product category, IT professionals use Inquiry.com to research their product direction and purchase decisions.

In the SQL Pro section of Inquiry.com, you can compare product offerings, features, and comparative research and get answers to your pressing questions. The list of Web-enabled database products is impressive in itself. I've found it to be a good starting point for general product research and technology purchasing decisions.

FIGURE 2.6.

Inquiry.com *offers the IT professional one-stop access to product information, comparisons, and technical research.*

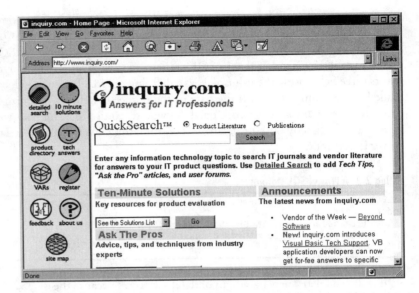

FIGURE 2.7.

The SQL Pro section of Inquiry.com *is an online excellent resource to the SQL language and products.*

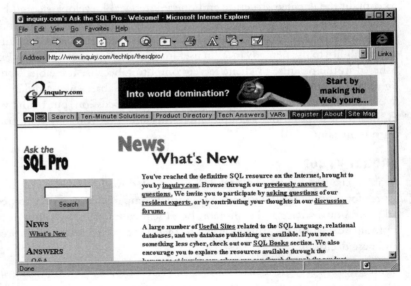

SQL Tutorial

If you are a novice or even an expert looking for a refresher course to SQL, you may find Jim Hoffman's online SQL Tutorial an interesting resource (see Figure 2.8). Located at http://w3.one.net/~jhoffman/sqltut.htm, Hoffman's tutorial is an excellent introduction to the world of ANSI-standard SQL. Concentrating on the SQL language proper without emphasis on individual vendors' implementations, it serves a useful purpose as an introduction. You'll find clear definitions as well as examples of standard SQL queries.

FIGURE 2.8.

An excellent introduction to SQL is Jim Hoffman's online SQL Tutorial.

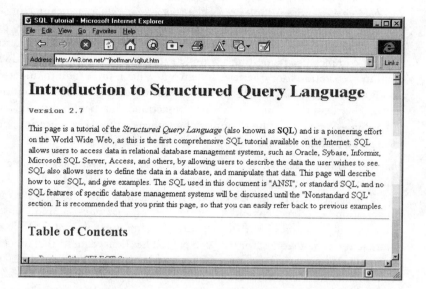

TIP

For more details on SQL syntax, consult Appendix F, "SQL Reference."

Client/Server

In our discussion about databases we asked some questions at the start, and we could do the same with the topic of client/server computing. What do you think of when you hear this term? Do you think of software like Windows NT Server and clients like Windows 95 or Windows NT Workstation? Or do you think of the Web and Web servers? Perhaps you have used a terminal to connect to a mainframe and are familiar with that client/server environment. Or you may be a developer who has created applications with both client and server components in one application. All these are examples of client/server computing, and reflect the way that this singular technology affects computing today. Prior to the popularity of the Internet and the Web, most people only encountered client/server computing in business computing environments. Today, though, client/server is becoming as popular in home computing as it is in businesses.

Client/Server Today

In the course of discussing client/server computing, we need to define a few terms. Like any other area of computing, client/server has its own terminology. Simple concepts like *front end* and *back end*, or more complex ones like *transaction management* enter any discussion. To begin with, the *client* in the equation is nothing more than an application, process, or piece of hardware that needs work done for it. The work could be simple like requesting a specific Web page, or complex like requesting a complete update of a company's worldwide financial statement in preparation for a quarterly statement. What is important to understand in this definition is that the client is typically unable to perform the operation without the assistance of the server. The client is the *front end* in this transaction. The client computer, application, or piece of hardware depends on the resources of another computer, application, or hardware to perform some useful function.

The server on the back end is the real worker bee. The server is responsible for performing the requested service for the client, or in many cases on behalf of the client. This is important to realize, because often the server component can actually be a client itself to another server. The conversation between client and server is called a *transaction*—a unique instruction or request that encapsulates a unit of work to be performed. In the example of the Web browser and server, a transaction is that request for the Web page. The client requests that the server send a specific Web page. When the server sends the page, that transaction is complete. What you may also begin to notice in these transactions is that some amount of so-called *middleware* is potentially involved in these processes. What is the middleware in a Web transaction? In this example, it is the underlying protocols that manage and transmit the data from server to client. In another instance, this middleware may be a discrete software component that somehow assists in the transaction.

An example of transaction management at a more complicated level could be the common act of transferring money from a savings account to your checking account through an ATM. Suppose you are traveling, and you find that you misjudged the amount of money you needed. When you make the electronic request from the remote ATM machine, the transaction that you request must be handled very carefully. The ATM (the client) must contact the bank's computers and verify that your savings account has the necessary funds to make the transaction. Then the funds must be transferred from your savings into your checking account. This happens so automatically that you may miss the subtlety of this transaction. If, for instance, some event occurs that prohibits the transfer to occur, or if the transfer does occur but it appears to have failed, the result is that money has been *created* by the transaction. Transaction-management software is involved that assures that the funds are committed and available in the checking account before completing the debit to the savings account balance. Note that any problems that occur with posting the changes to either account must be verifiable and reversible or, once again, money could be created by the transaction. The transaction-management software must have the capability to "back out" any change to assure that the request is completed correctly. Only after the state of the requested change is verified should the ATM report to you that the transaction was approved and update the printed statement. A common but complicated transaction indeed! You should appreciate the ATM more now, right? Imagine the same kind of transaction on a larger scale when a corporation transfers funds to an offshore subsidiary. The accidental creation or destruction of money could be catastrophic.

This example brings up another concept that we briefly need to consider. Transactions are themselves managed by a set of *business rules.* The transaction manager decides what to do about these kinds of situations by following a set of business rules that have been defined. Business rules are that set of defined cases that govern how the client/server transactions should proceed. You may see a practical example of business rules in evidence if your bank posts its rules for crediting an account when you make a deposit. At my bank, an out-of-state check is not immediately credited to my account, but is held for two days before the funds are available. The amount of the deposit is of course tabulated somewhere, but is not credited until the two days pass. This business rule is managed in the accounting software by an electronic form of the same business rule, and the money is credited at the allotted time.

Finally, we need to touch on the idea of states as it relates to computing. When we use the word *state*, we mean the condition or set of conditions that an application is in at any given time. Again, look at the typical ATM machine. The state of the machine at any moment in a transaction is clearly communicated to the user. When you first approach the machine, it is waiting for you to put in your ATM card. As soon as you enter your card, it requests a verification number to validate your use of the identification information transferred from the card. When the number is verified, the machine is then in a state for you to begin whatever transaction you came to conduct. What are some of the characteristics of this state at this moment? The computer knows your name, probably your account number, and also that you have not yet asked it to do any additional work. The state at this point in time may be pretty simple. When you press the appropriate button to withdraw some money, the ATM loads a different screen or set of screens. What happened to the identifying information? It still knows who you are, so the machine had some method of preserving the state between successive levels of the program. The programmer has carefully captured the necessary information for use throughout the program. This maintaining of the current state will continue until you complete all your business and the machine flushes its state memory for the next client.

All of these concepts—*front end, back end, transaction management, middleware, state,* and *business rules*—could conceivably exist in a single layer, but it is unlikely because of the resultant complexity. As an application becomes more complex, it begins to make sense to componentize the processes so that each layer only has to provide the function or set of functions that it was designed to handle. We've introduced a new concept in this paragraph, the concept of a layer. In simple terms, the layer could be considered synonymous with the front end/back end terminology. Thus our simple client/server has two layers or is termed *two-tier*, as it's increasingly being called. But as you may expect, a situation like the banking transactions that I described previously are more likely to be built using *three-tier* or *n-tier* architecture, with each tier representing one or more functions. A typical implementation you might see is the client composing the first tier, business rules residing on the middle tier, and a database on the third tier or back end.

Client/server computing is in use in every conceivable computing environment. As you can see, you use it every time you connect to the Web. When you use the ATM at your bank, you're using it. If you use a database application on the job, it probably is implemented using client/server concepts, especially if you are only one of many users of the same database.

> **NOTE**
>
> One of my co-authors discusses some of the same ideas in Chapter 15, "Introduction to Active Programming," in a little more detail.

Keep in mind that all the technologies developed for client/server computing were created to run over a known network. Most client/server technology was created to run over a corporate LAN or dedicated leased lines. The software and hardware are carefully defined and configured to optimum performance over the LAN. The security of the typical corporate LAN is such that it is reasonably certain that there is no reason to suspect an attempt to compromise corporate data. Even when a corporation expands and connects its affiliates into a WAN architecture, the applications that it runs are confined to a known network topology where every node on the route of any data is clearly defined. If there is a need to create direct connections between client and server, it can be fairly easily accomplished. Because the corporation owns the connections, it is just a matter of need and resources to make any adjustments necessary to make everything work well. Things are different on the Web!

Client/Server on the Web

The Web is the brave new world for client/server technology. You no longer own the wires and the connections that make up the network. The security concerns are entirely different; after all, outside your corporate LAN are your competitors! And because you can no longer guarantee the stability of the network and fix it yourself when it fails, you may have to change the way your applications run. Your applications may communicate with your back end through your own proprietary protocol. Unless you were very forward looking, your applications probably do not understand the protocols used on the Web at all. How exactly *do* you do client/server on the Web? It's not likely to be the same as any other type of client/server setup. These are the questions I hope to answer as I close this chapter. I'll discuss some of the problems that have arisen and how they are being overcome and look at the way client/server is being implemented on the Web.

The Problems Stated

Remember in Chapter 1 when I mentioned that HTTP is the language of the Web? Client/server communication on the Web must start with HTTP. And guess what? One of the most basic aspects of client/server cannot be accomplished at all without some serious programming. Remember that HTTP is a *stateless* protocol. It has no native way to remember what was on the page just before the current page. If you were using an online ATM, after you entered your validation information and clicked on the button to go to the next page, it would have no idea who you were at all on the next page! This is bad! How could you possibly maintain a client/server environment without knowing what state the client is in at a given moment? As I said, without some creative programming, you couldn't. What about the other critical concepts that are components of client/server? Can you see any problems with those concepts on the Web?

It seems that implementing tiers is a natural. It is quite easy to envision the typical three-tier setup being built with the client/server/database structure. What will happen to your transaction management? Are there new challenges when your transactions occur over the Internet instead of a dedicated corporate LAN? One of these is security. On the Internet, all or most of your communication with your tiers may need to be encrypted. If your clients are likely to perform financial transactions, you will probably need to use secure HTTP (HTTPS) for your communication. You may have to re-create your front-end application to utilize this new environment.

And what tools do you use to build these new front ends and back-end components? Are the tools you currently use "Web aware"? Does your application even lend itself to use on the Web at all? Ask yourself these questions and evaluate exactly how you get from your current configuration to running your client/server applications over the Web. Come to think of it, do you even want to run your application over the Web? What are the benefits?

No matter what tools you are using today, the odds are that your tool vendor is already looking at the ways to utilize the Web. Because of the ubiquity of the Web, there's no doubt that you'll find some tool vendor that has the solution you need. So, the tools probably won't be the impediment that you may have originally thought. Visual InterDev may be the only answer you need, both for your database access and to help you connect your existing applications to the Web. Because ASP enables you to access any ODBC-compliant database, you shouldn't have significant problems with that aspect of your application. And if your client/server applications are already running on Windows NT, you're probably not going to need to change much other than to hook up everything in a Web back end. A plus you will probably gain from your new application is that your remote users will now have the ability to run their needed applications from any browser anywhere. Remember that phone book application at the start of the chapter? What if that application were an online price book for a remote sales force? Suppose that you needed to create a new revision to accommodate a new field in your database? With a remote sales force, each person would have to get the new software, load it, and hope that it was installed and configured correctly. If you changed to a Web interface for the same information and needed to change *anything,* you would make all the changes on the Web server, and the next time the sales people connected they would immediately get the new interface. No new software to load, no need to worry about configuration; as long as your back end is running as it needs to, the users' front end will need no changes at all. That's the beauty of using the Web environment.

Client/Server Problems Overcome?

The problem of state changes is being partially overcome using cookies. As I mentioned in Chapter 1, cookies enable you to preserve any information needed on the user's machine. Cookies are limited, though, and have to be inspected and refreshed constantly to guarantee their validity. Cookies aren't automatic, and users can always deny accepting them, so they can't be depended on in every instance. Another way that people are saving state information is by attaching information about the current page in the URL for the next page (see Figure 2.9). Notice the convoluted string in the address window of the browser in this figure. Time Warner's Pathfinder uses the URL to pass state information. It's a complicated way to do it, but in the absence of a standard format, it is necessary.

FIGURE 2.9.

Time Warner's Pathfinder uses the URL to pass state information.

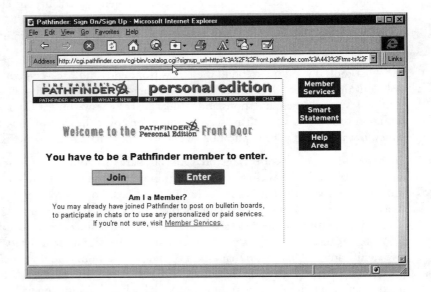

I mentioned CGI applications in Chapter 1 as well. You would use a CGI application to communicate with your back-end database. But you would likely have to preserve state information with this process as well, so the common way that people are overcoming this is by passing additional information to an intermediary program and then performing the database query as another part of the same application. The real problem with CGI is that CGI processes are expensive in the sense of server performance. Each CGI process that is created runs in its own memory space, with its own copy of the server's environment, and thus consumes more resources than just its own.

The combination of Visual InterDev and IIS means that you are no longer required to use such creative methods to manage state information. ASP has a `Session` object that maintains the state for the entire application represented by a client's access to a Web site. You can use

CGI and cookies if you want to do so, but state management is assured using the Session object. ASP keeps track of each unique client but leverages legacy techniques to create the best of both worlds.

Summary

In this chapter we looked at database technology, how it has evolved, and the creation of the SQL standard. We also looked briefly at client/server computing and how it is being translated to the Web.

In the next chapter we look at Microsoft's vision for the Web and how Visual InterDev expresses that vision.

2

RELATIONAL DATABASES AND TECHNOLOGY

Microsoft's Vision and Visual InterDev

by Glenn Fincher

IN THIS CHAPTER

CHAPTER 3

Bill Gates's famous statement of Microsoft's vision as voiced several years ago is *Information at your fingertips.*" It was meant to voice the intention to create applications that are easier to use, that enable new kinds of collaborative thinking, that, in effect, remove "*the one task, one application*" mode of computer usage. This slogan has taken on new meaning in the age of the Internet. Today, with the ubiquity of the Internet, the slogan could represent the entire computer industry with just a little change. "Information *in your face!*" could be the new slogan that best expresses not only Microsoft's but also the rest of the industry's present course. If you look at the largest or smallest hardware or software companies, you'll see them investing an incredible amount of money and effort into Internet-enabling their entire suite of products. The Web is clearly in the center of their business plans. With plans to "push" everything from up-to-the-minute news, product updates, or stock quotes directly to your PC, "Information in your face!" is closer to becoming a reality. With today's applications you are able to download product updates to your desktop, receive online technical support, or even play a computer game across the Internet with an opponent on the other side of the globe. Ordering software or clothes, collaborating on documents, building Web sites, or even talking on your Internet phone are more and more the way we work.

> **NOTE**
>
> Although it hardly seems possible, "Information At Your Fingertips" or IAYF was first propounded in a COMDEX keynote speech in 1990.

To survive in this kind of business climate, a company must constantly reevaluate its direction and make midcourse corrections. Microsoft has an incredible proclivity for reinventing itself every few years. It is extremely nimble and seemingly able to change course with an ease that other companies can only wish to imitate. Because of this ability to change so totally so quickly, Microsoft sometimes leaves the rest of the industry reeling with the changes. But, the outcome is usually a new level of compelling software for the masses of people running Windows. With the Internet as the center of the computing universe, Microsoft's development vision is no different. Microsoft is on a course to make the Internet the center of its software universe as well. In this chapter we will look at Microsoft's vision and how Visual InterDev fits that vision. Additionally, we'll see how Visual InterDev represents a new paradigm of applications—applications without walls. We'll look at Microsoft's

- Vision for the Web
- Illustrative sites
- Visual InterDev vision

You've seen in earlier chapters how traditional Web programming and database applications are accomplished today, and I hope that this chapter will be the necessary bridge from what you were able to do to what you can do with Visual InterDev. We'll look at each area listed previously and try to illustrate the problems Microsoft wants to solve. We'll see its vision for the area, and the solutions that Visual InterDev offers for this area. Finally, we'll take a quick look at the vision for Visual InterDev itself. What does Microsoft want you to do with Visual InterDev? After reading this chapter, I hope that you are challenged to rethink your development plans and delve into the rest of the book with a fresh view of the possibilities. What I hope to show you in this chapter is that Visual InterDev represents the best tool for you to accomplish your development goals. Along the way I hope to help you understand where Microsoft wants to take you when it asks, "Where do you want to go today?"

A Vision for the Web

Microsoft has attacked the Internet with a vengeance. Since its December 7, 1995 manifesto in which it announced a comprehensive corporate redirection, it has relentlessly revamped, recoded, and reorganized its vast software company around the Internet. With at least monthly announcements and developments to match them, it has moved from a company seemingly unaware of the Internet and the impact it could make on the future to a company leading the way with tools, applications, and programs. If you point your Web browser to any section of Microsoft's Web site (see Figures 3.1 through 3.3), you'll see that the Internet is driving much of what it does, and much of what it wants to enable you to do with your development.

3

MICROSOFT'S VISION AND VISUAL INTERDEV

FIGURE 3.1.

Microsoft's Press Release page always has news of new Internet-related developments.

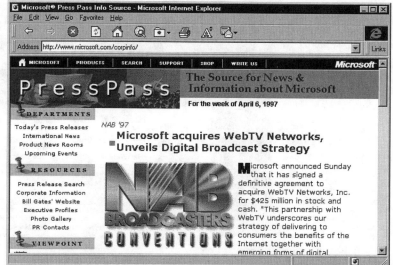

NOTE

Read the latest from Microsoft's corporate Press Release page (see Figure 3.1):

`http://www.microsoft.com/corpinfo/`

FIGURE 3.2.

Microsoft Visual Studio enables a new range of Internet development.

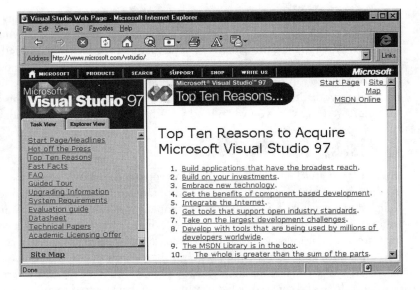

FIGURE 3.3.

Microsoft SiteBuilder Network is a virtual cornucopia of Web development resources.

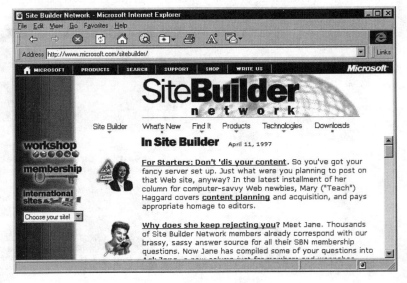

The Vision

The problems that people face using the Internet are as varied as the people using it. If you're a Web developer or Internet service provider (ISP) creating a commercial site for a customer, you're concerned about issues such as the visual layout, the content, the hardware, and the software. If you're a potential customer of that site, you might want only to be able to quickly navigate to the area of the site you are most interested in to purchase the good or service you were looking for. The site developer's problems boil down to how to make your visit to the site fulfilling for you. Issues such as bandwidth, coherent navigation, and secure access to online ordering are all important for these users. Online gamers have similar but slightly different concerns. They might also be interested in coherent navigation and, of course, bandwidth is also a concern. Online ordering is probably not an issue, but other issues such as communication with other players online will probably be a big one. All of these issues are real problems that sites face as they attempt to use the Web to provide compelling solutions for their users. Tim Berners-Lee simply did not expect all these uses of the Web when he first designed it.

Microsoft wants to provide the best tools for these different users. Whether it's the best browser to view the site, the best Web software to host the site, or the best coherent set of tools to build it, Microsoft wants to be there with its solutions. Along the way, the resulting experience for all those users should be exactly where *they* wanted to go. That's Microsoft's vision in a nutshell. End user applications, development tools, game environments, even hardware—all should give their users a compelling experience. And increasingly that experience is tied to the Internet and the Web.

> **NOTE**
>
> A recent addition to the Microsoft Web site is a site dedicated to the ISP (see Figure 3.4). This site offers quick access to everything the ISP needs to utilize Microsoft tools.

FIGURE 3.4.
Microsoft offers a one-stop site for ISPs.

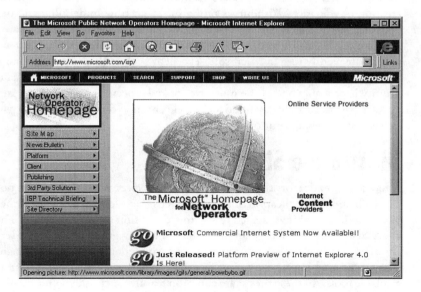

On July 16, 1996, Microsoft presented the WWLive event, which was simulcast across the world to approximately 20,000 Webmasters, developers, designers, and others. This event was created to showcase the wealth of tools, techniques, and creativity that goes into creating a leading edge Web site. Besides the wealth of generally good information that was presented, the show's producers distilled the day's instruction down to seven key concepts for creating compelling Web sites. They called these concepts the "Seven Steps To Highly Effective Web Sites":

- Define & Design
- Author & Manage
- Activate the Client
- Integrate into the Desktop
- Activate Your Server
- Create a Community
- Stay Connected

TIP

You'll find the entire WWLive event detailed online at
`http://204.203.124.10/wwlive/ie3/a_default.htm`

We won't take the time to detail each of these steps, but it should begin to be obvious how these statements reflect Microsoft's vision for the Web. The first two steps involve the initial creation of your site. Without spending sufficient time in defining and designing, authoring your site will be much harder. The authoring and management aspects are well met in Visual InterDev, as are most of the other steps. But implementing the last three steps probably are even more readily seen in Microsoft's excellent Web tools. Activating your server is done with ASP; you create a dynamic Web site using HTML + scripting + components. Creating a community is probably one of the most overlooked aspects of a site or even an application. But if you are able to successfully build a clientele around your Web site, you will be more likely to succeed at achieving your original goals.

Illustrative Sites

A few online endeavors that Microsoft has created serve as good cases in point of its vision for the Web and the application of the seven steps. Let's look at a couple of the more popular services that Microsoft has created to see how this vision drives the service. The sites we will look at are Slate—the E-Zine; Sidewalk—the online city guide, the SiteBuilder Network, and the Internet Gaming Zone—an online gamer's wonderland. All these are examples of the vision. They've created innovative extensive online experiences that fully illustrate the depth of the available tools. All these sites share common features such as dynamic content via Active Server Pages, personalized content and views, and interaction via community building forums.

The addresses are

SLATE—`http://www.slate.com/default.asp`.

Sidewalk—`http://www.sidewalk.com/`

SiteBuilder—`http://www.microsoft.com/sitebuilder/`

Internet Gaming Zone—`http://www.zone.com/`

> ### TIP
>
> The content of these sites is dynamic, changing constantly. We invite you to make frequent visits to discover new ideas for your own dynamic site construction.

Slate

Slate is the online magazine created by Microsoft in mid-1996 as a collaborative adventure with Michael Kinsley. It was originally slated (no pun intended!) to be an online subscription magazine, but instead the online edition remains free and is supported by advertising. When you connect to Slate, you'll immediately notice its somewhat clean, sparse graphics, and because the site is built using ASP, the pages are generated on-the-fly. Slate keeps its stories in a database, and the individual stories that comprise an edition are dynamically assembled into HTML by the Active Server Pages. Note that in Figure 3.5, at the top of the left column, you are given the option of clicking on Date to reorder the page. When you click on the word Date in the right-hand column, Slate reloads the page ordered as you requested as shown in Figure 3.6. Though this may be a minor change, the feature gives the user a feeling of control. This personalization is a real key to creating a compelling online experience.

FIGURE 3.5.

When you click on the word Date, *Slate dynamically reformats the page.*

FIGURE 3.6.

The same page reformatted and sorted by date instead of page number.

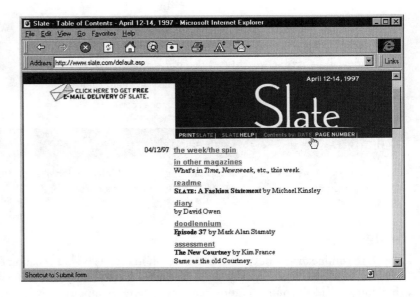

What's most interesting here is that the programmers of Slate decided it was important to give the user the choice. Using ASP, they implemented that choice as a POST method of the default.asp file. In other words, if the file is called via the "normal" method resulting in a GET method, the default sort algorithm is used—sort stories by page number. But if the user wants to see the articles sorted by date, the same default.asp is called again using the POST method while passing the ASP file the name/value pairs defined in the form to create the change. Listing 3.1 shows the HTML fragment used for the post.

Listing 3.1. Slate HTML fragment to change the article view.

```
<FORM METHOD=POST ACTION="default.asp">
<INPUT TYPE=hidden NAME="rand" VALUE=41521>
<INPUT TYPE=hidden NAME="toc" VALUE="date-short">
```

TIP

Don't worry about the code to do these kinds of things right now; there's plenty of time for that in the rest of the book! Chapter 15, "Introduction to Active Programming," will be a good place to start.

Another feature that Slate uses well is its reader forums (see Figure 3.7) to build community. "The Fray" reader forums give the user a chance to "sound off" in a real-time letter to the editor. As you can see, readers can directly enter their comments about a specific article and even engage in conversation with other readers. This feature is implemented using ASP pages as well, and is another example of Microsoft's vision for the Internet and how it is best accomplished. Users are invited to enter the discussion and log in to participate (see Figure 3.8). Once you are logged in, you can enter the discussion by posting in any area as seen in Figure 3.9.

FIGURE 3.7.

Slate's forums give readers an opportunity to discuss an article.

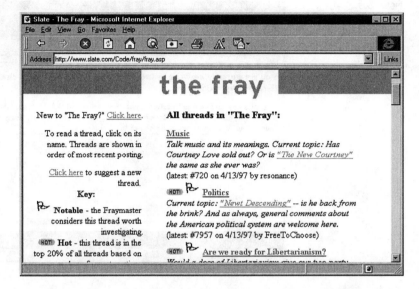

FIGURE 3.8.

Slate users first log in to be allowed to post a comment.

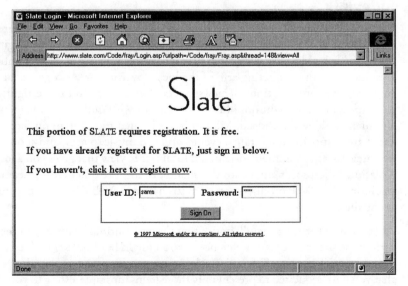

3

MICROSOFT'S
VISION AND
VISUAL INTERDEV

The combination of these features and the actual Slate content helped make Slate one of the most popular sites on the Web. Microsoft's vision is that features from sites like Slate will become the norm on the Web—using features that invite participation by the users instead of just static information. Compelling sites that invite frequent return visits are the goal of Microsoft. We'll look at another Microsoft site to see what we can glean from its layout and construction.

FIGURE 3.9.

When you want to post a comment, you enter it via a standard Web-based form.

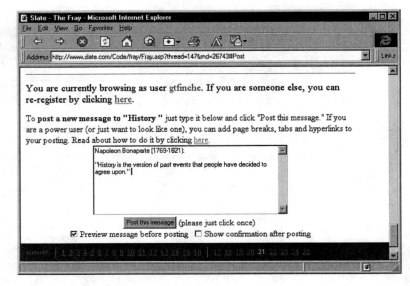

Sidewalk

Sidewalk is Microsoft's entry into the online city guide market (see Figure 3.10). Other companies with intents in this direction are Yahoo! and America Online Digital City. Many cities have established locally based Web sites under the auspices of the Chamber of Commerce, or in some cases, the marketing arm of the local government. Also typical are city guides created by local news organizations or newspapers. These sites tend to be tightly aligned with their local sponsor, and might not illustrate the locale with quite the same focus as an independent site such as Sidewalk. Indeed, Microsoft has limited the content on Sidewalk to six entertainment areas: movies, restaurants, events, arts and music, places, and sports and recreation. The one area not entertainment-oriented is local traffic view that gives you a local view of the traffic situation. Microsoft's entry into this market is, like the other areas, meant to showcase the capabilities of its Web products as well as to challenge Web site developers to create sites of similar quality.

As you navigate the site, you'll notice that the site continually offers you the opportunity to customize the site to suit your preferences, as you might have already noticed in Figure 3.10. When you customize the site, Sidewalk tracks your navigation and applies the customization features that you have requested to present only those items most interesting to you. Using the features of ASP and standard Web cookies, Sidewalk identifies you each time you enter the site without requiring a login form as Slate does. And with this identification via cookies come some expected changes to the information that the site offers. You'll notice that the next time you visit the site, Sidewalk displays a list of custom choices based on your preferences (see Figure 3.11).

FIGURE 3.10.

seattle.sidewalk.com
*offers a ready reference
to the sites and sounds
of Seattle.*

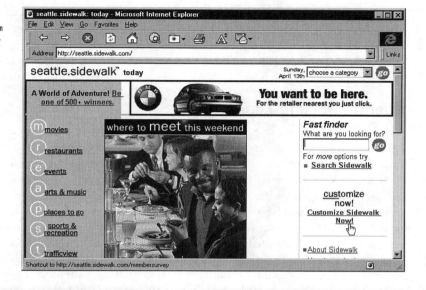

3

MICROSOFT'S VISION AND VISUAL INTERDEV

FIGURE 3.11.

*When you customize
your preferences,
Sidewalk shows you
personalized pages
based on your choices.*

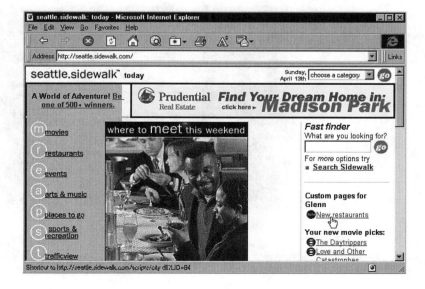

This kind of personalization is quite powerful. Using a combination of traditional Web programming and ASP, Sidewalk gives the site that personal touch that invites you back again and again. Visual InterDev allows you to create sites like Sidewalk, leveraging any and all current Web technology as needed. You'll learn more about utilizing these kinds of features of ASP in Chapter 15. Let's look at another site that illustrates the vision of Microsoft for the Web.

Internet Gaming Zone

The Internet Gaming Zone (http://www.zone.com/) is one of the more interesting sites that Microsoft programmers have created (see Figure 3.12). The Zone is an online gamer's paradise. The Zone allows you to connect with other game players across the Internet to play games such as Chess, Hearts, and *Monster Truck Madness*. When you register as a Zone member, you can play online games with other members all over the globe, conduct chats to share playing tips, or enter the Zone BBS with its interactive forums. A significant difference with the Zone registration and login usage is that the Zone uses an application that you download to your own computer and execute before you enter the Zone. This application illustrates a way to introduce a more familiar client/server application metaphor to your Web use. When you create a client/server application that utilizes Web technology, your users can literally be anywhere on the Internet. They are not limited to your own private LAN. But, it should also be obvious that these same technologies would work as well in an intranet. Figure 3.13 shows the Zone login dialog. When you enter your login name and password, the application attempts to connect to the login server to validate your credentials (see Figure 3.14).

FIGURE 3.12.

The Internet Gaming Zone illustrates Microsoft's vision in an innovative fashion.

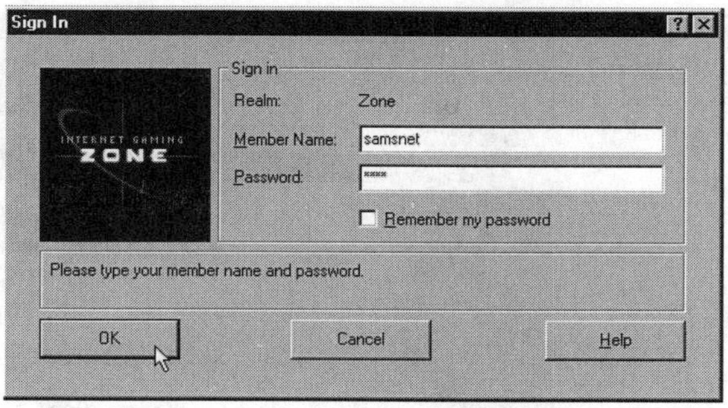

FIGURE 3.13.
The Zone uses a more traditional application to handle logging into the server.

FIGURE 3.14.
The Zone application contacts the dedicated login server to validate your credentials.

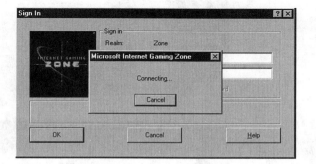

If you are implementing an intranet, or planning on using the PPTP to create a Virtual Private Network, these examples should help you see how you can utilize the Web to make these tasks easier. You don't have to create applications that run inside the browser if your users are already accustomed to using your existing client/server application. Just re-create that application to leverage the Internet and the Web in such a way that your users get all their benefits. I won't attempt to show you how to play any of the games on the Zone, but I invite you to look around and use this somewhat nontraditional site to challenge you to innovation.

SiteBuilder Network

The SiteBuilder Network (see Figure 3.15) is Microsoft's most significant contribution to the Web. I say that because the site attempts to show exactly how to use the Web to create any kind of site or application that you can envision. The reason that I find it so significant is that the information available on the SiteBuilder Network is not limited to Microsoft tools. When you join SiteBuilder as a member, you are able to download a number of tools to enhance your Web development. Figure 3.16 shows a partial list of downloads available in early April 1997. Many of these applications actually are demo or beta versions, but many more are full-fledged versions of the products for SiteBuilder users. If you really want to see Microsoft's vision for the Web, SiteBuilder is the place to go.

FIGURE 3.15.

SiteBuilder Network is Microsoft's dedicated Web development site.

FIGURE 3.16.

Members of the SiteBuilder Network are offered a wealth of Web development software downloads.

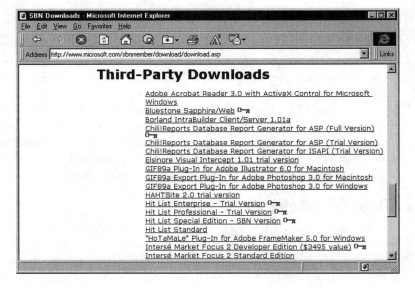

One new area of the SiteBuilder Network is an online magazine illustrating key technologies for Web development. Here you'll find the latest information on cutting-edge Web development comparable to what you'd expect to find in other online Web magazines such as *Web Developer* or *Web Review*. Look around for articles of interest such as the recent article on keeping your content up-to-date (see Figure 3.17), or the article about deciding on your Web server software and hardware (see Figure 3.18). These columns and others illustrate the state of Web development.

FIGURE 3.17.

The SiteBuilder Network magazine includes articles such as this one on updating content.

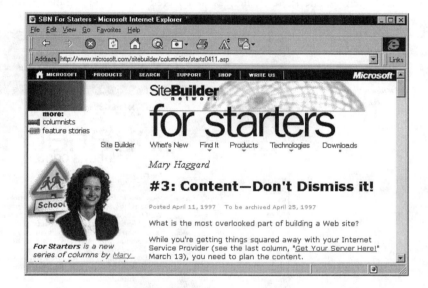

FIGURE 3.18.

Another recent article on SiteBuilder Network was the article on selecting a server.

Another area of SiteBuilder that illustrates Microsoft's vision for the Web is the Intranet Center (see Figure 3.19). One of the most compelling uses of the Web is the intranet. With many companies opening public Internet sites, it shouldn't be very surprising that many more companies are creating intranets. Without some of the inherent security problems faced on the Internet, intranets offer compelling uses for a corporation. Centralized information, easy client access, and the reduced need for paper distribution of such standards as employee manuals, job postings, and so on make an intranet an ideal medium. Intranets have unique problems and challenges, and these challenges are covered well in the Intranet Solutions Center.

FIGURE 3.19.

The Intranet Center of SiteBuilder Network contains a wealth of information about intranets.

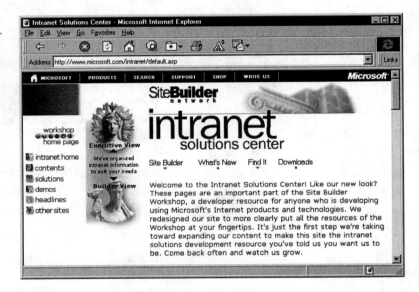

An example of the type of information available in the Intranet Center is a demonstration intranet for the fictitious Volcano Coffee Company (see Figure 3.20). This demo intranet gives you a good idea of the kinds of ways you could leverage the existing information your company already depends on to create your own intranet or ideas for a customer's intranet. Sample areas such as the one for the finance department (see Figures 3.21 and 3.22) illustrate the use of currently available data to add content to an intranet.

You should note that all this information simply views existing data that most finance departments already maintain. What this illustrates is that using the Web to allow access to existing data is a task accomplished fairly easily. Using ASP, you could even have all the data generated dynamically using ActiveX Automation on the server to automate the creation of the Web pages.

FIGURE 3.20.

A demonstration intranet for the fictitious Volcano Coffee Company.

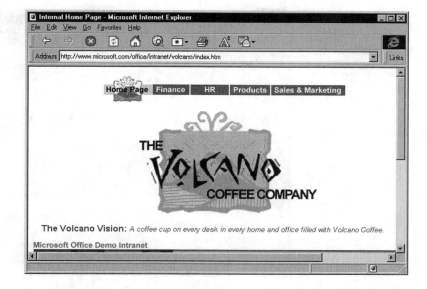

FIGURE 3.21.

The finance department of the Volcano Coffee Company.

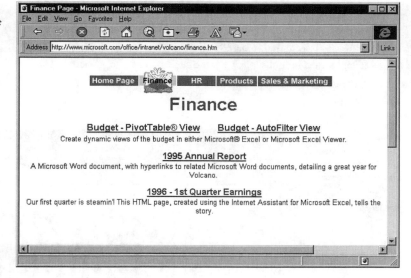

FIGURE 3.22.
Volcano Coffee quarterly earnings statement from the demonstration intranet.

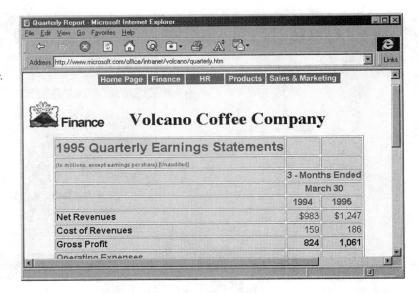

Another site you simply have to visit is *Unauthorized SiteBuilder* (see Figure 3.23)—an excellent independent site for Web development using Microsoft tools:

```
http://www.sitebuilder.net/
```

FIGURE 3.23.
The Unauthorized SiteBuilder *site is a must-see site for the ASP developer.*

Created by a convinced ASP user, the *Unauthorized SiteBuilder* site showcases the work of a number of other dedicated Web developers. These developers use all of Microsoft's Web tools and have created some of the best sites on the Web. In fact, another site that you'll find mentioned at the *Unauthorized SiteBuilder* site is one called the *Best & Brightest* (see Figure 3.24); it lists hundreds of other sites using ASP. These sites illustrate every level of site creation using ASP.

FIGURE 3.24.

Best & Brightest *highlights sites that use Microsoft ASP.*

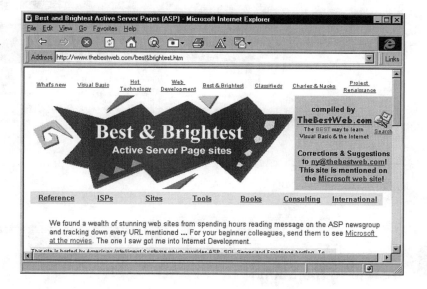

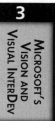

We've chosen to illustrate Microsoft's vision for the Web by using "live" illustration, believing that if a "*picture is worth a thousand words*" then it's possible that a live view of a site Web might be worth a similar amount. Make no mistake about it, Microsoft wants you to use its tools to create the best Web site anyone has ever visited. All these sites that we've illustrated demonstrate the capabilities of the tools in a visual way. To close this chapter, we will take a quick look at Visual InterDev to see how it might be used to illustrate *your* own vision for *your* Web.

The Visual InterDev Vision

Microsoft's vision for the Web as illustrated with Visual InterDev is to provide the best tools for rapid Internet development. Visual InterDev (see Figure 3.25) combines all the tools you need to create Web sites like those we've looked at earlier in this chapter. Each of those sites use client/server technology transformed by the Web to provide users with unique information sources. The range of tools that Microsoft has packed into Visual InterDev and the combined documentation on the CD-ROM will help you quickly become an expert Web developer. One thing I can highly recommend (besides reading the rest of this book!) is that you take the time to work through the ASP Roadmap tutorial. This tutorial is an excellent introduction to ASP development, and one that you are likely to overlook. We'll be looking at the Adventure Works sample site that ships with Visual InterDev to illustrate the way that Visual InterDev makes your Web development easier.

FIGURE 3.25.

Visual InterDev's integrated development environment.

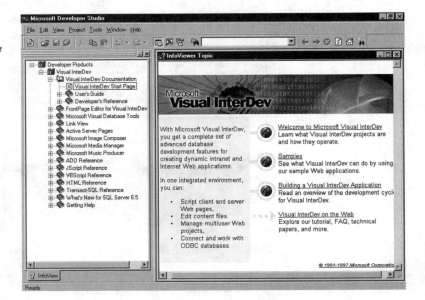

Installing the Samples

Microsoft would like to think that you installed all the sample files they so carefully created to accompany Visual InterDev, but that might not be the case. So we need to spend just a little bit of time showing you how to install these pieces of the software. You'll find sample code fragments throughout the documentation, but there are also several complete sample sites on your CD-ROM. When you installed Visual InterDev the first time, you were given the options to install the client and server pieces of Visual InterDev as seen in Figure 3.26. Some of the sample applications are delivered as part of the Active Server Pages selection, and other samples are installed along with Visual InterDev. To install all the sample files (you can always uninstall them at a later time), you will need to make sure you install both sets. We'll first look at the installation of the samples that are part of Visual InterDev.

Figure 3.26.

You install each of Visual InterDev's components from this setup dialog.

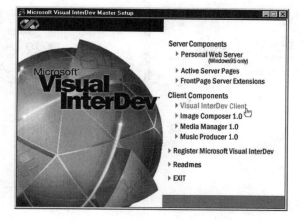

As you see in Figure 3.26, we've selected the Visual InterDev Client portion of the installation. If you installed Visual InterDev with the "Typical" mode of installation, the tutorial and sample applications are not installed. If that is the case, you will need to re-run setup to install those pieces. If you are installing Visual InterDev for the first time, choose the Custom mode as shown in Figure 3.27. Then you will be able to select the Sample Application Files (see Figure 3.28). This will install Visual InterDev and all the necessary tutorial and sample files.

Figure 3.27.

Choose the Custom mode of installation to be able to select the Sample files.

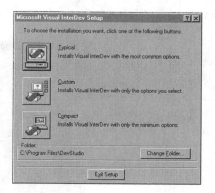

TIP

If you have already installed Visual InterDev without these files, re-running setup and choosing the Add/Remove button will show the same screen for you to make the necessary choices you saw in Figure 3.27.

3

MICROSOFT'S VISION AND VISUAL INTERDEV

FIGURE 3.28.

*Select Sample
Application Files from
the Custom dialog.*

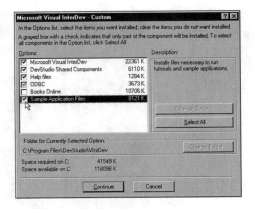

Once you have installed the sample files integrated into the Visual InterDev Client, you can install the ASP Roadmap and Adventure Work site. This part of the product is bundled with the Active Server Pages selection you might have noticed in Figure 3.27. If you have already installed ASP without these samples, you will need to first uninstall the ASP section and reinstall to select the sample files. When you reinstall ASP, make sure that you select the "On-line documentation, tutorial, Adventure Works sample site and collection of sample pages" selection as shown in Figure 3.29. This will install all the sample files for the ASP Roadmap and the Adventure Works content. With all the samples installed, you will be able to work through the ASP Roadmap and run the Adventure Works sample site.

FIGURE 3.29.

*Select "On-line
documentation,
tutorial,..." from the
ASP setup dialog.*

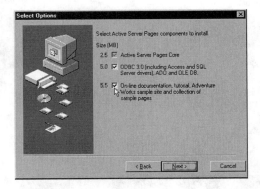

ASP Roadmap

The ASP Roadmap (see Figure 3.30) is a complete online reference library for ASP files. In addition to a tutorial with step-by-step lessons, the Roadmap files also include documentation on JavaScript, VBScript, the ASP object reference, and a programmer's reference. The lessons are worthwhile if you intend to master ASP, and offer one of the best ways to get up to speed quickly. Besides the Adventure Works site, there are a number of concise ASP Samples (see Figure 3.31) that illustrate single concepts or ideas.

Figure 3.30.

The ASP Roadmap is an excellent online tutorial for the use of Visual InterDev.

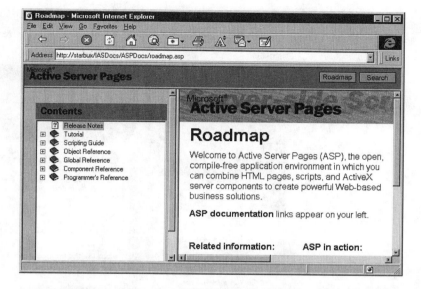

Figure 3.31.

Small ASP Samples illustrate single features or concepts.

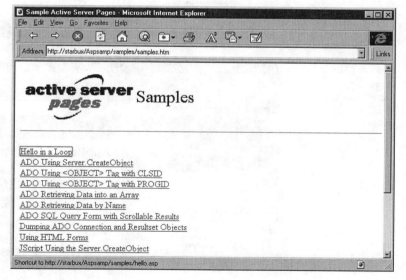

The Roadmap takes you through each aspect of the creation of a site and illustrates each concept with sample code. For example, the global.asa file (see Figure 3.32) is a global file that allows you to specify events or declare objects whose scope envelops the entire Web (or Application in Visual InterDev parlance). One of the available application-level events is the Application_OnStart (see Figure 3.33) event that appropriately enough executes its code when any user enters the site. Its use is fully detailed and examples are given. Within Visual InterDev, the global.asa file can be edited as you would edit any other text file (see Figure 3.34). From this brief foray, you should begin to see the benefits of investigating the Roadmap more fully. We'll look next at some of the features implemented within the Adventure Works site.

FIGURE 3.32.

The global.asa *file is fully documented within the ASP Roadmap.*

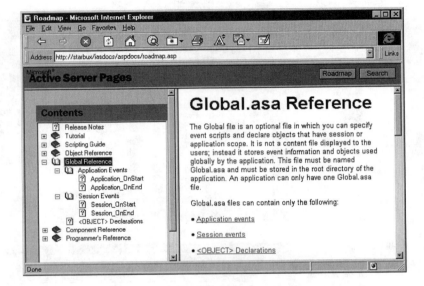

FIGURE 3.33.

Events such as the Application_OnStart *event are fully documented.*

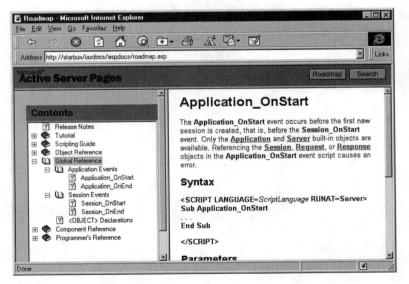

FIGURE 3.34.

Editing the global.asa *file is done within Visual InterDev.*

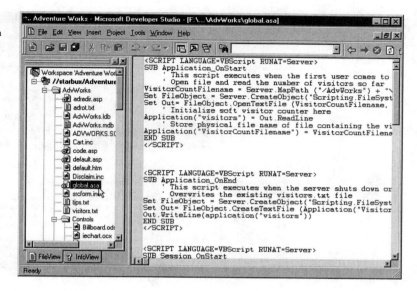

Adventure Works Site

Since we've looked briefly at the ASP Roadmap, let's look briefly at the Adventure Works site (see Figure 3.35). In some ways, this site is similar to the ones we looked at earlier, except that in this case, you have all the source code (see Figure 3.36) for the site! In the "old" days of the Web, unless you were doing everything using server-side scripting, your HTML and scripting source was available to anyone. Simply by using the View | Source option of his browser, anyone could peruse and/or steal your hard-written work. Even popular client-side scripting via JavaScript or VBScript is subject to the same danger. But when you execute your scripts on the server and then generate standard HTML, the client is going to see only the HTML you generated.

An especially interesting section of the sample site is the area implementing an intranet—the Inner Trail (see Figure 3.37). This section is a snapshot of the kinds of information that you might make available for your sales force. The data that is shown to the client is dynamically generated when the page is executed. A real-time illustration of a client/server database query, this type of application is exactly what you might be looking to build. Now you have the sample code, as well as detailed documentation on its use. Each section of the Inner Trail illustrates slightly different code to query the same database.

Another section of the site that is illustrative of the kind of site you might want to create is the "Geared Up" area. This is a live online catalog database that allows customers to browse through the site for the product of interest and buy it online. For example, if you wanted to purchase some Rock Shoes (see Figure 3.38), you'd navigate to the shoe section and place your order. A well-implemented site would show you exactly what you had ordered and give you a chance to cancel the order or shop for more (see Figure 3.39). The Adventure Works sample site contains a working implementation of a shopping cart application that you can use as a base for your own creation.

FIGURE 3.35.

Adventure Works is a complete sample Web site that ships with Visual InterDev.

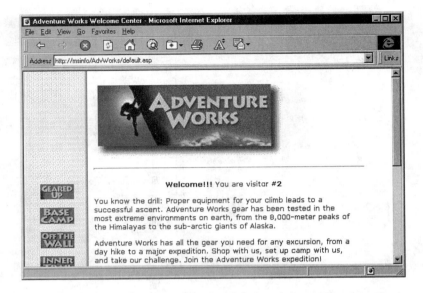

FIGURE 3.36.

You can view, edit, or browse the source code within Visual InterDev.

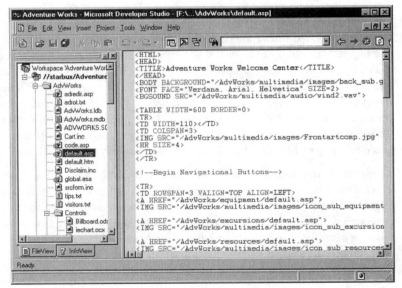

As you can see, there is more to Visual InterDev than you might have initially thought. The vision of Microsoft is to build state-of-the-art tools to allow *you* to create "Best-of-the-Web" sites. I think that by now you'll agree with me that it has accomplished its goal.

FIGURE 3.37.

If you are thinking of building an intranet, click on Inner Trail for a sample.

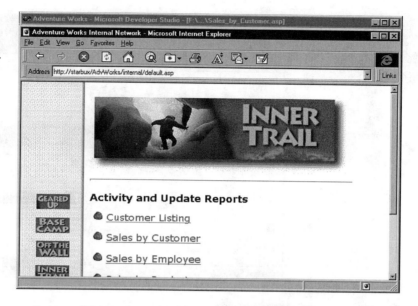

FIGURE 3.38.

The catalog section illustrates an online catalog similar to others you've seen on the Web.

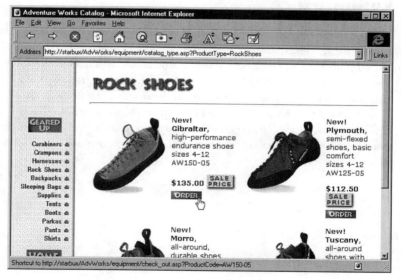

FIGURE 3.39.

The shopping cart application illustrates a common use on the Web.

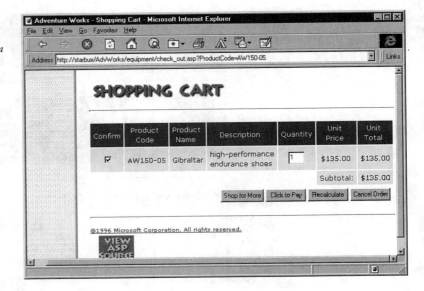

Summary

In this section of the book, we've looked at some of the issues that shape the Web today. In this chapter we've looked at several examples of Microsoft's vision for the Web by looking at several sample Web sites that best illustrate this vision. Microsoft hopes that its example in these diverse areas of the Web will "seed" the Web with innovation. By the use of community interaction and active or dynamic content, Web sites can capture users' interest and revitalize the Web. Visual InterDev is a great tool to help you build sites as innovative as these we've shown in this chapter, and will help you show *your* vision for the Web. In the next section of the book, you'll be treated to a detailed overview of each major feature of Active Server development using Visual InterDev.

II

PART

Getting Started with Visual InterDev

Client- and Server-Side Scripting

by Hei Lam

IN THIS CHAPTER

CHAPTER 4

Microsoft's Visual InterDev is an integrated visual development tool that provides a nice set of features for developing dynamic Internet and intranet Web-based applications. One of these features is ActiveX Scripting support. When I say *ActiveX Scripting,* I mean a scripting language that can be used with ActiveX controls and ActiveX components in the client-side Web page or the server-side page (Active Server Pages). Visual InterDev supports both VBScript and JavaScript, although VBScript is the default scripting language that is used for primary scripting. The default scripting language can be selected in the HTML tab of the Options dialog box of Visual InterDev. With this scripting support, the software developers have the choice to

- Pick their favorite scripting language
- Use client-side scripting, server-side scripting, or both
- Build programming logic, using functions within the HTML code
- Link and automate ActiveX controls and components such as Java applets

With these programming capabilities, an active, dynamic, and powerful Web-based application need not be a difficult task for software developers.

VBScript

VBScript is subset of Visual Basic for Applications (VBA) that was developed by Microsoft. It is designed to be a small, fast, secure, and lightweight interpreter language for use in Web application development. It is fully compatible with Visual Basic. If you know how to program in Visual Basic, you should have no problem writing VBScript code. Even if you have not used Visual Basic before, it is still a simple programming language to learn compared to programming languages such as C and C++.

JavaScript

JavaScript is an interpreted, easy-to-use, object-based scripting language designed for creating live online applications and compelling, interactive Web content for the Internet and intranets. JavaScript is analogous to VBScript. People with little or no programming experience can learn JavaScript easily. JavaScript is a product of Sun Microsystems, Inc. and Netscape Communications Corporation. Microsoft has its own version of JavaScript called JScript.

Client-Side Scripting

Before the invention of VBScript and JavaScript, the content of Web pages was written in Hypertext Markup Language (HTML), which has no processing power at all. HTML Web pages are used primarily for displaying information that is retrieved from the Web server. All the necessary processing is done on the server. If the Web application wants to process the data entered from the user, or needs to do a query against the back-end database, a server-side Common Gateway Interface (CGI) program must be involved. Furthermore, there is no chance to validate a user's input at the client side before it is sent to the server.

Client-side scripting, either VBScript or JavaScript, can solve those kind of problems. With embedded VBScript or JavaScript code in the HTML page, the input data of a Web page can be checked before being sent to the server. This client-side local processing eliminates some of the unnecessary steps that send data across the network. For example, a logon Web page that contains two data input fields for a user ID and a user password can be validated by the client-side VBScript logic. If a user forgets to enter either the user ID or password, his input data should not be sent to the server unless both input fields have been filled. The following example shows how VBScript validates the user's input data in a Web page:

```
*    <FORM NAME="LogOn">
     userid: <INPUT NAME="UserID" VALUE=""
     MAXLENGTH="10" SIZE=40>
     userpw: <INPUT NAME="UserPW" VALUE=""
     MAXLENGTH="10" SIZE=40>
     INPUT TYPE="BUTTON" VALUE="Log In" NAME="LOGON">
     </FORM>

     <SCRIPT LANGUAGE="VBScript">
     Sub LOGON_OnClick
     Dim LogOnForm
     Set LogOnForm=Document.LogOn
     If Rtrim(LogOnForm.UserID.Value="" or Rtrim(LogOnForm.UserPW.Value="" then
         MSgBox ("Log On", 64, "Please enter your user ID and password.")
     Else
         LogOn.Submit
     End If
     </SCRIPT>
```

When the Logon button is clicked, the VBScript subroutine LOGON is executed. If either the User ID field or Password field is missing data, the incomplete data will not be sent to the server. Instead, a warning message is displayed on the screen. Once these two input fields are filled and the Logon button is clicked, the data of these two fields will be submitted to the server through the environment variables.

> **NOTE**
>
> The client-side script is embedded in the Web page that is downloaded from the Web server.

The script code is executed by the ActiveX scripting engine within the Web browser.

Client-side scripting not only provides the capability to create variables, control logic, programming flow, and procedures in HTML pages, but it also can be used to "glue" the ActiveX controls and components. It is also valuable and useful in active and dynamic Web page development, especially when you consider that component software technology such as ActiveX controls and Java applets is going to play an important role in the future of computing. Client-side scripting can control and customize the behavior of the ActiveX controls and components by setting the object's properties, calling the object's methods, or firing the object's events. VBScript can also access the properties and methods of the Internet Explorer Web browser. The behavior of Internet Explorer can be controlled by the Web application through VBScript code as well.

In the Visual InterDev IDE, client-side scripting can be created easily from the Script Wizard. The Script Wizard enables you to quickly add ActiveX scripting to the controls in a Web page. To start the Script Wizard, select the Script Wizard command from the View menu on the main toolbar.

> **NOTE**
>
> See Chapter 15, "Introduction to Active Programming," for more details about client-side scripting programming.

Server-Side Scripting

The most interesting and exciting feature of the Web server-side development provided by Microsoft recently is the *Active Server Pages* (ASP), which is a new feature of Microsoft Internet Information Server (IIS) 3.0. This feature makes active Web content development much easier. Active Server Pages are based on the ActiveX scripting engine that is used for executing the server-side scripting such as VBScript and JavaScript code. Visual InterDev provides a visual, ease-to-use development environment to create Active Server Pages. As mentioned, Visual InterDev supports both VBScript and JavaScript in client-side or server-side scripting.

Before the evolution of Active Server Pages, Web server-side processing was based on CGI, which is an interface between an application and a Web server. This interface has been used in Web development since 1993. An application that follows the CGI specification and runs on the server-side machine is called a *CGI application*. As mentioned, a server-side CGI program must be involved when the Web application needs to access the back-end database. In a CGI application, the browser passes data to the server through environment variables. The server picks up the data and sends it to a separate executable that is executed. Once this server-side executable completes its processing, the expected result is sent back to the client side using the same mechanism. CGI applications can do a lot of things, such as respond to the Web client input, process forms, access the back-end database, and build HTML pages with data. However, a CGI program runs as a separate process in the server machine, which means that the CGI application needs its own CPU processing time and has its own overhead. For a busy Web server that may have thousands or even more hits daily, CGI will definitely generate enough overhead to reduce the server machine's performance. CGI is relatively slow and inefficient because of parameters passing between the client and server sides.

The server-side scripting technique in Visual InterDev is quite different. The scripting engine is tightly integrated with the Internet Information Server as an in-process component, which is a DLL. Obviously, a program that runs as in-process is faster than if it were to run out-of-process in the Web server. Also, there are no compilation or link steps for executing the server-side scripts. Compared to CGI executables, VBScript and JavaScript are easier to create, use, and modify. Therefore, instead of having to write CGI programs on the server, VBScript or JavaScript is the better solution for developing server logic.

Scripting functionality on the server side is similar to the client side. Both involve HTML and a scripting language, and both can add controls to the Web page. But server-side scripting has some unique characteristics:

- The server-side scripts are embedded in .asp files.
- The server-side scripts are processed on the server side; they are not sent to the client side.
- The server-side scripts can be used to modify the client-side script.

The following simple example shows how to embed a server-side script into the .asp file:

```
<HTML>

<%  If OrderAmount < 100 Then
        percent="5%"
    Elseif OrderAmount < 200 Then
        percent="10%"
    Else
        percent="15%"
    End if %>

<P> Thank you for your order.  Your discount will be <%=percent%> </P>

</HTML>
```

All the scripting logic within the server script tag (designated by the <%> tags) will be executed by the server script engine before this Active Server Page (.asp) being sent to the client machine. In this example, the discount percentage is calculated on the server side. The user in the client machine's Web browser can see the discount but not the logic to calculate the discount. From this example, we know that the business rules can be built, maintained, and modified in the server side by using server-side scripting technology. It is secure and transparent to the client-side users.

4

NOTE

In the Microsoft Visual InterDev environment, all server-side scripts are highlighted in yellow.

In Visual InterDev's integrated development environment, it is very easy to create an .asp file and embed scripting logic into it. Visual InterDev contains a simplified FrontPage97 HTML editor. Use this HTML editor to create a HTML file. Once the .htm file is created, rename it to an .asp file. In an .asp file, delimiters (<% and %>) are used to enclose the server-side scripts. Because the server-side scripts are not sent to the client side except to the HTML page, the Web application is not necessarily tied to any specific platform or Web browser. Also, the network traffic can be reduced because most of the processing is done on the server side.

Server-side scripting is suitable for developing intranet-based applications as well. The corporate MIS can use this technique to develop company-wide intranet applications, and yet have no need to distribute any client-side software except a Web browser. All the business rules, company policies, HR information, and so on are maintained on the server side. Any data, information, and policy updates needed occur on the server without any redistributed software for the client side.

In Visual InterDev IDE, server-side scripting can be automatically generated by Microsoft's new feature called design-time ActiveX controls. The detailed information of design-time ActiveX controls can be found in Chapter 13, "Working with Design-Time Controls."

> **NOTE**
>
> See Chapter 15 for more details about server-side scripting.

Summary

Client- and server-side scripting definitely give new blood to the traditional HTML-based Web development. For the client side, the scripting makes Web content much more dynamic and powerful by adding program logic and by utilizing ActiveX components and Java applets. For the server side, scripting makes back-end database access much easier and flexible without adding complex program logic and CGI's processing overhead. Because of Visual InterDev's support of VBScript and JavaScript, Java programmers and VB programmers can use their existing skills to develop Internet and intranet applications quite easily.

Connecting and Using Databases

by Keith Leavitt

IN THIS CHAPTER

With the ongoing growth of the Internet, the demand for content has spurred a major shift toward HTML and related development tools. Virtually every major tool developer has "webified" its flagship products. These tools provide an endless array of utilities designed to make content providers more productive. Among all the functions automated by recent tools, database connectivity through the Web has, in a sense, become the Holy Grail of tool development. The reasons are clear: by linking the browser with existing sources of information stored in standard legacy database tables, the user produces HTML dynamically as he traverses a Web site. Thus, by implementing database connectivity, a Webmaster can leverage the power of existing databases to free himself and the content provider(s) from the mundane task of developing and updating HTML files.

Although the utility of Web to database connectivity is substantial, so are the skills one must bring to bear on the task of implementing such a capability. HTML development, client- or server-side scripting, and an understanding of relational database management systems have been the basic requirements with which to start. Although several tools claim to make the task of developing a dynamic Web interface to a database "easy," this is likely so only for a developer with the aforementioned skills. Finding and retaining individuals with these skills will prove no small task today, because you will have no shortage of competition. As for the rest of us mortals, we have awaited a toolset that will completely shield us from the rigors of these demands. Of course, there is no free lunch, but the Web/database interfacing tools delivered with the Visual InterDev 1.0 represent a substantial gain on this most daunting task. For those who shudder at the sight of HTML tags, and wouldn't know JavaScript from VBScript to save their lives, it is possible to produce a Web site that dynamically produces pages providing two-way communications with databases on the server. And for those who are comfortable with the syntax of these and other languages, the Visual InterDev development environment offers a cohesive framework to leverage these capabilities to their fullest extent.

Installing and Setting Up Client- and Server-Side Components

Visual InterDev setup offers an array of components for both the server and client side of the HTTP equation. Establishing database to Web connectivity from the ground up on a Windows 95 machine requires all three server-side options and the Visual InterDev client. But before selecting any of these options, go straight to the bottom of the list and select the "read me" option. This is especially important if you have a beta release of the product (Internet Studio, for example) or expect to connect to an Oracle or SQL Server database. I know it's painful to read the instructions, but consider it an ounce of prevention.

Web Server Options: The Microsoft Personal Web Server for Windows 95

The first server-side option is the Microsoft Personal Web Server for Windows 95. This light-weight server is designed for development, testing, and demonstration purposes. For purposes of simplicity, this is the server used in the examples throughout the rest of this chapter. This simple support service is probably the most difficult option to install, primarily because it requires installation and configuration of a TCP/IP stack for Windows 95. One thing to note here is that following installation of this option, you might be hard pressed to find any indication of its presence on your desktop. The secret here is to look in the tray—that little indented box on the right side of your taskbar. As depicted in Figure 5.1, double-clicking the globe/computer icon in the tray brings up the Personal Web Server Properties, where you can start, stop, and generally administer the server very much like the IIS Internet Service Manager on NT Server installations.

> **NOTE**
>
> You can administer the Personal Web Server for Windows 95 from its icon in the Control Panel or in the tray, which is that little indentation on the right side of your taskbar.

FIGURE 5.1.

Installing the Personal Web Server for Windows 95 requires installation and configuration of the Windows 95 TCP/IP client, which can be tricky. The HTTP service administrator is accessed from the taskbar tray.

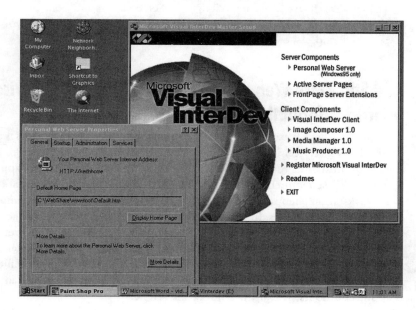

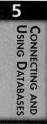

Running the Personal Web Server—or any other Web server for that matter—requires installation of the TCP/IP stack, such as the native Windows 95 stack. The TCP/IP stack can be installed and configured under the network icon in the Control Panel. This is a theoretically straightforward side requirement where you can get hung up indefinitely if you are not careful. Simply installing the stack and rebooting might be insufficient to get the Web server operating properly. If you're not connected to a TCP/IP network, you might need to specify an IP address under the TCP/IP properties dialog box in order for the computer name to map to an IP address when entered as a URL prefix in a Web browser. The TCP/IP stack that comes with Windows 95 installs to a default of `0.0.0.0.`, but this will not map as a valid IP address. Therefore, simply invent a valid one (as well as a subnet mask for good measure), and enter it in the IP address section of the TCP/IP properties dialog box. If you still have problems getting the server to respond, install the FrontPage Server Extensions. Although it is not yet documented in Visual InterDev, the FrontPage server utilities are installed with the Personal Web Server. These server utilities will be located on the path `<local drive>\Program Files\Microsoft FrontPage\Bin`.

> **NOTE**
>
> Operation of the Personal Web Server for Windows 95 will depend on your TCP/IP stack configuration. If you are logged in to a TCP/IP network and do not have a fixed IP address, you must select Use DHCP for WINS resolution on the WINS Configuration tab of the TCP/IP properties dialog box. If you are not logged in to a TCP/IP network, you need to specify a valid IP address, even if you have to make up a fake one.

And Still More Web Server Options: Peer Web Services and Internet Information Server for Windows NT

Like the FrontPage Personal Web Server, the Microsoft Peer Web Services is designed as a lightweight HTTP service primarily for development and testing purposes. Production servers designed for substantial traffic will likely require a more industrial strength approach. Microsoft's answers to these requirements are the two Web services for NT Workstation and Server. For NT Workstation clients, Peer Web Services provides a server engine compatible with all Visual InterDev capabilities. In Workstation 4.0, Peer Web Services can be activated in the Properties dialog under Network Neighborhood. Internet Information Server 3.0 is the current version of the high-end multiprotocol Web service that runs on NT Server 3.51 or better, and will provide the basis for most Active Server deployments. Microsoft demonstrates its confidence in IIS daily by running `www.microsoft.com` on it. Installation and administration of IIS is a subject unto itself, and I will not tackle it here.

Installing Active Server Pages

Installing Active Server Pages (ASP) is required for any of the server options previously discussed. The title here is a bit of a misnomer, because this option installs the ISAPI dynamic link library that makes active content possible on any of the three servers mentioned previously. Active Server Pages themselves are developed with the Visual InterDev client tools such as wizards and design-time ActiveX controls, which I cover later in this chapter. If you do not already have a FrontPage installation, installing the `isapi.dll` will add a Personal Web Server submenu to your Programs menu. This seems to be another misnomer, because it does not start any server utilities, but leads to two submenus: Active Server Pages Roadmap and Uninstall. The best feature of the ASP Roadmap is a tutorial that walks you through the creation of a functional Active Server Page. The sample page includes implementation of server-side script in a control loop that iteratively increases the font on a "Hello world" message to be displayed in a browser. In addition to the tutorial, the ASP Roadmap includes a scripting guide, an object reference, and a sample site, and is probably the best reference in the Visual InterDev toolset. The only drawback is that it is HTTP based, and so relies on a successful installation of both the server and ASP components of Visual InterDev.

The FrontPage Server Extensions: FrontPage Webs Versus Visual InterDev Projects

Installing FrontPage Server Extensions is the simplest of all the component options. These are required to use FrontPage for Web administration and development of Visual InterDev Web projects. Any Visual InterDev project can be administered and developed with FrontPage and vice-versa. FrontPage bots show up in the Visual InterDev edit panes, but can be installed only from the FrontPage editor. Similarly, VB and Java scripts show up in the FrontPage Editor as small icons, but ActiveX design-time controls produce script only in the Visual InterDev development environment. You can write and modify script in the FrontPage Editor, but text editing is all the functionality you'll find there. In general, FrontPage is the appropriate development environment for standard HTML with predefined interactive functions (bots). The more scripting you plan to use (server or client side), the more Visual InterDev becomes the appropriate environment.

Installation Options

When installing the Visual InterDev client, I strongly recommend you forego the default (typical) installation in favor of the custom option. If your hard drive can absorb the extra few megabytes, select all options including the books online and sample databases. The Dos Perros and 401K sample database applications provide examples of most major functions you can implement in a Web project with Visual InterDev. If you were (are?) one of those "gifted" children who disassembled every mechanical and electronic device in your home out of curiosity, the sample databases provide an invaluable opportunity to tear apart a working database web to see what makes it tick. And as for the help files, if you're like me, you'll need all the help you can get.

> **TIP**
>
> I'll say it again: Choose custom installation rather than default. Select all available options, because the extra assistance is well worth the disk space.

Selecting Your Back-End Database

Finally, if you intend to develop a Web interface to a real database other than the samples, you will need to have an ANSI SQL or at least ODBC-compatible database such as SQL Server, Oracle, or Access. The database should be installed on the server, within the Web space, and in a directory whose permissions will control read and write privileges on the database file. Most of the database functionality offered by Visual InterDev applies to SQL Server 6.5, but in keeping with our theme of simplicity, the databases used in all the examples throughout this chapter will be MS Access 7.0 files. I've created a simple Name Rank and Serial # `.mdb` database with three tables and a few predefined queries. The remainder of the installation options—the Image Composer, Media Manager, and Music Producer—offer substantial new content publication capabilities, but are not necessary for our Web connection.

The Visual InterDev Integrated Development Environment

The Integrated Development Environment (IDE) of this toolset is consistent with the new interface standard being implemented across the entire suite of Visual Studio tools. The same look and feel was first implemented in Visual C++, Visual J++, and soon will be in Visual Basic. Designed to leverage a developer's previous experience in other tools, the Visual InterDev interface implements the Info View (or help file system) in HTML, and makes extensive use of the right mouse button. Virtually every object in every IDE view produces a context-sensitive pop-up menu with a right-click. The help key (F1) produces help file pop-ups on the current view of the object selected on the IDE Info Viewer (left side). Place the cursor within VBScript in the source editing pane on the right side of the IDE, and F1 produces the language reference entry for the command selected. Clearly, the Visual InterDev developers went way out of their way to ensure assistance is never more than a keystroke away. The preview pane on the right side of the IDE is a container for the Internet Explorer, complete with the familiar URL, forward, back, and home buttons on the toolbar. Files can be added to any open Visual InterDev project simply by dragging and dropping into the File View of the IDE.

> **TIP**
>
> Right-click everywhere in the Visual InterDev IDE. Just about every object sports a context menu to guide you through its use.

Visual InterDev Learning and Productivity Tools

The Visual InterDev IDE offers a wide spectrum of tools to ease the learning curve of developing Active Server projects. These are CASE (computer aided software engineering) tools in the sense that they increase developer productivity by automating the generation of lines of code (or KLOC in software metric vernacular). From the command-level environment of the source code editor to wizards that do everything short of documenting your programs, the Visual InterDev IDE offers a broad range of tools to accomplish just about every conceivable development task. Either end of this spectrum has its advantages and disadvantages. The source editor has a code reference available at the tap of the F1 key, but by and large it requires familiarity with the scripting language you have chosen. At the other end, the most powerful wizards save huge amounts of time in development, but what goes on under the hood, and the insight that goes along with understanding this, is hidden from the developer. For ascending the considerable learning curve associated with Visual InterDev, I recommend starting with mid-level wizards that hold your hand through the production of Web projects, data forms, and other components. When you are familiar with the actions performed by the wizards, you can then choose lower-level tools to get down into the nuts and bolts to tweak them for your specific requirements. I have taken this path in the examples throughout this chapter to familiarize you with data connections, Web projects, and data forms.

ActiveX Data Objects

All database access through Active Sever Pages is accomplished through a new Microsoft data access component called ActiveX Data Objects (ADO). ADO runs on the Web server and is the basis for all Visual InterDev database connectivity. This component serves as an object layer between Active Server Pages and the application's back-end database. ADO is similar to RDO (Remote Data Objects) and DAO (Data Access Objects), but uses another new data access component: OLE DB. In addition to ODBC databases, OLE DB is designed to broker access to several types of data sources including e-mail systems. ADO has a relatively simple object model, exposing seven objects and four collections. Many development tools in the Visual InterDev IDE shield the user from the details of ADO, but any source-level database access development will require some understanding of the ADO object model and syntax. Those considering the development of data sources compliant with OLE DB should check out the latest scoop on OLE DB requirements at `http://www.microsoft.com/oledb`. Microsoft also has the requisite ADO information posted at `http://www.microsoft.com/ado`.

Building a Web Project and Making the Connection

Okay. So your Web server is up and running with the FrontPage Server Extensions and Active Server Pages (read `isapi.dll`) installed. The Visual InterDev client is running, and your database is sitting on the server just waiting for its first HTML action. What next? Well, it all has to do with workspaces, projects, `.asa` files, `.dsn` files, ActiveX controls, `.asp` files, and a bit of faith and persistence. Confused? So was I, and it is my sincere hope that the following saves you some, if not all, of the pondering, searching, experimenting, uninstalling, reinstalling, and sometimes downright thrashing around that I did trying to get my head around all this new stuff.

Visual InterDev Workspaces and Web Projects

The workspace is the basic framework in which individual developers or groups of developers can access one or more projects in the design-time mode. Workspaces and projects are stored as `<workspace name>.dsw` or `<project name>.dsp`, respectively, on the default path `<local drive>\Program Files\DevStudio\MyProjects\`. Workspaces are stored locally by default as they contain only development-environment information. New workspaces and projects can be established by choosing New from the File menu.

Like Visual Basic, Visual InterDev has both design-time and runtime environments and key files that determine which and how other files are associated with the Web application. The relationships between these files vary from runtime to design time. With a thorough understanding of the file structure of a Web project and command of a scripting language, one could develop these files in venerable tools such as Notepad ("Visual Notepad," as some developers like to quip...). Others might long for a simpler way to establish the framework for a Web project. For those of us in the latter group, the Projects tab offers a database project and several other wizards that build the basic file structures for several types of Web projects. For this example, I'll start with the Web Project Wizard, which will hold your hand through the development of the basic files required as a framework for the Web application. In the File View pane, select the workspace into which the project is to be inserted. Choose File | New, select the Projects tab, and then select Web Project Wizard. Enter a new project name and specify that the new project is to be added to the current workspace. In Step 2 of the wizard, you will be asked to specify a Web server, and whether the connection is to be established through Secure Sockets Layer (SSL). Selecting this option will encrypt all transmissions between the Visual InterDev client and server machines, and will require SSL to be enabled on your server. The last step of the wizard requests a name for the Web itself, and allows enabling of full text searching of the Web. Selecting this option will install a search page with a FrontPage search bot that supports basic Boolean (and/or/not) queries of the Web project. Upon completion, the wizard creates a new Web on the server, complete with FrontPage extensions, the `search.htm` page, and a file named `global.asa`.

The Global Active Server Application File

The global.asa file contains server-side VBScript and is loaded into memory the first time any user views a page in the Web application. This file defines global data and events for the entire Active Server application. Figure 5.2 depicts the global.asa file as viewed and edited in the Visual InterDev source editor environment. This editor is accessed by double-clicking the selected file under File View. The four events and their descriptions are commented at the top of the global.asa file. The Session events allow the server to retain information on a particular user's actions, and thus store state data throughout a session. This is a key capability of Active Server Pages, as it provides a method of overcoming the limitation of HTTP as a stateless protocol. It is in the first event procedure, Session_OnStart, where the database connection information will be stored. The Session_OnStart subroutine in the global.asa file in the Figure 5.2 has been generated by the Data Form Wizard, which you will see in detail later in this chapter. The global.asa file does not retain an open connection to the back-end database. It simply stores the session variables for establishing and tracking connections on the fly.

FIGURE 5.2.

The global.asa *file, as previewed in the source editor of the Visual InterDev IDE. Notice how the Web Project Wizard heavily comments all code in the files it generates.*

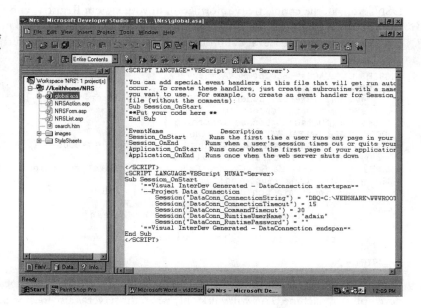

The Database Connection

The last little item you will need to add to your Web project is a connection to a database. The first step here is to place the database file on the server. The database file need not be in the Web space, or even on the same machine as the Web server. Because permissions are established by the Web project, the database can reside in any directory, volume, or even server with a connection to the Web project. Of course, if you should choose to implement a distributed system, server-to-server permissions must match those required in the Web project to edit the database. This final step is the biggest one yet, and once again I recommend resorting to a mid-level wizard to ease the pain of manual file creation, yet not so much as to leave you with a working connection and no idea just what was done to achieve this.

Using the Data Form Wizard to Create Data-Driven Web Applications

The wizard of choice here can be found in the Visual InterDev IDE by choosing File | New | File Wizards | Data Form Wizard. This wizard will step you through establishing the data connection and developing a basic set of Active Server files to access the database interactively. After specifying a filename, you will be prompted to select or develop a .dsn file. This is a local file that stores all the information needed to connect to a database, including driver type/version and path to the database file. ODBC 3.0 supports both system and file DSNs. System DSNs store all the connectivity information in your system Registry, and file DSNs store the same data in a single text file. The information in the DSN file is loaded into global.asa and expands the Session_On Start subroutine to include server-side script such as the following:

```
</SCRIPT>
<SCRIPT LANGUAGE=VBScript RUNAT=Server>
Sub Session_OnStart
    '==Visual InterDev Generated - DataConnection startspan==
    '--Project Data Connection
    Session("DataConn_ConnectionString") =
➥"DBQ=C:\WEBSHARE\WWWROOT\dp\<databasename>.mdb;
➥DefaultDir=C:\WEBSHARE\WWWROOT\dp;Driver={MicrosoftAccessDriver(*.mdb)};
➥DriverId=25;FIL=MSAccess;ImplicitCommitSync=Yes;
➥MaxBufferSize=512;MaxScanRows=8;PageTimeout=5;SafeTransactions=0;Threads=3;
➥UID=admin;UserCommitSync=Yes;"
        Session("DataConn_ConnectionTimeout") = 15
        Session("DataConn_CommandTimeout") = 30
        Session("DataConn_RuntimeUserName") = "admin"
        Session("DataConn_RuntimePassword") = ""
    '==Visual InterDev Generated - DataConnection endspan==
End Sub
</SCRIPT>
```

Note that the DBQ parameter hard-codes the path to the database as the local hard drive of the development machine. This will work only when the server is also located on the development machine. On a production server, the ODBC Driver Manager will look for the database on the Web server in the path specified by the DBQ connect string. To overcome this problem, you will need to manually change the DBQ path parameter to a UNC, or universal naming convention. In the preceding example, this can be accomplished by replacing the path segment "C:\WEBSHARE\WWWROOT\..." with the UNC equivalent "\\<servername>\...".

Back on Step 1 of the Data Form Wizard, select New (database connection), and the File Data Source tab in the resulting window. After specifying a new DSN name, you will be prompted to choose from a list of ODBC drivers for several popular Relational Database Management Systems including Access, SQL Server, and Oracle. You then can browse to the location where you choose to save the new `.dsn` file, specify the location of the database file, and connect as read/write or read only. Your new database connection will now be listed in the top combo box of the wizard, and this completes Step 1 (of 7!). Step 2 offers a choice of table or view (query) data from your database for the construction of HTML forms later in the wizard. You can also base these forms directly on a SQL statement. Wizard Step 4 (as shown in Figure 5.3) establishes the editing options your browsers will have including modification, deletion, and addition of records. From here you can also specify browser filtering capabilities and that the server return a feedback page after modifications. Wizard Step 5 establishes viewing options including form and list views, hot links on the resulting pages, and the number of records on each page. In Step 6 you finally get to do something fun by picking from several pre-designed page themes, and that completes your work. The wizard then grinds for a considerable amount of time, doing what would take your average Webmaster (an oxymoron, if ever there was one) with conventional tools and unconventional skills at least a couple days to complete.

FIGURE 5.3.

Interactive options in the Data Form Wizard. Imagine, if you will, the amount of script you would have to write to implement the functions in the checkboxes on just this one dialog box!

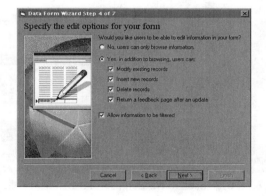

The Fruits of Your Labor

If you have successfully followed the steps to arrive at this point, and appreciate the previously substantial effort required to develop a flexible Web/database interface, you will undoubtedly be pleased with the results. So let's take our new Web project out for a test drive. When the wizard completes its machinations, you can view the fruits of your labor in the nearest Web browser. You can preview any of your new pages in the IDE, but if you are skeptical like me (hey, anyone can pass their own test!) you will want to see these pages work in the most obscure browser your users can dig up. So go find one other than IE, and take a look at your Web site. The wizard has created three new files with a user-defined prefix (as entered in the new filename text box prior to entering the wizard) and the suffixes `action.asp`, `form.asp` (as shown in Figure 5.4), and `list.asp`. Together, this system of forms provides all standard views of a relational database. The Form View presents one record at a time in Detail View. Field contents can be updated on the form, and changes posted to the back end with an Update button. From here, records can be added, deleted, or searched out with a filter. The Go to the right of the last field in the record is a live hyperlink to the URL listed in that record. The Data Form Wizard automatically generates this link for any field in the back-end table or query with a name beginning with URL_.

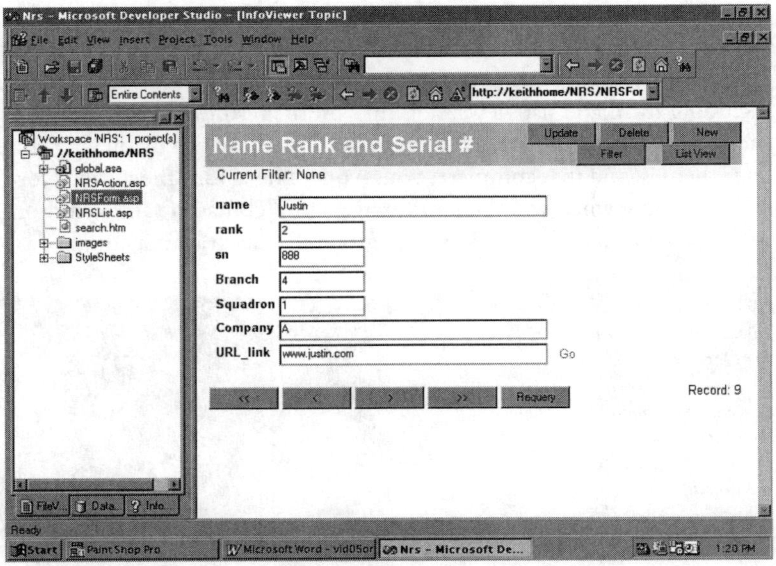

FIGURE 5.4.

The single record detail Form View of the Name Rank and Serial # database generated by the Data Form Wizard, as previewed in the browser container of the Visual InterDev IDE.

Switching to the List View (see Figure 5.5) produces a list of all records with hyperlinks from each record on the list back to the details in Form View. Selecting the ID # at the beginning of any record will return the browser to the Form View on that record.

As an added bonus, there are two currently undocumented features of the Data Form Wizard that augment the developer's capabilities. First, add a field to any table in your database, and begin the field name with URL_. Define the field data type as text, and enter a valid hyperlink URL in each record. The wizard will generate both form and list .asp files with live links to the location associated with each record. Define a field name beginning with IMG_, and the wizard will format the field as an inline image for the data form.

TIP

Create a field in your database table containing valid URLs and prefix the name of that field with URL_. The Data Form Wizard will automatically create hyperlinks on all forms containing that field.

Figure 5.5.

The List View of the Name Rank and Serial # database as generated by the Data Form Wizard. As previewed from IE 3.01, all hyperlinks from this dynamically generated .asp page are live.

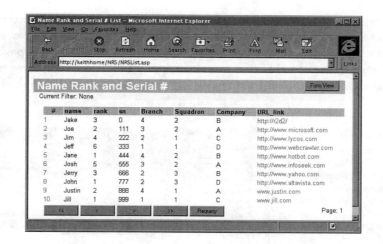

The third .asp file generated by the Data Form Wizard is Action.asp. This file contains all the error-handling routines for the functions in the other two .asp files.

Choosing a Scripting Language

One note on browsers before we move on: In general, a developer will have much greater control over the server configuration than that of the innumerable browsers his users will hit the server with. Visual InterDev offers VBScript or JavaScript as standard options for code generated by design-time ActiveX controls. Because the ISAPI.DLL will interpret either, the choice of server-side script is not critical. On the client side, however, JavaScript is still the only language interpreted by the vast majority of Web browsers, including Netscape Navigator. Unless you can ensure that your users will have Internet Explorer 3.0 or better, it is safest to stick with JavaScript on the client side.

What Goes On Under the Hood

Now that you have had your fun playing with your new creation in runtime mode, let's go back and look at the guts of this seemingly Rube Goldberg–inspired Web structure. When done, your Web project will be filled, not with the old familiar .html files, but with these somewhat alien .asp pages. Like HTML files, ASP files are simply text files with an extension that tells tools like browsers how to interpret them. The difference lies primarily in the server-side script embedded among the standard HTML head, body, and title tags. The three files produced by the Forms Wizard contain from 300 to more than 700 lines of HTML and Visual Basic server- and client-side script. The source code behind these files can be viewed and edited by right-clicking the file in the File View pane of the Visual InterDev IDE. Selecting Open will load the file into the Visual InterDev source-editing pane on the right side of the IDE. The source editor color-codes the various sections of the ASP file to make analysis and modification easier. Figure 5.6 shows the NRSform Active Server Page as viewed from the source editor.

Server-side script is delimited with `<%script%>` tags and highlighted in yellow. Client-side script is rendered in green font, such as the Data Range Footer control's `<Object>` tag in Figure 5.6. Wizard-generated scripts are heavily commented and offset with apostrophes, and scattered between standard HTML tags (seemingly few and far between) show up in purple, red, and blue font colors. Notice the Images and Style Sheets directories in the File View pane. These were automatically generated based on the template selected in the Data Form Wizard.

FIGURE 5.6.

Double-click on any file in File View to view and edit the code in the source editor. Server-side script is highlighted in yellow, client-side script is displayed in green font, and standard HTML tags in purple, red, and blue.

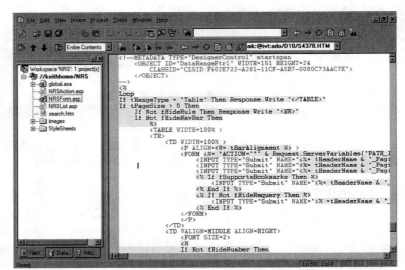

File-Viewing Options in the Visual InterDev IDE

In addition to viewing your pages in an external browser, the Visual InterDev IDE offers several tools to view the files both in runtime and design-time modes. Right-clicking the `.asp` document in File View produces a pop-up menu with links to these tools. Opening with the Active Server Page Editor allows the developer to view and edit the code behind the `.asp` documents. You can also preview the files in any browser on your computer, or even browse the interpreted `.asp` files in the InfoViewer. Each menu item offers options to add other external editing tools such as the FrontPage Editor. Viewing and editing the document in the FrontPage Editor is possible, but for documents that consist of mostly script (as pages designed to leverage the `isapi.dll` will tend to be), the Visual InterDev Source Editor is a much more useful tool. View Links provides a Web-like graphical view of all the links from the selected file, and is very reminiscent of the Hyperlink View in the FrontPage Explorer.

Re-entrant Code

Usually, modifications performed by wizards are one-way in that no further modification is needed or even possible after completion of the wizard. However, the ASP code produced by the Forms Wizard, like that of ActiveX design-time controls, is re-entrant, or fully modifiable within the source editing pane. Right-clicking within the script you want to modify produces yet another context-sensitive menu complete with a bevy of editing options including an HTML wizard, a script wizard, an ActiveX control, and an HTML layout. It is remarkable that even customizing the code at this level still does not require manual code writing, although this is always an option in Visual InterDev.

Gray icons in the File View (action, list, and search files, shown in Figure 5.6) indicate that those files only exist on the server. Colored icons indicate that a local working copy exists on the client in the IDE and must be loaded back to the server after editing. You can retrieve or release all working copies in a project by right-clicking the project and selecting either option from the pop-up menu. The Data Form Wizard places only the generated .asp files in the root directory of your Web. Once created, you can manually port the files to any other location in the Web, but before doing so, you must first disable the automatic link repairing function in the project. This is accomplished by right-clicking the project icon in the File View pane to open the Properties dialog box.

Visual Data Tools

Another change you will notice after the Forms Wizard does its work is the addition of a Data View tab to the right side of the Visual InterDev IDE. Double-clicking the cylindrical database icon exposes the Database objects through the ActiveX Data Objects layer, as depicted in Figure 5.7. These views comprise a subset of the capabilities of Visual Data Tools, as discussed in Chapter 12, "Database Management with the Visual Data Tools." Tables, views (queries), and stored procedures are available for modification in the results pane on the right by double-clicking the object in the Data View pane on the left. Clearly designed to leverage development experience with MS Access, the results pane can contain virtually every function and view of a database available in Microsoft's flagship desktop RDBMS. The database-management features of the Data View pane are extensive, and include creation and storing of tables, stored procedures, database diagrams, or entirely new database projects. The most powerful features are currently functional with ANSI SQL 92 databases (SQL Server 6.5), but most will work with any ODBC 3.0–compliant database.

FIGURE 5.7.

The Visual InterDev Data View offers a live view of all tables and queries in the connected database and is very reminiscent of the old MS Access Query-by-Example View.

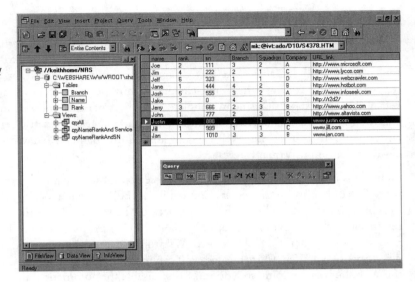

Using Design-Time Controls to Create Data-Driven Forms

Okay, so we have created a Web project and a system of Active Server Pages to access a database file through a Web interface using a high-level CASE tool such as the Data Form Wizard. As useful and instructive as the Data Form Wizard is, it still limits the range of content and layout to those built into a few Visual InterDev templates. Odds are, you will require more flexibility than the wizard offers, so let's take a look at some lower-level tools that give the developer more control over the format and content of a Web project and represent an evolutionary step up the Visual InterDev learning curve. You might have heard of ActiveX controls as the new nomenclature for lightweight versions of what old-school VB and VC++ programmers knew as VBX and OCX OLE custom controls. These were, and still are, self-contained OLE servers that eased the development of functions such as FTP automation by shielding the developer from nasty Windows API calls. Well, Visual InterDev introduces a new breed of these helpful little functions called *design-time custom controls*. True to their name, they are called at design time to hold the developer's hand through the creation of common client- or server-side functions. In the process, they insert VBScript or JavaScript on either the client- or server-side to implement these functions. The four design-time controls that Visual InterDev will install in the Registry of the development machine are the Data Command, Include, the Data Range Header, and the Data Range Footer. These offer a far greater range of possibilities, as they represent smaller building blocks than the wizards. Still they provide this capability without forcing the developer into the gory details of code development. The current implementation of design-time controls is through a wizard-like interface that steps you through the establishment of key properties or, for the brave, offers up the entire properties list. Rumor has it that the next release of Visual InterDev will contain a WYSIWYG design-time control interface. Like VB custom controls, there will likely soon be a huge market of third-party design-time controls to automate every conceivable development task, perhaps including the documentation of your programs!

The Data Range Header and the Data Range Footer

We will start our investigation of these controls with the Data Range Header and Footer. Together, we can use these to insert any range of database-stored content into browser-readable files. Start by selecting your project in the Visual InterDev workspace; then choose File I. New and the Files tab in the resulting dialog box. If old habits die hard, you might be tempted to select the HTML file option, like I did the first time. Forget that from now on. You are no longer developing HTML. You are now developing programs that develop HTML— Active Server programs specifically, and thus .asp extensions, will be replacing .html. Remember the first section of this chapter about letting the computer and existing databases do your work for you? Well, that's what we're going to do. Instead of HTML, select the Active Server Page option, give it a filename, and click OK. In the source editor on the right, you'll see a few lines of text that look suspiciously like a blank HTML file waiting for some content. And that's just what it is. The .asp extension is simply to tell the server that this file needs to be interpreted on the server side prior to shipping results to the browser on the requesting client. Just to make it painfully obvious what you need to do next, the file has a `"<!-- Insert HTML here -->"` comment highlighted in the center of it. Right-click this line and select Insert ActiveX control. Go to the Design-Time tab and select Data Range Header Control. On the control tab, select the name of your data connection as established in the previous wizard. Here is where things get slightly less than obvious. Select the Advanced tab. Anything that says "advanced" usually makes me nervous. I think they should hold a focus group in Redmond and consider other, less intimidating terms like "relax, take it easy" or "hey, this ain't rocket science." On the Advanced tab, set the cursor type to Keyset. This property specifies recordset membership and thus the type of movement possible within the recordset. The Keyset setting fixes membership and allows movement in all directions. Back on the Control tab, Bar Alignment will set where the navigation buttons will be placed, and Range Type determines whether the data will be displayed in a form, as text, or in a table. For our example, choose Table. You can select a record-paging alternative if you want the resulting recordset broken into several pages at a fixed number of records per page.

The SQL Query Designer

Now it's time to build the SQL statement that will query the database through the data connection. SQL gurus can enter the query statement directly into the command text box. The rest of us mortals will want to select the SQL Builder button and build the statement in the SQL Query Designer, a visual development environment very reminiscent of the Access Query-by-Example function. The SQL Query Designer consists of several panes, as shown in Figure 5.8. The Data tab on the left shows all objects in the database. The top section on the right is the diagram pane into which you can drag and drop tables, views, or other queries from the Data View on the left. You can also create joins by connecting fields between tables in the diagram pane. The next section down is the table pane where any fields selected from tables in the diagram pane are displayed. The SQL pane displays the live SQL resulting from any changes in the two panes above. You can even perform ad-hoc pass-through SQL queries to the connected ODBC database by typing directly into this pane. The SQL generated in this pane will vary from ANSI SQL 92 to ODBC SQL depending on the connected database. Changes will be reflected in the other three panes to the extent possible. The results pane is displayed at the bottom of the right side. The Query Designer does not supply a print routine, but you can copy to the clipboard from the Edit menu and paste results into another application.

Figure 5.8.

The Query Designer is invoked by the Data Range Header design-time control. SQL generated by the query builder will depend on the type of database you are connected to.

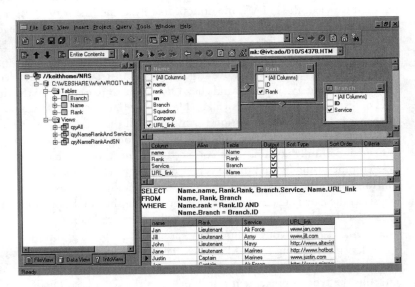

> **TIP**
>
> You can perform live SQL pass-through queries by typing directly into the SQL pane. Table graphics and results will be displayed automatically in the Query Designer.

Upon closing the Query Designer window, you will be asked whether you want to update the data range header. Select yes; then close the Data Range Header control property sheet. You should then be back in the source editor with about 80 new lines of both server- and client-side code in the new `.asp` file. Find the last line generated by the Data Range Header control. This should read `<!--METADATA TYPE="DesignerControl" endspan-->`. Right-click after this line, and insert another design-time ActiveX control. This time select the Data Range Footer control (remember to select the Design-Time tab first, as standard versions of the Data Range Header and Footer controls exist too!), and simply close the source editor and property sheet. No parameters require customizing, as this control simply closes the loop opened by the Data Range Header.

And Finally, We Actually Have to Write Some Good Old-Fashioned Code...

The last step requires a bit of source-level modification to build the table (remember selecting table display in the Data Range control property sheet?) and populate it with the fields specified in the SQL statement we built earlier. The table start tags should be inserted just below the HTML `<Body>` tag and before the `metadata` tag that starts the Data Range Header control. Three simple tags like `<div align="center"><center><table border="2" cellpadding="3">` should do the trick. Right-click the yellow highlighted server-side code generated by the Data Range Header control and select Edit design-time control. This will produce the Properties dialog box for that control, this time with the Copy fields button on the Control tab enabled. Selecting this yields a list of the fields available from the SQL statement, and you can copy any or all to the clipboard with the requisite server-side include script. Our Name Rank and Serial # database query example yielded the following:

```
<%= DataRangeHdr1("name") %><br>
<%= DataRangeHdr1("Rank") %><br>
<%= DataRangeHdr1("Service") %><br>
<%= DataRangeHdr1("URL_link") %><br>
```

But this will produce a vertical list of the results at runtime. To place them in table format, you must make the following slight modifications to the table tags:

```
<tr>
<td align = "center"><%= DataRangeHdr1("name") %></td>
<td align = "center"><%= DataRangeHdr1("Rank") %></td>
<td align = "center"><%= DataRangeHdr1("Service") %></td>
<td align = "center"><%= DataRangeHdr1("URL_link") %></td>
</tr>
```

Pasting these tags directly between the `endspan` tag from the Header control and the `startspan` tag from the Footer control will correctly format the display as a table. Finish off by inserting `</table></center></div>` immediately after the `endspan` tag from the Footer control and before the `</body>` HTML tag. Save your new file and preview it in a browser. Note that the URL field is not automatically rendered as a link as it was in the Data Form Wizard. You can easily create this function by modifying the `URL_link` tag to read as follows:

```
<td align = "center"><A HREF=<%= DataRangeHdr1("URL_link") %>><%=
➥DataRangeHdr1("URL_link") %></td>
```

Figure 5.9 shows the resulting table viewed on the client side. Although this file is not as flashy as the pages produced by the Data Form Wizard, you now see how design-time controls provide greater control over the pages you develop.

FIGURE 5.9.

A dynamically generated, database-backed HTML table built with design-time ActiveX controls.

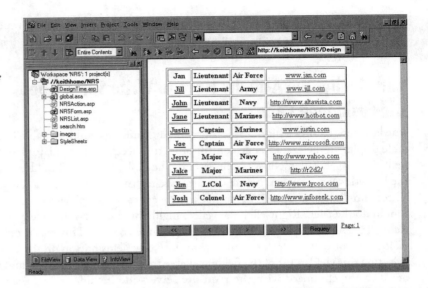

TIP

You can co-opt the Data Form Wizard's live URL trick by manually inserting an <HREF...> tag in the Data Range Header control's server-side script line referencing a field from your connected database with valid URLs.

Summary

It should now be clear that anyone who claims to have made Web/database connectivity easy from the developer's standpoint is exercising a considerable amount of poetic license with the adjective. Certainly though, Visual InterDev makes this task easier that previous tools. As a bonus, the Visual InterDev Integrated Development Environment leverages developer's experience with many—if not most—other major database and HTML development tools. In general, all development tools fit somewhere along a spectrum, with "powerful" at one end and "easy to use" at the other. Although Visual InterDev is a member of the Visual Studio suite of tools, it is truly a suite of tools in itself. As such, the Visual InterDev Integrated Development Environment successfully spans that spectrum with individual tools at either end of the range. A good approach to using Visual InterDev to establish Web/database connectivity is to start with some of the more powerful wizards such as the Data Form Wizard. When you are familiar with the files and code generated by these tools, you will be more prepared to apply tools and in turn ascend the Visual InterDev learning curve. You might have heard of the truth-in-advertising adage: "fast, cheap, good; pick two." Perhaps a modification of this would provide a useful rule-of-thumb regarding the use of Visual InterDev: "easy to use, powerful; start at one end and work your way to the other." Remember, there is no free lunch!

Developing the Application and Content

by Tarek El Abbadi

IN THIS CHAPTER

CHAPTER 6

This chapter discusses how to use Visual InterDev as it relates to creating a Web application and its content. You first see a more general overview of what Web projects are and how to work with them. Later, I focus on how to use Visual InterDev and, in the process, uncover many of its powerful features.

What Are Web Projects?

Web projects consist of all the files and directories that comprise a web, or Web site, in Visual InterDev. They are made up of two components: the server-side web and the client-side project.

Visual InterDev displays project files and file structures in what is known as the File View (see Figure 6.1). File View shows the Project Space, which shows the computer name (in this case, pharaoh), the project name (FirstProject), and the file structure. The same structure exists on both the Web server as well as the local machine. This directory structure is a replica of the master structure that resides on the server that hosts the Web project. When modifying files, a local version of the file on the server is created in a local working directory. When changes are made and saved, the server master copies are updated in the web directory. Whenever you view any of a part of your web with a browser, you are actually viewing the master copies located on the Web server.

FIGURE 6.1.

File View, showing the Project Space.

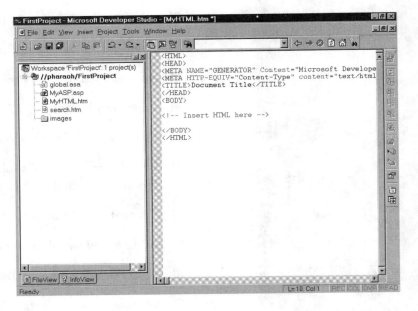

In a Web project, there are a number of available file formats. Some of the files types usually found in a Web project are HTML files, Active Server Pages, and HTML layout files. These files are the primary components that interact to form a Web site.

Creating an Application and Content

As discussed earlier, Web projects contain all the files comprising a Web site. Hence, the first step in creating a Web site is to create a Web project in Visual InterDev.

Creating a Web project involves a number of actions, both on the client side and the server side. This creation process is handled by the Web Project Wizard.

When a Web project is created, a working directory is created on the client side. This directory contains all the working copies of the master files that are located on the server. In addition to these working copies are project files that contain the information necessary to reopen a project. All these aspects of a Web project can be seen in the Project Workspace on the FileView tab.

On the server, creating a new Web project causes a new web with the same name to be created. The master files are contained in a web directory that is placed as a direct subdirectory to the root directory of the web server. With the proper settings selected, a Global.asa file and a Search.htm file are placed in the root directory. To change these settings, go to the Tools menu and choose the Web Projects tab in Options. Visual InterDev makes the building of a web application and the maintenance of the resulting Web site a fairly simple process.

New Project Types

Projects come in many different flavors. The following are the types of projects available in Visual InterDev:

- Database Project
- Departmental Site Wizard
- New Database Wizard
- Sample Application Wizard
- Web Project Wizard

Setting Up a Web Application

Here are the primary steps involved in setting up a web application:

1. Go to the File menu and choose New to bring up the new dialog box.
2. Click the Projects tab. (See Figure 6.2.)
3. Select the project type to be created by single-clicking Web Project Wizard.
4. In the Project name field, enter a name for the project.
5. Enter a path to the new project location in the Location field or click the [.....] button to browse.

FIGURE 6.2.

The Projects tab in the New dialog box shows the project types that can be created in Visual InterDev.

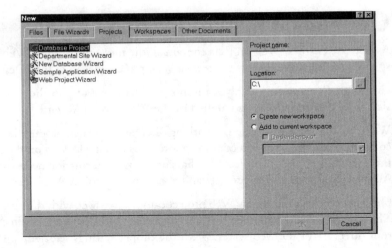

6. Click the OK button when you're done. This will bring up the Web Project Wizard.

In the Web Project Wizard—Step 1 dialog box, perform the following:

1. Enter the name of the server that will host the master web files.

2. If the server specified in step 1 supports SSL and SSL is active, click Connect Using SSL to enable Secure Socket Layer communication between that server and Visual InterDev. If the server selected in step 1 is not a secure web server, a message indicating that Visual InterDev is unable to contact the web server will appear. In such a case, uncheck this option.

3. To establish a connection with the server and go on to step 2, click Next. At this point, if the server cannot be found, a Cannot Contact Server error message appears, in which case you can click OK and either reenter a server or cancel the project-creation process.

In the Web Project Wizard—Step 2 dialog box, complete the project creation process with the following steps:

1. Select either Create a new Web or Connect to an Existing Web.

   If creating a new web, enter the name for the web and whether to create a Search.htm page to enable full text searches.

2. If you are connecting to an existing web, specify that Web project from the list of projects on that server. Click Finish when you're done.

At this point, Visual InterDev performs security checks such as administrator and authoring level permissions.

What Is the Project Workspace, and What Are Its Different Components?

At the left side of Visual InterDev you will find what is called the Project Workspace. This area is for organizing projects and is composed of three primary parts:

- File View appears when you have a project open. File View shows you the project, directory, and file structure in a hierarchical view that is much like the way Windows Explorer shows you your local file system.

- Info View (see Figure 6.3) is a hierarchical index of the documentation for Developer Studio. The InfoView tab is always visible unless you specify otherwise.

- Data View appears when a data source exists in the Global.asa file. Essentially, ODBC data source information is displayed in the Data View for database projects.

FIGURE 6.3.

Info View is an index of Developer Studio documentation. When you need help, click the InfoView tab and go to the desired topic.

WARNING

You must have a project open before you will see the FileView tab.

Adding Files to Your Project

Now that you have a project, you can add the components that will comprise your site—files. This can be accomplished in one of two ways.

■ If you want to create a new file, simply go to the File menu and click New. A list of file types will appear in the Files tab (see Figure 6.4).

FIGURE 6.4.

The Files tab in the New dialog box illustrates the file formats available in Visual InterDev.

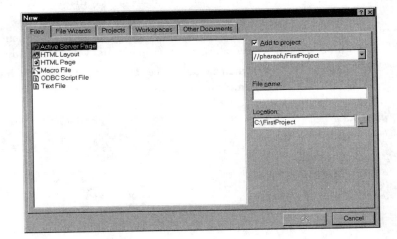

■ If you want to import a file from a directory on your hard drive to your current Web project, you can simply drag it from Windows Explorer or NT Explorer and drop it in the File View window of Visual InterDev.

> **TIP**
>
> Visual InterDev supports drag-and-drop from other applications such as Windows Explorer and NT Explorer. Just drag the file from one of these applications and drop it in the desired directory in Visual InterDev's File View.

The Visual InterDev File Types

The following are the various file types under Visual InterDev:

Active Server Page	An Active Server Page that can include server-side scripts. Ends with `.asp`.
HTML Layout	A file that contains only HTML layout. Ends with an `.alx` extension.

HTML Page	An HTML file. Ends with `.htm`.
Macro File	A macro file for Developer Studio. Ends with the `.dsm` extension.
ODBC Script File	A file containing SQL statements and commands. Ends with the `.SQL` extension.
Text File	Standard text—an unformatted ASCII file with a `.txt` extension.

Creating New Files in a Project

As mentioned earlier, you can create a new file in an open project quickly and easily in a number of steps:

1. In the Project Workspace, ensure that you are in File View. (If you're not, click on the FileView tab.)
2. From the File menu, select New.
3. Choose the Files, File Wizards, or Other Documents tab.
4. Select the file type you would like to create.
5. Give a name to the file in the File Name field.
6. To add the file to the active project, just check the Add to Project option.
7. Click OK when you're finished.

Once you create a new file, such as an HTML or ASP file, you can right-click it, select Open With... from the shortcut menu, and choose FrontPage. This action launches Microsoft FrontPage and opens the file there. After modifying the contents and saving in FrontPage, Visual InterDev automatically detects that the file has been modified and asks you whether you would like to load it into the current workspace.

Note that if you launch FrontPage on your own and create a new document, you *must* drag and drop the file each time you want to update the Visual InterDev copy. For example, say you open Windows Explorer or NT Explorer, launch FrontPage from its executable file, and then create a file called `MyPage.asp`. You then edit this file in FrontPage and save it when you are done. When you bring Visual InterDev into view, it knows nothing of your new file, `MyPage.asp`, because that file has no association with any project in Visual InterDev. You can now use one of the two methods outlined in the next section to add this file to your current project space. Keep in mind, however, that you will need to repeat these steps each time you modify `MyPage.asp`. If you want Visual InterDev to recognize a new file and keep track of the latest copy for you, you will have to either create the file from Visual InterDev at the very beginning or, alternatively, once it has been added to the current workspace, right-click the file and choose Open With... FrontPage. Now each time you work in FrontPage to modify this file and then bring Visual InterDev into view, it will prompt you whether you would like to load the latest version of that file.

Incorporating Existing Files in a Project

You can also add existing files to an open project.

1. In File View, right-click the project to which you want to add the file (see Figure 6.5).

FIGURE 6.5.

When open project is right-clicked, a handy shortcut menu appears.

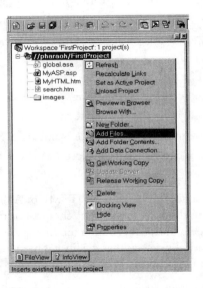

2. From the shortcut menu (from which you can choose Add Files or Folders, Preview in Browser, Refresh, or Get Working Copies), select Add Files.

3. Locate the file or files you would like added and click OK.

Here's another way to add existing files that is especially useful—one I prefer using: From Windows Explorer or NT Explorer, simply select the file or files you would like added and drag-and-drop them into the project directory in File View.

If you want to create a new file, simply go to the File menu and choose New; a list of file types appears in the Files tab.

If you want to import a file from a directory on your hard drive to your current Web project, you can simply drag it from Windows Explorer or NT Explorer and drop it in Visual InterDev's File View window.

Developing the Application and Content

CHAPTER 6

117

6

DEVELOPING THE
APPLICATION AND
CONTENT

> **WARNING**
>
> Avoid using FrontPage to create a new file. If you do, Visual InterDev will not automatically know that the file is associated with a project. In this case, you would need to add the file to the project in the method outlined previously each time you modify the file and save the changes. The proper method for adding existing files to a project is to right-click the file in File View, select Open With... from the shortcut menu and choose FrontPage from the available list of editors. If FrontPage is not a choice in the list, please see the section in this chapter titled "Adding a New Editor" to add FrontPage to your list of available editors.

Importing Folders

Visual InterDev also enables you to add the entire content of a folder to an open project as quickly and easily as adding a file. The following steps walk you through the process:

1. Make sure you are in File View; if you're not, click the FileView tab.
2. Place the pointer on the project or folder to which you would like to add the folder and right-click that item.
3. Choose Add Folder Contents from the shortcut menu.
4. Choose the folder.

The second method uses the drag-and-drop approach. Simply select the folder you would like to add from Windows Explorer or NT Explorer and drag and drop it into the project directory of your choosing.

Working with Existing Web Sites

Visual InterDev has the capability to grab the contents of a Web site, whether it is on a local machine or out on the Internet, and create a project out of it. It maintains the site's structure and links, no matter how large or complex. There are two types of Web sites: those created with FrontPage 97 and those created by other means. This distinction is important when importing Web sites into Visual InterDev.

For Web sites created with FrontPage 97, the following steps apply:

1. From the File menu, select New.
2. Choose Web Project Wizard from the Projects tab in the New dialog box.
3. Give a local name to the Web site.
4. Select Create New Workspace and click OK.
5. Enter the name of the web server where the Web site resides and click OK.

6. Click Connect to an existing web on Servername.

7. Use the list box to select the web you desire.

8. Click Finish for the Web site to be loaded into the current workspace. This imported web behaves exactly as any other created with Visual InterDev.

For Web sites not created with FrontPage 97 or Visual InterDev, use the following steps:

1. From the File menu, select New.

2. Choose Web Project Wizard from the Projects tab.

3. Give a local name to the Web site.

4. Select Create new workspace and click OK.

5. Choose the web server that will be hosting this Web site by typing its name in the appropriate field and click Finish.

6. In File View, right-click the project name and select Add Folders Contents from the shortcut menu.

7. Select the folder that contains the Web site you would like to import. Note that for the folder to be visible, you must have a network connection to the server that contains that data.

Introduction to the Visual InterDev FrontPage Editor

FrontPage is an HTML WYSIWYG editor (see Figure 6.6). It enables you to create Web pages quickly and easily without knowing HTML at all. For those who like to tweak their pages, it also enables you to get into the HTML code and change the code. First, I will discuss how to specify the FrontPage editor to be the default editor in Visual InterDev, and then I'll discuss how to use FrontPage to create Web pages.

To specify the FrontPage editor as the default HTML editor, follow these steps:

1. In the FileView tab in the Project Space, right-click the file you want to browse. The shortcut menu should appear.

2. Select Browse With... from the shortcut menu (see Figure 6.7).

3. A dialog box appears with the available browsers. If you don't see a browser that exists on your machine, you can click the Add button to add a new browser. Note that the default browser is set to Visual InterDev's InfoViewer. To change the default browser, simply select the desired browser and click Set as Default.

Selecting InfoViewer opens the chosen file in Visual InterDev and gives you full viewing and navigational facilities as Internet Explorer.

FIGURE 6.6.

The FrontPage Editor can be used to build WYSIWYG HTML pages. You can add links and place and resize graphics almost effortlessly.

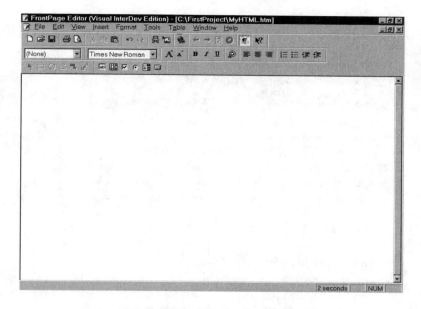

FIGURE 6.7.

The Browse With dialog box enables you to browse a file from a nondefault browser, add a new browser, or set the default browser.

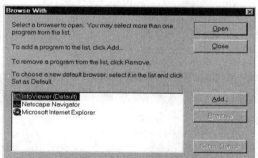

Content Development

When developing a web site, you could work in a team or individually. I will discuss a major issue that arises when working on files in a team, but first, let's get acquainted with master files, working copies, and the mechanics of how they interact. (See Chapter 7, "Managing the Site and Team Development," for more information about team development.)

What Are Working Copies?

Master web files are placed on the web server at the time of creation or inclusion into a project. When files are edited, Visual InterDev makes what is known as *working copies* on your local machine. The master file still resides on the web server. When the working copy is modified and saved, Visual InterDev updates the master file—the one associated with the working copy—on the server. By default, this is all done automatically by Visual InterDev whenever you open, edit, and save a file.

> **TIP**
>
> When working over a slow connection, you might want to disable automatic updating of master files when the working copies are saved on your local machine. To do this, from the Tools menu, click the Web Projects tab from Options.... Deselect Update server when files are saved, and click OK. Do not forget to manually update the server when you want to propagate the changes up to the server. This can be easily done by right-clicking the file whose master file you would like to update and selecting Update Server from the shortcut menu.

Getting and Releasing Working Copies

You can specifically request a working copy of the master file or folder on the web server. In File View, simply right-click the file or folder that you want to obtain a working copy of and select Get Working Copy. Visual InterDev then proceeds by placing a working copy on your local hard drive. When you want to remove the file or folder from your hard drive, just right-click the file or folder in FileView and select Release Working Copy. Now the only version is the master file or folder that resides on the web server.

> **NOTE**
>
> It's important to remember that the master file residing on the web server does not go anywhere. When you choose Get Working Copy, you only get a copy placed on your hard drive. When you choose Release Working Copy, the local copy of the file is removed from your hard drive. In both cases, the master file located on the web server does not move.

Note that Visual InterDev by itself does not provide source control. That means that Visual InterDev does not lock the files that are being edited by another user. This could be a problem, because it will accept the most recently updated version of a file. With Microsoft Visual SourceSafe installed on the server, a file is locked when a user is working on it.

Working on Projects in Teams with Visual SourceSafe

Under Visual SourceSafe, the mechanism by which you get and release working copies works in the exact same manner. The difference is that the master file or folder residing on the web server is locked when the first user requests a working copy. In this manner, another user is

Developing the Application and Content

CHAPTER 6

121

6

DEVELOPING THE
APPLICATION AND
CONTENT

prevented from getting another working copy on their machine until the first user releases their working copy, which unlocks the web server's master version. (See Chapter 9, "Effective Team Development Using Visual InterDev and Visual SourceSafe," for more information on Visual SourceSafe and team development.)

NOTE

When working in a group, if you are not running Visual SourceSafe, ensure that no two or more people are working on the same file simultaneously. Otherwise, the work of the first person who saves will be erased by a more current version of the file being saved by another user.

Various Methods of Opening Files

There are different ways to open files. To open files *residing on your local hard disk*, go to the File menu, select Open, navigate to the directory where the file is located, and select it. If you do not have working copies of the file you are looking for, this method of opening files will not work because the file does not exist on your hard drive. You must have first obtained a working copy of the file in order to be able to open it in this manner. Keep in mind though that when you save modified files that were opened in this manner, Visual InterDev does not update the master files located on the web server.

NOTE

The Open option of the File menu can only open files residing on the local hard drive. It cannot open files located on the server.

A more common method of opening files is performed from the FileView tab using the shortcut menu (see Figure 6.8) that appears when you right-click a file. This method opens files that are located on the web server.

In File View, simply right-click the file you want to open and select Open from the shortcut menu. This causes an editable copy to be opened with the default editor. If Visual SourceSafe is installed and running on the web server, Visual InterDev prompts you whether you would like a read-only copy or a write-enabled copy. For Visual SourceSafe to lock the file so that others cannot get working copies of that file, you would have to get a write-enabled copy.

To open a file with an editor that is not a default editor, right-click the file and select Open With from the shortcut menu (see Figure 6.9). The Open With dialog box lists the current editors you can use to open the file.

FIGURE 6.8.

Use the shortcut menu by right-clicking on the file you would like to open.

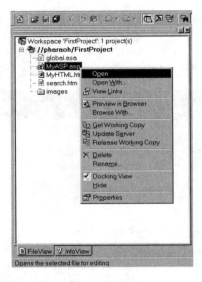

FIGURE 6.9.

The Open With dialog box enables you to open a file from a nondefault editor, add a new editor, or set the default editor.

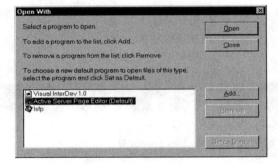

Adding a New Editor

You can add a new editor to edit a specific file type. The steps to do so are as follows:

1. Right-click the file of the same type for which you want to add an editor.

2. Select Open With from the shortcut menu.

3. In the Add Editor dialog box that appears, click the Add button to add the desired editor for that file type.

4. Give the editor a friendly name, a name that you will see when you choose from the list of available editors in the future.

After completing these steps, the editor you added should now be visible in the list of available editors.

Setting the Default Editor

Different file types are opened with different editors. Table 6.1 shows which editors are used to open the various file types.

Table 6.1. The default editors used with specific file types.

Default editor	File type
HTML Layout Editor	.alx
HTML Source Editor	.asa
	.asp
	.htm

The FrontPage editor may also be used to open .htm files.

You can set the default editor by doing the following:

1. Right-click the file of the same type for which you want to specify a default editor.
2. Select Open With from the shortcut menu.
3. Select the desired editor to be endowed with the privilege of being the default editor for that file type.
4. Click the Set as Default button.
5. Click Close when you're finished.

Saving Files

By default, a modified working copy of a file updates the master file on the server. Sometimes, you may want to disable this automated feature, especially if you are working over a slow connection.

To disable the automatic updating of master files, go to the Tools menu and select Options. Navigate to the Web Projects tab and deselect the Update server when files are saved option and click OK. Now every time you save, Visual InterDev does not automatically update the master files.

One word of caution is called for here. When viewing pages in your project with a browser using the Preview or Preview in Browser option in the shortcut menu, you will be browsing the server copy of the file. So if you have the automatic update option off, you must first select Update Server from the shortcut menu before the changes can be seen when browsed with the browser.

> **NOTE**
>
> If you are browsing a page that you know you modified but you do not see the changes, try clicking the Refresh button. If you still cannot see the changes you made, right-click the file and update the server from the shortcut menu to update the master copy with the latest version of the working copy. Keep in mind that the browser shows you the contents of the master copy, not the working copy.

The typical cycle employed in web page development can be summarized by these steps:

1. Working copies are obtained.
2. Files are opened and modified.
3. Changes are saved.
4. Working copies are released.

Viewing Web Pages in a Browser

Once a file has been saved on the web server, it can be viewed with a Web browser. To do this, in the File View pane, right-click the file and select either Preview in Browser or Browse With.... The former opens the file in the default browser. If you haven't set a default browser, Visual InterDev uses InfoViewer—a built-in browser. The latter enables you to choose a browser, add new browsers, and set the default browser that you would like to use. Alternatively, you can choose Preview in Browser from the File menu. This is the same as the first right-click option just described.

By viewing a web page using the procedure outlined in the previous paragraph, you can view Active Server Pages with server-side scripts. When previewing a page in this manner, you are actually viewing the master copy residing on the web server. It is for this reason that it is important to ensure that you save the latest changes and that the master files are updated on the server. You will still need to click the refresh button in the browser to see the latest modifications in effect.

> **TIP**
>
> To be able to preview the latest changes to a file in a browser, do not forget to save the changes *and* update the server. Remember, your browser shows you the master copy residing on the server, not the working copy on your local machine. Also, click the refresh button to see the latest changes.

Web Page Editing and Design

There are a number of built-in editors in Visual InterDev. Each editor is associated with the different file types supported by Visual InterDev. These editors are as follows:

■ **Source Editor**

Besides color-coding HTML code on-the-fly, Visual InterDev's built-in HTML Source Editor (see Figure 6.10) facilitates the HTML coding process in many ways. You can, for instance, quickly and easily insert ActiveX controls simply by right-clicking in the editor and selecting Insert ActiveX Control….

FIGURE 6.10.

Right-clicking in the source editor brings up a handy shortcut menu that allows you to insert HTML, insert ActiveX controls, or insert HTML layout.

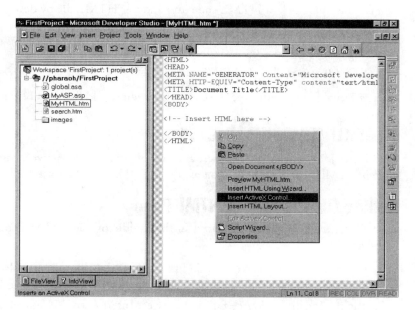

■ **FrontPage Editor**

A powerful editor that enables you to edit HTML files in WYSIWYG mode.

■ **Object Editor**

Allows you to add and modify objects including design-time controls and ActiveX controls in HTML pages.

■ **HTML Layout Editor**

The HTML Layout Editor enables you to design the architecture of your web pages from a bird's-eye view. This editor is especially useful when working with complex HTML pages that contain numerous controls. It also facilitates control sizing, placement, and layering. Place the cursor at the desired location to insert HTML Layout into the current HTML code, right-click in the editor window and select Insert HTML Layout….

■ **Script Wizard**

You can insert VBScript or JScript code in an HTML document in one of two ways. The first method just requires you to type in the code within the bounds of the <SCRIPT> tags (more on this later).

The second method of inserting VBScript or JScript code into your HTML code is to just use the Script Wizard, which automates the process and inserts the <SCRIPT> tags for you.

Inserting a Block of HTML Code

You can insert a block of HTML code into another HTML file by doing the following:

1. Place the cursor at the desired insertion location.
2. Right-click in the editor window.
3. Select Insert HTML Using Wizard.

Alternatively, you can just type the code where you would like it to be placed.

Working with Objects

Visual InterDev enables you to insert and edit objects such as ActiveX controls in the middle of your HTML code. To do this, you use the HTML Source Editor as well as the Object Editor.

Adding Objects to Your HTML Page

ActiveX controls can be easily placed in the middle of your HTML code in the following manner:

1. Open the HTML file you would like to insert the object in and place the cursor somewhere between the <HTML> tags, at the spot where you want to insert the object.
2. Right-click in the Source Editor and select Insert ActiveX Control from the shortcut menu (see Figure 6.11). This should bring up the dialog box for inserting ActiveX controls.

FIGURE 6.11.

You can insert a control or a design-time control from the Insert ActiveX Control dialog box.

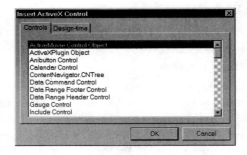

3. Choose the tab containing the type of object you want to add—control or design-time object—and select the specific object you desire.

4. Once the object is selected, the Object Editor appears inside the Source Editor. Use it to edit the control and specify its properties.

5. Close the Object Editor when you're done to automatically insert the object's code within the <OBJECT> tags.

Editing Objects

It is very easy to edit objects in Visual InterDev. The following steps outline the process:

1. Open the file that contains the object you would like to edit by right-clicking the file and selecting Open With….

2. Open the file with the HTML Source Editor.

3. Place the cursor within the confines of the <OBJECT> tags for the object you would like to edit.

4. Right-click inside the Source Editor window and select Edit ActiveX Control. This should cause the Object Editor to appear and load the object into it.

5. Edit the control and modify the properties as desired. When finished, close the Object Editor, and the object code will automatically be modified to reflect the changes you made.

Creating HTML Pages

To create an HTML page, choose New from the File menu to bring up the New dialog box. Select HTML Page in the Files tab and check Add to Project. This will add the new HTML file to the active project. Give the HTML file a name and specify its location. When you're done, click OK to open the file in the HTML Source Editor.

Editing HTML Pages

HTML pages are those that end with .asa, .asp, or .htm. To edit an HTML page, go to File View and double-click the HTML page you would like to edit. This opens the file with the default HTML Source Editor. If you would like to open it with another editor, right-click the file, select Open With… from the shortcut menu, and then select the editor you would like to use.

TIP

To edit an .htm file in WYSIWYG mode, open it with the FrontPage Editor. You can also use FrontPage to edit the HTML code. To do this, just go to the View menu and select HTML…. This opens a View or Edit HTML window with the current page's HTML code. When you are done making changes to the HTML code, click OK.

WARNING

It is recommended that you use the FrontPage Editor only for `.htm` files. Editing `.asa`, `.alx`, or `.asp` files with Microsoft FrontPage may cause undesired results.

Creating Active Server Pages

Active Server Pages are files that have the `.asp` extension. To create an Active Server Page, perform the following steps:

1. Select New from the File menu to bring up the New dialog box.
2. Choose Active Server Page and specify a filename and location where you would like the file to be added.
3. Click OK when you're done.

The new page appears in the Source Editor where you can right-click to add HTML code, ActiveX controls, design-time controls, and HTML layouts.

Introduction to HTML Layouts

HTML layouts are WYSIWYG `.alx` files in which you can easily place controls and specify their properties and locations. These files can be referenced from HTML or `.asp` files. In this manner, several web pages can share the same layout.

Creating, Inserting, and Editing HTML Layouts

Creating HTML layouts is a fairly straightforward process. The following steps outline the procedure:

1. Select New from the File menu.
2. In the Files tab, select HTML Layout.
3. Check the Add to Project option.
4. Specify the filename and location of the file.
5. Click OK to bring up the HTML Layout Editor (see Figure 6.12).
6. When the Layout Editor appears, right-click anywhere in the window and select properties from the shortcut menu to set such default properties as height, width, and color.

7. From the toolbox, select the control to be placed in the page and simply draw them in the HTML Layout window.

8. To change a control's properties, just right-click the control once it has been placed in the HTML layout and select Properties.

9. When you're done, choose Save from the File menu.

Figure 6.12.

The HTML Layout Editor permits you to add and edit such objects as command buttons, labels, and tabs. Simply drag them off the toolbar and drop them in the editor window.

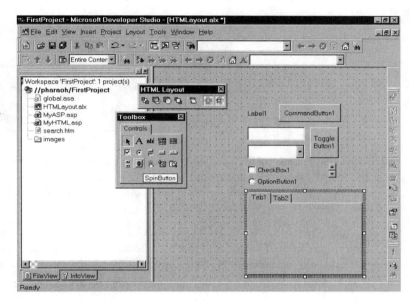

HTML layouts (see Figure 6.13) can be inserted in HTML files as well as Active Server Pages. If you thought *creating* HTML layouts is simple, I am sure you will find *inserting* them is a piece of cake! Here's how:

1. Open the .htm or .asp file into which you would like to insert the HTML layout.

2. Once the file has been opened in the Source Editor, place the cursor where you would like to insert the HTML layout. Note that you can insert it only between the <HTML> delimiters.

3. After placing the cursor, right-click in the Source Editor and select Insert HTML Layout.

4. Select the desired HTML layout or its URL, and you're done!

FIGURE 6.13.

The dialog box titled Select HTML Layout enables you to insert HTML layouts quite easily. Simply choose the desired HTML layout or its URL.

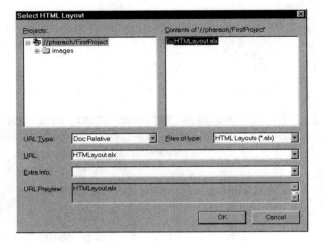

After you have created an HTML layout, you can edit it quite easily. In File View, simply right-click the HTML layout file you would like to edit and select Open; use Open With... if you would like to open the file with a non-default editor. Alternatively you can just double-click the file to open it in the default editor.

If you would like to edit an HTML layout that has already been placed in an HTML or ASP file, simply open that HTML or ASP file in the Source Editor and place the cursor between the <OBJECT> tags that contain the HTML layout you would like to edit. Right-click and select Edit HTML Layout from the shortcut menu. It's that simple.

Summary

Web projects contain files and directories that make up the web. To create a web site, select Web Project Wizard from the Projects tab in the New dialog box.

There are three convenient views in Visual InterDev: File View, Info View, and Data View.

When opening an .htm file with FrontPage, use the shortcut menu that appears when you right-click the file. Do not open the file from FrontPage.

Visual InterDev enables you to download a Web site and its structure into a project, whether that project was created with Microsoft FrontPage or another editor.

Working copies, which reside on the local machine, are replicas of master copies located on the server. Whenever you make changes to working copies, you should update the server's master copies and click refresh in the browser you are using to preview the pages. Microsoft Visual SourceSafe locks the master files at the server when a write-enabled working copy is granted to a user. This prevents multi-user saving conflict. When you're finished with working copies, release them.

You can add, remove, or set new default editors and browsers by selecting Open With... or Browse With... from the shortcut menu.

There are a number of editors for editing various file types. Visual InterDev automatically knows which editor to open for which file type.

Managing the Site and Team Development

by Matt Watson

IN THIS CHAPTER

CHAPTER 7

Whether you are developing a client/server application or a Web application, it is important to set up a project environment that will support the development, testing, and deployment of your application. There are several key concepts that your Web application project environment must support:

- Multiple developers
- Source code migration
- Source code version control
- Integration testing
- Ongoing maintenance of the application

Depending on the size and complexity of your project, some of these concepts may be more important than others. In this chapter, you will discover features of Visual InterDev that support creating a Web application in a team environment from development to deployment. In addition, you will learn about features of Visual InterDev that support managing the various Web sites that are needed during the development process.

What Is a Site?

In today's Internet-savvy world, the word *site* usually refers to a collection of HTML pages on the World Wide Web. A site can consist of any combination of static HTML pages, Java applets, ActiveX controls, graphical images, or dynamic HTML pages connected to a database. A Web site can represent a corporation, an individual, a service, or an organization. From an applications development standpoint, however, a Web site takes on a slightly different meaning. For our purposes, the word *site* will be used in the context of the environments required to develop your Web application. Three distinct environments are required during the application development process: development, testing, and production. In addition, you can add a fourth environment called application maintenance or post-production. It's a good practice to establish a corresponding Web site for each environment in the application development process. The following sections explain each of these site environments in more detail.

The Development Site

The development environment site should support the design, creation, and testing of the individual components that make up the Web application. The number of individuals involved in the development process will likely depend on the complexity and overall time frame of the project. The best practice is to establish a development site that supports multiple people in multiple roles working on the same project. Later in this chapter, you will learn about the various roles that are typically required when developing a Web application.

The Test Site

The testing environment site should support testing the components of the Web application together. Another term for the activity during this phase of the project is *integration testing*.

This includes testing interaction between the individual pages of the Web application, including the validity of links to other pages. Whereas the testing performed in the development environment focuses on the technical and functional implementation of an individual component, the testing performed at this stage should cover the overall functionality of the Web application. Separate test and development environments also enable you to ensure that code changes and works in progress do not deter your testing efforts. Think of this stage as a test drive for the Web application, simulating how the application will look and behave to the end users.

The Production Site

The final stage of the life cycle is the actual live version of the application on the Internet or your local intranet. At this point, your application and its functionality are accessible by the user community. Obviously, a separate production environment site must be established to support the use of your Web application by the end users. The production site will contain all the components necessary for execution and operation of your Web application.

The Post-Production Site

Once your Web application is deployed to the production environment, a different phase of the project life cycle begins. This phase is commonly known as the application maintenance or post-production phase. Maintaining your Web application involves incorporating changes to the application into the production environment. Depending on their frequency, you may choose to establish an environment that is similar to your development and test environment to make and test these changes. On the other hand, you may choose to simplify the maintenance environment by combining the development and testing environments into a single Web site. Figure 7.1 displays the sites involved in a typical Web application development effort.

FIGURE 7.1.
The different sites involved in developing a Web application.

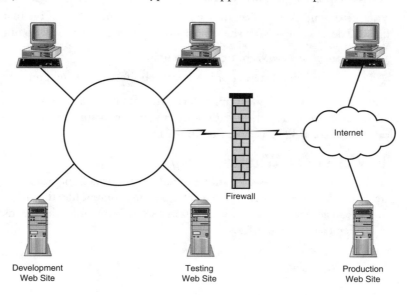

Developing the Web Application

Before you begin developing your Web application, it is important to plan your development environment. Although there are several things to consider during this planning process, a couple issues stand out. The first is the process of creating your Web development site. Earlier, you learned about a typical Web application project environment with a development, testing, production, and post-production Web site. The location of the development Web site depends on the size and complexity of your development effort. You basically have two options for setting up your development Web site:

- Create your development Web site on a centralized Web server.
- Allow each developer a Web site using Microsoft's Personal Web Server for Windows 95.

The second option is attractive if your developers are working remotely or spend their time away from your LAN or WAN. However, synchronizing multiple development Web servers can be an arduous task and should be avoided. Therefore, a better practice is using the centralized approach with a shared development Web site.

Another key issue to consider is source code control for your Web application. This item is important because of the number and variety of source files that will make up your Web application. In addition, you will probably have multiple developers working on your Web application. For this reason, you will need a mechanism for managing the source files among the members of your development team. Fortunately, the Visual InterDev architecture enables you to easily address both of these items.

Creating Your Development Site

When setting up your project development environment, one of the first tasks involves creating your development Web site. In performing this task, you will do one of the following:

- Create your new Web site from scratch.
- Use an existing Internet or intranet Web site as a starting point.

Visual InterDev includes features to facilitate both of these actions. Later in this chapter, you will discover Visual InterDev features for copying an existing Web site. In this section you will learn about creating your Web site from scratch.

The Web Project Wizard

Visual InterDev includes a wizard that guides you through the process of creating a new Web site. It also includes additional wizards for creating content files that are a part of your Web site project. To access the Web Project Wizard, select New under the File menu. You will see the dialog depicted in Figure 7.2.

FIGURE 7.2.
*Choosing the Web
Project Wizard.*

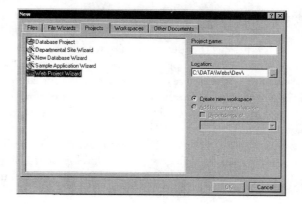

As you can see, the Projects tab offers several choices for creating a new Web site or application. For example, to create a blank Web site on a specified server, select the Web Project Wizard. Table 7.1 summarizes the features of each of the project wizards.

Table 7.1. The new project wizards.

Wizard	Description
Database Project Wizard	Creates a blank Web site with a specified database connection.
Departmental Site Wizard	Creates a shell Web site with typical HTML pages for a department including navigation between the generated HTML pages.
New Database Wizard	Creates a SQL Server database.
Sample Application Wizard	Installs a Web application on the specified Web server including database connections required by the application.
Web Project Wizard	Creates a new project with either a blank Web site or an existing Web site on a specified Web server.

Managing Your Components with Visual SourceSafe

Another key consideration in developing your Web application is source code control. There are two main reasons why source code control is critical to the success of your development efforts. The first is related to team development. Later in this chapter you will learn about the different types of roles involved in developing a Web application. For now, it is important to realize that your development Web site must be capable of supporting multiple developers, all working from a common set of source files. Source code control enables a developer to work with a source file such as an HTML file, multimedia file, or Active Server Page exclusively, without the fear of another developer working with the same file. The second reason why source code control is critical is the idea of saving each version of the source code as it goes through the development and revision process. By keeping a record of the revision history of a source file, prior versions of the source code can be recalled for later use. Used properly, this feature can be implemented to maintain different versions of your entire Web application. Visual InterDev provides for this requirement through its integration with Microsoft's Visual SourceSafe. In this section, you will get an overview of the features of Visual SourceSafe and its integration with Visual InterDev. You will learn more detailed information about Visual SourceSafe in Chapter 9, "Effective Team Development Using Visual InterDev and Visual SourceSafe." To use these features, you must install Visual SourceSafe on the Windows NT Web server containing your development Web site.

NOTE

Although you do not need to install Visual SourceSafe on your development workstations to use its features with Visual InterDev, you must select the Enable SourceSafe Integration option during the Visual SourceSafe installation process on the Web server.

In addition, you must set the appropriate permissions for your developers on the Web server and within the Visual SourceSafe database. Next, you will look at utilizing the features of Visual SourceSafe from within the Visual InterDev environment.

NOTE

If you do not have Visual SourceSafe installed, you must still address source code control issues in order to have a successful Web application development project. You may choose to use a different source code control program. You can customize the Tools menu by adding access to your chosen source code control program from within the Visual InterDev development environment. While this enables you to run the alternative source code control program from within the Visual InterDev development environment, you will not enjoy the integrated features offered by Visual SourceSafe.

Enabling Source Code Control

Once Visual SourceSafe is installed on your Web server, you are ready to utilize its source code control features. The first step in this process is putting your Web project under source code control. Under the Project menu, select the Enable Web Source Control item. Next, you should see a screen similar to the window displayed in Figure 7.3.

FIGURE 7.3.

*Enabling Web Source
Control in Visual
InterDev.*

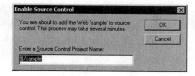

It's a good idea to accept the default for the source control project name. Once your Web project has source code control enabled, any new files created by your project team will automatically be added to the Visual SourceSafe project. Your Web site or application is now under source code control, and you are ready to begin using the features of Visual SourceSafe from within your development environment.

> **TIP**
>
> To disable source code control for your Web project, simply select Disable Web Source Control from the Project menu. Note that the Visual SourceSafe project created when you enabled source code control will still exist in the Visual SourceSafe database.

From a developer's perspective, the next step involves gaining exclusive access to the file or files he needs to work with. This process is commonly known as checking out the source code component. Once a source code component is checked out to a developer, only he can modify that file. Other developers can obtain a read-only copy of the file.

Checking Files Out

To check out a file, select the file in the File View pane and use the right mouse button to invoke the pop-up menu. Select the Get Working Copy menu item as depicted in Figure 7.4.

Checking Files In

Once you have completed working with the source code component, it's a good idea to check the file back into Visual SourceSafe. When making multiple changes to a file, you will have to use your best judgement on how often you should check in a copy of the file to Visual SourceSafe. Try to group your changes into logical units of work to create versions of the component that are meaningful. This will make your life much easier in the event that you have to backtrack and use a prior version of the source code component. To check a component back into Visual SourceSafe, select the file in the File View pane and use the right mouse button to invoke the pop-up menu. Select the Release Working Copy menu item, as depicted in Figure 7.5.

FIGURE 7.4.
Getting a working copy of a file.

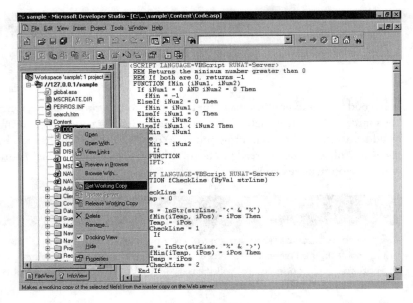

FIGURE 7.5.
Releasing a working copy of a file.

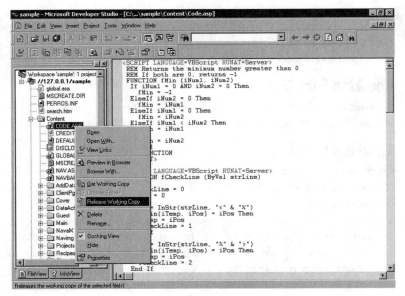

Additional Source Code Options

Visual InterDev offers you maximum flexibility in working with Visual SourceSafe integration and source code control. By accessing this option within Visual InterDev, you can utilize the full functionality of the Visual SourceSafe program for your development project. The Visual SourceSafe program itself can be accessed from the Project menu, as depicted in Figure 7.6.

FIGURE 7.6.

Accessing the Visual SourceSafe program.

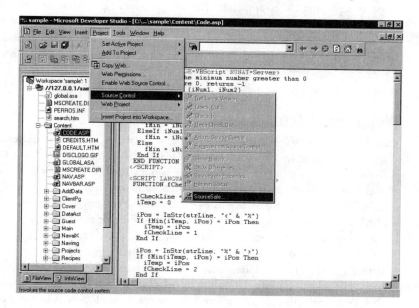

In addition, Visual InterDev enables you to customize the way it works and interacts with Visual SourceSafe. You can work with this customization feature by choosing Options from the Tools menu. You will be presented with a dialog like the one depicted in Figure 7.7.

FIGURE 7.7.

Setting options for Visual SourceSafe integration.

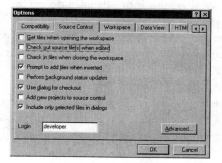

Using the Visual SourceSafe Program

If you have the Visual SourceSafe client installed on your development machine or you access Visual SourceSafe through the Project menu in Visual InterDev, you may want to take advantage of some of the features of the Visual SourceSafe application. In addition to the check-in/check-out functionality offered within Visual InterDev, there are several features in Visual SourceSafe related to Web application development. For example, Visual SourceSafe supports deploying a Web application into the production environment by allowing your project team to publish content to a Web server. You can also generate a map of your site from content files stored in a Visual SourceSafe project, as well as verify the hyperlinks within your Web project. Finally, Visual SourceSafe enables you to view a file's change history and differences between versions of a file. For more details on using Visual SourceSafe in an application development environment, see Chapter 9.

Web Project Team Roles

Thus far, you have learned about the proper environment needed for effective development of a Web application. In addition, you have learned about features of Visual InterDev that support the development phase of your Web application. At this point, you may be wondering why this is necessary. You may have created your own home page on the World Wide Web with little difficulty or assistance from others. However, any Web site or application with even a minimum of complexity usually requires the efforts of multiple people in a variety of roles. Depending on the complexity of your application, these roles may be filled by as few as three people or as many as 10. Each of these roles is equally important to the overall success of the project. Also, keep in mind that these roles apply to each phase of the application development process. Hopefully, an understanding of the typical roles involved with the development of a Web application will help you appreciate the team development features of Visual InterDev.

Application Designer

Someone who designs Web applications is primarily responsible for gathering user requirements for the functionality of the application and the appearance of the site. The application designer translates these requirements into a detailed design for the Web application. Many times, the same person or persons fill the designer and developer roles. In addition, there can be multiple types of designers on your project team. For example, you may require a database designer to create the logical and physical design of a relational database.

Functional Expert

The functional expert serves as the subject matter expert for the business function that is supported by the Web application. The exact type of person for this role will depend largely on the functionality supported by the Web application. This person will aid the design, development, and testing of the Web application.

Application Developer

Developers are responsible for creating a variety of Web-based content. This can include HTML files, Java applets, and Active Server Pages with VBScript. Depending on the complexity and technical architecture of your Web application, your development team might be responsible for creating stored procedures in a relational database, Active Server components, or Java servlets that support the functionality of the Web application. In addition, your developers are actively involved with the integration testing of the Web application.

Graphic Artist

The graphic artist is responsible for creating and integrating any multimedia content for the Web application, including graphic files and imagemaps for the Web site. In addition, the graphic artist should work closely with the application designers and functional experts to craft the look and feel of the Web application.

System Administrator

The system administrator role provides a catch-all for the roles needed to support the development, testing, and production environments. This role involves the management and administration of the tools involved in the development and testing processes. Examples of tools involved in the development process include Visual InterDev and Visual SourceSafe. This role also includes database administration responsibilities as well as the management of the platforms needed for both client and Web server development.

Webmaster

The Webmaster is responsible for managing the sites involved with the development of the Web application. This includes the development, testing, and production Web sites. This role requires deep knowledge of TCP/IP, the Internet, and the World Wide Web. This person or persons will work closely with the developers, graphic artists, and system administrators on all aspects of the Web application.

Project Manager

In describing this role, the name says it all. In order to have a successful development project, you must have someone who is capable from a technical and business-process standpoint leading your efforts. Communication and planning skills are a must for the project manager role.

Testing the Web Application

Two key issues to address during the testing phase of your project are source code migration and integration testing. Visual InterDev contains several powerful features that minimize the impact of these issues on your testing efforts.

Migrating Your Source

Code migration refers to the act of moving the source code and components that make up your application from one environment to another. During the testing phase of your project, you will migrate your application source code and components from the development environment to the testing environment. From the testing environment, your source will migrate to the production environment. With the number and variety of files that make up a typical Web application, this is not a trivial matter. Figure 7.8 displays the code migration process from the development site to the production site.

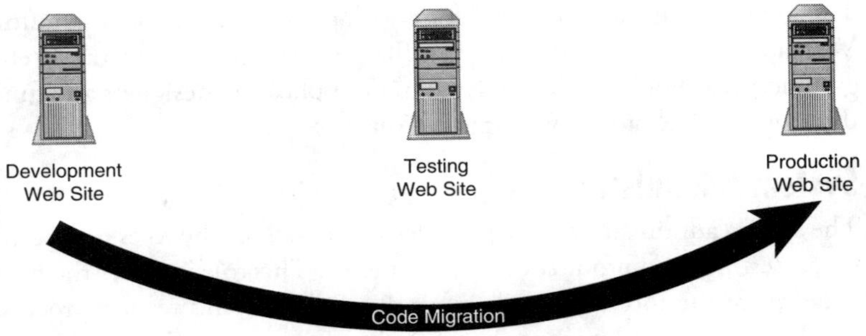

FIGURE 7.8.
The source code
migration process.

Development
Web Site

Testing
Web Site

Production
Web Site

Code Migration

Visual InterDev eases the source code migration process through the Copy Web feature.

Copy Web

Visual InterDev supports the movement of an entire Web site from one Web server to another through the Copy Web feature. For our purposes, there are two great uses for this feature:

■ Copying an existing web to use as a starting point for a new application.

■ Managing the code migration process from development to testing, testing to production, and so on.

You can find the Copy Web feature under the Project menu in Visual InterDev. Figure 7.9 illustrates the Copy Web dialog.

FIGURE 7.9.
Copying a web within
Visual InterDev.

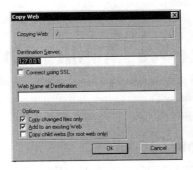

As you can see, the Copy Web dialog is straightforward and easy to use. From a security standpoint, Copy Web supports a Secure Sockets Layer (SSL) connection to the target or destination Web server. In addition, you have the option of only copying files that have changed since the last time Copy Web was executed for the destination Web site. From a development standpoint, this option is useful when you are refreshing your test site with the latest changes from the development site. By selecting this option, the test site will only receive the files that have changed since the last component migration. The other features enable you to add your site to an existing Web site on the destination Web server and copy child Web sites to the destination Web server if you are copying the root Web.

NOTE

Once you have used the Copy Web feature to copy a Web site, a new project must be created for the copied site before you can use it in Visual InterDev.

Working with Link View

One aspect of testing your Web application involves verifying the links that connect your site's content. Because most Web sites are made up of multiple files, individually opening each file and verifying the path to a hyperlink, graphical image, or Java applet could prove to be a tedious and time-consuming task. Fortunately, Visual InterDev enables you to graphically view the files or objects that make up your Web site or application. This site visualization feature is called the Link View. To access the Link View feature, select any file in the File View pane, right-click with the mouse, and select View Links. This operation is displayed in Figure 7.10.

FIGURE 7.10.

Accessing the Link View feature.

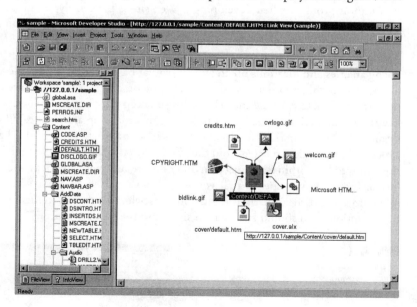

Link View uses different icons for each file type included in a Web site. Lines with arrows indicate the relationship between linked components and the selected file. Broken links are depicted in red, with the object's icon depicted in gray with part of the icon missing. Link View offers the user several options on the visual representation of the site. You can filter the types of components that are displayed in the Link View window. When the Link View is displayed, you can use the Filters menu item under the View menu to display components of a specific type. For example, you may choose to only display HTML pages or multimedia files. By using the right mouse button in Link View, you can further expand the view of the site to display additional layers of links to components. In addition, you can open the appropriate editor for the component or see a preview of the component in your default Web browser. As you can see, Link View gives your testing and development teams maximum flexibility in graphically viewing and interacting with the files and objects that make up a Web site.

> **TIP**
>
> You can use Link View to view sites on the World Wide Web. This feature is located under the Tools menu: View Files on the WWW. Once selected, a dialog appears containing a text box for the URL of the World Wide Web site you would like to see using Link View.

Repairing Broken Links

A common problem when developing a Web site is broken hyperlinks. A broken hyperlink occurs when a linked file's name or location changes. When working on a Web application with multiple developers, many changes take place to the structure of the Web site during the development phase. HTML source, multimedia files, and other content files will inevitably change names and locations on an almost regular basis. For example, a developer might insert a link to a file that another developer is working on and inadvertently use the wrong filename or URL. Fortunately, Visual InterDev helps you keep track of such occurrences. Visual InterDev keeps track of URL references within the files that make up a Web site. When a file is renamed or moved, Visual InterDev automatically takes action to repair the links that are broken in the process. When a file is deleted from the Web project, Visual InterDev will list the references to the removed file within the project. In order for the automatic link repair feature to work within Visual InterDev, you specify that you want links repaired within a Web project. Select your Web project and click the right mouse button. Select properties to turn on the automatic link repair option. You should see a screen similar to the one in Figure 7.11.

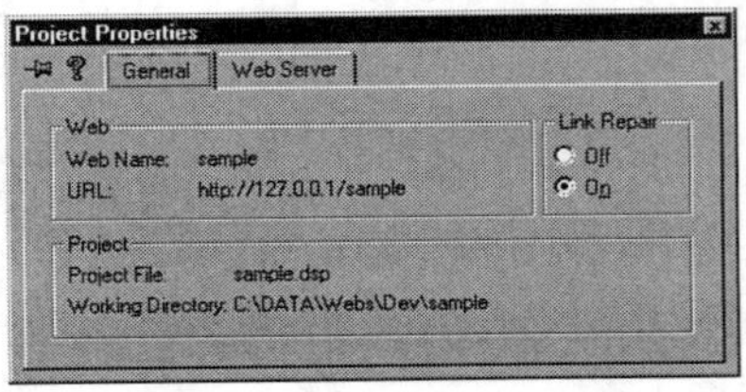

FIGURE 7.11.

Setting the automatic Link Repair property.

For more detailed information on the site management features of Visual InterDev, please see Chapter 11, "Managing the Site."

Deploying the Web Application

The final step of the Web application development process involves moving or deploying your application into the production environment. This is a big step in the life of any Web application. Many of the site-migration concepts discussed earlier apply to the deployment phase. However, your Web application should only be moved into the production environment after completing the testing phase. The move to the production Web site signifies a new phase in the life of your Web application: it is now accessible by its intended user community. In addition, you need to establish an application maintenance strategy and environment for any post-production changes that are made to your Web application.

Moving to Production

Earlier you learned about the features of the Copy Web function in Visual InterDev. You can use this same functionality to copy your Web application from the testing Web site to the production Web site. Again, it is important to realize that this is a significant step in the application development process for your Web application.

Summary

In this chapter, you discovered the features of Visual InterDev that support the development of a Web application in a team environment. In addition, you learned that a Web application requires distinct environments and Web sites for the development, testing, and deployment phases of your project. Visual InterDev offers several key features that facilitate managing the Web sites involved in the application development process. Visual InterDev contains wizards that enable you to quickly and easily create a Web site from scratch. The Copy Web function enables you to copy an existing site from your local intranet or the Internet and use it as a starting point for your Web application. In addition, the Copy Web function allows easy migration of your source code from the development Web site to the testing Web site, and so on. When testing your Web application, you learned the importance of testing the integration of your application content. Visual InterDev enables you to visualize the various documents that make up your Web application through the Link View. The Link View gives you a graphical representation of your Web site and the links that connect its documents. You also learned that it is common for such links to become broken during the development process. As a developer, you have the option of having Visual InterDev keep track of all of the hyperlinks within your Web application and automatically repair broken hyperlinks.

You learned about key issues involved with developing a Web application in a team environment. These issues include multiple developers working within a common environment and managing the source code within and between the development, testing, and production environments. Visual InterDev offers full integration with Visual SourceSafe, Microsoft's source code control application. Once source code control is enabled for your Web site, developers can utilize the check-in and check-out features to gain exclusive access to a component of the Web application. Thus, your developers are protected from inadvertently writing over one another's changes within a source code file. In addition, the Visual SourceSafe application enables your development team to maintain multiple versions of your Web application, track the change history of a file, and view differences between versions of a file. Finally, you learned about the different roles that are involved with the development of a Web application and their overall importance to the success of your project.

Integrating and Extending Visual InterDev

by Robert M. Niemela

IN THIS CHAPTER

In this chapter, I will discuss how to use Visual InterDev as it relates to extending the environment. To help you fully comprehend the power of Visual InterDev, I will talk first about the challenges facing developers today and the problems inherent with Web development tools. In the final segment, I will go over the finer essentials of an add-in and the key implements necessary to tap into the Visual InterDev world programmatically.

Overview: Technological Environment Continuum

There is little we can count on but change in life (and of course that statement starting a chapter). Technology is no exception, and has been moving ahead at a phenomenal rate where it has become a job just to keep up with our existing job. How does one stay on top? Software releases seem to perpetuate in beta and make it increasingly difficult to stay ahead. How do we grow along the technology continuum and face new technologies' advancements with a sigh of relief rather than the learning curve blues? There are three fundamental architectural structures available in Visual InterDev that are extremely powerful and that provide the mechanism for addressing these issues. First let me describe the problem that VI addresses head on.

The Problem: Lack of Extensible Tools

With the dawn of light-speed technological advancements and changing languages we have entered a new age of online development. This is an extremely exciting age in which the skill-sets have changed dramatically from two years ago. The underlying challenge today is trying to stay on top of new technologies while lacking appropriate tools to do so.

I strongly believe and stress that the answer to successfully adopting and staying abreast of any new technology is the set of tools that accompany it. The problem lies in that technology has changed and skill-sets have changed, but the tools have not. Faithful old Notepad remains the reigning winner for Internet developer sites. It is paradoxical to see that the new technologies of the future are still being built on rudimentary tools of yesterday.

And let's face it, Notepad, as simple as it is, doesn't lose much to its 16-bit, VBX-bloated competitors. We all have tried GUI/non-GUI HTML editors, and whether it be the primate nature of programmers wanting to know what is happening at the source level or that these editors rarely deliver their promised sanctuary, one can only speculate. GUI/WYSIWYG HTML editors serve a purpose, but given Java, JScript, VBScript, and the whole Active Server framework, the editors rarely meet the mark.

The primary reason HTML editors fall short of the challenge is due to their own existence—HTML. HTML doesn't provide database connectivity or scripting and thus neither do the large majority of editors within this Internet phenomenon.

In order to keep efficiently, effectively, and intellectually on top of technological advances, you must have the proper tools to support them. Otherwise, they just remain a white paper in the lost sea of brilliant ideas never pursued or adopted.

Static Web pages are now limited to personal home pages and time-insensitive data. We belong to a new age in online acquisitions: *dynamics*. We have entered a new stage of dynamics and to embrace this requires considerably more effort and planning than that of being statically existent. Dynamics is the primary thread of programming and is nothing new, but the dynamics of the Web in the past have been far too cryptic and debug intensive. The whole intranet/Internet development environment has changed considerably. We are now finding real needs and desires for attaining online goals but are not developing in a true manner due to tool scarcity. Much like relational database principles of normalization, so do we apply the same principles of development by reducing redundant coding efforts.

The bottom line still remains that tools will never keep up with technological change. Tools arise out of technological change. So there is this inherent continuum of technology and the tools that chase them on a scale of infinity. Several months ago, tools like Visual InterDev were not only out-of-sight, but also were out-of-mind. More precisely, to stay abreast, to maximize development efforts, and to be efficient, you must use the object exposures offered by the Visual InterDev development environment.

The Solution: $VI = EI^n$

Visual InterDev equals Environment Integration to the nth power. Visual InterDev enables you to meet the challenges of modern technology with and without the working environment. It provides this functionality by exposing its environment, thus allowing itself to be customized through the use of Web wizards, ActiveX design-time controls, and add-ins.

Add-Ins: Extensibility and Life Cycle Growth Solution

Being able to accommodate new technologies or to create them requires the flexibility of a development environment. Tools evolve at a much slower pace than technologies, and thus Visual InterDev has been created to provide this open architecture to build upon.

One of the most prominent development features that developers have used over the years is *add-ins*. Add-ins allow you to truly customize your development environment to meet any scripting need. Custom solutions for environment manipulation are ideally suited through add-ins. Repetitive tasks such as common scripting iterations are easy to incorporate by a simple button on the task bar. Any new Internet Engineering Task Force (IETF) approvals stronger than your basic 2 encapsulating tags that require considerable HTML coding (like writing a specific cascading style sheet or table layout) can be incorporated with Visual InterDev through the use of add-ins. Add-ins provide the mechanism to develop custom solutions that need to interact with the environment. In the case of an intranet scenario, suppose you have your own corporate client browser or server-side specifications that you repeatedly use on a consistent basis. Through the use of Visual InterDev add-ins, those custom navigates or object calls can be accomplished with relative ease.

Another weakness of most tools available today is that they lack the ability to provide in-process integration with their products. Most of the higher-end tools provide the ability to shell out to outside environments. But these outside environments provide little to no control to the actual process in which the development resides. Add-ins provide this functionality.

Add-ins have brought great solace to the programming world, thus it is a natural progression to bring the same benefits to the Web development world. Add-ins permit you to automate routine tasks in the Developer Studio environment as well as to customize programs to meet specific application development needs.

Add-ins use the framework known as Automation. Automation is formerly known as OLE Automation. Using Automation, you can manipulate the Developer Studio environment and its related components to truly customize the development experience.

Add-ins can be viewed and executed as toolbar icons, key sequences, or at the command line. The add-in is really the single most important efficiency giver within Visual InterDev. Many editors give the ability to add new tags, but none truly allows you the extensibility and flexibility that add-ins can provide.

At the end of the chapter I have created an add-in to determine the download time of a specific file based on its dependent graphics. The add-in calculates the required time of a particular file related to varying modem speeds.

Add-Ins Versus Macros

Add-ins differ greatly in functionality and deliverables from macros. Add-ins can achieve new heights of productivity simply through the underlying architecture: OLE Automation. The major difference and power between macros and add-ins is their development environment.

Macros are procedures written in Visual Basic Scripting Edition language. Macros are interpreted and extremely easy to create. You simply record a macro and then store it to be accessible as a toolbar icon, menu, or key combination. Macros provide a quick and dirty solution for most simple problems, but add-ins extend the environment to much higher proportions through file access and object-calling procedures.

Add-ins cover a much broader domain than macros and therefore by nature are much more powerful. Add-ins are not written within the environment itself but are written in a variety of different development tools. This allowance permits add-ins to access the Developer Studio Object model directly and therefore to manipulate its resources, methods, and properties.

Consequently, because add-ins can be developed in a wide variety of tools, the development solutions and possibilities are endless. Finally, as opposed to editors that simply use the x = shell command, an add-in can directly manipulate another executable application and maintain state. Add-ins can also provide a wide endless variety of GUIs compared to the infantile input-box macro feature.

Tools for Writing Add-Ins

Add-ins can be developed in tools such as Microsoft Visual C++, Microsoft Visual Basic 4.0, 5.0, or any tool that supports the Component Object Model. Because of the intuitive nature and syntax of Microsoft Visual Basic it is very advantageous to develop an add-in for it in version 5.0. VB 5.0 lends itself especially well to creating add-ins because it can handle events processed from the application as well as the new use of implements, which can make performance rise.

The Power of Add-Ins

In summary, add-ins are customizable, extensible, and life cycle promoting. Let's face it, developer tools will never fully keep pace with technology. Add-ins provide the vehicle for growth and expansion in an environment that allows them and in a technology that doesn't always. Add-ins can be simple extensions or large full-scale development solutions. The key to add-ins is manipulation through the COM. If your department is segmented into programmers and nonprogrammers, obvious benefits apply. Programmers develop custom solutions for the nonprogrammers to carry out tasks that are trivial to them and mundane to the programmers. The power comes from having the ability to access computer resources through sophisticated development tools and to appear as a simple part of the development shell.

ActiveX Design-Time Controls: Development and Automation

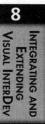

Another facet of development, which has made great strides in the development community, is the notion of ActiveX design-time controls. ActiveX design-time controls are the next step to automation and customization in the development process. ActiveX design-time controls use the object editor to assist their staging society, similar to ActiveX controls.

ActiveX Design-Time Controls Versus ActiveX Controls Versus Web Bots

ActiveX design-time controls are used only in the design-time environment. Conversely, ActiveX controls run within the Web browser at runtime. Design-time controls are never downloaded because they do not contain a binary runtime component. Therefore they are never seen by the browser/client directly because they are encapsulated within HTML comment blocks. There are controls that are used exclusively by the development environment. ActiveX design-time controls are most commonly used to generate source files in the design-time environment presented by a host container that can be used extensively to provide any authoring necessary including calling ActiveX server components. ActiveX components therefore live on the server or the development workstation rather than on the client workstation.

> **NOTE**
>
> No overhead is imposed directly on downloading pages that have used design-time controls to generate text.

Design-time controls are really standard ActiveX controls that have a built-in interface that allows them to generate text, whether it be VBScript, JScript, HTML, or plain text. Design-time controls provide the bridge to server-side development.

Web Bots are a technology specifically designed to work with Microsoft FrontPage and are not based on the COM model. They work only within Microsoft FrontPage and require the FrontPage editor to be used.

Tools for Writing ActiveX Design-Time Contols

These tools can be written in any COM-enabled tool. Tools such as Visual C++, Visual Basic, Borland Delphi, Microfocus COBOL, PowerBuilder, and the Component Object Model are standard for accessing exposed objects within Windows.

The Power of ActiveX Design-Time Controls

The power of ActiveX design-time controls lies within the fact that they can be developed to author a multitude of solutions. They are able to do this through the inherent format of HTML files: text. HTML is text; text is the ultimate universal denominator of formats. Design-time controls can generate text that, regardless of platform, is accessible. Client dependency is increasingly becoming less and less of an issue. The real focus becomes which development tool is the king. For example, a design-time control can be used to generate any form that is based on simple text. The generated text can be HTML content, VBScript, JScript, Java applets, ActiveX controls, or Active server components. Although design-time controls are available only within Microsoft InterDev, it is rumored to be part of Microsoft's master plan to have them incorporated in all Microsoft HTML editors. The potential of design-time controls dwells in the same rich contributive atmosphere that VBXs provided for VB 3.0, extensibility reaching its finest from third-party vendors. There is still a void of controls needed commercially and internally.

Web Wizards: True Customization

Aside from the powerful editing capabilities of Microsoft Access, Microsoft PowerPoint, and Microsoft Word, editors have succeeded very well due to the notion of wizards. Wizards promote user-friendliness in a product. Anything that can get the user involved more quickly in a product usually means a higher success rate. Wizards on the development side can be just as rewarding. Wizards are essentially aids that guide you step by step through a predetermined process to reach a final generated state. Wizards generally get you up-to-speed on a particular project by filling in information step by step and then generating an output based on the inputs. Wizards in VI are much more sophisticated in that they can generate on a much larger scale. Web wizards can be set to generate a few dynamic Web pages and scale up to an entire Web site. They aid in the automation of the production of high-quality, fully functional Web sites. They can generate one page or hundreds, depending on requirements. They can build pages that attach database functionality or even pages that call server-side components.

Web Wizards Versus ActiveX Design-Time Controls

Design-time controls and Web wizards are both COM-based components. Design-time controls can be used as steps within wizards and therefore provide more power. Web wizards have the ability to generate multiple pages, whereas design-time controls can generate only one. Because both components are, however, based on the COM model, they can be built in the same development environments. Finally, Web wizards can run as an entirely standalone application, whereas design-time controls cannot.

Tools for Creating Wizards

You can create Web wizards in tools such as Visual C++ or Visual Basic 5.0. The Web wizard framework is designed to be written optimally in VB 5.0 but can be written also in the following development tools:

Microsoft C++

Visual Basic 5.0

Borland Delphi

Borland C++

Symantec C++

TIP

There will be a Web Wizard Software Development Kit available from Microsoft in the near future, possibly by the time this book is released, so keep checking the Web site for releases.

The Power of Web Wizards

The power of Web wizards can be seen through their fine ability to run as a standalone executable application or DLL. Web wizards can be built in a variety of development tools as long as they can build OLE automation servers. Web wizards are not application specific. They can be compiled from a variety of tools. Webs wizards have the ability to incorporate design-time controls and produce an unlimited amount of pages. If a company is segmented with Internet programmers and non-Internet programmers, Web wizards can be the savior to bridge the development of the two. Graphics artists or content providers can come up quickly with the look and feel of the site, while the programmers can aid in the speed of complex development process. Complex scripting and controls can be developed using Web wizards to provide maximum utility. Wizards are by far the most powerful of all three, because they are not application specific.

Code Walkthrough

This example shows you how to build an add-in for Visual InterDev. You need the following to begin:

> Microsoft Visual Basic 5.0
>
> Microsoft Visual InterDev 1.0
>
> Add-in SDK
>
> Patience not to hack it away

Purpose

The add-in is meant to be a guideline to determine how heavy a given Web page is, related to its download time over a three-modem spectrum of 14.4, 28.8, and 57.6. The add-in appears as a button on the toolbar and, once clicked, calculates the active file's size and adds it to the total file sizes of its dependency objects (graphics). It performs this by first opening the active file in Visual InterDev and then reading through the file for HTML tags that use images. I have the code searching for BACKGROUND and SRC tags. Because those two tags can generally be found anywhere a graphic link is, it only searches for these key words.

NOTE

My download calculations are certainly debatable, but I am assuming the best possible connection environments. Keep in mind that the sole purpose is to show how easy it is to create an add-in and manipulate it in the VI environment.

Setting the Environment

I am not going to walk through each line of code but instead will highlight some of the places I used some of Visual InterDev's Objects. If you would like to view the code and compile the application yourself, you must begin by doing a few short environment steps.

Copy the sample code to a temporary directory and unzip the files. After you unzip them, open the file labeled `Performance.vbp`. After doing this we must begin addressing our references. Due to the wide assortment of setups, I purposely removed all project references so that the project can load. Select the Project menu and select References in the dialog (see Figure 8.1) specified in Listing 8.1. Select all the references to Visual Studio (there should be four).

> **NOTE**
>
> To set up the environment to create a Visual InterDev add-in from scratch, begin simply by starting VB and selecting from the startup dialog that you want to create a new ActiveX DLL. Select the appropriate references and begin coding.

Listing 8.1. References.

```
Reference = OLE Automation
WINNT\System32\STDOLE2.TLB

Reference = Visual Basic T-SQL Debugger
\Program Files\DevStudio\VB\Tsql\VBSDIADD.DLL

Reference = Visual Studio 97 HTML Editor
C:\Program Files\DevStudio\SharedIDE\bin\IDE\devhtm.pkg

Reference = Visual Studio 97 Shared Objects
C:\Program Files\DevStudio\SharedIDE\bin\devshl.dll

Reference = Visual Studio 97 Text Editor
C:\Program Files\DevStudio\SharedIDE\bin\devedit.pkg

Reference = Visual Studio 97 Web Projects
C:\Program Files\DevStudio\SharedIDE\bin\IDE\devisws.pkg
```

FIGURE 8.1.

The most important aspect of setting up a programming project to link VB and VI lies within the References dialog.

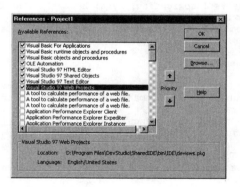

> **NOTE**
>
> The actual paths of your references will vary from computer to computer. The important fact to remember is that the filename is what you are searching for. In most cases the file can be found in your Windows/system/ directory or the directory in which you first installed Visual InterDev.

The Foundation Code

To begin with, in the general code (see Listing 8.2) to the `AppAddin` class, we ensure the `Implements` to the `IDSAddin` object is stated.

Listing 8.2. General section of AppAddin class.

```
Option Explicit
Dim m_intCookie As Integer
Dim m_cCommands As Commands
Implements IDSAddIn
```

The `IDSAddin` object implements a COM interface that makes it faster than the VB4, which would use the `IDDispatch` interface. The `IDSAddin` implement requires one function, one procedure, and one property.

When Visual InterDev first starts up it attempts to load all the add-ins specified in its customize dialog. Each add-in is instantiated by an `OnConnection` method, which is exposed by the add-in object. Listing 8.3 adds the necessary code to your `AppAddin` class to create it when Visual InterDev is loaded. The portion of the `OnConnection` method in Listing 8.3 sets up the command button and pointers to the code that executes the function.

Listing 8.3. The OnConnection and OnDisconnection functions.

```
Private Function IDSAddIn_OnConnection(ByVal pApp As
➥DSSharedObjects.IApplication, ByVal bFirstTime As Boolean,
➥ByVal dwCookie As Long) As Boolean
    Set m_cCommands = New Commands
    Set m_cCommands.m_app = pApp
    m_intCookie = dwCookie
    Dim instance As Long
    instance = App.hInstance
    m_cCommands.m_app.SetAddInInfo instance, m_cCommands, 1, 2, dwCookie
    m_cCommands.m_app.AddCommand "PerformanceMonitor" & Chr(10) _
        & "Performance Monitor" & Chr(10) _
        & "Displays performance information" & Chr(10) _
        & "Performance Monitor", _
        "PerformanceMonitor", 0, dwCookie
    If bFirstTime = True Then
        m_cCommands.m_app.AddCommandBarButton dsGlyph, "PerformanceMonitor",
        ➥dwCookie
    End If
IDSAddIn_OnConnection = True
End Function
Private Sub IDSAddIn_OnDisconnection(ByVal bLastTime As Boolean)
    Set m_cCommands.m_app = Nothing
    Set m_cCommands = Nothing
End Sub
```

TIP

Pay particular attention to the `m_cCommands.m_app.AddCommand` in Listing 8.3. This command sets up the Developer Studio shell to accompany the new command as a menu or button. For example, each command you want to have visible within the Visual InterDev development environment must incorporate an `AddCommand` method to create its existence. The syntax is as follows:

```
AddCommand <Command to execute>, <text displayed in menu>, <text displayed in
status bar prompt>, <text displayed in ToolTip>, <method name>, <toolbar bitmap>,
<cookie>
```

The property implemented is the `Description` property and appears at runtime in the bottom of the Add-in and Macro Files dialog within Visual InterDev when the particular add-in is selected. (See Listing 8.4.)

Listing 8.4. The `Description` property for `IDSAddin`.

```
Public Property Get Description()
        Description = "Add-in to determine the download times of
        ➥the current file."
End Property
```

The Add-In Code

In Listing 8.5, I implemented a command called `PerformanceMonitor`. The call to the procedure is there, so now we have to create the procedure to carry it out. At this point we need to create another class to handle the commands executed from the `IDSAddin` object.

The class is `Commands` and will be the object to handle all the commands we will execute specified in the `IDSAddin` class.

Listing 8.5. `PerfomanceMonitor` command specified in `IDSAddin` object.

```
Public Sub PerformanceMonitor()
'*********************************************************
'* Purpose : This is the main procedure that initializes the
'*           calculations and populates the frmPerformanceResults form.
'* Date :    04/27/97
'* Author :  Robert Niemela
'*********************************************************

    m_app.EnableModeless False
    Dim CurrentDocument As Document
    Dim varSize As Variant
    Set CurrentDocument = m_app.ActiveDocument
    Dim response
    'Since the Add-in calculates the filesizes and links
```

continues

Listing 8.5. continued

```
'on a disk file it must prompt the user to save any changes
'made to give an accurate reading.
If CurrentDocument.Saved = False Then
    response = MsgBox(CurrentDocument.FullName & " is not saved." & Chr$(10)
    ➥& "Performance Monitor needs it to be saved to give it an accurate
    ➥reading. " & Chr$(10) & "Do you want to save it now?", vbCritical +
    ➥vbYesNo)
    If response = vbYes Then
        CurrentDocument.Save CurrentDocument.FullName
    Else
        MsgBox "Readings from Performance Monitor will not be accurate.",
        ➥vbInformation, "Information"
    End If
End If
Dim i As Integer
Dim varFileSize
Dim varLinksize
'Calculate the original file size
varFileSize = get_FileSize(CurrentDocument.FullName, False)
'Calculate the total dependency file sizes
varLinksize = get_DependentsListAndSize(CurrentDocument.FullName,
➥CurrentDocument.Path)
'Populate the form
With frmPerformanceResults
    .Show
    .Caption = CurrentDocument.FullName
    .Text1 = CDec(varFileSize)
    .Text2 = CDec(varLinksize)
    .Text3 = CDec(varFileSize) + CDec(varLinksize)
    .Text4 = get_DownloadTime(CDec(.Text3), 14.4) & " sec(s)"
    .Text5 = get_DownloadTime(CDec(.Text3), 28.8) & " sec(s)"
    .Text6 = get_DownloadTime(CDec(.Text3), 57.6) & " sec(s)"
    'Populate the list control
    For i = 1 To m_strFiles.Count
     .List1.AddItem Mid(m_strFiles.Item(i), 1, 5) & "..." &
     ➥(Right(m_strFiles.Item(i) & " " & get_FileSize(m_strFiles.Item(i),
     ➥True), 25))
    Next i
End With
m_app.EnableModeless True
End Sub
```

Let's break down the code and understand how the Visual InterDev environment is being called.

In Listing 8.6 we declare `CurrentDocument` as a `Document` object so it exposes specific methods related to the Visual InterDev environment.

Listing 8.6. Declaring the Document object.

```
Dim CurrentDocument As Document
Dim varSize As Variant
Set CurrentDocument = m_app.ActiveDocument
Dim response
```

The add-in calculates file sizes and links based on a saved file. So the next few lines in the code (see Listing 8.7) poll the state of the currently active file to check whether the file is in a modified state (denoted by asterisks next to the filename in the VI caption bar). The Saved property is accessed through the CurrentDocument object and returns a Boolean data type. If the currently active file is not saved, prompt the user to save it and execute the Save method. The other important property to note being exposed from the CurrentDocument object is the FullName property. It is used simply for information to be presented to the user in the msgbox command.

Listing 8.7. Verify the state of the currently active file.

```
If CurrentDocument.Saved = False Then
        response = MsgBox(CurrentDocument.FullName & " is not saved." & Chr$(10)
        ➥& "Performance Monitor needs it to be saved to give it an accurate
        ➥reading." & Chr$(10) & "Do you want to save it now?", vbCritical +
        ➥vbYesNo)
        If response = vbYes Then
            CurrentDocument.Save CurrentDocument.FullName
        Else
            MsgBox "Readings from Performance Monitor will not be accurate.",
            ➥vbInformation, "Information"
        End If
    End If
```

Listing 8.8 shows the calculations being called by a variety of different functions. What is important to note here is that I am using the current document's path and filename to calculate its original size and its dependency file sizes. The calculations and the file searching are done in a common module called Common.bas. Listing 8.8 is the main launch point initialized by the IDSAddin object. This procedure carries out the calculation calls based on the Visual InterDev exposed methods and properties. It then populates the form with the calculated values and makes the form visible.

Listing 8.8. Populating the Performance form.

```
    varFileSize = get_FileSize(CurrentDocument.FullName, False)
    varLinksize = get_DependentsListAndSize(CurrentDocument.FullName,
    ➥CurrentDocument.Path)
With frmPerformanceResults
        .Show
        .Caption = CurrentDocument.FullName
        .Text1 = CDec(varFileSize)
        .Text2 = CDec(varLinksize)
        .Text3 = CDec(varFileSize) + CDec(varLinksize)
        .Text4 = get_DownloadTime(CDec(.Text3), 14.4) & " sec(s)"
        .Text5 = get_DownloadTime(CDec(.Text3), 28.8) & " sec(s)"
        .Text6 = get_DownloadTime(CDec(.Text3), 57.6) & " sec(s)"
        'Populate the list control
        For i = 1 To m_strFiles.Count
```

continues

Listing 8.8. continued

```
        .List1.AddItem Mid(m_strFiles.Item(i), 1, 5) & "..." &
        ➡(Right(m_strFiles.Item(i) & " " & get_FileSize(m_strFiles.Item(i),
        ➡True), 25))
        Next i
End With
m_app.EnableModeless True
```

To see the add-in in action, you must compile it to a DLL. After it's compiled, start Visual InterDev with any project loaded. Select Tools | Customize, choose the Add-ins and macro files dialog tab, and then select your DLL. You will most likely have to click Browse to locate your DLL and change the file type filter to DLL.

TIP

Place your DLLs in the `DevStudio\SharedIDE\Addins` directory if you want your add-ins to be automatically available in the Customize dialog.

Once you have selected the DLL, it will appear in a list (see Figure 8.2). Select the add-in `Performance.AppAddin` by clicking the checkbox next to it and close the dialog.

FIGURE 8.2.
The Customize dialog reports which add-ins are loaded.

NOTE

Back in Listing 8.3, the `OnConnection` code doesn't have to reload each time you make a programming change. To recompile the source simply release Visual InterDev's control of it by unchecking the listed name of the project you are compiling. After you close the dialog the DLL is free to rewrite itself by a compile command from VB.

Figure 8.3 shows the active file I have opened called `test.asp`. The open file contains a few dependent files, which are graphics and are contained in another directory.

Important Functionality Notes

To be realistic about developing such a tool, I could cover only one file structure setup. In order for the Performance Monitor to work, a few things have to be in place.

1. Any graphics files the active document links to must have a working copy available. To do this, select your graphics directory (in this case, Images), right-click, and select Get Working Copy.

2. Images and backgrounds specified within a Visual InterDev document must be specified only with relative pathnames.

3. The link files must be located in the same branch (for example, `<root>/doc/doc.htm` and `<root>/images/i1.gif`).

FIGURE 8.3.

The Visual InterDev environment with a file open and the Performance Monitor add-in loaded in a small floating button.

8

INTEGRATING AND EXTENDING VISUAL INTERDEV

NOTE

If nothing shows up in the list and you receive a negative number (-3) as the total link file size, then you violated one of the above three. Sorry, the structure can't possibly cover every situation.

Figure 8.4 shows the Performance Monitor at runtime. I opened a file test.asp, and it had several graphics tied to that page. The three files are listed in the lower list box with their respective file sizes. The top portion breaks down in bytes the size of the file and its total links.

FIGURE 8.4.

Performance Monitor in action! Don't go gambling on these figures. The Internet is an unpredictable beast.

Summary

The common powers of all three technologies overlap somewhat. Whether you work in a segmented environment of technical and nontechnical contributors, you're a sole developer, or you're even a hacker, all three available implementations offer something of great benefit to you. They allow you to focus on creating extensible tools to meet your development needs as you move across the continuum of technology. They also allow the roadwork to be built between the programmer and the content/graphic provider. Enhancement of this relationship provides the means to achieve collaboration in which the best of both worlds can apply. Add-ins provide the vehicle of custom inter-development environment tools, ActiveX design-time controls provide custom development of text generation, and Web wizards provide sequential custom file/task creation. Open architectures have always been the buzzword of technological creations; however, most often the hype usually smolders the promise into a proprietary environment. From a developer's perspective, Visual InterDev's strongest feature lies in having an environment that has no boundaries.

Following are some resources I found useful when researching Visual InterDev. Although numerous sites on the Internet provide information on Visual InterDev, I have compiled a specific list in order for you to research additional information on controls and the SDK for VI.

- Design-Time Control SDK

  `http://www.microsoft.com/intdev/sdk/dtctrl`

- ActiveX SDK Frequently Asked Questions

  `http://www.microsoft.com/support/products/developer/activexsdk/`
  `content/faq/default.htm`

- Microsoft Technical Support group

  `http://www.microsoft.com/support/products/developer/ActiveXSDK/`

■ The Internet Explorer team

`http://www.microsoft.com/iesupport/content/issues/`

■ Newsgroups

`news://msnews.microsoft.com`

■ Visual InterDev

`http://www.microsoft.com/VinterDev`

■ Design-Time Control Software Development Kit

`http://www.microsoft.com/intdev/sdk/dtctrl/dcsdk.htm`

■ Visual InterDev ActiveX Newsgroup

`news://microsoft.public.activex.vinterdev`

IN THIS PART

Visual InterDev Hands-On

Effective Team Development Using Visual InterDev and Visual SourceSafe

by L. Michael Van Hoozer

IN THIS CHAPTER

CHAPTER 9

Most organizations and corporations rely on the team concept to accomplish their purpose. The secret to success for the '90s involves the use of a team structure organized by projects. The dynamics of bringing together people of diverse backgrounds and expertise to achieve a project's mission is critical to an organization's success. A team's success hinges upon the team members possessing good interpersonal and relational skills as well as the implementation of effective tools and processes to enable the work of the team.

Most people think of the ability to work with others as a critical factor to the success of any team project. From a tool perspective, most developers think of source and version control software as the panacea for programming projects. Providing your team members with the right tool to perform their project roles is another key ingredient to the success of any project. The advancement of the Internet and the need for and popularity of Web-based applications has heightened the interest of a diverse set of people. The Web is not just for technical people anymore! Everyone in the organization is touting the virtues of the Internet, including graphic designers, marketing and public relations personnel, and the sales force, just to name a few. The very nature of an intranet suggests collaboration. More and more of these constituents are getting involved with the development of Web sites and Web-based applications. For this reason, it is crucial that the right people are paired with the right tools to perform their responsibilities.

In this chapter, you will receive a hands-on look at some topics that were covered in Chapter 7, "Managing the Site and Team Development." This chapter will help you understand how to use Visual InterDev, FrontPage 97, and Visual SourceSafe to effectively equip your team with the right tools. Microsoft has designed these tools with compatibility and integration in mind to aid in the development of your Web-based application. First, you will learn the relationship between FrontPage 97 and Visual InterDev. These complementary tools can be used together for Web-based development and are tailored to different audiences and people of varying degrees of expertise. Next, you will discover how to organize your project and application source code through the use of Visual SourceSafe. This software product enables you to maintain control over your source code as well as track multiple versions of your applications. In this section of the chapter, you will experience the Visual SourceSafe features that can significantly augment your team's productivity and help bring order to chaos. This part of the chapter will be divided into two sections—one section that covers how to use Visual SourceSafe to manage source control issues with library functions such as check in/check out, and another section that concentrates on how to manage multiple versions of your application. Finally, you will learn how to implement a security strategy that adequately addresses the needs of your team members.

Using Visual InterDev and FrontPage 97

The introduction of FrontPage revolutionized the way in which Web pages were developed. The laborious process of programming HTML tags and attributes was replaced with an easy-to-use interface. FrontPage 97, the latest version of this software, carries on the torch of this exciting WYSIWYG editor. The graphical interface of FrontPage 97 removes the monotony and complexity of developing Web pages and enables you to focus your attention on the design and the layout of the page.

Visual InterDev includes an implementation of the FrontPage Editor that enables you to quickly develop Web pages. The following sections will explore the relationship between the full, commercial version of FrontPage 97 and the FrontPage Editor for Visual InterDev. You will gain a solid understanding of how and when to use each tool for your Web-based application development.

> **NOTE**
>
> This chapter does not cover how to design and develop Web pages using FrontPage 97, but rather the virtues of each tool within the context of the experience of your team members. You will gain a thorough understanding of how to use FrontPage 97 to construct Web pages during Chapter 32, "Designing Web Pages with FrontPage 97and Extensions."

The Benefits of Using FrontPage 97

You may already be using FrontPage 97 as your editor of choice to develop the Web pages within your application. This product provides a WYSIWYG editor to easily design rich and robust Web pages. WYSIWYG denotes that what-you-see-is-what-you-get; in other words, the page that you view in the editor is the one that will display within the context of the browser. This visual metaphor is similar in nature to Microsoft Word, which also employs a WYSIWYG style. Similarly to Word, FrontPage 97 enables you to visually choose the features that you want and to receive instant feedback on the results. For example, if you want to create bold text, you highlight the text and click the Bold button on the toolbar. To insert a table, you can choose the Insert Table menu item and visually edit the contents of the table directly within the Web page. Previously, a developer had to use a series of <TH>, <TR>, and <TD> tags to create the table and insert the data. As you implement these formatting features, the FrontPage Editor will display your Web page as it will appear in the browser. Figure 9.1 displays the graphical nature of the FrontPage 97 Editor.

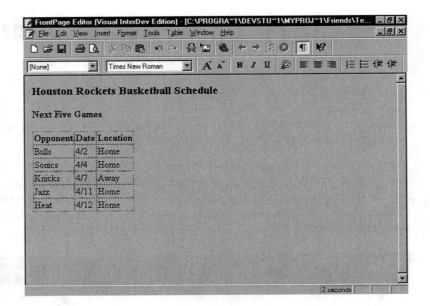

As you can see, the FrontPage Editor provides a user-friendly way for a person, technical or nontechnical, to design and develop a Web page in a short amount of time. Focus, again, is the key because the person can concentrate on how he wants the page to look versus the underlying HTML tag that should be utilized to produce the desired results.

> **NOTE**
>
> Both FrontPage 97 and the FrontPage Editor for Visual InterDev support the HTML 3.2 specifications for constructing Web pages as well as many Netscape and Microsoft extensions.

Developing Your Application with FrontPage 97 and Visual InterDev

If you have used Visual InterDev for any length of time, you know that the tool provides a very high-powered, integrated development environment to build robust Web-based applications. Visual InterDev consists of many tools and technologies that enable you to develop an interactive solution, including ActiveX controls, scripting language support, and database integration. The target audience for Visual InterDev includes a diverse set of audiences, as outlined in Table 9.1.

Table 9.1. Potential Visual InterDev users.

Team Member Role	Visual InterDev Tool
Graphic Artist	Image Composer
Content Author	FrontPage Editor for Visual InterDev
Application Developer	Visual InterDev development environment and tools
Database Developer	Visual Database tools

Although the main focus and attention are on the developer, Visual InterDev also provides the ability for a less-technical person to use the tool to produce the content of the Web site using the FrontPage Editor for Visual InterDev. Figure 9.2 depicts the various roles of a Web development team that are mentioned in Chapter 7.

FIGURE 9.2.
The ideal Web development team.

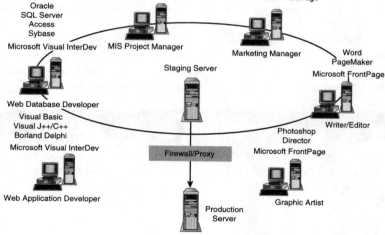

In this picture, you see an ideal Web development team and the tools they would be using to perform their responsibilities on the project. While you might not have the luxury of dedicating a single person to each of these roles, every Web-based development team will share the roles to build the application. The marketing manager and copy editor serve as the content authors and use the full commercial version of FrontPage 97 as their tool of choice. Their responsibility on the team is to ensure that the Web pages contain the proper content. The graphic artist utilizes the power of Image Composer to design high-quality graphics for the application. The application and database developers use Visual InterDev to complete the development of the application.

There are several important points to understand concerning the development process and this team. First, the content authors can construct the content for the Web site using a tool (FrontPage 97) that is targeted toward their level of expertise. Second, the files that are created using FrontPage 97 are incorporated into the project by the application developers using Visual InterDev. The key point to remember is that the files created with FrontPage 97 are completely compatible with Visual InterDev and its FrontPage Editor, and vice versa. The implication is that content authors can create and modify files and enable the application developers to further enhance the Web pages using Visual InterDev, which is more suited to their skill level. The synergistic relationship between FrontPage 97 and Visual InterDev enables your team to work in harmony and significantly increases the team's productivity.

Organizing Your Projects with Visual SourceSafe

With any project team, you must establish some semblance of order to produce the desired results. Version control software has been around for many years to provide order for application development projects that involve multiple team members. Visual SourceSafe is Microsoft's answer to the cumbersome task of maintaining order for your projects. Visual SourceSafe provides a very robust source code and version control software product. Moreover, you can integrate Visual SourceSafe with Visual InterDev to provide these integral functions for your project. Visual SourceSafe includes basic library functions such as the ability to exclusively reserve your code by checking it out as well as checking it back in to the project when you have completed your updates. Furthermore, you can institute a robust version control scheme that enables you to track multiple versions of your applications, view differences between the files, and merge the differences into one integrated version of the application.

> **NOTE**
>
> You can purchase Visual InterDev and Visual SourceSafe as individual products or as a part of Microsoft Visual Studio. The points that are covered in this section apply to both scenarios.

The Web Challenge

The rise in development of Web-based applications has posed a formidable challenge concerning management of content and files. As discussed earlier in this chapter, a Web development team can consist of multiple members who deliver varying files for the application. The challenge arises in trying to manage and maintain these files without having each member interfere with the other members' work. The need for dynamic and interactive applications has created an explosion of tools and technologies specifically geared for the Web. Also, the very nature of the Web enables you to incorporate numerous types of files including images, video, sound, and documents, not to mention the regular types of Web files such as HTML pages, ActiveX controls, and scripting code. The good news is that you can integrate tools such as Visual SourceSafe to handle this monumental task.

Integrating Visual SourceSafe and Visual InterDev

The benefit of using two complementary products from the same vendor is that, in theory, the tools should work well together. Microsoft delivers on this promise by providing seamless integration between Visual SourceSafe and Visual InterDev. When you set up Visual SourceSafe within your development environment, you can begin to immediately reap the benefits of this powerful product.

For a Web-based application, you may be using several different tools to build the various components and content. Visual SourceSafe offers integrated flexibility in enabling you to manage the different parts of your application. There are three basic models for controlling your source code for a Web-based application. First, you can use your Web server as a central point of control for your application. In this model, Visual SourceSafe is installed on the Web staging server, as depicted in Figure 9.3.

FIGURE 9.3.

Using the Web server to house your source control.

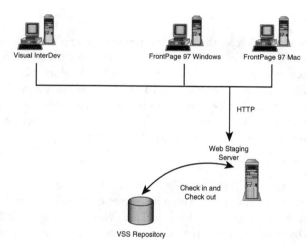

As you can see from Figure 9.3, the Visual SourceSafe repository database is stored on the Web server. All Visual SourceSafe operations are performed by the FrontPage Server extensions that you installed as a part of the Visual InterDev server installation. Also, the authentication security for developers is handled through the Web server. Notice that the team members consist of both content authors using FrontPage 97 (Windows and Macintosh versions) and Visual InterDev developers. This model does not require you to install the client version of Visual SourceSafe.

You may want to move your source code control to another dedicated server machine. Figure 9.4 illustrates the second model for source control.

FIGURE 9.4.
A dedicated source code control machine.

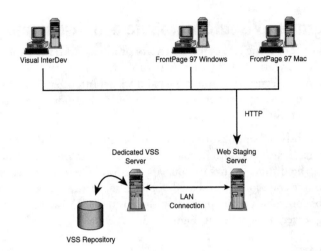

In this model, you have the same team members who utilize Visual SourceSafe to control the application source. The difference in this model is that the SourceSafe repository has been moved to a dedicated machine. The content authors and developers connect to the Web server through an HTTP connection, which in turn connects to the Visual SourceSafe machine through a LAN connection. The benefit of this model is that it enables you to logically separate the different functions of the two server machines. To configure a remote location for your SourceSafe repository, edit the following line in the SRCSAFE.INI file:

```
DATA_PATH = folder path
```

where `folder path` is the path of the data folder used by Visual SourceSafe. By default, this value is initially set to DATA, which instructs SourceSafe to search for the DATA subfolder in the path where the SRCSAFE.INI file is located. You can change this INI file to reference a remote location by providing a different server share and folder name. For example, the following update to the SRCSAFE.INI file changes the repository to point to the DATA folder on a remote server share named \\MYSERVER\DEVELOPERS:

```
DATA_PATH = \\MYSERVER\DEVELOPERS\VSS5\DATA
```

The final model extends the dedicated SourceSafe model to enable you to share the SourceSafe repository with other types of developers. Figure 9.5 demonstrates this kind of configuration.

FIGURE 9.5.
A shared model.

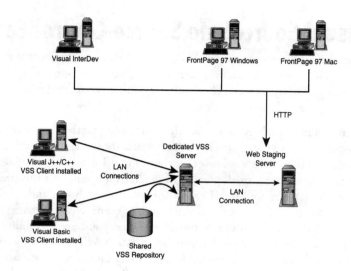

This model enables you to use the SourceSafe repository for other components of the Web-based application including Java applets, ActiveX controls, and Active Server components. As you can see in Figure 9.5, the component developers are using tools such as Visual J++, Visual C++, and Visual Basic to construct components for the application. These components are organized and controlled within the same SourceSafe repository as the other team members who are using Visual InterDev and FrontPage 97. This kind of configuration enables you to see the big picture and effectively manage every part of the application.

The integration of Visual InterDev and Visual SourceSafe enables you to place your Web projects under source control and take advantage of the services outlined in Table 9.2.

Table 9.2. Visual SourceSafe services.

Service	Description
Library functions	Ability to check-in/check-out code
History functions	Track multiple versions of an application and view/merge the differences
Security functions	Establish access rights to the files

The next three sections cover these services in detail.

9

EFFECTIVE TEAM DEVELOPMENT

Visual SourceSafe Source-Control Features

Source control revolves around basic library functions that enable a team of developers to re-serve their code in an unobtrusive manner. These functions are called *library services* because, like using a library, you can check out the book, or code, that you want to access and return, or check in, the code at a later time.

A more precise analogy might be with purchasing textbooks for college. As I get older, it be-comes harder and harder for me to remember those days. One thing I do recall from my col-lege days is that there were some textbooks that I could buy, highlight the text and write in, and then return for a small portion of the hefty amount that I initially paid for the book. For other books, I was told that I could not write in the book, and, at the end of the semester, I could still return the book for a measly sum of money. This scenario is analogous to the library services that Visual SourceSafe provides in that you have the ability to exclusively check out write-enabled copies of files that you can update as well as read-only copies that you can browse. These restrictions are configured in the Visual SourceSafe database using the Administrator tool. When you are finished updating or reading the file, you check the file back into a source control database that handles any file changes and makes them available to other team members.

The library features in Visual SourceSafe are an important component during the development and testing phase of your project. The next few sections guide you through the process of plac-ing a Visual InterDev project under source control and utilizing the library services within Visual SourceSafe.

Enabling Source Control for Your Projects

After you have installed Visual InterDev and granted access to the team members, you can en-able source control for your Web project from within the Visual InterDev development envi-ronment. For existing projects, open the project using Visual InterDev and select the Project menu, as shown in Figure 9.6.

The items that appear on this menu concern the overall project options and properties. To view the source-control options, choose the Source Control menu item. A list of submenu items will be shown, as in Figure 9.7.

> **NOTE**
>
> Most of the menu items that appear cannot be executed for Visual InterDev projects. These items appear as a part of the Developer Studio shell for other types of applications, such as Visual Basic and Visual C++ projects. For Visual InterDev projects, you can enable source control and launch the Visual SourceSafe Explorer.

Figure 9.6.

Viewing the Project menu.

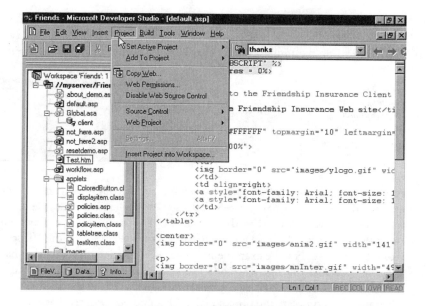

Figure 9.7.

Revealing the Source Control options.

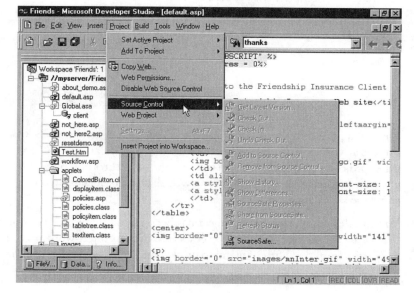

To enable source control for the project, select the Enable Web Source Control menu item from the list of Project menu items. After you select this command, a dialog window will display confirming the source-control enablement process, as shown in Figure 9.8.

FIGURE 9.8.

Enabling source control for your project.

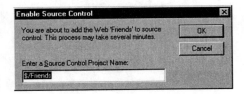

As you can see in Figure 9.8, a name is generated for your Visual InterDev project that is used as the entry into the Visual SourceSafe database. The name is composed of a $ (dollar sign) and a / (forward slash) along with the Visual InterDev project name. For example, a project entitled MyProject would have a default name of $/MyProject in the Visual SourceSafe Source Control database. For the example in Figure 9.5, the default name that has been generated is $/Friends. While you have the ability to change the name of the entry that will be placed in the Visual SourceSafe database, it is recommended that you accept the default name that is generated. To complete the process, click OK, and you will receive a message confirming that your project has successfully been placed under source control as shown in Figure 9.9.

FIGURE 9.9.

Completing the process.

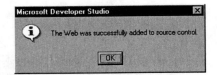

Once you have completed the process, all the source control services will be activated for this project as well as any other project within that particular web. When a developer opens another project within that web, the source control features will be enabled automatically. Also, any new projects that are created for a web that has been activated for source control will assume the same characteristics.

You can determine whether a project has been placed under source control by right-clicking the mouse on the name of the project located in the project workspace. You can then choose Properties from the shortcut menu to display the Properties dialog window, as depicted in Figure 9.10.

FIGURE 9.10.
Viewing the properties for the project.

From this window, you can view general properties about the project. When you click on the Web Server tab, you will uncover further information concerning your Web server for the project. Figure 9.11 reveals that the project in this example is a source-controlled project.

FIGURE 9.11.
Determining the true nature of the project.

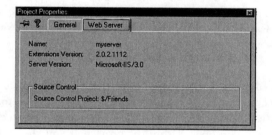

Checking-Out: The First Step

Most of the time, we think of checking in as the first step, as in checking in to a hotel or checking in for a conference. When you use source control, the converse is the first step—you need to check out the files that you will need. Based on your access privileges, you can check out files that are fully updateable, meaning that you are free to both view and change the files' contents. For other files in your project, you may be able to check out only a read-only copy of the file. This scenario exists either because you do not possess the proper permission to update the file or because someone else on the team has already checked out the file.

Visual InterDev enables you to open files within the project workspace using a variety of methods. First, you can click the right mouse button on the file and select Open from the list of shortcut menu items. Also, you can double-click on the desired file within the Visual InterDev project workspace. For source-controlled projects, all these methods represent ways to check out your files. Whatever method you choose to open a file, a dialog window will display as shown in Figure 9.12, prompting you to select a file-access method.

FIGURE 9.12.

Selecting a file-access method.

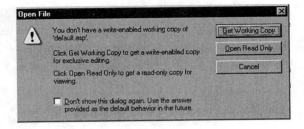

> **NOTE**
>
> For some files, you will not have a choice, and this dialog window will serve as a reminder notice about your access privileges. You can also right-click the mouse on the file and choose Get Working Copy from the shortcut menu. This method, by default, opens the file with full write access privileges unless the user does not have write privileges, in which case the file will automatically be opened as read-only.

From the dialog window displayed in Figure 9.12, you can choose to reserve a write-enabled or read-only copy of the file. The checkbox located at the bottom of the window enables you to assign the decision that you make for this file concerning access privileges as the default choice for all files that you open within the project. If you check this option, Visual InterDev will attempt to open all future files based on your initial preference, provided you have the correct access privileges as assigned in the Visual SourceSafe database. For example, you would want to select this option if you had the privileges and wanted to open all the files in the project as write-enabled. Then, you could avoid the hassle of being prompted for your preference each time you tried to access a file. After you indicate your preference for the access type, the file will be opened using its default editor. Figure 9.13 displays an ASP file that has been opened as write-enabled.

For this file, the user has full privileges to update the code. The icon located to the left of the filename in the project workspace is displayed in full color. This visual indicator serves as reminder that the file is a write-enabled working copy. If the developer had chosen to check out a read-only copy of the file, the icon would have appeared in gray, as depicted in Figure 9.14.

FIGURE 9.13.

Reserving the right to edit a file.

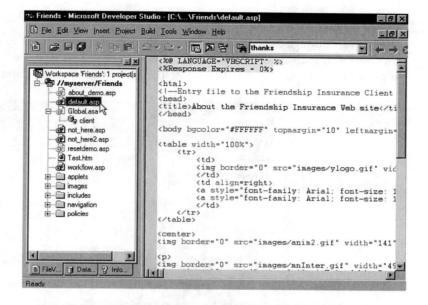

FIGURE 9.14.

Choosing a read-only copy.

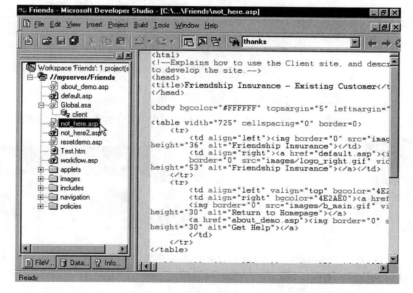

Checking In Your Files

When you are through using the copy of the file, you can check in the file by selecting it within the project workspace and clicking the right mouse button. This action will display the shortcut menu, enabling you to select Release Working Copy, as shown in Figure 9.15.

FIGURE 9.15.

Releasing the working copy.

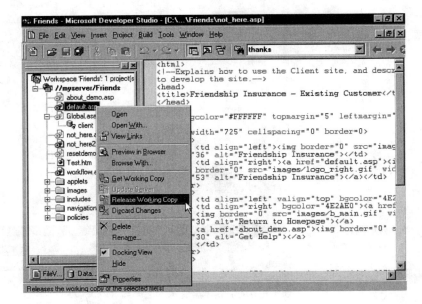

If you have made changes to the file, you will be prompted to document your changes by entering a comment describing the modifications, as shown in Figure 9.16.

FIGURE 9.16.

Documenting the change.

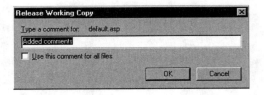

This process enables the team to track the type of change that was made and can be very useful for future reference. For example, suppose the change you make causes the application to crash. Now, this is purely a hypothetical situation, because we know your code would never contain bugs; but, just for the sake of argument, let's pretend that it did. Anybody on the team could refer back to the comment and use it to help locate the error.

The dialog window displayed in Figure 9.16 also provides an easy way for you to enter a comment that can be used for all files that you change in the project. This feature can be very helpful when you have to make the same type of change to a number of files within the project. By selecting this option, you can avoid having to type the same comment for each file that you change. Instead, because you have already chosen a default comment for the changes, you will be prompted to accept the default comment and click the OK pushbutton, as displayed in Figure 9.17.

FIGURE 9.17.

Saving the changes.

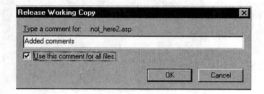

To cancel the changes to a file, you can click the right mouse button on the file and choose Discard Changes from the shortcut menu. This will release the working copy of the file and discard any changes you have made. When you choose this command, you will be prompted with a dialog window confirming this action, as shown in Figure 9.18.

FIGURE 9.18.

Confirming the cancellation of changes.

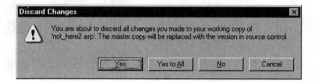

Visual SourceSafe Version Control Features

The influence of Visual SourceSafe does not end with managing and controlling the source during the development phase. Version control is also a very important part of an application development strategy. Visual SourceSafe offers a very solid set of services to help you maintain multiple versions of an application as well as to merge and track differences between files. These types of functions are commonly called history functions, because they are used after the files and application have been initially developed.

As mentioned previously in this chapter, these functions are not available from within the Visual InterDev environment. To execute these functions, you need to use the Visual SourceSafe Explorer, which is discussed in the next section.

9

EFFECTIVE TEAM
DEVELOPMENT

Exploring Visual SourceSafe

The Visual SourceSafe Explorer is very similar to the Windows Explorer and enables you to easily view and access your source-controlled projects and files. There are two basic ways to launch the Visual SourceSafe Explorer. First, you can activate the application from within Visual InterDev, as shown in Figure 9.19.

FIGURE 9.19.

Using Visual InterDev to launch the Visual SourceSafe Explorer.

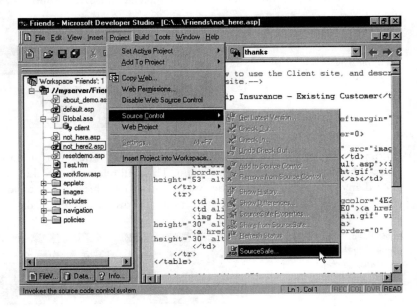

You can also start the Explorer from the Start menu in the more traditional fashion. Figure 9.20 displays the intuitive environment of the Visual SourceSafe Explorer.

The Visual SourceSafe Explorer consists of two panes—the project list and the file list. The project list is located in the left-hand window shown in Figure 9.20 and enables you to view all of your projects that have been enabled for source control. The projects are displayed as folders, and may consist of subfolders within the root folder that is listed at the top of the hierarchy tree. The file list is located to the right of the project list and displays all the files that are associated with the projects. Table 9.3 depicts the information that is displayed for each file in the list.

FIGURE 9.20.

The Visual SourceSafe Explorer.

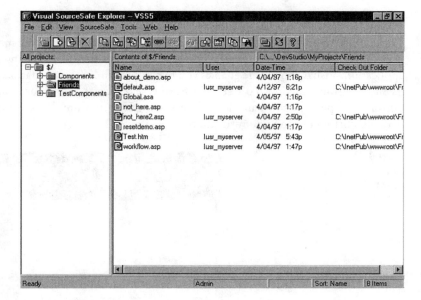

Table 9.3. File list columns.

Column	Description
Name	Name of the file
User	If applicable, the name of the user who has checked out the file
Date-Time	The date and time that the file was checked out or the date and time of the last modification for files that have been checked in
Check Out Folder	The name of the folder where the working copy was checked out to

The Visual SourceSafe Explorer supports the same metaphor as the Windows Explorer in that you can interact with the project folders and files by clicking and double-clicking on the files within the two panes. As you can see, the Explorer provides an intuitive and easy-to-use interface for interacting with your project files. The next sections cover two of the more important history functions that can be executed from within the Visual SourceSafe Explorer.

9

EFFECTIVE TEAM
DEVELOPMENT

Uncovering the History of a File

The ability to track the history of a file—including the updates that were made, who made the updates, and why they were made—is a very important part of managing the versions of an application. Visual SourceSafe enables you to comprehend this information through the use of its Show History function. To access this feature, select the desired file and click the right mouse button to display the shortcut menu. Select Show History from the list of menu items to display the History dialog window depicted in Figure 9.21.

FIGURE 9.21.

Viewing the history of a file.

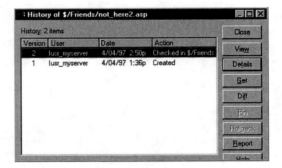

This dialog window presents a list box that contains the history of updates that have been made to the file. As you can see, a version number is listed in the first column enabling you to track the number of revisions that have been made to the file. Visual SourceSafe automatically generates the version number. Other columns include the user who made the revision and the date the change was made. The final column indicates the action that was taken regarding the change. For example, version 1 of a file will usually have an action of Created.

Several pushbuttons exist to the right of the list box in the History dialog window. Table 9.4 outlines these buttons and their functions.

Table 9.4. The Show History pushbuttons.

Pushbutton	Description
Close	Closes the window
View	Opens the file with a default editor
Details	Shows the history details of the file, including comments concerning the changes that were entered
Get	Retrieves a working copy of the file
Diff	Enables you to view the differences between the versions of the file
Pin	Enables you to associate a specific version of the file with the current version of the project

Pushbutton	Description
Rollback	Enables you to roll back to a previous version of the file
Report	Creates a report of the details and differences concerning the file versions
Help	Displays the online help

Valuing the Differences Between Files

In the last section, I mentioned that you can see the differences between versions of a file. This feature is very important from a historical perspective when you want to track every change that is made to the files within your application. Along with this concept, you can also manage and merge the differences between the file versions. This feature is especially useful when multiple developers have made changes to the same file and you want to include all the changes within the release of the application.

To activate this function, select the desired file from within the file list and display the Show History window. Next, select the files that you want to compare from the list box, as shown in Figure 9.22.

FIGURE 9.22.

Choosing the files.

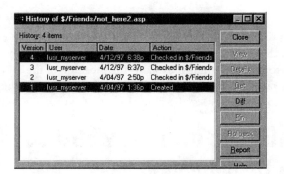

9

EFFECTIVE TEAM
DEVELOPMENT

NOTE

For noncontiguous files, you can use a combination of the Ctrl (Control) key and the left mouse button to select these files in the same manner that you select these types of files from within the Windows Explorer. For contiguous files, use the Shift key and the left mouse button.

Once you have chosen the files that you want to compare, click the Diff pushbutton. A dialog window will display similar to the one shown in Figure 9.23.

FIGURE 9.23.

Viewing the differences.

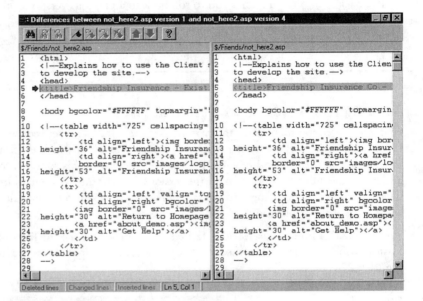

From this window, you can examine the differences between the files. Every difference is highlighted in the code panes and is distinguished by a different color based on its type. The legend at the bottom of the window explains the meaning of the different colors. The types of differences between files include deleted, inserted, and changed lines. This color-coded syntax enables you to very easily see the differences that exist between the versions.

Establishing a Security Strategy for Effective Team Development

The final section of this chapter outlines some guidelines to follow when devising an effective security strategy for your development team. The implementation of a Web-based application must involve the proper use of security to facilitate your development. You can utilize these suggestions to properly segment the development of your application while giving the developers access to the files they need. These considerations are covered in the following list:

- **Implement a group permission strategy using Windows NT security.** Set up groups within the NT User Manager that cover the basic types of users of your Web. For example, you could establish groups such as Site1_Authors, Site1_Admin, Site1_Developers, and so on.

- **Use FrontPage permissions to establish security for your groups.** Configure the FrontPage Web permissions to match the user groups that you set up in Windows NT. In other words, set up Web permissions for authors, administrators, and so on.

- **Configure your security per project using FrontPage 97 or Visual InterDev.**

- **Use NTFS security to establish Access Control Lists (ACLs) on files and folders within a Web project.** This strategy enables you to restrict access to certain folders within your project thereby providing more granular control. For example, you could configure one author to have full access to the project content and other authors to only have access to certain directory folders.

Summary

Effective team development means the difference between successful and unsuccessful projects. People must learn to work together if they want to achieve this success. While personalities often factor into the successful meshing of a team, the integration of Visual InterDev, FrontPage 97, and Visual SourceSafe can provide key enabling tools to achieve harmony among your team members. Visual InterDev and FrontPage 97 provide two powerful tools that are appropriately tailored to unique audiences. These tools complement the strengths of the other to provide an effective solution to your development needs.

Visual SourceSafe enables you to maintain balance and order regarding your development effort. Using Visual SourceSafe, your team members can work in peace and isolation until they are ready to share their work with the other team members.

The final thought concerning effective team development involves the proper use of security controls. Using NTFS and a group permission strategy, you can effectively isolate your team members without having them feel as if they were on an island. The security strategy considerations that were discussed in this chapter are more analogous to fifty states that join to together as one nation. Sound familiar?

9

EFFECTIVE TEAM
DEVELOPMENT

CHAPTER 10

Using the Visual InterDev Editors for Scripting and Layout

by L. Michael Van Hoozer

IN THIS CHAPTER

It has become almost anticlimactic to state the need for dynamic and interactive Web-based applications. Users have already made their demands known, and developers have responded in a revolutionary way. The importance of ActiveX controls and scripting languages has created the need for tools to ease the process for developing Web-based applications. Visual InterDev is one of the tools that has simplified the task of building interactive applications for the Web by providing several features to meet the developer's need.

This chapter focuses on how to design and develop an effective layout for your application using several editors that are included within Visual InterDev. Specifically, you will learn about the Object Editor and the HTML Layout Editor. The Object Editor enables you to insert individual ActiveX controls into your Web pages, and the HTML Layout Editor enables you to create an application interface using multiple ActiveX controls. You will also gain an understanding of how to make your interface come alive through the use of scripting code.

> **NOTE**
>
> This chapter serves as a hands-on overview of how to use the editors and add script for your Web-based applications. A more in-depth discourse on client-side script and programming with controls and objects is covered later in Part IV, "Programming with Visual InterDev."

Overview of Visual InterDev Editors

Visual InterDev includes several editors that increase a developer's ability to design and develop effective applications for the Web. Since the Web metaphor has shifted from the passive act of reading information to a more interactive style of doing and buying, the need for a more expansive set of tools has increased. The developer's toolbox used to include only a good HTML editor such as "Visual" Notepad. Now, we have Visual InterDev that provides other editors in addition to the basic HTML editor to enable us to accomplish our mission: to build the killer app for the Web. Table 10.1 summarizes the basic editors that are included as a part of Visual InterDev.

Table 10.1. The Visual InterDev editors.

Editor	*Purpose*
HTML Source Editor	Color-coded HTML source editor
FrontPage Editor	WYSIWYG HTML source editor
Object Editor	Enables you to insert ActiveX controls into your Web pages
HTML Layout Editor	Enables you to build an application interface composed of multiple ActiveX controls
Script Wizard	Automates the process of adding scripting code for your ActiveX controls and HTML

As you can tell, Visual InterDev brings together many tools and technologies for the Web into one integrated development environment. The rest of the chapter focuses specifically on how to use the Object Editor, HTML Layout Editor, and Script Wizard to build an interactive interface for your application.

ActiveX Controls 101

Any developer who has built or used a client/server or Web application is familiar with the concept of controls. Controls are the cornerstone of any application, because they enable you to interact with the system. Microsoft and many third-party vendors have led the charge in developing many controls to support developers in their never-ending quest to build the killer application. First, there were Visual Basic controls, or VBXs. Next, OLE controls, or OCXs, entered into the technology revolution, opening new possibilities. These OLE controls were built on Microsoft's Component Object Model (COM) and allowed developers to take advantage of the 32-bit computing model. OLE controls also provided for a more seamless integration of multiple applications such as Microsoft Word and Excel. With the explosive popularity of the Web, Microsoft constructed a lightweight version of these OLE controls to support the capability to transfer the controls across the Web. ActiveX controls have entered the scene in record numbers and provide for rich and robust functionality without the overhead of their OLE control cousins.

> **NOTE**
>
> Many arguments have ensued involving the security of ActiveX as well as other Internet technologies. Microsoft has continued to update ActiveX technology to address these security issues. As a developer, you need to be aware of the security issues and weigh the benefits of ActiveX to your application. Choosing ActiveX will definitely provide more flexibility and integration on the desktop with other applications. The additional flexibility, however, provides the potential for more issues to arise regarding the security of your application. As a final thought, ActiveX does not pose any more of a threat to the security of your application than any other technology that you might use.

Understanding ActiveX Controls

ActiveX controls are based on COM-like OLE controls. They can be used to build both client/server and Web-based applications. ActiveX controls come in three basic flavors. First, there are those controls that have transformed from VBX controls to OLE controls and now to ActiveX controls. Examples include the push button and the radio button. Second, many vendors have created Internet-specific controls such as the Marquee control that enable you to display scrolling text across a Web page. The final type includes new controls based on the ActiveX and COM model. Table 10.2 outlines some of the more typical ActiveX controls that can be used with Visual InterDev.

Table 10.2. Popular ActiveX controls.

Control	Description
Check Box	Enables the user to select one or more choices
Combo Box	Enables the user to enter text or select item from a list
Command Button	Push button that the user can press to initiate an event
Hot Spot	Represents an area on a page that can trigger an event
Image	Displays an image to the user
Label	Text typically used to describe other controls
List Box	Enables the user to choose one or more items from a list
Marquee	Enables you to place scrolling text onto a Web page
New Item	Enables you to denote new items on a page
Preloader	Enables you to load a control's URL into the client computer's cache and download the control when necessary
Radio Button	Enables the user to select one choice from a group of items
Scroll Bar	Enables the user to set the value of another control by scrolling in some direction
Spin Button	Enables the user to change a number by clicking one of the arrows
Stock Ticker	Provides a stock ticker for the Web page that downloads dynamic data
Tab Strip	Presents a tabbed dialog window to the user that groups related controls
Text Box	Enables the user to enter a single line of text
Toggle Button	Displays whether a control is selected

The list in Table 10.2 only scratches the surface concerning the plethora of available choices of ActiveX controls. The basic purpose of ActiveX controls is to enable you to build a bridge between the user and the computer. The proper use of ActiveX controls and other objects enables the user to effectively utilize and, at the same time, enjoy your application. The most effective application interfaces are those that, like a good leader, get out of the way and let good people do their jobs. As more new and exciting controls are developed, the tendency is to treat everything like a nail and pound people over the head with the controls. For this reason, design and layout are an important and crucial factor in constructing your Web-based application. The next two sections focus on the Object Editor and the HTML Layout Editor that help you to build intuitive (that is, unobtrusive) interfaces.

Exploring the Object Editor

The Object Editor is one of the Visual InterDev editors that enables you to insert ActiveX controls onto your Web pages. This visual editor enables you to work with individual ActiveX controls and is good for situations when you are going to place only one or two controls on the Web page. The Object Editor is limited in that it does not enable you to place multiple controls on top of one another. For these types of scenarios, you need to use the HTML Layout Editor that will be covered later in this chapter. You can, however, visually establish the properties and attributes of individual controls to help construct an effective Web page. The next few sections will guide you through the process of using the Object Editor.

Using the Object Editor with ActiveX Controls

To insert an ActiveX control into a Web page, click the right mouse button at the desired spot on the Web page. The shortcut menu will be displayed as shown in Figure 10.1.

FIGURE 10.1.

Inserting an ActiveX control.

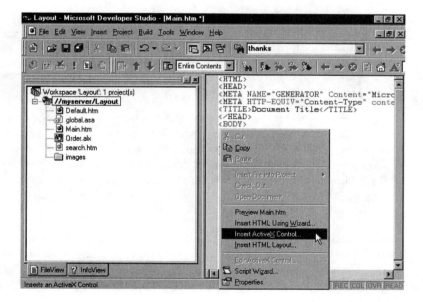

From the shortcut menu, you can select Insert ActiveX Control from the list. A dialog window will be displayed like the one pictured in Figure 10.2, allowing you to choose the preferred ActiveX control.

10

USING THE VISUAL
INTERDEV EDITORS

FIGURE 10.2.

Choosing the right ActiveX control.

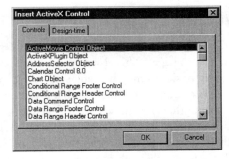

> **NOTE**
>
> The list of ActiveX controls that displays in the dialog window is based on the ActiveX controls that have been installed and registered for your client machine.

This dialog window consists of two tabs—one tab that contains a list of available ActiveX controls and another tab that displays the available design-time controls.

> **NOTE**
>
> Design-time controls are a special form of ActiveX control. These special controls enable you to visually set the properties and attributes for the control while you are designing the application and Web page. When you run the application, the only remnant of the design-time control that persists is runtime text that contains special instructions for the application. The runtime text can include HTML, scripting code, and text. Design-time controls will be covered in detail in Chapter 13, "Working with Design-Time Controls."

The next decision involves selecting the ActiveX control from the list of available choices. The controls that appear in the list have been configured and registered for use on your machine. After you select the desired control and press OK, the Object Editor activates and displays the chosen ActiveX control. In Figure 10.3, the Object Editor displays a pushbutton that has been chosen for a sample Web page.

Setting the Properties of the Control

As previously stated, the Object Editor enables you to visually set the properties and attributes of the ActiveX control. From within the Object Editor, you can select the control and right-click the mouse to display a shortcut menu for the control. Choosing Properties from the list of menu items will display a Properties dialog window for the control. Figure 10.4 displays the Properties window for a pushbutton.

FIGURE 10.3.
Viewing the control with the Object Editor.

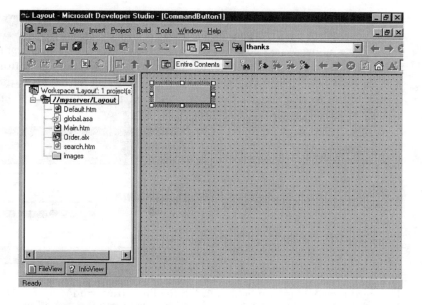

FIGURE 10.4.
The Properties window.

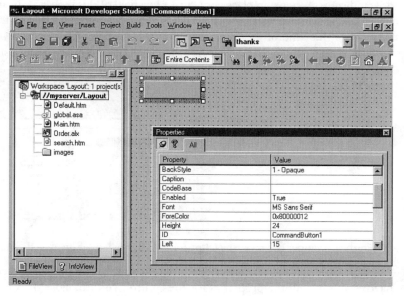

The Properties window enables you to establish the behavior of the control by setting its initial properties. For example, one of the key properties for a pushbutton is the caption that will be displayed to the user. The Properties window lists all of the design-time properties for the control on the left-hand side of the window. You can provide a value for each property in the space on the right-hand side of the window. For some properties, a default value is provided. The property value fields will consist of text boxes, combo boxes, and dialog window indicators. These three types are the most common forms of fields found in the Value column on the Properties window. A text box field will enable you to enter free-form text in the field such as the caption for a pushbutton. A combo box field enables you to select from a list of options such as True/False. When you place your cursor in a field of this type, the down arrow will appear indicating that you can choose a value from a list as illustrated in Figure 10.5.

FIGURE 10.5.

Picking a property value from the list.

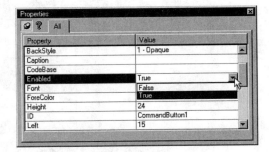

The third type of common field found in the Properties window is the ellipsis, or dialog window indicator. When you place your cursor in a field of this type, an ellipsis appears indicating that a dialog window will be displayed for you to choose the value of the property. A good example of this kind of property is the background color for a control. For example, Figure 10.6 shows the ellipsis that appears for the BackColor property for a pushbutton.

FIGURE 10.6.

Placing the cursor in an ellipsis field.

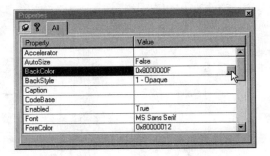

When the developer clicks on the ellipsis, the Color palette is displayed, as shown in Figure 10.7.

The developer can then choose a background color for the control and click OK. When you have established all the properties for the control, you can close the Object Editor to reveal how the ActiveX control appears within the Web page. For example, Figure 10.8 demonstrates how a pushbutton appears within a Web page using the HTML Source Editor.

FIGURE 10.7.
Displaying the Color palette.

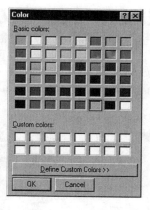

FIGURE 10.8.
A nonvisual way to look at objects.

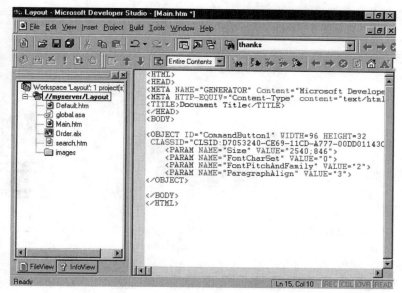

Notice the HTML `<OBJECT>` tags that surround the control. You will also notice that some of the properties and their values have been set for this control and appear within those tags. If the Object Editor had not been used to visually insert this control, the developer would have had to use a more archaic approach involving the typing of these cryptic codes. Thank goodness for advances in modern technology. Sometimes, it is the simple things in life that mean so much.

Using the Object Editor to Edit the Control

You might be wondering how you get back to the friendly, visual environment of the Object Editor after you have initially set the properties for the control. From within the Web page, place your cursor anywhere between the <OBJECT> tags for the control that you want to see, and right-click the mouse to display the shortcut menu. Choose Edit ActiveX Control from the list of menu items as illustrated in Figure 10.9.

FIGURE 10.9.

Editing the ActiveX control.

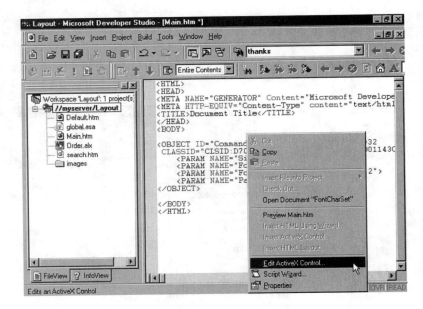

The control will be displayed within the Object Editor, allowing you to make any changes to its properties. After you have made the updates, the Web page will reflect the new properties of the control.

So far, you have learned about ActiveX controls and how to use the Object Editor to manipulate individual controls on a Web page. But, what if you want to construct a robust user interface for your application comprised of multiple controls? The next section reveals the answer to this mystery.

Unleashing the Power of the HTML Layout Editor

The HTML Layout Editor provides the other means for working with ActiveX controls. This editor was first introduced as an individual product named the ActiveX Control Pad. You might have used this tool or other tools such as Visual Basic that enable you to work with ActiveX controls. The HTML Layout Editor enables you to place multiple controls onto a form that can then be inserted into your Web page. The main benefit of using the HTML Layout Editor is that it enables you to construct an effective interface for your application. Unlike the Object Editor, the Layout Editor enables you to place ActiveX controls on top of one another. This feature is especially useful when you need to organize and group several controls such as radio buttons or checkboxes. You can use a frame to house these controls, thereby providing a more intuitive interface.

Similar to tools such as Visual Basic, the HTML Layout Editor enables you to insert ActiveX controls onto a form. You can move and position these controls to create an effective interface. When you have designed the layout, you can then set the properties for the controls to define their behavior and characteristics. Each control possesses a unique set of properties. As with the Object Editor, you can set the values for the control's properties using the Layout Editor.

The next section will guide you through the process of designing and developing an application interface using the HTML Layout Editor. You will learn how a control's properties can be utilized to affect the behavior of the interface.

Creating the HTML Layout

This section focuses on how to use the HTML Layout Editor to design and build an effective interface for your Web-based application. You can create an HTML layout by selecting New from the File menu. The New dialog window will be displayed as shown in Figure 10.10.

FIGURE 10.10.
The New dialog window.

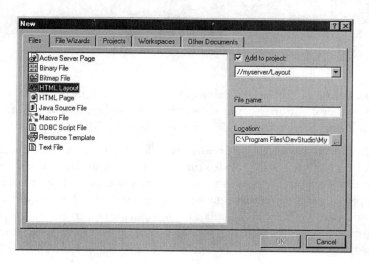

From this window, you can click the File tab and choose HTML Layout from the list of options. You will also need to enter a name for the layout, as illustrated in Figure 10.11.

FIGURE 10.11.
Creating the HTML layout.

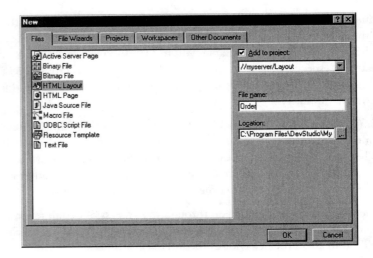

By default, the Add to Project checkbox will be selected, and the name of the current project will be displayed. These defaults enable you to add the HTML layout to the current Visual InterDev project. In addition, the Location field defaults to the directory for the current project.

> **NOTE**
>
> Although you will typically accept the defaults when creating an HTML layout, you can change any of these default values to create a layout independent of the current project.

After you have entered the name of the layout and verified the default choices, you can press the OK pushbutton to confirm the creation of the layout. The HTML layout will be activated displaying a blank form, as demonstrated in Figure 10.12.

The HTML Layout Editor reveals a basic form that serves as the house for your ActiveX controls. A toolbox is also provided that includes the available ActiveX controls. Similar to other visual tools, you can select these controls and place them on your form. A floating toolbar also appears providing toolbar options regarding the overall layout of the controls. The project workspace in Figure 10.12 displays the name of the new layout file that was added to the project. Notice that this file is distinguished by its .ALX extension that denotes the file as an HTML layout file.

FIGURE 10.12.

Viewing a form using the Layout Editor.

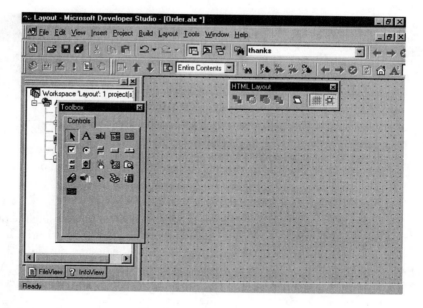

Establishing the Properties of the Form Layout

The first step to creating the interface for your application is to set the properties of the form layout. You can display the Properties window for the layout by clicking the right mouse button anywhere on the form and choosing Properties from the shortcut menu. Figure 10.13 depicts the Properties window for a sample HTML layout.

FIGURE 10.13.

Setting the properties for the layout.

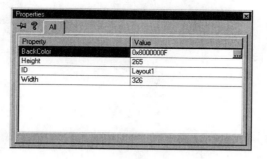

As you can see from this example, you can adjust the ID, height, width, and background color of the form. It is recommended that you change the ID property to a more descriptive name for identifying the layout. For example, if you construct a Web page that includes multiple HTML layouts, you will want to create descriptive names that enable you to easily identify the different layouts.

> **NOTE**
>
> If you use multiple layouts on a Web page, you need to insert them into the Web page in the order that you want them to appear.

You can also adjust the height and width for the layout to properly position the layout within the context of the Web page. The background color property enables you to define an effective background for your controls. For this property, you can enter the cryptic code for the desired color, or you can click the ellipsis and choose a color from the Color palette dialog window.

Integrating ActiveX Controls into Your Layout

The next step to building an effective user interface involves choosing the proper controls. To place a control onto the form, click the left mouse button on the control in the toolbox. After the control has been selected, move your cursor to the desired position on the form and click the left mouse button. The control will be inserted using its default size. You can also move your cursor to the starting position on the form and drag the mouse to customize the size of the control. When you have defined the appropriate size for the control, you can release the left mouse button to complete the process. Figure 10.14 depicts a text box that has been placed on a sample layout form.

FIGURE 10.14.

The text box control.

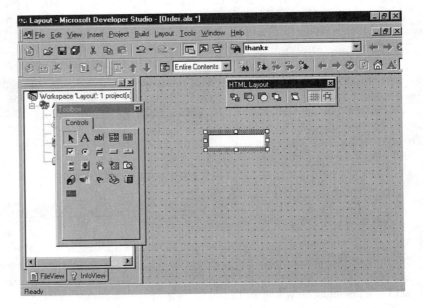

You can set the properties for the control by double-clicking the left mouse button on the control. An alternative method involves selecting the control, right-clicking the mouse to display the shortcut menu, and choosing Properties from the list of items. Figure 10.15 shows the Properties window for the Text Box control.

FIGURE 10.15.

Setting the properties for the text box.

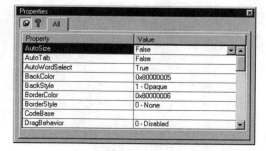

The Text Box control provides various properties that you can configure to define its characteristics and customize its behavior. These properties include the ID, height, width, text, and maximum length just to name a few. Again, you will want to define a unique name for each control using the ID property. A common standard for naming text box controls includes using the txt prefix. For example, the ID for the name text box should be defined as txtName. You can then use this unique name to refer to the Name text box within your scripting code.

> **NOTE**
>
> You will learn how to manipulate the behavior of controls through the use of script in the final section of this chapter.

After you have inserted a control onto the form, you can repeat the same process of selecting the control in the toolbox and clicking the correct position on the form. You might want to select the controls and arbitrarily place them on the form. You can then move the controls by selecting the control and dragging them into the correct position. You can also resize the controls by dragging the corners of a control. You might have a need to move multiple controls as a group. In these cases, select the first control and then hold down the Ctrl key and click the other controls. When you have selected all the appropriate controls, you can move the controls as a group.

For related controls such as multiple labels on a form, you can set the common values for the control properties by selecting the controls and right-clicking the mouse to display the shortcut menu. From the list of menu items, select Properties to display the common Properties dialog window for the controls. Figure 10.16 shows the Properties window for a group of labels.

10

USING THE VISUAL INTERDEV EDITORS

FIGURE 10.16.

Setting the properties for multiple labels.

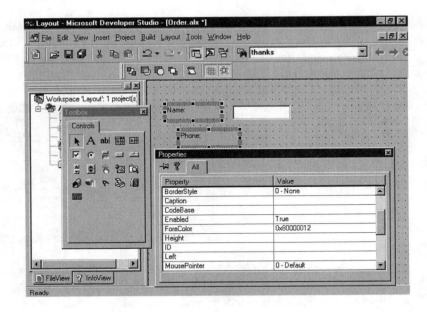

The property values that you set for a group of controls apply to all of the controls. For example, you could set the `Left` property to a certain value to properly align all of the labels on your form. Figure 10.17 shows the results of setting a common value for the `Left` property for the set of labels displayed in Figure 10.16.

FIGURE 10.17.

Aligning multiple labels.

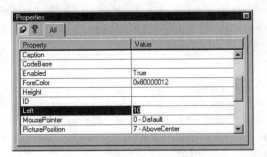

After you finish designing your interface with the appropriate controls, select Save from the File menu to save the HTML layout.

Adding Controls to the Toolbox

The initial toolbox that appears when you create your first HTML layout includes the default ActiveX controls that are registered and included with Visual InterDev. You can customize the controls that appear on the toolbox by right-clicking the mouse and choosing Additional Controls from the shortcut menu. This action will display a dialog window similar to the one pictured in Figure 10.18.

FIGURE 10.18.

Customizing the toolbox.

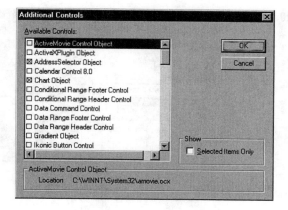

The Additional Controls dialog window reveals all of the ActiveX controls that have been registered for your client machine. You can select the controls by clicking the checkbox to the left of the desired control. Notice, as you highlight the individual controls, that the field at the bottom of the window shows the actual location of the control on your machine. To hide controls in the toolbox, deselect the checkbox next to the desired control.

You can also delete controls that appear in the toolbox by selecting the control, clicking the right mouse button, and choosing Delete from the list of menu items. To customize the appearance of the control on the toolbox, right-click the mouse on the control and choose Customize from the list of options. Figure 10.19 demonstrates the dialog window that appears as a result of this action.

FIGURE 10.19.

Customizing the appearance of the control.

The control that appears in Figure 10.19 is a command button as indicated by the Tool Tip Text field. This text represents the description that will display when the mouse is placed over the control in the toolbox. You can customize the text that appears in this field as well as the appearance of the icon for the control.

If you want to further organize the controls in the toolbox, you can create new tabs in addition to the default Controls tab. You can accomplish this task by clicking the right mouse button on or near the Controls tab. Figure 10.20 displays the shortcut menu options that appear as a result of this action.

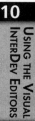

FIGURE 10.20.
Manipulating the tabs in the toolbox.

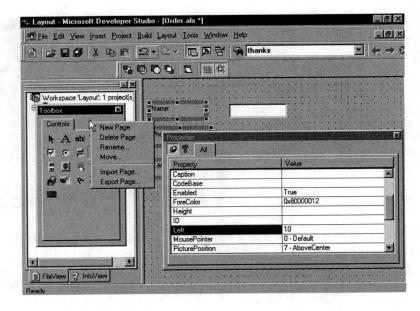

Table 10.3 outlines these menu options and their meaning.

Table 10.3. HTML Layout toolbox options.

Menu Item	Function
New Page	Creates a new tab for the toolbox
Delete Page	Deletes the current tab in the toolbox
Rename	Enables you to rename the current tab
Move	Moves the order of the tabs
Import Page	Imports a predefined tab page from a file
Export Page	Saves a tab page to a file

So far, you have learned how to work with the HTML Layout Editor and all of its features. The next section shows you how to insert the HTML layout into your Web page.

Inserting the Layout into Your Web Page

To use the layout within your application, you must insert it into the appropriate Web page. You can accomplish this task by placing your cursor at the desired position in the Web page document and right-clicking the mouse button. From the shortcut menu, select Insert HTML Layout, and a dialog window will be displayed similar to the one shown in Figure 10.21.

FIGURE 10.21.

Choosing the HTML layout for your Web page.

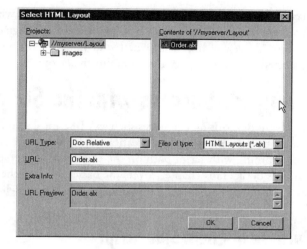

This dialog window enables you to choose an HTML layout from the list to insert into your Web page. Notice that the list box, by default, displays the available ALX, or HTML layout, files. After you select the file from the list and click OK, the layout will be inserted into your Web page, as demonstrated in Figure 10.22.

FIGURE 10.22.

Viewing the layout within the Web page.

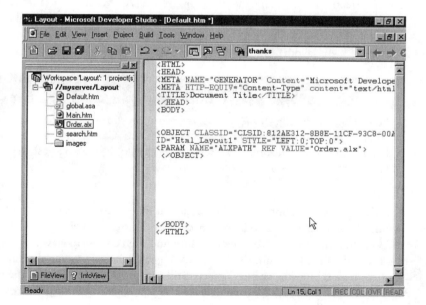

You can edit this layout by right-clicking the mouse anywhere within the <OBJECT> tags for the layout. You can then visually manipulate the properties and design of the layout using the HTML Layout Editor. After you have completed your updates, save your changes, and the updates will be reflected in the Web page that contains the layout.

Scripting for Success with the Script Wizard

With the advent of scripting languages such as VBScript, JScript, and JavaScript, many possibilities have opened concerning the creation of dynamic and interactive applications for the Web. Programming with script both on the client and the server will be covered in detail in Part IV of this book. This chapter covers the basics of using the Script Wizard within Visual InterDev to automate and simplify the process of developing client-side script for your application.

The Purpose of Client-Side Script

The main function of client-side script involves validating user input and responding to user-initiated events. For example, you could use client-side script to validate that the user entered the right type of data for certain fields on a form. Another example would be displaying a message to the user to confirm that an order had been submitted successfully.

You have learned two specific methods for inserting ActiveX controls into your Web page. First, you learned about the Object Editor that enables you to insert individual controls into a Web page. For Web pages that include these types of ActiveX controls (that is, pages not associated with an HTML layout), the script code can be added directly into the HTML or ASP file.

> **NOTE**
>
> Remember, ASP stands for Active Server Page. You were first introduced to ASP files in Chapter 4, "Client- and Server-Side Scripting." Also, Chapter 19, "Creating Active Server Pages," provides an exhaustive discourse on how to develop and use this new and exciting functionality within your Web-based application.

For Web pages that contain an HTML layout, you must associate the code with the ActiveX layout file in order for the code to impact those controls. To view this code, you need to open the ALX file with the HTML Layout Editor and then choose to view the script instead of viewing the code directly within the HTML Web page. This process only concerns script that affects controls within the layout. You can still add general script code to the HTML Web page. The next section provides a good overview of how to add script for your ActiveX controls using the Script Wizard.

Using the Script Wizard

Like most wizards from Microsoft, the Script Wizard serves as a visual guide for adding script to your application. The Script Wizard offers flexibility in allowing you to add scripting logic through a point-and-click interface that is very intuitive. You can also take more control of this task by customizing and adding your own code.

The following example guides you through the process of adding script for a sample HTML layout. From within the Web page file, click the right mouse button within the <OBJECT> tags for the HTML layout to display the shortcut menu, as shown in Figure 10.23.

FIGURE 10.23.
Editing the HTML layout.

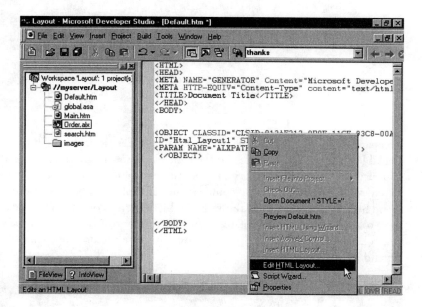

Choose Edit HTML Layout from the list of menu items. After you have activated the HTML Layout Editor, you can right-click the mouse and select Script Wizard from the shortcut menu. The main Script Wizard window will appear as shown in Figure 10.24.

The List View is the default view for the Script Wizard and displays the controls, events, and actions that are available for the selected layout or control. You can use this view to visually associate controls and events with the appropriate actions. From Figure 10.24, you can see that the List View is divided into several panes. The pane located in the top left of the window is the Event pane. This pane enables you to view all of the controls for the layout and their associated events. For example, if you included a command button as a part of your layout, it would appear along with its associated events such as the Click event.

FIGURE 10.24.

Script Wizard—List View.

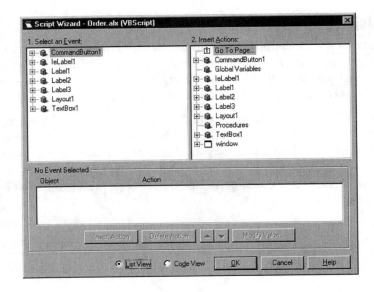

The pane to the right of the Event pane is called the Actions pane. This pane displays all of the available actions and properties for the controls. Also, any pertinent procedures for the layout appear in this pane. From this pane you can set the properties and actions to execute for a selected event. For example, you could set the value of a text box when the user clicks the command button. To accomplish this task, double-click the command button control in the Event pane to expand the list of available events for the control. Then, select the Click event for this control. You can then move over to the Actions pane and double-click the Text Box control to expand its properties.

> **TIP**
>
> You can also expand items listed within the Event and Actions panes by clicking the + (plus) sign located to the left of each item in the list.

Locate the Text property and double-click to display a dialog window, as shown in Figure 10.25.

From this dialog window, you can enter the value that will be displayed in the text box when the user presses the command button. The results will appear in the bottom pane that is also referred to as the Script pane. This pane shows the actions for an event listed in the order that they will take place.

You can see from this example that the List View enables you to easily establish basic functionality for your application. When you want to assume more control over this process, you can use the Code View. The Script Wizard provides two radio buttons at the bottom of the main window that easily enable you to switch between the two views. In Figure 10.26, the developer has selected the Code View by clicking the appropriate radio button.

FIGURE 10.25.

Setting the value of a text box.

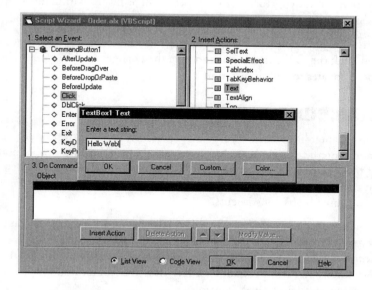

FIGURE 10.26.

The Script Wizard— Code View.

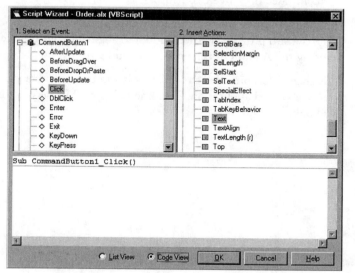

From this window, you can enter the scripting code directly into the Script pane. The Script Wizard can assist you in this process by allowing you to select events and actions from the top panes of the window. For example, when you double-click a property within the Actions Pane, the name of the control and the property will be placed within the Script pane, allowing you to use it within your custom code.

After you have developed your scripting logic for the application using the Script Wizard, you can click the OK pushbutton and save the changes to the layout. The Web page will reflect these updates for the application.

Summary

This chapter has provided you with a hands-on look at how to design and develop your application interface using ActiveX controls and HTML layouts. Proper usage and implementation of these exciting new objects from Microsoft can make or break an application. Many times, an effective interface can be the critical success factor in determining how much the application is used by its constituents.

You learned about two Visual InterDev editors that enable you to organize and integrate ActiveX controls into your Web pages—the Object Editor and the HTML Layout Editor. The Object Editor is a very useful tool for handling individual controls on a Web page. The HTML Layout Editor, on the other hand, is a very effective tool for building a powerful application interface composed of ActiveX controls.

The ability to make the controls come alive provides a dynamic experience for your users. The Script Wizard provides a powerful tool to augment your productivity during development by reducing the amount of time it takes to add scripting logic to your application.

This chapter has provided the basic tools and concepts that you need to develop the logic for your Web-based application. This knowledge will be very useful when you get to Part IV of this book.

Managing the Site

by L. Michael Van Hoozer

CHAPTER 11

IN THIS CHAPTER

The concept of a Web site has become a loosely used term that needs some clarification. The term *site* used to refer to HTML files and possibly a CGI script or two. Nowadays, a *site* refers to a plethora of parts, including documents, Web pages, scripts, components, and objects. The reason for this ever-expanding definition of a site can be traced to the popularity of interactive, dynamic Web-based applications. These applications include both Internet-based, electronic commerce systems as well as corporate intranets. It is definitely an exciting time to be developing applications for the Web. The tools and technologies are continuing to be unveiled at a rapid pace. In fact, Microsoft has declared 1997 as the Year of the Developer.

While these times are definitely intriguing for the developer, they have exponentially raised the stress level of the Web site administrator. The administrator now has to be concerned with not only a larger number, but also many different types of files. Tools and processes are continuing to emerge in this area to aid in managing all the pieces that come together to form a Web-based application. This chapter explores the capabilities of Visual InterDev concerning the proper management of files within your Visual InterDev projects.

First, you will learn how to use the Link View to get a handle on all the various pieces of your Web site puzzle. This chapter also explores how to properly manage your files using Visual InterDev's features. After explaining the file-management capabilities of Visual InterDev, the chapter unveils the powerful Copy Web function that simplifies the process of deploying your Web. Finally, the chapter shows you how to repair broken links that can occur throughout your Web site.

Unleashing the Power of the Link View

Visual InterDev includes a Link View feature that provides the functions of a site-visualization tool. By using the Link View, you can logically explore the components of your Web site. Specifically, you can view all the Web pages within your Web site graphically, and view the relationships that exist between the pages. Moreover, all the documents, objects, script, and other ancillary pieces of your Web pages are also displayed. You can expand or contract the view to see different details about the file relationships. For large Web sites, this ability can provide a way to drill down on certain aspects, or sections, of your Web site.

The Link View provides a lot of flexibility in enabling you to choose the appropriate view for your needs. It also enables you to explore further details about the files that are displayed. For example, the Link View provides the name and type of file indicated by a visual icon. You can also place your cursor over the icon to display the location of the file. Every file that is a part of your Web page and site is displayed within the Link View including HTML pages, Active Server Pages, GIF and JPG images, ActiveX controls, Java applets, HTML layout files, and so on.

Viewing the Links for a File

You can view the links for a file within your Visual InterDev project by selecting the file in the project workspace and clicking the right mouse button to display the shortcut menu, as demonstrated in Figure 11.1.

FIGURE 11.1.

*Choosing the Link
View for a file.*

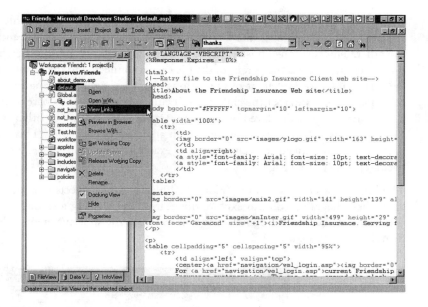

From the shortcut menu, you can choose View Links to display the Link View for the selected file. Figure 11.2 depicts an example of the power of the Link View.

FIGURE 11.2.

The Link View.

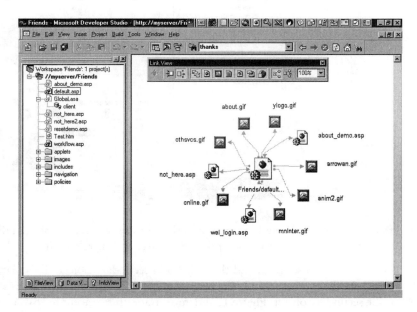

The page in this example is the default page for a sample Web site. This Web page is an Active Server Page (ASP), as denoted by the .asp extension. The page includes several GIF images as well as links to other ASPs within the Web site. The lines between the files depict their relationships. Notice that for some files, the line consists of a circle on one end and an arrow on the other. This relationship is described as a parent/child relationship in which the file that is located by the circle is the parent of the file that is connected to the arrow. In Figure 11.2, the `default.asp` file is the parent of the various GIF files, such as `online.gif`. The parent/child relationship indicates that the child file is included as a part of the parent file. In this case, the `online.gif` image is displayed on the `default.asp` Web page. The other type of relationship shown in Figure 11.2 consists of a line with an arrow at both ends. This type of line denotes that the files are linked to each other. For example, the `default.asp` Web page links to the `about_demo.asp` Web page.

The Link View enables you to explore the links for other objects that are contained within a Link View diagram. You can explore this feature by selecting a secondary object within the diagram and clicking the right mouse button. From the shortcut menu, select View Links, as demonstrated in Figure 11.3.

FIGURE 11.3.

Selecting another object.

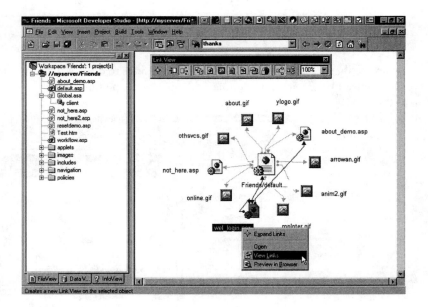

After you select the View Links menu option for the secondary object, a diagram will be displayed that enables you to explore the new object and its related files.

You can also choose to expand the links for a secondary object. This feature enables you to expand the diagram to include the originally selected objects and its links along with the links for the secondary object. Figure 11.4 demonstrates this concept for two related objects within a Web site.

FIGURE 11.4.

Expanding the links.

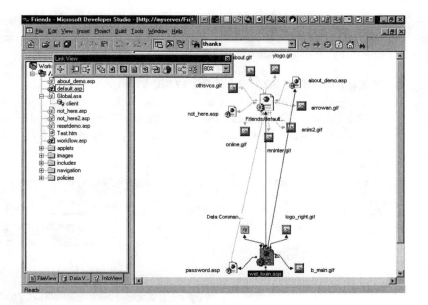

As you can tell from Figure 11.4, a Link View diagram can become quite large as you continue to expand the links. To enable you to see all the files, Visual InterDev provides a feature that allows you to customize the display of the diagram. The Zoom Link View appears on the View Link toolbar and enables you to select different display percentages for the diagram. This option is illustrated in Figure 11.5.

FIGURE 11.5.

Zooming in on your diagram.

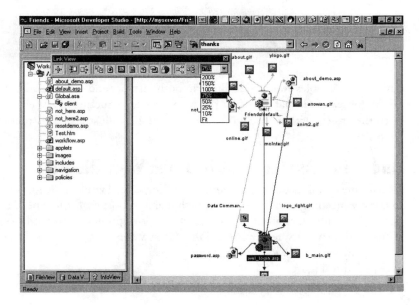

The Zoom Link View is a combo box that enables you to enter a custom percentage or choose a predefined value from the list. You can also select Fit from the list of combo box options to automatically tailor the size of the diagram to the size of the display.

Viewing the Links on the World Wide Web

Link View provides a feature for you to view the links for Web pages located on the World Wide Web (WWW). To use this feature, select the Tools menu and choose View Links on WWW. A dialog window will display that enables you to enter a URL address for the Web page, as depicted in Figure 11.6.

FIGURE 11.6.

Creating a Link View for a URL address.

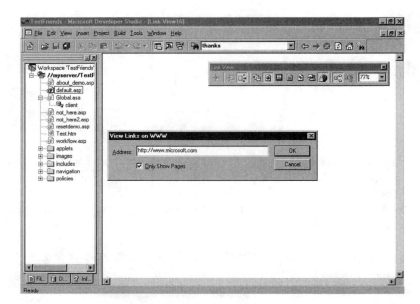

This feature enables you to view links on both intranet and Internet addresses. The basic benefit of this feature is that it enables you to explore the structure of a Web site without having to open the project within Visual InterDev. Figure 11.7 illustrates the structure of the Microsoft Web site.

Understanding the Icons in a Link View Diagram

Visual InterDev lives up to its name in providing several visual indicators within the Link View to convey meaning to the user. First, each icon symbolizes its file type. This feature helps the developer or administrator understand what type of program was used to create the file. Also, Visual InterDev activates a verification process when a Link View is created. As the files included with the Link View undergo this process, their icons progress through a series of states, as depicted in Figure 11.8.

FIGURE 11.7.
Viewing the links for an external site.

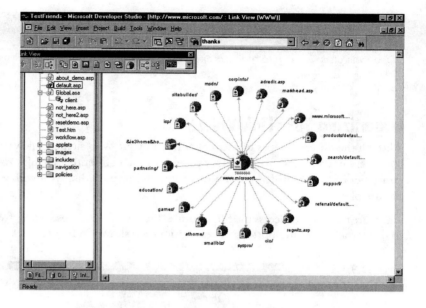

FIGURE 11.8.
The natural progression of a file.

Link View Verification Process

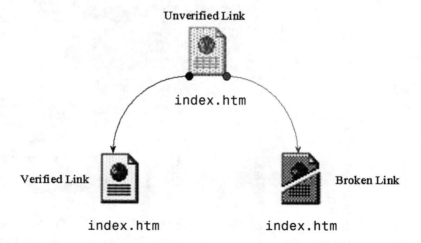

Unverified Link

index.htm

Verified Link

Broken Link

index.htm

index.htm

The first icon appears in gray, indicating that its link has not been determined or verified. If Visual InterDev determines that the file contains a valid link to the primary object in the diagram, Link View will display the file's icon in its natural color. If, however, the file represents a broken link, the icon for the file will appear broken and in red.

> **NOTE**
>
> You will discover how to repair broken links in the section titled "Reconciling Broken Links," later in this chapter.

Organizing Your Link View

With all the different types of files contained in your Web site, a Link View diagram can become very unwieldy. Visual InterDev provides a useful filter that enables you to view only certain types of files. This feature can be very useful in providing you with a more manageable picture of your Web site.

There are two ways to access the filter feature. First, you can choose Filters from the View menu to display a list of filter options. These options are shown in Figure 11.9.

FIGURE 11.9.

Available filter options.

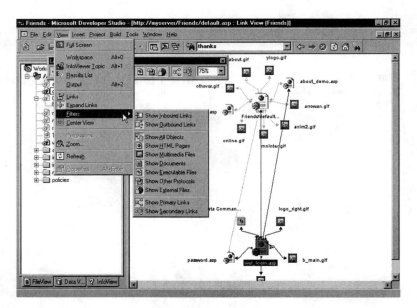

You can also select a filter option from the Link View toolbar. The icons on the toolbar correspond to the icons displayed to the left of the Filter menu's options portrayed in Figure 11.9. Table 11.1 explains the functions of these options.

Table 11.1. Filter categories.

Icon	Category	Description
	Inbound Links	Displays the inbound links; in other words, the children of the parent object
	Outbound Links	Displays the outbound links; in other words, the objects that the parent links into (the parent's parent)
	All Objects	Displays all objects
	HTML Pages	Displays HTML Web pages
	Multimedia Files	Displays images and multimedia files
	Documents	Displays document files (MS Word, PowerPoint, and so on)
	Executable Files	Displays program files such as EXEs and DLLs
	Other Protocols	Displays links to non-HTTP objects such as news servers, Mail, and Telnet
	External Files	Displays objects external to the project
	Show Primary Links	Displays the links to and from the primary, or expanded, object
	Show Secondary Links	Displays links between the secondary, or unexpanded, objects on the diagram

All these options are selected by default when a Link View diagram is created. When you click on an option, the filter will be toggled on or off depending on its state. If you wanted to show only the HTML or ASP pages for a site, you would need to turn off the other filter options on the Link View toolbar. Figure 11.10 displays the results of this action.

FIGURE 11.10.

*Viewing the Active
Server Pages.*

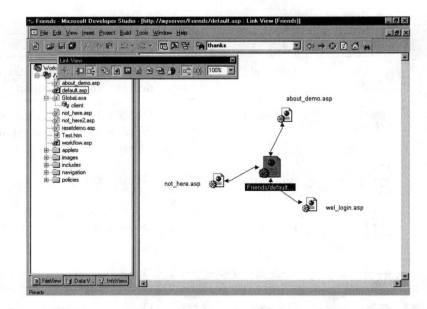

TIP

The Show All Objects option enables you to easily return to the default state of the
diagram.

Editing an Object

Link View enables you to explore all the many pieces of your Web site and understand the
relationships of the files. After examining the site, you may have occasion to edit or view a file
contained within the site. Visual InterDev enables you to accomplish this action directly from
within a Link View diagram by selecting the object and clicking the right mouse button. From
the shortcut menu, you can then select Open from the list of menu items, as demonstrated in
Figure 11.11.

After you select the Open menu item, the object will be opened using its default editor. Figure
11.12 depicts an ASP file that has been opened from within a Link View diagram.

The example in Figure 11.12 displays an ASP file that has been opened using the HTML Source
Editor, which is the default editor for HTML and ASP files. If the file had been of another file
type, such as an HTML layout, the HTML Layout Editor would have been activated to open
the file.

FIGURE 11.11.
Choosing to open the object.

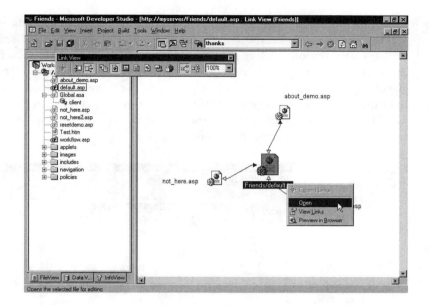

FIGURE 11.12.
Editing an ASP file.

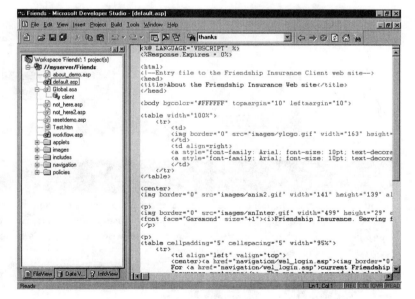

You can also select multiple files to open and explore from within a Link View diagram. To accomplish this task, select the first object and then hold down the Ctrl (Control) key and click the left mouse button to select additional objects in the diagram. You can choose the same or different types of files. For example, you might want to open both a Web page and its HTML layout. By executing the previous instructions to select these objects, you can then click the right mouse button and choose Open from the shortcut menu that is displayed for these objects. The files will then be opened in the order they were selected. Figure 11.13 illustrates the process of choosing multiple files to open.

FIGURE 11.13.

Opening multiple files.

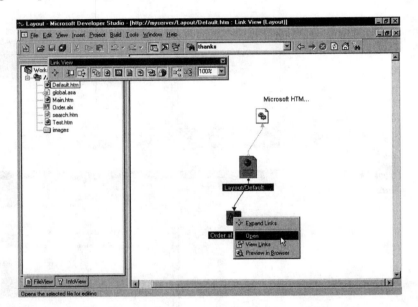

TIP

You can also click the left mouse button and drag the mouse over the files that you want to select. A rectangle will display as you drag the mouse to serve as a visual guide concerning the objects that you are selecting. After you release the left mouse button, all the objects contained in the rectangle will be chosen.

Exploring the Object Shortcut Menu

Visual InterDev provides some other options to enable you to work with Link View objects. These options are summarized in Table 11.2.

Table 11.2. The Object shortcut menu options.

Menu Item	Description
Expand Links	Expands the diagram to include the links of the selected object
Open	Opens the object using its default editor
View Links	Creates a new Link View diagram for the object
Preview In Browser	Enables you to preview the Web page using the default browser

Using Visual InterDev to Manage Your Files

Visual InterDev takes advantage of the file-manipulation features within Windows to simplify the management of your project files. These features can save significant development effort when you are working with multiple files from multiple sites. Similar to the Windows Explorer, the Visual InterDev File View enables you to easily interact with your project folders and files. For example, File View enables you to add, edit, delete, and rename any file or folder that is contained in the project workspace. These functions are available from the shortcut menu after you have selected the appropriate file or folder. Figure 11.14 depicts the available options for a sample ASP file.

FIGURE 11.14.

Viewing the editing options for a file.

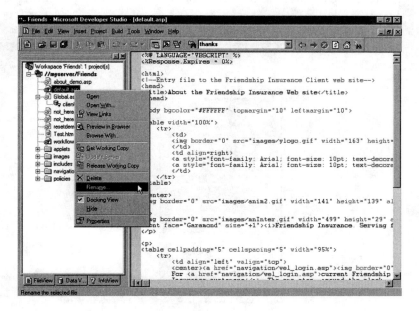

For the sample ASP file shown in Figure 11.14, the options include opening and editing the file, renaming it, and deleting it from the project. To rename the file, select Rename from the list of menu items and a dialog window will display, enabling you to enter the new name for the file. To delete the file, you can choose Delete from the shortcut menu, and a message will display that enables you to confirm your decision, as shown in Figure 11.15.

FIGURE 11.15.

Confirming the deletion of a file.

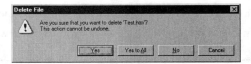

If you choose multiple files in the project workspace and select Delete, you have the option of confirming one file at a time or deleting all the files at once.

Adding Files from Other Projects

You might want to reuse files from previous Web sites. There are two basic ways to accomplish this task. The first method, which is covered in this section, involves adding files and folders from within the project workspace. The second method involves using the Copy Web function and is explained in the next section of this chapter.

To add files or folders to a Visual InterDev project, you can select the root directory for your project and click the right mouse button to display the shortcut menu, as depicted in Figure 11.16.

FIGURE 11.16.

Adding content to your project.

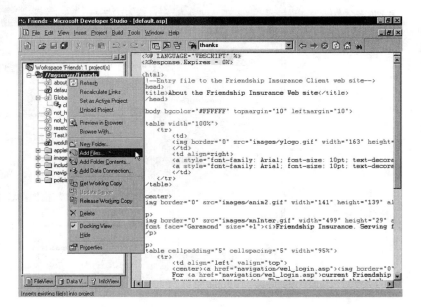

To add files to the project, select the Add Files menu option. A dialog window will display, enabling you to select the files that you want to add to the project. (See Figure 11.17.)

FIGURE 11.17.

Selecting the files to add to your project.

You can also choose Add Folder Contents to add all the files within a folder. In this scenario, the Browse for Folder dialog window will display, enabling you to choose a folder to add to the project. This dialog window is illustrated in Figure 11.18.

FIGURE 11.18.

Adding the contents of a folder.

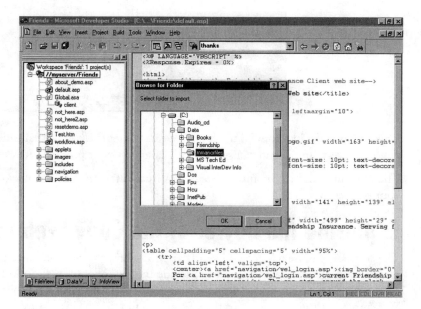

The files and folders that you copy into a project become a part of that particular project. Any changes that are made to the files pertain to the new project. The updated files are saved as a part of the new project and do not affect the behavior of other projects because you have made a copy of the files for the new project.

Another way to add files and folders to a Visual InterDev project workspace involves dragging and dropping the objects from within the Windows interface. For example, you can select a file or folder within the Windows Explorer and drag the object over to the Visual InterDev project workspace, as demonstrated in Figure 11.19.

FIGURE 11.19.

Dragging a folder into Visual InterDev.

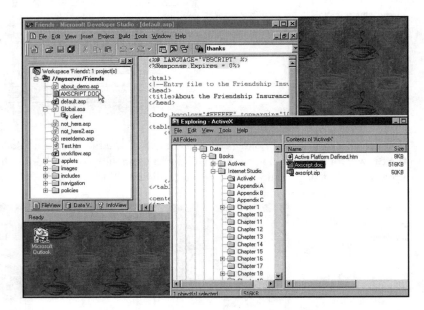

This action will add a copy of the folder and its contents to the Visual InterDev project. This method is very simple and can significantly augment your productivity.

These features add to the intuitiveness of Visual InterDev and enable you to easily manage your project files.

Exploring the Power of the Copy Web Function

The concept of reuse has been diligently applied to everything from object-oriented programming to recycling. The basic notions include the reduction of waste and the ability to create once and reuse over and over again. Visual InterDev enables you to apply this model to your Web projects through the use of the Copy Web function. This feature can save you development time for a specific project as well as increase your productivity across multiple projects.

Enhancing a Single Project Effort

Chapter 7, "Managing the Site and Team Development," covers the basic environments for a Web project. These environments include development, testing, production, and post-production. You may have one or all of these environment sites for your Web project. The basic premise is that each of these environments provides a unique area for you to implement your Web-based application. Each site is tailored to the specific needs and evolutionary stage of your project. For example, the testing environment represents an area that enables you to test the application once all the pieces have been developed. The Copy Web function supports your needs for each of these stages and environments by enabling you to migrate the Web site to each environment. You can use the Copy Web function to copy the site to another directory on the same machine or on a different machine.

Using the Copy Web Function

To use this powerful feature, you must have administrator privileges on the destination location. Open the Web project that you want to copy and choose Copy Web from the Project menu. The Copy Web dialog window will display, as shown in Figure 11.20.

FIGURE 11.20.

Copying a Web site.

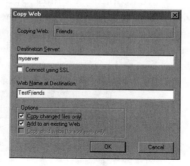

The name of the Web site that is being copied displays in the top field of this window. The destination server defaults to the current Web server, but you can change this field to point to another Web server. A checkbox enables you to select a Secure Sockets Layer (SSL) connection for the site. The next field, in the middle of the window, enables you to enter a name for the new project at the destination location. The remaining options provide customization options that enable you to tailor the material being copied. For example, the first option enables you to copy only the files that have changed. This option can be very helpful during the development and testing phases of your project, when you are constantly testing and fixing different parts of your application. You might not want to copy the entire Web site to the testing environment every time an update is made. Instead, you can use this option and migrate only the files that have been updated. The Add to an existing Web option enables you to copy the Web site as a child to an existing Web parent. If you do not select this option, the site will be added to the root web for the destination server. The Copy child webs option is enabled only for root webs. This option enables you to copy all the child Web sites that exist within a root web.

After you enter the appropriate options and click OK, the Web site will be copied to its intended destination. Figure 11.21 illustrates the confirmation message that is displayed upon completion of this process.

Figure 11.21.
Confirming the process.

Accessing the New Web

Once the Web site has been copied, you must create a Visual InterDev project to utilize its contents. The newly copied Web site will inherit the security settings of the root web at the destination location. To create a project using the copied Web site, select New from the File menu. You can then click on the Projects tab and select the Web Project Wizard from the list of options, as shown in Figure 11.22.

Figure 11.22.
Initiating the Web Project Wizard.

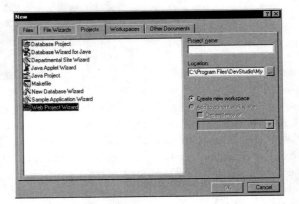

In the text box pictured in Figure 11.22, you need to enter a name for the new project. The location will default to the current location for your projects. You can accept this location or change it to another directory. The Create new workspace option will be selected by default, enabling you to create a new project workspace for the project. You can accept this default and click OK to begin the process of creating a new Web project. Figure 11.23 depicts the Web Project Wizard dialog box that appears as a result of this action.

FIGURE 11.23.

Creating a project—
Step 1.

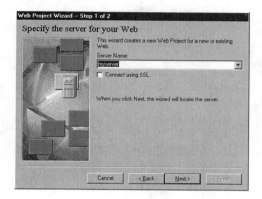

This box enables you to specify a server for your Web project as well as to make a decision concerning the type of connection for the server. After you make your selections, you can click the Next button to proceed to the next step in the process. From this box, you can choose to create a new web or connect to an existing one. For Web projects that you have copied, you want to choose the latter option, as portrayed in Figure 11.24.

FIGURE 11.24.

Creating a project—
Step 2.

In this example, the option to connect to an existing Web server has been chosen, and the name of the copied Web project has been selected. The final step in the process is to click the Finish button, which will create a new project for the copied site, as shown in Figure 11.25.

FIGURE 11.25.

Reuse at its finest.

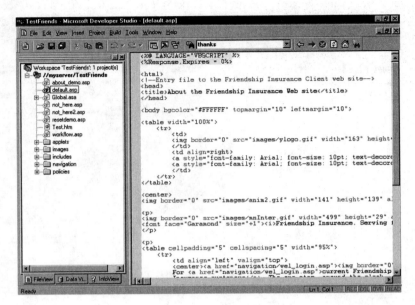

Visual InterDev provides a very straightforward process to enable you to copy a Web site and reuse its contents. This feature can definitely save valuable development time and enable you to capitalize on previous investments.

Reconciling Broken Links

Visual InterDev enables you to automatically monitor the links within your Web site. For example, if you move or rename a file, you will receive a warning message similar to the one displayed in Figure 11.26.

FIGURE 11.26.
Noticing a problem.

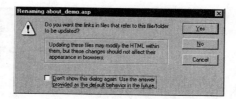

This warning dialog box enables you to update the references to this file to reflect the change and avoid a broken link. To receive this proactive warning message, you must have previously activated the automatic link repair feature for the project. You can do this by selecting the project name in the project workspace and choosing Properties from the shortcut menu. From the General tab, choose On for the Link Repair option, as shown in Figure 11.27.

FIGURE 11.27.
Choosing to repair the links automatically.

For those occasions when you choose not employ this feature for your Web projects, Visual InterDev provides an alternative manual process for resolving the links. When you notice a broken link in your Link View diagram, you can place your cursor over the broken icon until a ToolTip message is displayed. Figure 11.28 displays a sample message describing the reason for a broken link.

In this example, the file has been renamed, and, therefore, the file (or object) cannot be found. You need to manually change the name of the file back to its original value. Then, you can select the project name in the project workspace and right-click the mouse to display the shortcut menu. From the list of menu items, pick Recalculate Links, as shown in Figure 11.29.

The links will be recalculated and present a more harmonious relationship between the files in your project, as depicted in Figure 11.30.

FIGURE 11.28.
Discovering the reason for a broken link.

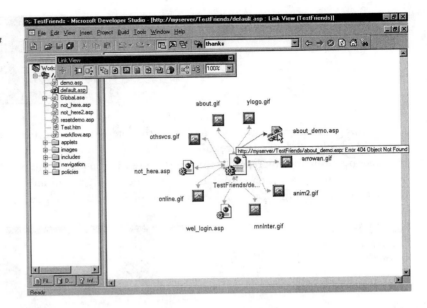

FIGURE 11.29.
Recalculating the links.

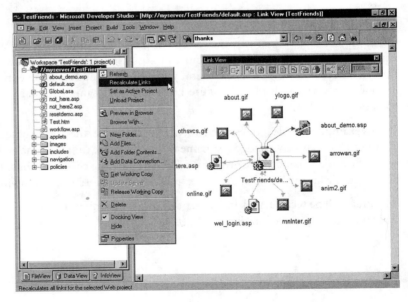

FIGURE 11.30.
*A reconciled
relationship.*

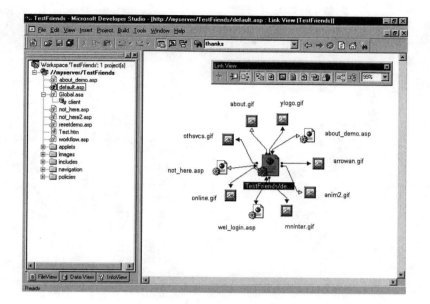

Summary

The proper management of a Web site is very important to its continued use and success. The Webmaster's expertise and skills are critical to the success of this effort, but skills alone will not suffice. This person must have tools at his disposal to be able to effectively carry out his responsibilities. Visual InterDev provides some key tools to aid in this process.

This chapter has demonstrated some of the Visual InterDev features that enable you to properly manage a site. Link View provides a very intuitive and easy-to-use site-visualization tool that enables you to examine the structure of your site. The Copy Web function provides a solid method for reusing the content of existing Web sites as well as maintaining order throughout the development life cycle. Visual InterDev also assists you during development by automatically maintaining the relationships and links between your Web site files.

CHAPTER 12

Database Management with the Visual Data Tools

by Kevin Jullion

IN THIS CHAPTER

Before reading this chapter, you should be familiar with basic relational database concepts, including the use of tables and queries, and you should have some understanding of relational database normalization practices, including joins. For an overview of relational databases see Chapter 2, "Relational Databases and Client/Server Technology." If you need more information on the Query Designer, see Appendix A, "Query Designer Primer."

Dynamic Web Sites: An Overview

As more tools become available to create Web-based content, you will have noticed that publicly accessible Web sites (that is, Internet sites) are becoming more and more dynamic in nature. By dynamic, I mean that the pages are constructed on the fly as the user is navigating the Web site, as opposed to the pages being constructed by individual content authors. Not even 12 months ago most Web sites were statically authored sites, requiring a great deal more maintenance. The vast majority of the data that is included in today's dynamically constructed Web sites is, of course, coming from a relational database management system (RDBMS).

For example, customers of a Web site could place an order online and have the Web server add the order to the database, and the Web server would then construct and display the confirmation page back to the requesting customer confirming the order. The sample confirmation Web page shown in Figure 12.1 will help to illustrate where the dynamic data might be coming from.

FIGURE 12.1.

Confirmation Page example.

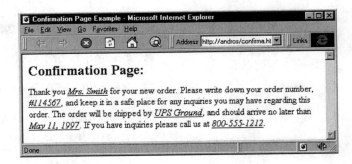

In this example, the underlined text is dynamic data read from the database, and is created as part of the order process. The Web server creates the page and sends the page back to the customer; it does not exist otherwise.

Dynamic Web Pages Are Distributed Client/Server Applications

Because dynamic Web pages are actually constructed by a program on the Web server, and only the results of the program are returned to the requesting client browser, database-driven Web sites are actually distributed client/server applications. The intensive calculations and output are done on the high performance Web servers and the client browsers only receive the resulting HTML code that is necessary to show well-organized, accurate, and attractive Web pages. As an additional benefit to this model, because the pages are constructed on the fly they do not require persistent storage on the Web server's hard disk.

Also, because the database does not have to reside on the same physical machine as the Web site, you can further distribute the processing of queries against the database(s) to additional machines on your network, thus achieving load balancing. This is what is called an *n-tier* client/server application. It is n-tier because you can have any number of machines involved in the persistent storage of the data and any number of other machines doing the processing of your result sets. Sites with a high volume of hits/visitors should consider using this n-tier model to prevent bottlenecks or slowdowns on the Web server.

The inclusion of Visual Data Tools within the Visual Studio Integrated Design Environment (IDE) gives developers a very tightly integrated database development and database administration workspace. There are four major components included with the Visual Data Tools, and all are interrelated to some degree.

Data View

The Data view shows a graphical, hierarchical view of the objects (including tables, fields, database diagrams, stored procedures, and views) in the databases that your Visual InterDev project is connected to. The connection is live, meaning that the developer can use the Database Designer and the Query Designer to develop, maintain, and administer these databases without having to leave the Visual InterDev IDE.

The Database Designer

The Database Designer enables you to manage the objects in the database, including creating and editing tables, views, stored procedures, triggers, database diagrams, and so on. For more information on creating queries, stored procedures, and triggers, see Chapter 21, "Creating and Debugging Queries, Stored Procedures, and Triggers."

The Query Designer

The Query Designer enables you to drag tables onto the Query Designer pane and graphically create and run complex queries, including those with joins. For an overview of the Query Designer tool, see Appendix A.

The Source Code Editor

The Source Code Editor is much like the editor that Visual InterDev includes to enable you to modify HTML source directly. However, in the Visual Data Tools area, the Source Code Editor will enable you to create and edit triggers and stored procedures.

Creating a Database-Aware Web from Within Visual InterDev

With the advent of Microsoft Internet Information Server 3.0 (IIS) there was an update to the functionality of the Open Database Connectivity (ODBC) layer. As part of the ODBC 3.0 specification, you are now able to create what is called a file Data Source Name (DSN). A file DSN stores connection information in a file that contains the location and other properties, including username and password, for accessing a database. A system or machine DSN is stored in the registry of the machine in which the DSN is created, and as a result, system DSNs are much less portable to other machines. A system DSN allows the Web server to communicate with and make changes to the data stored in the relational database that the DSN points to.

Connectionless DSN

When you add your first data connection to a Visual InterDev project you will notice that a `global.asa` file is created. This file is a simple ASCII text file that you can manually edit if you need to. In the `global.asa` file you will find all the database connection references needed for the Web that you are working on. File-based DSNs are recommended because they do not involve the registry of the Web server, they can be moved from staging server to production server, and are autonomous.

If you already have a data connection established, any subsequent data connections that you create are appended to the `global.asa` file. It is even possible to create data connections to heterogeneous relational databases within the same Web project. These databases can even reside on separate physical machines, as long as the RDBMS is ODBC 3.0 compliant. By default these data connections are pooled by the Internet Information Server, which means that Web sites created with Visual InterDev will scale from a few concurrent users to hundreds or even thousands of concurrent users or more. In addition, when adding a data connection, the IIS server generates connection caching and time-out values by default. The developer can change these default values, however, if desired.

Creating a Data Connection

You connect your Visual InterDev project to an RDBMS by way of a data connection. To add a data connection to your Visual InterDev project follow these steps:

1. In File view, on the Project menu, click Add To Project, and then click Data Connection.
2. In the Select Data Source dialog box, either choose an existing DSN or create a new DSN.
3. Log on to the data server if required.

Alternatively, you can create a new project using the Database Project Wizard, and this will create a data connection for you for this new project:

1. In File view, on the File menu, click New.
2. Select the Project tab, and then choose New Database Project.
3. You will be prompted to provide the DSN.
4. In the Select Data Source dialog box, either choose an existing DSN or create a new DSN.
5. Log on to the data server if required.

Once you have a data connection established, you will notice that a new tab appears in the Workspace pane; the tab is labeled Data View. From the Data View tab you can access the tables, views, database diagram, and stored procedure within the RDBMS that you selected (assuming the RDBMS supports all of these objects).

Having a data connection included within your Visual InterDev project means that you can make design changes, query tables, and populate databases without leaving the Visual InterDev Integrated Development Environment (IDE). The documentation refers to this as a *live connection* to the database, because you can make real-time updates to the data and the database structure—if you have sufficient administrative rights to the objects in the database—while creating your Web application.

12

MANAGEMENT
WITH VISUAL
DATA TOOLS

Table 12.1. Comparison of available features among ODBC-compliant databases.

Database	View, edit data	Create, execute, save queries	Create, edit stored procedures and triggers	Design tables, database diagrams	Create new databases
Microsoft:					
Access 7.0	Yes	Yes			
Access 8.0	Yes	Yes			
SQL Server 4.2	Yes	Yes			
SQL Server 6.0	Yes	Yes	Yes		
SQL Server 6.5	Yes	Yes	Yes	Yes	Yes
Visual FoxPro	Yes	Yes			
Oracle:					
Version 6.x	Yes	Yes			
Version 7.x	Yes	Yes	Yes		
Other ODBC databases	Yes	Yes			

SOURCE: Visual InterDev Online Help: "Visual Database Tools Features for ODBC Databases."

NOTE

Microsoft created a high-performance ODBC driver for Oracle, and it ships in the box with Visual InterDev.

NOTE

The ODBC drivers for Informix that shipped with Visual InterDev were found to have some problems; to read up on these issues or locate the service pack that addresses this issue, visit the following site:

http://www.microsoft.com/support/vinterdev

Creating a New Table in an MS SQL Server Database

To create a new table from the Visual Data Tools in a SQL Server database, go to the Data View tab, right-click the Tables folder, and select New Table. You will be prompted for the name you want to give this new table.

On the right side of the IDE, the Database Designer pane gives you a table in design mode—much like the SQL Enterprise Manager New Table window. You can now add columns to this table and create all of the required column property entries necessary to define and maintain the entity and domain integrity of the table. Such properties include Column Name, Datatype, Allow Nulls, Identity, Identity Seed, and so on. (For more information on these table properties see the discussion later in this chapter on Database Designer.)

Changing the Design or Data in an MS SQL Server 6.5 Table

To modify the design of an existing table, right-click the table in the Data View pane and select Design. The Database Designer will open the table in design mode on the right-hand side of the IDE. This feature is only available for Microsoft SQL Server 6.5 databases.

If you want to insert, update, or delete records in one of your existing tables, double-click the table in the Data View pane and the Database Designer will open the table showing all of the columns and all of the records. You can make changes to these records only if you have the necessary security privileges assigned on that table.

What If I Am Not Using MS SQL Server 6.5?

The only way to change the design of a table that is not part of a SQL Server 6.5 database is to modify the design of that table through the individual RDBMS's native methods. For example, in Microsoft Access you would open the .MDB file and change the properties of your tables using the Microsoft Access development environment. It should be noted though that even without the RDBMS engine installed on your local machine you *can* insert, update, and delete records in these other database engines from within the Visual InterDev IDE as long as that relational database is ODBC compliant.

Query Designer

The Query Designer is a visual design tool that enables you to create Structured Query Language (SQL) statements that query or modify tables in any ODBC-compliant database. If you are familiar with creating a query using either MS Query or Microsoft Access's Query By Example grid, you will immediately recognize the functionality of the Query Designer. The Query Designer that comes with Visual InterDev, however, is vastly more powerful and easier to navigate with than either of those tools. See Appendix A for a look at the Query Designer basics.

In order to create queries in Visual InterDev, you will first need to create a data connection. Refer to the section "Creating a Data Connection."

Creating a New Query

There are three ways to launch the Query Designer, and how you do so will depend on the specifics of the project you are working on. First, if you have created a database project, you can right-click the Data Connection in File view and select New Query. This will bring up the Query Designer; refer to the section on using drag and drop to populate this query with tables. If you create a query this way it is saved as a standalone file; it is not stored in the database. Instead it becomes part of the project you are working in and appears in the File View tab for the data connection you are querying.

Second, if you have not created a database project but one of the files in your project uses either the Data Range Header or the Data Command design-time controls, you can view the properties of these ActiveX controls and click the SQL Builder button in the property sheet. To do this, open the file that contains the ActiveX control in the Visual InterDev Source Editor, right-click the control, and select Edit Design-time Control. Choose the Control tab on the Properties dialog box and then select the SQL Builder button. The Query Designer will open with the SQL query as it was last saved as part of this ActiveX control. (For more information on design-time controls, see Chapter 13, "Working with Design-Time Controls.")

> **NOTE**
>
> By definition, for an ActiveX control to be included in a Web page the file must be an HTML server-side script file (.ASP). Simply renaming an .HTM file to .ASP is not sufficient. You will also need to add server-side script tags to the .HTM file. (For more information on server-side scripting, see Chapter 23, "Using Active Server Scripting with Databases.")

Third, if you do not have a database project and you have not used the two aforementioned design-time ActiveX controls, you can simply double-click any of the tables in the Data View tab, which will immediately execute a SELECT * FROM <tablename> query against that table. From the result set that is generated you can use the Query toolbar (see Figure 12.2) to show the Diagram, Grid, SQL, and or Results panes, or use the View menu and select Show Panes. Unfortunately, there is no way to have all of the panes appear with a single click.

TIP

Whenever you create a query based on a data connection you are given a read-only Data Connection Properties dialog box. If you find this to be an annoying feature, click the small x in the top-right corner to remove it from your workspace.

FIGURE 12.2.
Query toolbar.

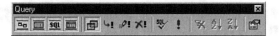

Query Designer Panes Will Alleviate Your Pains

Once you have opened the Query Designer window, you can drag tables from the Data View tab and drop them onto the Diagram pane. Drag and drop all of the tables you need to create the desired result set. The action of selecting the checkbox next to any of the columns in the table in the Diagram pane will begin the process of actually creating a SQL query. As an alternative method, you can drag columns from the Diagram pane onto the Grid pane and achieve the same results.

As with most of the tools in this product you can find many ways to accomplish the same thing. The Diagram, Grid, and SQL panes are aware of changes you make in any of them, so you can create your SQL statement by making changes in a way that is most comfortable for you, and automatically the Query Designer will synchronize the other panes. (For a more detailed description of these panes see Chapter 21.)

Not sure what datatype underlies the columns you are interested in? You can simply use your mouse to hover over the top of the column name in the Diagram pane, and a tooltip will appear telling you the datatype and size properties for that column. If the datatype is a numeric or a currency you may want to consider using some of the built-in convert functions to enhance the look of the output.

Creating and Changing Joins

If your database contains tables that have relationships defined, the Query Designer will recognize these joins and depict them graphically in the Diagram pane and in the SQL pane when you add these related tables to the Diagram pane. The SQL pane writes the WHERE clause using the INNER JOIN ANSI style. Again, you can modify these joins in either place, or create new joins that haven't been defined as part of the table structure.

Specifically, you can modify the joins to be left outer joins, right outer joins, or full outer joins. To do this right-click the line that depicts the join and select Properties. From the Properties dialog box you can determine how the join is configured. See Appendix A for more information on using the Query Designer and creating joins.

Perfecting Your Result Set: Aliasing Your Column Names

If you are unhappy with the column name that is in the table, you can have your result set return a friendlier name by using the Alias feature. Using a column alias enables you to make the result set column titles read exactly the way you want them to. For example, we could alias the column au_lname as Author's Last Name as follows:

```
SELECT  au_lname AS "Author's Last Name"
```

Sorting Your Results

The best way to quickly change the sort order of a query is to either use the Sort Type column in the Grid pane and select the sort order as ascending or descending, or right-click the column name in the Diagram pane and select Sort Ascending or Sort Descending. The Sort Order column simply determines which column gets ordered first, in the SQL ORDER BY clause. You will notice that this creates an A to Z or Z to A icon next to the column name in the Database pane, depending on which sort method you selected.

As with all the methods presented here, if you are a SQL syntax guru, you can always choose to edit the ORDER BY clause of a SQL statement directly in the SQL pane.

Grouping Records

To add a GROUP BY clause to your SELECT statement, you can right-click the gray area of the Diagram pane and select GROUP BY. GROUP BY clauses must be applied to all of the columns used in the result set, by definition.

Using the Group By column in the Grid pane enables you to create other oft-used queries like finding the total number of authors in the Authors table.

```
SELECT Count(*) FROM Authors
```

Simply choose All Columns from the table and then click the combo box in the Group By column in the Grid pane and choose Count. In the same way, you can create other queries, like Max, Min, Sum, or Avg queries.

Using Criteria

If you want to limit the records returned in your result set you do so by specifying a criteria on your columns. To add a criterion, add a constant or a variable in the Criteria column of the Grid pane. Constants are great for testing and debugging but are really used in a dynamic application; most of the time you will use a variable here. If you are going to use a variable, start by including an = sign in the criterion, then surrounding the variable name with square brackets (for example, =[MyVariable]). (See Figure 12.3.)

FIGURE 12.3.

Creating a parameter query.

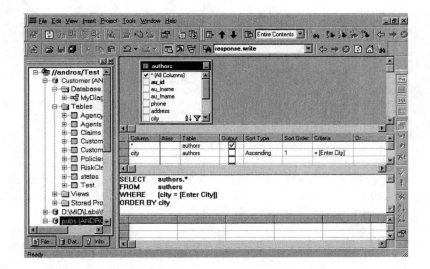

12

MANAGEMENT
WITH VISUAL
DATA TOOLS

You will notice that this creates a Filter icon next to the column name in the Database pane. Setting criteria is typically used in the context of creating a search or lookup function from a Web page. In this scenario the Web page will pass a variable that the user has included as his search criterion to the SQL query and only those records that match that criterion will be returned.

To extend this functionality, you can set the criterion to be a LIKE clause, by including the word LIKE in front of the bracketed criterion variable, then appending through your application's code a trailing % character to the variable that is being passed. The % character is SQL Server's reserved wildcard character.

By executing a query that has a variable parameter as its criterion from the Visual InterDev IDE you are presented with a Define Query Parameters dialog box (see Figure 12.4), which in many ways resembles the functionality that Microsoft Access uses to prompt for parameter values. This is great for testing and debugging your SQL result sets.

FIGURE 12.4.

Executing a parameter query in the IDE.

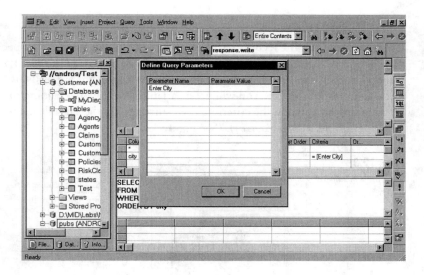

Once you have successfully created the correct SQL syntax to get the desired results, save your design-time control and use your scripting language (VBScript or JScript) syntax to pass the user-specified search criteria from the Web page to the SQL query. (For more information on scripting see Chapters 16 and 17, "An Introduction to Scripting Languages," and "Extending Pages with Controls and Objects.")

DISTINCT

Using the DISTINCT keyword, you can limit result sets to unique values. For example, if we wanted to know what states were represented by at least one author, we would use a DISTINCT query:

```
SELECT DISTINCT state FROM Authors
```

If you want to add a DISTINCT clause to your SELECT query, you can right-click the gray area of the Diagram pane and select Properties; in the Properties dialog box, choose the Query tab, and set the Distinct Values option. Otherwise, edit the SQL pane and add the word DISTINCT after SELECT.

Verifying SQL Syntax

Visual InterDev's Visual Data Tools also provides a SQL syntax checker, so you can test the validity of your SQL statement without having to run the query. This will prove especially useful for queries that return large result sets, or when working remotely on a Web site over a slow modem connection. To check your SQL syntax click the Verify SQL Syntax button on the Query toolbar.

> **TIP**
>
> As you manipulate and perfect your result set, it is possible that you will find the columns in your result sets are coming out in the wrong order. If this happens, click the column selector bar in the Grid pane, and drag the columns back to the order you want them to appear in.

Database Designer Versus SQL Enterprise Manager

The Database Designer tool is equivalent in many ways to the SQL Enterprise Manager that comes with SQL Server. There are still many things that you will have to do in SQL Enterprise Manager, such as creating the initial database devices that will house the database files. However, Visual InterDev's Database Designer tool does give you some new features that are not available in SQL Enterprise Manager. Let's take a closer look at some of these new features.

Changing Script and DDL Statements

Whether you are creating a new SQL Server 6.5 table or modifying the design of an existing table, you will find this aspect of the Database Designer tool to be an invaluable resource. By right-clicking on a table in Data view you can select the Design menu option, and the table will be opened in the Designer pane on the right-hand side of the IDE. Here you can *graphically* alter all of the table properties. For example, you can modify the name of the column, the datatype of the column, what size the column's data should be, and any defaults that the column should include when new records are added and no value is specified for that column. Also, you can specify whether the column should allow nulls as well as establish all of the identity properties for an identity-type column: the identity seed and the identity increment.

Better yet, as you make design changes to your tables if you modify a column's datatype and that column is part of an existing relationship with another table, you will actually be given the opportunity to ripple, or cascade, your changes down (or up) to those related tables. Datatype conversions are handled for you automatically.

What the Database Designer tool is actually doing for you behind the scenes while you are making these design changes is creating a *change script*. The change script can be viewed and saved, and is nothing more than an ASCII text file consisting of the Data Definition Language (DDL) statements that the SQL Server database engine understands and can respond to. With the change script you can apply the changes immediately by exiting the design window and answering Yes in the Save Change Script dialog box. (See Figure 12.5.) Or, if you don't have the required database object change permissions, you can save this change script to a file and give it to your database administrator (DBA) to implement for you.

FIGURE 12.5.

*Save Change Script
dialog box.*

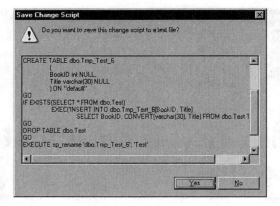

In our example, we have made a change to the datatype of the Book column. We have changed the datatype from being a type char to a type varchar. As the graphic shows, the change script includes a significant amount of DDL syntax necessary to make this seemingly simple change. Having to manually type these DDL statements would be far more time-consuming and much more susceptible to errors than having the Database Designer tool do it for you. In our simple scenario we can look at what the DDL statements are doing and what will happen when these statements are applied to the database. The change script will perform the following steps:

1. Create a new table with the new column definitions
2. Insert all of the records from the old table into the new table, including conversions that have to be made, if any
3. Drop the old table
4. Rename the new table to the old table's name

In addition, these change scripts automatically include the syntax needed to wrap the DDL statements in a *transaction*. Using a transaction means that if any one of the statements should fail during execution for whatever reason, the whole transaction set will be rolled back in its entirety. Generally speaking, transactions ensure that the database objects, such as tables, are left in a complete and usable state.

The change script feature alone makes Visual InterDev an attractive tool for database administrators to complete their database management tasks faster and more completely. Power users, too, will now have the ability to attempt the design changes they see as necessary and produce the DDL statements needed to effect that change. The DBA no longer has to get bogged down in the details of a table change. The DBA need only confirm the accuracy of the changes, and their impact, and then implement those changes.

To implement a change script the DBA can open the .SQL file in SQL Enterprise Manager's SQL Query tool or the ISQL/W tool, and execute it there.

Database Diagrams

A new feature in SQL Server 6.5 databases makes it possible for you to create database diagrams. A database diagram is a graphical representation of the relationships that exist between the tables in a relational database. Other database tools may refer to these as schemas, or entity relationship diagrams. The ability to create database diagrams is especially useful in large databases with many tables; a subset of individual tables can be added to a database diagram and can be viewed as a set, giving a smaller representation of the database as a whole.

Database diagrams are actually stored in the database in a table called `dtproperties`, so this is an attractive feature for team-based development. Database diagrams can be created and when saved are available for all of the developers to view. These diagrams are especially useful for giving developers a high-level view of the interrelationships that exist between all of the tables in a database and they can be printed.

Creating a Database Diagram

To create a new database diagram, right-click the Database Diagrams folder in Data view, and select New Diagram. You will be prompted for a name for this diagram after you have finished adding all of the tables, relationships, and so on. The Database Diagram toolbar even has a button to let you create new tables to add to your database. (See Figure 12.6.)

FIGURE 12.6.
*Database Diagram
toolbar.*

Next, drag and drop tables from the Data View tab onto the Database Diagram pane. As you drop related tables the database diagram will recognize these relationships and will depict these relationships graphically. To remove a table from the Database Diagram click the table name of the table you want to remove and then click the Remove Table From Diagram button on the toolbar.

If you need to add a primary key to an existing table, you can click the Set Primary Key button on the Database Diagram toolbar. (Remember, primary key columns cannot have their `Allow Nulls` property set to `True`.) From the toolbar you can also choose to view only the table names, view all of the column properties of the tables, or view only the primary key columns.

Within your database diagram you can zoom in to get an exploded view of the tables or zoom out by choosing a Zoom percentage from the combo box on the Database Diagram toolbar. As your diagram starts to get cluttered with more and more tables you can collapse the tables to show only column names, only key columns, only table names, or you can explode the view to include all column properties.

By choosing the Properties button on the toolbar you get a complete picture of all of the relationships, indexes, keys, and constraints that are present among the tables that make up this database diagram.

Relationships, Indexes, and Constraints

To create a relationship between two tables in a database diagram, click the column selector of one table and drop it onto the related column in the other table. The standard method here is to start the process on the table that is on the one-side of the many-to-one relationship. You will then be prompted with the Create Relationship dialog box. Here you can name the relationship you have just created, as well as apply constraints to the relationships, such as when the relationship should be enforced and whether or not the index should be clustered. These properties are not usually represented graphically in database diagrams.

Finally, if you want to enforce a constraint on a column or combination of columns you can create a check constraint. Check constraints restrict the type of data that can be added to a column; for example, verifying that the `ReturnDueDate` of a movie rental must be greater than or equal to the `MovieRentDate`.

Views

You can think of a *view* as a virtual table. For example, you could create a view on a table that selects two out of the six columns in a table. Views are often used in SQL Server databases to assign permissions; in this way users can be assigned permissions to access the view and do not need to have permissions to the underlying tables. Data modifications are possible through views.

Views Versus Queries

If you are familiar with Microsoft Access, a query (or more accurately a `QueryDef`) in Access is equivalent to a view in SQL Server terminology. In fact, if you have an Access database in your Visual InterDev project, you will have noticed that the Views folder in Data view actually contains the queries found in your Access `.MDB` file.

This is an important distinction here between queries and views. Queries in Visual InterDev terminology are actually the `SELECT` statements that we have been referring to with respect to the ActiveX design-time controls. Views, on the other hand, are actual objects that are stored in the database.

Creating a View

To create a new view you can edit the SQL statement in the SQL pane of the Query Designer, and add the syntax:

```
Create View <viewname> as
```

in front of the `SELECT` statement. The Query Designer will warn you that the SQL statement can no longer be depicted graphically in the Diagram and Grid panes; choose Yes to continue, then run the query (see Figure 12.7). If you have specified the correct syntax you will receive a message that the query executed successfully. In order to see your new View under the Views folder in Data view you will have to refresh the data connection. To refresh your data connection, right-click the root level of the project and select Refresh.

Editing and Testing a View

Because there is no interface for directly editing a view, it is preferable to perfect your query before turning it into a view. If you need to make changes to an existing view in your database, you will have to do so using the database engine's native methods.

Stored Procedures

Stored procedures are another feature that SQL Server users will be able to take advantage of with Visual InterDev's Visual Data Tools. (For more information on stored procedures see Chapter 21.)

What Are Stored Procedures?

Stored procedures are collections of SQL statements intermixed with control-of-flow language to provide quick execution of logic. A stored procedure has more functionality and flexibility than an ordinary SQL SELECT statement. Using stored procedures, the developer can create complex programs that will allow for parameters to be passed to a SQL statement and the results obtained from running the stored procedure can then be used or passed on to additional stored procedures.

There are two major benefits that the developer gains by making use of stored procedures. One, the stored procedures themselves are compiled; their execution plan is stored in the SQL Server procedure cache and therefore they execute much faster than normal SELECT statements. Two, using stored procedures, the developer can actually have a single procedure execute multiple SELECT statements. If needed, procedures on remote machines can also be executed; these are called remote stored procedures. Remote stored procedures can also be configured to run as distributed transactions. If this option is set, SQL Server implicitly initiates an MS Distributed Transaction Coordinator transaction. Although this feature is out of the scope of this book, it serves to point out that using SQL Server with Visual InterDev is a powerful scalable solution.

Anatomy of a Stored Procedure

Let's take a closer look at how to create and edit stored procedures from within Visual InterDev's Visual Data Tools. First, as with views, it is best to create a SQL SELECT statement and make sure that you are getting the correct result set back. Once you have a satisfactory SELECT statement, add the text

```
CREATE PROCEDURE <ProcedureName> AS
```

in front of the SELECT statement, and run the query. Again, you will be warned with the Query Definitions Differ dialog box that the statement cannot be depicted graphically by the Query Designer. Choose Yes to continue (see Figure 12.7). You will get a message box stating that the Query ran successfully.

FIGURE 12.7.
The Query Definitions Differ dialog box.

Alternatively, you can right-click the Stored Procedures folder in Data view and select New Procedure, and the Source Editor will be opened with a shell of the stored procedure syntax completed for you. If you prefer this method, simply paste in your SQL statement and execute the stored procedure to complete the process. (See Figure 12.8.)

FIGURE 12.8.
Stored procedure open in Source Editor.

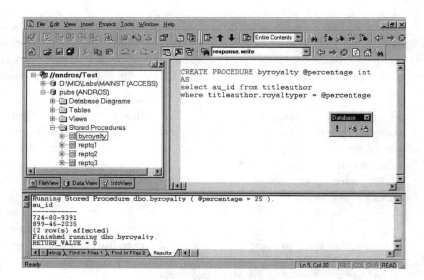

Example

Included in the pubs database that comes with SQL Server is a stored procedure called byroyalty. If you run a stored procedure that requires parameters to be passed you will get a Run Stored Procedure dialog box (see Figure 12.9).

FIGURE 12.9.
Run Stored Procedure dialog box expecting a parameter.

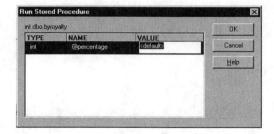

Triggers: An Overview

Triggers are special stored procedures that are fired-off or triggered when records in a table are modified. INSERT, UPDATE and DELETE triggers can be created and the actual trigger that is fired will depend on the type of data modification. When triggers fire they are automatically wrapped in a transaction with the change event that fired them. Thus, triggers actually fire right after the data modification event, and if for some reason an error occurs, the entire transaction is rolled back. (For more information on triggers refer to Chapter 21.

INSERT, UPDATE, and DELETE Triggers

UPDATE and DELETE triggers are often used to enforce referential integrity, because they can cascade changes to related tables. It is preferred that referential integrity be implemented using primary key and foreign key constraints.

Summary

We have looked at what are arguably Visual InterDev's most powerful tools, collectively referred to as Visual Data Tools. Extraordinary depth is built into some of these tools, particularly the Query Designer. Without having to leave the Visual InterDev IDE, the developer can design his Web content, create a connection to a live database, update records in the Web's database, and even modify the design of the tables in that live database.

It should be fairly obvious that the Visual Data Tools are very heavily tailored toward those developers who use the SQL Server 6.5 database engine. But at the same time, developers using other RDBMs can still find enough functionality to treat Visual InterDev as a viable Rapid Application Development (RAD) tool for generating powerful, fast, and dynamic Web sites that can scale from a few concurrent users to thousands of connected users. Perhaps future releases of Microsoft Access and Visual FoxPro will enable the developer to make design changes without leaving the Visual InterDev IDE.

With Visual InterDev Visual Data Tools, it is expected that there will be a major shift in the way both Internet and intranet sites are created over the next year.

Working with Design-Time Controls

by Susie Adams

IN THIS CHAPTER

CHAPTER 13

In much the same way that an embedded FrontPage wizard enables you to compose static HTML forms, the design-time control enables you to create complex Active Server Pages (ASPs) and HTML Web pages. These controls save the developer time by providing a visual tool that can generate complex scripting logic that would have normally taken hours, in a matter of minutes. This chapter talks about this new technology and the four controls Microsoft has chosen to introduce with Visual InterDev.

What Is a Design-Time Control?

Design-time controls are standard ActiveX controls that have been modified to include a new COM interface that enables them to generate text directly into a document. They are similar to standard ActiveX controls in that they provide a graphical user interface that lets the developer reopen and change control properties at design time. However, there are some fundamental differences. Standard ActiveX controls have a binary component that exists at runtime. Design-time controls do not. When the user browses a document that contains text generated by a design-time control, he or she only sees the HTML output it created; there is no visible evidence of the control that generated it.

To better understand the importance of the design-time control, let's compare the visual creation of a window-based Visual Basic form to that of a similar form created as a browser-independent Active Server Web page. To create the form in Visual Basic is fairly simple. You create a new form, drag a data control onto the window, and set its properties. You then drag a data-bound ActiveX table control onto the window and set its properties to reference the data control you just created.

The Web alternative also begins with the creation of a new form, or in this case an .ASP file. But now what? In the past you would have had to open the file in what looks like little more than a text editor and start coding. You could have opened the page using a WYSIWYG HTML editor, but this would not have addressed the Active Server Scripting component. Visual InterDev's standard source code editor, while Web developer friendly, would also require you to compose the script. Drag-and-drop visual controls that help the developer design Web-based Active Server content were simply not available. This posed a fairly serious productivity problem.

To solve this problem, Microsoft developed the design-time ActiveX control. This new control was designed to automatically generate the scripting logic that a developer created by hand. The control can be reopened again and again, preserving the state of the properties the developer sets at design time, while at the same time enabling the developer to modify the text in an editor after it has been generated.

So how does all this work? Design-time controls generate two types of text, design-time and runtime text. The design-time text is used by the ActiveX control to visually re-create the property dialog settings when the user opens the control in the host editor. This text is wrapped in an HTML comment so that it is invisible to the user's browser. The runtime text contains the HTML or text content that is displayed to the user when he opens the file in a browser. This content usually consists of JavaScript, VBScript, and/or HTML that can be processed by the client or server at runtime.

Using Design-Time Controls to Author Runtime Text

Design-time controls can author almost any type of text you can imagine into an HTML or Active Server .ASP file. The controls that exist today generally focus on the generation of complex dynamic content. For example, have you ever tried to create an .ASP page that connects to a database and then displays records from that database in an HTML table? If you have, you know that the script you need to compose includes procedures to connect to an ODBC database, create a recordset, and then loop through records, thus dynamically generating the HTML rows and columns to visually display the records. This is a lot of work for developers who are used to writing client/server–based applications and even to those who aren't. The Microsoft design-time controls simplify this process by allowing you to use a visual control to create most of this script and HTML content for you. These controls can be used to author HTML content as well as client- and server-side script. This includes script that references ActiveX server components, Java applets, and ActiveX control <OBJECT> tags.

Anatomy of the Text Generated by Design-Time Controls

As I mentioned earlier, a design-time control generates both design-time and runtime text. This generated text is included between two METADATA comments. These comments are responsible for telling the host application what portion of the HTML file belongs to the control. The first METADATA comment contains an <OBJECT> tag, very similar to that of a standard ActiveX control. The <OBJECT> tag contains the property settings that allow the host application to re-open the control and make changes to the values that were set previously.

An example of the METADATA comment script follows:

```
<!--METADATA TYPE="DesignerControl" startspan
    <OBJECT ID="DataRangeHdr1" WIDTH=151 HEIGHT=24
    CLASSID="CLSID:F602E721-A281-11CF-A5B7-0080C73AAC7E">
        <PARAM NAME="_Version" VALUE="65536">
        <PARAM NAME="_Version" VALUE="65536">
        <PARAM NAME="_ExtentX" VALUE="3969">
        <PARAM NAME="_ExtentY" VALUE="635">
        <PARAM NAME="_StockProps" VALUE="0">
        <PARAM NAME="DataConnection" VALUE="Customer">
        <PARAM NAME="CommandText" VALUE="SELECT Customers.Customer_ID,
➥Customers.First_Name, Customers.Last_Name FROM Customers">
        <PARAM NAME="CursorType" VALUE="1">
        <PARAM NAME="LockType" VALUE="3">
        <PARAM NAME="PageSize" VALUE="8">
        <PARAM NAME="CacheRecordset" VALUE="1">
    </OBJECT>
-->
```

The following line of script designates the end of the design-time control text.

```
<!--METADATA TYPE="DesignerControl" endspan-->
```

Working with Design-Time Control Hosts

Visual InterDev is the first of the Microsoft editors to embrace the design-time ActiveX control technology. In time, the Microsoft FrontPage and Trident editors will also support them. Because the controls are based on Microsoft's COM technology, they are fairly simple to build and host, making them a very attractive discipline for third-party HTML vendors as well. Third-party vendors will leverage this new technology to create features that will extend their editors' current functionality. For example, a third-party control developer could write a design-time control that could visually create a data-bound HTML table. This vendor could then distribute this control to give its product the new functionality, even though the original editor executable does not specifically support it.

Creating Your Own Design-Time Control

The easiest way to create a design-time control is with the Visual Basic Control Creation Edition 5.0. Building design-time controls consists of first creating a standard ActiveX control and then implementing the IActiveDesigner interface. Design-time controls can be created by any development tool that can create an ActiveX control, including Microsoft's Visual C++ 4.1 or later, Visual Basic Control Creation Edition version 5.0, Borland's Delphi or C++, and Symantec's C++.

For more information on building design-time ActiveX controls, see Chapter 38, "Creating Design-Time Controls for Visual InterDev."

Working with Visual InterDev's Design-Time Controls

The current release of Visual InterDev comes packaged with four design-time controls: the Include control, the Data Command control, the Data Range Header control, and the Data Range Footer control. The first control inserts the contents of a file into a second file at runtime. The last three controls use the ActiveX Data Object (ADO) technology to link an .ASP file to an ODBC data source.

About the Controls

The Data Command control enables the developer to visually create a query against a project data connection. When you save the control, it automatically generates the script necessary to create a database connection and recordset object based on that query.

The Data Range Header and Data Range Footer design-time controls extend the functionality of the Data Command control. Using the ADO technology, they work together as a team to display and navigate through a multirecord recordset that's been created from a SQL query or stored procedure. The Data Range Header control writes the script that connects to a database, creates a recordset, and begins a loop. The Data Range Footer control creates the server script that creates the record navigational buttons and finishes the loop begun by the Data Range Header control.

The Include control enables you to insert the contents of one file into another file at runtime. Developers would typically use this control if they needed to insert a common element into several different pages. This control enables the developer to update one page instead of 10 when content changes. The include file usually consists of items like headers, footers, and common script functions and procedures.

How to Insert a Design-Time Control

To insert a design-time control, open an `.ASP` file and right-click just below the line of text in the Source Editor where you want the control placed. When the menu appears, choose the Insert ActiveX Control option, as shown in Figure 13.1.

FIGURE 13.1.

Inserting a design-time control.

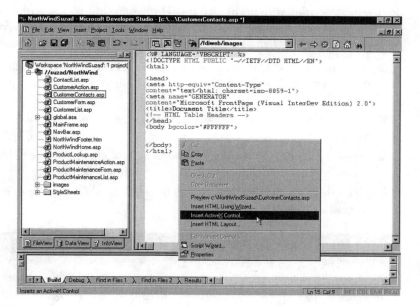

In the Insert ActiveX Control dialog box that appears, choose the Design-time tab and select a control (see Figure 13.2). The Object Editor that opens will contain two windows, the Control Design window and the Properties window. On the Control tab of the Properties window, modify the property values to manipulate the script that is generated by the control. You save the updates to your control by closing all the Object Editor design windows. The specifics of inserting a control are discussed in greater detail in the sections that follow.

FIGURE 13.2.

*The Design-time tab of
the Insert ActiveX
Control dialog window.*

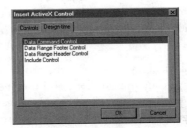

Modifying the Text Generated by a Design-Time Control

When you open a file that contains a design-time control, you'll notice that the text it generates does not look any different than the HTML and script you create yourself, as a developer. You can easily modify any part of the runtime text with little or no effect on the design-time control itself. You can also modify the design-time text; however, there is a chance you could destroy its association with the host editor. The design-time text can either be modified manually or by reopening the design-time control (see Figure 13.3). A list of a few of the situations you might encounter when you begin to manually modify design-time text follows:

- If you strip the METADATA comments from the file, the host editor will no longer recognize the control. You will no longer be able to modify the control's properties at design time.

- If you delete the endspan METADATA comment, one will be implied at the end of the file for you.

- If you try to modify the value of a PARAM tag, the change will be reflected in the control's Properties dialog window the next time it is edited.

- If you delete the runtime text, it will be regenerated for you the next time the control is saved.

NOTE

If you edit the runtime script created by a control, be careful; your changes will be overwritten if you reopen the control in edit mode. If you want to modify the code, you should first delete the METADATA comments.

FIGURE 13.3.

Editing the design-time control.

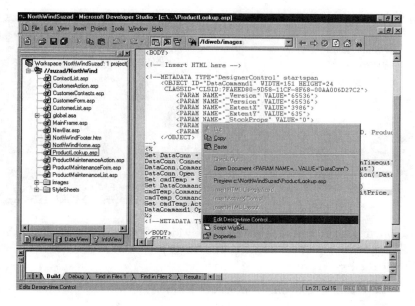

Using the Data Command Control

You should use the Data Command control when you need to look up or modify a record in a database table. It will create the script you need to execute a query against a database and return a result set.

Inserting a Data Command Control

You can insert the control just like any other ActiveX control by right-clicking in the Source Editor (refer to Figure 13.1). When the pop-up menu appears, choose the Insert ActiveX Control option. From the Insert ActiveX Control dialog (refer to Figure 13.2), choose the Design-time tab's Data Command Control option and set the control properties. There are several types of properties that can be set from this window. The following sections discuss each of these properties in detail.

Setting Up the Control Tab

The Control tab enables you to modify the key properties of a control. From this tab you can modify the control name, the database connection, the command type, and the SQL query. This tab contains the properties that are required to instantiate a control (see Figure 13.4).

FIGURE 13.4.
The Data Command design-time control Properties window.

The `ID` property enables you to uniquely identify a control. You will use this name to reference a control's properties throughout the script you create in the `.ASP` file. The ID name must follow these syntax rules:

- It cannot contain an embedded period.
- It must begin with an alphabetic character.
- It cannot exceed 255 characters.
- It must be unique within the scope of the `.ASP` file.

The `DataConnection` property enables you to select the active data connection for the control. The connection will be used to build the control's `Command` property.

> **NOTE**
>
> If the drop-down data connection list box is empty, first check to see whether there are any active data connections defined in your project. Second, check to see whether the current `.ASP` file has been saved to the project; the list box will not display the list if the current `.ASP` file doesn't exist in the project.

The `CommandType` property enables you to select the type of command the control will implement. The four available types are `SQL`, `StoredProcedure`, `Table`, and `View`. The value of your command type will determine the type of command text you can create.

The `SQL` type enables you to create a SQL expression. You can do this by either manually composing a SQL query in the edit box or by selecting the SQL Builder button. The SQL Builder button will open the Visual InterDev Query Builder (see Figure 13.5). This tool enables you to visually drag and drop database tables into a design pane that can create and execute SQL queries. The SQL Builder button is disabled for all other command types. For detailed discussions about the Query Builder, refer to Chapter 12, "Database Management with the Visual Data Tools."

FIGURE 13.5.
The Query Builder.

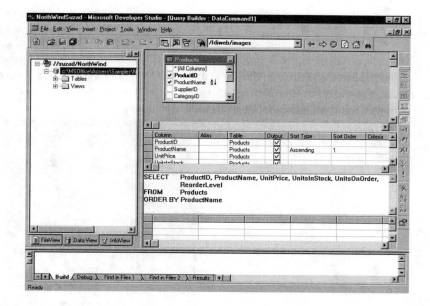

The `Table` command type enables you to generate a query from one specific table. It populates the `CommandText` property with a list of tables from the database selected in the `Data Connection` property.

The `View` command type enables you to create a query from a selected view. This option populates the `CommandText` property with a list of views found in the database.

The `StoredProcedure` command type populates the `CommandText` property with the list of stored procedures maintained in your database. If the stored procedure you select has parameters, the Parameters tab of the Properties dialog window is also enabled. The Parameters tab enables you to enter the values of the parameters the stored procedure is expecting. The Parameters tab is displayed in Figure 13.6.

FIGURE 13.6.
The stored procedure Parameters tab.

Setting Up the Advanced Tab

The Advanced tab contains properties that manipulate cursor management and command configuration settings (see Figure 13.7). In most situations these parameters are kept at their default values. The cursor parameters include `CursorType`, `LockType`, and `CacheSize`. The command parameters consist of the `Prepared`, `CommandTimeout`, and `MaxRecords` properties.

FIGURE 13.7.

The Advanced tab of the Data Control Properties dialog.

The `CursorType` property enables you to select the type of cursor you want a Data Command recordset to use. Your cursor choice depends on the types of activities your user needs to accomplish. The available cursor types are shown in Table 13.1.

Table 13.1. Cursor types.

Cursor Type	Description
Forward Only	Supports `MoveNext` recordset navigation only. (Default)
Keyset	Fixed-membership recordset that supports navigation in all directions. Displays record modifications made by other users.
Dynamic	Dynamic-membership recordset that supports navigation in all directions. Displays record modifications and additions made by other users.
Static	Snapshot that supports fixed membership and recordset navigation in all directions.

For further discussions on ADO recordset properties, see Chapter 22, "Integrating ActiveX Database Components."

The `LockType` property controls the type of lock placed on a recordset when the script creates it at runtime. The lock type characteristics can vary depending on the database provider. Table 13.2 is a list of the available lock types and their general definitions.

Table 13.2. Lock types.

Lock Type	Description
ReadOnly	Allows read-only access to the recordset.
Pessimistic	Record locks are placed on each record at edit time.
Optimistic	Record locks are placed on each record at update time.
BatchOptimistic	Allows Optimistic batch updates of the recordset.

You should use the Prepared property for those commands you need to execute frequently. The Prepared property enables you to request that the server create a compiled version of a query or command the first time it is executed. All subsequent executions of the command will then use this compiled version instead of recompiling it each time the command is executed.

The commandTimeout property enables you to tell the server how long to wait before terminating an ADO command. You should use this property to control how a server handles the cancellation of a database command in situations where the server is experiencing delays due to increased network traffic or heavy server use. If the time elapses before the command is executed, an error occurs and ADO cancels the command. If you set the property to zero, ADO will wait indefinitely for the command to execute.

Use the MaxRecords property to limit the number of records a server returns from a database. The default setting for this property is zero, which means the database server will return the entire result set.

The Server-Side Script Generated

The script shown in Figure 13.8 was generated by a Data Command design-time control with a command type of SQL.

The Data Command control first creates and opens a database connection object. A Connection object represents an open connection to an ODBC data source.

```
Set DataConn = Server.CreateObject("ADODB.Connection")
DataConn.ConnectionTimeout = Session("DataConn_ConnectionTimeout")
DataConn.CommandTimeout = Session("DataConn_CommandTimeout")
DataConn.Open Session("DataConn_ConnectionString"),
➥Session("DataConn_RuntimeUserName"), Session("DataConn_RuntimePassword")
```

The control then creates a Command object and a Recordset object. The Command object will define the specific command you are going to execute against the database. The Recordset object will contain the results of that command after it is executed:

```
Set cmdTemp = Server.CreateObject("ADODB.Command")
Set DataCommand1 = Server.CreateObject("ADODB.Recordset")
```

13

WORKING WITH
DESIGN-TIME
CONTROLS

Finally, the `Recordset` and `Command` objects are created from properties that were set at design time by the developer:

```
cmdTemp.CommandText = "SELECT ProductID, ProductName, UnitPrice,
➥UnitsInStock, UnitsOnOrder, ReorderLevel FROM Products"
cmdTemp.CommandType = 1
Set cmdTemp.ActiveConnection = DataConn
DataCommand1.Open cmdTemp, , 0, 1
```

FIGURE 13.8.

The Data Command –
generated text.

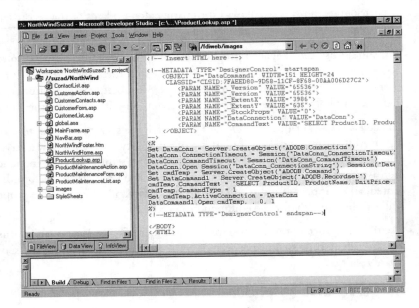

Working with Data Range Controls

If you're familiar with building Web applications, I'm sure you've already run into the situation in which you need to create a page that contains a multirecord recordset. If the recordset was large, the resulting physical size of the page probably increased user access times beyond acceptable levels. The obvious solution to this problem is to compose a record paging or filtering procedure to restrict the number of records displayed per page. Well, in theory this sounds like a great idea, but how do you go about implementing it? Creating the script to build this type of procedure is quite complicated and would probably take hours to code and debug. Recognizing this problem, Microsoft has simplified the process by creating the Data Range Header and Footer design-time ActiveX controls.

Using Data Range Controls to Create a Data-Bound Web Page

The Data Range controls allow you to visually create a database query and then designate how you want to display the results. The Header control asks you to specify whether you want to display the result set as text, as a table, or as a data input form. The script the Data Range controls create works to create looping logic that cycles through the recordset and displays one or more dynamically constructed HTML pages. The Data Range Header control creates the script that defines the property variables, builds the data recordset, and begins the loop. The Data Range Footer control ends the loop and provides the navigation buttons that allow the user to manipulate the recordset. The Data Range controls do not, however, create all the script you'll need to complete the page. To create the script to display field values, you have to either manually code the script yourself or use the Copy Fields option located on the Data Range Header control's Properties window to create the script for you.

The Data Range Header and Data Range Footer design-time controls can also be used independently. If your recordset is small and you want to display the result set as a table or as text, you probably will not need to insert the Data Range Footer control. If you do not use it, you have to manually insert the Loop command to terminate the looping logic created by the Data Range Header design-time control.

Using HTML Tables with Data Range Controls

To display recordset data in an HTML table, you need to compose most of the HTML table tags yourself. The ending table tag `</TABLE>` will be created for you, if you set the `RangeType` property to `Table`. To create the table column headings you need to insert the following text before the Data Range Header control text:

```
<table border="1" cellpadding="0" cellspacing="0" width="95%">
<tr>
<th width="20%" bgcolor="#800000"><font color="#FFFFFF">
➥Customer Id</font></th>
<th width="20%" bgcolor="#800000"><font color="#FFFFFF">
➥Customer  Name</font></h>
<th width="20%" bgcolor="#800000"><font color="#FFFFFF">
➥Contact  Name</font></th>
<th width="20%" bgcolor="#800000"><font color="#FFFFFF">
➥Title</font></th>
<th width="20%" bgcolor="#800000"><font color="#FFFFFF">
➥Phone</font></th>
</tr>
```

The row and column definitions can be created manually, or you can use the Copy Fields button on the Data Range Header control's Properties window to generate the script for you. The Copy Fields dialog is discussed in detail later in this chapter. You insert the HTML table row and column definitions between the script generated by the Data Range Header and the Data Range Footer design-time controls:

```
<tr>
<td><%= DataRangeHdr1("CustomerID") %></td>
<td><%= DataRangeHdr1("CompanyName") %></td>
<td><%= DataRangeHdr1("ContactName") %></td>
<td><%= DataRangeHdr1("ContactTitle") %></td>
<td><%= DataRangeHdr1("Phone") %></td>
</tr>
```

13

WORKING WITH
DESIGN-TIME
CONTROLS

In our example, the Data Range Header `RangeType` property is set to `2-Table`; therefore, the Data Range Footer script will provide the `</TABLE>` tag. If you had set the property to `1-Text` or `3-Form`, you would have needed to insert the `</TABLE>` tag manually or set the `RangeType` variable to `Table` before the Data Range Footer script.

The Data Range Header Control

The Data Range Header control takes the Data Command control one step further by allowing you to create and manipulate a recordset that returns multiple records. It creates the beginning of a loop that will cycle through each record in a recordset and then implement record paging, if requested.

Inserting a Data Range Header Control into an ActiveX Server Page

To insert a Data Range Header control, right-click in the source editor and choose the Insert ActiveX Control menu option, as shown in Figure 13.1. In the Insert ActiveX Control dialog box that appears (refer to Figure 13.2), choose the Design-time tab and select the Data Range Header Control option. The section that follows discusses the control parameters shown in Figure 13.9.

FIGURE 13.9.

The Data Range Header design-time control Properties window.

Setting Up the Control Tab

The Data Range Header Control tab contains the parameters needed to create a Data Range Header control. Many of the properties on this tab are duplicated on the Data Command Control tab. For details on the properties not discussed here, refer to the section "Setting Up the Control Tab," earlier in this chapter.

The `CacheRecordset` and `CacheSize` properties are employed to optimize recordset performance by controlling the number of records returned from a server into local memory. The recordset is cached as a `Session` object that enables the client and server to avoid re-execution of the query each time a user requests a new page of data. This property becomes extremely important when you are required to manipulate large recordsets. For example, if your query returns a recordset with 1,000 records and your CacheSize is set at 25, the first time you execute the query only the first 25 records will be sent to the client, not all 1,000. When you navigate past the 25th record in the cache, the server will retrieve the next 25 records.

You can adjust the CacheSize property value at runtime; however, the change will only affect subsequent retrievals from the database. You cannot set a CacheSize to 0. A CacheSize of 0 will cause the server to return an error. The cache property values are displayed in Table 13.3.

Table 13.3. Cache properties.

Cache Property	Description
CacheRecordset = True	Caching is on—better browsing performance.
CacheRecordset = False	Caching is off—better if you have a large number of concurrent users. (Default)
CacheSize = Number of Records	Number of records to cache. (Default = PageSize)

Although caching records can improve performance, it does consume both Web and database server resources, so if you expect a heavy server load you might want to optimize for the server.

> **NOTE**
>
> Records retrieved from the cache do not reflect the changes made by other users while they are cached. To force an update of the cached data, use the Resync method or requery the recordset.

The Bar Alignment property enables you to align the record-navigation button bar (see Figure 13.10) left, right, or centered below the data.

FIGURE 13.10.
The record-navigation button bar.

The Range Type property is used by the Field List and Copy Fields dialog boxes to determine how to compose the script they generate. If the RangeType property is set to Table, the Data Range Footer script generates the </TABLE> tag at runtime. If the RangeType property is set to Text or Table, the HTML generated for the Customer_Name field selected in the Copy Fields dialog box would appear as

```
<%= DataRangeHeader1("Customer_Name") %><BR>
```

If `RangeType` is set to `Form`, the HTML for the `Customer_Name` field selected in the Copy Fields dialog box would appear like this:

```
<INPUT TYPE="Text" SIZE=25 NAME="Customer_Name" VALUE="<%=
➥DataRangeHeader1("Customer_Name") %>"><BR>
```

The `RecordPaging` property enables you to specify whether or not you want to have all of the records in a recordset output to a page at once, or a page at a time. You alter the `PageSize` property to control the number of records displayed on each page. For example, if a Footer control is inserted after a Header control with a `PageSize` property greater than `0`, the Footer control will automatically generate the script to create the record navigation buttons. It will also display a page number, based on the `Absolute_Page` variable, in the lower-right corner of the page.

The default `PageSize` property of `0` will output the entire recordset to the Web page. In this case you do not need to insert a Data Range Footer control. For example, the following script, included after the Data Range Header script, displays the value of the `Customer_Id` field for each record in a recordset named `DataRangeHeader1`:

```
<!-- METADATA TYPE="DesignerControl" endspan -->
<%=DataRangeHeader1("Customer_Id") %>
<% Loop %>
```

Setting Up the Advanced Tab

The Data Range Header Advanced tab is identical to the Data Command Advanced tab Properties window. Figure 13.11 displays the Data Range Header control's Properties window.

FIGURE 13.11.

The Data Range Header control's Properties window.

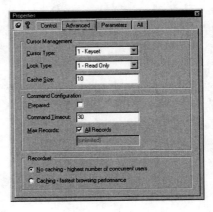

The Server-Side Script Generated

The Data Range Header control first loads the script variables with default settings or values of properties specified at design time.

```
fHideNavBar = False
fHideNumber = False
fHideRequery = False
fHideRule = False
stQueryString = ""
fEmptyRecordset = False
fFirstPass = True
fNeedRecordset = False
fNoRecordset = False
tBarAlignment = "Center"
tHeaderName = "DataRangeHdr1"
tPageSize = 6
tPagingMove = ""
tRangeType = "Table"
tRecordsProcessed = 0
tPrevAbsolutePage = 0
intCurPos = 0
intNewPos = 0
fSupportsBookmarks = True
fMoveAbsolute = False
```

The script then checks to see if Session variables for the page move and recordset parameters exist. If they do, the script loads them into their local variable counterparts.

```
If Not IsEmpty(Request("DataRangeHdr1_PagingMove")) Then
    tPagingMove = Trim(Request("DataRangeHdr1_PagingMove"))
End If
```

If a recordset Session variable is not found, one is created from the CommandText property:

```
If IsEmpty(Session("DataRangeHdr1_Recordset")) Then
    fNeedRecordset = True
Else
    If Session("DataRangeHdr1_Recordset") Is Nothing Then
        fNeedRecordset = True
    Else
        Set DataRangeHdr1 = Session("DataRangeHdr1_Recordset")
    End If
End If
If fNeedRecordset Then
    Set DataConn = Server.CreateObject("ADODB.Connection")
    DataConn.ConnectionTimeout = Session("DataConn_ConnectionTimeout")
    DataConn.CommandTimeout = Session("DataConn_CommandTimeout")
    DataConn.Open Session("DataConn_ConnectionString"),
➡Session("DataConn_RuntimeUserName"), Session("DataConn_RuntimePassword")
    Set cmdTemp = Server.CreateObject("ADODB.Command")
    Set DataRangeHdr1 = Server.CreateObject("ADODB.Recordset")
    cmdTemp.CommandText = "SELECT CustomerID, CompanyName, ContactName,
➡ContactTitle, Phone FROM Customers ORDER BY CompanyName"
    cmdTemp.CommandType = 1
    Set cmdTemp.ActiveConnection = DataConn
    DataRangeHdr1.Open cmdTemp, , 1, 1
End If
On Error Resume Next
If DataRangeHdr1.BOF And DataRangeHdr1.EOF Then fEmptyRecordset = True
On Error Goto 0
If Err Then fEmptyRecordset = True
DataRangeHdr1.PageSize = tPageSize
fSupportsBookmarks = DataRangeHdr1.Supports(8192)
```

13

WORKING WITH
DESIGN-TIME
CONTROLS

If the filter Session variable is present, a filter is applied to the recordset:

```
If Not IsEmpty(Session("DataRangeHdr1_Filter")) And Not fEmptyRecordset Then
    DataRangeHdr1.Filter = Session("DataRangeHdr1_Filter")
    If DataRangeHdr1.BOF And DataRangeHdr1.EOF Then fEmptyRecordset = True
End If
```

The current record and page are calculated.

```
If IsEmpty(Session("DataRangeHdr1_PageSize"))
➥Then Session("DataRangeHdr1_PageSize") = tPageSize
If IsEmpty(Session("DataRangeHdr1_AbsolutePage"))
➥Then Session("DataRangeHdr1_AbsolutePage") = 1

If Session("DataRangeHdr1_PageSize") <> tPageSize Then
    tCurRec = ((Session("DataRangeHdr1_AbsolutePage") - 1) *
➥Session("DataRangeHdr1_PageSize")) + 1
    tNewPage = Int(tCurRec / tPageSize)
    If tCurRec Mod tPageSize <> 0 Then
        tNewPage = tNewPage + 1
    End If
    If tNewPage = 0 Then tNewPage = 1
    Session("DataRangeHdr1_PageSize") = tPageSize
    Session("DataRangeHdr1_AbsolutePage") = tNewPage
End If


If fEmptyRecordset Then
    fHideNavBar = True
    fHideRule = True
Else
    tPrevAbsolutePage = Session("DataRangeHdr1_AbsolutePage")
```

If the page was called from a navigation button, the calling action is applied to the recordset:

```
    Select Case tPagingMove
        Case ""
            fMoveAbsolute = True
        Case "Requery"
            DataRangeHdr1.Requery
            fMoveAbsolute = True
        Case "<<"
            Session("DataRangeHdr1_AbsolutePage") = 1
        Case "<"
            If Session("DataRangeHdr1_AbsolutePage") > 1 Then
                Session("DataRangeHdr1_AbsolutePage") =
➥Session("DataRangeHdr1_AbsolutePage") - 1
            End If
        Case ">"
            If Not DataRangeHdr1.EOF Then
                Session("DataRangeHdr1_AbsolutePage") =
➥Session("DataRangeHdr1_AbsolutePage") + 1
            End If
        Case ">>"
            If fSupportsBookmarks Then
                Session("DataRangeHdr1_AbsolutePage") =
➥DataRangeHdr1.PageCount
            End If
    End Select
    Do
```

```
        If fSupportsBookmarks Then
            DataRangeHdr1.AbsolutePage =
➡Session("DataRangeHdr1_AbsolutePage")
        Else
            If fNeedRecordset Or fMoveAbsolute Or DataRangeHdr1.EOF Then
                DataRangeHdr1.MoveFirst
                DataRangeHdr1.Move (Session("DataRangeHdr1_AbsolutePage")
➡- 1) * tPageSize
            Else
                intCurPos = ((tPrevAbsolutePage - 1) *
➡tPageSize) + tPageSize
                intNewPos = ((Session("DataRangeHdr1_AbsolutePage")
➡- 1) * tPageSize) + 1
                DataRangeHdr1.Move intNewPos - intCurPos
            End If
            If DataRangeHdr1.BOF Then DataRangeHdr1.MoveNext
        End If
        If Not DataRangeHdr1.EOF Then Exit Do
        Session("DataRangeHdr1_AbsolutePage") =
➡Session("DataRangeHdr1_AbsolutePage") - 1
    Loop
End If
```

The loop is started that will cycle through the recordset.

```
Do
    If fEmptyRecordset Then Exit Do
    If tRecordsProcessed = tPageSize Then Exit Do
    If Not fFirstPass Then
        DataRangeHdr1.MoveNext
    Else
        fFirstPass = False
    End If
    If DataRangeHdr1.EOF Then Exit Do
    tRecordsProcessed = tRecordsProcessed + 1
%>
<!--METADATA TYPE="DesignerControl" endspan-->
```

The Data Range Footer Control

The Data Range Footer control creates HTML navigation buttons that allow a user to move through records in a recordset a page at a time. The script it composes works in conjunction with the script the Data Range Header control generates to dynamically display and manipulate multiple records from a recordset on one or more Web pages.

Inserting a Data Range Footer Control into an ActiveX Server Page

To insert the Data Range Footer control, right-click in the Source Editor of an open .ASP file and select the Insert ActiveX Control option. From the pop-up menu that appears, select the Design-time tab's Data Range Footer Control option. The properties for this control are usually kept at their default values; however, they can be modified. The Data Range Footer control Properties window is shown in Figure 13.12.

13

WORKING WITH
DESIGN-TIME
CONTROLS

FIGURE 13.12.

The Data Range Footer control Properties window.

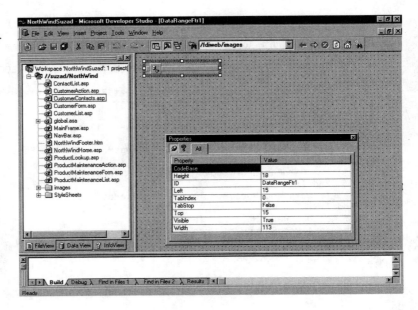

Customizing Data Range Footer

You can customize the visual appearance of the footer components by manipulating the Data Range Footer's properties. (See Table 13.4.) The script to set these property values must be inserted before the Data Range Footer script. There are four properties that can be toggled on (`True`) and off (`False`).

Table 13.4. Data Range Footer variables.

Variable	Description
fHideRule	Hides the horizontal rule. (Default = `False`)
fHideNavBar	Hides the navigation button bar. (Default = `False`)
fHideNumber	Hides the page number in the lower-left corner of the page. (Default = `False`)
fHideRequery	Hides the Requery button in the navigation bar. (Default = `False`)

The Server-Side Script Generated

The generated script first finishes the loop that was started by the Data Range Header generated script:

```
<%
Loop
```

If the RangeType property was set to Table in the Data Range Header Properties window, an ending `</TABLE>` tag is created:

```
If tRangeType = "Table" Then Response.Write "</TABLE>"
```

If there is more than one page, the navigation bar and current page number are displayed:

```
If tPageSize > 0 Then
    If Not fHideRule Then Response.Write "<HR>"
    If Not fHideNavBar Then
        %>
        <TABLE WIDTH=100% >
        <TR>
            <TD WIDTH=100% >
                <P ALIGN=<%= tBarAlignment %> >
                <FORM <%= "ACTION=""" & Request.ServerVariables("PATH_INFO")
➥& stQueryString & """" %> METHOD="POST">
                    <INPUT TYPE="Submit" NAME="<%= tHeaderName & "
➥PagingMove" %>" VALUE="    &lt;&lt;    ">
                    <INPUT TYPE="Submit" NAME="<%= tHeaderName & "
➥PagingMove" %>" VALUE="    &lt;    ">
                    <INPUT TYPE="Submit" NAME="<%= tHeaderName & "_
➥PagingMove" %>" VALUE="    &gt;    ">
                    <% If fSupportsBookmarks Then %>
                        <INPUT TYPE="Submit" NAME="<%= tHeaderName & "_
➥PagingMove" %>" VALUE="    &gt;&gt;    ">
                    <% End If %>
                    <% If Not fHideRequery Then %>
                        <INPUT TYPE="Submit" NAME="<% =tHeaderName & "_
➥PagingMove" %>" VALUE=" Requery ">
                    <% End If %>
                </FORM>
                </P>
            </TD>
            <TD VALIGN=MIDDLE ALIGN=RIGHT>
                <FONT SIZE=2>
                <%
                If Not fHideNumber Then
                    If tPageSize > 1 Then
                        Response.Write "<NOBR>Page: " & Session(tHeaderName &
➥"_AbsolutePage") & "</NOBR>"
                    Else
                        Response.Write "<NOBR>Record: " & Session(tHeaderName
➥& "_AbsolutePage") & "</NOBR>"
                    End If
                End If
                %>
                </FONT>
            </TD>
        </TR>
        </TABLE>
    <%
    End If
End If
%>
</center>
</div>
<!--METADATA TYPE="DesignerControl" endspan-->
```

Displaying Field Values

You need to manually insert Active Server script to display field values from a recordset in an .ASP page. If you are using Data Range controls, this script needs to be inserted between the script generated by the Data Range Header and the Data Range Footer controls. For example, to display values from a recordset named DataRangeHdr1, you must insert the following script after the script generated by the Data Range Header control:

```
<%= DataRangeHdr1("CustomerID") %>
<%= DataRangeHdr1("CompanyName") %>
<%= DataRangeHdr1("ContactName") %>
<%= DataRangeHdr1("ContactTitle") %>
<%= DataRangeHdr1("Phone") %>>
```

Using the Copy Fields Dialog

If you're still a little uncertain about creating your own Active Server script you can use the Copy Fields button in the Data Range Header Properties window (refer to Figure 13.9) to help you. When you open the Copy Fields dialog (see Figure 13.13), it will prompt you to select fields from a field list box. The list of fields was compiled from the SQL you generated in your DataCommand property. When you exit the dialog, the script to display these fields is copied to the clipboard. To paste the script into the .ASP page, place your cursor in the Source Editor and choose the Paste command from the Edit menu. The section on the Data Range Header control's RangeType property shows examples of the script the Copy Fields dialog generates.

FIGURE 13.13.
The Copy Fields dialog.

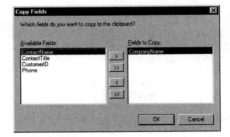

Using the Data Range Builder

You can use the Data Range Builder to insert both the Data Range Header and Footer controls into a Web page at once. The builder is really a wizard that takes you through a series of two steps. In the first step you will be asked to specify whether or not you want to display all of the records at once, or a page at a time. If you choose by page, you will be prompted to enter the number of records per page and the position of the record navigation toolbar (left, right, or center) relative to that page. The second step asks you to enter the name of the Data Range controls. The wizard steps are displayed in Figures 13.14 and 13.15.

FIGURE 13.14.
Step 1—The Data Range Builder.

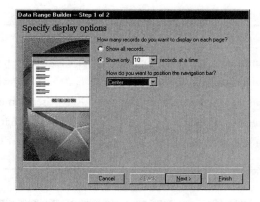

FIGURE 13.15.
Step 2—The Data Range Builder.

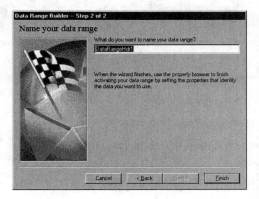

Extending the Use of Design-Time Control Properties

The Data Range design-time controls utilize variables stored as Session properties (see Table 13.5). Because of this, you can change the properties at runtime to further customize their behavior. These properties can be set at design time and runtime to alter the functionality of the Active Server script.

Table 13.5. Data Range control properties.

Property Name	Description
DataRangeHeader1_ConnectionString	String containing the database connection parameters
DataRangeHeader1_ConnectionTimeout	Length of time to wait before ending a connection attempt
DataRangeHeader1_CommandTimeout	Length of time to wait before ending an ADO command execution attempt

continues

Table 13.5. continued

Property Name	Description
DataRangeHeader1_RuntimeUserName	Database username
DataRangeHeader1_RuntimePassword	Database password
DataRangeHeader1_Recordset	Recordset name
DataRangeHeader1_Filter	SQL string that contains a WHERE clause
DataRangeHeader1_AbsolutePage	Current recordset page displayed in the browser

> **NOTE**
>
> All Data Range control properties are prefaced with the control name. For example, the following property name assumes a DataRangeHeader name of DataRangeHeader1:
>
> DataRangeHeader1_Recordset

Changing a Recordset Dynamically at Runtime

You may want to modify the Recordset object at runtime. You can accomplish this by using this sample script:

```
<% Set Session("DataRangeHeader1_Recordset") = rsEmployee %>
```

Let's examine the script generated by the Data Range Header control to better understand this process. The script first checks to see if the Recordset object exists as a Session variable. If the recordset is stored as a Session variable, the script will begin to reference that recordset. If the Session Recordset does not exist, the control will create a local recordset. If the CacheRecordset property is set to True, it will store the local recordset as a Session variable:

```
...
If IsEmpty(Session("DataRangeHdr1_Recordset")) Then
    fNeedRecordset = True
Else
    If Session("DataRangeHdr1_Recordset") Is Nothing Then
        fNeedRecordset = True
    Else
        Set DataRangeHdr1 = Session("DataRangeHdr1_Recordset")
    End If
End If

If fNeedRecordset Then
    Set Customer = Server.CreateObject("ADODB.Connection")
    Customer.ConnectionTimeout = Session("Customer_ConnectionTimeout")
    Customer.CommandTimeout = Session("Customer_CommandTimeout")
    Customer.Open Session("Customer_ConnectionString")
    Set cmdTemp = Server.CreateObject("ADODB.Command")
```

```
    Set DataRangeHdr1 = Server.CreateObject("ADODB.Recordset")
    cmdTemp.CommandText = "SELECT Customers.Customer_ID From Customers "
    cmdTemp.CommandType = 1
    Set cmdTemp.ActiveConnection = Customer
    DataRangeHdr1.Open cmdTemp, , 1, 3
End If
...

If fNeedRecordset Then
    Set Session("DataRangeHdr1_Recordset") = DataRangeHdr1
End If
...
```

The Data Range Filter Property

In many situations you might need to filter a recordset on a value a user selects at runtime. You can do this by setting the `DataRangeHeaderName_Filter` variable at runtime to a valid `WHERE` clause for the recordset object. For example, the following code sets a filter on the `DataRangeHeader1` recordset to display only those records that have a `Company_Id` equal to `'22'`.

```
<% Session("DataRangeHeader1_Filter") = "[Company_ID] = '22'" %>
```

Once again, let's look at the script generated by the Data Range Header control to better understand this process. The following script first checks to see if a Data Range filter `Session` variable has been initialized. If it has, the filter string is applied to the recordset. If it exists but the string is empty, the filtering on the recordset is removed. If it is not found, nothing is done with filtering.

```
<%
  If Not IsEmpty(Session("DataRangeHdr1_Filter")) And Not fEmptyRecordset Then
    DataRangeHdr1.Filter = Session("DataRangeHdr1_Filter")
    If DataRangeHdr1.BOF And DataRangeHdr1.EOF Then fEmptyRecordset = True
End If
%>
```

Retrieving a Recordset Page Dynamically

If your application is complicated or if you jump between windows and pages frequently, you might want to employ the ability to dynamically set the page number of a recordset displayed in a Web page at runtime. You can control the page that's displayed by setting the `AbsolutePage` `Session` variable at runtime. The following example uses an input field on a page to determine which page in the recordset to jump to:

```
<FORM METHOD=POST ACTION="SetPage.asp">
<INPUT  TYPE="text" SIZE="5" MAXLENGTH="20"  NAME="PgNo">
<INPUT TYPE=SUBMIT NAME=SUBMIT VALUE="Submit">
</FORM>
```

The script in the `SetPage.asp` then sets the `AbsolutePage` property to the value the user selects and redirects the user to `Employee.asp`, where that page of records is displayed:

```
<%
Session("DataRangeHeader1_AbsolutePage") = Request("PgNo")
Response.Redirect "Employee.asp" %>
```

The Server-Side Include Directive

During the Web application development process you decide on things such as standard fonts and background and headers and footers, all of which need to be implemented on every page of the Web application. Up until now, you would have needed to copy and paste the script from a default page to each one of the application's pages. If a modification was made to the default page, you would have needed to make the same change to each page that contained it.

The Server-Side Include (SSI) `#INCLUDE` directive simplifies this process by allowing you to copy the contents of one file into another file at runtime. For example, you might have created a standard header that contains a company logo and some HTML text that needs to be displayed on the top of each page. If the text is modified frequently, you'll want to be able to update it in one place and have that modification cascaded to every page that contains the script. You can use the server-side include to do this by saving the file header as a separate page and then inserting the `#INCLUDE` directive that references that page into each page that requires it.

Microsoft's newest version of SSI also supports special preprocessing directives. These directives are listed in the Table 13.6. To learn more about these directives, review Microsoft's IIS documentation.

Table 13.6. SSI preprocessing directives.

Directive	Definition
`#FLASTMOD`	The time of the last modification to the file.
`#FSIZE`	The size of the file.
`#CONFIG`	Enables you to specify how variables and commands are displayed.
`#ECHO`	Displays CGI system environment variables.
`#EXEC`	Executes CGI system commands.

The Design-Time Include Control

You use the Include design-time control to add the `#INCLUDE FILE` or `#INCLUDE VIRTUAL` directives to an `.ASP` file. The `#INCLUDE` directive inserts the contents of the text file it references into the text file that contains it. The `#INCLUDE FILE` directive references a file by its relative path. The `#INCLUDE VIRTUAL` directive references a file by its virtual path. The following is an example of the script the Include control generates.

```
<!--#INCLUDE FILE="myfile.asp"-->
<!--#INCLUDE VIRTUAL="/myfile.asp"-->
```

Inserting the Include Design-Time Control into an ActiveX Server Page

To insert an Include design-time control, right-click an open page in the Source Editor and select the Insert ActiveX Control menu option. From the Insert ActiveX Control dialog's Design-time tab, select the Include Control option. The dialog that opens is called the URL Builder. It requests that you enter the URL (Universal Resource Locator) of the file you want to include. Figure 13.16 displays the Include control's Properties window.

FIGURE 13.16.

The Include control's Properties window.

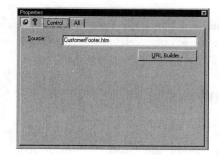

The Graphical URL Builder

You can specify that a URL point to a file from your current Web project, or from any site that is Web accessible. To create the URL, you first select the type of URL you want to build from the URL Type box. You can choose to have the URL path relative to the root of the IIS server (Root Relative), relative to the current document (Doc Relative), or relative to the IIS operating system (Absolute). You can alter the URL that is created by modifying the text displayed in the URL box. You can also use the URL box to enter the URL of a file that is maintained by a site external to your Web. If you need to specify a parameter, you can do so in the Extra Info edit box. The URL Builder window is displayed in Figure 13.17.

FIGURE 13.17.

The Graphical URL Builder.

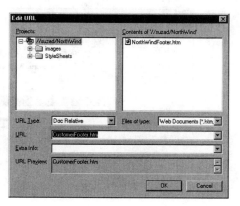

Sharing Script Libraries

You can use the INCLUDE directive to insert files that contain Active Server subroutines and functions into a Web page at runtime. For example, the following function resides in a file named `myname.inc`:

```
<!--myname.inc-->
<%
Function MyName( cFirstname, cLastName)
    NameString = "'" & cFirstName & " " & cLastName & "'"
End Function
%>
```

Instead of copying this script into every file that needs to call the function, you can add the Include directive to each page referencing that file. An example of this follows:

```
<!--#INCLUDE FIL="myname.inc"-->
```

The Finished Product

Figure 13.18 displays a page that was composed using three of the four design-time controls. The Data Range Header and Data Range Footer were used to create the customer recordset and display the recordset field values. The Include control was used to insert the copyright information at the bottom of the `CustomerContact.asp` file.

FIGURE 13.18.

*The Customer
Contact List.*

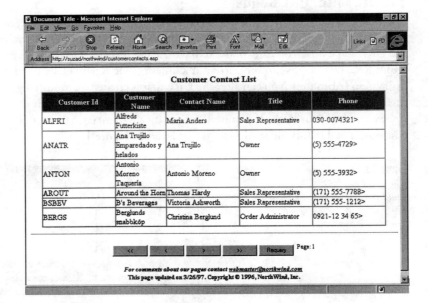

Learning More About Design-Time Controls

Microsoft is currently working with third-party vendors to provide support for building ActiveX design-time controls. If you would like to pursue building your own design-time controls, you should consider downloading the Microsoft Web Design-time Control SDK. The documentation included contains tutorials and sample design-time applications. There is also some information regarding integration with host services. Microsoft has also started a developers newsgroup named `activex.programming.control.Webdc`.

Summary

The design-time controls give developers the flexibility they need to create complex Web applications by enabling them to create standard objects visually, while at the same time enabling them to view and modify the source code that is generated. They save the developer time by providing a visual tool that can generate complex scripting logic that would have normally taken hours, in a matter of minutes. As the Web tool arena matures, so, too, will the tools that facilitate the visual creation of active content Web pages, making the Visual InterDev design-time controls the first of what I'm sure will be a flood of third-party extensions introduced to the marketplace.

Using Microsoft Script Debugger to Eliminate Problems

by Michael Marsh

IN THIS CHAPTER

After programming within Visual InterDev for a while, you will become aware of a major weakness: the lack of a debugger. This can make life a little tedious when chasing down anything other than the most trivial bug. Back in the old days, I used to use `printf()` to output variable states and to signal that my code had reached a certain point during execution. Well, here I am again, only this time I'm using `Response.Write()`!

As with the weather in certain parts of the world, if you don't like the state of your development environment, wait a while and it will change. Microsoft has recently released the Script Debugger for client-side scripting, which may be a preview of things to come for Visual InterDev.

> **NOTE**
>
> The version of the Script Debugger that I'm using for this chapter is 1.0 (Beta 1). Because this is a beta version of the app, things can and probably will change by the time it is released. (See Figure 14.1.)

FIGURE 14.1.

The About box from the Script Debugger showing the version number.

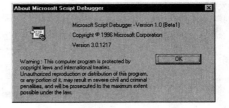

Mind you, this is not a debugger for Visual InterDev's server-side scripting; it is solely built for use with client-side Active Scripting languages such as VBScript and JScript. If you use client-side scripting in your site's pages, this debugger will make your life a lot easier. But as I'll show you, there are some weird interactions between client-side and server-side scripts within the Visual InterDev environment.

Active Scripting

Before I get into the details of using the Script Debugger, I'll give a brief introduction to the languages at which the debugger is targeted. If you're already familiar with Active Scripting, you can safely skip or skim this section.

Active Scripting is a method for providing script languages to browsers using COM. An Active Scripting script engine is a COM object that can execute script code based on various sources of input (direct script parsing, calls to the engine's exposed COM interfaces, or calls to the host application). Using COM as the glue enables you to use several languages uniformly in your code. For example, the code in Listing 14.1 implements two buttons activated by scripting. BUTTON1 uses VBScript, and BUTTON2 uses JScript. Any language implemented with Active Scripting could be used interchangeably in this way.

Listing 14.1. A sample page that uses two scripting languages.

```
<HTML>
<HEAD>
<TITLE>Two Script Languages Page</TITLE>
</HEAD>
<BODY>
<H1>VBScript and JScript, together at last!</H1>
<HR>
<INPUT TYPE="Button" NAME="BUTTON1"  VALUE="VBScript">
<INPUT TYPE="Button" NAME="BUTTON2"  VALUE=
➥"JScript" LANGUAGE="JScript" onClick="OnClick()">
<SCRIPT LANGUAGE="VBScript">
<!--
Sub BUTTON1_OnClick()
    MsgBox("VBScript Clicked!")
End Sub
-->
</SCRIPT>
<SCRIPT LANGUAGE="JScript">
<!--
function OnClick()
{
    alert("JScript Clicked!");
}
-->
</SCRIPT>
</BODY>
</HTML>
```

> **NOTE**
>
> Notice the comment identifiers around the actual code, both for VBScript and JScript. If you leave these out, browsers that can't interpret these scripts will print the code as text on the page.

VBScript

VBScript is a subset of Visual Basic designed for scripting applications within Web pages. Safety and size concerns meant that certain parts of Visual Basic were not included in the script version. For example, none of the file functions are included, so that you may not access the file system from within your scripts.

For more information on VBScript, try Microsoft's VBScript site at http://www.microsoft.com/vbscript/. This is the main site for information about VBScript at the time of this writing. Another great resource is Sams.net's own *VBScript Unleashed*, by Petroutsos, Schongar, et al.

JScript

JScript is to Java what VBScript is to Visual Basic. That is, JScript is a safe and small subset of Java. It should be said that JScript is Microsoft's implementation of Netscape's JavaScript, and there are some differences.

Microsoft maintains an active information site for JScript at `http://www.microsoft.com/jscript/`.

Other Script Languages

Although I have not heard of any other languages that have been ported to Active Scripting, I wouldn't be surprised to see more additions in the near future. Some good candidates are Perl, Tcl/Tk, Python, Pascal, and Eiffel. I don't mean to slight by exclusion any language here, and Microsoft certainly doesn't: Any language can be ported. For more on porting languages to Active Scripting, check out the `http://www.microsoft.com/support/activescript/` page.

Java

Java is obviously not a scripting language. I include it here because the Script Debugger is supposed to be able to debug Java applet code seamlessly alongside any Active Scripting language within your page. As I write this, the Java VM with ActiveX debugging is not yet available.

Pain: Debugging Before Script Debugger

As I mentioned in the introduction, the old days of debugging by writing variable states and location points to the screen or file system seem to be upon us again. In those days, the lack of a debugger meant writing more code to find bugs in code you already wrote. I humbly admit to chasing bugs in C programs that were actually caused by misuse of the `printf` statement. And, though this *never* happened to *me*, I've heard stories of debug code actually making it into a released product.

Many of us used client-side scripting on our pages before the advent of server-side scripting and Visual InterDev. I used ActiveX Control Pad because it had good support for creating scripts and for ActiveX controls (see Figure 14.2). But there was no debugger, so I had to resort to old habits.

The `MsgBox` Statement

In lieu of `printf()`, the old `MsgBox` statement serves well. Look at the following code fragment:

```
<!--
Option Explicit
Sub BUTTON1_OnClick()

    Dim x

    x = 2
    Select Case x
```

```
        Case 1
            ' do something real here
            MsgBox("Case " & Format(x))
        Case 2
            ' do something real here
            MsgBox("Case " & Format(x))
        Case Else
            MsgBox("Bad Case!")
    End Select

End Sub
-->
```

If you get unexpected results from code such as this, putting MsgBox statements in judicious places will help illuminate what is really going on. Often this is an iterative process, whereby you continually refine where you place your MsgBox until that magical moment when you realize what the mistake is. The process is slow and cumbersome, prone to deceiving you into following red herrings, and occasionally inadequate for finding bugs. Plus, you have to click through all those message boxes.

FIGURE 14.2.
The ActiveX Control Pad application.

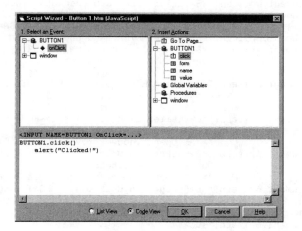

The document.Write() and document.WriteLn() Statements

There are times when you want to dump a bunch of information, perhaps too much to fit reasonably within a message box. In those cases, the document.Write() and document.WriteLn() methods are very helpful. Listing 14.2 is an example of this technique; Figure 14.3 shows the output from the code. Note that using document.Write() and document.WriteLn() has consequences that are unexpected when using the debugger; I'll touch on this shortly.

Listing 14.2. Using the `document.Write()` and `document.WriteLn()` methods for dumping information.

```
<HTML>
<HEAD>
<META NAME="GENERATOR" Content="Microsoft Developer Studio">
<META HTTP-EQUIV="Content-Type" content="text/html; charset=iso-8859-1">
<TITLE>Document Information Window</TITLE>
</HEAD>
<BODY>
<H1>Error!</H1>
<HR COLOR="RED">
<SCRIPT LANGUAGE = "VBScript">
<!--

Option Explicit
Sub window_OnLoad()
    Dim x
    document.Open
    document.WriteLn("<H1>Document Information </H1>")
    document.WriteLn("<HR>")
    document.WriteLn("<B>Title: </B>" & Opener.document.title & "<BR>")
    document.WriteLn("<B>Last Modified: </B>" & _
                     Opener.document.lastModified & "<BR>")
    document.WriteLn("<B>Cookie: </B>" & Opener.document.cookie & "<BR>")
    document.WriteLn("<B>Link Color: </B><FONT COLOR = " &_
                     Opener.document.linkColor & _
                     ">" & Opener.document.linkColor & "</FONT><BR>")
    document.WriteLn("<B>Active Link Color: </B><FONT COLOR = "  &_
                     Opener.document.aLinkColor & _
                     ">" & Opener.document.aLinkColor & "</FONT><BR>")
    document.WriteLn("<B>Visited Link Color: </B><FONT COLOR = " &_
                     Opener.document.vLinkColor & _
                     ">" & Opener.document.vLinkColor & "</FONT><BR>")
    document.WriteLn("<B>Background Color: </B><FONT COLOR = " &_
                     Opener.document.bgColor & _
                     ">" & Opener.document.bgColor & "</FONT><BR>")
    document.WriteLn("<B>Foreground Color: </B><FONT COLOR = " &_
                     Opener.document.fgColor & _
                     ">" & Opener.document.fgColor & "</FONT><BR>")
    document.WriteLn("<OL>")
    document.WriteLn("<LH><B>Controls</B><BR>")
    For x = 0 To Opener.document.forms(0).elements.length - 1
        document.WriteLn("<LI>" & Opener.document.forms(0).elements(x).name)
    Next
    document.WriteLn("</OL>")
    document.Close
End Sub
-->
</SCRIPT>
</BODY>
</HTML>
```

FIGURE 14.3.
The results of the code in Listing 14.2.

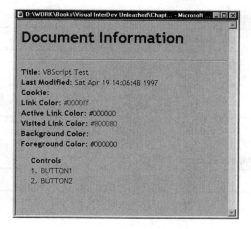

Trapping Errors Using the Err Object and the On Error Resume Next Statement

The two previous techniques work fine just as long as there is nothing in the code that causes a runtime error. If there is, you get the error message box as shown in Figure 14.4, and execution halts.

FIGURE 14.4.
The runtime error message box.

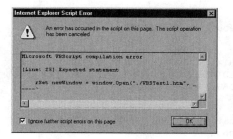

Sometimes the information in this error message box is sufficient to correct a bug from, as with syntax errors. Often it is not, and in those cases, you need a method to override the display of the error message box and halt execution. Use the On Error Resume Next statement to continue past a runtime error and the Err object to display information about the error. Table 14.1 shows the Err object's properties, and Table 14.2 shows its methods.

Table 14.1. Properties of the Err object.

Property	Description
Description	Text description of the error
HelpContext	Topic index from the help file, if available

continues

Table 14.1. continued

Property	Description
HelpFile	Applicable help file, if available
Number	The number that corresponds to the error
Source	Describes what originated the error

Table 14.2. Methods of the Err object.

Method	Parameters	Description
Clear	None	Resets the Err object
Raise	The error number	Forces an error to occur

Listing 14.3 shows how the On Error Resume Next statement and the Err object can be combined to produce useful debugging output. Figure 14.5 shows the output of the code in Listing 14.3.

Listing 14.3. Using On Error Resume Next and Err for dumping debug information.

```
<HTML>
<HEAD>
<TITLE>Err Debugging</TITLE>
</HEAD>
<BODY>
<H1>Error!</H1>
<HR COLOR="RED">
<SCRIPT LANGUAGE = "VBScript">
<!--

Option Explicit
Sub window_OnLoad()
    On Error Resume Next
    Err.Raise 6
    document.Open
    document.WriteLn("<H1>Err Object Information </H1>")
    document.WriteLn("<HR>")
    document.WriteLn("<B>Number: </B>" & Err.Number & "<BR>")
    document.WriteLn("<B>Description: </B>" & Err.Description & "<BR>")
    document.WriteLn("<B>Source: </B>" & Err.Source & "<BR>")
    document.WriteLn("<B>Help File: </B>" & Err.HelpFile & "<BR>")
    document.WriteLn("<B>Help Context: </B>" & Err.HelpContext & "<BR>")
    document.Close

End Sub
-->
</SCRIPT>
</BODY>
</HTML>
```

FIGURE 14.5.

Debugging with the On Error Resume Next *statement and the* Err *object: the results of the code in Listing 14.3.*

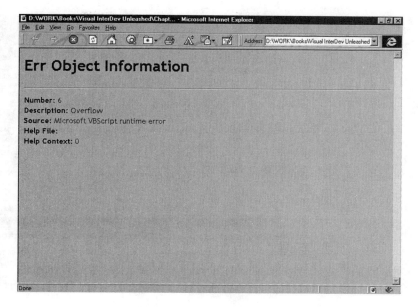

Pain Relief: The MS Script Debugger

A doctor asks his patient, "Why do you beat your head against the wall?" The patient replies, "Because it feels so good when I stop." Likewise, the techniques that I've just described are pretty effective, although actually quite painful. Just how painful is only evident when you stop! The Script Debugger enables you to debug your code painlessly, without extra coding or other gyrations (see Figure 14.6).

It bears repeating here that this debugger is intended for use with client-side scripting. It does not work with server-side code within Visual InterDev. In fact, the debugger behaves somewhat strangely when debugging client-side code within the Visual InterDev environment, although this may be due to the debugger's beta status as of this writing. That much said, it is still an immensely useful tool for those projects that include client-side scripting and Java.

As of this writing, you can download the Beta 1 version of the script debugger from http://www.microsoft.com/workshop/prog/scriptie/. Follow the included installation instructions, and you should be ready to use the debugger.

14

**USING
MICROSOFT
SCRIPT DEBUGGER**

FIGURE 14.6.

The Microsoft client-side Script Debugger.

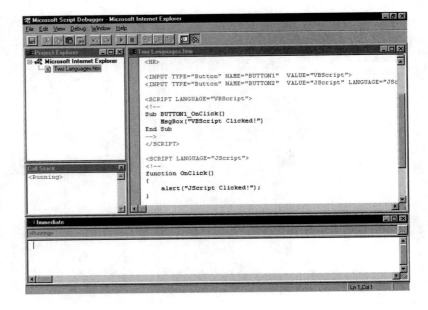

Features

Here is a list of some of the major features of the debugger. I'll explore most of these in detail later.

- Seamless integration with the browser: Once installed, you call the debugger by choosing View | Source from the browser menu. The debugger also pops up when a runtime error occurs.

- Debug multiple languages in the same session: As you can see in Figure 14.6, the debugger recognizes that there are two scripting languages present in the code. You can debug both in the same session. Any language that is ported to Active Scripting will theoretically work within the debugger. The debugger will also debug Java applets, once a new Java VM is installed.

> **NOTE**
>
> The new Java VM that includes support for ActiveX debugging was not yet available for download at the time of this writing. Consequently, I was unable to review this functionality of the debugger.

- Breakpoints: The debugger enables you to set breakpoints in your script code, as you would with other debuggers. When execution reaches a line with a breakpoint, execution halts and control is given to the debugger. You can then view variables, use the Immediate window, step through the code, or use any of the other features that assist in your debugging effort.

- Language extensions for debugging: Both VBScript and JScript have support for debugging built into the language. Table 14.3 shows the VBScript extensions, and Table 14.4 shows the JScript extensions.

- Stepping through code: The Script Debugger supplies three ways of stepping through code: Step Into, Step Over, and Step Out.

- Integrated call stack: The call stack shows the call structure of a routine. Both the VBScript and JScript call stacks are combined, giving the appearance of a single call stack.

- Immediate expression evaluation: You can use the Immediate window to evaluate any expression in any Active Scripting language.

- Editor features: Code coloring, undo, split windows, and sophisticated searching are all part of the editor's feature list.

- View structure of a page's links: Another cool feature of the debugger enables you to view the link structure of the current page. The Project window shows you this view in a tree-list format. When the page changes, so does this display.

Starting the Debugger

As I mentioned previously, there are several ways to start the debugger. One is to simply hit a runtime error in your code. This pops up the debugger, with the cursor of the Code View window at the offending line. The second way is to choose View | Source from the main browser menu. Within Visual InterDev, right-click the Topic Viewer window that contains your executing code; then select View Source from that menu. Finally, if you have used any of the debugger extensions for halting execution (Stop for VBScript and debugger for JScript), the debugger will start when this code is hit.

The User Interface

The user interface for this debugger is not substantially different from other debuggers you might have used. This is an MDI application; that is, multiple windows are contained within the application, each with a dedicated purpose. The main menu enables access to many functions, some of which are mirrored on the toolbar for speedy access. The Help system is HTML based, allowing for easy updates in the future. This is a good thing, because the information currently provided is not adequate.

Menus

Here is a rundown of the menu structure of the debugger:

- **File menu:** Enables you to save and save as, as well as exit the debugger.
- **Edit menu:** Enables you to do the standard copying, pasting, and selecting, plus searching.
- **View menu:** Enables you to display three windows: Project Explorer, Immediate window, and Call Stack.

■ **Debug menu:** Controls aspects of the debugging process such as stepping and setting breakpoints. Two commands are of note here: Break at Next Statement and Show Next Statement. The former will halt execution when the code reaches the very next statement, and the latter will highlight the line that will be executed next.

■ **Window menu:** Enables control over the child windows in the application for arranging, splitting, and activating.

■ **Help menu:** Launches the help system (see Figure 14.7) and presents an About box (refer to Figure 14.1).

FIGURE 14.7.

The Script Debugger help system.

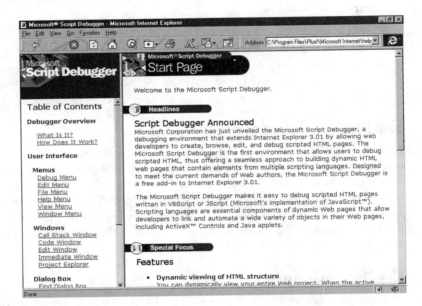

Windows

Figure 14.6 shows most of the windows for this application. The windows are

■ **Project Explorer:** Shows the hierarchy of the current page's links.

■ **Code window:** Displays the code that is currently executing. Note that you cannot edit the code in this window. Attempting to do anything that the debugger perceives as editing will bring up a dialog box (see Figure 14.8) that asks if you want to edit the code. If you answer positively, a new window opens within which you are allowed to edit. In my view this is cumbersome, and something that I hope will be corrected in future versions.

■ **Edit window:** Enables you to modify the code. Although I've already complained about how you get to this window, the fact that you can modify and save code *within* the debugger is a tremendous boon to productivity. The color coding and split window features of the editor are particularly nice.

- **Call Stack window**: Shows a trace of the call stack. Again, this call stack display integrates both VBScript and JScript (and, reportedly, Java) calls.
- **Immediate window**: You can use this window to evaluate expressions within a debugging session. You can evaluate expressions from any Active Scripting language in this window. Figure 14.9 shows an example of immediate expression evaluation.

FIGURE 14.8.

You cannot edit in the Code window!

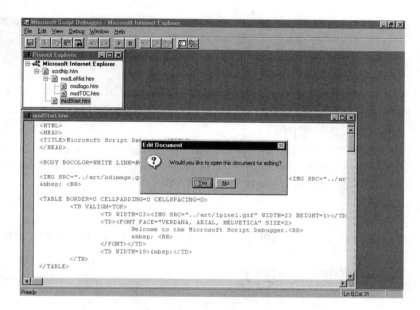

FIGURE 14.9.

Using the Immediate window.

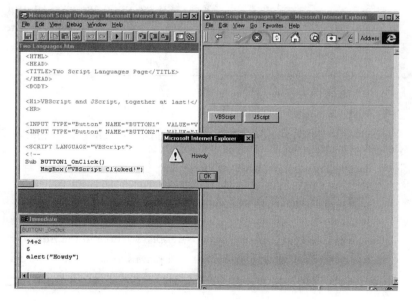

■ **Find dialog box**: Enables you to search your source files. It has some relatively sophisticated options, as shown in Figure 14.10. You can search within the current script only, within just the selected text, or across all files within the set contained in the Project window. You can control the direction of the search, and apply filtering based on case, pattern matching, and whole word only.

FIGURE 14.10.

The Find dialog.

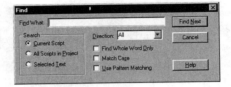

Language Support

Both VBScript and JScript contain special language extensions provided to help with debugging chores. Other Active Scripting languages may or may not provide the same services. However, the Debug object will be available to all.

VBScript

The following table describes the debugging support included in the VBScript language.

Table 14.3. VBScript debugging language extensions.

Statement	*Parameters*	*Description*
Stop	None	Halts execution and gives control to the debugger.
Debug.Write	String *string*	Displays *string* in the Immediate window.
Debug.WriteLn	String *string*	Displays *string* in the Immediate window with a new line.

JScript

Table 14.4 shows the language extensions added for debugging support in JScript.

Table 14.4. JScript debugging language extensions.

Statement	*Parameters*	*Description*
debugger	None	Halts execution and gives control to the debugger.
Debug.Write	String *string*	Displays *string* in the Immediate window.
Debug.WriteLn	String *string*	Displays *string* in the Immediate window with a new line.

A Sample Debugging Session

All these features look and sound terrific. Let's fire up a session and see how well they are implemented. Once again, I would caution you again that I am using the first beta of the Script Debugger, and some of the trouble we find along the way may well be due to immaturity.

The Sample Scripted Page

The code in Listings 14.2 and 14.4 make up the sample application we will debug. Listing 14.4 shows code that presents the user with two buttons: one to display a window with further information and another to close that window. Figure 14.11 shows the result of the code in Listing 14.4, and of clicking the Show Doc Info Window button.

CAUTION

You can't run these pages from within the Visual InterDev environment. The window.Open statement gives a runtime error to the effect that Open is not a method of the Window object. I believe that the parser of the browser within the Visual InterDev environment has trouble distinguishing between client- and server-side scripts. This is one of several strange behaviors I've seen trying to explore the Script Debugger within the Visual InterDev environment.

One more thing to be aware of: If you install the Script Debugger, you will get it popping up on runtime errors in the Visual InterDev environment's Topic Viewer. It's tempting to use the editor of the debugger to correct the mistake and continue, but that doesn't work well. I wasn't able to reliably save changes within the debugger and have them appear in the Visual InterDev editor. A complicating factor is that before you release code, the source lives in two places: locally and on your Web server. The best thing to do when the debugger pops up within the Visual InterDev environment is to close it immediately and work within Visual InterDev's own tools.

Listing 14.4. Code for the Document Information page.

```
<HTML>
<HEAD>
<META NAME="GENERATOR" Content="Microsoft Developer Studio">
<META HTTP-EQUIV="Content-Type" content="text/html; charset=iso-8859-1">
<TITLE>Document Information</TITLE>
</HEAD>
<BODY>
<H1>VBScript Test</H1>
<HR COLOR="BLUE">
<FORM>
<INPUT TYPE="SUBMIT" VALUE="Show Doc Info Window" NAME="BUTTON1">
<INPUT TYPE="SUBMIT" VALUE="Close Document Info Window" NAME="BUTTON2">
</FORM>
<SCRIPT LANGUAGE = "VBScript">
<!--
```

continues

Listing 14.4. continued

```
Option Explicit
Dim newWindow
Dim strFile
Sub BUTTON1_OnClick()
    StrFile = "./VBSTest1.htm"
    Set newWindow = window.Open(strFile, "newWindow", _
                               "toolbar=no", "menubar=no", _
                               "resizeable=no")

End Sub
Sub BUTTON2_OnClick()

    newWindow.Close
End Sub
-->
</SCRIPT>
</BODY>
</HTML>
```

FIGURE 14.11.

*The Document
Information page.*

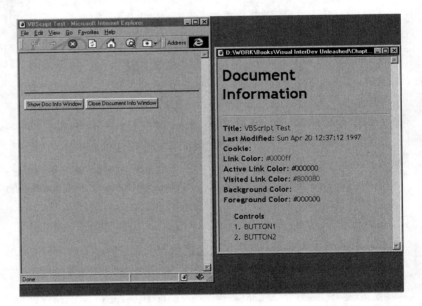

Tracing Execution

Let's trace the execution of these pages. Start by bringing up the code into the browser by double-clicking the file DocInfo.htm. The browser will look like the left side of Figure 14.11. Select View | Source from the main menu or right-click the page and select View Source from the popup menu. The debugger will come up. Select Debug | Break on Next Statement from the debugger's main menu. Now go back to the browser and click the Show Doc Info Window button. The debugger will regain control, and the cursor will be at the line that is about to be executed. This line is highlighted as well. Click the Step Over button on the toolbar. The second window pops up, but as yet has no information in it. Click the button twice again, and the information window fills out.

Notice that the Project window now shows two pages, `DocInfo.htm` and `DocInfo1.htm`. If you double-click `DocInfo1.htm` in the Project window, you'll see the source code for the Document Information window. The source is not exactly what appears in Listing 14.2 because the debugger only sees the source that gets to the browser. Because we've used `document.WriteLn` statements to produce this page, only the results of those statements get to the browser. This is a limitation of this debugger; I would like to see the full source. As it stands I cannot debug that second page as it is written.

The Call Stack

If, when you selected Debug | Break on Next Statement and regained control of the debugger by pressing the Show Doc Info Window button, you also had displayed the Call Stack window, you would have seen something similar to Figure 14.12. The Call Stack will show you how you got to where you currently are by describing each function call. Remember that this stack is integrated, so calls from various languages would appear in the same window.

FIGURE 14.12.

The Call Stack for the Document Information page.

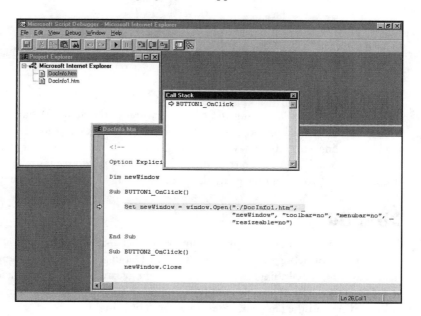

Looking at Variables

In the debugger, put a breakpoint at the line that begins `Set newWindow =`. Now return to the browser and click the Show Doc Info Window button. The debugger will gain control, and you will be stopped at your breakpoint. Open the Immediate window, if it is not already available. Type ?strFile in the Immediate window and press Enter. Immediately below what you typed you will see the string ./DocInfo1.htm, the contents of the strFile variable. Figure 14.13 illustrates this.

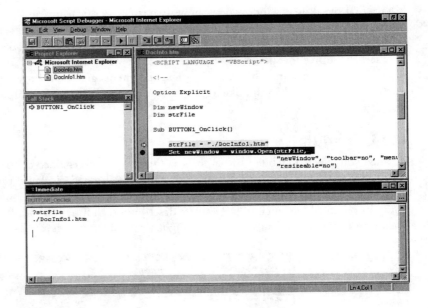

Last Words

The combination of debugging and editing features of the Script Debugger makes it a powerful tool in the war against bugs. I've described these features in some detail, but there is nothing like tackling a real problem with a debugger to get intimately familiar with it. Another useful application of a debugger is to trace through your code just to see if it works the way you think it does. Even if you don't have any (known!) bugs, this is still a useful quality measure.

Summary

If you're using client-side scripting, some real relief is available when you are faced with the painful chore of debugging. Microsoft's Script Debugger is a gem, although it requires, perhaps, a little more polishing. All the usual debugging features are available, and Microsoft throws in a few extras. The ability to modify code within the debugger is extremely valuable, as are color-coding and the language extensions for debugging.

Are we glimpsing at the future of Visual InterDev debugging? I sure hope so. As great an environment as Visual InterDev is, the missing debugger can make it truly painful at debugging time. Integrating a debugger that includes the features of Script Debugger into Visual InterDev would complete an otherwise fabulous development environment.

Programming with Visual InterDev

IV

PART

Introduction to Active Programming

by John J. Kottler

IN THIS CHAPTER

CHAPTER 15

A New Era

There was a time when the Internet was merely a distribution mechanism—a place where users could browse to a particular computer resource and either examine the data online or copy it to their computer. If you have been involved with Internet development for longer than a year, chances are you remember the days when a Web site consisted of simply text, graphics, and hyperlinks spattered throughout. In the recent past, it was plausible for a single person to do it all: set up a Web server, design HTML pages, add graphics, and manage some content.

However, times have changed rapidly in the Internet world. Such simple Web sites are now seen rarely. With new technologies that have been introduced within the past year, it's possible to add animation, database connectivity, high security, and truly interactive applications to Web pages. And with the Internet becoming more of an advertising and marketing vehicle, these technologies become highly necessary to maintain an edge over the competition. To create a truly successful site today, you may be required to fill multiple roles: a server administrator, security expert, graphic artist, navigation and layout expert, content manager, programmer, and database administrator, to name a few.

Because of the drive to have successful Web sites on the Internet, companies are using the newest technologies to make a user's experience at the site as engaging and valuable as possible. After all, viewers are bored easily and flip between Web sites almost as easily as they change television stations when nothing interests them. However, it is not just the work done on the Internet that is spurring these new technologies and the demand for truly interactive sites. Intranet and extranet technologies, which are based on Internet technologies, give corporations the ability to use the standard and inexpensive Internet technology easily within their own personal organizations or with select outside organizations. As more and more companies implement intranets, the developers who used to program mainframe and PC-based applications are finding a shift toward creating these same applications, but to be viewed through the intranet. Therefore, to create robust intranet applications that rival the database systems of the past, capabilities such as transaction management, security, database access, and scaleability need to be addressed with Internet technologies.

Although the technologies are being developed and perfected for use within intranets or the Internet, developers are finding that creating Web-based applications is difficult. Even with all the technologies in place, a developer often finds that many tools are required to complete the job. For example, to create a robust Web-based application, you may require database connectivity on the Web server and programs to be executed within the client's Web browser, as well as security measures for preventing unauthorized access. Using typical Internet tools, you would need a Web page designer tool, a separate utility for adding client-side applications such as Java applets, another technology for compiling server-side programs, the capability to manage all the changes being done, and countless other tools for database connectivity and security.

As you can see, developing and maintaining a Web application that was built using a plethora of tools and countless different languages can be a daunting experience. The goal of Microsoft's Visual InterDev product is to consolidate many of these separate tools into one application. This in turn makes the Web application developer's life less hectic and allows for more efficient and timely changes to Web sites.

Client/Server Meets the Web

There is clearly a shift from classical computer program development toward networked, Web-based development. The popularity of the Internet alone verifies this fact. Therefore, traditional technologies such as client/server also need to be re-created to find their niche in the networked world of the Internet.

The reality is that the Internet is already a type of client/server environment. Remember, the Internet is simply a collection of computers networked together. Typical Web pages are similar to client/server in that a client application (in this case a Web browser) requests information from a server (a Web server). Once the data has been found and prepared by the server, it is sent back to the client. The client then displays the content given by the server. The Internet clearly relies on both client- and server-side technologies to accomplish the task of distributing data. You may also think of this as a two-tier architecture, one tier for the client and one for the server.

But because of the advent of more powerful Web browsers with the capability to execute commands on the client computer and the capability to display rich controls such as Java applets or ActiveX controls, it has become increasingly difficult to decide where the processing should be done. Should programming for an application reside and execute on the server or the client computer? Unfortunately, there is no easy solution for picking where to execute code; the decision rests in a conclusion obtained only after thoroughly evaluating a series of issues, which I will review shortly. To make matters worse, technically, this two-tier architecture can be expanded into three tiers or more. A commonly referenced buzzword in the computer industry today is *N-tier architecture,* implying an infinite number of computers and that application code can execute on any of those machines.

You can imagine that deciding where your programmed code should exist in this type of environment can be very intimidating. Just understanding what N-tier architecture means is difficult. Even if you think you have no idea what N-tier architecture is, chances are you have been exposed to it. Let's look at an example to help further clarify N-tier. Let's assume that you are visiting a typical Web site that accesses data from a database. In this scenario, you are using a three-tier architecture: the client, the Web server, and the database server. In reality, the developer of such a site would not place all application code on any one of these tiers. Instead, the programming would be divided between the three for the most optimized, secure, or capable code. Figure 15.1 depicts a possible three-tier environment.

FIGURE 15.1.
Web-based applications can contain programs that run on the client, on the Web server, or on other servers.

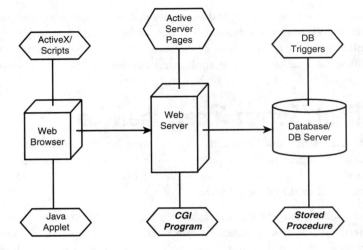

Choosing Sides

As I have reviewed client/server and multi-tier architectures, I have found that it is difficult to decide where to best place components of a Web-based application. The benefit of multi-tier systems is the same as the divide and conquer strategy. With multiple systems involved, a single problem can be solved more quickly with three brains than one. Although there are no given rules that clearly dictate where you should place independent application components, there are some general guidelines you can follow to ease your decision. Ask yourself the following questions to help you decide where to best place your application code:

■ Will users with limited browsers be accessing your site?

If you are creating an external Web site and do not want to manage multiple versions for different browsers with varying capabilities, you may want to design for the lowest common denominator. Don't forget you may have users with devices such as handheld PCs that can browse the Web but can't run Java, ActiveX, or client-side scripts. If either of these points is the case, you should probably avoid dynamic programming code to be executed on the client, because not everyone will be able to run it. Look at doing most of the dynamic page creation, data verification, and other programming chores on the server.

The drawback to placing more code on the server is the apparent slowness of the application to the user, largely due to the constant passing of data over the network.

■ Are a majority of the users of your Web application going to be using more robust browsers?

If most of your users will be using higher-powered Web browser software, chances are they will have the advanced capabilities that Java, ActiveX, and client-side scripting offer. Therefore you can offload some of the programming chores to be accomplished on the client computer. Obvious benefits to this approach include immediate responses to actions made by the user and more flexibility through the use of Java or ActiveX controls than standard HTML. A good example of when to use client-side applications is when performing entry field validations or calculations.

■ Is your application connecting to other systems such as database servers or mainframes?

Once you move into the world of database applications, there is a shift toward including applications on the server. Typically the databases that will be accessed through Web applications are large. A user will not want to download megabytes of information to be viewed on his local computer. The actual scripts that control program flow, the searching of data, security checking, and transaction management should be handled on the server. Then the compact result set can be returned to the client.

Connecting to databases, however, automatically introduces the three-tier architecture. Now, instead of simply a Web client and server, there is a database server that often can be programmed as well. In general, activities that a server specializes in should be fully utilized. In the case of database Web applications, you could write server programs that actually query the data and perform actions on the data. But chances are, the database server is more efficient at doing these tasks through SQL commands or stored procedures and triggers.

One drawback, however, with this approach is that when multiple servers are involved, there are also multiple languages, technologies, and file types to manage.

■ Will your application require high levels of security?

Applications that require user authentication or page flow should be created on the server. It is still difficult today to implement security in the Web client. Sure, there are technologies such as the Secure Sockets Layer (SSL) that help encrypt and decrypt data sent over the network, but there isn't much help in preventing users from changing an HTML file and resubmitting data to the server.

Another good example is user access verification. For instance, it's impossible to determine a user and allow only particular portions of an HTML file to be available to that user using just the Web client. But that user could easily change the HTML file or scripts to see the restricted information. Also, a Web application cannot control the flow of HTML pages presented to the user. A user can easily type a different URL, choose a favorite or bookmark, or click the Back button in his browser. The Web browser software allows all these options without question, even though your particular application in theory requires a user to view certain pages in a particular order.

Because every HTML page is requested from the server, to ensure proper security, these requests can be sent to a server program. This server program, which cannot be viewed or altered by the user, can verify user access and page flow and then return the appropriate page.

As you can see, choosing where to place the functionality of a Web-based application is a difficult task. Lest you think there's a light at the end of the tunnel, let's examine a few more problems associated with Web applications. Don't worry, there will be a light at the end of this tunnel; you just need to be prepared before you see it.

Web Client/Server Problems

With all the development groups flocking to Web-based application development, it's hard to believe that there are actually problems with implementing Web-based client/server applications. There are, however, several factors that don't make client/server on intranets or the Internet impossible, but more challenging.

Too Many Options

For quite some time, developers were lacking a truly integrated development environment that encompassed all aspects of client/server on the Web. Microsoft's Visual InterDev attempts to solve this dilemma by enabling a developer to control server- and client-side programming as well as database connectivity and programming within one self-contained environment. However, before Microsoft's Visual InterDev, truly interactive, client/server Web applications required knowledge in many development languages and tools.

CGI

Another problem with client/server development on the Web in the past was the actual server-side programs themselves. There was a time when all Web server applications that communicated with Web clients were required to be written using the Common Gateway Interface (CGI). Although a simple and useful mechanism for exchanging data between the client and the server, CGI is not the most efficient.

The primary problem with CGI is that in order for it to work, data from the Web client is passed to an instance of a server program. Although this sounds fine in theory, in reality this means that each time a Web browser requests data from a server-side program, a separate copy of that program must run. For every request to run a program, there is a copy of that program running in memory. When only a few users are browsing the same Web page and requesting data from server-side programs at once, CGI works fine. However, when several hundred or more users are accessing server programs with CGI, there are hundreds of applications running on the server. Obviously, the more programs that are executed simultaneously, the more strain there is on the server, and the result is a sluggish if not unstable environment. This is not desirable in a world where hundreds or thousands of users can be performing activities at the same time. Certainly you wouldn't trust your banking on a system that could potentially crash because too many programs are running at once!

In an attempt to solve this problem, the companies that wrote Web server software began to create server Application Programming Interfaces (APIs) that were more suited to this demanding environment. These APIs allow programs on the server to communicate with the Web browser like CGI does, but more efficiently. Microsoft introduced such an API for its Internet Information Server (ISAPI), and Netscape also offers an API for its servers (NSAPI). The benefit of ISAPI and NSAPI programming is that each server program only executes once, but is multithreaded. Therefore, each user who executes a server-side application demands a thread to that application, not a full copy of that application running. In this case, one instance of the program is physically running on the server, although multiple users may be using personal threads of it. Many of today's technologies, such as Microsoft's Active Server Pages, make use of ISAPI for optimum performance.

Stateless Environment

The Internet was designed to be accessed for short bursts of time. Think about it; each time you access a Web page, the following events occur: You connect to a server and request data, the data is passed down to the browser, the data is displayed, and the connection is closed. Now when I talk about connections in this case, I am not referring to the physical connection between a client and a server such as your modem connection at home or high-speed T1 access at work. In the case of a modem at your home, you remain physically connected to your Internet service provider. But when you browse a Web site, you do not maintain an open connection dedicated to that Web server. The server needs to handle many users at once; it does not keep one connection open and dedicated to an individual for the length of time it visits the site.

Because there is no sustained connection, the server does not inherently remember who you are. Each time you connect to the server, you are using a potentially different connection and instance. Imagine for a moment an automatic teller machine (ATM). If ATMs were designed like Internet Web sites and each screen of the machine represented an individual Web page, you would need to connect to the server each time a new screen displayed. In reality, this would also require you to re-authenticate who you are.

In order to prevent inconveniences in using transactional or database applications on the Web, it is necessary for the programs running on the Web server to "remember" each user who is logged in for the duration he is accessing resources on that server. The server in this case is remembering the settings that were used during a user's session. Therefore it is important for the server programs to remember the *state* the server was in last. For a user who is logged into a system, the programs must remember who that person is as he accesses different data on the system.

Internet technology, however, as mentioned earlier, does not maintain an open conduit for each user who is accessing server resources. In addition, the server does not remember its last state. Therefore the Internet, by nature, is *stateless*. If you've been following along, you can clearly see the problem with creating transactional or complex Web applications on the Internet. The technology is stateless by default, but traditional client/server requires that states be managed during a user's session. Until recently, Web-based applications required custom programs to be written that managed state manually, typically through the use of cookies or CGI parameters, as you will see shortly.

Security

The stateless trait of the Internet makes other components of application development difficult as well. Let's assume you are creating a Web site that contains information that is specifically tailored for each individual. This could be confidential information that other users should never see. Therefore you instinctively decide to include IDs and passwords as part of your security measures for this site. But because of the stateless nature of Internet technology, the Web server does not remember information between pages that are requested by a user. If your server application relies on a user ID to determine which information to display back to the client, the server would need to continuously request the ID from the user for each protected page.

If state was somehow maintained, however, it would be possible for a user to log in once, and for that user's ID to be stored as a global variable that can be constantly queried as necessary. Server programs in the past needed to implement this kind of security manually as well, through cookies or CGI parameters. Yet these techniques are, in themselves, not the most secure methods, mainly because this type of data can either be found on the client computer or be altered by the client.

To make security more robust in the Internet environment, many tools and technologies today are employing security measures on the server. Once the programs and data tables that implement security are placed on a server, a user cannot access or change that data in an attempt to hack into the system. Microsoft's Active Server Pages (ASP) technology implements session variables that are internal to Internet Information Server and the embedded ASP libraries.

Transaction Management

The management of transactional systems is imperative to a successful Web- or client/server–based application. Transaction-based systems enable developers to create applications that succeed or fail completely. With transaction management, there is never a state in which an activity or event only partially completes. You can see why this type of technology is important. Assume that you would like to change your personal information in a Web-based database application. After completing all personal, address, and contact information, you would like to submit all the changes. You wouldn't want the Web application to only store your address information without your name and contact information as well.

Transaction management also safeguards against system faults. In our example of personal information updates through a Web-based system, an interruption such as a disturbance in your physical connection could occur that would prevent all information from being updated. If someone ran over your modem telephone line with a vacuum cleaner in your house, both you and the Web application developer would rather have none of the information come across than incomplete information.

Although the personal information update example seems a bit trite, expand the example to something most people care more about than keeping their personal information up to date. Imagine a Web-based ATM application for your bank. In our example, let's assume that you can pay for an item directly from this Web application. All you need to do is type in a code number that identifies that item, its price, and from where you are ordering it. When you click on the Purchase button, this banking application should deduct money from your account and credit the money to a second account. But let's say that the server application crashes in the middle of the transfer. Money was deducted from your account, but never credited to the store's account. In this case, both you and the store lose. You lost the money from your account, and the store never received it. Obviously you want either the entire transaction to either succeed or fail, not just independent portions of that transaction.

Transaction management has existed for quite some time in database and mainframe systems. But this type of technology is just being introduced for Internet servers.

Message-Oriented Middleware

Perhaps this section of this book has covered more computer acronyms and buzzwords than any other! *Message-Oriented Middleware*, or MOM, is a technology that helps guarantee that particular actions are accomplished. This technology can best work with transaction management software to create a complete solution.

MOM is simply a technology that builds a queue for receiving and dispatching messages. As you use a Web-based application, each of your actions causes events to occur on the server. These events can be translated as messages to be performed, particularly on other servers. For instance, if a Web server wanted to retrieve information from a mainframe, the Web server application may send a message to the mainframe requesting that data. MOM servers take those messages and queue them, usually in the order in which they were received, to be dispatched to their appropriate destinations.

But what's the advantage of Message-Oriented Middleware? There are many advantages to using this technology, but two examples stand out in particular. One example is load-balancing the work to be performed. Sometimes complex applications routinely request services from a server. Sometimes these requests are so frequent that multiple servers of the same type are installed to handle the incoming load of requests. If this is the case, it is possible to divide the work evenly between these multiple servers to save time and not backlog any particular machine. MOM technology can examine the destination of messages from its queues and find the server best suited for handling the request before dispatching it.

Another distinct advantage is that MOM can help guarantee that actions occur. You'll recall that transaction management controls whether the entire set of actions completes successfully. If there is a failure, it is up to the user to resubmit the action. However, when bundled with MOM, it is possible to guarantee the delivery of data or actions. For instance, let's assume you are using a Web browser client to complete a form of data that you would like to send to the banking application. You click on the Submit button and receive some type of confirmation that the data was sent. As far as you know, your request has been processed. In reality, however, there may be many more complex actions that first need to be followed on the back end of the site. This Web server, for instance, might need to connect to a database server to update the transaction in a database. But what if that connection fails for a particular reason? If MOM technology is utilized between the Web and database servers, the data being updated is first submitted to a MOM queue. If the database server is down or the connection is lost, the message will remain in the queue until connectivity is re-established. The MOM server will then dispatch the message automatically after the connection is restored.

Again, this is a powerful technology that is necessary for guaranteed delivery of information in complex client/server applications. With the remote nature of the Internet, this technology has become more necessary for creating Web-based applications.

The Old World

So how were applications created before these server-side technologies became more prevalent? In the past, state management was commonly accomplished through one of two mechanisms: CGI programs with common parameter passing or cookies.

You'll remember that the key to maintaining states on the Web server is to store particular information to be accessed between pages. Developers are familiar with this concept as global variables for their applications. These variables are available to an entire application. The same concept can be applied to server applications to maintain state. Several key variables can be defined as global variables that are available to the server application time and time again.

Yet these global variables are a little more specific. Each of these variables must be dedicated to individual users for custom settings during a session. In the past, this was accomplished using CGI parameters or cookies. The key to maintaining state using these techniques is to pass the unique ID to the client so that the client can pass it accurately back to the server the next time a page is requested.

CGI programs that run on the server can execute without input data or may accept parameters that define what actions the program can take. For instance, if a CGI program exists on a Web server that retrieves information based on a query constructed by the user, the information provided by the user can be passed as parameters to the CGI program. You may have noticed some Web sites on the Internet that contain long and somewhat cryptic URL lines. Chances are these URL lines were generated by a CGI program on the server as a unique ID to identify your own personal session at that site. Some sites may use more logical parameters such as your unique ID for the system.

In either case, each Web page that is to be included in state management must be generated somehow by a CGI program. This program would read parameters such as the user ID from the CGI command line and execute instructions based on that data. It would then return that information to the client, but dynamically create the resulting HTML. This dynamic creation of the HTML file is necessary to update all appropriate links within the file with the unique ID information. A link to another page, for instance, may actually link to a CGI program, passing in the page to link to as a parameter as well as the unique ID information again. Because the CGI program is constantly being used on the server and all links point to that program passing in the common identifier, the identifier is never lost during the session. This identifier is created by the CGI program, passed to the browser indirectly through parameters to CGI program links, and passed back to the server in subsequent hits by the same CGI parameters.

A second technique for storing variables locally is to use cookies. Cookies in a cookie file are similar to settings that you would find in your `windows.ini` file. With cookies, it is possible to store a piece of data from the server on a client machine. Then, when the client requests subsequent pages from the server, the server can access and use the previously stored cookies. In this way, cookies are easier to use for maintaining state because the actual process of storing and updating state information is somewhat automated by the nature of cookies.

A great example of where cookies are used today to maintain information about your visits to Web sites can be found at sites such as MSN (The Microsoft Network) that request and store particular information about what interests you. Your personal information is stored on their site's server, and a unique key is passed to your client computer. This unique key identifies your personal settings for the site and is passed to the server each time you re-enter that site so that the custom information may be gathered.

In any case, you can see how creating a site that maintains information about the state of your session during your visit to a site can be difficult. In both methods discussed, a large amount of manual labor and programming is required to accomplish this task.

The Not-So-Old World

Creating Web-based client/server applications using the older technologies is surely not an efficient way for companies to use technology. Therefore, many companies such as Microsoft are introducing or have introduced strategies to address the headaches associated with developing Web applications.

Microsoft, as you will see later in this section and throughout this book, has introduced a technology referred to as *Active Server Pages*. This technology originated from another technology that was bundled with its Internet Information Server Web server product. The Internet Database Connector (IDC) was a technology that allowed site developers easy access to databases through ODBC and simple template files. IDC was so simple to use when creating sites that it quickly gained popularity, and Microsoft recognized the need to expand upon this functionality. As a result, Active Server Pages are similar to the older IDC technology; however, its functionality has been expanded considerably and the language is now based on the popular Visual

15

INTRODUCTION
TO ACTIVE
PROGRAMMING

Basic Scripting language. A major improvement in this technology, as you will see shortly, is the inclusion of a session-management object that maintains state for an individual user on the server.

IDC

If you're not familiar with the IDC, it's a fairly simple way to get connected to databases and exchange data with the Web browser. The technology uses two main files to instruct the actions to be performed on a database: the .IDC file and the .HTX file. If you combine IDC with your Web pages, you need at most three text files and a single database to implement IDC.

An HTML Form

Let's say you wanted to create an entry form that allowed the user to enter a name of a product to search for. You're probably already familiar with the plethora of <INPUT> tags available for data entry, as well as the CGI programs that are usually written to capture data and retrieve information from data stores. With IDC, however, you do not need to create custom CGI programs. The .IDC file that you create is used in place of the <FORM> tag's ACTION attribute. In reality, this .IDC file is associated with a library on the Web server that parses the data in the .IDC file and performs the requested actions. Listing 15.1 demonstrates a simple HTML form that can pass data to an .IDC file on the Web server.

Listing 15.1. Connectivity to Internet databases often starts with an HTML file to retrieve query data.

```
<FORM ACTION="getname.idc" METHOD="GET">
Enter a product name to search for:<BR>
<INPUT NAME="product_name" SIZE=30>
</FORM>
```

The .IDC File

To begin database connectivity using IDC, you must create a text file on your IIS Web server that ends with an .IDC extension. This file is fairly simple and contains some basic information. Listing 15.2 demonstrates a simple .IDC file.

Listing 15.2. This getname.idc file defines what SQL statements to use and which databases are affected.

```
  Datasource: ODBC_ProductDB
    Template: results.htx
SQLStatement: SELECT Product_Name, Price FROM products
             WHERE name='%product_name%'
```

First of all, there are many additional attributes that you may set in the `.IDC` file, however, the three listed in Listing 15.2 are the basic, required attributes. Each of these attributes is necessary to create the connectivity you require:

- `Datasource`—This attribute enables you to specify which database you want to connect to. Valid information for this attribute is the names of the database connections as defined in the ODBC Data Source Administrator found in the operating system's control panel.

- `Template`—When data is requested from a data source, you will undoubtedly want to tailor the output to match your design. This attribute enables you to specify which template file to use. This template is essentially an HTML file with placeholders for the database data to be inserted into, as well as some basic programming commands.

- `SQLStatement`—With thousands or millions of records of information available in a database, you will need to issue a SQL statement to extract only appropriate data or to perform other database functions.

NOTE

Notice that you can substitute data from the HTML form into the `.IDC` file by enclosing the input field's internal name from the HTML with % characters. In Listing 15.2, whatever the user enters into the entry field from the HTML form will replace the variable as part of the SQL statement. For instance, if a user types in `laptop` as a product to search for, the IDC SQL statement will be translated as `SELECT Product_Name, Price FROM products WHERE name='laptop'`.

Get accustomed to seeing the % sign used to distinguish variables or programming scripts from standard HTML. Active Server Pages are based on IDC technology and inherit the use of the % character.

The `.HTX` File

Once the query has been issued, the data needs to be returned to the Web browser. But you probably do not always want the results in a standard tabular format. In fact, you may also want to only display particular information as defined by a program script. The `.HTX` template file enables you to define HTML to be returned to the browser as well as data to be substituted into that HTML file.

There are many options for defining the `.HTX` file, but I will simply cover a basic example here to give you a flavor of how the Internet Database Connector works completely. Listing 15.3 displays a simple `.HTX` file that returns a table of information based on the query.

Listing 15.3. The `results.htx` file defines how results from the database query are to be formatted.

```
<HTML>
<TITLE>Product Results</TITLE>

<BODY>
Here's the products that match your description:<P>
<TABLE>
<TR>
<TD>Product Name</TD>
<TD>Product Price</TD>
</TR>
<%BeginDetail%>
<TR>
<TD><%Product_Name%></TD>
<TD><%Price%></TD>
</TR>
<%EndDetail%>
</TABLE>
</BODY>
</HTML>
```

Listing 15.3 is an extremely terse example of what can be placed within an .HTX file. As you can see, it is mostly straightforward HTML. However, you will notice the additional tags: <%BeginDetail%> and <%EndDetail%>. The product database in discussion will contain hundreds of records, with each individual record corresponding to a single product. As the SQL statement is executed in the .IDC file, a result set of several records will be returned. In the resulting HTML file that is passed back to the Web browser, you want to display all of that data. But because you are using dynamic database queries, you do not know exactly how many records will be returned, and that number will constantly change. Therefore, the <%BeginDetail%> and <%EndDetail%> tags indicate that all text and tags between these two is to be included repeatedly with each record of information from the database.

You will also notice two additional tags that represent the data returned in the SQL statement of Listing 15.2. This SQL statement extracts the Product Name and Price columns of information from the product database. These two information column names may then be substituted in the .HTX file, to be replaced with actual data when the .IDC file is executed.

The final result of the IDC process yields a table of information similar to that found in Listing 15.4.

Listing 15.4. The results from the IDC query can be formatted for your Web site.

```
Here's the products that match your description:

Product Name          Product Price
100MHz Laptop         $1200
120MHz Laptop         $1500
133MHz Laptop         $1800
Laptop Case           $45
Laptop 8MB Memory     $79
```

> **NOTE**
>
> Only a small portion of the IDC specification has been covered here to give you a flavor for the technology. It's important to have an appreciation for this technology, because it is the foundation for Active Server Pages technology, which I cover later in this section. If you research IDC further, you will find that it contains conditional logic statements and many more variables. You will also notice, however, that it uses a language similar to VBScript, but is not quite completely compatible.

As nice as the Internet Database Connector is for retrieving data from databases and potentially storing information in databases, it does not include capabilities for facilitating state management. As you will see later in this section, Active Server Pages continue where IDC left off and include capabilities for state management. For more information on IDC, see Microsoft's Web site or see other books from Sams.net Publishing such as *Internet Information Server Unleashed.*

A Whole New World

You have seen how CGI programs can be written (in theory) to handle state management as well as IDC programs that can control data in databases. Likewise, you have seen that neither of these technologies alone solves all the problems outlined earlier with client/server development on the Web. Microsoft's Active Server Pages, on the other hand, help developers to conquer some of the hurdles placed in their path with traditional Web-based client/server development. There are many features of Active Server technology that ease development:

- Active Server Pages, like their predecessor IDC, use the ISAPI interface to optimize connectivity between the client and server applications.

- The languages used for Active Server Pages are VBScript and JScript (Microsoft's implementation of JavaScript), which are more widely known languages.

- The architecture for Active Server Pages is extensible. With Active Server Pages it is possible to include server objects (ActiveX controls) in server applications. Even additional languages may be used within the server pages and intermixed.

- Session management is possible through a `Session` object that stores state information for a user during that user's visit to the site.

- A similar syntax to IDC is used for substituting data within the returned pages as well as for performing programming code during the preparation of the results.

- The classic `.IDC` files required previously have been replaced with the more robust ActiveX Data Objects (ADO). These objects can easily be included and accessed by any Active Server Page.

- It is possible to lock files with Active Server Pages in order to prevent anomalies from occurring when multiple users are attempting to read or write the same file at once.
- Certificates installed on client browsers can be read and utilized to strengthen security in server-based applications.

In Chapter 19, "Creating Active Server Pages," you will learn how to create Active Server Pages of your own.

Summary: Settling the New World

With all the new capabilities of Active Server Pages, it has become apparent that a single tool should be developed to help coordinate the efforts of creating a client/server Web application. Microsoft has introduced Visual InterDev as a product that provides a single environment for creating and managing source code for the client, server, and database. Besides a common environment, Visual InterDev provides support for scripting languages and the incorporation of objects and controls in a project. The tool also supplies a simple utility for working with objects as well as a scripting wizard to guide you through creating simple programmatic functions.

In the following chapters, you will learn more about Active Server Pages, VBScript, JavaScript, programming with controls and objects, and how Visual InterDev supports all these technologies. In the final chapter we will examine a fictitious, yet plausible Web site for selling computer systems. It will review the source code, tips, and tricks necessary for creating a fully functional Web-based application. So get ready to check out the newest additions to client/server programming on the Web.

An Introduction to Scripting Languages

by John J. Kottler

IN THIS CHAPTER

CHAPTER 16

Following the Script

The world of Internet application development is complex and, as you saw in Chapter 15, "Introduction to Active Programming," requires numerous technologies. To fashion a complete, interactive Web application, you need to consider creating application code that can run in a variety of ways. This code may be compiled Java applets that are downloaded to the Web browser, server-side code that is written in languages such as Perl or C, or client-side scripts such as JavaScript or VBScript. Whatever the choice, it is important to note the need to distribute the task of executing code on both the server and the client.

Traditional server-side programming has been accomplished through the use of compiled applications written in languages such as C or interpreted languages such as Perl. However, with newer technologies such as Microsoft's Active Server Pages, which you will learn more about in Chapter 19, "Creating Active Server Pages," it is possible to use scripting languages that are gaining in familiarity and popularity.

In this chapter, you will gain an overview of two scripting languages that are supported by Visual InterDev and that have become commonplace in the Internet world: JavaScript and VBScript. These two languages have become popular and are gaining support because they are languages that are easy to use and are based on other languages that have been in the computer industry for years. They are also scripting languages that, as you will learn shortly, do not need to be compiled and are therefore easier for developers to implement.

Speaking the Same Language

If you've developed applications for computers before, you are clearly familiar with what a language is. Computers understand instructions in their own language, which is made up of a series of 1s and 0s that is difficult for a human being to translate and comprehend. In the beginning of computers and software development, programmers needed to know how to program computers using the computer's native language.

As software development software progressed, new languages were introduced to the computer. These languages are not really understood by the computer, but are translated for the computer. Languages such as BASIC (Beginner's All-purpose Symbolic Instruction Code) made an English-like language available for developers to write in. The computer would then take these English words and translate them into the appropriate functions that it could understand.

Just as computer technology has grown exponentially in the past, the languages and tools for programming computers have grown. Many new languages have been introduced to solve unique programming problems. Some languages are very simple to understand, while others are very complex and can perform just about anything. Each language also varies in how quickly it executes commands or in how optimized the native computer code is. The actual instructions may also be executed differently, depending on the model used by the programming language.

Language technology hasn't changed much with the Internet. Even though there are new languages that were introduced because of the presence of the Internet, many of the languages execute code in one of the following ways: interpreted, compiled, or scripted.

Interpreted

When a Spanish-speaking person gives instructions to another person who understands only English, chances are nothing will be accomplished. The only way this problem can be rectified is by including an interpreter who understands both languages and can translate between the two individuals.

Believe it or not, there are interpreters for your computer, although sometimes you'll never understand why your computer doesn't work correctly! Every computer program written in a language other than the computer's native language requires an interpreter. This interpreter converts the English-like commands of a language such as BASIC into statements that the computer can understand and execute.

Although all languages are interpreted to a point, the term *interpreted languages* today often implies code that is interpreted by the computer as the program is running. For example, as each line of instructions is read by the computer, it is translated immediately at that point and executed.

There are many languages available today that are based on this technology. Languages such as BASIC work on this principle. In fact until recently, popular languages such as Visual Basic were strictly interpreted languages as well. Even Java applications, although optimized, are interpreted as the code is executed.

There is some benefit to using interpreted languages. Interpreted languages often are more portable; that is, they can be executed on different computer systems with differing hardware and software. As long as the right translator is on the computer, any computer can read and execute the commands of an interpreted language. This is the founding concept of Java and is why Java code is interpreted, so that it can run on any system as long as the Java interpreter is written for that system.

But there is also a drawback to interpreted languages. Because there is a translation step necessary for every line of code that is to be executed, interpreted languages are often slow. The computer is doing about twice the work by translating instructions before executing them. Some of today's newer interpreted languages optimize the instructions to be interpreted before they are executed. Usually this is accomplished by compiling the application to an optimized file that can be translated more quickly. For example, although Java applets are interpreted for use across multiple platforms, the applets are compiled to an optimized code language for maximum speed during interpretation.

Compiled

Because interpreted languages are not fast enough for some applications, other languages utilize the concept of a compiler. Compilation software takes all of the instructions written in languages such as C and translates them into computer code at once. The final result is written to a file that the computer understands naturally, so it does not need to impose a translator.

Although compiled applications are considerably faster than interpreted applications, they are not as portable. Because the program is compiled to a computer's native language, there's a problem when you try running that same program on a completely different computer with different hardware and operating system software. A Macintosh and a Windows PC do not execute software the same way. In order to make your application run on both, you must compile and distribute multiple versions of your software for each computer platform.

Scripting

Scripting languages are based on interpreted languages and therefore suffer from the same limitations and gain the same benefits. Scripting languages are nearly identical to interpreted languages with a few minor exceptions.

The first exception is that scripting languages are often limited in their capabilities. They are commonly designed to automate tasks in software such as word processors or to perform simple actions. They usually do not contain the robust features of their sibling interpreted languages.

Scripting languages are also rarely compiled. Instead, they are left in their native format and are always translated when executed. Because they are not compiled languages or even optimized interpreted languages, scripting languages often run slower. Usually the source code for scripting languages is not hidden or jumbled by the compilation process. Therefore, it is easy for others to view, modify, or copy the program code that you write.

The Advantages of Scripting Languages

Scripting languages have become a popular way to enhance a user's visit to a Web site, so there must be obvious advantages to using these languages. Indeed, there are several positive reasons for using scripting languages such as VBScript or JavaScript.

- **Distributed**—Scripting languages such as VBScript and JavaScript can be executed on either the client or the server. When executed on the client, scripting languages can perform actions on local data or objects and process information more quickly than constantly sending data over the Internet to the server. However, if the security, capability, or power of the Web server is required, that same language can be used to accomplish the task. Between the two ends of client/server, you can create a highly complex application that can execute different portions either locally or on the server for optimal performance.

■ **Portable**—The code that is written using scripting languages is highly portable. As long as there is a translator for a scripting language available on the computer that is reading the language, the program will execute. The code you write doesn't need to be compiled for every platform it will run on.

■ **Interpreted**—Because applications written with scripting languages are interpreted and not compiled, you can easily include application code in your Web site. You can insert scripting commands directly into HTML pages or Active Server Pages without additional compilers. You can also make immediate changes to your source code without recompilation. In addition, if you are designing Web sites for which you cannot control the server environment, you can still program applications using client-side scripting.

■ **Common Language**—Scripting languages for Internet development are based on other common development languages such as those found in Visual Basic and Java. Both of these languages have been exceedingly popular choices for developing applications. If you know one of these languages, you should be able to adapt rather easily to the scripting versions of these languages. Also, because they are becoming popular and standard development languages, you can be sure to find numerous tools such as Visual InterDev to support these languages as well as language libraries and support.

Disadvantages to Scripting

Sure scripting languages are easy to learn and implement. They offer many of the capabilities that you require for creating complex client/server applications for the Web. However, it is important to note that there are several capabilities that these languages lack.

■ **Portability**—In theory, Internet scripting languages can be executed on any Web browser that contains the scripting engine for translation. In reality however, this is not as tidy as it seems. For instance, since its inception JavaScript has never been released as an open language for inclusion in other browsers. Therefore, companies such as Microsoft had to implement JavaScript as best as they could without knowing all of the intricate implementation details of the language when they developed Internet Explorer. The result in this case was JScript, a highly compatible language to JavaScript, but not entirely compatible. In fact, many JavaScript-enriched Web pages will not execute properly when viewed with Internet Explorer for this very reason.

■ **Browser Support**—There is also a battle raging over which languages to develop with. Although Internet Explorer supports both VBScript and JavaScript, Netscape does not support VBScript directly. Therefore, if you are designing pages that require scripting languages on the client Web browser, you may be limited to using the common language of JavaScript (or JScript). Or you may need to create two versions of your Web page, one JavaScript enhanced and another VBScript enhanced. In either case, this is terribly inconvenient and is reminiscent of the days of specialized HTML tags supported by only particular browsers.

> **TIP**
>
> You can include both JavaScript and VBScript interchangeably in your scripting applications. One portion can be written in VBScript while another is in JavaScript. Given the current state of turmoil over which scripting languages to support, however, you may want to include tests in your Web site that detect which browser is viewing the site. You may perform these tests locally via client-side scripting or on the server. By testing the browser version, you can return Web pages that are optimized for the capabilities of that browser, including JavaScript or VBScript application code.

- **Not Compiled**—Although non-compiled code is easier to maintain and implement in certain cases, the trade-off is in speed. Scripts are interpreted and therefore require more time to complete than optimized, compiled applications.

- **Insecurity**—Sometimes you may not want others to see the program code that you designed for verifying data or performing other confidential actions. You probably will not want others modifying that program code to submit incorrect data. Scripts written in VBScript or JavaScript for the Web browser are insecure; that is, the source code for the entire script is available for review. If users save these scripts to their local hard disks, they can modify the scripts or reuse them in their own Web pages. Worse yet, if a client-side script is the only means of preventing illegal data from being entered into a system, a user can change the validity checks and submit invalid information without alarm.

- **Low-Powered**—Although scripting languages provide you with a complete feature set for most needs, they do lack the robustness and features of other technologies such as Java or ActiveX. When creating local applications that perform very complex actions or require high amounts of interactivity, scripting languages cannot provide all of the capabilities you need.

Client- and Server-Side Scripting

As you have already seen, it is possible to use scripting languages on both the server and the client. It is important to notice the similarities and differences when developing scripts to be executed on either side. Although the same language can be used for either client or server scripts, there are varying capabilities and thus variations in the language for both platforms. For more information on choosing when to develop on the server or client, see Chapter 15 .

Local Scripting

Clearly there are times when you want to perform actions locally on the client computer. If you are doing simple calculations, verifying the format of entered data, or controlling the actions of clicked buttons on a form, you will probably want to place the script in the Web page

An Introduction to Scripting Languages

CHAPTER 16

333

16

AN INTRODUCTION
TO SCRIPTING
LANGUAGES

that is executed by the Web browser. These types of actions can be executed more quickly because a connection to the Web server isn't required just to perform a simple math calculation.

It is also possible to use scripting functions more interchangeably with the Web page. Whenever you ask the Web server to return a result to the Web browser, it typically returns the entire page—not just the answer. With script functions, data can be returned immediately without intervention or disturbance to the appearance of the Web page.

Adding Scripts to Web Pages

Because HTML pages are downloaded to be formatted and displayed by the Web browser, source code for scripts is also embedded in the HTML files. When a Web browser downloads a page with embedded scripts, the data is displayed within the Web browser window and the scripts are executed.

To add scripts that run on the client side of the connection, you can embed scripting commands by surrounding those commands with the <SCRIPT> and </SCRIPT> tags. Any text within those tags will be treated as scripting language commands.

The following is the syntax for the <SCRIPT> tag:

```
<SCRIPT LANGUAGE="language name">
... scripting statements
</SCRIPT>
```

You may recall that it is possible to use either the JavaScript or VBScript scripting languages within your Web sites. The LANGUAGE parameter enables you to specify for which language the commands between the <SCRIPT> tags are written.

> **NOTE**
>
> You may notice that as you use Visual InterDev to create your client-side scripts, the script that you add is surrounded by the <SCRIPT> tags as well as HTML comment tags (<!-- and -->). Surrounding your script code with comments will ensure that browsers that do not understand scripting languages will not display the script as text within your Web document.

Remember that different capabilities are available for developing local scripts and server scripts. Client scripts can access, query, and control objects specific to the client. For example, client scripts can use objects such as those provided by the browser to control the browser or interactive objects such as form objects. In any case, these capabilities are unique to the client and are not available for use on the server. Because the server runs by itself without human intervention, there typically is no Web browser in use on the server and certainly no data forms that require user input.

Because the scripts are executing on the client, they can interact with all objects that are usually available to the client. These objects include components of the Web browser, form fields within an HTML file, Java applets, and ActiveX controls.

Server Scripting

Often when there are large databases to access or other resources on the Web server, you will typically want to create scripts that run on the server. The advantage of using scripting languages opposed to CGI programs is that the scripting language is often common between the client and server software. Therefore, you need to understand only the differences between server and client capabilities, not different languages. Most often you will find capabilities on the server that address some of the issues that were raised in Chapter 15. With server-side scripts it is possible to access database reserves, manage transactions, and perform session management for users of your site.

Adding Server Scripts

As you will see in Chapter 19, "Creating Active Server Pages," it is also fairly straightforward to add these same scripting languages to server-side applications. Although the languages are the same for pieces of an application that run on both the client and the server, they clearly execute in different locations. Scripts that run on the server have access to databases and other capabilities that a client might not have. Server scripts exist in Active Server Pages and execute only on the server. They typically execute before the page is sent to the browser, unless they are initiated by user actions such as completing a form.

To distinguish server-side scripting commands from client-side scripts or HTML that is to be returned to the browser, Active Server Pages extensively use <% and %> characters surrounding server commands. Just as you specify which language to use with your client-side pages, you can also choose your server language using the following line in your Active Server Page:

```
<%@ LANGUAGE="language" %>
```

After you have selected your language of choice for server-side scripts, you may then use similar commands as you would with client scripting languages. To indicate which portions of the HTML file are to be treated as server-side scripting commands, you simply enclose the code with the matching <% and %> characters.

```
<%
... some server-side scripting statements
%>
Some HTML<BR>
<%
... some more scripting statements
%>
```

Later in this book when you learn about Active Server Pages in more detail, you will also see that there is one additional tag, the <%= tag. This special tag instructs the Web server to assign actual values of variables to the output stream to be returned to the Web browser.

> **NOTE**
>
> When creating server-side pages or Active Server Pages, you will be creating both the client and server scripts in a single file. Although you will see scripts for both sides of the connection in a single file, the server-side scripts are substituted with results when the server page is processed. In other words, all script that appears between the <% and %> tags will be removed and not viewable on the client computer. These tags are replaced with actual data based on the script's instructions.

Script Language Overview

Like most computer languages today, scripting languages such as VBScript and JavaScript are object-oriented in nature. Each language has its own specific syntax for performing looping, condition checking, and other functions. But in addition, each language can work with objects by setting properties, invoking methods, or acting on events. To begin an introduction to the JavaScript and VBScript languages, let's first examine the general syntax for both. You will quickly find that the capabilities of both languages are very similar; the differences lie in their exact implementation of these capabilities.

What's Your Function?

Assume that you are writing an application and you need to determine sales tax. If you have multiple forms on a Web page, you may need to calculate the tax several times. Because the code for calculating sales tax is always the same, you wouldn't want to retype that block of code each time you wanted tax calculated, would you? Instead, you would want to create a *function*. A function is a block of code that you write and group together. That block can be given a name so that it can be identified by other parts of your application, and it can accept values or return results. Listing 16.1 is an example of a valid function in both JavaScript and VBScript.

Listing 16.1. A function for calculating tax can be created in both JavaScript and VBScript.

```
JavaScript:
function CalculateTax(amount, percent){
    if (percent < 1)
        percent = percent + 1;
    if (percent < 0)
        Alert ("Illegal tax amount");
    else
        return amount * percent;
}
VBScript:
function CalculateTax(amount, percent)
    if percent < 1 then
        percent = percent + 1;
```

continues

Listing 16.1. continued

```
    if percent < 0 then
        MsgBox ("Illegal tax amount")
    else
        CalculateTax = amount * percent
end function
```

> **TIP**
>
> You should place functions for scripting languages in the <HEAD> section of your HTML files and not the <BODY> section.

You will notice immediately from Listing 16.1 that the functions do the same thing. They read the tax variable passed to the function and make certain that 1 is added to its value if the variable is a decimal number ranging between 0 and 1. If a percentage is passed that is less than zero, an error message occurs; otherwise, the final amount with tax is calculated and returned.

JavaScript

JavaScript or JScript functions require that the following format be followed for declaring functions:

```
Function FunctionName(variable 1, variable 2, ...){
    ... statements
    return return_value
}
```

The block of code is surrounded by the { and } characters, and resulting values are returned via a return statement with that value.

VBScript

VBScript expects functions to be declared using the following format:

```
Function FunctionName (variable 1, variable 2, ...)
    ... statements
    FunctionName = return_value
End Function
```

The block of code to be treated as a function starts with the Function definition and ends with the End Function statements. Values that are to be returned are done so by assigning the name of the function to the value you would like to return.

Calling Functions

After you have defined functions that you will use multiple times in your application, you can invoke them anywhere else within your application. To invoke a function, you simply use it as part of your script. If the function returns a value, then it should be used in the script you write

An Introduction to Scripting Languages

CHAPTER 16

337

16

AN INTRODUCTION
TO SCRIPTING
LANGUAGES

that invokes the function. Also, if a function is expecting variable parameters, you must pass those parameters as well. Both VBScript and JavaScript invoke functions in the same way. The following is a brief demonstration of the CalculateTax function being invoked:

```
new_total = CalculateTax(total_amt, 1.06)
```

VBScript's Subroutines

It is possible to create a function that does not return a value in JavaScript; however, VBScript has specific keyword statements for identifying "functions" that do not return results. Blocks of code that do not return values are considered *subroutines* and are identified by the Sub and End Sub statements in VBScript.

```
Sub RoutineName (variable 1, variable 2, ...)
    ... statements
End Sub
```

What If?

In the CalculateTax function, you saw a few statements such as if and else. These statements help applications written in JavaScript or VBScript to "test" for particular values or actions. If the value returned by this test is true or equivalent, one block of code can be executed. If it is false, another block of code can be executed. The if...then...else statements are among the most powerful and give the computer its intelligence when processing functions. Listing 16.2 shows some examples of valid conditional checking in both JavaScript and VBScript.

Listing 16.2. if statements add power to functions by invoking appropriate blocks of code after a comparison is made.

```
JavaScript:
if (a == 1){
    Alert ("Everything's fine.");
    Results = MissionStatus(a);
}
else if (a == 2){
    Alert ("Things are OK, but could be better.");
    Results = MissionStatus(a);
}
else {
    Alert ("Houston, we have a problem...");
    Results = MissionStatus(-1);
}
VBScript:
If a=1 then
    MsgBox ("Everything's fine.")
    Results = MissionStatus(a)
ElseIf a=2 then
    MsgBox ("Things are OK, but could be better.")
    Results = MissionStatus(a)
Else
    MsgBox ("Houston, we have a problem...")
    Results = MissionStatus(-1)
End If
```

> **NOTE**
>
> Notice that when testing for equivalence in JavaScript, you must use two = characters. This is an important and often overlooked requirement, particularly for first-time developers. If you do not put the ==, you may experience problems later on. Along with the opening and closing braces ({ and }), these syntax formats show JavaScript's relationship to Java and to C/C++.

JavaScript

You will notice immediately that the JavaScript (JScript) version of the if statement follows this format:

```
if (comparison #1) {
    ... Statements to execute if condition is TRUE
}
else if (comparison #2) {
    ... Statements to execute if second condition is TRUE
}
else {
    ... Statements if both conditions are FALSE
}
```

Blocks of code that are to be executed between the condition checks are clearly distinguished by surrounding braces.

VBScript

VBScript, although very similar, follows a slightly different syntax:

```
if comparison #1 then
    ... Statements to execute if condition is TRUE
else if comparison #2 then
    ... Statements to execute if condition is TRUE
else
    ... Statements if both conditions are FALSE
end if
```

> **NOTE**
>
> To implement if statements, you do not need to include the entire if, else...if, else syntax. If your program logic simply requires a simple if condition without capturing the else portion, simply leave out the else...if or else portions.
>
> If there is more than one line of code to be executed when a comparison is true, that block of code must still be clearly indicated by the braces in JavaScript or the If...End If pair in VBScript.

An Introduction to Scripting Languages

CHAPTER 16

339

16

AN INTRODUCTION
TO SCRIPTING
LANGUAGES

Loop-de-Loop

Let's say that you are creating a database system and want to display every record in the database. How would you do this? If there were *always* five records of information in that database, you could write your scripting code five times, once for each record. But if there were 500 records, would you want to copy and paste your code 500 times? Even if you invoked a function that displayed the record's information, would you want 500 function calls in a row? What if there weren't always the same number of records in this database? To perform actions numerous times, you can employ loops in both the JavaScript and VBScript scripting languages.

A *loop* is simply a mechanism for indicating a block of code that is to be executed any number of times. An additional benefit of loops is that you can also do conditional loops. These loops can execute a number of times based on whether a condition remains true. For example, in the database example, a conditional loop would be used because you want to display each line of data and stop the loop only when you've reached the last record in the database. Listing 16.3 shows the most common loop, the `for` loop, in both JavaScript and VBScript.

Listing 16.3. The `for` loop is a simple method for executing a block of code for a given number of times.

```
JavaScript:
for (loop=1; loop<=5; loop++){
    ...Statements to repeat
}
end_point=5;
for (loop=1; loop<=end_point; loop++){
    ...Statements to repeat
}
VBScript:
for loop=1 to 5
    ...Statements to repeat
next
end_point=5
for loop=1 to end_point
    ...Statements to repeat
next
```

As you can see from Listing 16.3, `for` loops have a starting point and an ending point. In this example, a block of code repeats five times. Loops consist of three portions: the starting point, the ending point, and the loop index. The starting and ending points for the loop can be either definite numeric values or may be variables that change based on other criteria, as shown in Listing 16.3.

You can think of the loop index as a counter or an accumulator. During each pass of the loop, the loop index is incremented automatically by a value of 1. Therefore, in Listing 16.3, the loop index starts at 1, updates to 2, 3, and 4, and stops at 5. Loop indices are useful in your code to traverse through multiple properties or array values and are used as a pointer to an individual element.

Although the default is to increase a loop index by a value of 1, you can change the index to increase by 2, 4, -8, or any other amount. This can be handy in certain circumstances where the loop index is used to point to other objects or array elements.

JavaScript

The JavaScript implementation of for loops is as follows:

```
for (loop_index = starting point;
    stop condition;
    loop_index increment){

    ... Statements to be looped
}
```

The *starting point* is the first value that the *loop_index* is set to. The loop will continue to execute until a condition is met as defined by the *stop condition*. As long as the evaluation of this condition is true, the loop will continue. Any valid conditions may be performed like those used with the if statement.

The *increment* value instructs how the *loop_index* is to be updated. Using the default ++ indicates that the value should be increased by 1. Likewise, you could use -- to decrease the value by 1 or another shortcut syntax such as += or -= to add or subtract a particular amount to the *loop_index*. Valid operators are shown in Table 16.1, later in this chapter.

VBScript

VBScript uses the following syntax to implement loops:

```
for loop_index = starting point to ending point step increment value
    ... Statements to be looped
next
```

Similar to the JavaScript version of loops, VBScript indicates a starting and ending point for the loop. The loop will continue to execute until the *loop_index* exceeds the *ending point* value. Like the JavaScript version, you may control how the *loop_index* is updated by specifying an increment value after the step statement. This value can be only a positive or negative number and is added to the *loop_index* during each iteration of the loop.

It is important to note that although you can substitute variables for the start point, end point, or increment value, the for loop in VBScript does not make use of conditions to terminate the loop.

While...Wend Loops

Loops are useful for traversing through code for a given number of times. The for loop enables you to specify beginning and ending points for the loop. There will, however, be occasions when you would like to perform some actions while a condition is true. Listing 16.4 demonstrates a while loop that executes a block of instructions until the variable z is less than 10.

16

Listing 16.4. It is possible to loop while a condition is met.

```
JavaScript:
while (z<10){
    z++;
}
VBScript:
while z<10
    z=z+1
wend
```

JavaScript

In JavaScript, you simply need the following format for a while loop:

```
while (condition){
    ...Statements to repeat
}
```

> ### TIP
>
> Avoid circumstances where you can cause the application to go into an *infinite loop*. Infinite loops are loops that never terminate because the condition to terminate is never met. An example of a loop that never terminates is
>
> ```
> while (1){
> }
> ```
>
> Because the condition is always true, the loop will never terminate and your code will never continue. To avoid infinite loops, be sure that the conditions for your loops will always be met.

VBScript

VBScript follows a similar syntax for while loops as does JavaScript:

```
while condition
    ... Statements to repeat
wend
```

Unlike JavaScript, however, VBScript denotes code to be looped by the while... wend pair. wend in this case stands for "While END."

Do While...Until Loop

Although while loops are popular methods for repeating commands an unknown number of times, VBScript encourages the use of the do loop. This loop is available only within VBScript and essentially replaces the while loop. In fact, the do loop is more powerful and flexible.

> **NOTE**
>
> VBScript still supports the `while` syntax for seasoned Visual Basic or Visual Basic for Applications developers who are accustomed to that syntax. The preferred method for VBScript, however, is the do loop.

The general syntax for `do` loops is as follows:

```
Do While ¦ Until condition
    ... Repeated Statements
Loop
Or,
Do
    ... Repeated Statements
Loop While ¦ Until condition
```

First, notice that this loop is different from other loops because it denotes the block of code to be repeated in the loop with the `do` and `loop` statements. You will also notice that the loop can be executed either `while` or `until` a condition is true, as well as that the placement of this condition can be at the start or the end of the loop.

While or Until

Basically the difference is in the logic. You can create a `do` loop that works just as effectively with either the `while` or `until` statements, but one command may appear more logical than another. In general, one typically causes the loop to repeat while the condition is true, and the other causes the loop to repeat while the condition is *not* true.

The `while` syntax does exactly what it implies: It executes the loop while the condition holds true. Take the following example:

```
z=0
do while z<10
    z=z+1
loop
```

In this case, while the variable z is less than 0 the loop will repeat, causing z to be increased by 1. When z is greater than or equal to 10, the loop will stop because the condition is no longer met.

`until` statements also repeat statements in a loop until a condition is met. However, it is a subtle difference. `while` loops repeat when a condition is true, but `until` loops execute when a condition is false and stops once the condition is met (hence, `until` a condition is met). The following example will help clarify the difference:

```
z=0
do until z=10
    z=z+1
loop
```

An Introduction to Scripting Languages

CHAPTER 16

343

16

AN INTRODUCTION
TO SCRIPTING
LANGUAGES

In this example, z is not equivalent to 0 when the loop starts. Therefore, the loop repeats, increasing the value of z by 1. Once the value of z reaches 10, the loop stops, but not until then.

Loop Placement

With the do loop, it is possible to do the condition checking for the termination of the loop either directly after the do statement or after the corresponding loop statement. At first, you may think that there is no difference, but in reality there is a very subtle one. Let's start by looking at the example in Listing 16.5.

Listing 16.5. An incorrect position of the condition in this example could cause an error to occur.

```
Set fs = CreateObject("Scripting.FileSystemObject")
Set a = fs.OpenTextFile("c:\testfile.txt")
do
    j = a.ReadLine
loop until a.AtEndOfStream
a.Close
```

Listing 16.5 is a simple script that opens a file on the hard drive and attempts to read each line at a time from the file. However, there is a potential problem with this application. It is possible for the computer to try reading a line from the file although there are no lines left to read in the file. This could occur because the condition that checks for the presence of the end of the file falls after the actual reading from the file. Because the loop won't terminate until this condition is met, the loop will repeat once more even though the end of the file has been reached. In this case, it would be safer to place the condition in the do portion of the loop in order to test for the condition before performing a potential erroneous action.

There are other times, however, when you might want to place the condition at the end of the loop. For example, suppose the condition should be checked only after a variable in that condition has been initialized by a function call that is embedded in the loop. You would want the loop to execute at least once before checking the condition to stop. Listing 16.6 shows a good example of where placing the condition after the loop makes sense.

Listing 16.6. In this example, the value of result must be set first before testing.

```
do
    result=GetInformation("user",z)
    z=z+1
loop until result="VALID"
```

Instead of,

```
result=GetInformation("user",1)
z=2
do until result="VALID"
    result=GetInformation("user",z)
    z=z+1
loop
```

Building Nests

So far you have seen basic examples of conditional and looping statements. In reality, it is possible to place loops within other loops, conditions within conditions, conditions within loops, or loops within conditions. Just remember to clearly indicate which blocks of code are to be treated as part of the condition or loop. In JavaScript this means placing an adequate number of braces ({ and }), and in VBScript, this means matching the appropriate keyword. Listing 16.7 shows an example of nested loops and condition statements.

Listing 16.7. Placing loops within loops, conditions within a condition, or loops/conditions within loops/ conditions is referred to as *nesting*.

```
for z=1 to 10
    if myData(z)>100
        for a=1 to 2
            MsgBox myResults(a)
        next
    end if
next
```

> **TIP**
>
> You can probably tell that once you start nesting within a complex application, it becomes hard to find which blocks of code are affected by which statements. You should try to indent your code as shown in Listing 16.7 to make it more legible.

Hello...Operator?

Throughout this section, you have seen that there are operators used to assign information to variables and operators for performing condition testing. You're probably familiar with the common ones, such as addition (+), subtraction (-), multiplication (*), and division (/). But there are several additional operators that are valid for both JavaScript and VBScript. Tables 16.1 and 16.2 list valid operators for JavaScript. Table 16.3 lists similar operators for VBScript.

Table 16.1. The JavaScript assignment operators.

Operator	Function	Description
++	Increment	Increments a value by 1. In a sense, adds 1 to a value.
- -	Decrement	Decrements a value by 1 or subtracts 1 from a value.
+=	Addition Assignment	Example: x += 5 is equivalent to x = x+5, which simply adds 5 to the current value of x.

An Introduction to Scripting Languages

CHAPTER 16

345

16

AN INTRODUCTION
TO SCRIPTING
LANGUAGES

Operator	Function	Description
-=	Subtraction Assignment	Example: x -= 5 is equivalent to x = x-5, which subtracts 5 from the current value of x.
*=	Multiplication Assignment	Example: x *= 5 is equivalent to x =x*5, which multiplies the current value of x by 5 and assigns that result to x.
/=	Division Assignment	Example: x /= 5 is equivalent to x = x/5, which divides the current value of x by 5 and assigns that result to x.
-	Negation	The negation operator negates a value. Example: If x=5, -x would yield -5. If x=-5, -x would yield 5.
%	Modulus	This operator returns the remainder when two values are divided integrally. Example: 16 % 5 returns 1.
<<	Bitwise Shift Left	Converts a value to its binary equivalent and shifts the bits one place to the left. The result is converted back to a value.
<<<	Bitwise Double-Shift Left	Converts a value to its binary equivalent and shifts the bits two places to the left. The result is converted back to a value.
>>	Bitwise Shift Right	Converts a value to its binary equivalent and shifts the bits one place to the right. The result is converted back to a value.
>>>	Bitwise Double-Shift Right	Converts a value to its binary equivalent and shifts the bits two places to the right. The result is converted back to a value.
&	Bitwise AND	Converts both values to their binary equivalents and compares each bit by ANDing their values. The result is converted back to a value. Example: 10001000 & 11001010 would yield 10001000.
¦	Bitwise OR	Converts both values to their binary equivalents and compares each bit by ORing their values. The result is converted back to a value. Example: 10001000 ¦ 11001010 would yield 11001010.

continues

Table 16.1. continued

Operator	Function	Description
^	Bitwise Exclusive OR	Converts both values to their binary equivalents and compares each bit by XORing their values. The result is converted back to a value. Example: `10001000 ^ 11001010` would yield `01000010`.

Table 16.2. JavaScript conditional operators

Operator	Function	Description
==	Equal	TRUE is returned if the two operands in a condition are equal.
!=	Not equal	If the two operands are not equivalent, TRUE is returned.
>	Greater than	TRUE is returned if the first operand is greater in value than the second.
>=	Greater than	When the first operand's value is greater than or equal to the second's or equal to value, TRUE is returned.
<	Less than	The result is TRUE if the first operand is lesser in value than the second.
<=	Less than	If the first operand's value is less than or equal to the second operand's value, TRUE is returned.
&&	Logical AND	When comparing multiple conditions, && returns TRUE when the first condition's result is TRUE *and* the second condition's result evaluates to TRUE.
¦¦	Logical OR	If multiple conditions are compared, ¦¦ will return TRUE if either the first condition *or* the second condition evaluates to TRUE. If one condition is TRUE, the condition of another is basically ignored.
¦	Logical NOT	The NOT¦ operator will invert an operator's value. For instance, if an operator is TRUE, the NOT¦ operator will cause it to evaluate to FALSE.

Table 16.3. The VBScript assignment and conditional operators.

Operator	Function	Description
&	Concatenation	Appends a second string onto the end of the first.
-	Negation	Example: if x=5, -x=-5; if x=-5, -x=5.
+	Addition	Sums two numbers together.
-	Subtraction	Subtracts the second number from the first.
*	Multiplication	Multiplies two numbers together.
/	Division	Divides the first number by the second.
\	Integer Division	Divides the first number by the second and returns a result rounded to the nearest integer.
Mod	Modulus	Divides the first number by the second and returns the remainder.
^	Exponentiation	Raises the first number to the power of the second number. Example: $2^2=2^\wedge2=4$, $2^3=2^\wedge3=8$.
And	Logical AND	When comparing two values, And returns TRUE if the first condition is TRUE and the second condition is TRUE.
Or	Logical OR	When comparing two values, Or returns TRUE if either condition is TRUE or both conditions are TRUE.
Not	Logical NOT	Logically inverts a value. Example: if x=TRUE, Not x=FALSE.
Xor	Logical XOR	When comparing two values, Xor returns TRUE only if one condition is TRUE at once.
Eqv	Logical Equivalence	Two conditions are considered equivalent if either both conditions are TRUE or both conditions are FALSE.
Is	Object Comparison	If two variables being compared point to the same object, the result is TRUE.

Commenting Your Code

Within the scripting languages, it is possible to add text that has nothing to do with scripting commands. This text is documentation that you write within your code to help you and others understand the logic that is taking place in the scripts. It is essential that you write comments for your code in order for others to understand your workmanship. Others cannot possibly read your mind and follow your train of thought for coding the application the way you did.

Even if they could, you could save them a lot of time just by adding a few descriptions throughout your source code, describing what it is doing.

Comments do not have to be verbose. They should be kept concise so that another developer can understand what is being accomplished in the script without reading a novel. You also do not need to comment every line of code that you write. You should comment lines that appear confusing and add general comments to a section of code.

In JavaScript you can denote comments by using either a // character at the beginning of a single line, or the /* and */ pair of characters surrounding multiple lines of comments. VBScript also allows you to comment your code; however, you can comment only a single line at a time via the ' character at the beginning of the line.

Bug Zappers

As you design your JavaScript and VBScript applications, undoubtedly you will come across instances where your scripts do not appear to be functioning correctly. Or worse, unexpected results are occurring. When these events arise you need to debug your application, finding possible problems in the application and repairing them.

JavaScript and VBScript are simple extensions to the HTML Web page. A standard Web page does not contain any functionality for testing or debugging HTML files, so there is even less support for debugging scripts. Tools such as Visual InterDev that help you write complex scripts should be able to help you figure out what has gone wrong with them. Visual InterDev provides debugging capabilities by returning error messages with exact line numbers at which the script failed. Often, you will need more information to fix problems, however. Therefore, here are a few suggestions to help you figure out what is working or not working with your own custom scripts. Incidentally, more detailed coverage of script debugging can be found in Chapter 14, "Using Microsoft Script Debugger to Eliminate Problems."

What to Debug

Every problem with source code is related to its own unique design. It is impossible to suggest a guideline for debugging your applications, but here are a few things to consider:

- Insert debugging points throughout your code. Make an educated guess as to where the script is failing, and place debugging statements just before and after that section of the script. If both debugging statements appear when you run the script, chances are the problem is further down in the script. If neither statement appears, then the problem lies at the beginning of the script. If only the first debug statement appears, the problem lies somewhere in the block of code between the two debug points.

- You can place debugging points around larger sections of code, but keep in mind that you may need to narrow the focus in order to find the exact line that is causing the problem.

An Introduction to Scripting Languages

CHAPTER 16

349

16

AN INTRODUCTION
TO SCRIPTING
LANGUAGES

- Usually debug points are messages such as "executed search successfully." But instead of simply indicating how far the script executed, you will probably need to return variables. More often than not, scripts don't execute correctly because the programmer thinks that a variable is set to a particular value when in reality it is not. Be sure to place the values of variables in question into the debug messages.

- Consider using message boxes for client-side scripts and log files of errors and variables for server-side scripts.

MsgBox or Alert

It's not the most elegant method, but you can learn a lot by reading messages that appear on the client side of the application. If a client script is not functioning properly, you can embed VBScript MsgBox or JavaScript Alert commands to display content in a message box. The advantage to this approach is that program execution suspends until you dismiss that dialog box. Therefore, you can never miss the information that is being displayed.

As convenient as message boxes are, you should never use them to display information within server-side scripts. Sometimes message box commands will display their content on the server computer's screen, which you can't read unless the machine is nearby. To make matters worse, you cannot dismiss that message box if you can't see it!

Another disadvantage with messages is that you must dismiss each message box in order for the program to continue. If you have many message boxes scattered throughout, this can become annoying very quickly.

Log Files

Another approach is to write log files of the debug statements instead of displaying message boxes. These ASCII text files simply contain messages that you would normally display in message boxes, only they are written sequentially to the file.

With logged debug statements you can allow the entire program to execute without constant, annoying message boxes. You can also review all debug information, whereas you may "miss" seeing the data in a message box if you dismiss it too quickly by mistake. Listing 16.8 demonstrates how you can write data to a file using VBScript.

Listing 16.8. You can write debug information to a file for later review.

```
Set fs = CreateObject("Scripting.FileSystemObject")
Set a = fs.OpenTextFile("c:\debug.txt", ForAppending, TRUE)
a.WriteLine("Search completed successfully.")
a.Close
... some more functionality
Set a = fs.OpenTextFile("c:\debug.txt", ForAppending, TRUE)
a.WriteLine("Some more functionality completed successfully.")
a.Close
```

In Listing 16.8, you might notice that each time a debug line is to be added to the debug log file, the file is reopened and then closed. Sometimes when working with files, not all information is written to the file until the file is closed. The information is sometimes stored in a cache until committed via a `close` command. If this is the case and the file is opened only once at the beginning of the script code and then closed at the end, then some information might not be captured to the file. For example, if the script crashes somewhere in the middle of the script, the `close` statement will never be reached and the cache may never be written to the file. Constantly opening and closing the file between script code will help ensure that the cache is constantly flushed.

Summary

It is difficult to cover all of the nuances of two programming languages as complete as VBScript and JavaScript within one chapter. If you would like additional information on programming in these languages, you may want to consult other books such as *JavaScript Unleashed* or *VBScript Unleashed* by Sams.net Publishing.

I hope this chapter has covered the basics for you and introduced you to the fundamentals of programming scripts using the VBScript and JavaScript languages. In the next chapter, you will build on your scripting knowledge and learn how to integrate scripts with objects such as ActiveX or Java applets.

Extending Pages with Controls and Objects

by John J. Kottler

IN THIS CHAPTER

CHAPTER 17

This chapter picks up where the previous one left off by showing you how to put scripting languages to work. In this chapter you learn how to use VBScript and JavaScript—along with objects such as Java applets and ActiveX controls—to add interactivity to previously bland Web pages. You also find out all about HTML form objects and browser objects, and how they are used in conjunction with scripting languages to perform practical functions in the context of a Web page.

You may be surprised to find out that the scripting you learn about in this chapter is presented outside the context of Visual InterDev. This is done specifically to show you what is happening behind the scenes of a script. When you finish the chapter, you'll be better prepared to let Visual InterDev handle some of the dirty work and automate the scripting process. You'll also appreciate it much more!

What Are Objects and Controls?

If you are familiar with object-oriented programming (OOP), chances are you are already intimately familiar with the concepts of objects, properties, methods, and events. Object-oriented programming has become exceedingly popular, particularly with the advent of graphical user interfaces in operating systems such as Windows and Windows 95. The architecture surrounding object-oriented programming lends itself nicely to integrating within other environments. With object-oriented technology, it's easy to change components of an application without changing the entire application. OOP shields developers from the intricacies of the object and its functionality and enables the developer to simply use that object.

For instance, when Visual Basic was introduced, the concept of Visual Basic controls was introduced as well. These controls allowed the Visual Basic developer to expand the capabilities of Visual Basic. If Visual Basic did not contain a control that was required by the developer, the developer could find another suitable third-party control that could be used. These controls could be thought of as objects. It is possible to include the objects in your own application, change the appearance and functionality of the object via its exposed properties, invoke actions that the object could perform through its exposed methods, and even be notified when particular actions affect the object via events. With these objects, it is possible to use the objects without knowing exactly how these objects work. For instance, in the case of an image-editing object, you would want to use a color balance function, but you wouldn't really care how that function was actually implemented.

Although it was initially intended for traditional software development on a computer, object-oriented technology has found its way as a natural fit into Internet development. Today's numerous sites on the Web are more interactive than they were a year ago. Partially, this is because of the increased use of databases and server scripts; however, part is due to the use of client-side objects that users can interact with. Java applets and ActiveX controls are examples of objects that can be used on your Web pages. The use of these controls enables you to create more robust, user-friendly, and interesting Web sites. In this section, you will learn how to use objects such as ActiveX controls within your Web pages.

Client Versus Server

Again, as with everything covered in this section of the book, there is a question of when to use objects on the server and when to use client-side objects. There are many objects that VBScript and JavaScript can utilize on both the client and server. As with everything, the choice of which objects to use and where to use them depends partially on the application that you are building.

Visual InterDev includes several controls that are particularly useful for server-side development. Chapter 19, "Creating Active Server Pages," covers the controls that are available on the server in more detail. These controls range from banner-ad rotators to database connectivity controls.

As you create your site, you will find that the server-side objects will typically be used on the server for performing database actions or other server-related tasks. You will also find that session management and dynamically generated pages will be accomplished via server-side controls. But there will be times when you want to implement client-side controls as well. For instance, if you are creating an application where the user must specify a date, you might want to use a calendar control that draws a calendar object in the client's window. With such a control, you do not need to write routines to verify that valid dates are chosen, nor do you need to write code that formats the calendar views. Your scripts merely need to take advantage of the calendar object's features.

> **TIP**
>
> You should not use controls with a server-side application if that control *requires* user interaction. Most server applications are written to execute without any intervention. Just as you would not want to display message boxes on a server computer because they can't be dismissed, your application should not use controls that require a user at the server computer.

Scripting Languages and Objects

Both the JavaScript and VBScript languages enable you to write code that interacts with objects and controls such as a calendar control. These objects can be either Java applets, ActiveX controls, or other objects inherent to the Web browser or Web server. Different objects are available depending on whether you are writing client- or server-based code. In general, there are three things you can do with objects. You can set the attributes or *properties* of objects, invoke functions or *methods* of objects, and design scripting functions that handle *events* triggered by the objects. But before you do any of these, you must specify to include the object with your Web page.

Embedding Objects

Just like in VBScript or JavaScript coding, objects must be embedded within your HTML or Active Server Pages in order to function. If you are creating an HTML page for the client computer, you can use objects that require user intervention such as the calendar control. When designing server-side Active Server Pages, you can make use of the special server controls that are available. In either case, the method for embedding controls is the same for client and server pages.

> **NOTE**
>
> In Chapter 18, "Using Visual InterDev to Create Scripts," you will learn more about adding and editing objects using the Visual InterDev interface. But it is still important to understand what Visual InterDev is doing. Because although Visual InterDev makes the insertion of objects easier, you still will see the HTML code that Visual InterDev generates in your application.

Inserting ActiveX Controls

As you are aware, ActiveX controls are different than Java applets. Therefore, a separate syntax is used for embedding ActiveX controls from that used for Java applets. To insert an ActiveX control on a client or server Web page, you use the <OBJECT> tag. The <OBJECT> tag expects the following attributes:

```
<OBJECT
    classid = "CLSID:ActiveX Class ID"
    id = Object Name for use on page
    width = Width of the object in pixels
    height = Height of the object in pixels
    data = URL for data to be used by ActiveX control
    type = Internet MIME type for the data being used
    standby = Text to display while the object and data are loaded
    server = URL to use to obtain control if not already local
>
</OBJECT>
```

ClassID

Every ActiveX control that is created can be uniquely identified by a GUID, a Globally Unique ID. This sequence number is generated when the ActiveX control is created and stays with that object forever. This unique ID is guaranteed to be unique for every ActiveX control created. Therefore, when you embed an object, you indicate the unique identifier that is interpreted to the actual corresponding control. Each type of ActiveX control contains its own unique ID, yet that unique ID is used on all computers to identify that specific control. Therefore, the first step to embedding an ActiveX control is to identify which control you want to embed via its ClassID, which is the object's GUID.

Let's take an example of the Internet Explorer Web browser, which almost every Windows 95 user should have installed on his or her computer. The Internet Explorer Web browser window itself is in reality an ActiveX control, so you can reuse the browser in your own custom applications or in the Windows 95 operating system itself. The unique number that is used to identify the Internet Explorer browser control is {0002DF01-0000-0000-C000-000000000046}. If you used this ID number as the ClassID parameter for the <OBJECT> tag, you would embed the Internet Explorer Web browser window.

So now you're wondering, "Just where did that GUID number come from?" No, most people do not memorize these IDs, and there is no documentation in any help files that show these IDs. You need to find these IDs on your own. However, there is a tool that helps you find them: the Registry Editor that comes with Windows 95.

As you know, the system Registry for Windows 95 is the main database that contains all information about the computer system. In addition to containing hardware information or personal settings, it also holds the information about all registered ActiveX controls. Each ActiveX control that is registered has its unique ClassID or GUID registered in the Registry as well.

To find a ClassID for a particular object, you must follow these steps:

1. Run the Registry Editor (regedit.exe).
2. Find the control you want to embed within the My Computer\HKEY_CLASSES_ROOT directory.
3. Use the ClassID listed in the system Registry for that control with the ClassID attribute of the <OBJECT> tag.

Figure 17.1 depicts a typical Registry screen. In this example, the ClassID (CLSID) for the Internet Explorer control is highlighted. You can quickly see that the number in the right pane of the Registry Editor is the same number mentioned earlier for the Internet Explorer browser control.

FIGURE 17.1

The Registry Editor can be used to find objects and their associated ClassIDs.

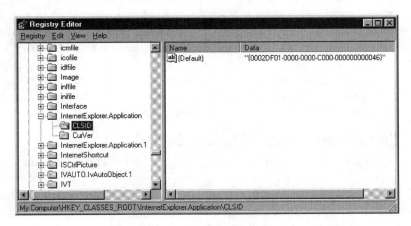

This is certainly not the easiest or least painful method for inserting objects on a Web page! Fortunately, tools such as Microsoft's Visual InterDev list all of the controls you can choose from and automatically find and insert these unique IDs into your Web documents for you.

It's in the Name

The `id` attribute of the `<OBJECT>` tag is highly important if you want to do something with the object after it has been embedded on a Web page. If you want to change any of the attributes of the object or invoke its functions, you need to name the object so that it can be addressed by your scripts later. Each object on a page must be assigned a unique name so that no objects are confused by the script engine. It's possible to have multiple objects of the same type on a single page, but you must give each instance of that object a separate name.

Downloading Controls

Not all users browsing your Web site will necessarily have the ActiveX control that you use on their local computer. If they don't have the control, they cannot experience the Web page as it was designed to be used. Fortunately, it is possible for a user to download ActiveX controls that are necessary for viewing a Web page. Although the process of downloading controls is automatic, it is sometimes useful to specify a particular URL to use when retrieving the control. If you want to specify the exact URL at which an ActiveX control can be found, you can use the `server` attribute of the `<OBJECT>` tag.

Data and Types

Some ActiveX controls are simple controls that provide enhancements to the browser or Web page. Other controls require particular data files in order to function. If the ActiveX control being used requires a file, the data file as well as the type of file can be specified using the `data` and `type` attributes of the `<OBJECT>` tag.

An example of when you might want to use these attributes would be with a video playback control such as ActiveMovie. With this control, you might want to specify the location URL for the movie to play in the `data` property. The `type` attribute is the MIME (Multipurpose Internet Mail Extension) type for the data being transferred. This type is used within Internet documents to indicate the format of the data being transferred. Typically data is transferred using the `text/html` type, but when other forms of data such as audio files are transferred, the data is indicated by another identifier, such as `audio/wav`. These types can be defined in Internet Explorer within the Programs | File Types... option.

Default Parameters for ActiveX Controls

When you first insert a control on a Web page, you will probably want to specify some default settings for the control. The settings, also referred to as the properties for the control, can be set by standard HTML within the `<OBJECT>` tag. Until now you have noticed the `<OBJECT>` and associated `</OBJECT>` tag, but you did not find any information between the two. The `<PARAM>` tag is one tag that is valid between these `<OBJECT>` tags.

Most ActiveX controls enable you to change their attributes. A calendar control, for instance, enables you to change the current year displayed by the control. Attributes that can be modified are referred to as the object's *properties*. As you will see shortly, these properties can be changed by scripting languages such as VBScript or JavaScript, but they can also be set by the <PARAM> tag. The <PARAM> tag accepts two attributes:

```
<PARAM    NAME = Name of property to change
          VALUE = Value to change property to
>
```

Therefore, to set the current year for your calendar control to 1998, you could use the following <PARAM> tag:

```
<PARAM    NAME = year
          VALUE = 1998
>
```

Embedding Java Applets

As powerful as ActiveX controls are, it is also nice to know that you can use Java applets on your Web pages and connect these applets to JavaScript or VBScript scripts. Sun's Java applets have been used on the Net for a slightly longer time than Microsoft ActiveX controls. The benefits and drawbacks of both ActiveX controls and Java applets have been widely discussed and have become a type of feud between proponents of either technology. Microsoft ActiveX fans dismiss Java, and Java supporters are often against Microsoft. Whatever the result of these battles, the ultimate decision is based on a developer's personal preference as well as the targeted audience for the site. For instance, although ActiveX controls are powerful, you might find that you need to rely on Java applets because you cannot be sure that all browsers accessing your external site are ActiveX-aware.

In any case, the following syntax is used to insert a Java applet in a client-side application or a Java servelet in a server-side application:

```
<APPLET   CODE = Java Applet (.class file)
         WIDTH = Width in pixels
        HEIGHT = Height in pixels
          NAME = Name used for Java applet in scripts
>
</APPLET>
```

Applets are a little simpler to embed than ActiveX controls. To place an applet on your page, you use the <APPLET> and corresponding </APPLET> tags. Within the <APPLET> tag itself are several attributes that you can set.

Break the Code

The CODE attribute of the <APPLET> tag enables you to specify the Java applet that you want to be displayed within the Web browser or invoked by the server-side application. This attribute basically holds the name of the Java class that you want to display. Whenever a Java applet is created, it is compiled as a `.class` file. This file is used to identify which Java applet to download. This technique is just a tad simpler than embedding a GUID for an object after finding it in the system Registry! Java is like ActiveX in that, if the Java applet does not already exist in the local client's cache, the applet will be transferred to the machine before it is run.

Name

Again as with ActiveX controls, if you plan on changing properties or invoking functions of a Java applet, you need to give each applet its unique name within your Web page. Then you can reference that Java object in your custom scripts by its name. Like ActiveX, you can have multiple Java applets on a single Web page. Also like ActiveX, you should name each instance of a Java applet by a separate name so that the script engines do not confuse the objects.

Properties

Now that you understand objects such as ActiveX controls and Java applets and how to include them on your pages and in server scripts, you will want to learn how to control them via script languages such as JavaScript or VBScript. Objects such as ActiveX controls often contain several variables that you can set to determine the characteristics of that object. These attributes or properties can easily be set via VBScript or JavaScript and can also be read by either language. Properties for an object can be anything such as a background color for the object, how far a progress bar should show, the year to display in a calendar control, or simply the text to be displayed with the object.

In both JavaScript and VBScript, you can denote object properties by using the name of the object in your source code, followed by a dot (.) and then the name of the property. If you are setting a value for an object's property, you can assign the numeric or string value by using the standard assignment operator (=). You can also examine the values of a property by simply using the `object.property` syntax in your expressions. In Listing 17.1, a progress bar is added to a Web page and named `ProgressBar1`. The code in Listing 17.1 demonstrates how to assign or query properties of the progress bar.

Listing 17.1. Properties can easily be set or queried in VBScript or JavaScript.

```
<OBJECT ID="ProgressBar1" WIDTH=100 HEIGHT=20
    CLASSID="CLSID:0713E8D2-850A-101B-AFC0-4210102A8DA7"
    DATA="DATA:application/x-oleobject">
</OBJECT>
<SCRIPT LANGUAGE="VBScript">
' Check the value of ProgressBar1
' If it's less than 50% full, make it 50%
if ProgressBar1.value < 50 then
    ' Make the Progress Bar 50% full
    ProgressBar1.value=50
end if
</SCRIPT>
```

> **TIP**
>
> Don't forget to assign names to the objects on your Web page. If you want to reference these objects in your custom scripts, each object must have a unique name on the page. This name will be used in your scripts to identify which exact object you want to work with.
>
> When embedding ActiveX objects, the names of these controls are determined by the ID parameter of the <OBJECT> tag. To address Java applets by name, you can assign names via the NAME parameter for the <APPLET> tag.

Methods

You'll remember that you can create functions for common actions that you want to execute multiple times from separate sections of your application. Objects have functions of their own as well. These functions are referred to as *methods* for the objects. Just as you can change the attributes of an object via its properties, you can instruct objects to perform actions by invoking their methods.

Object methods are accessible in both JavaScript and VBScript and follow a similar notation to properties. To invoke a method, you simply use the `result = object.method(parameters)` syntax. Because methods are just like functions, they can accept parameters for defining the actions in the method, and they can return results to the statement that called the method. However, depending on the object, some of an object's methods might not require parameters at all or might not return results. These are optional parameters for some methods of objects.

> **NOTE**
>
> If you choose to invoke a method that does not return a result, you must use the `call` statement in VBScript. The `call` command instructs VBScript to execute a method or function that does not return data. If you are using the method as a function and your code uses the returned value, you can simply do the assignment within your code.

Listing 17.2 demonstrates how a method is invoked for a Web browser ActiveX control. This example actually places an Internet Explorer Web browser window within your normal Web browser window! This Web browser control supports several methods, including the `GoHome()` method, which displays the browser's home page.

Listing 17.2. Methods such as GoHome() can be invoked using the JavaScript and VBScript languages.

```
<OBJECT ID="WebBrowser1" WIDTH=300 HEIGHT=151
    CLASSID="CLSID:EAB22AC3-30C1-11CF-A7EB-0000C05BAE0B">
    <PARAM NAME="Height" VALUE="150">
    <PARAM NAME="Width" VALUE="300">
    <PARAM NAME="AutoSize" VALUE="0">
    <PARAM NAME="ViewMode" VALUE="1">
    <PARAM NAME="AutoSizePercentage" VALUE="0">
    <PARAM NAME="AutoArrange" VALUE="1">
    <PARAM NAME="NoClientEdge" VALUE="1">
    <PARAM NAME="AlignLeft" VALUE="0">
</OBJECT>
<P>
<INPUT LANGUAGE = "VBScript"
            TYPE = BUTTON
           VALUE = "Go Home"
         ONCLICK = "call WebBrowser1.GoHome()">
```

Events

So far you've learned how you can control objects and applets from JavaScript or VBScript code. However, there will be occasions when you want your script to react to an action that a user performs on other objects. For instance, when a user clicks on a spin button to increase an entry value, you want to update a variable within your script.

When an action such as a mouse click is performed on an object, that object can send a message to the VBScript or JavaScript code, instructing the script that an action occurred on the object. This passing of messages to signal particular actions to other objects is common in object-oriented technology. The code that you write to do something when it receives one of these messages is referred to as an *event*. For each action that is possible on the object, you could write an event to handle that action in your script. For instance, if a "clicked" script is available for a button object, you could write a script event that is triggered when a user clicks on that button.

Two types of events are available for the Web browser: events that are triggered from objects such as ActiveX controls embedded on a Web page and events that are triggered from form objects. Although similar in theory, there are slight differences between the two.

> **NOTE**
>
> Currently, VBScript can act only on events triggered by ActiveX controls and not Java applets. Likewise, JScript/JavaScript does not adequately support ActiveX controls. In the future, these limitations should be eliminated. However, in the meantime, if your applications require the processing of events, consider using JavaScript with Java applets and VBScript with ActiveX controls.

ActiveX Events and VBScript

To begin the discussion of handling events in your scripts, let's first talk about handling events triggered by objects such as ActiveX controls. When a user clicks on an object such as a spin button control, events are fired by the object to be received by a script within the Web page. The scripts that act on events fired by an object are referred to as *event handlers*. In the case of the spin button, two events that can be triggered by the actual spin button control are SpinUp and SpinDown. The appropriate event is triggered for when the user clicks on the up arrow or the down arrow of the button control. Both of these events can be handled by VBScript code to perform different actions.

To look further at implementing event handlers, let's first examine some source code. Listing 17.3 displays a simple HTML page with a spin button control and some VBScript for handling that control.

Listing 17.3. Embedding a simple control such as a spin button requires that you first insert it with the <OBJECT> tag and then implement the SpinUp and SpinDown events.

```
<HTML>
<SCRIPT LANGUAGE = "VBScript">
value = 0
Sub MySpinButton_SpinUp()
    value = value + 1
    if value>10 then value=10
End Sub
Sub MySpinButton_SpinDown()
    value = value - 1
    if value<1 then value = 1
End Sub
</SCRIPT>
<BODY>
Click on the spin button:
<P>
<OBJECT
    ClassID = "B16553C0-06DB-101B-85B2-0000C009BE81"
        ID = MySpinButton
     WIDTH = 15
    HEIGHT = 19
>
<-- Set background color of control to white -->
<PARAM  NAME = "backcolor"
      VALUE = "16777215"
>
If you had an ActiveX-capable browser, you'd see a spin button.
</OBJECT>
</BODY>
</HTML>
```

As you can see from Listing 17.3, two VBScript subroutines have been added to accommodate for the two events that will be triggered when a user clicks on the up and down arrows of the spin button MySpinButton control. Whenever a user clicks on the up arrow, the SpinUp event is triggered and `value` is incremented by one. Likewise, when the down arrow is clicked, the `SpinDown` event is triggered and `value` is decremented by one.

In general, you can implement event handlers within your VBScript code by using the following syntax:

```
Sub ControlName_ControlEvent(Event Parameters)
... some VBScript code
End Sub
```

Each subroutine that handles events can be identified by the name of the control, followed by an underscore (_) and the name of the event that will be sent by the control to the script. In addition, some events will pass additional information about the control as part of the event. A fictitious `ColorChanged` event for a color control, for instance, could send the value of a color selected by the user.

> **TIP**
>
> Valid properties, methods and events for controls are often documented somewhere in the help files that accompany those controls. However, tools such as Visual InterDev also display valid control information via their development environment. In Chapter 18, you will see just how to select properties and methods from ActiveX controls and create events without any knowledge of the control.

HTML Form Events

Earlier I mentioned that there are two different types of events that can be handled by VBScript: ActiveX events and HTML form object events. Let's now examine how to handle events triggered by objects such as buttons or fields on a form.

You are probably familiar with creating HTML forms by now. You know that you can embed objects within a form such as buttons, entry fields, radio buttons, and checkboxes. You may also already have some experience with reading the results of these controls as input to server-side scripts such as CGI applications. However, it is also possible to do a great amount of work with these controls locally. In a little while, you will be introduced to the object hierarchy for form controls. For right now, let's review what forms of events are available as a result of using these controls on a Web page HTML form. With VBScript or JavaScript, it is possible to attach logic to these objects as well to make HTML forms even more powerful.

Just as the spin button control creates an event called `SpinUp` when a user clicks on that button, form objects on an HTML page send events of their own. Table 17.1 lists some valid events that are available for form objects as well as the objects to which these events apply.

TIP

Why would you want to handle events triggered by HTML form objects? Well, more than once you will probably create an interface for other ActiveX controls or Java applets on your Web page. You somehow need to know when a user selects something such as a button on your Web page in order to update the other objects appropriately. You can also use the onBlur event to perform validation checks on data entered into forms. As you develop Web pages that are more interactive on the client side, you will find many uses for these events.

But don't think that events are valid only on the client. Server objects can create events that could be handled by VBScript or JavaScript as well. For instance, with a database, your server script could invoke a method for the database object that compacts the database, which may take a few minutes. When the database has finished compacting, the database control could trigger a finished event. This event could be handled by the script for a Web page and in turn continue processing or invoke other scripts.

Table 17.1. Several events are available for programmatic control by HTML form objects.

Event	Description	Applies To
onFocus	This event is triggered whenever a user clicks on the form object or presses the Tab key to select that object.	Text Fields Text Areas Selections
onBlur	Code will be executed for this event when a user either presses the Tab key to move off of an object or clicks on an object other than the current object on the form.	Text Fields Text Areas Selections
onSelect	Just as you can highlight text with your mouse in a word processor, you can highlight text in an entry field on a form. When you select that text, this event will be triggered.	Text Fields Text Areas
onChange	Whenever contents in a field change, this event is executed.	Text Fields Text Areas
onClick	As its name implies, whenever you click on an object with the mouse, this event is triggered.	Buttons Radio Buttons Check Boxes Submit Buttons Reset Buttons

continues

Table 17.1. continued

Event	Description	Applies To
onSubmit	It is possible to execute script code when the Submit button is clicked on a form. This event is triggered when that button is pressed.	Form Submission

Capturing Form Events

To capture events fired by form objects, you first need to assign the events for each object. If you've worked with HTML forms in the past, you are already quite familiar with the <INPUT> tag. This tag enables you to create input controls within an HTML form such as buttons, text objects, radio buttons, or checkboxes. The same tag also provides additional support for associating scripts to be executed on particular events that affect these form objects.

You will recall that the <INPUT> tag usually follows this format:

```
<INPUT  NAME = Field Name
        TYPE = "text, checkbox, button or radio"
       VALUE = Default Value
        SIZE = Display Size
       Event = "custom script"
    LANGUAGE = "VBScript or JavaScript"
>
```

Immediately you should recognize the addition of two attributes to the <INPUT> tag: *Event* and LANGUAGE. With these two attributes, it is possible to specify scripting code that is to execute when a user performs an action on the object.

> **LANGUAGE:** The LANGUAGE attribute in this case is identical to the LANGUAGE attribute of the <SCRIPT> tag. It enables you to specify which scripting language you will be using for your custom code. When used with the <INPUT> tag, it instructs which language is to be used to interpret instructions found in the *Event* attribute.
>
> *Event*: This attribute specifies one of the valid event names listed in Table 17.1. You can use any of the event names listed in Table 17.1, depending on the action you want to take. For instance, if you are creating a button object with the <INPUT> statement, you probably want to use the onClick event. The onClick event will then allow you to create script to execute when a user clicks on the button. After specifying the event you want to handle with script, you can code your script immediately after the *Event* attribute, or you could instruct the event to pass control to a VBScript or JavaScript function that you create to handle the event.

Listing 17.4 demonstrates how to use an event to validate a user's input when the user presses the Tab key to move to another entry field.

Listing 17.4. Data that a user enters can be easily verified by using event handlers such as onBlur.

```
<HTML>
<SCRIPT LANGUAGE = "VBScript">
Sub CheckAmount()
    if document.MyForm.TotalAmount.value<10 then
        Msgbox "You must enter a value greater than 10."
    end if
End Sub
</SCRIPT>
<BODY>
<FORM ACTION = "commit.cgi" NAME = "MyForm">
Enter the total number of people attending this meeting:<P>
<INPUT     NAME = "TotalAmount"
           SIZE = 4
       LANGUAGE = "VBScript"
         onBlur = "CheckAmount()">
</FORM>
</BODY>
</HTML>
```

TIP

Although you could write all of your script code within the *Event* attribute of the <INPUT> tag, it is recommended that you place these scripts within other functions and only invoke the functions from the <INPUT> tag. Embedding large amounts of JavaScript or VBScript source code within the *Event* attribute of the <INPUT> tag can make the code difficult to read and understand.

NOTE

Sometimes you will need to include functions or variables within the *Event* attribute of the <INPUT> tag. In these cases you might need to work with string expressions, which are typically denoted by double quotation marks (") around the text to be treated as a string. However, you might notice that to include information separated by spaces for attributes of HTML tags, you must enclose that information in double quotes.

Both JavaScript and VBScript can be easily confused by embedding double quotation marks within other double quotation marks. One quotation mark indicates the beginning of a string, while the second indicates the conclusion of that same string, not the start of an embedded string.

To avoid confusion, you can use the single quotation marks (') to surround strings within strings. For instance, if CheckItem is a function that expects a string of text and is invoked on a button's onClick attribute, you could use the following syntax:

```
<INPUT    TYPE = BUTTON
        onClick = "CheckItem('Monitor')"
          VALUE = "Check on Monitor Availability"
    >
```

HTML Form Object Hierarchy

You've learned about the capabilities offered by VBScript and JavaScript for handling events triggered by objects on an HTML form such as text fields or buttons. Although only events have been discussed so far, these objects are very similar to other ActiveX controls or Java applets in that they also contain properties or methods of their own. The actual number of properties and methods available for each of these form controls is quite robust, and a complete discussion would extend beyond the scope of this book. However, this section gives you a brief look at the object hierarchy offered by the Web browser and an example of how to access and control these object properties.

Web Browser Object Hierarchy

Both Netscape's and Microsoft's Web browsers enable scripting languages such as JavaScript and VBScript to retrieve and set properties for the Web browser itself as well as any controls associated with the browser. This includes elements of a Web document such as the form controls. In the previous section, you learned how these form objects generate events. In this section, you will see that these same objects contain attributes that can be controlled programmatically.

The Web browser itself can be referenced by VBScript or JavaScript. Actually, every item within that Web browser window is somehow related. You're familiar with your Web browser, whether it is Netscape Navigator or Microsoft Internet Explorer. Regardless of the browser you use, several components are similar in each. Think about a standard Web page. When you view a Web page, there is information within the browser regarding the current URL that you are viewing, navigational information such as what page was before or after this page in the history list, the actual data for the page you are viewing, and possibly additional windows or frames of Web page information. Figure 17.2 outlines the multiple components available as objects to scripting languages.

FIGURE 17.2.

Controls designed on an HTML form page can be referenced via VBScript or JavaScript as well.

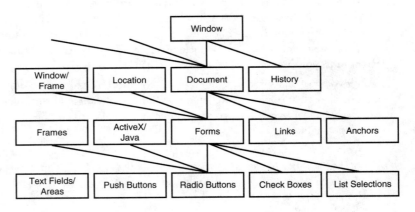

Referencing Browser Objects

With the object model displayed in Figure 17.2, it is easy to determine how to reference any component that exists on a Web page. You can reference any object that is a descendent of the root Window object by incorporating that object's name in your script for identifying that object. For instance, let's assume you want to access a form called MyForm within a Web page document. This object could be referenced in your VBScript or JavaScript application using the following syntax: document.MyForm. You will notice that any objects that exist lower than the Document object must be referenced by names that you assign to those objects. In the example, MyForm was assigned to a form object attached to the Document object.

To reference objects that exist in the lower layers of the chart in Figure 17.2, you must explicitly state the path to be traversed to access these objects. Each object that exists along the hierarchical path between the root and the object you want to reference must be included in the statement you build. Each object between the root and the destination object is separated by the dot (.) character. For instance, let's assume that you want to update text in a text field on a form. Let's call that field MyField and have it be on a form named MyForm. To reference this object in your script, you could use the following syntax:

To set the value of MyField:

```
document.MyForm.MyField.value = "New Text"
```

To read the value of MyField:

```
Alert (document.MyForm.MyField.value)
```

As you can see, after you have properly identified the object you want to modify, you may also indicate which property you want to work with or which method to invoke. Listing 17.4 gives an example of how object properties can be used to validate user input.

There are numerous methods and properties available for browser objects. Fortunately they can be easily viewed and edited using Visual InterDev. In Chapter 18, you will learn just how to adjust these properties or invoke these methods by making selections with the Visual InterDev tool. For more on objects, along with their properties and methods, see Appendix D, "VBScript Reference."

> **NOTE**
>
> Notice that it is quite possible for a window to be embedded within another window. This is typical with many Web sites, particularly those that use frames to divide the main browser window. Keep in mind that each subwindow of the main window also contains the same object hierarchy displayed in Figure 17.2. But each subwindow contains unique information specific to that subwindow's objects.

Summary

In this chapter you learned how to embed objects such as ActiveX controls and Java applets into your Web pages. You also learned how to control those objects dynamically via VBScript or JavaScript, as well as how to create event handlers for ActiveX controls. This chapter demonstrated how to do many of these tasks manually. In fact, Visual InterDev was not required to create the pages or source code discussed in this chapter. However, in the next chapter, you will see how the features of Visual InterDev make application development much faster and easier.

Using Visual InterDev to Create Scripts

by John J. Kottler

IN THIS CHAPTER

So far you have learned quite a bit about developing dynamic Web sites. You now know the concepts behind active programming, you have a basic knowledge of two popular programming languages for the Internet, and you even understand how to expand the capabilities of your Web site via controls or Java applets. However, as you have learned these technologies, you have found out how to implement these capabilities manually. You've probably already guessed that some tasks are quite tedious and have probably asked yourself, "Isn't there a better way?"

For quite some time, creating dynamic Web sites took a special talent. The ability to integrate graphics and content with cleverly written programs that handle the logic of the site is the skill necessary to create a successful site. You saw for yourself in the past few chapters that it is not the easiest task to insert ActiveX controls if you don't visit through the system registry first. You saw that it is possible to write scripts that handle some logic on both the client and server side, but that it is also possible for that logic to go awry or for you to forget about a particular function and code your application incorrectly because of an oversight. Manually inserting scripts and objects can be a real chore, and it takes a lot of time during initial development as well as during testing and debugging.

Fortunately, Microsoft's Visual InterDev development tool helps you to write scripts, insert controls, and manage your Web site more effectively. The tool handles many of the tedious tasks for you, enabling you to concentrate more on the site itself instead of how to make the technology work within your site. In this chapter, I review how Visual InterDev makes life easier for you by examining how to embed ActiveX controls, create HTML layouts, use the Script Wizard to create your code, and even work with design-time controls that make server-side development easier.

Inserting ActiveX Controls

In Chapter 17, "Extending Pages with Controls and Objects," you were introduced to the concept of object-oriented programming, especially as it is related to ActiveX controls or Java applets. You also quickly learned that to embed ActiveX controls by hand is not the most intuitive process. You'll recall that inserting an ActiveX control requires the use of the <OBJECT> tag, which in turn relies on a particular classid attribute. This attribute holds the *Globally Unique ID* (GUID) for an ActiveX control, which uniquely identifies a particular ActiveX control on any system. The benefit of a GUID is that such an ID is associated with only one type of control, such as a spin button, but that ID uniquely identifies that same control for any computer system on which that control is installed. The drawback of this approach is that these IDs are rather large and cannot be easily found anywhere but in the system registry files of either the Windows 95 or Windows NT operating systems. As you saw in the last chapter, finding, extracting, and using these IDs to identify controls within your Web pages became quite an arduous process.

Visual InterDev makes the use of ActiveX controls incredibly simple when creating Web pages within the Visual InterDev environment. With Visual InterDev, you can choose the ActiveX control you want to add to your Web page from a list of controls. After you have selected the control, you can make modifications to the properties of that control and save the information directly into your Web page.

Choosing Controls

To choose a control to add to your Web page, first make certain that you have the Web page source code selected in the Visual InterDev editor to which you want to add the ActiveX control. This can be any HTML page to which you want to add the control within your project. After you have selected the file to add the control to, position your text cursor within that file at a point where you would like to insert the control. Typically you will insert controls within the `<BODY>` portion of a Web page, because they appear in the final Web page at the spot where you inserted them. Therefore, if you are creating a Web page and would like to have text surrounding the control, you would position your cursor at the spot between the text where you would insert the control.

After you have chosen the spot to insert an ActiveX control, you can insert the control using one of two methods. You can insert a control by selecting ActiveX Control… from the Insert | Into HTML menu of the Visual InterDev menu bar, or you can right-click within the HTML file itself to choose Insert ActiveX Control… from a pop-up menu, as shown in Figure 18.1.

FIGURE 18.1.

You can easily insert ActiveX controls into your Web pages with the Visual InterDev editor.

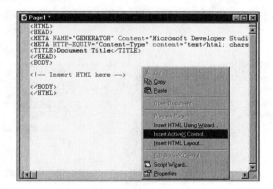

In either case, after you have invoked the command to insert a control, another window will appear within the Visual InterDev editor, prompting you to pick a control to insert. An example of this window is shown in Figure 18.2.

FIGURE 18.2.

Any ActiveX control registered on your development system can be inserted into a Web page.

The list of controls displayed in the Insert ActiveX Control window is the list of ActiveX controls that are registered in the system registry of the computer you are working on to create the Web page.

> **NOTE**
>
> It is important to note that Visual InterDev lists only those controls that are available on the same machine on which Visual InterDev is installed. Therefore, not every possible control in the world is displayed. If you want to use a control that is not found in the list, you must first install the control on your Visual InterDev computer system to make it available to other applications on that computer.

Setting Control Properties

After you have chosen the control to insert on your Web page, you will be presented with a small window that displays the control as well as a Properties window that will enable you to change its attributes. In Figure 18.3, the Progress Bar control was chosen to be placed on a Web page. Therefore, a small window displays how that control will appear on a Web page, while a Properties sheet opens for all the attributes of the Progress Bar.

FIGURE 18.3.

The Properties window enables you to set attributes for the ActiveX control you are adding to your Web page.

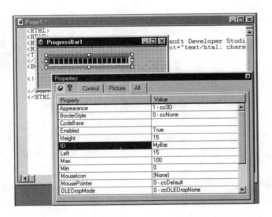

Notice that the Properties window contains three separate tabs. These tabs may change, depending on the control being inserted onto a Web page. Some controls make use of these tabs, and others might not implement separate tabs at all. These tabs help to break up large quantities of properties into more manageable sets or provide for custom dialog boxes that might be necessary in specifying complex properties.

In any case, you can display properties for an ActiveX control by clicking the All tab, which displays all the control's properties. There are numerous properties for every type of control, and the actual properties vary depending on the type of control being used. For example, our Progress Bar contains properties such as Max and Min values. Other controls, such as calendar controls, will contain properties such as Day, Month, or Year. Each control uses properties that are relevant to that control.

> **TIP**
>
> No matter what an ActiveX control does, chances are that each control will contain at least one property in common: the ID property. This property is used to set the control's name as it will be identified on the Web page and referenced by other scripts or controls. Make sure that you name each of your controls. Visual InterDev will automatically give a name to new controls that are created, but you will want to rename these controls to more appropriate names that you will remember when creating your Web site.

After you have set the properties for the control you are placing on your Web page, simply close the window that contains the preview of the control. Closing this window automatically closes the respective Properties window, but if you close the Properties window first, you will need to close the actual control window yourself.

Setting and Getting Properties with Scripts

Although it is simple to review and set properties for ActiveX controls with the Properties window, you will find it necessary to be able to retrieve and assign these properties using scripts. To assign properties via a scripting language such as VBScript, you could use the following syntax:

```
ActiveXControlID.property = value
```

Therefore, to set the value of the Progress Bar control, or how far the progress bar should be filled, you could set the value property of the control with the following statement:

```
MyBar.value = 25
```

This would fill one quarter of the progress bar, assuming that the maximum value for the progress bar is 100 and the minimum is 0.

Likewise, to retrieve property information from a control, you can simply use the ActiveX control name followed by the property in an expression, such as

```
Msgbox(ProgressBar.Value)
```

Invoking Methods

Each ActiveX control you place on a Web page may have properties or attributes that you can set, but it may also contain methods or functions that you can invoke. To invoke these methods, you can simply type scripts that activate methods or receive event information for the controls you add to a Web page. To invoke a method for an ActiveX control, you can use the following VBScript syntax:

```
ActiveXControlID.method(parameters...)
```

For example, if you were using a calendar ActiveX control and wanted to change to a particular date within that control, you would call a setDate method in which the parameters for that method would be the day, month, and year to change the control to.

Receiving Events

A large number of ActiveX controls are interactive; that is, an end user can click on the control with the mouse, and something happens as a result. In addition to an action actually being performed in the ActiveX control itself, it is possible to trap this action and have a script written in VBScript perform an additional action based on the event. To add events for an ActiveX control in VBScript, you can use the following:

```
Sub ActiveXControlID_EventName(parameters)
    ... Some VBScript
End Sub
```

With our Progress Bar control, it is possible for a user to click on the progress bar. Although clicking on the bar doesn't make the ActiveX control do anything by itself, we could write an event that traps that action and does something based on the action of clicking on the bar. For instance, let's make a dialog box appear that displays the current percentage complete when a user clicks on the progress bar. To do so, we could use the following script:

```
Sub MyBar_Click()
    Msgbox(MyBar.value)
End Sub
```

HTML Layout Controls

If you have developed Web pages in the past, you are already used to being restricted by what you can place within an HTML form as well as not being able to precisely place controls on a Web page. In addition, you cannot hide or disable controls within a Web page or maintain which controls are placed on top of others. Fortunately, HTML layout files enable you to do all these things you have been previously restricted from doing.

HTML layout files can be created within Visual InterDev quite easily, and are very similar to creating windows in Visual Basic or other similar Windows development tools. These layout files preserve everything about the placement of the control as well as its *Z-order attribute*, or how far under or above other controls it is. With HTML layout files, you can be quite granular with the placement of controls within the form area. In addition to using the basic form controls such as buttons, fields, radio buttons, and checkboxes, you can add a plethora of additional controls such as tab strips, toggle buttons, captions, hot spots, spin buttons, scrollbars, and even Web browsers!

Creating an HTML Layout

To start creating an HTML layout with Visual InterDev, you can choose New... from the File menu to display a window that contains five tabs for creating new files, new files based on wizards, new projects, new workspaces, and other new documents. Clicking on the Files tab reveals several different file types that Visual InterDev can create, including HTML documents, Active Server Pages, and HTML layouts. To create an HTML layout, choose HTML Layout from the New Files window. After you have selected to create a new HTML layout, several windows will appear within the Visual InterDev editor that are similar to those found in Figure 18.4.

FIGURE 18.4.

The HTML Layout editor in Visual InterDev allows you greater precision over the placement of ActiveX controls.

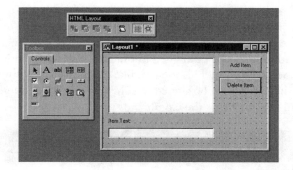

> **NOTE**
>
> If you already have a project, you might want to add a new HTML layout file directly to the project instead of creating a standalone file and adding it to the project later. To do this, simply choose New... from the Project | Add to Project menu.

The main window, which is labeled Layout1 * when you first create a new layout file, is a screen that allows you to preview exactly what the layout screen will look like on your final Web page. This window allows you to place controls within the window that can interact with each other or with other components of the Web page that are not included in the layout file. It is your canvas, if you will, for painting controls in the exact placement you desire.

The window labeled Toolbox is another extremely important window when it comes to designing layout files. This window contains icons of all controls that you can place on the layout window you are designing. By default, several components are included in the toolbox, such as buttons, text areas, list boxes, and the like. However, the tools shown in the toolbox window are simply ActiveX controls that you add to the HTML layout window. Therefore, it is possible to include additional ActiveX controls in your HTML layout toolbox.

To add or remove controls from the toolbox window, right-click on one of the controls in it. A pop-up menu will appear, allowing you to specify additional controls, delete the currently selected control, or customize the selected control. If you choose Additional Controls from the pop-up menu, another window will appear, listing all the ActiveX controls registered in the system. To include any of those controls in your standard HTML Layout tool palette, simply check the boxes next to the controls you want to include. To remove a control from the toolbar, choose the Delete option from the pop-up menu. Otherwise, to change the ToolTip text or icon for a tool on the toolbar, choose Customize from the pop-up menu.

The final window you will notice when you create a new HTML layout file is the HTML Layout window. This window is actually a toolbar within Visual InterDev that can be docked along the sides of the editing window or remain free-floating. The options in this toolbar allow you to specify options for each control, such as how far behind or in front of other controls it should be or whether it should be aligned to the grid displayed within the Layout window, or to invoke the Script Wizard. This toolbar, like other toolbars within the Visual InterDev development environment, can be altered to suit your needs by choosing Customize from the Tools menu and then selecting the Commands tab.

> **TIP**
>
> Like other controls, the HTML Layout control itself contains numerous properties that can be set. One property in particular that you might want to change is the ID property. This property specifies the name of the HTML Layout control and will be used to identify that control in scripts that you write on a Web page that interacts with that control.

Adding Controls

After you have created a new HTML layout, you'll notice that the initial window is blank. You will need to add controls to the window such as buttons, text boxes, or other controls to make the layout file truly useful. To add a control to the Layout window, simply click once in the toolbox on the control you want to add. If you then move the mouse cursor over the Layout window, you will notice that the cursor changes from a standard arrow to a cross-hair, with the graphic for the control you are adding in the lower-right corner of the cross-hair.

At this point, you may draw the control on the Layout window. To draw the control, simply hold down the left mouse button at the position where you want to start drawing the control and drag the mouse to specify the size of the control. A rubber-band outline will appear, showing you the size and position of the control you are placing as you move the mouse. When you have decided on the right location and size, release the left mouse button to drop the control into place. When you release the mouse button, you will see the control appear within the Layout window.

Just like the Layout window itself and all other ActiveX controls that you place within a Web page, you can change properties for the controls placed on a layout page. When you right-click on a control, a pop-up menu will appear, presenting the familiar Properties choice at the end of the menu list. Because controls on a layout page are ActiveX controls, their properties and values range just as ActiveX controls do. However, just like every other control I have discussed so far, the ActiveX controls in an HTML layout file contain the ID property, which should be set to a logical value in order to be referenced within your custom scripts or by the Script Wizard.

Saving and Using the Layout

After you have finished creating your layout, you will need to save the HTML layout file. You can do this at any time by choosing Save or Save As… from the File menu. Or, when you close the layout window, a message will prompt you asking if you want to save the file. HTML layout files are saved using the .alx extension. If you created the layout file without adding it to a project, you will need to remember the name of the layout file in order to include it later in your scripts.

TIP

When creating new files such as HTML files, Active Server Pages, or HTML layout files, consider adding them directly to the project you are working on. If you add them via the Project | Add to Project | New menu, these files will automatically be associated with the project and will make selection of these files for inclusion in your scripts or Web pages easier in the future. Including files within projects also makes the copying of the Web site from a local source to a remote server easier.

To use the HTML layout file that you just created in your Web pages, begin by finding the spot you want to insert the layout file within your HTML or Active Server Page (ASP) file. Like ActiveX controls, the results of HTML layout files appear within the Web page at the exact location where you add them, so make certain that the text cursor is at the position you want to add the layout. To embed the layout within your Web page, either choose HTML Layout from the Insert | Into HTML menu or right-click within the Web page editor to display a pop-up menu with the choice Insert HTML Layout. Either way, after you have chosen to insert an HTML layout in your Web page, a dialog box will appear, prompting you to select the HTML layout file to include. If you designed the layout file and saved it separately, you will need to choose the actual layout file. If you created the layout file as part of the project, a different dialog box will appear, displaying the HTML layouts available within the project. Figure 18.5 shows an example of this dialog box and a sample HTML layout file included in the current project.

FIGURE 18.5.

A list of available files in a project is available to facilitate the insertion of files such as HTML layouts within a Web project.

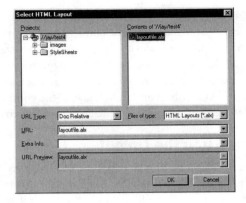

After choosing the HTML layout file to include in your Web page, you will notice that Visual InterDev will automatically place the correct <OBJECT> tags within your Web page that identifies the layout file you selected.

Control Properties and Scripts

Of course, HTML layout files add tremendous flexibility in the layout and design of Web pages, but they also require scripting in order to be truly effective. Fortunately, the Script Editor, which you will learn about shortly, supports HTML layout files and can create script easily for those controls or help you to write your own custom scripts. In general, as you are designing scripts to be executed within the HTML layout file, you will use the name of the individual controls in the file, followed by the dot (.) character and the property you want to examine/set or method you want to invoke. This approach is valid only when you are creating scripts within the HMTL layout file itself. If you are creating scripts that are in the Web page that need to access or set properties for a specific control within an HTML layout file, you will also need to specify the name of the actual HTML Layout control itself in your scripts.

Let's take a quick example to explain this further. Let's say that you have a simple text field (TextBox1) within an HTML layout file (Layout1) that you want to read in your Web page's VBScript function. In order to access the text field, you will need to specify the HTML layout object that was added to the page and then the control itself. Listing 18.1 gives a quick example of how to create a script in a Web page that displays contents of a Layout control.

Listing 18.1. Controls within an HTML layout file can be addressed within scripts of a Web page.

```
<OBJECT ID="Html_Layout1"
     CLASSID="CLSID:812AE312-8B8E-11CF-93C8-00AA00C08FDF">
        <PARAM NAME="ALXPATH" VALUE="layoutfile.alx" REF>
    </OBJECT>

<SCRIPT LANGUAGE="VBScript">
'   Display the contents of the TextBox control in the Layout File
    MsgBox Html_Layout1.TextBox1.text
</SCRIPT>
```

Why Use HTML Layouts?

As you have seen, creating HTML layout files is similar to creating Web pages. You simply place ActiveX controls within the layout that are to be displayed and connect the code between the controls via scripts. So how does using HTML layout pages differ from embedding ActiveX controls on a standard Web page?

First of all, HTML layout pages are not suitable for large volumes of text or graphics, such as documents. Although there are controls that allow you to add pictures and text areas to HTML layouts, neither offers the same robust capabilities of HTML Web pages. Also, although you can add complex controls to layout files that may contain HTML capabilities or more, it is still difficult to import data into those controls. If you are planning on creating Web pages with content, stick to traditional technologies such as HTML files and to editors such as FrontPage. HTML layout files are suitable for creating small portions of a Web page that are embedded within that Web page. The capabilities of HTML layout files enable you to create many controls that act together and can be positioned exactly within a Web page.

> **TIP**
>
> Remember that an HTML layout file is simply treated as an ActiveX control within your Web page. There is no reason why you can't add as many HTML layouts to a Web page as you like.

HTML layout files are embedded as ActiveX objects within Web pages. Therefore, in order to display content within a HTML layout page, all necessary controls must be transferred from the server to the end user's client browser when the page is viewed for the first time. If you are creating Web pages that are going to be used by low-bandwidth or diverse browsers, you may find that the ActiveX HTML Layout object may not be suitable and that you may need to use other technologies.

A definite benefit to ActiveX objects, however, is that the scripting code that you add to an HTML layout file is not readily available to viewers of your Web page. Even though the layout file is embedded within your Web page, a user can choose to view the Web page's source and will only find the HTML layout file as an object reference. The source code that was constructed within the HTML layout file is safely embedded within the .alx file that defines the HTML layout file.

> **TIP**
>
> If you are creating scripts that should not be viewed or edited by clients browsing your Web site, you might consider writing those scripts and storing them within HTML layout files. Clients viewing your Web page will not be able to view the contents of these scripts unless they can view the actual layout files themselves.

> **NOTE**
>
> HTML layout files (.alx) are simple text files that exist somewhere on the Web server where they can be referenced by Web pages. These files are simple text files and typically contain just basic HTML object definitions for ActiveX controls and scripts that you create for the layout file. These files are not complete HTML files, but rather fragments that are inserted into the Web page when the page is requested by a client.

Design-Time Controls

So far you have seen how Visual InterDev can help you create your Web projects by assisting you with the addition of ActiveX controls and HTML layout files. Although both of these assistants are helpful, they don't really aid you in creating your application, just in adding components to your application. In a moment you will learn about the Script Wizard, which truly helps you with the creation of scripts within your Web site. But there is another type of helper within Visual InterDev that helps you write scripts: design-time controls.

Design-time controls are very similar to other ActiveX controls that you embed on a Web page. They are controls that can have properties and settings just like ActiveX controls, but the key difference is that design-time controls embed actual script within your Web page. These controls are used to aid developers in writing scripts while a Web site is being designed, whereas ActiveX controls are displayed when the site is viewed.

Although you can make choices in design-time controls and set properties, these selections are translated to actual statements that are included within your Web page script. To understand this further, let's take a look at a design-time control included with Visual InterDev, the Data Range Wizard.

Inserting Design-Time Controls

There are two ways by which you can add design-time controls to your Web page in a project. First you must view the HTML page or Active Server Page into which you want to insert the design-time control. Again, as with other controls embedded within these pages, you must position the text cursor at the point in your HTML or ASP file where you want to insert the design-time control. After you have selected that point, you can choose to insert a design-time control; either select Use Wizard from the Insert | Into HTML menu or right-click within the file you are viewing and choose the Insert HTML Using Wizard option from the pop-up menu.

In either case, you will be presented with a window prompting you to choose the design-time control that you want to insert. Figure 18.6 illustrates a sample of this window with the Data Range Wizard control. From this window, you can choose the design-time control that you want to insert into a Web page.

FIGURE 18.6.
*There can be more than
one design-time control
available to insert into
your Web page.*

After you have selected the appropriate control, you may be presented with a window with attributes for that control, or a wizard may appear that prompts you for specific information. In the example of the Data Range Wizard, a wizard window will appear, asking you a few questions before inserting the results into your Web page. Figure 18.7 illustrates the first step of the Data Range Wizard.

FIGURE 18.7.
*Design-time controls
may feature wizards to
ease the setup of these
controls.*

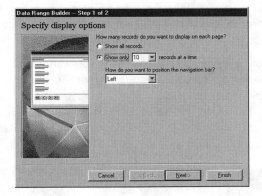

18

Properties for Design-Time Controls

After you have stepped through any questions posed by the design-time control's wizard, you will be presented with two windows, one containing a sample of the control you are embedding on the Web page and the other containing a full list of properties that you can set for the control. You also might notice that in the Web page that you are working on in the background, several statements have been added to include the design-time control in your Web page. You will also see script commands built in that window after you set properties for the control. Figure 18.8 shows a sample of the Data Range Wizard with its associated Properties window.

FIGURE 18.8.

Design-time controls, like other ActiveX controls, contain many properties that can be set.

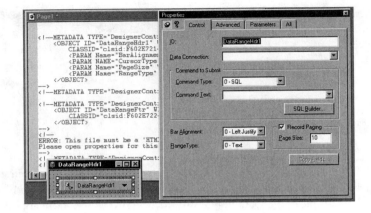

In the case of the Data Range Wizard control, you can choose among numerous settings that enable you to connect to a database and return the results in pages. The advantage of this control is that it automatically creates the script necessary for the database connection as well as appropriate script for controlling Page Forward, Page Backward, and other navigational buttons.

Once you have determined the properties you want to use for your page, the respective script for your choices will be updated in the window of the original HTML or ASP file when the control's windows are dismissed. The Data Range Wizard expects to write scripts to an Active Server Page. Therefore, the Active Server Page window that was being edited when the control was first inserted will contain the appropriate server-side Active Server script that controls database connections and record results.

> **NOTE**
>
> It is possible for you to place a design-time control in the wrong type of Web page for a site. For instance, the Data Range Wizard expects to create scripts within an Active Server Page, yet it is quite possible for you to insert the control within a standard HTML file. Watch the scripts that are built within the Web page file carefully. If there were any problems while the script was being generated by the control, these errors will appear within the Web page that you are working on, as will a suggestion for fixing the problem.

Design-time controls are useful because they can create a large number of script commands for you automatically. Often these controls will be useful ones that will encompass many capabilities that you would otherwise need to implement manually. But don't think that you are restricted to just the script that is automatically generated by the design-time control. You can, and often will need to, insert your own commands within the scripts generated to make the Web page truly useful.

The Script Wizard

You've learned quite a bit about controls and how to embed them within your HTML or Active Server Pages. But you haven't really seen how Visual InterDev can help you develop scripts, other than pre-made scripts that can be generated by design-time controls. But Visual InterDev does offer a helper for creating original scripts as well. The Script Wizard within Visual InterDev can create some basic scripts for handling events triggered by objects, updating properties, invoking methods of objects, or creating and maintaining custom subroutines or variables.

Developing Scripts

To understand the Script Wizard better, let's first take a look at a very simple application within a Web page. Let's say you want to create a Web page that contains an entry field and a button. The purpose of this page is to display the text Script Wizard! in the text field whenever a user clicks on the command button. (I told you this was a really simple example!) Listing 18.2 shows the code necessary for creating the entry field and command button in HTML.

Listing 18.2. A simple HTML application can be automated with the Script Wizard.

```
<HTML>
<HEAD>
<META NAME="GENERATOR" Content="Microsoft Developer Studio">
<META HTTP-EQUIV="Content-Type" content="text/html">
<TITLE>Document Title</TITLE>
</HEAD>
<BODY>

<INPUT SIZE=60 NAME="TextEntry"><BR>
<INPUT TYPE="BUTTON" VALUE="Set Text" NAME="SetIt">

</BODY>
</HTML>
```

Listing 18.2 simply paints the entry field and command button within an HTML page, so now let's invoke the Script Wizard to add the functionality to this application.

To start the Script Wizard, simply right-click somewhere within the Web page to display the common pop-up menu that you have seen numerous times already in this chapter. You will notice a Script Wizard choice toward the end of the menu. Clicking on this option will display a window similar to the one shown in Figure 18.9.

In this example, we want to update the text field whenever someone clicks on the SetIt button. So to start our script, we want it to be triggered whenever someone clicks on the button. Therefore, you want to select the Click event from the SetIt button in the leftmost column of the window. Because the action of clicking on the SetIt button will reset the value of the text field, the second step is to choose an object to affect by picking the Value property of the TextEntry field in the right column. The script is almost finished, but the final action must be set. In this case, we want `TextEntry.value` to be updated to the text `Script Wizard!` when the SetIt button is clicked. The action in this case would be the assignment of `TextEntry.value` to `Script Wizard!`. When you click the Insert Action button at the bottom of the window, a separate window will appear, prompting you for the text you want to assign to the text entry field. You can then type in the words `Script Wizard!` to complete the script. When you have finished, click OK at the bottom of the window to dismiss the Script Wizard window and update the scripts in the HTML page.

FIGURE 18.9.

The Script Wizard displays all objects on a Web page with their respective properties, methods, and events.

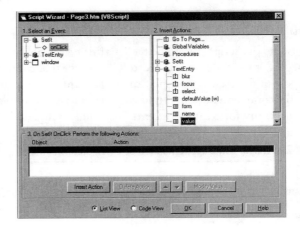

Listing 18.3 illustrates the new scripts that were created automatically by the Script Wizard to handle the events and actions that we defined. Notice in particular the addition of the ONCLICK and LANGUAGE attributes to the <INPUT> tag for the command button.

Listing 18.3. The scripts that were created automatically by the Script Wizard.

```
<HTML>
<HEAD>
<META NAME="GENERATOR" Content="Microsoft Developer Studio">
<META HTTP-EQUIV="Content-Type" content="text/html">
<TITLE>Document Title</TITLE>
</HEAD>
<BODY>

<INPUT SIZE=60 NAME="TextEntry">
<BR>
<INPUT LANGUAGE="VBScript"
       TYPE=BUTTON
       VALUE="Set Text"
      ONCLICK="TextEntry.value = &quot;Script Wizard&quot;"
        NAME="SetIt">

</BODY>
</HTML>
```

NOTE

Although a simple text string was set using the Script Wizard, the window that appears prompting for that string also features two additional buttons: Custom and Color. By clicking on the Custom button, you can include a VBScript expression or variable in place of static text. Likewise, in some cases you will be setting color properties and will need to click on the Color button to display a palette of colors to choose from.

TIP

More often than not, you will not be able to complete a script with just a single action. With the Script Wizard, you may add as many actions as you would like to a particular event. The actions will simply be executed in the order in which they appear.

Creating Routines

In Chapter 16, "An Introduction to Scripting Languages," you learned how subroutines could be used for repeating blocks of VBScript code within an application. But subroutines are also particularly useful for easing code written in events for HTML form objects. In the preceding example, the simple task of changing the text field's value was accomplished with one line of script within the ONCLICK event of the HTML button. But if there were a more complex script to be executed, you probably would not want to see it all on one line in the editor. You could just as easily create a subroutine that contains the script you want to execute and simply call that subroutine from within the ONCLICK event.

To create subroutines or procedures using the Script Wizard, you must first select the Code View option at the bottom of the Script Wizard window. Then, to create a procedure, simply right-click in the Insert Actions pane on the right side of the window. A pop-up menu will appear, allowing you to create a new global variable or a new procedure. When you choose New Procedure, a third pane will appear at the bottom of the Script Wizard window with some text in the first line defining a new procedure. Figure 18.10 illustrates this code window.

Within this window you can type any scripting commands that you want to have associated with the subroutine. You can also rename the subroutine itself and add parameters to the line, as shown in Figure 18.10. Notice that although there is a Sub statement automatically defined, you do not need to write the corresponding End Sub statement. This is generated automatically for you. You will find the code generated automatically and inserted within <SCRIPT> and </SCRIPT> tags somewhere near the top of your HTML page.

18

USING VISUAL INTERDEV TO CREATE SCRIPTS

FIGURE 18.10.

The Script Wizard allows you to create custom scripts.

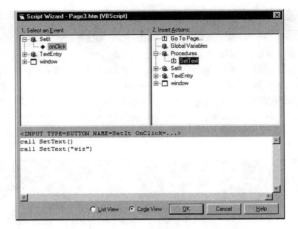

After you have created subroutines, they will be listed in the future under the Procedures section of the Insert Actions pane in the Script Wizard window. Therefore, when you are creating events and actions for those events in the future, you can just as easily select a procedure that you have written as you would another object on the page.

> **NOTE**
>
> If you don't see the procedures you created right away in the Script Wizard window, don't be alarmed. Make certain that the View Code option is selected at the bottom of the window first.

Global Variables

As you write scripts you will undoubtedly use variables to hold information. In addition to simple variables within scripts or subroutines, you may also define global scripts in Visual InterDev. Global variables are just like regular variables except that they can be seen and changed from anywhere within the Web page. Often variables are used just within a particular script or procedure and once the script is finished, those variables are released. Global variables, on the other hand, are available continually until the Web page is unloaded. Likewise, variables defined in one procedure are not readable by other procedures, but global variables are available to all procedures.

Global variables are defined within <SCRIPT> sections toward the beginning of an HMTL page. These variables can also be created via the Script Wizard in Visual InterDev. After opening the Script Wizard window, you will see the section Global Variables within the Insert Actions pane on the right side of the window. To add a new global variable, simply right-click in that pane to display a pop-up menu. When the menu is available, click on the New Global Variable option.

A window will appear, prompting you to type in the name of the global variable you would like to define. After you have entered the variable name, it will be added to the Global Variables list in the right pane. From there it can be set or used in any scripts that you create with or without the Script Wizard.

Summary

In this chapter you have learned some of the basic ways in which Visual InterDev can aid you in your Web application development. You learned about the capabilities that the tool offers for embedding ActiveX controls, HTML layouts, design-time controls, and scripts with the Script Wizard. Although many of these capabilities make the development of script code easier for developers, they are by no means a complete substitution for coding by application developers. As much as Visual InterDev helps with the creation of scripts, you will still need to invest in learning the scripting languages and practice writing scripts on your own in order to maximize the capabilities of your Web sites.

In the next chapter, you will learn about server-side scripting via Microsoft's Active Server Pages technology. This capability enables you to create truly dynamic Web sites by offering the power of server-side scripts that can be written as easily as client-side scripts.

18

USING VISUAL
INTERDEV TO
CREATE SCRIPTS

Creating Active Server Pages

by John J. Kottler

IN THIS CHAPTER

In the preceding chapter you learned how to use scripts on the client side of a Web application to perform different tasks. Although client-side scripts are powerful and very useful in certain situations, there are also situations when it becomes necessary to place the responsibility of performing tasks on the Web server. Microsoft's Active Server Pages provide a means of using the familiar scripting technologies you've learned about thus far to embed functionality on the server side of a Web application.

In this chapter, you will be introduced to the concepts behind creating Active Server Pages. You will also see that Active Server Pages feature truly powerful scripting engines such as VBScript and JScript that enable you to accomplish many complex tasks. In addition, the scripting languages that are used with Active Server Pages provide the capability to insert and work with objects of varying types. Included with Active Server Pages are many built-in objects for maintaining Web applications as well as many controls that can be embedded to provide additional functionality such as database connectivity or file system control.

What Are Active Server Pages?

If you have ever attempted to create a robust Web site, complete with database connectivity or server generated Web pages, chances are you have used languages such as Perl to create CGI programs. Creating server-side programs has not been easy or much fun in the past. Typically a separate language was required and some routines were necessary for parsing user input or attaching to databases. Of course, there was no easy interface for controlling the entire development of such a complex site. Maintaining all the code became a challenge, and it was easy for a site to grow wildly out of control. To do anything constructive with server-side scripts often required a tremendous amount of manual effort and creative programming.

Fortunately, Microsoft has introduced a new technology for creating server-side scripts. *Active Server Pages* (ASPs) are pages that you design to execute on the server but may contain additional information to be passed to the browser. In general, Active Server Pages are very similar to HTML pages that your client browser views. In fact, Active Server Pages can include HTML to pass back to the browser. But in addition to standard HTML, Active Server Pages can interpret instructions such as those written in languages like VBScript or JScript. It is possible to embed both client-side scripts that are passed to the browser for execution as well as scripts that run entirely on the server. Therefore, Active Server Pages are the closest to encompassing client, server, and HTML development into a single, manageable file.

Even though ASP files have improved the capabilities for client/server development by themselves, Visual InterDev enhances the creation and maintenance of these files. As you can imagine, holding client-side scripts, server-side scripts, and HTML in a single file can become confusing. With standard ASP files it is sometimes difficult to distinguish client or server actions. With Visual InterDev, it is possible to more easily manage your code. The editor provides numerous features such as color-coded text to clearly indicate which sections are server-side tasks. As you will see later in this chapter, Visual InterDev also offers the capability to insert common HTML functions for server tasks via design-time controls.

How ASP Works

As we have already mentioned, Active Server Pages are basically HTML files with additional, server-side commands embedded within the file. Therefore, Active Server Pages are simply text-based files just as HTML is. All Active Server Page files end with the .ASP extension. In addition to standard Active Server Page files, there is one global Active Server Page file that is denoted with the .ASA extension. These global files enable you to control particular events for the Web application as well as create global variables to be shared across multiple pages. Each Web application that you build with Visual InterDev can contain one ASA file in its project.

These files, like all data on a Web site, exist first on the Web server and are downloaded as required to the Web browser for interpretation and display. Active Server Pages are slightly different from other traditional files, however, in that they are first analyzed by the Web server before they are downloaded to the client.

This pre-download analysis is required in order for any functions to execute on the server that may affect the results sent to the browser. Any server-side functions are parsed out of the ASP file by the Web server and executed. Depending on the nature of the commands within the ASP file, those commands may be stripped out of the final resulting file sent to the browser or replaced by actual data.

For instance, let's say you are developing a Web site that contains information in a database. In order to retrieve information from the database that exists on the Web server, you need to use server-side scripts; therefore, Active Server Pages are appropriate. This Active Server Page will probably contain HTML to be sent to the browser for displaying information and some server-side commands for opening the database, retrieving information, and sending the information back to the Web browser. In this case, any commands that instruct the Web server to open a database and read information from the database should not be passed back to the client. There really is no need for this information to be passed to the client because it is all executed on the Web server. In addition you probably would not want to send these commands to the client because the client will not understand how to interpret them and you probably would not like others to know what your server is doing for security reasons.

In this database example, the commands for retrieving data are stripped from the final HTML sent to the Web browser. But in addition to stripping commands, numerous statements that instruct the Web browser to insert values into the final HTML result must be interpreted and replaced by their actual values. To understand these concepts further, it is easier to first examine a sample ASP file and its respective results.

A Sample ASP File

Figure 19.1 shows a rather simple HTML page, displaying inventory for an online computer store that we will examine more in Chapter 20, "Putting It All Together—Creating an Interactive and Dynamic Application." This is a simple HTML page that any HTML-savvy developer can create. But the trick is to embed actual data into the table that is generated from a database, not static information.

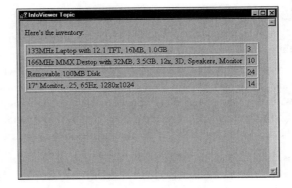

Listing 19.1 illustrates how to create the results painted in Figure 19.1 by using an Active Server Page. You will quickly realize that there are special commands inserted into the Active Server Page that instruct the server to open the database, retrieve values, and return the values to the Web browser. However, you never see these commands in the final HTML that is displayed by the browser, nor the source code for that HTML file. In fact the actual data in the table, although generated dynamically from a database, appears as static text in the resulting HTML file.

Listing 19.1. Commands in the Active Server Page are replaced by actual values to create the final HTML file displayed by the browser in Figure 19.1.

```
<%@ LANGUAGE="VBSCRIPT" %>
<HTML>
<HEAD>
<META NAME="GENERATOR" Content="Microsoft Visual InterDev 1.0">
<META HTTP-EQUIV="Content-Type" content="text/html; charset=iso-8859-1">
<TITLE>Document Title</TITLE>
</HEAD>
<BODY>
<%
Set Conn=Server.CreateObject("ADODB.Connection")
Conn.Open "DataConn"
Set rs=Conn.Execute("select * from inventory")
%>
<H1>Here's the inventory:</H1><P>
<TABLE BORDER=1>
<% while not rs.eof %>
<TR>
    <TD><%= rs("Description")%></TD>
    <TD><%= rs("Quantity")%></TD>
</TR>
<% rs.MoveNext
wend
rs.close
Conn.close
%>
</TABLE>
</BODY>
</HTML>
```

You can easily see that there are server-side script commands embedded within HTML tags in the Active Server Page that are not displayed in the final result page painted by the browser. You will also notice that the language used for database connectivity commands is very similar to VBScript. That's because it is VBScript! A distinct advantage to using Active Server Pages is that you can specify any Active Scripting engine that you prefer to use to write your code. In Listing 19.1, it is possible to embed server-side commands that are written using JScript just as easily as VBScript.

Let's dissect the source code in Listing 19.1 and see exactly how the source code displays the results in Figure 19.1. If you skip down halfway through the source code, you will find that a database connection is opened to a `DataConn` object. You will learn more about database connectivity shortly when we discuss ActiveX Data Objects (ADO) later in this chapter. Shortly after the opening of this database connection, a SQL statement is issued to select particular data from the appropriate table in the database. The results from this SQL statement are stored in a result set that is used to display the actual data. The data is displayed by using a combination of VBScript, HTML, and some additional data object commands. In this example, a `while` loop is used to step through each record of the database. Within that loop are HTML commands that format the table appropriately, including table cells which contain instructions to print the actual Description and Quantity columns from the database. The final resulting HTML is assembled by the Web server and sent to the Web browser, with all of the commands executed and stripped from the result file and all values embedded where specified.

Changing the Language

You might have noticed that the first line in each example we have examined is `<%@ LANGUAGE=Script Language %>`. This line indicates to the Web server that any scripting code found within an Active Server Page is to be treated as statements for the specified language. In the examples we have looked at, the language of choice has been VBScript. It is just as easy to modify the default script to be another script language such as JScript.

If you decide to use the `<SCRIPT>` tags within an Active Server Page, it is possible to specify different languages for code that exists between those tags. It is perfectly legal to mix languages, as long as they are properly specified for each section of code in the application's page.

19

CREATING ACTIVE SERVER PAGES

> **NOTE**
>
> The default language to be used in Active Server Pages can be chosen via the Tools | Options menu. The Options dialog box features a tab marked HTML which contains a Default Languages section for changing the initial language to be used in Active Server Pages.

Programming Active Server Pages

The simple example that we have examined so far quickly demonstrated the capabilities of Active Server Pages and Listing 19.1 featured some of the syntax for programming Active Server Pages. With HTML, client scripts, and server scripts all existing in a single file, it is imperative that each type of code be separated in order for the server to perform actions on the correct sections and pass others through to the Web browser.

In Chapter 16, "An Introduction to Scripting Languages," you learned about creating scripts that can execute on the client computer. With Active Server Pages, you can embed these client scripts, but you also have the ability to create scripts that execute on the server. Because both client- and server-side scripts can use the same scripting languages, it is highly important to distinguish between the different sets of code. In Visual InterDev, server scripts are color-coded in a default black-on-yellow text to distinguish server code from HTML or client scripts. However, because Active Server Pages are simply text files, the Web server requires more than just color coding in the editor to distinguish what should be run at the server.

There are three unique ways to indicate that blocks of script are to be executed on the server. One method is to surround commands with the <% and %> tags. In this case, any text between these tags is treated as server-side scripting commands, based on the language defined at the beginning of the Active Server Page. In addition to specifying commands to execute on the server, you can clearly indicate variables that are to be replaced by actual values by using the <%= *variable* => syntax. Finally, because it is possible to create subroutines within the Active Server Pages just as you would with client scripts, you can specify blocks of code using the <SCRIPT> tag, as long as the tag contains the RUNAT=Server attribute.

Blocks of Server Code

Anything that exists within the Active Server Page file is sent to the browser, unless it is denoted at server-side commands. To indicate server-side commands within an Active Server Page, you can use the following syntax:

```
<%
... Server-side commands
%>
```

Any text that exists between the <% and %> tags is considered server-side script. You can type any valid VBScript statements between these tags and include server-side objects and actions as well. Whatever commands exist between these tags are executed when the page is read by the server. If the statements between these tags affect the output of the page to the Web browser, the modifications are made and sent in place of, or as a result of, these statements.

> **NOTE**
>
> A block of server-side code does not need to be contiguous. It is possible to have multiple blocks of server-side code spattered throughout the Active Server Page and even have HTML or client code embedded between blocks of server-side code.

The <% and %> tags can be used anywhere within an Active Server Page to indicate code that is to run on the server and potentially modify the resulting HTML. Listing 19.2 gives a simple example where VBScript for executing a loop is embedded within the Active Server Page. The result is simply an HTML page with the phrase I am repeating myself. displayed 10 times.

Listing 19.2. A simple Active Server Page with VBScript commands surrounded by <% and %> tags.

```
<%@ LANGUAGE="VBSCRIPT" %>
<HTML>
<HEAD>
<META NAME="GENERATOR" Content="Microsoft Visual InterDev 1.0">
<META HTTP-EQUIV="Content-Type" content="text/html; charset=iso-8859-1">
<TITLE>Document Title</TITLE>
</HEAD>
<BODY>
<% for z=1 to 10 %>
    I am repeating myself.<BR>
<% next %>
</BODY>
</HTML>
```

As you can see from Listing 19.2, it makes logical sense to insert text other than just server-side scripting commands between statements that are server-side script commands.

> **NOTE**
>
> When placing non-script text between sections of an Active Server Page that does contain script commands, make certain that any statements before or after that non-script text is adequately encompassed with the <% and %> tags. In Visual InterDev, any script commands should be highlighted in the appropriate color in the editor. Any text that is not scripting commands between server-side statements should appear in the default HTML text colors for the editor.

Embedding Variables

No programming language is complete without the capability to handle variables and scripting languages for Active Server Pages is no exception. When programming server-side scripts, you define and manipulate variables of different types just as you would with the client-side scripting languages such as VBScript and JScript. However, when you want the value of a variable to be output to the HTML result stream, you can identify values to output by surrounding the results with <%= and %> tags. The = character in the opening tag instructs the Web server to substitute an actual value for a variable or function into the output stream to the Web browser. Listing 19.3 demonstrates how these tags can be used to change the size of the output font as well as display the numbers 1 through 6. The results of Listing 19.3 are shown in Figure 19.2.

Listing 19.3. Variables can be used and interpreted for inclusion in the HTML output stream.

```
<%@ LANGUAGE="VBSCRIPT" %>
<HTML>
<HEAD>
<META NAME="GENERATOR" Content="Microsoft Visual InterDev 1.0">
<META HTTP-EQUIV="Content-Type" content="text/html; charset=iso-8859-1">
<TITLE>Count It!</TITLE>
</HEAD>
<BODY>
<H1>Count It!</H1>
<% for z=1 to 6 %>
    <% if z<4 then %>
        <FONT SIZE=<%= z%> COLOR=#000080>
    <% else %>
        <FONT SIZE=<%= z%> COLOR=#800000>
    <% end if %>
    Number: <%= z%></FONT><BR>
<% next %>
</BODY>
</HTML>
```

FIGURE 19.2.

Font size can be changed via variables and the content of variables can be sent to the resulting HTML file.

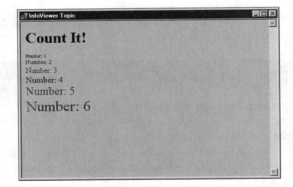

As you can see from Listing 19.3, the <%= z %> syntax substitutes the value of the variable z at a particular given point in time. In this example, z is the loop index for a loop that extends from 1 to 6. Therefore, the font size is changed to z, or 1 through 6, and the text Number: is generated followed by the appropriate index number. As the loop executes, the values of z are replaced with 1, 2, 3, 4, 5, and 6, respectively. To make the example more interesting, the value of z is analyzed via an if statement, which changes the output text color to red if the value of z is greater than or equal to 4. As you can see, the `<%= z %>` syntax can be used anywhere in the Active Server Page file where values should be placed.

Where to RUNAT

So far you have seen how to embed script commands and variables into your Active Server Page. But there are times when you will want to create subroutines to perform routine tasks. To create subroutines, you can use the `<SCRIPT>` command to help determine which scripts run on the server and which run on the client. The `<SCRIPT>` command, as you may already know, contains the LANGUAGE attribute which enables you to specify which language the script code will be written in.

In addition to this attribute, a RUNAT attribute controls whether that script executes on the server or on the client. If you want to have a script run on the server, you merely need to include the `RUNAT="server"` attribute in the `<SCRIPT>` tag. Client-side scripting does not require the RUNAT attribute to be set. To define a block of code that executes as a function, you can surround that block with the `<SCRIPT>` and `</SCRIPT>` tags. Listing 19.4 demonstrates a function that is written to execute on the server.

Listing 19.4. The `<SCRIPT>` tag can be used to specify code that executes on the server as well.

```
<%@ LANGUAGE="VBSCRIPT" %>
<HTML>
<BODY>
<% Call HelloWorld %>
</BODY>
</HTML>
<SCRIPT LANGUAGE="JScript" RUNAT="Server">
function HelloWorld()
{
    for (j=0;j<5;j++){
        Response.write("Hello World!<BR>");
    }
}
</SCRIPT>
```

19

CREATING ACTIVE
SERVER PAGES

> **NOTE**
>
> It is possible to define subroutines within blocks of server-side code that is distinguished by the surrounding `<%` and `%>` tags. Script for those subroutines must be in the same language as the default language for the Active Server Page as defined by the `<%@ LANGUAGE %>` statement at the start of the file. By using the `<SCRIPT>` tags however, you may specify sections of code that use other scripting languages.

Functions and subroutines can be invoked via scripting languages on the server just as they are invoked within client scripting languages. In the example shown in Listing 19.4, the `call` statement invokes the appropriate subroutine, as required by VBScript.

Application ASP Files

In addition to typical Active Server Pages, each project that you build for a Web site contains a separate ASA file. This file is a global file that holds global variables for the entire Web application as well as objects and events relevant to the Web application itself. It is important to notice that this file does not generate content to be displayed to the Web browser, but rather only maintains information internally to the Web application. Only one ASA file is allowed for every Web application that is created, and if you create a Web application using the project wizards in Visual InterDev, this ASA file is created automatically for you. In some cases you might not require an ASA file for your application, which is completely acceptable because this file is optional for Web applications. But for the times you will require the use of an ASA file, let's review the capabilities this file offers.

> **NOTE**
>
> Any text within an ASA file that is not enclosed within <SCRIPT> tags is ignored by the Web server.

Because these global Active Server Page files do not export results to a Web client, they can only contain scripting commands from a valid scripting engine to perform actions internally on the Web server. Within these scripts you can add code to handle several different events for the Web application, create objects, or declare global variables. Whatever is developed within the ASA file is available on all other Active Server Pages throughout an application.

Application Events

Within the ASA file, it is possible to trap events particular to an application. There are two application events: `Application_OnStart` and `Application_OnEnd`. An application is considered to be the entire set of pages that exist in the root Web directory and any pages within subdirectories of that directory. Whenever a Web page in any of those directories is opened, the application is started. Once a user has finished using the Web application, the `Application_OnEnd` event is triggered. The following syntax is used to define application events within the ASA file:

```
<SCRIPT LANGUAGE="Script Language" RUNAT="Server">
Sub Application_OnStart
... Script statements
End Sub
</SCRIPT>
```

or,

```
<SCRIPT LANGUAGE="Script Language" RUNAT="Server">
Sub Application_OnEnd
... Script statements
End Sub
</SCRIPT>
```

Session Events

Application events are triggered for all users. It doesn't matter who the user is that is using the application, an application event is triggered and any data made available within those events is available to all users. Session events, on the other hand, are triggered before a Web page is processed and is dependent on the user viewing the Web site. Any specific information defined in a server session is available to respective users and not anyone else. Therefore, it is possible to store information about individual users or to use the `Session` objects to control user access into the system.

Another common use for the `Session` object is to create an environment that *maintains state*—that is, the server application knows who you are as a user for each page you access, without asking you to re-authenticate. With session management, it is possible to more accurately create traditional client/server applications on the Web. The following syntax is used to determine when a user has initiated a session or closed a session of the Web application:

```
<SCRIPT LANGUAGE="Script Language" RUNAT="Server">
Sub Session_OnStart
... Script statements
End Sub
</SCRIPT>
```

or

```
<SCRIPT LANGUAGE="Script Language" RUNAT="Server">
Sub Session_OnEnd
... Script statements
End Sub
</SCRIPT>
```

19

CREATING ACTIVE
SERVER PAGES

Object Declarations

In addition to defining routines to execute for the session or application, it is possible to define global objects within the ASA file. Objects declared in this application can be made available for the scope of either a user session or the entire Web application. This is particularly useful if you are planning on using a similar object on many server pages. For instance, a connection to a single database from many Active Server Pages could be established once in the ASA file instead of each individual .ASP file.

Defining objects for use in Active Server Pages is very similar to adding objects to be used on Web pages displayed within the browser. The following syntax is used to declare objects within the global ASA file:

```
<OBJECT    RUNAT="Server"
           SCOPE="Scope"
              ID="Identifier"
          PROGID="progID"
Or       CLASSID="ClassID">
</OBJECT>
```

SCOPE—Objects defined in the ASA file can be made available throughout the entire application, or can be generated and used per user session. You can specify what type of object to create by using either the Application or Session value for this attribute.

ID—Just as you define names for objects that you want to control via script in client-side applications, you need to specify a unique ID name for each object defined on the server. If you want to invoke an object later in your Active Server Pages, you would use this ID name followed by the appropriate object method or property.

PROGID—When inserting objects within Active Server Pages, you must define either the program ID that uniquely identifies that object, or the object's class ID. If you are using the object's program ID, the format is typically *vendor.component.version*.

ClASSID—If a program ID does not exist to adequately define an object to embed, then you may use the class ID for an object. Class IDs are globally unique IDs that identify each object in the system and are listed in the system registry of Windows 95 and Windows NT operating systems.

Using Built-In Server Objects

It is easy to include server-side objects within your Active Server Pages, and shortly you will learn how to include additional server-side components. But fortunately there are many objects that are available for use by Active Server Pages that are inherent to the Web server. These objects will help your application read requests from HTML forms, post results to the Web browser, and control the server.

NOTE

In the next several sections of the chapter, you will learn about some of the more important objects that can be used with Active Server Pages. Although this chapter presents an overview of each object, you should refer to Appendixes E, "Active Server Pages Scripting Reference," G, "Visual InterDev Design-Time ActiveX Control Reference, "and H, "COM Reference," for a more detailed object reference.

The Application Object

You may recall that there are events that are directly related to the start and end of the entire Web application. These events were made available in the global Active Server Page file because there exists an Application object. Just as with any object, the Application object contains additional properties that may be invoked by your scripts. The following is a list of valid methods for the Application object and their functions:

- Lock—Whenever you want to change a global variable for the Web application, you want to make sure that it is only changed by one user at a time. If variables were left open many users could be changing the same variable at the exact same time, causing the wrong results to occur. Instead you want to lock a variable, have one user update it, and then unlock it again. This will prevent multiple users from affecting a variable at once.

- Unlock—After you have modified application-specific information, you will want to unlock the information to instruct the server that a user has finished modifying it. Once unlocked, that global information is now available for modification by other users.

TIP

A good place to use the application Lock and Unlock methods is for recording users who accessed your site. Let's assume that you want to update a variable in the global application file (.ASA) that keeps track of the number of visitors at your site. When a user enters the application, a variable could be updated by adding 1 to it. However, you want it to be updated accurately by each user who enters the site. By locking the variable first, a second user will not be able to touch that variable until the first is finished. This way the information in that variable will be accurate.

The Request Object

The Request object contains information passed to the server-side application from a Web browser. Typically this type of information results from an HTML form that a user completes or cookies that are stored on the client computer. There are many collections associated with the Request object. For instance, because a form can contain many fields, a collection of form properties is available to the Web server.

The Response Object

Just as you can examine information passed to the server from the client, you can format data sent from the server back to the client. The Response object enables you to send information directly to the client or set particular objects in the client such as cookies.

The Server Object

The Server object contains properties and methods for creating objects on the server or for encoding information passed between the client and the browser.

The Session Object

Earlier you learned about Session and Application events within the ASA file. In addition to these events, you can also control several properties and methods for a user session.

Active Server Components

In the previous section, you were introduced to objects that are included with the Active Server Pages server technology. However, the real power of Active Server Pages and its respective objects lies in the fact that you can include additional objects or components to expand the capabilities of Active Server. Some server components are included with Active Server, but there will undoubtedly be additional components available by other companies as well. There are several additional server components that are included with Active Server and Visual InterDev; in this chapter we will examine only a few. Another component, ActiveX Data Objects, is reviewed in Chapter 20.

Ad Rotator

You've seen it on just about every commercial Web site today: ads for everything from computer peripherals to investment firms. Everyone is trying to grab your attention to visit their site and hopefully purchase their product or service. In the past, custom scripts were necessary on the server in order to display the correct banner ad and provide the appropriate links to an advertiser's Web site. With the Ad Rotator component, it is easy to include banner ads in any site you create with Active Server Pages.

TIP

Ads do not have to be used only to advertise products, services, or other sites. Users who come to visit your site may just be interested in learning about the newest features or content added to your site. Use the Ad Rotator to rotate messages containing new information about your site.

Browser Capabilities

If you have ever created a Web site that is available on the Internet, chances are you've experienced the frustration at one time or another of creating a site that was optimized for different Web browsers. Although not quite as significant an issue today, not so long ago each browser featured different capabilities that may or may not have been available in other browsers. Often browsers such as Netscape's Navigator pioneered new capabilities such as tables or frames, while others such as Microsoft Internet Explorer introduced multimedia extensions and advanced font control. In the past, you needed to determine what browser was accessing your site in order to tailor the results appropriately.

With the consolidation of standards in the Internet arena, this is becoming less of an issue for typical computers accessing the Web. However, you must remember that there are other factors today that can influence how your site should be displayed. Devices such as WebTV and handheld PCs are creating a new type of browser for the Internet. These browsers typically do not contain identical features as their computer rivals; therefore, Web sites can be optimized for these separate devices.

The Browser object enables you to retrieve information about the computer that is browsing your Web application. With this information, you can optimize the data that is sent to the browser.

Content Linking

A lot of Web sites consist of pages of information that should appear in a particular order. For instance, a story site may contain stories where each chapter of the story is a separate HTML page. But you don't want to read the story out of order. You want to be able to click on a Next link to move to the next chapter, a Previous link to move back a chapter, and a Table of Contents link to display a list of all chapters in the story. With traditional HTML files, this would require the developer to insert links manually to control page flow and the table of contents. This is fine except when new information is added, such as a new chapter in the story. Adding new information would require a site developer to update all necessary links that should point to the new file.

With the Content Linking control, it is possible to create a single control file of all HTML pages that are related to each other. Once this file has been created, you can use the Content Linking control in your Active Server Pages to perform Next and Previous links automatically, and generate a dynamic Table of Contents.

Summary

In this chapter you have been introduced to Active Server Pages and the concepts behind creating applications that execute on the server. You also learned how to distinguish between what is processed on the server and what is passed directly to the Web client. You saw that Active

19

CREATING ACTIVE
SERVER PAGES

Server Pages can also contain global variables or objects that are available for entire Web application or individual sessions. Finally, you were introduced to a plethora of objects that are included with Active Server for adding productivity to your Web applications.

In the next chapter, you will see how all the technologies you have learned about in this section can be combined to create a Web-based application. You will see how client and server scripting are important to complete a Web site, and you will be introduced to connecting to databases for retrieving and storing information.

Putting It All Together—Creating an Interactive and Dynamic Application

by John J. Kottler

IN THIS CHAPTER

CHAPTER 20

In the past five chapters, you have learned a lot about Visual InterDev, and particularly how to create dynamic Web sites with ActiveX controls, Active Server Pages, and scripts. But how do all these features work together to create a world-class Web site? In this chapter, I'll review the creation of a fictitious Web site and examine the techniques used for the site. You'll quickly see how client scripts, server scripts, ActiveX controls, and more can help make sites interesting and dynamic. I'll touch briefly on each technology that was covered within the past five chapters as it relates to the project we are creating in this chapter.

Making Sense of It All

So what type of Web site should we create? Although there is a myriad of possibilities for Web sites, let's take a fairly simple example. Let's create an online store for computer equipment. This online store, CompuShop, will give visitors to the site the ability to view computer hardware and software that is available for purchase, determine whether particular items are in stock, and order items. In addition, users will be able to view items based on particular criteria and search through the content of the Web site. In addition to this functionality, the main Web page for the site will contain an advertisement section where new products or specials can be displayed on a rotating basis.

Now, what types of technology are needed to create this type of Web site? To determine what is required, let's examine each portion of the site in a little more detail. To begin, let's consider the main page, or *home page*, for the site. More than likely, this will be an introductory page with information such as the store's name, a logo, and possibly some other artwork. In addition, you will probably add links on the main page to other sections of the site, such as product browsing or ordering, and searching capabilities. In addition, at the bottom of the main page, advertisements will rotate displaying the current items on sale or hot deals. The main page therefore requires standard HTML and graphics, but also some server-side scripts. In this case, a server-side script would be beneficial for determining what type of browser is accessing the site or to display the rotating ads.

A primary function that users will expect is a search capability. Searching in this instance can be performed in one of two ways. Because all inventory items will be found in an online database, searches can be made through the contents of the database for particular products. In addition, users might want to search the entire Web site for keywords. In the first scenario, simple SQL statements can be issued that retrieve appropriate information from the database. As far as site searches go, this capability is included automatically with certain Web projects that you create with Visual InterDev. Each item in the database might or might not contain additional detailed information that can be held in a separate Web page. This information, although available through the database and any query screens, should also be made available to full-text searches of the Web site.

But in addition to finding particular products, a user will (we hope) also want to order items. To do this, a separate data-entry screen must be made available in order for the user to specify things such as quantity and delivery address. The information entered on this screen can then be updated in a separate order-entry database that exists on the Web server. To accomplish this data-entry screen, an HTML form can be used to create the entry form, and database connectivity to the server will be used to insert new rows of data into a database table. Although validation on user input can be performed on the client, in this particular instance it will be verified on the server for the sake of a complete example.

Setting Up Shop

The CompuShop Web site is shaping up into a fairly complex application. So where do you begin creating such an application? To start, you should already have some basic HTML pages and graphics prepared before starting the site. You will need to create the overall appearance of the Web site and some static HTML pages. To create graphics, you can use the Image Composer application that is included with Visual InterDev, and you can use Visual InterDev itself to compose standard HTML Web pages with the FrontPage Editor. After creating some of the basic Web pages and graphics that the CompuShop Web site will require, we can begin creating the CompuShop project in Visual InterDev.

Creating the CompuShop Project

To get started creating our Web site in Visual InterDev, we need to create a new project for this site. To create a new project, choose New from the File menu and make certain that the Projects tab is selected in the resulting window that is displayed. Because we are creating a fairly basic Web site, let's choose the Web Project Wizard from the list and specify a destination directory of CompuShop on our personal Web server. The options that should be selected are illustrated in Figure 20.1.

FIGURE 20.1.
The CompuShop Web site starts first with a brand-new project.

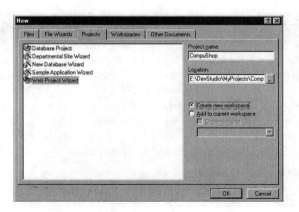

After you have created the new Web project, you will find yourself viewing a new Visual InterDev project with the list of files available in the Workspace window along the left side of the application.

20

CREATING A
DYNAMIC
APPLICATION

The first thing you will probably want to do after creating a new project in Visual InterDev is to add any HTML files or graphics that you have already created to the currently selected project. You must add these files to the project in order for them to be viewed in the Workspace window and for them to be used by other Visual InterDev components and editors. To add files to the current project, select Project | Add to Project | Files… to display a dialog box that enables you to specify which files to include in the project.

Creating the Default Page

After you have imported all necessary graphics, HTML documents, and other files that you have prepared before starting the project, you are ready to begin creating the CompuShop application. Let's start by creating the introductory page that will act as a menu for the Web site. This first page will basically contain HTML text and some graphics, and it is natural to think that you will be adding an HTML file to the site. But we want this site to be smart enough to check to make sure that the browser accessing the site is capable of viewing tables. If the browser is not table-aware, a message should be sent back to the client mentioning this fact and recommending that a table-savvy Web browser be used instead. We also want to create a rotating advertisement at the bottom of this initial screen. To check browser capabilities and establish a rotating ad, we will need to use two server-side components: the Browser control and the Ad Rotator control.

Because we are going to be using some server-side components, we must create a server-side Web page or an Active Server Page. To add a new page to the project, choose Project | Add to Project | New…, select Active Server Page from the resulting window, and make certain that you typed `default.asp` for the name of this new file. After the new file has been created, you are ready to add ActiveX components to the file for the Browser and Ad Rotator controls.

TIP

Whenever you add new HTML files or even Active Server Pages to a project, chances are you will want to add *some* amount of static content to that page as well. Although you can laboriously add content via traditional HTML tags in the Active Server Page file that is displayed in the Visual InterDev editor, you will probably rather add it with a tool such as FrontPage. Although the version of FrontPage that is included with Visual InterDev is automatically associated with HTML files for editing those files, it is not associated with Active Server Pages, even though those pages return HTML as well.

To add FrontPage as a suitable editor for Active Server Pages, right-click on an Active Server Page in the Workspace window. A pop-up menu will appear with an Open With… choice. Select this option to display a window with possible tools to use with the particular file you selected in the Workspace. Although FrontPage is not listed as a suitable editor for Active Server Pages, you can click on the Add button in the resulting Open With… window to add a new editor for the Active Server Page file type.

After you have added FrontPage as a valid editor for ASP files, you can later open these files with FrontPage directly from Visual InterDev. However, remember that Active Server Pages frequently contain numerous scripts and commands that might not be readable by other tools such as FrontPage. Make certain that while you are using tools such as FrontPage del you do not inadvertently remove crucial lines from the Active Server Page file.

Adding Server Controls

In Chapter 19, "Creating Active Server Pages," you learned a great deal about the coding conventions used for creating server-side scripts and about the many controls that are available to be executed on the server. We will be using two of the controls that are covered in that chapter to detect information about the browser accessing the Web site and to create advertisements that rotate at the bottom of the page.

The Browser Control

After you have tweaked the Active Server Page with the content you want to display in typical HTML format, you can add the Browser control. In this case you simply want to instruct the user that if he is using a browser that does not support tables, he should obtain a browser that does. Although tables are not really necessary to view this site, some of the information that will be returned by scripts that access the database later in this chapter will be better viewed if the browser supports tables. To add the Browser control to the Active Server Page, you can use the following syntax:

```
<% Set BrowserObject = Server.CreateObject("MSWC.BrowserType") %>
```

Remember that, because this is code that should execute on the server and not be part of the Web page when displayed in the client, you must enclose this statement and others like it within the <% and %> tags. In any case, this line creates a Browser control and assigns it the name BrowserObject, which can be used to reference the object later in our script.

After creating the object, you will want to test whether the browser accessing the CompuShop Web site is capable of displaying tables. Fortunately, the Browser control features a property named Tables that is set to TRUE if the browser accessing the site supports tables, and is set to FALSE otherwise. Therefore, the Active Server Page can send different text back to the Web browser based on whether it supports tables by using the following code:

```
<% if BrowserObject.Tables=FALSE then %>
    You better get a browser with table support to view this site!
<% else %>
    Good, you've got a browser that handles tables!
<% end if %>
```

20

When you are creating your official site, you might want to do more with this information than simply post a message back to the user. You might want to set global variables for the project, for instance, so that further pages of the site can send back information to the Web browser that is optimized for that particular Web browser's capabilities.

> **NOTE**
>
> As you might recall from Chapter 19, global variables are declared in the .ASA file for an application and are available to all Web pages that comprise the application.

The Ad Rotator Control

You'll recall that an Ad Rotator control presents multiple advertisements at a specific location in an Active Server Page, based on a control file. In addition to this control file, a redirect file can be implemented. And, of course, all the graphics for an ad must be created. To add an Ad Rotator control to our CompuShop Web project, we must first create some graphical advertisements and include them in the CompuShop project. In this case we are going to create three graphic ads for a notebook computer, a modem, and a desktop system. Only the first ad for the notebook computer, however, will have a link to an actual HTML file in our project that describes the notebook in more detail.

Once the graphics have been created and added to the Web project, the Ad Rotator control must be added to the Active Server Page that creates the home page for this Web site, default.htm. The following lines can be added to include the Ad Rotator control in the Web page:

```
<% Set AdRotatorObject = Server.CreateObject("MSWC.AdRotator") %>
<%= AdRotatorObject.GetAdvertisement("adfile.txt") %>
```

But in order for this Ad Rotator to work correctly, there must be a control file that specifies which ads to display, the hyperlinks that an ad links to, and the frequency with which an ad will appear. These parameters can be specified in a control file (adfile.txt). Listing 20.1 shows the control file used at the CompuShop online computer store to display three different advertisements.

Listing 20.1. A control file is used to specify advertisements to be displayed by the Ad Rotator control.

```
REDIRECT adredir.asp
HEIGHT 25
*
http://jay/CompuShop/images/ad1.jpg
http://jay/CompuShop/133Notebook.htm
Special this week: 133MHz Notebook!
50
http://jay/CompuShop/images/ad2.jpg
-
Looking for a new Desktop System?
30
```

```
http://jay/CompuShop/images/ad3.jpg
-
$49 28.8 modem! Blast through the Internet!
20
```

You will also recall that when a user clicks on a link for an ad, another Active Server Page may be invoked first before passing the user to the resulting link. This is necessary on occasion to warn the user that he is leaving the host site or to tally the number of times visitors chose to visit a sponsor for an advertisement. In either case, the logic for this can be processed by another Active Server Page. In the case of CompuShop, the `adredir.asp` page simply redirects a user to a specific link, because most of the advertisements on the site will be for products within the site. Because no tracking is being performed on advertisements, a simple redirect statement is used in the `adredir.asp` page. This statement retrieves the URL that an advertisement points to and simply displays that page:

```
<% Response.Redirect(Request.QueryString("url")) %>
```

This statement functions correctly because the links in the Ad Rotator control file for an advertisement are passed to this Active Server Page via a CGI parameter, and follow the URL behind the ?. Figure 20.2 demonstrates the complete default Web page for the CompuShop Web site, complete with a browser-detection statement `Good, you've got a browser that handles tables!` and the rotating advertisement `HOT Deal on 133MHz Notebook`.

FIGURE 20.2.

The home page for the CompuShop Web site contains script for detecting browser capabilities and displaying rotating ads.

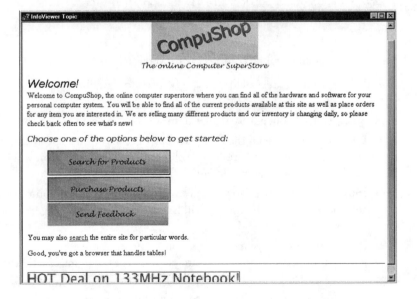

> **NOTE**
>
> Make sure there are no spaces after the redirect filename in the Ad Rotator control or unnecessary spaces before any URL in that file. Extra spaces might be transferred to the query portion of future URLs and might cause errors in your application because the exact URL cannot be found.

Searching for Products

In our simple sample Web site, we will have a database on the Web server that contains the inventory of products available for ordering. In this fictitious example, we will create a site with a simple Access database. The database will contain two tables: an Inventory table that will contain information about current inventory, and an Orders table that will track orders submitted by customers on the Web site.

> **TIP**
>
> When you create robust online databases, you may want to consider a stronger database system such as SQL Server or Oracle servers. Although Access is suitable for personal and small-scale database applications, it is not appropriate for thousands of users who want to access data at the same time.

This inventory table will be composed of several fields:

- Description—A text field that can be used to describe the product being sold at the Web site.

- Stock Date—When a particular item was last received at the online computer store.

- URL—Some items in the database may have additional specification sheets or advertisements for the product. If this additional information is in an HTML format, the URL can be referenced via this field.

- Information in other formats may also be referenced, but you must make a judgment call about whether the format will be supported by your target audience's Web browser.

- Part Number—Every item in the computer store must be uniquely identified. The part number ensures that there are no two types of items exactly the same in the store.

- Quantity—Each time stock is delivered to the online computer store, the number of units for each product is increased. This quantity can be checked to ensure that products are available for ordering.

- Price—A store would not be very effective if it didn't actually sell something! But each item can range in price, so that price is stored in this field.

- Type—More often than not, many items are similar in one way or another and can be grouped together. For instance, although there are 15- and 17-inch monitors and different brands of those monitors, they are all still monitors and can be grouped by that keyword.

After we have established this database with these key fields, we're ready to create a Web page that allows users to search for items. In this example, let's create a simple page that prompts the user to choose what type of computer equipment he is searching for. In this case, our simple Web page will contain a single drop-down menu to choose a particular type of product and a Search button that will submit the data from the form to the server for processing. Figure 20.3 illustrates a sample page for searching through the Products database.

> **NOTE**
>
> Although the sample search page in the CompuShop Web site searches only for products based on a particular type, it is possible to expand the capabilities to search on any criteria and return any information. You'll quickly find that Active Server Pages can be quite powerful for database information retrieval.

FIGURE 20.3.

A simple product search for the CompuShop Web site will display products based on their product type.

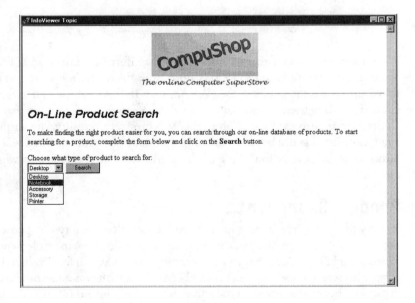

20

CREATING A
DYNAMIC
APPLICATION

After a user clicks on the Search button, a second Web page will be presented, displaying the results of the search within a table. The items in the resulting product list that is returned should all be of the type that the user selected. In the example shown in Figure 20.3, the resulting products should all be laptops or notebook computers. Figure 20.4 gives you an example of such a returned list of products.

FIGURE 20.4.

After a user has selected products to view, the resulting Web page will display products in the database that match the user's product choice.

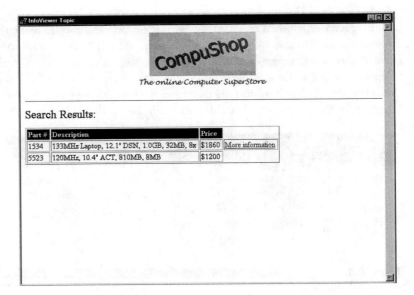

It is important to notice that in order to process information from an HTML form, an Active Server Page is required to receive the input from the form, invoke scripts that perform functions, and return the results to the Web browser. In this case, the Active Server Page retrieves a choice made by a user, queries data from a database to find information that matches that user's choice, and returns the final result to the Web browser. In reality, the scripts on the server add a tad more intelligence by understanding that not every product listed will contain additional information that can be found at a URL and lists More information only when additional pages are available.

ProductSearch.htm

So now that you understand what the product-search capability is supposed to accomplish in the CompuShop Web site, you can begin understanding how to implement it. The first step is to create an HTML page that will be referenced by the Search for Products button on the main page. This search page will contain an HTML form with two items on the form: a drop-down menu for choosing a product type and a submission button. Listing 20.2 contains the source code for creating the search page displayed in Figure 20.3, which was generated using FrontPage.

Listing 20.2. The `ProductSearch.htm` file is used to allow users to select what types of products to view.

```html
<html>

<head>
<meta http-equiv="Content-Type" content="text/html">
<meta name="GENERATOR"
   content="Microsoft FrontPage (Visual InterDev Edition) 2.0">
<title>Product Search</title>
</head>

<body bgcolor="#FFFFFF">
<CENTER><img src="../CompuShop/images/compushop.jpg" width="266"
height="116"></CENTER>

<hr>

<p><font size="5" face="Arial"><em><strong>On-Line Product Search
</strong></em></font></p>

<p>To make finding the right product easier for you, you can
search through our on-line database of products. To start
searching for a product, complete the form below and click on the
<strong>Search</strong> button.</p>

<form method="POST"
      action="http://jay/CompuShop/searchit.asp"
        name="ProductSearch">

    <p>Choose what type of product to search for:<br>
    <select name="SearchBy" size="1">
        <option>Desktop</option>
        <option>Notebook</option>
        <option>Accessory</option>
        <option>Storage</option>
        <option>Printer</option>
    </select>
    <input type="submit" name="SearchIt" value="Search"></p>

</form>
</body>
</html>
```

You will quickly see that the <FORM> tag contains two attributes that must be completed in order to send data filled in the form to the Web server. The first attribute, METHOD, allows you to choose between GET and POST. Because a user will be sending data from the Web browser to the Web server, he will be posting information to the Active Server Page. Specifically, the results from this page will be sent to the application on the server that is specified in the ACTION attribute. In this case, the results of this Web page will be sent to an Active Server Page on the server named SearchIt.asp.

An important point to remember while creating your HTML forms that will be sending data to the server is that the names for each entry field must be specified. Assigning the form's entry fields logical names allows you to easily access the information from server-side scripts in the future.

20

CREATING A
DYNAMIC
APPLICATION

SearchIt.asp

The Web page that displays the standard search form for choosing a particular product type is fairly straightforward and can be easily created. When you have that form defined, you will want to connect fields in that form to a server-side application that can do something with the choices made. In this case, we want to search a database for all items of a particular product type. The SearchIt.asp file that was defined in the form in Listing 20.2 will perform the server-side scripts that are necessary to connect to a database and format the results. Listing 20.3 demonstrates the SearchIt.asp file.

Listing 20.3. SearchIt.asp is a server-side file that actually performs the search against the product database, based on the product choice made by the user and the ProductSearch.htm file.

```
<%@ LANGUAGE="VBSCRIPT" %>
<!DOCTYPE HTML PUBLIC "-//IETF//DTD HTML//EN">
<html>

<head>
<meta http-equiv="Content-Type"
content="text/html; charset=iso-8859-1">
<meta name="GENERATOR"
content="Microsoft FrontPage (Visual InterDev Edition) 2.0">
<title>Product Search Results</title>
</head>

<body bgcolor="#FFFFFF">
<% Set DB=Server.CreateObject("ADODB.Connection")
   DB.Open "CompuShop"
   SearchString = "select * from inventory where Type='" &
                  Request.Form("SearchBy") & "'"
   Set DB_Results = DB.Execute(SearchString)
%>
<p align="center">
<img     src="http://jay/CompuShop/images/compushop.jpg"
      width="266"
      height="116"> </p>

<hr>

<p><font size="5">Search Results:</font><br>
</p>
<table border="1">
    <tr>
        <td bgcolor="#000080"><font color="#FFFFFF"><strong>
           Part #
        </strong></font></td>
        <td bgcolor="#000080"><font color="#FFFFFF"><strong>
           Description
        </strong></font></td>
        <td bgcolor="#000080"><font color="#FFFFFF"><strong>
           Price
        </strong></font></td>
    </tr>
```

```
<% while not DB_Results.eof %>
    <tr>
        <td>
            <%= DB_Results("Part Number") %>
        </td>
        <td>
            <%= DB_Results("Description") %>
        </td>
        <td>
            $<%= DB_Results("Price") %>
        </td>
      <% if DB_Results("URL")<>"" then %>
        <td>
            <a href="<%= DB_Results("URL") %>">More information</a>
        </td>
      <% end if %>
    </tr>
    <% DB_Results.MoveNext
wend
%>

</table>
<% DB_Results.Close
    DB.Close %>

</body>
</html>
```

Database Connectivity

The most important thing that the SearchIt.asp file does, however, is connect to a database in order to return current results to the Web browser. This Active Server Page accomplishes connectivity to the Inventory database through a server-side ActiveX control, referred to as ADO or the ActiveX Data Object. The ADO control provides database connectivity through ODBC to other databases on your computer system or on the network. ADO encapsulates the connection, use, and record handling of databases with straightforward methods and properties similar to other ActiveX controls. For more information on the ActiveX Data Object and its functions, see Chapter 22, "Integrating ActiveX Database Components."

To start using results from the Inventory database, first the control must be added to the Active Server Page. The following statement, found near the start of Listing 20.3, adds the control for use within the page:

```
Set DB=Server.CreateObject("ADODB.Connection")
```

The object is created and is named DB so that it can be referenced throughout the Active Server Page. Once the ADO object has been created, the database used in the Web page must be opened for access. The ADO control features an Open method that enables you to specify a database connection to open. The following line opens a database connection that is defined in Visual InterDev for the CompuShop database:

```
DB.Open "CompuShop"
```

Making a Connection

Data connections are links to actual database files and are stored as part of a Visual InterDev project for a Web site. Because it is important to have this connection created before implementing database commands in an Active Server Page, let's first see quickly how to create a data connection in Visual InterDev.

To add a database connection to a Web project in Visual InterDev, you can either choose Project | Add to Project | Add Data Connection... from the menu or right-click on the project name in the workspace to present a pop-up menu. Near the middle of that pop-up menu, you can select the option Add Data Connection... The resulting Select Data Source window displays possible file and system data sources to which you can connect. This window is pictured in Figure 20.5 and might look familiar, because it is a subset of the 32-bit ODBC Control Panel that is commonly found in Windows 95.

FIGURE 20.5.

Before working with databases, a data connection to a data source must be created for the Web project.

> **TIP**
>
> If the database you want to connect to is not presently listed in the Select Data Source window, you might want to verify that it doesn't exist in the listing under another tab. If you know for sure that the connection has never been established before, you may want to create a new ODBC entry by clicking on the New button in the Select Data Source window and following the instructions for adding a new entry.

After you have selected the data source to create a connection to, Visual InterDev will add the connection to your Web project as part of the `global.asa` file. In reality, Visual InterDev is creating connectivity scripts for using the data source you specified and is storing these scripts as part of the `global.asa` file, which is accessible from any other page in the Web project. The information in these scripts is tweaked based on some properties you specify through the Data Connection Properties window that displays shortly after you connect to a data source. These properties may include database-specific properties or additional settings such as a login ID or password. Figure 20.6 illustrates some of the properties that are changeable for an Access database.

FIGURE 20.6.

Data Connections in Visual InterDev support properties of their own that can be modified.

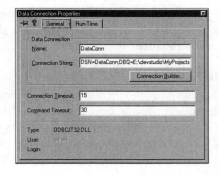

Retrieving Results

After you have created the ADO control to an Active Server Page, added the appropriate data connection to the Web project, and opened that connection via the Open method, you are ready to retrieve data from or add data to the database. Basically, all data is either inserted, edited, or retrieved from a database table. These functions, as well as many others, are accessible via commands for the database system. Although different database systems may have varying database commands, every database system on the market today supports a common set of commands referred to as *SQL* (Structured Query Language). This basic database language is English-like in nature and instructs the database engine to perform particular actions. Coverage of the SQL language is far beyond the scope of this chapter, but you can find additional information in Appendix F, "SQL Reference."

To execute a SQL statement via ADO, you use the Execute method for the ADO object that you create as a result of connecting to the database. In Listing 20.3, this would be the DB object. The Execute method expects the instructions to execute as parameters to the method.

To retrieve all information from the Inventory table in the CompuShop database, we could use the following SQL statement:

```
select * from inventory
```

But this would return all items in the Inventory table. In our Product Search page, we want to return only those entries that match the product type the user selected in the previous HTML form. To restrict entries that are returned in SQL you can use the where clause, which can be treated as an if condition. Records of information are returned only if they match the condition you specify after the where statement. Therefore, to restrict the returned data to only those type of products that are notebook computers, you could use the following SQL statement:

```
select * from inventory where Type='Notebook'
```

Any information returned as a result of a database query is often stored in a *result set*. A result set is a miniature table that is created, updated, and removed automatically by the database management system (DBMS). These result sets are useful for application developers because the application does not need to maintain this information; the DBMS does it already. You can then write application code that analyzes this smaller, faster, and more manageable table. The result set in Listing 20.3 is defined as DB_Results and is set to contain the results of the SQL statement that is executed.

Displaying the Result Set

Our Web page for displaying products is really beginning to shape up now. The work of connecting and retrieving information from the database has already been accomplished, and the results are sitting in a result set that can be accessed by DB_Results. Now we just need to format the results to look presentable within a Web page. The easiest way to accomplish this is to create a table. We're already used to looking at information provided to us in reports that are basically columns of information. Therefore, a table would be suitable for presenting all products, their prices, and part numbers. Each column in the table will represent the data for each individual product that is displayed in a row of the table.

Because we used a where clause in the SQL statement that retrieved the product information, the results are already narrowed, and we can simply display all information in the result set without using too much logic in the script. The script will basically walk through the contents of the result set, starting at the beginning and displaying each item and its relevant information in an HTML tabular format. Therefore, the script can loop through the information in the result set while the script is not at the end of the result set:

```
<% while not DB_Results.eof %>
<% wend %>
```

The result set object, which in this case is DB_Results, contains a property named eof, or end-of-file. Whenever the end of the result set is reached, this property is set to TRUE. Therefore, the while loop is set to execute as long as the eof property is not TRUE, or as long as there are records in the result set.

Of course, simply looping through a result set will add no value to the results displayed in the Web browser. You must actually instruct the Active Server Page to print results of a particular field in the Inventory table to the Web browser. To display information from a result set you can simply use the result set's name followed by the name of the field you want to display. For instance, to display the description of a product, we can use the following statement in the Active Server Page:

```
DB_Results("Description")
```

Because simply printing the information would produce an unwieldy screen, the results are made more legible by incorporating the use of HTML tables.

Finally, if the script that we have created so far simply looped through the result set and displayed values, the script would run forever. Why? Because there is no instruction in the loop to advance to the next row of information in the result set. You may think that implementing the loop alone will physically cause the result set to advance row by row. However, in order to physically advance through the result set to the next row, you must instruct this advancement via the MoveNext method that is available to the result set object (DB_Results).

Smarter Than the Average Script

Typically, a simple while loop will suffice for exporting information from the result set to the appropriate HTML for a Web browser. But there will be times when you will need to add a little more intelligence to the script. In the case of the Product Search page, some products might contain a URL that points to an additional file for more information about the product. But not every product will contain a URL. For those products that do, however, we would like to display the words More information as a hyperlink next to the product and connect that hyperlink to the actual file that contains the additional information.

In the Active Server Page that generates the results for the product search, an if statement is used to check the validity of the URL field for each product being displayed. If the URL contains information, the text More information is created as a hyperlink to the URL contained in the URL field. If it does not, that column of the table is skipped entirely. The following section of code illustrates this logic:

```
<% if DB_Results("URL")<>"" then %>
      <td>
          <a href="<%= DB_Results("URL") %>">More information</a>
      </td>
<% end if %>
```

Closing It Up

After all the results have been passed to the browser and the loop has terminated, there is no longer any need for database connectivity in this Web page. Therefore, the result set and data connection are both closed. It is good practice to close connections that are not in use and to verify any connections that are left open. Some database-management systems might limit the number of concurrent users to a database, and you certainly will not want to waste any of these connections.

To close connections, each ActiveX Data Object used in this page features a Close method. The following lines of code demonstrate how to close a database connection when finished:

```
<% DB_Results.Close
   DB.Close %>
```

Ordering Products

Now that you have totally reviewed how to add the ability to search for products to the CompuShop Web site, let's take a few minutes to review the process of adding information to

20

CREATING A
DYNAMIC
APPLICATION

a database through an Active Server Page and ActiveX Database Objects. Our CompuShop Web site is set to take orders, or in this case, simply allow updates of order information. To create an order-entry system, two files are again required, just as they were for searching products. Both an HTML file for creating the actual form to be filled by the user and an Active Server Page to handle information from that form are required to successfully update information to the Orders table of the CompuShop database.

Many of the techniques for connecting to and retrieving information from a database has already been reviewed in the previous section. A similar approach is used for connecting to the Orders table as was used for connection to the Inventory database. However, in this Active Server Page, we want to verify that information was entered into the data form and actually insert that data into the Orders table. The PurchaseForm.htm file is a simple HTML file with a form and standard input fields for data. The PurchaseIt.asp page is used to retrieve information from that form and update the Orders table. Like the ProductSearch.htm file before, PurchaseForm.htm uses the ACTION attribute of the <FORM> tag to specify which Active Server Page will be handling information from the HTML form.

PurchaseIt.asp

The PurchaseIt.asp file performs validation checks on data input on the purchase form and updates the content in the Orders database. Listing 20.4 shows the PurchaseIt.asp file, including all the validations performed on incoming data and the database commands for updating the database.

Listing 20.4. When adding information to a database, you should perform validation checks to ensure that the data entered is correct.

```
<%@ LANGUAGE="VBSCRIPT" %>

<HTML>
<HEAD>
<META NAME="GENERATOR" Content="Microsoft Visual InterDev 1.0">
<META HTTP-EQUIV="Content-Type" content="text/html">
<TITLE>Order</TITLE>
</HEAD>
<BODY BGCOLOR=#FFFFFF>
<CENTER><IMG SRC="http://jay/compushop/images/compushop.jpg"></CENTER>

<%  dim errors
    errors=0
    dim ErrorList
    ErrorList="<H1>ERROR</H1>"

    if Request.Form("Name")="" then
        errors=1
        ErrorList=ErrorList & "<BR>You must fill in your name!"
    end if

    if Request.Form("Address1")="" then
        errors=1
```

```
        ErrorList=ErrorList & "<BR>You must fill in your address!"
    end if

    if Request.Form("City")="" then
        errors=1
        ErrorList=ErrorList & "<BR>You must fill in your city!"
    end if

    if Request.Form("State")="" then
        errors=1
        ErrorList=ErrorList & "<BR>You must fill in your state!"
    end if

    if Request.Form("Zip")="" then
        errors=1
        ErrorList=ErrorList & "<BR>You must fill in your zip!"
    end if

    if Request.Form("PaymentType")="" then
        errors=1
        ErrorList=ErrorList & "<BR>You must fill in a payment type!"
    end if

    if Request.Form("PaymentType")<>"Check" and
        Request.Form("CardNumber")="" then
            errors=1
            ErrorList=ErrorList &
                    "<BR>You must fill in your card number!"
    end if

    if Request.Form("ProductNumber")="" then
        errors=1
        ErrorList=ErrorList & "<BR>You must fill in a product number!"
    end if

    if Request.Form("Quantity")="" or Request.Form("Quantity")<"0" then
        errors=1
        ErrorList=ErrorList & "<BR>You must specify a quantity!"
    end if

    if errors then %>
        <%= ErrorList %>
<%  else
        Set DB=Server.CreateObject("ADODB.Connection")
        DB.Open "CompuShop"
        InsertString = "INSERT INTO Orders VALUES ('" &
                    Request.Form("Name") & "', '" &
                    Request.Form("Address1") & "', '" &
                    Request.Form("Address2") & "', '" &
                    Request.Form("City") & "', '" &
                    Request.Form("State") & "', '" &
                    Request.Form("Zip") & "', '" &
                    Request.Form("Phone") & "', '" &
                    Request.Form("PaymentType") & "', '" &
                    Request.Form("CardNumber") & "', '" &
                    Request.Form("Quantity") & "', '" &
                    Request.Form("ProductNumber") & "')"
```

continues

20

CREATING A
DYNAMIC
APPLICATION

Listing 20.4. continued

```
        DB.Execute(InsertString)
        DB.Close
%>
        <H1>Thank you for your order!</H1>
<%  end if %>

</BODY>
</HTML>
```

The source in Listing 20.4 is fairly straightforward and doesn't require much analysis. The script basically verifies that all the information entered on the HTML form is valid before submitting it to the database. Most of the `if` statements simply verify that the field is not blank, while some check for other invalid entries. In any case, you might notice that the variable `ErrorList` accumulates all errors and displays them all at once at the end of the script only if an error was generated, which is identified when `Errors` is set to `1`.

You will also notice the familiar ActiveX Data Object commands for opening a connection, executing a SQL statement, and closing the connection. You might notice, however, that a different SQL command is executed. In this case, we want to add information to a database table, not just retrieve data from the table. Therefore, we can use the SQL `INSERT INTO` statement, which allows you to specify which table you want to insert information into as well as the actual data to insert.

> **NOTE**
>
> When inserting information into a database table with the `INSERT INTO` SQL command, make certain that the data specified by the `VALUES` clause is listed in the same order in which it was created in the table into which the data is being inserted. If you are not sure about the order of fields in a particular table, you can view the table's properties by clicking on the Data View tab of the Workspace window in Visual InterDev if you have the data connection added to your project.

The `INSERT INTO` statement expects the name of the table to insert data into as well as a single entry of data. The actual values for the new entry in the database table are defined by information that follows the `VALUES` clause. The basic format for the `INSERT` statement is as follows:

```
INSERT INTO table_name VALUES ('field1_data', 'field2_data', ..., 'fieldn_data')
```

In this page, the actual information passed by the HTML form is obtained by the `Request` object and is substituted for each of the fields to be inserted into the `Orders` table.

Summary

In this chapter you saw how to combine Active Server Pages, ActiveX controls, scripts, and databases to create a simple, yet potentially powerful, Web site. Everything that is covered in this chapter helps illustrate how to apply the knowledge you have gained in this section of the book. With this basic understanding, you are now ready to tackle more complicated tasks and more robust Web sites. In the next part, "Creating Database Applications with Visual InterDev," you will learn more about databases, database connections, and programming Visual InterDev applications to interact with these databases. You will build on the knowledge you have learned in this section and learn how to apply your skills to create truly robust database applications on the Web.

V

PART

Creating Database Applications with Visual InterDev

CHAPTER 21

Creating and Debugging Queries, Stored Procedures, and Triggers

by Craig Eddy

IN THIS CHAPTER

This part of the book describes creating a database application with Visual InterDev. Earlier chapters covered some of the basics. This includes Chapter 5, "Connecting and Using Databases," and Chapter 12, "Database Management with the Visual Data Tools." This part of the book, Part V, "Creating Database Applications with Visual InterDev," builds upon the knowledge gained in these previous chapters.

This chapter discusses how to create and manage the queries, stored procedures, and triggers. Using the Visual Data Tools, you can manipulate the components of a database specified by a Visual InterDev database connection. Creating the database connection is covered in Chapter 5.

This chapter does not go into much technical detail about why queries, stored procedures, and triggers are important to a database. Nor does this chapter explain how these elements should be designed in your particular database. This chapter does provide you with the information necessary to implement these database components using Visual InterDev.

The sample database used in this chapter was created using the Visual Data Tools. Included on the accompanying CD-ROM is a SQL script file that you can run against SQL Server to create this database. If you want to work along with the text, install this script using ISQL/W or SQL Enterprise Manager.

The remaining chapters in this part of the book go into more detail about creating database applications. Topics include the following:

- Using ActiveX database components such as the Active Data Objects, which is discussed in Chapter 22, "Integrating ActiveX Database Components."
- Using server-side VBScript to connect to databases, which is discussed in depth in Chapter 23, "Using Active Server Scripting with Databases."
- Transaction and state management, which is discussed in Chapter 24, "Implementing Transactions and State Management."
- Combining all of the information from these chapters and creating a database application. This is accomplished in Chapter 25, "Putting It All Together—Creating a Web Database Application."

Limitations of the Visual Data Tools

You can use Visual InterDev's Visual Data Tools to open a database connection on any ODBC-compliant source. This includes SQL Server, Oracle, Microsoft Access, Microsoft Excel, and even text files. However, the full capabilities of the Visual Data Tools are only realized when used with Microsoft SQL Server 6.5.

With data sources other than SQL Server 6.5, you will be able to open tables and execute queries. You will not be able to modify the design of a table or to add new tables. However, you will be able to see a list of the table's fields and their properties. The same holds true with the Views tree item in the DataView tab. This tree item displays the queries in a Microsoft Access database. The DataView tab for a Microsoft Access database is shown in Figure 21.1.

FIGURE 21.1.

The DataView tab of a Microsoft Access database.

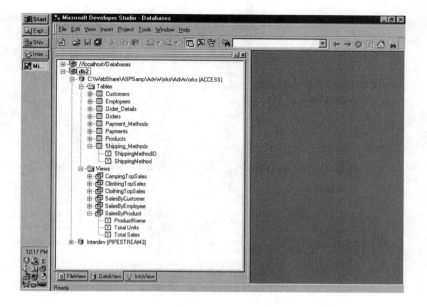

Also, you won't be able to create triggers and stored procedures on databases other than SQL Server 6.5. This is usually because the database does not support such components. However, even older versions of SQL Server are not fully supported with the Visual Data Tools.

Working with the Query Designer

As a programmer who learned about databases by using Microsoft Access, I was always disappointed with the tools that were available for SQL Server. Access provides a very visual user interface for designing and working with databases. The tools provided with SQL Server have a more text-based look and feel to them. For example, there is no grid for modifying the data stored in a table. Access has one. There was also no database diagramming for tasks such as query definition and relationships.

The Visual Data Tools Query Designer provided with Visual InterDev removes those user interface constraints. Using the Query Designer you can visually create SQL statements for querying or updating your database. You can also view and, in some cases, edit the data returned by a query. You can even create parameterized queries, which require some values be provided for each execution of the query.

The Query Designer is shown in Figure 21.2. You can start the Query Designer in one of several ways. First, on the FileView tab you can select a database connection and use the shortcut menu's New Query menu item. Second, you can open the Query Designer by double-clicking a table name on the DataView tab. You will then need to use the Query toolbar to activate all of the panes.

FIGURE 21.2.

The Query Designer.

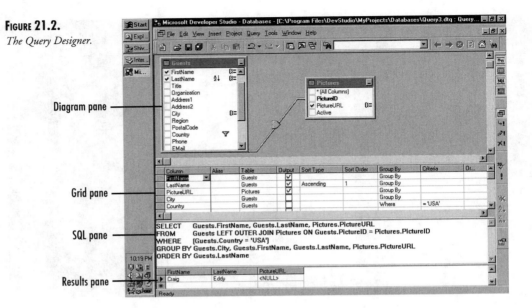

Diagram pane

Grid pane

SQL pane

Results pane

The Four Panes of the Query Designer

As you can see in Figure 21.2, the Query Designer consists of four panes: the Diagram pane, the Grid pane, the SQL pane, and the Results pane. You can have any or all of these panes active at a given time. The top four buttons on the Query toolbar show and hide each of the panes.

The top three panes, the Diagram, Grid, and SQL panes, are synchronized. When you make a change in one pane, the Query Designer updates the other two appropriately to reflect this change.

The Diagram Pane

The Diagram pane displays the tables and views being used in the query. Each table and view gets its own window within the Diagram pane that displays the field names and shows how each field is being used in the query. The title bar of each window displays the table or view name. There is a minimize button that will minimize the window down to just the title bar. This can be useful when you have many tables involved in a single query.

The checkboxes to the left of the field names indicate whether the given field is returned in the result set. There is a special row labeled *(All Columns) that will cause all of the fields to be returned in the result set. Only a field with its box checked will be returned. That does not mean, however, that the field cannot be used in specifying query criteria or grouping.

In Figure 21.2 there is a symbol to the right of the LastName field in the Guests table. This symbol indicates that the query results will be sorted based on the contents of that field. You can specify that a field should be sorted upon by right-clicking the field's name and selecting the appropriate sort order from the shortcut menu.

The symbol to the right of the City field in the Guests table indicates that the results will be grouped by city. As you can see, the City field is not going to be returned by the query (whether this is a good practice is a topic for another discussion). The funnel symbol next to the Country field indicates that the field is being used to define the criteria for the query.

Notice the line connecting the two tables. This line indicates that there is a join between these two tables. The line connects the fields that define the join, but the field in the Guests table is near the bottom of the field list and not visible in the table's window at this time. Joins are used to connect the data in one table with corresponding or related data in another table. For this database, records in the Guests table can have a corresponding record in the Pictures table. The join between these tables defines this relationship.

The join line also displays the type of join being used between the tables. The possible choices are INNER JOIN, OUTER JOIN (in either direction), and FULL OUTER JOIN. The definition of these types of joins is left to a treatise on relational database design. Basically, the type of join determines, based on data in the related fields, which rows will be returned from each table.

The Grid Pane

The Grid pane is where you can set various properties for the fields in the query. The Grid pane is set up like a spreadsheet having one row for each field that takes part in the query. Note that the field does not have to be included in the query's result set in order for it to have a row in the Grid pane.

Each column of the Grid pane represents an attribute of the field for that particular query. You can set an alias for the field, specify whether it is returned in the result set, and specify whether the results are sorted based on the field. You can also specify the grouping to be used for the query, if any, and the criteria that will be used to determine which rows belong in the result set.

To add a field to the Grid pane, you can check the field's checkbox in the Diagram pane, you can drag the field from the Diagram pane into the Grid pane, or you can specify the field using the Column and Table columns of the grid. If you use the Table drop-down first, the Column drop-down will contain only those fields that belong to the specified table. If the Table column is empty, the Column drop-down will contain all fields available to the query.

This pane operates almost identically to other grids found in Microsoft products. You can select an entire row by clicking the row header. Then you can use the shortcut menu to perform various editing tasks.

The SQL Pane

The SQL pane is where the SQL statement for your query is displayed and edited. SQL stands for Structured Query Language, which is the standard language used for creating queries using SQL databases.

The Query Designer takes what you enter in the SQL pane, parses it, and updates the Diagram and Grid panes appropriately. To assist you in editing the SQL statement, the Query Designer will automatically format the statement for you. There is a Verify SQL Syntax button on the Query toolbar that allows you to check the syntax of the query before you attempt to execute it. Although not necessary, it's always a good idea to verify this beforehand.

You can use the SQL pane to modify the SQL statement generated based on changes in the Diagram and Grid panes, or you can enter your own statement. There are cases where the necessary SQL statement cannot be represented in the other two design panes. In these cases, such as with a UNION query, you must enter the SQL statement directly into the SQL pane. If the Query Designer cannot represent the query in the other two panes, those panes will be disabled.

The Results Pane

Finally, the Results pane is where the resulting data is output. This is another grid that displays one column for each field and one row for each record in the result set. If the query's result set is updatable, you can edit the data within the grid. You can add and delete rows as well.

Creating a New Select Query

The steps to create a new query are quite simple. You can open the Query Designer in one of two ways. First, if you're on the FileView tab you can select the appropriate database connection, right-click, and select New Query from the shortcut menu. Second, if you're on the DataView tab, double-click the name of one of the tables or views that will be used in the query.

Here are the steps you'd use in creating a new query using the first method:

1. On the FileView tab, select a database connection. Right-click and select New Query. A blank Query Designer is opened, as shown in Figure 21.3, and the workspace area switches to the DataView tab.

2. Using the DataView tab, drag and drop any tables or views that will be used in your query to the Diagram pane. You can also select specific fields and drag those to the Diagram pane. This will cause the Query Designer to set those fields to be returned in the query's results.

3. In the Diagram pane, click the checkbox on the fields that should be returned by the query. Notice that the Grid and SQL panes adjust accordingly, as shown in Figure 21.4.

FIGURE 21.3.
The empty Query Designer.

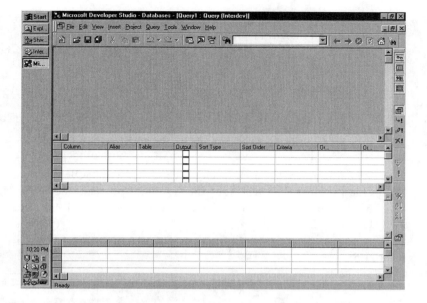

FIGURE 21.4.
The Query Designer with some fields selected.

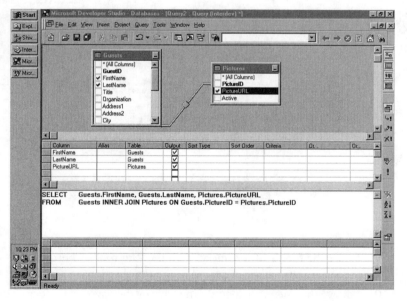

4. If you want to sort the returned data, select the field or fields to sort on, right-click, and select the appropriate sort order from the shortcut menu. Again, notice how the other two panes change as well.

5. If there are any criteria to limit the records returned, enter them in the Criteria columns on the Grid pane. If there is more than one possible value for a given field, use the Or columns as well. If the field in question isn't already in the Grid pane, use the Column and Table columns to add it.

6. If you want to rename a field when it is returned, enter the new name in the Alias column. The Results pane column heading for a field will use the Alias if specified. Otherwise, the string shown in the Column cell for the field will be used.

7. If you have multiple tables and want to change the join type, right-click the join line and select the appropriate type of join in the shortcut menu.

8. When the query has been specified, click the Verify SQL Syntax toolbar button on the Query toolbar. This will verify the SQL that appears in the SQL pane. Any problems will be reported in a message box. Otherwise, you'll receive the message box shown in Figure 21.5.

FIGURE 21.5.

The syntax verified message box.

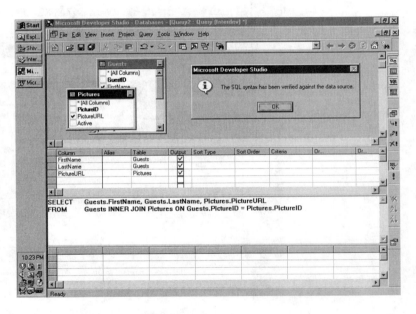

9. To see the results of the query, click the Run toolbar button. The query will execute and the results will be displayed in the Results pane.

10. To save the query, click either the Save or the Save All toolbar button, or use the File | Save or File | Save All menu option. The File Save dialog will activate. Specify a folder and a name for the query file. Click the Save button.

Creating and Debugging Queries, Stored Procedures, and Triggers

CHAPTER **21**

437

21

CREATING AND
DEBUGGING
QUERIES

Creating a New Action Query

So far we've dealt only with Select queries. The Query Designer also allows you to create action queries that will perform some activity upon the data in a table. You can create insert, update, and delete queries. All of these use the top three panes only. The Results pane is not used.

To create an insert, update, or delete query, click the appropriate button on the Query toolbar. The Diagram and Grid panes change slightly depending on which type of query you've chosen. Otherwise, the queries are created exactly as in the previous section.

When you click the Run button, the Query Designer will inform you of the results of the query using a message box. Note that there is no way to Undo an action query. Once you've executed it, the effects are permanent. To save the query, use the File | Save or File | Save All menu option or toolbar buttons.

Debugging Queries

Now that your query has been designed and saved, it's time to execute and, if necessary, debug the query. Queries that perform SELECT statements are much easier to test and debug than action queries. Because action queries usually make changes to the data in the tables, you'll have to restore the original data or at least get the database into a condition that will allow you to test the query. For this reason, this section will cover only SELECT queries.

The amount of time it will take to debug a query is directly related to the number of tables involved. This is due to the often complex nature of the joins among the tables, particularly if more than two related tables are involved in the query. In the case of joined tables, if the query is returning too many or too few records, the problem may lie in the type of join specified between the tables. To change the join type, right-click the line joining the tables in question and use the shortcut menu to alter the type of join.

For example, the join between the Guests and Pictures tables of the sample database can be Select All Rows from Guests, Select All Rows from Pictures, both, or neither. The first two options specify which table will be the "master" table in the relationship. The other table is then a subordinate or lookup table to the first. In the Guests and Pictures relationship, I've chosen Select All Rows from Guests because I want to return all of the rows from the Guests table even if there is no corresponding row in the Pictures table. The InfoViewer topics on SQL Server do a good job of discussing joins.

If you're confident your joins are correct, the next possible source of trouble in a query is in the criteria. Make sure your specified criteria completely model the data you want to return. If the query returns too many rows, the criteria are not specific enough. If not enough rows are returned, the criteria are too specific.

Finally, if your query involves any aggregate functions such as SUM or AVG and the data isn't correct, check your GROUP BY clause to ensure that it contains the proper fields. If you add incorrect fields to the grouping, the aggregate functions will return incorrect values or an incorrect number of rows. If too few rows are returned, you don't have enough fields specified in the GROUP BY clause. If too many rows are returned, you have too many fields.

Working with Stored Procedures

Stored procedures are similar to queries but much more powerful. You program stored procedures using a language called Transact SQL (TSQL), which is a procedural language similar to Microsoft's Visual Basic.

Using TSQL you can execute multiple SQL statements within a stored procedure. You can also use IF...THEN and other familiar constructs to control the flow of execution within the stored procedure. Unlike queries, however, stored procedures are compiled within the database. This allows them to execute much faster than standard queries.

The stored procedures available within a database are displayed in the DataView tab under the Stored Procedures folder. Expand the folder to see all of the currently defined stored procedures for that database. You can also expand a stored procedure entry to see the procedure's list of parameters.

To open a stored procedure for editing, right-click the procedure's name and select Open on the shortcut menu. The procedure opens in a text editor where you can view and modify the TSQL contained within the stored procedure. To execute a stored procedure, select it in the DataView, right-click and choose Run on the shortcut menu. The results are displayed in the Output window.

Creating a New Stored Procedure

To create a new stored procedure, perform the following steps:

1. Select the proper database on the DataView tab. Open the database's folder and right-click Stored Procedures. Select New Stored Procedure on the shortcut menu.

2. A shell for the new stored procedure is created in a text editor window, as shown in Figure 21.6.

3. Replace the text /*Procedure Name*/ with the name of your new stored procedure.

4. Complete the remainder of the stored procedure using Transact SQL.

5. When the stored procedure is completed, click the Save toolbar button or use the File | Save menu option to save the stored procedure into the database. Stored procedures must be saved before they can be used. The process of saving a stored procedure includes parsing its syntax and compiling it on the SQL Server.

FIGURE 21.6.

*The New Stored
Procedure editor.*

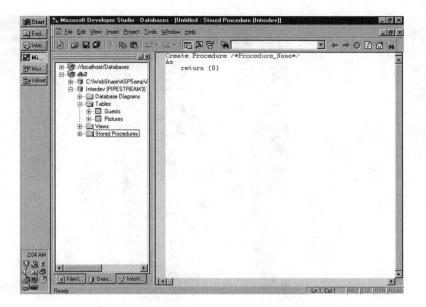

6. If the Transact SQL syntax is incorrect or if the stored procedure references unknown entities within the database, an error will occur when you attempt to save the stored procedure. These errors are displayed in a Server Errors dialog box. The error messages should point you in the right direction to correct the syntax in the stored procedure.

When all of the problems have been removed from the Transact SQL code, the stored procedure will appear in the Stored Procedures folder for the database. You can now use this stored procedure as described in the rest of this section.

Creating Parameterized Stored Procedures

Typically your stored procedures will require some input data in order to execute. These input items are called parameters. For example, you may want to list all of the Guests records in a particular region. To do so, you would create a stored procedure that takes the desired region as a parameter and returns all of the Guests records having that region. Such a stored procedure is shown in Figure 21.7.

This stored procedure takes one parameter, @Region. This parameter is defined as a Varchar data type with a maximum length of 30 characters. If no value is supplied, SQL Server will use NULL as the default value. This is all specified by the line @Region varchar(30) = NULL.

The only block of Transact SQL code is an IF...ELSE block. For those accustomed to reading Visual Basic code, the THEN is implied. If the @Region parameter is not supplied or is passed as NULL, the procedure will return all rows from the Guests table. Otherwise, only those rows having the value specified by @Region in the Region field will be returned.

FIGURE 21.7.

The
`GetGuestsInRegion`
stored procedure.

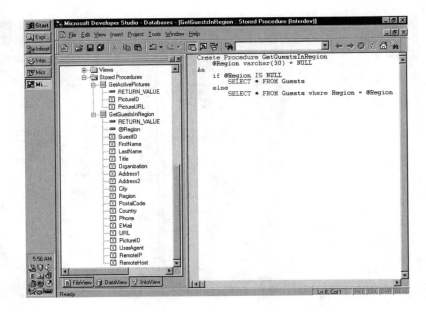

When parameterized stored procedures are executed, Visual InterDev displays the Run Stored Procedure dialog shown in Figure 21.8. This is where you enter values for the parameters of the stored procedure. You can also instruct InterDev to use the parameter's default, if one is available.

FIGURE 21.8.

The Run Stored Procedure dialog.

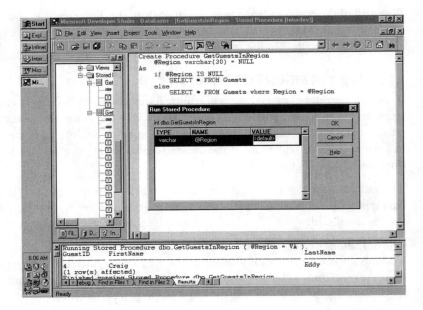

Creating and Debugging Queries, Stored Procedures, and Triggers

CHAPTER 21

441

21

CREATING AND
DEBUGGING
QUERIES

Notice that in the DataView tab the stored procedure has been expanded. The top two items beneath the stored procedure name are the procedure's parameters. The items that follow are the fields that the procedures will return. You can use the shortcut menu on any of these items to view their properties (data type and size).

Executing Stored Procedures

To execute a stored procedure, select the procedure in the DataView and use Run from the shortcut menu or use Tools | Run from the main menu. The Results pane will open if it's not currently visible. The results of the stored procedure's execution will be output to this window, as shown in Figure 21.9.

FIGURE 21.9.

How Visual InterDev looks after running a stored procedure.

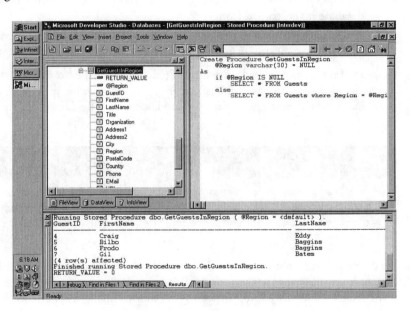

The first line in the output specifies what parameter values were passed to the procedure. The next line is the field header. This shows the name of each field returned by the procedure. Next come the returned rows, one line per row. This is followed by a row count and, finally, the execution finishes by telling us the return value.

NOTE

As you can see from this example, every stored procedure has a return value whether you specify one or not. The default data type for the return value is int and the default value is 0.

Copying, Renaming, and Deleting Stored Procedures

You can make a copy of a stored procedure to use in creating a new stored procedure. You can also copy a stored procedure to another database. The steps are simple:

1. Select the original stored procedure in the DataView tab.
2. Use the Edit | Copy menu option or select Copy from the shortcut menu.
3. Select the Stored Procedures folder of the destination database (either the current database or another SQL Server database).
4. Use Edit | Paste or select Paste from the shortcut menu. Visual InterDev saves and compiles the stored procedure, giving it a unique name if it is pasted to the same database it was copied from.
5. If necessary, edit the stored procedure by opening it. When your edits are completed, click the Save button or use the File | Save menu to recompile the stored procedure.

You can also rename a stored procedure. To do so, select the stored procedure and use the File | Rename menu option or select Rename from the shortcut menu. A dialog appears requesting that you input the new name. Enter it and click OK. The database is updated with the new name.

> **NOTE**
>
> If the stored procedure is opened in an edit window you will not be able to rename it from the menu. Instead, activate its edit window and change the stored procedure name there. Make sure you save the stored procedure after changing its name in this manner.

To delete a stored procedure, select it in the DataView tab and use either Edit | Delete or select Delete from the shortcut menu. A confirmation dialog appears asking you to verify that you want to delete the procedure. Answering yes on this dialog will permanently delete the procedure from the database.

> **NOTE**
>
> If the stored procedure is opened in an edit window you will not be able to delete it. The Delete items will be disabled in the menus. You must close the edit window containing the stored procedure before you can delete it.

Working with Triggers

Triggers are specialized stored procedures that, if defined for a table, are automatically executed every time data in the table changes. Triggers are useful for enforcing complex business rules on the data in the table. If the updated data does not satisfy the business rules, the changes can be rolled back, or canceled. Triggers can also be used to perform lookups or updates on other tables.

You can define triggers for insert, update, and delete actions on a given table. You can define one trigger for all three actions or any combination of the actions. For example, you may have one trigger that handles inserts and updates on the table and another trigger that handles deletions from the table.

To view the contents of an existing trigger, expand the table folder in the DataView tab. Triggers appear after the fields in the expanded tree. Either double-click the trigger's name or select the trigger and use the Open item on the shortcut menu.

Creating a Trigger

To create a trigger, follow these steps:

1. Select any table in the Tables folder of the DataView tab. Use the shortcut menu and select New Trigger.

2. An edit window opens with the skeleton of a trigger, as shown in Figure 21.10.

FIGURE 21.10.
The edit window of a new trigger.

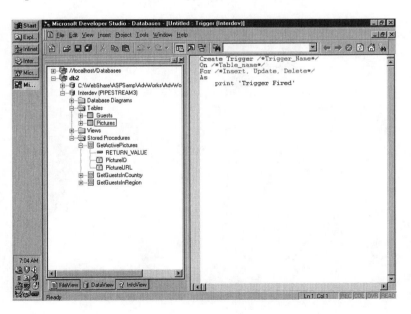

3. Replace /*Trigger_Name*/ with the name for the trigger, /*Table_name*/ with the name of the table to which this trigger will belong, and /*Insert, Update, Delete*/ with any combination of Insert, Update, and Delete, depending on the nature of the new trigger.

4. Add Transact SQL code to the body of the trigger (the portion after AS).

5. When you have finished coding the trigger, click the Save button or use the File | Save menu item. The trigger will be compiled into the database. If there are any errors within the trigger code, they will be displayed within a Server Errors dialog.

Removing Triggers

To remove a trigger, select it in the DataView tab and use Edit | Delete or select Delete from the shortcut menu. If the trigger is open in an edit window, the Delete items will be disabled. You must close the edit window in order to delete the trigger.

Summary

This chapter discussed the creation and usage of queries, stored procedures, and triggers with Visual InterDev. The remaining chapters in this section will discuss advanced database topics and how to utilize Active Server scripting to access your databases. In the final chapter of Part V, we'll create an Active Server application based on the database we've used in this chapter.

Integrating ActiveX Database Components

by Craig Eddy

IN THIS CHAPTER

CHAPTER 22

In the previous chapter, you learned all about using the Microsoft Visual Data Tools to create queries and access SQL Server stored procedures and triggers. While the information was certainly useful in general, the topic of the Visual Data Tools is not specific to Web programming or to Visual InterDev. This chapter, however, does contain such specific information.

The topic of this chapter is integrating ActiveX database components into your Active Server Pages. Using Visual InterDev as your development tool, you'll learn all about the use of the ActiveX Data Objects. You'll also learn about some design-time database controls that can perform some of the otherwise tedious database coding tasks for you. I end this chapter with an example of how all of these components come together to form an interactive database query and updating tool.

These database components include the ActiveX Data Objects, or ADO, which are high-speed, lightweight data-access objects specifically designed for use with Microsoft OLE DB providers. ADO, as you'll see in this chapter, has a very flat object model. This makes it particularly easy to program in the Active Server environment because you do not have to traverse an entire object model to get your database work accomplished.

In the second half of this chapter I cover some of the ActiveX design-time controls provided with Visual InterDev. These controls are useful only at design-time. They will do the grunt work of inserting script or HTML code into your Active Server Pages for you. They have no effect on the runtime characteristics of your Active Server Pages. Design-time controls, as you'll see in this chapter, are inserted and have their properties adjusted just like any other ActiveX control you'd insert into your Active Server Pages. The script or HTML generated depends on how the control's properties are set.

Introducing the ActiveX Data Objects

In the flurry of development tools and Web server tools that Microsoft introduced in 1996 and 1997 came the introduction of a new database technology called OLE DB. OLE DB is a set of OLE interfaces that provide a consistent means of access to many different types of data sources. OLE DB is similar to (and rides on top of) the Open Database Connectivity (ODBC) platform in that it is intended to provide a common means of accessing a variety of diverse data service providers.

The ActiveX Data Objects provided for use with Active Server Pages and Visual InterDev are optimized for use with OLE DB. The ActiveX Data Objects provide several key advantages to the Active Server developer:

- Objects can be created independently of one another. The flat object model does not require you to create and maintain an entire hierarchy of objects.
- Support for batch updates.
- Support for stored procedures, including those that return multiple result sets.
- Support for many different cursor types, including some server-side cursors.
- Free-threaded objects, which are more efficient for use in Web server applications.

The ADO Object Model

As mentioned earlier, the ActiveX Data Objects utilize a flat object model. You do not have to create objects that are the children of other objects. Instead, you can create independent objects and then associate them using properties such as `ActiveConnection`, which relates a `Recordset` object with a `Connection` object. Another advantage of the ADO model is that it provides you with the full capabilities exposed by the underlying data provider, but also provides quick methods of performing command operations.

A diagram of the ADO object model is shown in Figure 22.1. If you're familiar with the Data Access Objects or the Remote Data Objects included with Microsoft Visual Basic, you'll immediately appreciate the simplicity of the ADO model.

FIGURE 22.1.
The ADO object model.

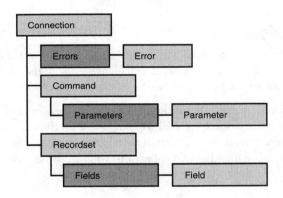

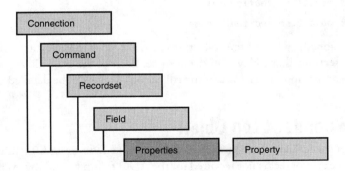

Although the object hierarchy is flat, Figure 22.1 seems to imply that the `Command` and `Recordset` objects are children of the `Connection` object. This is not the case, however. What Figure 22.1 illustrates is that the `Command` and `Recordset` objects cannot do their work without a corresponding open `Connection` object. If a `Command` or `Recordset` is created independent of an active connection, however, the ADO engine will create a `Connection` object but won't assign that object to an object variable.

> **NOTE**
>
> If you will be creating multiple Recordset and/or Command objects that will access the same Connection object, you should explicitly create a Connection object. You will then use this Connection object as the source for creating the Recordset and/or Command objects.

Another aspect of the simplicity of the ADO model is that it contains only a few objects. This set of objects, though, can be used to completely model any imaginable data source. The fact that there are fewer objects in the collection makes it easier to code your Active Server Pages—you can get the same work done while having to learn and remember the usage and syntax of fewer objects.

ADO Collections

In the remainder of this section I will introduce you to the various objects within the ADO model. While this can't be considered an exhaustive study of the ADO objects and collections, it will provide you with a base upon which to use the ADO within your Active Server Pages.

All of the ADO collections contain the Item and Count properties found in most OLE object collections. The Item property is used to reference a specific member of the collection. The Count property evaluates to the number of member objects currently defined on the collection. To reference a specific member of a collection, you can use any of the following:

■ *object.collection.*Item(0)

■ *object.collection.*Item("*name*")

■ *object.collection.*(0)

■ *object.collection.*("*name*")

Additionally, a few of the collections provide other means of accessing their member objects. The sections that follow will detail these. Each of the collections has its own set of methods, depending upon the nature of the collection. These will be detailed individually in the following sections as well.

The Connection Object

The Connection object provides an open connection to an OLE DB data source. An explicit Connection object is not required for the ADO to function. However, if an explicit Connection object is not created, the ADO will create an implicit one whenever a Recordset object is opened or a Command object is executed. The hierarchy of the Connection object is shown in Figure 22.2.

FIGURE 22.2.
The ADO Connection *object.*

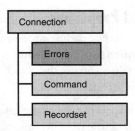

Each open Connection object represents a connection to the underlying data source. You can establish and break the physical connection using the Open and Close methods, respectively. These methods will be discussed in the upcoming section "Using the ActiveX Data Objects."

The type of physical connection used to access the data depends, of course, upon what the data source is and where it is located relative to the machine on which the ADO connection is instantiated. The connection may be attached to a local Microsoft Access database or to a remote server database residing on a SQL Server machine on the other side of the continent.

The Execute Method

In addition to the Open and Close methods, the Connection object also has an Execute method. This method allows you to run a query against the underlying data source. The query can either turn results into a Recordset object or it can perform some action upon the underlying data. The syntax for the Execute method takes either of the following forms:

```
Set recordset = connection.Execute(CommandText, [RecordsAffected], [Options])
```

or

```
connection.Execute CommandText, [RecordsAffected], [Options]
```

The CommandText parameter is a string representing the query, table name, or stored procedure to be executed. The format of this string is specific to the underlying OLE DB data source. The RecordsAffected optional parameter provides a means for the data source to return the number of records that were affected by the operation. The data type for this variable is Long. Finally, the Options parameter provides a means of instructing the data source how it should interpret the contents of the CommandText parameter. The available choices are

- adCmdText (1): The CommandText parameter contains a textual command.
- adCmdTable (2): The CommandText parameter contains a table name.
- adCmdStoredProc (4): CommandText contains a call to a stored procedure.
- adCmdUnknown (8): (Default) The type of the command is not known.

Connection Object Properties

The Connection object has several useful properties. However, you'll probably find that in practice you'll use them infrequently. This is due to the fact that the most useful property, ConnectionString, is set when you use the object's Open method. Some of the more useful properties are outlined in this section.

The ConnectionString property contains the information necessary to actually open a connection to the underlying data source. This information includes a username and password for access control, the data source name if ODBC is being used, a provider-specific filename used to identify the exact source of the data, and the name of the OLE DB provider. Not all of this information is required for every OLE DB provider, however.

The ConnectionTimeout property indicates how long the ADO engine should wait while attempting to establish a connection. Should this time period expire without a successful connection, an error will be generated. This time is specified in seconds, and the default value is 15.

The CommandTimeout property is similar to the ConnectionTimeout property. It specifies the length of time to wait for a command to complete before generating an error. This property also specifies seconds, and the default value is 30.

The Mode property is a read/write property that specifies what kinds of modifications can be made to the underlying data in a connection. This property must be set only when the connection is closed.

Transaction Management

The Connection object also provides methods that allow you to use transaction-based processing on the data source. These methods are BeginTrans, CommitTrans, and RollbackTrans. More information about transaction processing is provided in Chapter 24, "Implementing Transactions and State Management."

Transactions are used to group commands together. If any one of the commands fails, the entire group of commands can be rolled back and their effects undone. Likewise, if all commands succeed, the entire group can be committed to the data source at one time. If no transaction processing is used, the OLE DB provider will commit the operations to the data source as soon as they are performed.

The BeginTrans method starts a new transaction. From the point that BeginTrans is executed, all operations against the data source are wrapped together in the transaction. The CommitTrans method instructs the OLE DB provider to actually commit the transactions to the data source and to end the current transaction. On the opposite side, RollbackTrans informs the provider that the transaction should be cancelled. All operations that took place since the BeginTrans method was invoked will be wiped out.

Integrating ActiveX Database Components

CHAPTER 22

451

22

ACTIVEX
DATABASE
COMPONENTS

The Recordset Object

The Recordset object is used to view and manipulate the data in an underlying data source. The Recordset's data can be derived from a base table or an executed query. Using a Recordset, you can perform a variety of operations on the data, including updating, deleting, and inserting records, providing the data source and the query executed permit such functions. This section doesn't provide an exhaustive reference to the Recordset object, but it will get you started in using it effectively.

As you can see in Figure 22.3, the Recordset object requires a Connection object in order to function. You can, of course, create a Recordset independent of a Connection, but in doing so the ADO engine will create an implicit Connection object. This Connection object just won't be assigned to an object variable.

FIGURE 22.3.
The Recordset *object.*

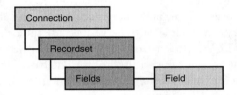

The Fields Collection

Each Recordset object has a Fields collection that contains a Field object for each column in the underlying data. Using the Field object's Value property, you can set or return the data in the current record for the specified column. Use any of the following to retrieve the value for a specific field:

- recordset.Fields.Item(0)
- recordset.Fields.Item("*name*")
- recordset.Fields(0)
- recordset.Fields("*name*")
- recordset(0)
- recordset("*name*")
- recordset![*name*]

In addition to the Value property, the Field object also sports a number of other useful properties. These include the Type, Precision, and NumericScale properties, which provide you with some basic attributes about each field. There are also properties for DefinedSize and ActualSize, which return the declared size of a field and the size of the data stored in the field for the current record, respectively.

Navigating the Recordset's Data

The ADO model provides several methods for navigating the data in a Recordset object. These consist mainly of MoveFirst, MoveNext, MovePrevious, and MoveLast. There are also two properties, AbsolutePosition and AbsolutePage, which can be used to move to different records in the recordset.

The MoveFirst method moves to the first record in the recordset. MoveNext moves the record pointer to the record following the current record. MovePrevious moves the record pointer to the record preceding the current record. MoveLast moves the record pointer to the last record in the recordset. There is also a Move method that allows you to move a specified number of records, either relative to the current record or relative to a record bookmark specified by the method's optional second parameter.

The AbsolutePosition property sets the current record pointer to a specified record number within the recordset. Normally you would not discuss absolute positioning with a database management system such as SQL Server because the concept of a numeric record pointer is nonexistent. This is especially true of dynamic recordsets whose membership can be changed based upon the actions of other users of the database. However, the AbsolutePosition property allows you to specify that for the current sort order on the current recordset, move to record number *x*. This is a 1-based property, meaning that to move to the first record in the recordset, you would use

```
Recordset.AbsolutePosition = 1
```

The upper limit to the AbsolutePosition property is the value of the recordset's RecordCount property.

Using the ADO's paging feature, you can divide a recordset into pages, each containing the same number of records. The number of records contained in a page is controlled by the PageSize property. Using the AbsolutePage property, you can specify which page, from 1 to PageCount, to set as the current page. The first record on that page then becomes the current record.

While navigating a recordset, you can check the BOF and EOF Boolean properties to determine whether you've reached the beginning or end, respectively, of the recordset. When the record pointer is positioned at the first record and you execute the MovePrevious method, the current record will become invalid and the BOF property will be set to True. Likewise, if the record pointer is positioned at the last record in the recordset and you execute MoveNext, the record pointer becomes invalid and the EOF property is set to True.

Miscellaneous Recordset Methods and Properties

The Recordset object has far too many properties to explain all of them in the context of this chapter. However, this section will introduce you to some of the more important of these properties.

First, the `CursorType` property determines what type of cursor is created for the `Recordset` object. The property is read/write when the recordset is closed and read-only after the recordset is opened. You can specify a value for this property using the property itself or by setting the `CursorType` parameter when you invoke the recordset's `Open` method. The possible values for `CursorType` are

- `adOpenForwardOnly (0)`—A forward-only cursor. Similar to a static cursor, but enables you to move through the recordset in the forward direction only. This type of cursor is ideal when you need to make a single pass through the records in the recordset. This is the default value for the `CursorType` property.

- `adOpenKeyset (2)`—A keyset cursor. Similar to a dynamic cursor except that records added by other users are not visible to the recordset. Data changes to records in the recordset are visible, however, and records deleted by other users become inaccessible to the recordset.

- `adOpenDynamic (3)`—A dynamic cursor. Any modifications, additions, or deletions made by other users are visible in the recordset. Also, every form of record navigation is available. Bookmarks are only available if the OLE DB provider supports them.

- `adOpenStatic (4)`—A static cursor. Produces a static copy of the recordset. No additions, deletions, or modifications are visible to the recordset.

To determine which operations an opened `Recordset` object will allow, you can invoke the `Supports` method. This method's syntax is

```
SET boolean = recordset.Supports(CursorOptions)
```

where `CursorOptions` is any of the constants specified by `CursorOptionEnum`. The method returns `True` if the specified cursor option is valid for the recordset.

The possible `CursorOptions` values are as follows:

- `adAddNew (16778240)`—`AddNew` method is available.

- `adApproxPosition (16384)`—The `AbsoluteRecord` and `AbsolutePage` properties are available.

- `adBookmark (8192)`—The `Bookmark` property can be used to access specific records.

- `adDelete (16779264)`—The `Delete` method is available.

- `adHoldRecords (256)`—You can retrieve more records without committing all pending changes and releasing all currently held records.

- `adMovePrevious (512)`—You can use the `MovePrevious` or `Move` methods to move backward in a recordset.

- `adResync (131072)`—You can update the recordset's data with the data currently available in the database.

- adUpdate (16809984)—You can invoke the Update method to commit record changes to the database.
- adUpdateBatch (65536)—You can use batch updating to commit changes to the database in groups.

The ActiveConnection property allows you to create a recordset independent of a Connection object. You can create one Recordset object that will be used with multiple Connection objects, for example. To assign the Recordset to a Connection, set the ActiveConnection property to a reference to the Connection object. The syntax is

```
Set recordset.ActiveConnection = connection
```

This property is read/write when the recordset is closed. It is read-only after the recordset has been opened or the Source property has been set to a valid Command object.

The Source property is where the source for the data is set. This can be set to a Command object, a SQL statement, a table name, or a stored procedure name. Like most recordset properties, Source is read/write when the recordset is closed and read-only when the recordset is opened. If you set the value to a valid Command object, the recordset inherits the ActiveConnection property from the Command object. Viewing the Source property in this case does not return the name of the Command object, but rather the Command object's CommandText property.

The Command Object

The final ActiveX Data Object discussed in this chapter is the Command object. A Command object is created to hold a command you wish to execute against a data source. They are typically used with parameterized queries or stored procedures, thanks to the availability of the Parameters collection (discussed later in this chapter).

You can create a Command object that returns results to a Recordset object, performs a batch process on the data, or makes changes to the database structure. Like a Recordset, Command objects can be created independent of a Connection object. Like the Connection object, the CommandText property can be a SQL statement, a table name, or a stored procedure.

Properties and Methods of the Command Object

The Command object has only a few properties and methods. These are introduced in this section.

The CommandText property holds the text of the command to be executed and indicates what this text is. As mentioned with the Connection object, the CommandType property can take one of four values:

- adCmdText (1): The CommandText parameter contains a textual command.
- adCmdTable (2): The CommandText parameter contains a table name.

■ adCmdStoredProc (4): CommandText contains a call to a stored procedure.

■ adCmdUnknown (8): (Default) The type of the command is not known.

The ActiveConnection property is identical to the Recordset object's ActiveConnection property. Setting it to a valid Connection object will associate the Command object with that Connection object.

The CommandTimeout property behaves identically to the Connection object's CommandTimeout property—it specifies the amount of time the ADO engine will give a command to complete its execution.

Finally, the Prepared property specifies whether the provider should prepare (compile) the command before executing it. If this is set to False, the provider should execute the command directly, without compiling it. If set to True, having a compiled version of the command will allow subsequent executions of that command to operate faster (though the *first* execution may be a little slower due to the time it takes to compile the command).

There are only two methods for the Command object: CreateParameter and Execute. The Execute method executes the SQL query or stored procedure specified by the CommandText property. If the query returns results, a Recordset object can be created to hold them. The syntax for the Execute method is either

```
Set recordset = command.Execute(RecordsAffected, Parameters, Options)
```

or

```
command.Execute RecordsAffected, Parameters, Options
```

where *RecordsAffected* is an optional variable to hold a count of the number of records affected by the Command object, *Parameters* is an optional variant array of parameter values, and *Options* is an optional parameter used to specify the CommandType property for the Command object.

The CreateParameter method is used to create a new Parameter object, as discussed in the next section.

The Parameters Collection

The Parameters collection is used to specify any parameters that may be required during the execution of a Command object. The Parameters collection is made up of Parameter objects. The necessary Parameter objects are defined by the query or stored procedure being executed.

The Parameters collection has the standard properties and methods: Count and Item properties and Append, Delete, and Refresh methods. The Append method is used to add a parameter created with the Command object's CreateParameter method to the Parameters collection. The syntax for the CreateParameter method is

```
Set parameter = command.CreateParameter(Name, Type, Direction, Size, Value)
```

The Parameter object has properties that correspond to the parameters for the CreateParameter method. They describe the parameter and its usage in the current Command object. These properties include Name, Type, Value, Direction, and Size. To define a parameter for a Command object, use the following code:

```
Set myCommand = Server.CreateObject("ADODB.Command")
Set myParameter = myCommand.CreateParameter
➥("Param1", adVarChar, adParamInput, 50, "Parameter Value")
MyCommand.Parameters.Append myParameter
```

Using the ActiveX Data Objects

Now that you've been introduced to the ActiveX Data Objects, it's time to put them to use. This section will provide some brief examples of opening an ADO Connection object and creating an ADO recordset.

Opening an ADO Connection

A simple example illustrating how to open an ADO Connection object is provided in Listing 22.1. The results of this page are shown in Figure 22.4.

Listing 22.1. An ADO connection example.

```
<%@ LANGUAGE="VBSCRIPT" %>

<HTML><HEAD><TITLE>Connection Properties</TITLE></HEAD>
<BODY>
<%
set conn = Server.CreateObject("ADODB.Connection")
conn.open "DSN=WebGuest;UID=sa;DATABASE=Interdev", "sa", "secret"
%>
<font face="Comic Sans MS">
<CENTER>
<H2>Connection Properties</H2>
<table border=1>
<tr><td align=right>Provider:</td><td><%=conn.Provider %></td></tr>
<tr><td align=right>Connection Timeout:</td><td> <%=
➥conn.ConnectionTimeout %></td></tr>
<tr><td align=right>Command Timeout:</td><td> <%=conn.CommandTimeout %></td></tr>
<tr><td align=right>Isolation Level:</td><td> <%=conn.IsolationLevel %></td></tr>
<tr><td align=right>Mode:</td><td> <%=conn.Mode %></td></tr>
</table></CENTER></font>
<% conn.close %>
</BODY></HTML>
```

The script code begins by creating an object to hold the Connection object, conn. The Open method is then invoked, providing an ODBC data source name, a username, and a password. Following this is the HTML to create a table where we'll output some of the properties of the newly opened Connection object. The properties being displayed are Provider, ConnectionTimeout, CommandTimeout, IsolationLevel, and Mode. The connection is then closed.

FIGURE 22.4.
The ADO Connection sample Web page.

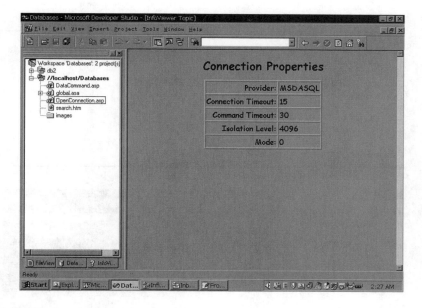

Creating an ADO Recordset

Now let's look at returning some results with a recordset. Doing so is not much more difficult than the previous example. The code is presented in Listing 22.2. An example of the resulting Web page is shown in Figure 22.5.

Listing 22.2. The recordset sample code.

```
<%@ LANGUAGE="VBSCRIPT" %>

<HTML><HEAD><TITLE>Registered Guests</TITLE></HEAD><BODY>
<%
set conn = Server.CreateObject("ADODB.Connection")
set rs = Server.CreateObject("ADODB.Recordset")
set cmd = Server.CreateObject("ADODB.Command")
conn.open "DSN=WebGuest;UID=sa;DATABASE=Interdev", "sa", "secret"
cmd.CommandText = "SELECT FirstName, LastName, Title FROM Guests"
cmd.CommandType = 1
Set cmd.ActiveConnection = conn
rs.Open cmd, , 1, 1
%>
<font face="Comic Sans MS">
<CENTER>
<H2>Registered Guests</H2>
<table border=1>
<tr><th>First Name</th><th>Last Name</th><th>Title</th></tr>
<%while not rs.eof %>
<tr><td><%=rs("FirstName")%></td>
    <td><%=rs("LastName")%></td>
    <td><%=rs("Title")%></td>
```

continues

Listing 22.2. continued

```
</tr>
<%
    rs.MoveNext
wend
%>
</table>
<%
rs.close
conn.close
%>
</BODY></HTML>
```

Figure 22.5.

The output page from the recordset example.

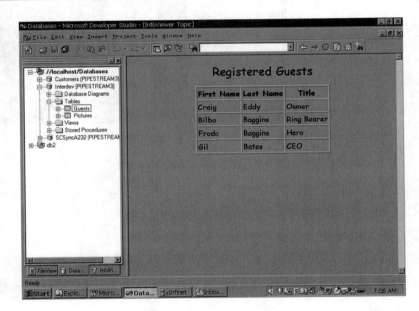

This example starts out similarly to Listing 22.1. The first task is to create several objects that will be used in the page. A Connection, a Command, and a Recordset object are created. The Connection object is then opened as in the previous example.

Next, some of the Command object's properties are set to define the query that we're going to execute. The SQL statement being used to return results is placed in the CommandText property, and the CommandType property is set to indicate that CommandText contains a SQL string. Finally, the Command object's ActiveConnection property is set to the connection opened earlier.

Next, the recordset is opened using the Open method. Here the Command object is specified as the Source parameter, an ActiveConnection parameter is not necessary (recall that the recordset will inherit the command's ActiveConnection value), the CursorType is set to 1 (a keyset cursor), and the LockType is also set to 1 (a read-only recordset is produced).

Now that the recordset is opened, the code can start to navigate the recordset's returned rows. The page is going to display the results in a table, so the HTML defining the table's header row is output first. Then the code uses a While loop to step through each record in the recordset. Each field returned by the query is placed into a different column of the table. After all columns have been output to the HTML, the recordset's MoveNext method is invoked to move the current record to the next record in the recordset. When the loop reaches the end of the recordset, signified by the EOF property becoming True, the table definition is ended. Finally, the code closes down the Recordset and Connection objects.

One possible extension you might want to make to the code in Listing 22.2 is to add a check on the possibility that the query returns no results. Instead of outputting a table with only a header row, you should output a message to the effect that there are no results for the current query.

Design-Time ActiveX Controls

In the previous sections we've discussed the ActiveX Data Objects. These are OLE Automation objects accessible only through coding with some sort of scripting engine. In this section I introduce you to some of the design-time ActiveX controls provided with Visual InterDev.

A design-time ActiveX control is a control that you embed into your script files just like you would embed an ActiveX control into a standard HTML page. The difference is that a design-time control will produce HTML and script code, depending upon the properties that you set at design-time.

There are three design-time ActiveX controls relevant to this chapter. One is the *Data Command* control, which can create script code similar to the second example in the previous section. The other two are the *Data Range Header* and *Data Range Footer* controls. These are used to embed script into the page that performs the tasks of field and record navigation. All three of these controls will be discussed in the remainder of this section.

Inserting the Control

Inserting the Data Command control into an Active Server Page is a simple process. Simply select the spot in your page where you'd like to insert the control (preferably near the top of the file), and use the Insert | Into HTML | ActiveX Control menu item. The Insert ActiveX Control dialog, shown in Figure 22.6, appears.

When you insert a design-time control into your Active Server Pages, the control's OBJECT tag and script output will be bracketed by specially formatted comments. These comments allow Visual InterDev to identify those portions of the script page that relate to a specific design-time control. When you choose to edit the design-time controls properties, InterDev will highlight the portion of the script that appears between these comment tags. This section will be replaced with the updated script that results from your property changes. You should not edit these comment tags, which appear as

```
<!--METADATA TYPE="DesignerControl" startspan
<OBJECT>...
...</OBJECT>
-->
```

and

```
<!--METADATA TYPE="DesignerControl" endspan-->
```

FIGURE 22.6.
*The Insert ActiveX
Control dialog.*

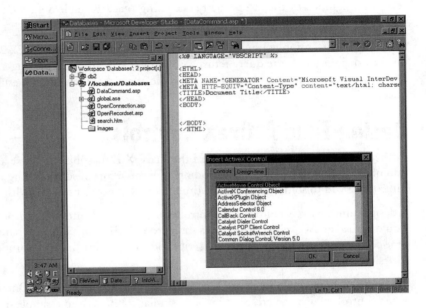

Editing the Control's Properties

To edit the control's properties, open the edit window for the page in question. Click in the script code anywhere between the `startspan` and the `endspan` comments for the control to be edited. You then have two choices. First, you can right-click and select Edit Design-Time Control on the shortcut menu. Or, you can use the Edit | ActiveX Control in HTML menu item from the main menu. The control's designer will appear, as shown in Figure 22.7.

Once you have finished editing the control's properties, close the designer window to update the script code on the Active Server Page that relates to the control.

WARNING

If you edit the control's script directly in the script edit window, your changes will be lost the next time you use the control's designer window to edit its properties. Likewise, if you change the name of the control in the <OBJECT> tag, you should change the code associated with the control to reflect the new name as well.

FIGURE 22.7.

The Data Command designer and property dialog.

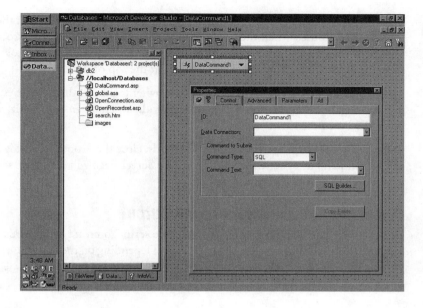

Using the Data Command Control

The Data Command control creates script code that will allow you to browse or modify data pointed to by an InterDev project's data connection. Depending on the properties you set on the control, it will set up script code that creates all the objects necessary to query the database. The properties of these objects will be set according to the properties you specify for the Data Command control.

Setting the Control's Properties

The properties for the Data Command control are set using one of the four tabs on the Properties dialog shown in Figure 22.7.

On the Control tab, you specify the name to use for the Data Command as well as the data connection to use. Using the Command To Submit frame you can specify the `CommandText` and `CommandType` properties. If you choose SQL in the Command Type drop-down list, the SQL Builder button activates. You can click this button to use the Query Builder window. This will allow you to construct a new query based upon existing tables and queries in the database.

On the Advanced tab you can set such properties as the cursor and lock types, as well as the command timeout time and the maximum number of records returned by the resulting data set. You can also specify the size of the data cache used by the ADO by specifying the number of records to cache on the network drive. If you want the command compiled before it is executed, check the Prepared box.

On the Parameters table you specify the properties of any parameters that the Data Command is using. This is used when the CommandText property refers to a stored procedure. The name, type, and size of each parameter is provided. You can fill in the Value column by selecting a specific parameter and typing in the text box at the top of the tab.

The All tab is where you can use a property browser to edit all the properties of the Data Command control. This does not include the individual parameters, however, which must be set using the Parameters tab.

Once you've set the properties to suit your needs, close the Properties dialog and then close the Data Command designer window. The Active Server Page will now have script code added to it to match the properties you specified.

Dissecting the Control's Script Output

Once you've closed the control's designer, the script to create the recordset specified by the properties is placed into the Active Server Page. Depending on the CommandText and CommandType properties, you may have more or fewer ADO objects. A sample of some code generated is provided in Listing 22.3.

Listing 22.2. The recordset sample code.

```
<!--METADATA TYPE="DesignerControl" startspan
    <OBJECT ID="DataCommand1" WIDTH=151 HEIGHT=24
    CLASSID="CLSID:7FAEED80-9D58-11CF-8F68-00AA006D27C2">
        <PARAM NAME="_Version" VALUE="65536">
        <PARAM NAME="_Version" VALUE="65536">
        <PARAM NAME="_ExtentX" VALUE="3969">
        <PARAM NAME="_ExtentY" VALUE="635">
        <PARAM NAME="_StockProps" VALUE="0">
        <PARAM NAME="DataConnection" VALUE="Interdev">
        <PARAM NAME="CommandText" VALUE="dbo.&quot;GetGuestsInCountry&quot;">
        <PARAM NAME="CommandType" VALUE="1">
        <PARAM NAME="ParamCount" VALUE="2">
        <PARAM NAME="Param0" VALUE="Return Value,,4,4,4">
        <PARAM NAME="Param1" VALUE="@Country,,12,1,20">
    </OBJECT>
-->
<%
Set Interdev = Server.CreateObject("ADODB.Connection")
Interdev.ConnectionTimeout = Session("Interdev_ConnectionTimeout")
Interdev.CommandTimeout = Session("Interdev_CommandTimeout")
Interdev.Open Session("Interdev_ConnectionString"),
➥Session("Interdev_RuntimeUserName"), Session("Interdev_RuntimePassword")
Set cmdTemp = Server.CreateObject("ADODB.Command")
Set DataCommand1 = Server.CreateObject("ADODB.Recordset")
cmdTemp.CommandText = "dbo.""GetGuestsInCountry"""
cmdTemp.CommandType = 4
Set cmdTemp.ActiveConnection = Interdev
Set tmpParam = cmdTemp.CreateParameter("Return Value", 3, 4, 4)
cmdTemp.Parameters.Append tmpParam
Set tmpParam = cmdTemp.CreateParameter("@Country", 200, 1, 20)
```

```
cmdTemp.Parameters.Append tmpParam
DataCommand1.Open cmdTemp, , 0, 1
%>
<!--METADATA TYPE="DesignerControl" endspan-->
```

The code can be divided into three basic chunks. The first chunk creates a `Connection` object and assigns its properties using the values from some session properties found in the `GLOBAL.ASA` file. The second chunk creates a `Command` object and sets its properties. The Parameters collection for this `Command` object is then populated. Finally, the last chunk of code opens the `Recordset` object using the objects defined.

You can then do whatever you want with the `Recordset` object. The Data Command control has quickly placed code in your Active Server Page that sets up the `Recordset` for you. You didn't even need to know the material from the first half of this chapter—Visual InterDev can do it all for you.

Using the Data Range Controls

The Data Range controls insert script into your Active Server Pages that will do most of the grunt work necessary to output a recordset's data onto the Web page. There are the Data Range Header and Data Range Footer controls. The two controls work in tandem, but, depending on how the data is to be displayed on the page, you can use the Data Range Header by itself.

In this chapter I will introduce you to these controls. Chapter 23, "Using Active Server Scripting with Databases," will use them in more depth.

Using the Data Range controls, you can simplify the tasks of

- Outputting an entire recordset's data onto a Web page.
- Outputting a recordset's data using a paging methodology, where only a certain number of records are displayed on each page.
- Quickly generating tabular data from your recordset.
- Optimizing paging through the use of record caching on the Web server.

The Data Range Header Control

The Data Range Header control provides the script that appears at the top of the page. The script generated by the control depends on the properties you set when the control is in edit mode. For the purposes of this chapter, we'll consider two simple cases: outputting the entire recordset at one shot and using paging.

The control's default property settings will create a script designed to output the entire recordset on a single page. The `Recordset` object will be defined to most efficiently output the records onto the page. This is done by choosing the proper `CursorType` (Forward Only) and `LockType` (Read Only) for the `Recordset` object.

To control whether the entire recordset is output in one shot or paging is used, check the Record Paging checkbox that appears on the Control tab of the Property dialog on the control's designer window. Then set the PageSize property to the number of records that should appear on each page.

To support paging you must choose an appropriate CursorType that supports paging, such as Keyset or Static. Forward Only and Dynamic cursors do not support paging because they do not support bookmarks. You must also choose a record source that will support scrollable cursors. This includes tables, SQL statements, views, and stored procedures, which contain only a single SELECT statement. Also, the stored procedure can't have a return value because the ActiveX Data Objects consider this to be an additional SELECT statement.

> **NOTE**
>
> If your CursorType and LockType properties do not support paging, Visual InterDev will display a message box informing you of this fact when you attempt to enable record paging. You must modify these properties before you can turn on record paging.

Also on the Control tab is a Range Type drop-down list box. This controls how the scripting will be generated to assist in outputting the data. If you choose 2 - Table and use the Data Range Footer control, it will output the closing </TABLE> tag for you. If you want to use a table to format your data and you do not use the Data Range Footer or you do not set the Range Type to 2 - Table, you will have to insert the closing </TABLE> tag yourself.

The Copy Fields button will copy to the clipboard script code to output the recordset's fields. The setting in Range Type determines what code is copied to the clipboard for each field. If the Range Type is 0 - Text or 2 - Table, the code looks like

```
<%= DataRangeHdr1("Name") %><br>
```

If the Range Type is 1 - Form, the code looks like

```
<INPUT TYPE="Text" SIZE=25 MAXLENGTH=30 NAME=Name VALUE="<%=
➥DataRangeHdr1("Name") %>"><br>
```

> **NOTE**
>
> The MAXLENGTH element in the <INPUT> tag is set to the size of the Database field.

Once you have set the properties appropriately for your desired recordset, close the control's designer window. The Active Server Page will be updated with script code that reflects the properties you have set.

Now simply add script code to display the recordset's fields, such as

```
<%= DataRangeHdr1("Name") %>
```

immediately following the `endspan` comment tag for the header control. If you are not using paging, you also need to close the `Do` loop that the header control's script has started. Do so by placing the code `<% Loop %>` immediately after the last field is output. If you are using paging, the Data Range Footer control will insert the loop for you.

The Data Range Footer Control

If you are using paging to display the records in your recordset, you must insert a Data Range Footer control into your script. The only property that's useful on the designer window for this control is the `ID` property. The script code generated uses the values of the variables created by the Data Range Header control. The Data Range Header control is where your data range's properties should be defined.

The Data Range Footer's code creates a series of buttons that are used to navigate the pages. These include moving one record at a time and moving to the first and last record of the recordset. The script code takes care of keeping track of which page is currently being viewed and resubmitting the page whenever a navigation button is clicked.

A Quick Example Using the Data Range Controls

As a quick example, the page shown in Figure 22.8 was created by the Active Server Page provided in Listing 22.3. The Data Range Header is set to use record paging with a page size of one record. The `form` method was used to display the data even though no data update buttons are provided. I did this to provide a consistent look with other pages for this particular site. The form input tags are contained within a table to provide proper alignment of the fields.

FIGURE 22.8.

A quick example of the Data Range controls in action.

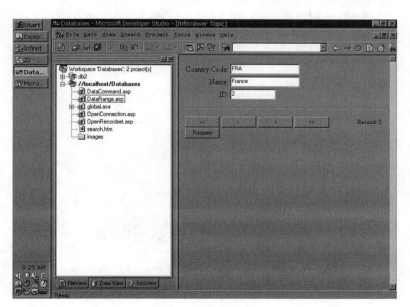

Listing 22.3. A quick example of using the Data Range controls.

```
<%@ LANGUAGE="VBSCRIPT" %>

<HTML>
<HEAD>
<META NAME="GENERATOR" Content="Microsoft Visual InterDev 1.0">
<META HTTP-EQUIV="Content-Type" content="text/html; charset=iso-8859-1">
<TITLE>Document Title</TITLE>
</HEAD>
<BODY>


<!--METADATA TYPE="DesignerControl" startspan
    <OBJECT ID="DataRangeHdr1" WIDTH=151 HEIGHT=24
     CLASSID="CLSID:F602E721-A281-11CF-A5B7-0080C73AAC7E">
        <PARAM NAME="_Version" VALUE="65536">
        <PARAM NAME="_Version" VALUE="65536">
        <PARAM NAME="_ExtentX" VALUE="3986">
        <PARAM NAME="_ExtentY" VALUE="635">
        <PARAM NAME="_StockProps" VALUE="0">
        <PARAM NAME="DataConnection" VALUE="SCSyncA232">
        <PARAM NAME="CommandText" VALUE="dbo.&quot;spc_GetCountryList&quot;">
        <PARAM NAME="CommandType" VALUE="1">
        <PARAM NAME="CursorType" VALUE="1">
        <PARAM NAME="ParamCount" VALUE="1">
        <PARAM NAME="Param0" VALUE="Return Value,,4,4,4">
        <PARAM NAME="RangeType" VALUE="1">
        <PARAM NAME="PageSize" VALUE="1">
    </OBJECT>
-->
<%
fHideNavBar = False
fHideNumber = False
fHideRequery = False
fHideRule = False
stQueryString = ""
fEmptyRecordset = False
fFirstPass = True
fNeedRecordset = False
fNoRecordset = False
tBarAlignment = "Left"
tHeaderName = "DataRangeHdr1"
tPageSize = 1
tPagingMove = ""
tRangeType = "Form"
tRecordsProcessed = 0
tPrevAbsolutePage = 0
intCurPos = 0
intNewPos = 0
fSupportsBookmarks = True
fMoveAbsolute = False

If Not IsEmpty(Request("DataRangeHdr1_PagingMove")) Then
    tPagingMove = Trim(Request("DataRangeHdr1_PagingMove"))
End If

If IsEmpty(Session("DataRangeHdr1_Recordset")) Then
    fNeedRecordset = True
```

```
Else
    If Session("DataRangeHdr1_Recordset") Is Nothing Then
        fNeedRecordset = True
    Else
        Set DataRangeHdr1 = Session("DataRangeHdr1_Recordset")
    End If
End If

If fNeedRecordset Then
    Set SCSyncA232 = Server.CreateObject("ADODB.Connection")
    SCSyncA232.ConnectionTimeout = Session("SCSyncA232_ConnectionTimeout")
    SCSyncA232.CommandTimeout = Session("SCSyncA232_CommandTimeout")
    SCSyncA232.Open Session("SCSyncA232_ConnectionString"),
➥Session("SCSyncA232_RuntimeUserName"), Session("SCSyncA232_RuntimePassword")
    Set cmdTemp = Server.CreateObject("ADODB.Command")
    Set DataRangeHdr1 = Server.CreateObject("ADODB.Recordset")
    cmdTemp.CommandText = "dbo.spc_GetCountryList"
    cmdTemp.CommandType = 4
    Set cmdTemp.ActiveConnection = SCSyncA232
    Set tmpParam = cmdTemp.CreateParameter("Return Value", 3, 4, 4)
    cmdTemp.Parameters.Append tmpParam
    DataRangeHdr1.Open cmdTemp, , 1, 1
End If
On Error Resume Next
If DataRangeHdr1.BOF And DataRangeHdr1.EOF Then fEmptyRecordset = True
On Error Goto 0
If Err Then fEmptyRecordset = True
DataRangeHdr1.PageSize = tPageSize
fSupportsBookmarks = DataRangeHdr1.Supports(8192)

If Not IsEmpty(Session("DataRangeHdr1_Filter")) And Not fEmptyRecordset Then
    DataRangeHdr1.Filter = Session("DataRangeHdr1_Filter")
    If DataRangeHdr1.BOF And DataRangeHdr1.EOF Then fEmptyRecordset = True
End If

If IsEmpty(Session("DataRangeHdr1_PageSize")) Then
➥Session("DataRangeHdr1_PageSize") = tPageSize
If IsEmpty(Session("DataRangeHdr1_AbsolutePage")) Then
➥Session("DataRangeHdr1_AbsolutePage") = 1

If Session("DataRangeHdr1_PageSize") <> tPageSize Then
    tCurRec = ((Session("DataRangeHdr1_AbsolutePage") - 1) *
➥Session("DataRangeHdr1_PageSize")) + 1
    tNewPage = Int(tCurRec / tPageSize)
    If tCurRec Mod tPageSize <> 0 Then
        tNewPage = tNewPage + 1
    End If
    If tNewPage = 0 Then tNewPage = 1
    Session("DataRangeHdr1_PageSize") = tPageSize
    Session("DataRangeHdr1_AbsolutePage") = tNewPage
End If

If fEmptyRecordset Then
    fHideNavBar = True
    fHideRule = True
Else
    tPrevAbsolutePage = Session("DataRangeHdr1_AbsolutePage")
    Select Case tPagingMove
```

22

ActiveX
Database
Components

continues

Listing 22.3. continued

```
            Case ""
                fMoveAbsolute = True
            Case "Requery"
                DataRangeHdr1.Requery
                fMoveAbsolute = True
            Case "<<"
                Session("DataRangeHdr1_AbsolutePage") = 1
            Case "<"
                If Session("DataRangeHdr1_AbsolutePage") > 1 Then
                    Session("DataRangeHdr1_AbsolutePage") =
➥Session("DataRangeHdr1_AbsolutePage") - 1
                End If
            Case ">"
                If Not DataRangeHdr1.EOF Then
                    Session("DataRangeHdr1_AbsolutePage") =
➥Session("DataRangeHdr1_AbsolutePage") + 1
                End If
            Case ">>"
                If fSupportsBookmarks Then
                    Session("DataRangeHdr1_AbsolutePage") =
➥DataRangeHdr1.PageCount
                End If
        End Select
        Do
            If fSupportsBookmarks Then
                DataRangeHdr1.AbsolutePage = Session("DataRangeHdr1_AbsolutePage")
            Else
                If fNeedRecordset Or fMoveAbsolute Or DataRangeHdr1.EOF Then
                    DataRangeHdr1.MoveFirst
                    DataRangeHdr1.Move (Session("DataRangeHdr1_AbsolutePage")
➥- 1) * tPageSize
                Else
                    intCurPos = ((tPrevAbsolutePage - 1) * tPageSize) + tPageSize
                    intNewPos = ((Session("DataRangeHdr1_AbsolutePage")
➥- 1) * tPageSize) + 1
                    DataRangeHdr1.Move intNewPos - intCurPos
                End If
                If DataRangeHdr1.BOF Then DataRangeHdr1.MoveNext
            End If
            If Not DataRangeHdr1.EOF Then Exit Do
            Session("DataRangeHdr1_AbsolutePage") =
➥Session("DataRangeHdr1_AbsolutePage") - 1
        Loop
End If

Do
    If fEmptyRecordset Then Exit Do
    If tRecordsProcessed = tPageSize Then Exit Do
    If Not fFirstPass Then
        DataRangeHdr1.MoveNext
    Else
        fFirstPass = False
    End If
    If DataRangeHdr1.EOF Then Exit Do
    tRecordsProcessed = tRecordsProcessed + 1
%>
```

```
<!--METADATA TYPE="DesignerControl" endspan-->

<!-- ************************************** -->
<TABLE>
<TR><TD ALIGN=RIGHT>Country Code:</TD><TD><INPUT TYPE=
➥"Text" SIZE=25 MAXLENGTH=8 NAME=CC
VALUE="<%= DataRangeHdr1("CountryCode") %>"></TD></TR>
<TR><TD ALIGN=RIGHT>Name:</TD><TD><INPUT TYPE="Text"
➥SIZE=25 MAXLENGTH=30 NAME=Name
VALUE="<%= DataRangeHdr1("Name") %>"></TD></TR></TD>
<TR><TD ALIGN=RIGHT>ID:</TD><TD><INPUT TYPE="Text"
➥SIZE=15 MAXLENGTH=15 NAME=GAF_ID
VALUE="<%= DataRangeHdr1("GlobalAddrFormatID") %>"></TR></TD>
</TABLE>
<!-- ************************************** -->

<!--METADATA TYPE="DesignerControl" startspan
    <OBJECT ID="DataRangeFtr1" WIDTH=151 HEIGHT=24
     CLASSID="CLSID:F602E722-A281-11CF-A5B7-0080C73AAC7E">
         <PARAM NAME="_Version" VALUE="65536">
         <PARAM NAME="_ExtentX" VALUE="3986">
         <PARAM NAME="_ExtentY" VALUE="635">
         <PARAM NAME="_StockProps" VALUE="0">
    </OBJECT>
-->
<%
Loop
If tRangeType = "Table" Then Response.Write "</TABLE>"
If tPageSize > 0 Then
    If Not fHideRule Then Response.Write "<HR>"
    If Not fHideNavBar Then
    %>
     <TABLE WIDTH=100% >
     <TR>
         <TD WIDTH=100% >
         <P ALIGN=<%= tBarAlignment %> >
         <FORM <%= "ACTION=""" & Request.ServerVariables("PATH_INFO") &
➥stQueryString & """" %> METHOD="POST">
             <INPUT TYPE="Submit" NAME="<%= tHeaderName &
➥"_PagingMove" %>" VALUE="    &lt;&lt;    ">
             <INPUT TYPE="Submit" NAME="<%= tHeaderName &
➥"_PagingMove" %>" VALUE="    &lt;    ">
             <INPUT TYPE="Submit" NAME="<%= tHeaderName &
➥"_PagingMove" %>" VALUE="    &gt;    ">
             <% If fSupportsBookmarks Then %>
                 <INPUT TYPE="Submit" NAME="<%= tHeaderName &
➥"_PagingMove" %>" VALUE="    &gt;&gt;    ">
             <% End If %>
             <% If Not fHideRequery Then %>
                 <INPUT TYPE="Submit" NAME="<% =tHeaderName &
➥"_PagingMove" %>" VALUE=" Requery ">
             <% End If %>
         </FORM>
         </P>
     </TD>
     <TD VALIGN=MIDDLE ALIGN=RIGHT>
         <FONT SIZE=2>
         <%
```

continues

Listing 22.3. continued

```
                If Not fHideNumber Then
                    If tPageSize > 1 Then
                        Response.Write "<NOBR>Page: " & Session(tHeaderName &
➥"_AbsolutePage") & "</NOBR>"
                    Else
                        Response.Write "<NOBR>Record: " & Session(tHeaderName &
➥"_AbsolutePage") & "</NOBR>"
                    End If
                End If
                %>
                </FONT>
        </TD>
    </TR>
    </TABLE>
    <%
    End If
End If
%>
<!--METADATA TYPE="DesignerControl" endspan-->
</BODY></HTML>
```

The only code that was added to the page manually appears between the

```
<!-- ************************************** -->
```

comment tags. Everything else was generated by the Data Range Header and Data Range Footer controls.

Summary

In this chapter you've learned a lot about the components available for creating database applications using Active Server Pages and Visual InterDev. This chapter should serve as a reference for Chapter 23, which will go into great depth on creating Active Server Pages that access a database.

The final chapter in this section, "Putting It All Together—Creating a Web Database Application," will use these components to create an entire database application running on the Active Server platform.

CHAPTER 23

Using Active Server Scripting with Databases

by Craig Eddy

IN THIS CHAPTER

Chapters 21 and 22, "Creating and Debugging Queries, Stored Procedures, and Triggers" and "Integrating ActiveX Database Components," introduced you to using Visual InterDev and Active Server components with your database-management system. This chapter expands on those chapters. The chapter at hand doesn't cover one specific topic; instead, it's a smattering of different topics related to using Active Server scripting with databases. You'll learn how to retrieve data from the database, how to set up a search form for a relational database, and how to create a data-editing form.

Microsoft's vision for the Internet has long been that the Internet is nothing more than a worldwide client/server database application. Even the simplest of Web sites, using only static HTML pages, matches this model: The client (browser) retrieves a record (an HTML file) from the server for presentation to the human user. In the case of Active Server Pages, a "real" client/server system can be created. In fact, with the help of Visual InterDev and the ActiveX Data Objects (ADO), it's possible to convert an entire Windows-based application to an Active Server application with minimal effort.

This chapter assumes you've read Chapters 21 and 22. If you have not done so, you should at least make sure you're familiar with the concepts presented in those chapters. The ADO, in particular, plays a prominent role in this chapter. This chapter also provides a concrete example of using the Data Range controls presented in Chapter 22. You should also have a basic understanding of database programming concepts, because that's what this chapter is really all about.

This chapter covers the following topics:

- Setting up a database connection
- Opening and using recordsets
- Creating a database search form
- Using the Data Range design-time controls
- Creating a database editing form

 You'll find all the Active Server script files on the CD-ROM accompanying the book. There's also a SQL script file for creating the database that's used in this chapter.

Setting Up the Database Connection

One of the first steps in any database application is to make contact with the database-management system. This can require a network connection or being on the machine running the application. The same holds true for database applications created using Active Server scripting.

Typically the Web server running the Active Server application and the database server or file holding the data are on different machines, but this is not always the case. The good news here is that to the Active Server Pages, it doesn't matter where the data physically resides because the ADO uses ODBC to connect to the data. In the ODBC data source, you'll set the parameters necessary to point the ADO engine to the physical data.

In this section you'll learn all about creating a database connection that you can use with your Active Server applications. There are two steps you should take to do so: Use the Visual InterDev New Database Connection function and then add code to your Active Server Pages to open the Connection objects.

Creating the ODBC Data Source

The first step necessary to use the ActiveX Data Objects (ADO) is to have a proper ODBC data source created. The data source tells the ODBC driver manager how to connect to the physical data. This includes which database-management system (DBMS) the database uses, where the data physically resides, and which transport mechanism (if applicable) should be used to access the data.

> **NOTE**
>
> The data source must be created on the machine that is running the IIS 3.0 server software. Likewise, if you are using other machines to develop the Web projects for this server, you should set up an identical data source on those machines. This will enable you to use the database features of Visual InterDev on those machines.

When you provide the ADO engine with a data source name while opening a connection, the ADO engine passes off this name to the ODBC driver manager. The driver manager then uses the settings from the data source to attempt the connection to the database.

To create an ODBC data source, you must first gather several key pieces of information. First and foremost, you must know which DBMS the database resides on. This will determine which ODBC driver you must use to connect. The second piece of information is the name of the server (if you're using a client/server DBMS such as SQL Server or Oracle) on which the database resides. Third, you need to know the name of the database. In the case of an Access or other file-system database, this is either the filename or directory name. Finally, if the database has any security implemented, you'll need to have the proper logon credentials handy. This is typically a combination of a logon name and password.

After you've gathered the necessary information, you can create the data source. The steps vary depending on the needs of the DBMS and the ODBC driver that connects to it, as well as the version of the ODBC driver manager you have installed, but they'll probably follow the general path presented here:

1. Start the Control Panel application by clicking the Windows Start button and selecting Settings and then Control Panel.
2. Double-click the 32bit ODBC icon. The ODBC Data Source Administrator application appears, as shown in Figure 23.1.

FIGURE 23.1.

The ODBC Data
Source Administrator.

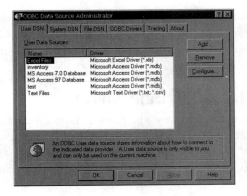

3. Select the System DSN tab. You need to create a system DSN as opposed to a user DSN because the Web server, either IIS or Personal Web Server, runs as a system service, not as a logged-in user. A system DSN is valid for every user of the particular system as well as any service running on the system.

4. Click the Add button. The Create New Data Source dialog, shown in Figure 23.2, appears.

FIGURE 23.2.

The Create New Data
Source dialog.

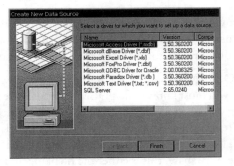

5. In the list box, select the ODBC driver that matches the database you're connecting to. Then click the Finish button.

6. The ODBC data source setup dialog for the driver you chose in step 5 appears. Although this dialog is different for each driver, they all have two things in common: a data source name and a database location. Some drivers may require additional information to complete the definition of the data source. Figure 23.3 shows a sample data source configuration for a SQL Server database being accessed using TCP/IP. If you need help defining the data source, click the Help button. The driver-specific help file will be displayed.

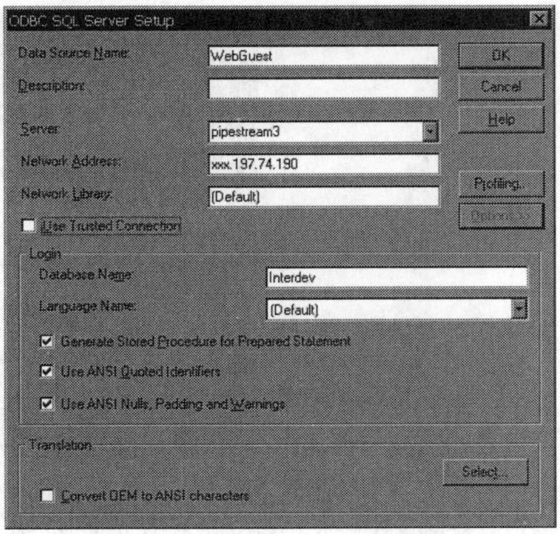

FIGURE 23.3.
The ODBC SQL Server Setup dialog.

7. Once you've entered the necessary information, click the OK button to save the data source information and return to the ODBC Data Source Administrator.

Now that you've created the data source, you can use it in any application or development environment capable of accessing ODBC data sources. If you're familiar with opening Access databases using the Data Access Objects, opening any ODBC data source won't be tricky for you. In fact, the ADO `Connection` object makes it completely painless, as you'll see in the upcoming sections.

Adding a Database Connection with Visual InterDev

Visual InterDev provides a facility called the *database connection* to assist you in connecting your Active Server project to an ODBC data source. When you add a database connection to a Visual InterDev Web project, code to connect to the ODBC data source is placed into the `GLOBAL.ASA` file for the project. In this section, you'll learn how to use this facility as well as how to access the `Connection` object that's created in the `GLOBAL.ASA` file.

To add a database connection using this feature, follow these steps:

1. Start InterDev and load the project to which you want to add the connection.
2. In the FileView tab of the Workspace window, right-click on the project in question. Select Add Data Connection from the shortcut menu. Alternatively, you can use the Project | Add to Project | Data Connection main menu item.
3. The ODBC Select Data Source dialog, shown in Figure 23.4, appears. Click on the Machine Data Source tab to view the available system data sources.

FIGURE 23.4.

*The ODBC Select
Data Source dialog.*

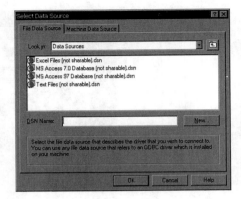

4. In the list box, select the desired data source. If the necessary data source does not exist, click the New button to create a new data source. After the data source is selected, click the OK button.

5. If any logon credentials are required for ODBC to connect to the data source, the appropriate logon dialog for the ODBC driver will be displayed. Enter the appropriate information on this dialog and click OK.

6. If your selected project is a Web project, the GLOBAL.ASA file will be updated with code that sets the values for several Session properties. The Data View tab will now be available no matter which type of project you have opened in InterDev.

The Session properties created in GLOBAL.ASA are named based on the name of the database specified in the data source. For example, if the database name is InterDev, the Session properties would be named InterDev_xxxx.

The Session properties created are xxxx_ConnectionString, xxxx_ConnectionTimeout, xxxx_CommandTimeout, xxxx_RuntimeUserName, and xxxx_RuntimePassword. Using these properties throughout your Active Server application will provide a consistent database connection. Listing 23.1 shows an example of the code created for a SQL Server database.

Listing 23.1. An example of the GLOBAL.ASA code for a SQL Server database connection.

```
<SCRIPT LANGUAGE=VBScript RUNAT=Server>
Sub Session_OnStart
'==Visual InterDev Generated - DataConnection startspan==
'--Project Data Connection
Session("Interdev_ConnectionString") = "DSN=WebGuest;UID=sa;
➥APP=InterDev;WSID=CRAIGEDD;DATABASE=Interdev"
Session("Interdev_ConnectionTimeout") = 15
Session("Interdev_CommandTimeout") = 30
Session("Interdev_RuntimeUserName") = "sa"
Session("Interdev_RuntimePassword") = "secret"
'==Visual InterDev Generated - DataConnection endspan==
End Sub
</SCRIPT>
```

You are at liberty to change the names of the Session properties if you want to, but if you do so and then attempt to view the properties of the data connection from the Workspaces window, InterDev won't be able to match your new names to the names it assigns to the properties of the data connection.

You can use these Session properties to open connections to the database. Doing so is covered in the next section.

Adding the Code for the Database Connection Objects

Now that the Session properties for the data connection have been defined in GLOBAL.ASA, you can use them to open a Connection object in any Active Server Page in your project. These properties make it easy to code both the creation and the opening of these connections.

The first step in creating and opening a database connection is to actually create the Connection object. This object is a class of the ADODB object. You create a Connection object named MyConn using the script code

```
Set MyConn = Server.CreateObject("ADODB.Connection")
```

The next step is to set the properties of the Connection object. This is where the Session properties created in the GLOBAL.ASA file come into play. You can use the following code to set the properties for the Connection object:

```
MyConn.ConnectionTimeout = Session("Interdev_ConnectionTimeout")
MyConn.CommandTimeout = Session("Interdev_CommandTimeout")
```

This code assumes that the Session properties are named *Interdev_xxxx*. You can also set the ConnectionString property explicitly using

```
MyConn.ConnectionString = Session("Interdev_ConnectionString")
```

but this isn't necessary because, as you'll see in a moment, the connection string can be specified when you use the Connection object's Open method.

Finally, you establish the connection to the data source using the Open method, as in

```
MyConn.Open Session("Interdev_ConnectionString"), _
            Session("Interdev_RuntimeUserName"),
➥Session("Interdev_RuntimePassword")
```

Note that you do not have to use the Session properties in order to create and open the Connection object. Doing so, however, makes your code more consistent and easier to maintain. Should the ConnectionString property for an ODBC data source change, you'll only have to make the change in the GLOBAL.ASA file. If you hard-code ConnectionString properties throughout your application, you'll have to change it on every Active Server Page on which it's used.

> **WARNING**
>
> According to the ADO Reference Guide, you should not pass username and password information in *both* the ConnectionString argument and the optional username and password arguments of the Open method. Doing so can cause unpredictable results. You should pass such logon credentials in one place or the other.

Opening and Using Recordsets

Now that you have a Connection object created and opened, you can retrieve some data from the database using a Recordset object. This section discusses creating, opening, and using an ADO Recordset with Visual InterDev.

Creating the Recordset Object

The first step in using a recordset is to actually create an instance of a Recordset object. After the instance is created, you then set its properties and open the recordset using the object's Open method.

To create an instance of a Recordset object, you don't need to have an opened Connection object. This is in stark contrast to other data access object models you might be familiar with. For example, Microsoft's Remote Data Objects (RDO) and Data Access Objects (DAO) both require that you create a recordset using an existing, open database connection. The ActiveX Data Objects model lets you create and use its objects independent of one another.

The code for creating an instance of a Recordset object is simple:

```
Set MyRS = Server.CreateObject("ADODB.Recordset")
```

That's all there is to it. You now have a Recordset object which can have its properties set and can, eventually, be opened with the help of an existing, open Connection object.

Setting the Recordset's Properties

Several properties should be set before you actually use the recordset. Like the Connection object, the Recordset object also has several properties that can be automatically set when the Open method is invoked. Some of the properties that can be set before opening are illustrated in the following code:

```
MyRS.CacheSize = 10
MyRS.MaxRecords = 100
MyRS.PageSize = 10
```

These are all properties that affect the number of rows returned at specific times during the life of the recordset.

Opening Recordsets Using SQL Statements, Table Names, and Stored Procedures

You can use table names, stored procedures, or SQL statements as the record source for the data returned by the recordset. These are all text source types. You can also use a valid Command object as the record source.

If the recordset has not yet been opened, you could specify the record source using the Source property. It is common practice, however, to specify the record source as a parameter of the Open method.

In addition to specifying the record source, you must also provide a Connection object through which the recordset's data will be retrieved. This is done either by setting the recordset's ActiveConnection property to a valid Connection object, as in

```
Set MyRS.ActiveConnection = MyConn
```

or by specifying the appropriate Connection object as a parameter when the Open method is invoked.

Next, you must decide the cursor type and lock type to use for the recordset. The type you should choose depends on what the recordset will be used for. If it is just going to output records one after another (the typical case), you should use a read-only lock and a forward-only cursor.

Finally, you need to construct the text command that will produce the data you want to return in the recordset. This can be either a SQL statement, a table name, or a stored procedure name. If you're using a stored procedure that requires parameters, you should create a Command object to use as the source for your recordset. This is discussed in the next section.

Let's look at some examples for each method. First, suppose you had a table named Guests and wanted to return all of the records using the recordset MyRS. The following code would accomplish this:

```
MyRS.Open "Guests", MyConn, 0, 1, 2
```

The first parameter is the table name. The second parameter is the Connection object that was opened on the database. The third and fourth are the cursor type (forward-only) and lock type (read-only). Finally, the last parameter is the command type and specifies that the command is a table name.

Next, a stored procedure would be used with

```
MyRS.Open "spc_GetGuests", MyConn, 0, 1, 4
```

where spc_GetGuests is the name of the stored procedure, and the last parameter specifies that a stored procedure is being used.

Finally, a SQL statement would be used with

```
MyRS.Open "SELECT * FROM Guests", MyConn, 0, 1, 1
```

where the final parameter specifies that a SQL statement is being used to open the recordset.

> **TIP**
>
> When your query will return values from TEXT or LONGVARBINARY fields, you can improve the query's performance by placing these fields at the end of the field list in the SQL SELECT statement.

Opening Recordsets Using Command Objects

If the source for your recordset is a stored procedure requiring parameters or if the same source will be used repeatedly, you will want to create a Command object. This section discusses the creation of a Command object and its Parameters collection.

A Command object is a way of encapsulating the details of a query or database action within an ADO object. The object can then be used (repeatedly if necessary) to either return results through a Recordset object or to perform its action upon the database. Command objects are typically used with parameterized stored procedures, but this is not necessarily always the case.

To create a Command object, you need to know the following details:

- What is the source of the command? That is, what SQL statement or stored procedure will be used when the command is to be executed?
- What parameters, if any, does the command require?
- Does the command return records, or does it perform some action on the database?
- Will the command be compiled by the OLE DB provider?

When these facts are known, you can begin to construct the Command object. The first step, as always, is to create an instance of a Command object. This is done using the code

```
Set myCommand = Server.CreateObject("ADODB.Command")
```

You can then begin to set the properties for the Command object. See Chapter 22 for more details on the properties of the Command object.

The first property to set is the ActiveConnection property, as in

```
Set MyCommand.ActiveConnection = MyConn
```

where MyConn is a valid Connection object.

The most important property is the CommandText property. This is where you specify the text of the command. This can be a SQL statement, a stored procedure name, or a table name. Along with the CommandText property is the CommandType property. This property specifies exactly what the `CommandText` property represents: a SQL statement or other text, a stored procedure name, or a table name. Using this property is not mandatory, but will improve the performance of the `Command` object. This is due to the fact that the ADO engine will not have to determine what the `CommandText` property represents; it will assume it represents exactly what the `CommandType` property says it does.

You may also need to specify parameters for the command. This is done using the `Command` object's `CreateParameter` method to create a `Parameter` object for each required parameter. You then use the `Append` method of the `Command` object's `Parameters` collection. The following code illustrates this in action:

```
Set MyParam = MyCommand.CreateParameter("@Country",200,1,20,"USA")
MyCommand.Parameters.Append MyParam
```

This code creates a new parameter named @Country. Its data type is varchar. It's an input parameter whose length is 20 characters, and the value provided for the parameter is USA. A more intuitive way of providing the value is accomplished using the code

```
Set MyParam = MyCommand.CreateParameter("@Country",200,1,20)
MyCommand.Parameters.Append MyParam
MyCommand.Parameters("@Country") = "USA"
```

The only difference here is the way the parameter's value is specified. Instead of specifying it in the `CreateParameter` method, it is explicitly set after the parameter is added to the `Parameters` collection. The two code snippets accomplish the same task, but the second example is easier to read and understand.

After all of the necessary parameters, including output parameters and return values, have been defined, you can use the `Command` object. The object has a method called `Execute` that can be used for an action query or to create a `Recordset` object. The code

```
MyCommand.Execute
```

will execute the command. The code

```
Set MyRS = MyCommand.Execute
```

will execute the command and place any records returned into the `MyRS` recordset.

You can also use the `Command` object as the source parameter when you invoke a recordset's `Open` method, as in

```
MyRS.Open MyCommand, , 0, 1
```

Here the second parameter, `ActiveConnection`, is left blank. This is because the recordset will inherit the `Command` object's `ActiveConnection` property. Note also that the `CommandType` parameter is not used. Because the source parameter is set to a `Command` object, the command type is not necessary.

Returning the Results to the Web Page

Now that you've opened the recordset, it's time to output its results to a Web page. This is perhaps the most amazing feat that Active Server applications perform. Back in the old days of Web server applications, you had to write and compile an entire executable just to retrieve the results of a simple query. Using Active Server Pages, you can accomplish the same feat in a few lines of code, with no compilation required.

Let's look at a very straightforward example of placing all the code to output a recordset's results in one section of an Active Server Page. This is illustrated in Listing 23.2. The code assumes that the Connection object, MyConn, has already been defined and opened elsewhere.

Listing 23.2. A simple Active Server Page to return a query's results.

```
<%
Set MyRS = Server.CreateObject("ADODB.Recordset")
MyRS.Open "Guests", MyConn, 0, 1, 2
while not MyRS.EOF %>
Last Name: <%= MyRS("LastName") %>
First Name: <%= MyRS("FirstName") %>
EMail: <%= MyRS("EMail") %>
<HR>
<%      MyRS.MoveNext
wend %>
```

That's all there is to it! This will output the LastName, FirstName, and EMail fields for each record in the Guests table. The records will be separated by a horizontal rule, as specified by the <HR> tag. Don't forget to put in the MyRS.MoveNext code, or you'll just create an endless loop! If your Active Server Page never returns, look for this right off the bat. It's a common mistake!

You can also wrap HTML table tags around the output of your field values to format the data into a table. You would code the header information for the table before you started the while...wend loop. Typically, each row in the recordset's results would represent a row in the output table. This is done by wrapping all the field values with <TR>...</TR> tags. Finally, each field typically represents a single column in the table. These are wrapped with <TD>...</TD> tags. Listing 23.3 demonstrates how the data can be output into a table.

Listing 23.3. A query's results displayed in an HTML table.

```
<TABLE border="1"><TR><TH>Last Name</TH>
<TH>First Name</TH><TH>E-Mail</TH></TR>
<%
Set MyRS = Server.CreateObject("ADODB.Recordset")
MyRS.Open "Guests", MyConn, 0, 1, 2
while not MyRS.EOF %>
<TR><TD><%=MyRS("LastName")%></TD>
<TD><%=MyRS("FirstName")%></TD>
<TD><%=MyRS("EMail")%></TD>
</TR>
<%      MyRS.MoveNext
wend %>
```

Creating a Database Form

Another use for Active Server Pages is to create database forms. These forms can be used for searching, viewing, or inserting/updating data in the database. The pages containing the database forms are created using HTML form tags with Submit buttons that activate other Active Server Pages that contain the actual database interface. The steps in creating a database form manually are

1. Decide which data will be displayed or modified with the form.

2. Create the page containing the HTML form. This can be either Active Server script or straight HTML.

3. Code the script to interface with the database.

4. Code the page to display the results. This can be either Active Server script or straight HTML.

The following section, "Using the Data Range Controls," demonstrates how you can use ActiveX design-time controls to assist you in coding database forms.

Creating the HTML Form

The first step in creating the database form is to decide which data will be displayed or edited using the form. Once this is decided upon, you can begin to create the HTML form to be used. You can use either strictly HTML or you can add some Active Server scripting to create a dynamic form.

All HTML forms begin with a `<FORM>` tag that contains information about the form. This information includes the action that will be taken when the form's Submit button is clicked, as well as the protocol to be used to pass the form's data to the submission application. For our purposes here, the action will be to load an Active Server Page that will service the data entered into the form. So, a typical `<FORM>` tag used in an Active Server environment probably looks something like

```
<FORM ACTION="submit.asp" METHOD="POST">
```

Each input field will have some sort of `<INPUT>` tag (for text boxes, checkboxes, and radio buttons) or `<SELECT>` tag (for selecting items in a list of some sort) associated with it that defines how the data is entered into the form. Finally, there will be a Submit button and probably a Clear button on the form. The Submit button activates the resource defined in the `ACTION` element of the `<FORM>` tag and passes the data entered into the form to the resource. For our discussion, the `ACTION` refers to an Active Server Page.

Listing 23.4 shows a typical page containing an HTML form. This page is shown in a browser window in Figure 23.5.

TIP

The easiest way to create a page with an HTML form is to use the FrontPage editor. Even if your page will eventually contain Active Server script or some of InterDev's design-time controls, use FrontPage to do all the tedious work for you. You can then add the Active Server script code using InterDev's source editor.

Listing 23.4. A simple HTML form.

```
<html>
<head>
<meta http-equiv="Content-Type"
content="text/html; charset=iso-8859-1">
<meta name="GENERATOR"
content="Microsoft FrontPage (Visual InterDev Edition) 2.0">
<title>Document Title</title></head>
<body>

<h2>To search, please supply any of the following information:</h2>

<form action="submit.asp" method="POST">
<div align="center"><table border="0" cellspacing="5">
<tr><td align="right">First Name:</td>
<td><input type="text" size="30" maxlength="40" name="FirstName">
</td></tr>
<tr><td align="right">Last Name:</td>
<td><input type="text" size="30" maxlength="40" name="LastName">
</td></tr>
<tr><td align="right">Phone:</td>
<td><input type="text" size="30" maxlength="40" name="Phone">
</td></tr>
<tr><td align="right">Company:</td>
<td><input type="text" size="30" maxlength="40" name="Organization">
</td></tr>
<tr><td align="right">Address:</td>
<td><input type="text" size="30" maxlength="40" name="Address">
</td></tr>
<tr><td align="right">City:</td>
<td><input type="text" size="30" maxlength="30" name="City">
</td></tr>
<tr><td align="right">State/Prov:</td>
<td><input type="text" size="30" maxlength="30" name="State">
</td></tr>
<tr><td align="right">Zip/Postal:</td>
<td><input type="text" size="30" maxlength="30" name="PostalCode">
</td></tr>
<tr><td align="right">E-Mail Address:</td>
<td><input type="text" size="40" maxlength="40" name="EMail">
</td></tr>
<tr><td align="right">Operating System:</td>
<td><select name="OS" size="1">
    <option selected>Windows 95 </option>
    <option> Windows-NT </option>
```

```
    <option> Windows 3.1 or 3.11 </option>
</select> </td></tr>
<tr><td align="center" colspan="2">
<input type="submit" value="Submit Entry">
<input type="reset" value="Clear Fields">
</td></tr>
</table></div></form>
</body>
</html>
```

FIGURE 23.5.
A sample HTML form.

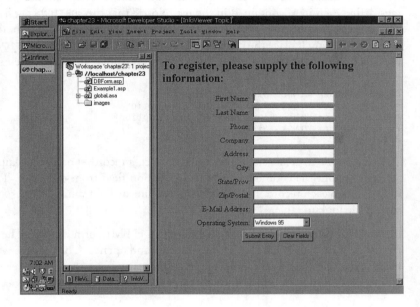

Filling a List or Combo Box

One of the necessities you'll run into when you're building a database form is the need to display the data from a lookup table. A *lookup table* is a table that is used to translate code values stored in a field in a base table. For example, you might have an Action field in a table that stores activities. In the `Activity` table, the Action field is a coded value that corresponds to a row in an `ActionCode` table. The `ActionCode` table has a row for each `ActionCode` that provides a description of the `ActionCode`. This way, if a description should happen to change, you can simply change one row in the `ActionCode` table instead of multiple rows in the `Activity` table. This is the power of relational databases in action.

The problem with lookup tables from a database form perspective is that you don't want the user to have to remember the `ActionCode` values. The user should only be concerned with the description of the action, not the code. So, to create an HTML form that contains plain language instead of coded values, you'll have to do some extra work.

Fortunately, Active Server scripting and the ActiveX Data Objects make this task quite simple. Instead of using a static HTML page for the database form, you're going to use an Active Server Page that will generate a drop-down list filled with the possible choices for the lookup field.

The HTML for a drop-down list looks like this:

```
<select name="OS" size="1"><option value="WIN95">Windows 95</option>...</select>
```

where the <SELECT>...</SELECT> tags define the entire list box and the <OPTION>...</OPTION> tags define each item contained in the list. Notice that the <OPTION> tag has a VALUE element. This is used to specify the data that will be submitted when the form's Submit button is clicked. This is where you'll place the code field. Between the <OPTION> and </OPTION> tags, you'll place the description field. So, a list box that contains possible operating systems would look like

```
<select name="OS" size="1">
<option value="WIN95">Windows 95</option>
<option value="WINNT40">Windows NT 4.0</option>
<option value="WINNT35">Windows NT 3.5x</option>
<option value="WIN31">Windows 3.1x</option>
</select>
```

The script code to create such a list will first open a recordset on the lookup table. It will need to retrieve both the code field and the description field from this table. The script will then loop through each record in this table and output the field values to the <OPTION> tag, one per row in the lookup table.

Listing 23.5 provides sample code for filling an HTML form list box. The code assumes that the connection MyConn has already been created and opened. The OpSystems table contains two fields: OSCode and Description. The HTML source when this code is executed should look identical (with the exception of the data in the table) to the HTML snippet shown previously.

Listing 23.5. Filling an HTML form list box.

```
<%  set RS = Server.CreateObject("ADODB.RecordSet")
    RS.Open "OpSystems", MyConn, 0, 1, 2
    If not(RS.EOF) then %>
<SELECT NAME="OS" SIZE="1">
<%      while not(RS.EOF) %>
<OPTION VALUE="<%=RS("OSCode")%>">
<%=RS("Description")%> </OPTION>
<%        RS.MoveNext
      wend %>
</SELECT>
<%  end if %>
```

Creating the Search Results Page

Now that the HTML form is created, it's time to create the Active Server Page that will service the form. How this page is coded depends on the purpose the HTML form serves. If the form is a search form, the Active Server Page will perform a query on the database based on the data entered on the form. A results page will be returned to the user. If the form is a data-entry form, the Active Server Page will insert into or update the database and provide some sort of feedback to the user detailing the success or failure of the operation.

For this chapter, we're building a search page. Chapter 25, "Putting It All Together— Creating a Web Database Application," covers both inserting and updating records as well as searching the database.

The first step in creating the results page is to retrieve the data that was entered into the HTML form. This is accomplished using a feature of the global `Request` object that enables you to access members of the object's collections using the syntax

```
Request("variable")
```

The collections we're concerned with in this chapter are the `Form` and `QueryString` collections. The `Form` collection is populated when the HTML form's `<FORM>` tag specifies a `METHOD` of `POST`. The `QueryString` collection is populated when the HTML form's `<FORM>` tag specifies a `METHOD` of `GET`.

If the `GET` method is used, the data will be passed to the Active Server Page using the query string portion of the URL, in the format

```
http://www.myhost.com/submit.asp?LastName=Jones
```

To retrieve the data in your script code and assign it to a variable `strLastName`, you could use either

```
strLastName = Request("LastName")
```

or

```
strLastName = Request.QueryString("LastName")
```

If the `POST` method is used, the data is passed to the Active Server Page encapsulated within the HTTP request message that the browser sends to the Web server when the user clicks the Submit button. To retrieve the data in your script code and assign it to a variable `strLastName`, you could use either

```
strLastName = Request("LastName")
```

or

```
strLastName = Request.Form("LastName")
```

Notice that if you use the first syntax to retrieve the data, it doesn't matter which method (`GET` or `POST`) is specified on the HTML form. Either method can be retrieved.

The next step in producing the results page is to build the recordset that will be used to retrieve the records matching the data entered into the form. By now you're probably sick of opening `Recordset` objects, so I won't explain the details. Basically, you're going to construct a SQL statement that's based on the data that the user entered into the HTML form. This SQL statement will then be used as the source parameter for the Recordset object's Open method. Listing 23.6 shows one way to open this recordset. It's what I call the "brute force" method because each field is individually coded. You could also iterate through the Form or QueryString collection and build the SQL statement that way.

Listing 23.6. The SUBMIT.ASP Active Server Page.

```
<%@ LANGUAGE="VBSCRIPT" %>

<HTML><HEAD>
<META NAME="GENERATOR" Content="Microsoft Visual InterDev 1.0">
<META HTTP-EQUIV="Content-Type" content="text/html; charset=iso-8859-1">
<TITLE>Search Results</TITLE></HEAD><BODY>

<%   strWhere = ""
    if Len(Request("FirstName")) > 0 then
        if len(strWhere) > 0 then strWhere = strWhere & " AND "
        strWhere = strWhere & "FirstName = '" & Request("FirstName") & "'"
    end if
    if Len(Request("LastName")) > 0 then
        if len(strWhere) > 0 then strWhere = strWhere & " AND "
        strWhere = strWhere & "LastName = '" & Request("LastName") & "'"
    end if
    if Len(Request("Phone")) > 0 then
        if len(strWhere) > 0 then strWhere = strWhere & " AND "
        strWhere = strWhere & "Phone = '" & Request("Phone") & "'"
    end if
    if Len(Request("Organization")) > 0 then
        if len(strWhere) > 0 then strWhere = strWhere & " AND "
        strWhere = strWhere & "Organization = '"
        strWhere = strWhere & Request("Organization") & "'"
    end if
    if Len(Request("Address")) > 0 then
        if len(strWhere) > 0 then strWhere = strWhere & " AND "
        strWhere = strWhere & "Address1 = '" & Request("Address") & "'"
    end if
    if Len(Request("City")) > 0 then
        if len(strWhere) > 0 then strWhere = strWhere & " AND "
        strWhere = strWhere & "City = '" & Request("City") & "'"
    end if
    if Len(Request("State")) > 0 then
        if len(strWhere) > 0 then strWhere = strWhere & " AND "
        strWhere = strWhere & "Region = '" & Request("State") & "'"
    end if
    if Len(Request("PostalCode")) > 0 then
        if len(strWhere) > 0 then strWhere = strWhere & " AND "
        strWhere = strWhere & "PostalCode = '" & Request("PostalCode") & "'"
    end if
    if Len(Request("EMail")) > 0 then
        if len(strWhere) > 0 then strWhere = strWhere & " AND "
        strWhere = strWhere & "EMail = '" & Request("EMail") & "'"
    end if
```

```
        if Len(Request("OSCode")) > 0 then
            if len(strWhere) > 0 then strWhere = strWhere & " AND "
            strWhere = strWhere & "Guests.OSCode = '" & Request("OSCode") & "'"
        end if

        'construct the SQL statement
        strSQL = "SELECT FirstName, LastName, Organization, Address1, "
        strSQL = strSQL & "City, Region, PostalCode, Phone, Email, "
        strSQL = strSQL & "OpSystems.Description FROM Guests LEFT OUTER JOIN "
        strSQL = strSQL & "OpSystems ON Guests.OSCode = OpSystems.OSCode "
        if Len(strWhere) > 0 then strSQL = strSQL & "WHERE " & strWhere
        set MyConn = Server.CreateObject("ADODB.Connection")
        MyConn.Open Session("Interdev_ConnectionString"), _
                    Session("Interdev_RuntimeUserName"), _
                    Session("Interdev_RuntimePassword")
        set RS = Server.CreateObject("ADODB.RecordSet")
        RS.Open strSQL, MyConn, 0, 1, 1

        'if no records found, display a message and exit
        if RS.EOF then
            Response.Write "<CENTER><H2>No matching records found!</H2></CENTER>"
            Response.Write "<P><H3>The SQL string was: " & strSQL & "</H3>"
            Response.write "</BODY></HTML>"
            Response.End
        end if

    'construct the table for the output %>
<table border="1">
    <tr>
        <th align="left">First Name</th>
        <th align="left">Last Name</th>
        <th align="left">Organization</th>
        <th align="left">Address</th>
        <th align="left">City</th>
        <th align="left">State</th>
        <th align="left">Postal</th>
        <th align="left">Phone</th>
        <th align="left">EMail</th>
        <th align="left">Op. System</th>
    </tr>
<%  while not(RS.EOF)
        Response.Write "<tr>"
        For Each Field in RS.Fields
            Response.Write "<td>"
            if Len(Field.Value) then
                Response.Write Field.Value
            else
                'make sure the cell shows up empty
                Response.Write " "
            end if
            Response.Write "</td>"
            Response.Write "</tr>"
            RS.MoveNext
        Next
    Wend %>
</table>
</BODY></HTML>
```

After the recordset is opened, the data is output into a table. If no records were found that match the criteria entered on the form, a message to that effect is displayed. Each field is output by iterating through the recordset's Fields collection instead of hard-coding a reference to each field. This makes the code not only smaller, but also easier to maintain. If we add or remove a field from the SELECT statement and table header, we won't have to change the code that displays the field's values. However, if there are any fields that the recordset should contain but that shouldn't be displayed within the table, some additional code will have to be added to remove those fields from consideration here.

Notice the line inside the while loop that reads Response.Write " ". This is instructing the browser to put an empty cell within the table in place of any data. This is used because otherwise the cell would be omitted by the browser, making the table look strange.

Using the Data Range Controls

Now that you've seen how to create a database search page using nothing but Active Server script, let's throw in some ActiveX design-time controls and see if we can't make our task a little easier. As introduced in the previous chapter, Visual InterDev ships with a few useful design-time controls. These controls are used while you're creating your Active Server Pages. They assist you in doing menial, grunt-work tasks that usually require lots of code that doesn't change much from application to application.

We're going to rework our search results page using the Data Range controls. InterDev comes with two such controls: the Data Range Header and the Data Range Footer. The Header control can be used by itself if your results page will not use recordset paging. The Footer control, which is used if you want to output the records onto multiple pages, requires the use of the Data Range Header control in order for it to operate correctly.

This section will discuss both options: First, all records will be output onto a single page; then we'll use the Data Range Footer and create multiple pages, each containing a fixed number of records. The second of the two following sections builds on the first, so be sure to read them in order.

Creating a Single Page Recordset Output

Using the Data Range Header control will enable you to remove a lot of the code we used in Listing 23.6. Some of the code we'll reuse, though, because it still applies. The Data Range Header will code the following tasks for you:

- Create and open a Connection object to the database.
- Create and open a Command object based on a query, stored procedure, or table name you provide.
- Create and open a Recordset object using the Command object.
- Provide the ability to filter the Recordset object's data.
- Provide the initial logic necessary to loop through the recordset's returned records.

We will, of course, take advantage of all these features of the Data Range Header. As a basic outline to using the control, follow these steps:

1. Create a new Active Server Page in your current project. Name it `submit-drh.asp`, or at least something different than the page you saved from Listing 23.6.

2. Copy the script code from Listing 23.6. Begin at `<%  strWhere = ""` and copy down to the line preceding the comment `'construct the SQL statement`.

3. Because we'll be using the `Recordset` object's `Filter` property, which works with straight field names, not fully qualified *table.field* names, modify the section that starts with `if Len(Request("OSCode")) > 0 then` to read

```
if Len(Request("OSCode")) > 0 then
        if len(strWhere) > 0 then strWhere = strWhere & " AND "
        strWhere = strWhere & "OSCode = '" & Request("OSCode") & "'"
end if
```

4. Immediately following this code, insert the following code:

```
if Len(strWhere) > 0 then
    Session("DRH_Filter") = strWhere
elseif len(Request("DRH_PagingMove")) = 0 then
    Session("DRH_Filter") = ""

end if
```

The `Session` property `Session("DRH_Filter")` will be used by the Data Range Header control to filter the recordset.

5. Next, copy the code from Listing 23.6 that starts with `'construct the table for the output %>` down to and including the line that contains the first `</tr>` tag. This will set up the table, just as in the previous example.

6. Insert a Data Range Header control by selecting Insert | Into HTML | ActiveX Control from the menu bar. Click on the Design-time tab, select Data Range Header Control, and click OK.

7. The Data Range Header build screen will appear. In the Properties dialog, set the ID to `DRH`. Use the SQL Builder button to construct the SQL statement. Include the `Guests.OSCode` field in the query because we'll be using that field in the `Filter` property, and the ActiveX Data Objects require a specific reference to any field that appears in the `Filter` property. We didn't need this in the previous example because we were using the SQL statement's `WHERE` clause to do our filtering.

8. Close the build screen. Notice that the amount of code in the Active Server Page just increased dramatically. All the code between the lines `<!--METADATA TYPE="DesignerControl" startspan` and `<!--METADATA TYPE="DesignerControl" endspan-->` was added by the design-time control. Do not modify any of this code. You can edit the design-time control's properties by right-clicking anywhere in this section and selecting Edit Design-time Control from the shortcut menu.

9. Immediately after the endspan line, enter the following code:

```
<%  Response.Write "<tr>"
    For Each Field in DRH.Fields
        if Field.Name <> "OSCode" then
            Response.Write "<td>"
            if Len(Field.Value) then
                Response.Write Field.Value
            else
                'make sure the cell shows up empty
                Response.Write " "
            end if
            Response.Write "</td>"
        end if
    Next
    Response.Write "</tr>"
Loop %>
</table>
```

This is basically a copy of the table output code from Listing 23.6, but we've added some code to remove the OSCode field from the output and renamed the recordset to DRH, which is the name assigned to the Data Range Header control.

10. Save the page and open the page that contains the form being submitted. Change the <FORM> tag's ACTION element so that it references the Active Server Page you've just saved (submit-drh.asp, if you followed my advice in step 1).

11. Test the new form page to display the records. If you have any trouble, the best troubleshooting mechanism is to disobey my rule about not modifying the design-time control's code and place Response.Write statements to display debugging information. You should remove these when the problem is solved, however.

Using Recordset Paging and the Data Range Footer Control

Now it's time to convert the results page to display the records in pages. This is done by modifying some of the Data Range Header's properties, removing a few lines of the existing script code we added, and adding the Data Range Footer control.

To create the script using record paging, follow these steps:

1. Make a copy of the Active Server Page created in the previous section. This needs to be done using Windows Explorer because InterDev does not have a File Copy feature. Name it submit-drf.asp. Return to InterDev and add the new file to the current project.

2. Open the file in the source code editor. Right-click anywhere within the code for the Data Range Footer and select Edit Design-time Control from the shortcut menu.

3. Change the Bar Alignment property to 2 - Centered and the Range Type to 2 - Table. Go to the Advanced tab and change Cursor Type to 3 - Static. Then return to the Control tab, check the Record Paging checkbox, and modify the Page Size if you like.

> **NOTE**
>
> The design-time control will not allow you to enable Record Paging if you haven't changed the Cursor Type to `Static` or `Keyset`. This is because the other cursor types do not support the properties necessary to utilize the paging features.

4. Scroll to the code we added after the Data Range Header's endspan line. Remove the word `Loop` inside the script code (the Data Range Footer will add a loop statement for us) and the `</table>` tag (which the Data Range Footer will also add for us because the Range Type is set to `2 - Table`).

5. With the cursor positioned where the `</table>` tag was located, insert the Data Range Footer design-time control by selecting Insert I Into HTML I ActiveX Control from the menu bar. Click on the Design-time tab, select Data Range Footer Control, and click OK.

6. When the build screen appears, simply close it because there are no properties that are set on the Data Range Footer.

7. Back on the script code, notice the new code inserted for the Footer control. The `Loop` has been put in place, and there is a line that reads

```
If tRangeType = "Table" Then Response.Write "</TABLE>"
```

This is the line that closes the table for us. Within the Data Range Header's code, the value of `tRangeType` is set based on the setting of the Header control's Range Type property.

8. Save the page. Return to the HTML form file and change the `<FORM>` tag's `ACTION` element to point to the new ASP file (`submit-drf.asp`). Preview this page and click the Submit button.

9. Notice that along the bottom of the results page are a series of buttons. These are the page-navigation buttons. They should be centered beneath the table, thanks to the setting of the Bar Alignment property of the Header control. You can click the buttons to move from page to page. If only one page is available based on the data you have in the database, you can change the Header control's Page Size property to a smaller value. This property sets the number of records that will be displayed on each page.

Summary

In this chapter you've learned how to use Active Server scripting to perform a variety of database access functions. Although the chapter is not an exhaustive study of every possible database activity you can perform using Active Server scripting, it should provide you with a springboard to experimenting on your own. The topics in this chapter can be easily adapted to perform other database-maintenance activities.

23

USING ACTIVE SERVER SCRIPTING WITH DATABASES

In Chapter 24, "Implementing Transactions and State Management," you'll learn everything you want to know about maintaining session state and implementing database transactions. In Chapter 25, you'll create a real-world database application using Active Server scripting and combining all the topics from the chapters in this section.

Implementing Transactions and State Management

by Craig Eddy

IN THIS CHAPTER

CHAPTER 24

When you write a real-time database application, no matter what your environment, you should implement some sort of transaction management. Using transactions, you can ensure that all of the data involved in a transaction is valid and also that all of the database actions have been successful before any are actually committed to the data store.

The first half of this chapter discusses transaction management using the ActiveX Data Objects (ADO), starting with a brief introduction to database transactions. Then you'll learn how to use the ADO's transaction-management features to implement transaction management with OLE DB data sources.

One of the biggest drawbacks of the Hypertext Transfer Protocol (HTTP), the communications protocol that Web browsers and servers use to talk to one another, is that it is a stateless protocol. This means that there is no way to track a user from page to page in a Web site. Likewise, there is no way to know when a user starts or ends a session on the Web site.

The second half of this chapter deals with the Active Server solution to the statelessness of HTTP: the Session object and cookies. Although the Session object will not solve all of the state management problems discussed in the preceding paragraph, it does take Web server state management to a new level.

Introduction to Database Transactions

Database transactions serve as a wrapper around a series of operations. A transaction ends in one of two ways: either the transaction is successful and all of the operations are committed to the physical storage, or the transaction is not successful and all of the operations are aborted (or rolled back, in database terminology) and their effects are undone.

The classic example used to illustrate transaction processing is the transfer of funds from one bank account to another. The transfer involves two distinct operations: a debit from one account and a credit to another account. If either of these operations were to fail, the other one should not take place either. But imposing an order on these operations does not solve the problem because either operation could fail. The answer is to wrap the transfer of funds within a transaction. If either operation fails, the transaction is aborted and both operations are rolled back.

Typically, if you perform a database operation without starting a transaction, the data provider commits the operation instantly. After you begin a new transaction, however, the data provider will stop instantly committing operations. Instead, the provider will wait for the transaction to be committed before saving the changes to the physical storage.

Transactions can also be nested; that is, you can start a new transaction within an existing transaction. Each nested transaction is committed or rolled back individually but is governed by the transaction in which it is nested. When committing or rolling back nested transactions, you must work backward from the innermost transaction to the outermost transaction. In other words, there must be as many commits or rollbacks as nested transactions. Nesting of transactions is typically only an issue when stored procedures or triggers make calls to other stored procedures.

In many database-management systems (Microsoft Access in particular), using transactions for your database updates will greatly improve performance because the entire operation is stored in local memory until committed. At that time, the database management system (DBMS) uses a sort of burst mode to commit the data to the physical storage. This increases performance because the physical storage device that the database resides on only has to be opened and written to once per transaction, not once per operation. By far the slowest part of a database operation is the actual writing of the data to a physical device such as a hard disk. With transactions, you need to write the data to a physical device less frequently.

ActiveX Data Objects and Transaction Management

As with most data access objects, the ActiveX Data Objects provide the necessary complement of tools for using database transactions. These include several methods and a property. The transaction occurs at the `Connection` object level and so all of these methods and the property belong to the `Connection` object.

This section discusses the methods first and finishes up with a brief discussion of the `Attributes` property.

The ADO Methods Supporting Transactions

Three methods are used to support database transactions: `BeginTrans`, `CommitTrans`, and `RollbackTrans`. All of these methods operate on a `Connection` object. The `Connection` object must be opened before the methods are invoked. Likewise, you cannot call `CommitTrans` or `RollbackTrans` without first calling `BeginTrans`. Doing so will produce a runtime error.

The syntax for the `BeginTrans` method is

```
[level = ]connection.BeginTrans
```

where *level* is a Long variable into which the method can place the nesting level of the transaction. This is only necessary if you have a nested transaction and want to keep track of the nesting level. The first transaction returns a level of 1. The second transaction (which would be the first nested transaction) returns a level of 2.

The syntax to commit or roll back the transaction is

```
connection.(CommitTrans ¦ RollbackTrans)
```

24

TRANSACTIONS AND STATE MANAGEMENT

Neither of these methods returns a value. Invoking `CommitTrans` commits the operations performed and ends the transaction. Invoking `RollbackTrans` reverts the database to its state at the time `BeginTrans` was invoked and ends the transaction.

Listing 24.1 provides an example of how to use these methods with some of the ActiveX Data Objects. The code has no basis in fact, but it demonstrates the concepts and usage of the transaction processing methods.

Listing 24.1. Using transaction processing with ActiveX Data Objects.

```
<%  set MyConn = Server.CreateObject("ADODB.Connection")
    MyConn.Open Session("DSN"), Session("Username"), Session("Password")
    MyConn.BeginTrans
    On Error Resume Next
    strSQL = "UPDATE BaseTable SET FirstField = '" & strFirstField & "' "
    strSQL = strSQL & "WHERE BaseTableID = " & Session("BaseTableID")
    MyConn.Execute strSQL
    If Err.Number <> 0 then
        MyConn.RollbackTrans
        Response.Write "An error occurred: " & Err.Description
        Response.End
    End If
    strSQL = "UPDATE TrackTable SET LastUpdate = GetDate() "
    strSQL = strSQL & "WHERE BaseTableID = " & Session("BaseTableID")
    MyConn.Execute strSQL
    If Err.Number <> 0 then
        MyConn.RollbackTrans
        Response.Write "An error occurred: " & Err.Description
        Response.End
    End If
    MyConn.CommitTrans
    Response.Write "Updates were successful!"
    Response.End %>
```

In Listing 24.1, the first step is to create and open the `Connection` object. Next, a transaction is started using the `BeginTrans` method. Immediately after this, the error trapping is enabled.

Using the `On Error Resume Next` makes it possible to check for runtime errors within the Active Server code. If this line is not put in place, the Active Server engine will be required to handle the runtime error. It handles such errors by returning an all-but-meaningless HTML page to the browser. Instead, we're going to handle the errors ourselves.

A SQL statement is then constructed and executed using the `Connection` object's `Execute` method. If this produces an error (which a trigger might raise if the update operation is invalid, for example), the value of `Err.Number` is set to something other than `0`. In this instance, we invoke the `RollBackTrans` method and display a message to the browser. The script code then exits via the `End` method of the `Response` object.

This is then repeated for another SQL statement. Again, if an error occurs, the `RollbackTrans` method is called. This time, it not only rolls back the most recent SQL statement, but also the preceding one.

Finally, if no errors occur with either `Execute` method, the transaction is committed using the `CommitTrans` method. Now, both SQL statements are commited to the database, the transaction ends, and a nice message is provided to the browser.

Using the Connection Object's `Attributes` Property

What happens after a transaction is ended (either committed or rolled back) is determined by the data provider. Some providers immediately and automatically begin a new transaction when an existing transaction is ended. Most providers, however, do not implement this feature.

The ADO provides a property of the `Connection` object that you can query to determine whether or not the data provider utilizes this feature. The property is named `Attributes`. For `Connection` objects, the property takes one of three values:

- ■ `0` (default)—A new transaction is not started upon `CommitTrans` or `RollbackTrans`.
- ■ `131072`—A new transaction is started when `CommitTrans` is invoked.
- ■ `262144`—A new transaction is started when `RollbackTrans` is invoked.

Maintaining State with the `Session` Object

As mentioned in the introduction to this chapter, the HTTP protocol that Web browsers and Web servers use to talk to one another is a stateless protocol. Each time a resource is requested, a new connection is opened between the browser and the server. The Web server has no way of relating the current request it is servicing to any other request it has received. However, you cannot really develop a robust user-sensitive application without keeping track of the user's current and past states. The Active Server model provides two ways to accomplish this: the `Session` object and client-side cookies.

This section discusses the `Session` object and its use in maintaining a user's state. The `Session` object is a built-in server object that does not need to be created using the `CreateObject` method. A particular instance of the `Session` object is valid for a particular user from the time a page is opened in your application until the session is either abandoned (through the invocation of the `Session` object's `Abandon` method) or times out. A timeout occurs if the user does not refresh the current page or request a new page within the number of minutes specified by the `Session` object's `Timeout` property.

> **NOTE**
>
> The Session object is scoped to the Active Server application level. An Active Server application consists of any Active Server or HTML pages that reside within a particular virtual directory on the Web server. If the user wanders outside of this particular directory, even into one of its subdirectories, a new session is started and the preceding session's objects are unreachable. If this is a possibility on your server, you must devise some workaround. For example, if the new virtual directory resides on the same server, you can use the built-in Server object, but keep in mind that this is global and shared by all applications open on the server at the time. You can also use client-side cookies to maintain the data that needs to transfer from application to application.

Session Events

The Session object has two events that you can utilize in your efforts to maintain state. These events can be used to set up and tear down information about a user's state and about the application. The events are named Session_OnStart and Session_OnEnd. The code for these events is placed in the GLOBAL.ASA file that should be present in every Active Server application directory on your server.

Session_OnStart

The Session_OnStart event is the first piece of code that each user is guaranteed to execute. There is also an Application_OnStart event, but that is only executed by the first user who happens to start a new instance of the Application object, not necessarily every user. It is here that you can set up all of the Session properties to be used throughout your Active Server application.

The code in this event is executed before any code on the requested page. All of the built-in server objects (Application, Request, Response, Server, and Session) are available during the execution of Session_OnStart.

If you've used InterDev to add any data connections to your project, the Session_OnStart event will already have some code in place. An example of this code is shown in Listing 24.2. This is where the Session properties that are used by the data connection get their values. (Refer to Chapter 22, "Integrating ActiveX Database Components" and Chapter 23, "Using Active Server Scripting with Databases," for examples of using these Session properties.)

Listing 24.2. Setting up data connections in Session_OnStart.

```
<SCRIPT LANGUAGE=VBScript RUNAT=Server>
Sub Session_OnStart
'==Visual InterDev Generated - DataConnection startspan==
'--Project Data Connection
```

```
Session("Interdev_ConnectionString") = _
    "DSN=WebGuest;UID=sa;APP=ASP;WSID=CRE;DATABASE=Interdev"
Session("Interdev_ConnectionTimeout") = 15
Session("Interdev_CommandTimeout") = 30
Session("Interdev_RuntimeUserName") = "sa"
Session("Interdev_RuntimePassword") = "secret"
'==Visual InterDev Generated - DataConnection endspan==
End Sub
</SCRIPT>
```

The Session_OnStart event is also where you'd want to do any incrementing of page hit counters. The code provided in Listing 24.3 implements a page counter. It combines the Application_OnStart, Application_OnEnd, and Session_OnStart events to do its work.

Listing 24.3. Implementing a page hit counter.

```
<SCRIPT LANGUAGE=VBScript RUNAT=Server>
SUB Application_OnStart
' Open file and read the number of visitors so far
HitCountFile = Server.MapPath ("/") + "\visitors.txt"
Set objFile = Server.CreateObject("Scripting.FileSystemObject")
Set Out= objFile.OpenTextFile (HitCountFile, 1, FALSE, FALSE)
' Initialize soft visitor counter here
Application("hits") = Out.ReadLine
' Store physical file name of file containing the visitor count
Application("HitCountFile") = HitCountFile
END SUB
</SCRIPT>

<SCRIPT LANGUAGE=VBScript RUNAT=Server>
SUB Application_OnEnd
' Overwrites the existing visitors.txt file
Set objFile = Server.CreateObject("Scripting.FileSystemObject")
Set Out= objFile.CreateTextFile (Application("HitCountFile"), TRUE, FALSE)
Out.WriteLine(application("hits"))
END SUB
</SCRIPT>

<SCRIPT LANGUAGE=VBScript RUNAT=Server>
SUB Session_OnStart
' Increase the visitor counter
Application.lock
Application("hits")= application("hits") + 1
t_hits = application("hits")
Application.unlock
' Periodically, save to file
If t_hits MOD 15 = 0 Then
    SET objFile = Server.CreateObject("Scripting.FileSystemObject")
    Set Out= ObjFile.CreateTextFile (Application("HitCountFile"), TRUE, FALSE)
    Application.lock
    Out.WriteLine(t_hits)
    Application.unlock
End If
END SUB
</SCRIPT>
```

24

TRANSACTIONS
AND STATE
MANAGEMENT

The third thing that can be done inside the Session_OnStart is to transfer any client-side cookies your application utilizes to Session properties. Listing 24.4 shows an example of how this is accomplished. The last section of this chapter, "Using Client-Side Cookies to Maintain State," provides more details about using client-side cookies.

Listing 24.4. Retrieving client-side cookies.

```
<SCRIPT LANGUAGE=VBScript RUNAT=Server>
SUB Session_OnStart
Session("CustomerID") = Request.Cookies("CustomerID")
Session("ShowGraphics") = Request.Cookies("ShowGraphics")
Session("FriendlyName") = Request.Cookies("FriendlyName")
END SUB
```

Session_OnEnd

The Session_OnEnd event is called whenever the user's current session is abandoned (through the use of the Session.Abandon method) or times out. The only built-in objects that are accessible in this event are Application, Server, and Session. This event really isn't useful for much except possibly closing secure database connections or logging the end of session to a database. The user's Web browser probably isn't even connected to the server anymore (except possibly in the case of the Session.Abandon method), so the Response and Request objects are invalid and, therefore, client-side cookie manipulation is out of the question. In addition, the Server object's MapPath method is also invalid during this event, further restricting the amount of work you can do here.

Using the Session Object

The Session object is capable of storing data within a collection it maintains. You can store any type of data within the Session object's collection, even other objects. However, you cannot store a reference to the other built-in server objects (such as Application or Server).

To store a value in the Session object's collection (and create what is referred to as a Session property), use either of the following:

```
Session("variable") = value
Set Session("variable") = object
```

To access the value of a Session property, use

```
Variable = Session("variable")
```

If you are storing an object reference within a Session property, you can access any of the object's properties or methods using the syntax:

```
Session("variable").(property ¦ method)
```

To retrieve a copy of the object stored in a `Session` property, use

```
Set object = Session("variable")
```

You cannot use the `Session` properties as an array because the data is already stored in a collection. Instead, create a local array and assign the `Session` property to be the array itself, as in

```
Dim strArray(3)
strArray(1) = "Red"
strArray(2) = "White"
strArray(3) = "Blue"
Session("TheArray") = strArray
```

You then must retrieve a local copy of the array before referencing the elements at a later time:

```
strLocalArray = Session("TheArray")
Response.Write "The colors in the flag are "
Response.Write strLocalArray(1) & ", " & strLocalArray(2)
Response.Write ", and " & strLocalArray(3)
```

You should modify the array elements using the local copy of the array and then store the array back to the `Session` property when you've finished modifying its elements.

Using Client-Side Cookies to Maintain State

The `Session` object does not provide a persistent storage mechanism for tracking users. When the user's session times out or is abandoned, the `Session` object is destroyed and all of the data it contains is lost. If you need a way to persist the state or user data while the user's session is active, you can use client-side cookies.

Client-side cookies are data elements that Web browsers and Web servers pass back and forth as pages on a site are requested by and returned to the user. Cookies are maintained and stored by the Web browser application on the user's hard disk. Although much has been made recently about the use of cookies and concerns for privacy, they are still the best mechanism Web programmers have at their disposal for storing information about individual users. Cookies have the following (and possibly several more) advantages:

- They are automatically handled by the HTTP protocol, meaning that your Active Server script does not have to specifically request them.

- They are much faster to access than data stored within a database. There is a built-in collection to handle cookies. You do not have to use the ADO to open a database connection and a recordset.

- They are stored on the user's machine. This means that if a user never visits your site again, you're not wasting database space storing information about that user. Instead, far fewer bytes are stored on the user's hard disk (cookies have much less storage overhead than database records).

- Cookies have an expiration date that causes the Web browser application to automatically remove them after a certain date.

This section provides a brief introduction to the use of client-side cookies. The next chapter, "Putting It All Together—Creating a Web Database Application," provides more detail on using cookies within an application.

Setting Cookies

When your Active Server script needs to store a value in the user's cookie file, you use the `Response` object's Cookies collection. This collection, like most collections used in Active Server applications, is used with the following syntax:

```
Response.Cookie("cookie") = value
```

You can also create a cookie dictionary by specifying

```
Response.Cookie("cookie")("key") = value
```

as in

```
Response.Cookie("MyCookie")("Type1") = FirstType
Response.Cookie("MyCookie")("Type2") = SecondType
```

This is just another mechanism for storing structured information within the cookie.

When using cookies, you should enable response buffering. Enabling response buffering forces the server to process all of the script code and HTML before returning any data to the Web browser. You enable buffering by using the statement

```
Response.Buffer = True
```

The data is sent whenever the script ends or either `Response.End` or `Response.Flush` is invoked.

Cookies also have several properties that you can set using the syntax

```
Response.Cookie("cookie").property = value
```

Accessed via the `Response` object, these properties are write-only. The properties include

- `Expires`. The date on which the cookie is to expire.
- `Domain`. If specified, the cookie will be sent only when the page requested is in the domain specified.
- `Path`. Similar to `Domain`. If specified, the cookie will be sent only when the page requested is in the path specified. If not specified, the application's path is used.
- `Secure`. Specifies whether or not the cookie is secure.

There is also a read-only property named `HasKeys` that you can use to determine whether a particular cookie is a dictionary.

Reading Cookies

If cookies have been written for a particular domain and path, they are returned to the Web server by the Web browser whenever a page in the domain and path is to be requested. The Active Server engine parses the cookie from the HTTP request message and stores the data into the Request object's Cookies collection. You can then reference the cookie value using the syntax

```
Request.Cookies("cookie")[("key")]
```

You can also iterate through all of the cookies using the For Each construct.

The Request object's Cookies collection has one property, HasKeys. This property, which is read-only, specifies whether or not a particular cookie is a cookie dictionary. If it is, you must use the key name when accessing the cookie.

Summary

In this chapter you've learned about some mechanisms that are necessary when creating a real-world database application using Active Server scripting. Database transaction processing is necessary to ensure the integrity of the data within your database as well as to enhance performance. The mechanisms for maintaining state within your application and within a particular user's session are necessary to provide the user with the feeling that there is some intelligence behind your Web application. They also enable you to make some choices about how to handle the user throughout the application.

In the final chapter of this part of the book, Chapter 25, "Putting It All Together—Creating a Web Database Application," you'll build an entire database application from the ground up. The concepts learned in this chapter will be put to rigorous use during that process.

24

TRANSACTIONS
AND STATE
MANAGEMENT

CHAPTER 25

Putting It All Together—Creating a Web Database Application

by Craig Eddy

IN THIS CHAPTER

The time has finally come to put all the pieces together and create a Web database application. The preceding chapters have shown you how to

- Create database queries, stored procedures, and triggers (Chapter 21, "Creating and Debugging Queries, Stored Procedures, and Triggers")
- Use ActiveX database components with Visual InterDev (Chapter 22, "Integrating ActiveX Database Components")
- Use Active Server scripting to perform database tasks (Chapter 23, "Using Active Server Scripting with Databases")
- Implement transaction processing and state management (Chapter 24, "Implementing Transactions and State Management")

In this chapter we're going to wrap a lot of these concepts together and create a full-fledged application using Active Server scripting, ActiveX design-time components, and Visual InterDev. The application we'll create is called WebGuest. It's a full-featured Web site registration application that captures information from Web surfers and enables you to search on and maintain that data. All these entry, searching, and maintenance functions are done using only a Web browser; so, as long as your operating system sports a graphical Web browser, we're going to create a truly platform-independent application.

There are several parts to our application. The first is the Switchboard, the page where users first enter the site. This page contains links to all the other pages in the application. Next, you'll be introduced to the Data Form Wizard, which we'll use to create some generic maintenance forms for some of the tables in the database. Then we'll create the data entry form and the Active Server Page that actually adds the records to the database. Finally, we'll modify the search form used in Chapter 23 to fit the graphical style used in the WebGuest site. This will then become our database search form.

The Preliminaries

The first step in creating the WebGuest application is to create the Visual InterDev workspace and project. To do so, follow these steps:

1. Start Visual InterDev. Select File | New and move to the Projects tab in the New dialog.
2. Select Web Project Wizard in the list of project types. Enter a suitable name in the Project name text box. A good choice is WebGuest. Verify the directory location shown in the Location text box. Click OK.
3. When the Web Project Wizard appears, use its dialogs to create a new web on your Web server.
4. After you've finished with the Web Project Wizard, you'll have a web that contains a global.asa file and an Images directory.

You're now ready to begin creating the Active Server content for the WebGuest application.

Creating the Database

The first step in creating the content for the WebGuest application is to create the database. This is the same database used in previous chapters, but I'll repeat the steps here for creating this database in Microsoft Access 97 format. By combining an Access 97 database with the Personal Web Server, you can create, test, and debug your application from a Windows 95 machine and not have to have an active connection to the Internet or even a local area network. This is the quickest and safest route to take when you're in the early stages of your application's development cycle.

To create the database, start Access 97 with a blank database. Name the database GUESTS.MDB and store it in the project directory created in the preceding section. Add the three tables as specified in Table 25.1, Table 25.2, and Table 25.3. For our purposes, there's no need to create any relationships or utilize any validation rules. All Text data type fields should have the Allow zero length strings property set to Yes. Fields marked with an asterisk (*) are the primary keys for the table in which they appear.

> **NOTE**
>
> The GUESTS.MDB file, as well as all the source code and images used in this chapter, is included on the CD-ROM that accompanies this book.

Table 25.1. The Guests table.

Field Name	Data Type	Length
GuestID (*)	AutoNumber	
FirstName	Text	50
LastName	Text	50
Organization	Text	50
Address1	Text	50
City	Text	50
Region	Text	30
PostalCode	Text	30
Country	Text	20
Phone	Text	20
EMail	Text	255
URL	Text	255
PictureID	Number	Long Integer
OSCode	Text	8

Table 25.2. The Pictures table.

Field Name	Data Type	Length
PictureID (*)	AutoNumber	
img_PictureURL	Text	255
Active	Text	1

Table 25.3. The OpSystems table.

Field Name	Data Type	Length
OSCode (*)	Text	8
Description	Text	20

NOTE

The img_PictureURL field is given the img_ prefix to take advantage of some of the features of the Data Form Wizard, discussed later in this chapter.

After the tables are created, you should populate the OpSystems table. The data in Table 25.4 should be used to stay consistent with the text of this chapter.

Table 25.4. The OpSystems table's data.

OSCode	Description
WIN95	Windows 95
WINNT40	Windows NT 4.0
WINNT351	Windows NT 3.51
WIN31	Windows 3.1x
OTHER	Other

After you've created the database, you'll need to add a database connection to the project. To do so, follow these steps:

1. Make the menu selections Project | Add To Project | Data Connection.
2. When the Select Data Source dialog appears, select the Machine Data Source tab and click the New button.

3. The Create New Data Source Wizard appears. Select the System Data Source option button and click Next.

4. Select `Microsoft Access Driver (*.mdb)` in the list box that appears on the next dialog. Click Next and then click Finish.

5. On the ODBC Microsoft Access 97 Setup dialog, enter a name for the data source (`WebGuest` is a good choice) and select the database you just created using the Select button in the Database frame. Click OK.

6. When you return to Visual InterDev, the `global.asa` file now has a plus sign in its tree entry on the FileView tab of the Workspace window. Click this plus sign and you'll see the data connection you just created. Because we'll be using ASP files from earlier chapters, we'll need to rename this connection to be consistent with those files. Select the connection and click the right mouse button. Select Rename from the shortcut menu and rename the data connection to Visual InterDev.

That's all there is to it! You now have a database and a database connection ready to go.

Designing the Switchboard

The next step in the application is to design and code the Switchboard page. This will be the default or startup page that surfers see when they start the WebGuest application. There won't be any Active Server code on this page, so you should name it so that it is the default page for your Web server. This is typically `default.asp`, `default.htm`, `default.html`, `index.htm`, or `index.html`. For my Personal Web Server setup, the default page is `default.asp`, so that's what I've named my Switchboard page.

The Switchboard contains links to all the other pages in the WebGuest application. The HTML code for this page is provided in Listing 25.1. There's nothing out of the ordinary here except for the reference to the style sheet. When we get to the Data Form Wizard in the next section, we'll choose a style for our data form. When we do so, the wizard will install a cascading style sheet into the Web site. This style sheet should be used on every page within the site to provide a consistent look and feel. This is accomplished using the `<LINK>` tag, which should appear before the `<BODY>` tag in the pages.

Listing 25.1. The Switchboard page (`default.asp`).

```
<%@ LANGUAGE="VBSCRIPT" %>
<!DOCTYPE HTML PUBLIC "-//IETF//DTD HTML//EN">
<html>
<head>
<meta http-equiv="Content-Type"
content="text/html; charset=iso-8859-1">
<meta name="GENERATOR"
content="Microsoft FrontPage (Visual InterDev Edition) 2.0">
<title>WebGuest Switchboard</title></head>
```

continues

Listing 25.1. continued

```
<LINK REL=STYLESHEET HREF="./Stylesheets/Redside/Style2.css">

<body background="Images/Redside/Background/Back2.jpg">

<h2 align="center">Welcome to the WebGuest Switchboard!</font></h2>
<ul>
    <li><h3><a href="EntryForm.asp">Enter a new Guest</a></h3></li>
</ul>
<ul>
    <li><h4><a href="searchForm.asp">Search for a Guest</a></h4></li>
</ul>
<ul>
    <li><h4><a href="GuestList.asp">Guest Maintenance</a></h4></li>
</ul>
<ul>
    <li><h4><a href="pictList.asp">Picture Maintenance</a></h4></li>
</ul>
</body></html>
```

The results of this HTML are shown in Figure 25.1. Note that the style sheet has not yet been added to this site. Therefore, Figure 25.1 does not show the final look of this page, but does show how the page looks at this point in the site's development.

FIGURE 25.1.

The Switchboard page in Browser Preview.

Using the Data Form Wizard

The Data Form Wizard is a fantastic tool for quickly creating generic database-maintenance forms. Using this wizard, you can create an entire database-maintenance application without writing any Active Server script or HTML yourself. The wizard will literally create all of it for you.

However, the script files generated by the Data Form Wizard are not very customizable. They contain an enormous amount of Active Server code but are easily generated. For these reasons, I won't even provide listings for these files. (They are, of course, available on the CD-ROM.)

The following section describes how to use the Data Form Wizard to create maintenance pages for the Pictures and Guests tables. There will be separate forms for surfers to search and enter data into the Guests table, but the maintenance pages will be useful from a back-end standpoint.

Creating a Data Form

Creating a data form using the Data Form Wizard is a very simple process. You'll decide which table, view, stored procedure, or query will be used as the record source for the data form and then decide on a style for the form. That's all there is to it. The wizard does the rest of the work. When you've finished creating the form, you'll have set of fully functional pages you can use to maintain the data in your database.

To create a data form using the wizard, follow these steps:

1. Open the WebGuest project. Select Project | Add To Project | New menu from the menu. The New dialog appears.

2. Select the File Wizards tab. In the list box, select Data Form Wizard. Enter a name in the Filename text box. For this form, enter Guest. Click OK.

3. The first dialog of the wizard appears, as shown in Figure 25.2. The available data connections are contained in the drop-down list box. The only connection we have in this project is already selected, so we'll leave the default. You could add a new connection, if necessary, by clicking the New button. In the title text box, enter Guest Maintenance. Click Next.

4. The next dialog is where you choose the type of the recordset to be used. In this case, a table is being used. This is the default selected in the list box. Click Next.

5. In this dialog, shown in Figure 25.3, you'll select the table and fields to be used in your data form. The drop-down list box contains the names of all the tables in the database. Select Guests in the list box.

FIGURE 25.2.

The first dialog of the Data Form Wizard.

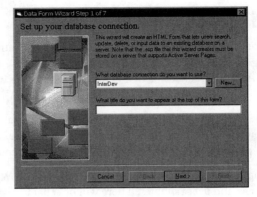

FIGURE 25.3.

The table and field selector dialog of the Data Form Wizard.

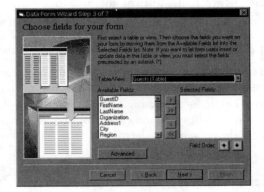

6. The Available Fields list box contains the names of the fields in the selected table. You can select all fields by clicking the button labeled >>. After a field is in the Selected Fields list, you can remove it by clicking the button labeled <, or you can remove all fields by clicking <<. For this application, select every field except the GuestID field.

7. After all necessary fields have been moved to the Selected Fields list, click the Advanced button. This displays the Advanced Field Options dialog, shown in Figure 25.4. Here you can change the label used when a field is displayed. You can also create a look-up field similar to that found in Access 97 by using the Look-up table drop-down and its associated drop-down lists. Make the changes detailed in Table 25.5.

FIGURE 25.4.

The Advanced Field Options dialog of the Data Form Wizard.

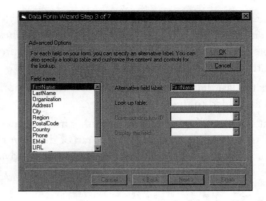

Table 25.5. Changes to make on the Advanced tab for the Guests table.

Field	Alternative Label	Look-up Table	Key ID	Display Field
FirstName	First Name			
LastName	Last Name			
Organization	Company			
Address1	Address			
Region	State			
PostalCode	ZIP			
PictureID	Picture	Pictures	PictureID	img_PictureURL
OSCode	Op. System	OpSystems	OSCode	Description

8. After these changes are made, click OK; then click Next. The next dialog is where you set the options available on your data form. You can specify that the form is for browsing only, or you can allow the user to also edit data. You can also specify whether the filtering of data should be supported. Leave the defaults selected (all modifications allowed, filtering allowed) and click Next.

9. On this dialog you specify the types of forms to be created. You can create a Form View, a List View, or both. In addition, if you have selected both Form View and List View, you can specify whether the List View should have a link to the Form View for each item (using the checkbox labeled Hotlink items in list to Form View). You can also specify whether List View should use paging and, if so, how many records should be displayed on each page. Leave the defaults (all items selected, page size of 10) and click Next.

25

CREATING A WEB DATABASE APPLICATION

10. The next dialog is where you choose the theme or style for the pages. You can select the theme desired from a list box containing all the installed Visual InterDev themes. The picture box on the left of the dialog provides a preview of the theme you select. Select the Redside theme and click Next.

11. This is the last dialog, so click Finish, and the appropriate pages, images, and style sheets are added to the WebGuest site.

12. Repeat the preceding steps to create some maintenance pages for the Pictures table. Name these Pict on the File Wizards tab of the New File dialog. Use all fields from the Pictures table, and you don't need to use the Advanced Field Options dialog. Be sure to select the Redside theme when you reach the Themes dialog in the wizard.

Using the Data Form

 Now that you've created the data forms, you can use them to enter information for the Pictures table. The first step is to add the pictures to your Web site. Choose Project | Add To Project | Files from the menu. Select the files to be added in the Insert Files Into Project dialog that appears. The images I used in creating the WebGuest application are included on the CD-ROM. You can insert them directly from the CD-ROM.

After you've added the images, you should create a Pictures record for each one. Do this by opening PictForm.asp in a browser. Click the New button. The page should look similar to Figure 25.5. Enter the information and click the Insert button. A feedback form should appear, informing you that the insert was successful. To insert additional records, click the New button. Otherwise, click the Form View button.

FIGURE 25.5.

The Pictures table's insert data form.

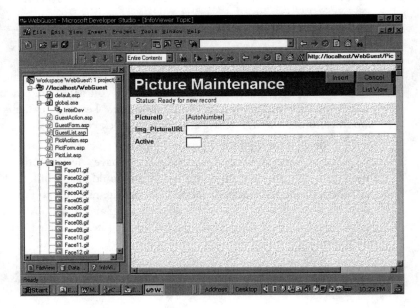

When you've finished entering data, click the List View button or open `PictList.asp` in the browser. The List View form should appear similar to Figure 25.6—but with the data you entered, of course. You can click in the # column to view and edit the particular `Pictures` record in Form View. You can use the navigation buttons at the bottom of the screen to move forward and backward a page at a time or to move to the first or last page. You can also query the database again by clicking the Requery button. This will refresh the data in the List View.

FIGURE 25.6.

The Pictures *table's List View data form.*

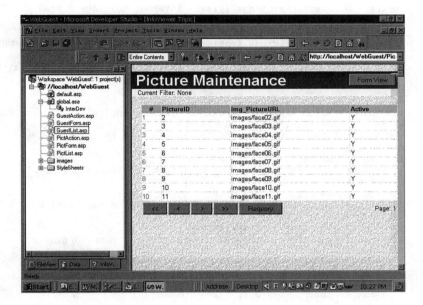

Creating the Search Form

For the search form, we're going to use a modified version of the form created in Chapter 23 and presented in Listing 23.4. We'll also use a slightly modified version of the Active Server Page that returned the search results using the Data Range Footer. The version of the search form for the WebGuest application appears in Listing 25.2. This file must be named `SearchForm.asp`, or the link to this file must be renamed in the `default.asp` file.

> **NOTE**
>
> If you have not already done so, you should read Chapters 22 and 23 before proceeding. These chapters provide the background information necessary to understanding how the Data Range controls work.

Listing 25.2. The search form (SearchForm.asp).

```asp
<%@ LANGUAGE="VBSCRIPT" %>
<!DOCTYPE HTML PUBLIC "-//IETF//DTD HTML//EN">
<html>
<head>
<meta http-equiv="Content-Type"
content="text/html; charset=iso-8859-1">
<meta name="GENERATOR"
content="Microsoft FrontPage (Visual InterDev Edition) 2.0">
<title>Search For A Guest</title></head>
<LINK REL=STYLESHEET HREF="./Stylesheets/Redside/Style2.css">
<BODY BACKGROUND="./Images/Redside/Background/Back2.jpg" BGCOLOR=White>

<center><h2>To search, please supply any of the following information:
</h2></center>

<form action="submit-drf.asp" method="POST">
<div align="center"><table border="0" cellspacing="5">
<tr><td align="right">First Name:</td>
<td><input type="text" size="30" maxlength="40" name="FirstName">
</td></tr>
<tr><td align="right">Last Name:</td>
<td><input type="text" size="30" maxlength="40" name="LastName">
</td></tr>
<tr><td align="right">Phone:</td>
<td><input type="text" size="30" maxlength="40" name="Phone">
</td></tr>
<tr><td align="right">Company:</td>
<td><input type="text" size="30" maxlength="40" name="Organization">
</td></tr>
<tr><td align="right">Address:</td>
<td><input type="text" size="30" maxlength="40" name="Address">
</td></tr>
<tr><td align="right">City:</td>
<td><input type="text" size="30" maxlength="30" name="City">
</td></tr>
<tr><td align="right">State/Prov:</td>
<td><input type="text" size="30" maxlength="30" name="State">
</td></tr>
<tr><td align="right">Zip/Postal:</td>
<td><input type="text" size="30" maxlength="30" name="PostalCode">
</td></tr>
<tr><td align="right">E-Mail Address:</td>
<td><input type="text" size="40" maxlength="40" name="EMail">
</td></tr>
<tr><td align="right">Operating System:</td>
<td><select name="OSCode" size="1"><option value="">(none)</option>
<%  set MyConn = Server.CreateObject("ADODB.Connection")
    MyConn.Open Session("Interdev_ConnectionString"), _
                Session("Interdev_RuntimeUserName"), _
                Session("Interdev_RuntimePassword")
    set RS = Server.CreateObject("ADODB.RecordSet")
    RS.Open "OpSystems", MyConn, 0, 1, 2
    If not(RS.EOF) then
    while not(RS.EOF) %>
<OPTION VALUE="<%=RS("OSCode")%>">
<%=RS("Description")%> </OPTION>
```

```
<%        RS.MoveNext
      wend
      end if %>
</SELECT>
</td></tr>
<tr><td align="center" colspan="2">
<input type="submit" value="Submit Entry">
<input type="reset" value="Clear Fields">
</td></tr>
</table></div></form>
</body></html>
```

The differences between Listing 25.2 and Listing 23.4 are minimal. First, a `<LINK>` tag is used to reference the style sheet installed when we used the Data Form Wizard. The `<BODY>` tag was also modified to specify the background graphic and color. Finally, script code was added to read the available operating systems from the OpSystems table and place them into the Operating System drop-down list box. (In Listing 23.4, the values in the list box are hard-coded.)

The script code for submit-drf.asp is presented in Listing 25.3. Again, this is slightly modified from the file created in Chapter 23. Most of this code is, of course, produced by the Data Range Header and Footer controls. If you haven't already done so, you should follow along with the steps outlined in Chapter 23, beginning in the section "Creating the Search Results Page," to create the Active Server Page.

> **NOTE**
>
> Recall from Chapter 23 that you do not manually add any of the code between the lines
>
> `<!--METADATA TYPE="DesignerControl" startspan`
>
> and
>
> `<!--METADATA TYPE="DesignerControl" endspan-->`
>
> This is all added when the design-time control is placed onto the page.

Listing 25.3. The Active Server Page to return search form results (submit-drf.asp).

```
<%@ LANGUAGE="VBSCRIPT" %>

<HTML>
<HEAD>
<META NAME="GENERATOR" Content="Microsoft Visual InterDev 1.0">
<META HTTP-EQUIV="Content-Type" content="text/html; charset=iso-8859-1">
<TITLE>Search Results</TITLE></HEAD>
<LINK REL=STYLESHEET HREF="./Stylesheets/Redside/Style2.css">
<BODY BACKGROUND="./Images/Redside/Background/Back2.jpg" BGCOLOR=White>
<center><h2>Search Results</h2></center><p>
<%   strWhere = ""
```

continues

Listing 25.3. continued

```
    if Len(Request("FirstName")) > 0 then
        if len(strWhere) > 0 then strWhere = strWhere & " AND "
        strWhere = strWhere & "FirstName = '" & Request("FirstName") & "'"
    end if
    if Len(Request("LastName")) > 0 then
        if len(strWhere) > 0 then strWhere = strWhere & " AND "
        strWhere = strWhere & "LastName = '" & Request("LastName") & "'"
    end if
    if Len(Request("Phone")) > 0 then
        if len(strWhere) > 0 then strWhere = strWhere & " AND "
        strWhere = strWhere & "Phone = '" & Request("Phone") & "'"
    end if
    if Len(Request("Organization")) > 0 then
        if len(strWhere) > 0 then strWhere = strWhere & " AND "
        strWhere = strWhere & "Organization = '"
        strWhere = strWhere & Request("Organization") & "'"
    end if
    if Len(Request("Address")) > 0 then
        if len(strWhere) > 0 then strWhere = strWhere & " AND "
        strWhere = strWhere & "Address1 = '" & Request("Address") & "'"
    end if
    if Len(Request("City")) > 0 then
        if len(strWhere) > 0 then strWhere = strWhere & " AND "
        strWhere = strWhere & "City = '" & Request("City") & "'"
    end if
    if Len(Request("State")) > 0 then
        if len(strWhere) > 0 then strWhere = strWhere & " AND "
        strWhere = strWhere & "Region = '" & Request("State") & "'"
    end if
    if Len(Request("PostalCode")) > 0 then
        if len(strWhere) > 0 then strWhere = strWhere & " AND "
        strWhere = strWhere & "PostalCode = '" & Request("PostalCode") & "'"
    end if
    if Len(Request("EMail")) > 0 then
        if len(strWhere) > 0 then strWhere = strWhere & " AND "
        strWhere = strWhere & "EMail = '" & Request("EMail") & "'"
    end if
    if Len(Request("OSCode")) > 0 then
        if len(strWhere) > 0 then strWhere = strWhere & " AND "
        strWhere = strWhere & "OSCode = '" & Request("OSCode") & "'"
    end if
    if Len(strWhere) > 0 then
        Session("DRH_Filter") = strWhere
    elseif len(Request("DRH_PagingMove")) = 0 then
        Session("DRH_Filter") = ""
    end if

'construct the table for the output %>
<table CELLSPACING=1 CELLPADDING=1 BORDER=0 WIDTH=100%>
    <tr align="center" valign="TOP">
        <td WIDTH=20> </td>
        <th BGCOLOR=Silver><h4>First Name</h4></th>
        <th BGCOLOR=Silver><h4>Last Name</h4></th>
        <th BGCOLOR=Silver><h4>Company</h4></th>
        <th BGCOLOR=Silver><h4>Address</h4></th>
        <th BGCOLOR=Silver><h4>City</h4></th>
```

```
                    <th BGCOLOR=Silver><h4>State</h4></th>
                    <th BGCOLOR=Silver><h4>Postal</h4></th>
                    <th BGCOLOR=Silver><h4>Phone</h4></th>
                    <th BGCOLOR=Silver><h4>EMail</h4></th>
                    <th BGCOLOR=Silver><h4>Op. System</h4></th>
                    <th BGCOLOR=Silver><h4>Picture</h4></th>
                    <td WIDTH=20> </td>
            </tr>

<!--METADATA TYPE="DesignerControl" startspan
        <OBJECT ID="DRH" WIDTH=151 HEIGHT=24
         CLASSID="CLSID:F602E721-A281-11CF-A5B7-0080C73AAC7E">
                <PARAM NAME="_Version" VALUE="65536">
                <PARAM NAME="_Version" VALUE="65536">
                <PARAM NAME="_ExtentX" VALUE="3986">
                <PARAM NAME="_ExtentY" VALUE="635">
                <PARAM NAME="_StockProps" VALUE="0">
                <PARAM NAME="DataConnection" VALUE="Interdev">
                <PARAM NAME="CommandText" VALUE="SELECT Guests.FirstName,
                 Guests.LastName, Guests.Organization, Guests.Address1, Guests.City,
                 Guests.Region, Guests.PostalCode, Guests.Phone, Guests.EMail,
                 OpSystems.Description, Guests.OSCode, Pictures.img_PictureURL
                 FROM ((Guests LEFT OUTER JOIN OpSystems ON Guests.OSCode =
                 OpSystems.OSCode) LEFT OUTER JOIN Pictures ON Guests.PictureID
                 = Pictures.PictureID )">
                <PARAM NAME="CursorType" VALUE="3">
                <PARAM NAME="RangeType" VALUE="2">
                <PARAM NAME="BarAlignment" VALUE="2">
                <PARAM NAME="PageSize" VALUE="10">
        </OBJECT>
-->
<%
fHideNavBar = False
fHideNumber = False
fHideRequery = False
fHideRule = False
stQueryString = ""
fEmptyRecordset = False
fFirstPass = True
fNeedRecordset = False
fNoRecordset = False
tBarAlignment = "Center"
tHeaderName = "DRH"
tPageSize = 10
tPagingMove = ""
tRangeType = "Table"
tRecordsProcessed = 0
tPrevAbsolutePage = 0
intCurPos = 0
intNewPos = 0
fSupportsBookmarks = True
fMoveAbsolute = False

If Not IsEmpty(Request("DRH_PagingMove")) Then
    tPagingMove = Trim(Request("DRH_PagingMove"))
End If
```

continues

25

CREATING A WEB DATABASE APPLICATION

Listing 25.3. continued

```
If IsEmpty(Session("DRH_Recordset")) Then
    fNeedRecordset = True
Else
    If Session("DRH_Recordset") Is Nothing Then
        fNeedRecordset = True
    Else
        Set DRH = Session("DRH_Recordset")
    End If
End If

If fNeedRecordset Then
    Set Interdev = Server.CreateObject("ADODB.Connection")
    Interdev.ConnectionTimeout = Session("Interdev_ConnectionTimeout")
    Interdev.CommandTimeout = Session("Interdev_CommandTimeout")
    Interdev.Open Session("Interdev_ConnectionString"), _
                  Session("Interdev_RuntimeUserName"), _
                  Session("Interdev_RuntimePassword")
    Set cmdTemp = Server.CreateObject("ADODB.Command")
    Set DRH = Server.CreateObject("ADODB.Recordset")
    cmdTemp.CommandText = "SELECT Guests.FirstName, Guests.LastName, " & _
        "Guests.Organization, Guests.Address1, Guests.City, Guests.Region, " & _
        "Guests.PostalCode, Guests.Phone, Guests.EMail, " & _
        "OpSystems.Description, Guests.OSCode, Pictures.img_PictureURL " & _
        "FROM ((Guests LEFT OUTER JOIN OpSystems ON Guests.OSCode = " & _
        "OpSystems.OSCode) LEFT OUTER JOIN Pictures ON Guests.PictureID " & _
        "= Pictures.PictureID )"
    cmdTemp.CommandType = 1
    Set cmdTemp.ActiveConnection = Interdev
    DRH.Open cmdTemp, , 3, 1
End If
On Error Resume Next
If DRH.BOF And DRH.EOF Then fEmptyRecordset = True
On Error Goto 0
If Err Then fEmptyRecordset = True
DRH.PageSize = tPageSize
fSupportsBookmarks = DRH.Supports(8192)

If Not IsEmpty(Session("DRH_Filter")) And Not fEmptyRecordset Then
    DRH.Filter = Session("DRH_Filter")
    If DRH.BOF And DRH.EOF Then fEmptyRecordset = True
End If

If IsEmpty(Session("DRH_PageSize")) Then Session("DRH_PageSize") = tPageSize
If IsEmpty(Session("DRH_AbsolutePage")) Then Session("DRH_AbsolutePage") = 1

If Session("DRH_PageSize") <> tPageSize Then
    tCurRec = ((Session("DRH_AbsolutePage") - 1) * Session("DRH_PageSize")) + 1
    tNewPage = Int(tCurRec / tPageSize)
    If tCurRec Mod tPageSize <> 0 Then
        tNewPage = tNewPage + 1
    End If
    If tNewPage = 0 Then tNewPage = 1
    Session("DRH_PageSize") = tPageSize
    Session("DRH_AbsolutePage") = tNewPage
End If
```

```
If fEmptyRecordset Then
    fHideNavBar = True
    fHideRule = True
Else
    tPrevAbsolutePage = Session("DRH_AbsolutePage")
    Select Case tPagingMove
        Case ""
            fMoveAbsolute = True
        Case "Requery"
            DRH.Requery
            fMoveAbsolute = True
        Case "<<"
            Session("DRH_AbsolutePage") = 1
        Case "<"
            If Session("DRH_AbsolutePage") > 1 Then
                Session("DRH_AbsolutePage") = Session("DRH_AbsolutePage") - 1
            End If
        Case ">"
            If Not DRH.EOF Then
                Session("DRH_AbsolutePage") = Session("DRH_AbsolutePage") + 1
            End If
        Case ">>"
            If fSupportsBookmarks Then
                Session("DRH_AbsolutePage") = DRH.PageCount
            End If
    End Select
    Do
        If fSupportsBookmarks Then
            DRH.AbsolutePage = Session("DRH_AbsolutePage")
        Else
            If fNeedRecordset Or fMoveAbsolute Or DRH.EOF Then
                DRH.MoveFirst
                DRH.Move (Session("DRH_AbsolutePage") - 1) * tPageSize
            Else
                intCurPos = ((tPrevAbsolutePage - 1) * tPageSize) + tPageSize
                intNewPos = ((Session("DRH_AbsolutePage") - 1) * tPageSize) + 1
                DRH.Move intNewPos - intCurPos
            End If
            If DRH.BOF Then DRH.MoveNext
        End If
        If Not DRH.EOF Then Exit Do
        Session("DRH_AbsolutePage") = Session("DRH_AbsolutePage") - 1
    Loop
End If

Do
    If fEmptyRecordset Then Exit Do
    If tRecordsProcessed = tPageSize Then Exit Do
    If Not fFirstPass Then
        DRH.MoveNext
    Else
        fFirstPass = False
    End If
    If DRH.EOF Then Exit Do
    tRecordsProcessed = tRecordsProcessed + 1
```

continues

25

CREATING A
WEB DATABASE
APPLICATION

Listing 25.3. continued

```
%>
<!--METADATA TYPE="DesignerControl" endspan-->
<%  Response.Write "<tr valign=""TOP"">"
    Response.Write "<td WIDTH=20> </td>"
    For Each Field in DRH.Fields
        if Field.Name <> "OSCode" then
            Response.Write "<td BGCOLOR=""White"">"
            if Len(Field.Value) then
                if Field.Name = "img_PictureURL" then
                    Response.Write "<IMG SRC=""" & Field.Value & """>"
                else
                    Response.Write Field.Value
                end if
            else
                'make sure the cell shows up empty
                Response.Write " "
            end if
            Response.Write "</td>"
        end if
    Next
    Response.Write "<td WIDTH=20> </td>"
    Response.Write "</tr>"
%>

<!--METADATA TYPE="DesignerControl" startspan
    <OBJECT ID="DataRangeFtr1" WIDTH=151 HEIGHT=24
     CLASSID="CLSID:F602E722-A281-11CF-A5B7-0080C73AAC7E">
        <PARAM NAME="_Version" VALUE="65536">
        <PARAM NAME="_ExtentX" VALUE="3986">
        <PARAM NAME="_ExtentY" VALUE="635">
        <PARAM NAME="_StockProps" VALUE="0">
    </OBJECT>
-->
<%
Loop
If tRangeType = "Table" Then Response.Write "</TABLE>"
If tPageSize > 0 Then
    If Not fHideRule Then Response.Write "<HR>"
    If Not fHideNavBar Then
    %>
    <TABLE WIDTH=100% >
    <TR>
        <TD WIDTH=100% >
            <P ALIGN=<%= tBarAlignment %> >
            <FORM <%= "ACTION=""" & Request.ServerVariables("PATH_INFO") & _
                               stQueryString & """" %> METHOD="POST">
                <INPUT TYPE="Submit" NAME="<%= tHeaderName & "_PagingMove" %>"
                    VALUE="   &lt;&lt;   ">
                <INPUT TYPE="Submit" NAME="<%= tHeaderName & "_PagingMove" %>"
                    VALUE="   &lt;   ">
                <INPUT TYPE="Submit" NAME="<%= tHeaderName & "_PagingMove" %>"
                    VALUE="   &gt;   ">
                <% If fSupportsBookmarks Then %>
                    <INPUT TYPE="Submit" NAME="<%= tHeaderName & _
                    "_PagingMove" %>"   VALUE="   &gt;&gt;   ">
                <% End If %>
                <% If Not fHideRequery Then %>
```

```
                          <INPUT TYPE="Submit" NAME="<% =tHeaderName & "_PagingMove" %>"
                                 VALUE=" Requery ">
                     <% End If %>
                </FORM>
                </P>
           </TD>
           <TD VALIGN=MIDDLE ALIGN=RIGHT>
                <FONT SIZE=2>
                <%
                If Not fHideNumber Then
                     If tPageSize > 1 Then
                          Response.Write "<NOBR>Page: " & _
                                    Session(tHeaderName & "_AbsolutePage") & "</NOBR>"
                     Else
                          Response.Write "<NOBR>Record: " & _
                                    Session(tHeaderName & "_AbsolutePage") & "</NOBR>"
                     End If
                End If
                %>
                </FONT>
           </TD>
      </TR>
      </TABLE>
<%
      End If
End If
%>
<!--METADATA TYPE="DesignerControl" endspan-->
</BODY></HTML>
```

The differences between the Active Server Page created in Chapter 23 and the one presented in Listing 25.3 are as follows:

■ The <LINK> tag was added and the <BODY> tag was modified to match the theme chosen for the Web site.

■ The output table was modified to match the List View's. This was done first near the top of the page within both the opening <TABLE> tag, the first (header) row's <TR> tag, and each of the <TH> tags. Also, two additional columns that provide spacing to the left and right of the table were added to the header row.

■ The Data Range Header's CommandText property was modified. The Data Range Header control starts immediately after the first row's closing </TR> tag. Click anywhere between the beginspan and endspan comment lines for the Header control (see Chapter 23 for more details on using the Data Range Header control). Right-click and select Edit Design-time Control in the shortcut menu. When the Properties dialog appears, click the SQL Builder button. Add the Pictures table and set the join to Select all rows from Guests. This is done by right-clicking the join line (the line connecting the Guests and the Pictures table) and choosing Select all rows from Guests on the shortcut menu. Add the column img_PictureURL to the output list by clicking its checkbox in the Pictures table. Save the query; then close this window and the Data Range Header's window.

■ The code immediately following the Data Range Header's `endspan` line is where the data is output to the table. This has been modified to match the site's Redside theme (including the spacing left and right of the table) and to include the picture in the table. The picture was added using the HTML `<IMG>` tag.

After these changes have been made, you should save the file. No changes were required to the Data Range Footer's properties because, as explained in Chapter 23, this control uses the property settings for its corresponding Data Range Header control.

Creating the Guest Entry Form

Creating the guest entry form is even easier than creating the search form. To create the form, follow these steps:

1. Make sure you have a local copy of the file `SearchForm.asp` in the project's directory. If you do not, select the file in the Workspace window, right-click, and select Get Working Copy from the shortcut menu.

2. Using Windows Explorer, copy the file and rename the copy to `EntryForm.asp`.

3. Add the file to the project using the Project | Add To Project | Files menu selections. Locate `EntryForm.asp` and click OK. The file is now added to the web and to the project's Workspace window.

4. Open the file in Visual InterDev's source editor.

5. Change the `<FORM>` tag's `ACTION` element to `guest-entry.asp`.

6. Between the lines that read

```
</SELECT>
</td></tr>
```

and

```
<tr><td align="center" colspan="2">
```

add the following code:

```
<tr><td align="center" colspan="2">You may choose a picture to
represent yourself:</td>
</td></tr>
<tr>
<%  RS.Open "Select * from Pictures where Active = 'Y'", MyConn, 0, 1, 1
      If not(RS.EOF) then
          leftright=0
          while not(RS.EOF) %>
              <td align="right" border="1"><input type="radio"
              name="PictureID" value="<%=RS("PictureID")%>">
              <img SRC="<%=RS("img_PictureURL")%>"
              align="absmiddle">
              </td>
<%            leftright = leftright+1
              if leftright = 2 then
                  leftright=0
                  Response.write "</tr><tr>"
```

```
                end if
                RS.movenext
            wend
        end if %>
    </tr>
```

This displays each active picture with a radio button and allows the surfer to choose a picture that best represents himself or herself. The pictures are displayed two across. This is done by using the variable leftright to keep track of which picture is being output, the one on the left or the one on the right. After the picture on the right is displayed, a new row is added to the table.

Next we need to create guest-entry.asp. This code will take the data entered on the guest entry form and create a new record in the Guests table. A feedback page will then be presented, informing the surfer of his/her GuestID. If any errors occur, they will also be displayed, and the surfer will have the opportunity to retry the form or to e-mail the site's Webmaster. Of course, more robust error tracking could easily be added using a variety of techniques, but those are beyond the scope of this chapter.

The code for guest-entry.asp is presented in Listing 25.4. The code opens a connection to the database, creates a recordset based on the Guests table, invokes the AddNew method, sets the field values based on the Request object (which contains the values entered onto the guest entry form), and performs an Update. If everything is successful, the surfer will see a feedback page containing the GuestID for his/her Guests record. Otherwise, the on error resume next lines will trap any errors that occur. A message is displayed on the Web browser that provides a description of the error and a course of action for the surfer.

Listing 25.4. The code for guest-entry.asp.

```
<%@ LANGUAGE="VBSCRIPT" %>
<HTML><HEAD>
<META NAME="GENERATOR" Content="Microsoft Visual InterDev 1.0">
<META HTTP-EQUIV="Content-Type" content="text/html; charset=iso-8859-1">
<TITLE>Document Title</TITLE>
</HEAD>
<LINK REL=STYLESHEET HREF="./Stylesheets/Redside/Style2.css">
<BODY BACKGROUND="./Images/Redside/Background/Back2.jpg" BGCOLOR=White>
<%  set MyConn = Server.CreateObject("ADODB.Connection")
    MyConn.Open Session("Interdev_ConnectionString"), _
                Session("Interdev_RuntimeUserName"), _
                Session("Interdev_RuntimePassword")
    set RS = Server.CreateObject("ADODB.RecordSet")
    RS.Open "Guests", MyConn, 1, 3, 2
    on error resume next
    RS.AddNew
    if err then
        Response.Write "<center><h1>An error occurred attempting to add "
        Response.Write "your record to the database:</h1>"
        Response.Write "<h2>" & err.description & "</h2><p>"
        Response.Write "<h2>Use the Back button to return to the form and "
        Response.Write "try again, or contact the Web master at "
```

25

CREATING A
WEB DATABASE
APPLICATION

continues

Listing 25.4. continued

```
        Response.Write "<a href=""mailto:webmaster@mydomain.com"">"
        Response.Write "webmaster@mydomain.com</a></h2></body></html>"
        Response.end
    end if
    RS("FirstName")=Request("FirstName")
    RS("LastName")= Request("LastName")
    RS("Phone") = Request("Phone")
    RS("Organization") = Request("Organization")
    RS("Address1") = Request("Address")
    RS("City") = Request("City")
    RS("Region") = Request("State")
    RS("PostalCode") = Request("PostalCode")
    RS("EMail") = Request("EMail")
    RS("URL") = Request("URL")
    RS("OSCode") = Request("OSCode")
    RS("PictureID") = Request("PictureID")
    on error resume next
    RS.Update
    if err then
        Response.Write "<center><h1>An error occurred attempting to add "
        Response.Write "your record to the database:</h1>"
        Response.Write "<h2>" & err.description & "<p>"
        Response.Write "<h2>Use the Back button to return to the form and "
        Response.Write "try again, or contact the Web master at "
        Response.Write "<a href=""mailto:webmaster@mydomain.com"">"
        Response.Write "webmaster@mydomain.com</a></h2></body></html>"
        Response.end
    end if
%>
<center><h1>Thank you for registering!</h1>
<h2>Your GuestID is <%=RS("GuestID") %><h2>
<p>Return to the <a href="default.asp">SwitchBoard</a></center>
</BODY></HTML>
```

Testing the Application

Testing the application is when you'll have the most fun. Select the file default.asp (or what-ever you named the Switchboard page) in the Visual InterDev Workspace window. Right-click and select Preview in Browser. You should see a page like that shown in Figure 25.7.

If you haven't already done so, create some records in the Pictures table using the Picture Maintenance section.

Next, select Enter a New Guest and add a Guests record. If you have any trouble, first verify that the form is correct by double-clicking EntryForm.asp in the Workspace window. If the form appears to be in order, open the guest-entry.asp file and verify it against Listing 25.4. If you're still having trouble, check the database design to make sure it's correct.

FIGURE 25.7.
The Switchboard page in Browser Preview.

After you've entered a few records in the Guests table, use the Search for a Guest link to verify those pages. Again, if you have any trouble, start with the HTML form page and work back to the database design. A common source of errors here is the CommandText property of the Data Range Header control. Make sure all required fields are specified and that the joins between the tables are properly formed.

Finally, use the Guest Maintenance section to modify some of the Guests records, delete a few records, and insert a record or two. Because we haven't modified any of the code that was created by the Data Form Wizard, any problems will be due to improperly using the wizard when the pages were created, or possibly to a bug in the wizard. The best course of action is to delete the pages created by the wizard and start over. Fortunately, this hardly takes any time at all because the wizard does the majority of the grunt work.

Summary

This chapter presents the WebGuest application. It's a complete application you can use today to create a guest-registration application for your Web site. There are plenty of ways to extend this application, however. For example, you could add some timestamp fields, more demographic data, and the ability to create usage charts and graphs based on this information. All this and much more is possible thanks to Active Server technology. As you have learned throughout this section of the book, Active Server scripting makes Web-based access to databases extremely easy to program and implement.

25

CREATING A WEB DATABASE APPLICATION

The next part of this book, Part VI, "Implementing Security with Visual InterDev," discusses another topic of interest to database programmers: security. You'll learn all about creating a secure Web site, as well as how to use digital certificates and user authentication.

VI
PART

Implementing Security with Visual InterDev

Securing the Web

by Michael Marsh

IN THIS CHAPTER

CHAPTER 26

Visual InterDev is all about allowing users controlled access to your data. The operative word for these next four chapters is *controlled*: I'll show you how to protect data that may be part of your site but that is not for public consumption.

Securing your Web site is something of an arms race between whatever measures you can put in place and whatever attacks can be used against them. Intruders are always creative when trying to hack your site! You can also be creative in preventing these attacks, but you can go too far. Security is necessarily a trade-off between level of security and ease of use. The chapters in this part of the book provide you with measures that will ward off most attacks while not putting undue burdens on your legitimate users or on you as the administrator of the site.

Security might not be the most exciting subject in this book, but it is essential. If you're reading this section, chances are you already know this. If you are just browsing, I encourage you to read the following case histories in hopes of convincing you to read all four chapters. Not only do these true stories make interesting reading, but they should also illustrate just how important security is for your site.

Why Secure Your Site?

Your data is your business! Isn't this obvious? Your data should mean a great deal to you and your site. If you are publishing information, it is your responsibility to ensure its integrity. Certainly secrecy is one aspect of data integrity, but consider also the data's availability: Your site will have little value if legitimate users cannot access appropriate information.

An attack on your site can damage your reputation. Your data can be vandalized, rendered offensive, and left visible to the public. Existing sites have been "customized" with pornography, foul language, political ranting, and other such nonsense.

Attackers can hide their identities by co-opting yours. In a famous case, e-mail with racial slurs was sent using the account of a professor at Texas A&M University. The damage to his reputation was great, and it took a considerable amount of time and effort to handle the consequences.

Your hardware is also at risk of attack. Intruders have been known to hijack disk space and CPU time for their own use. This can obviously affect your system's performance. If you sell your computer's resources, an attack like this can cause lost revenue.

Here are a few hypothetical situations for you to consider:

■ Your site sells media for use by other sites or in other forms of publication. If a user can access the media files without paying for them, you lose revenue.

■ Your site is a company intranet containing information intended for your employees only. If competitors can get to that information, your business may be damaged.

■ A company intranet may have data intended for individual use, such as salary and benefits information. If the wrong employee can access this information, you could have a legal problem on your hands.

Case History 1: The CIA and DOJ Web Site Incidents

On September 18, 1996 the CIA Web site home page (http://www.odci.gov/cia/) was modified by an intruder. Figure 26.1 shows the hacked site. A similar attack was effected on the Department of Justice home page a month earlier. The intruders have not yet been identified. These incidents beg the question: If government security agencies can't prevent attacks of this sort, how can you and I?

FIGURE 26.1.

The hacked CIA home page.

These attacks were made by gaining access to the files that make up the page. If you can protect these files, you can protect your site from this kind of attack. Fortunately, as you will see, protecting your site's files is straightforward using NT and IIS.

Case History 2: The Kriegsman Furs Incident

As you can see from Figure 26.2, this site was hacked by an animal rights activist. Reading the text shows that the individual involved believed that this was a good thing to do. The attacker claims to have meant no harm to the administrators of the site. However, the damage to the company was likely very real, and it is the administrator's responsibility to protect the site.

FIGURE 26.2.

The hacked Kriegsman Furs site.

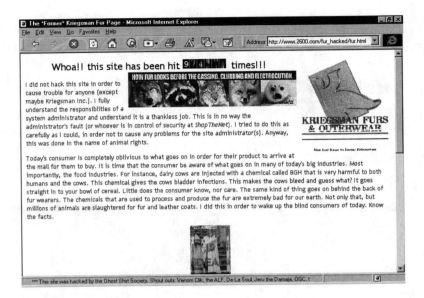

Case History 3: The Web Communications Incident

Early on the morning of Saturday December 14, 1996, an attacker in British Columbia initiated an SYN flood attack against Web Communications' network. Web Communications provides Web hosting for about 3,000 commercial sites. The attack swamped the network with false service connection requests, denying access to legitimate users. The result was that the commercial sites hosted by Web Communications could not do business because they lost contact with their customers. This happened on a weekend just before the holidays when the sites were expecting significant traffic. The attack held Web Communications and its customers hostage for nearly 40 hours.

Any machine running TCP/IP is vulnerable to this kind of attack. For a fix to this problem for NT, see article Q142641 on Microsoft's Knowledge Base at `http://www.microsoft.com/kb/`. Attackers never rest, and neither should your security plan!

Web Site Security Overview

The measures I'll soon discuss are a combination of host security and network security. The host security model depends on the host operating system to provide security, and the network security model works across operating systems. The first two sections cover topics generic to any security installation. Those that follow apply to sites using Visual InterDev. For the specific examples, I will assume that you are running NT Server 4.0 and Internet Information Server 3.0.

Hardware Security

This section discusses hardware-based security components. A secure site needs to implement at least one of these; more likely, your site will use them in some combination. Each of these components has consequences for level of security, ease of use, performance, and ease of administration.

Firewalls

A firewall is a system that separates two networks. Of specific interest here is that firewalls separate your internal network from the Internet (see Figure 26.3). Firewalls control access to your network through a single point of entry and exit (a *choke point*). This allows the firewall to scrutinize the traffic and ensure that it is within the acceptable parameters defined by your security plan. That is, you configure the firewall to accept or reject traffic based on criteria you select.

FIGURE 26.3.

A firewall separates two networks: yours and the Internet.

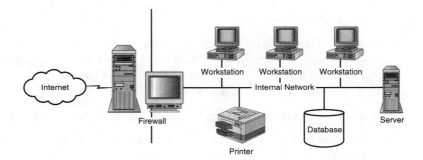

Firewalls are usually some combination of computers, routers, and software. They can be purchased as a system, or built from scratch. These days, a commercial firewall usually comes in one box, making installation somewhat easier. Building a firewall from scratch is more difficult, but may be necessary to achieve custom configurations.

Firewalls are powerful tools, but they do have some drawbacks:

- They cannot protect data that does not pass through the firewall.
- They cannot protect from inside attacks.
- The data filtering through a firewall slows access, sometimes significantly.
- Some Internet services will not be available to users through a firewall.
- Firewalls are expensive to implement and maintain.

Still, there is no better protection for your data against attacks from an outside network available today. If your site must be on the Net and it needs the absolute best security, a firewall of some sort is your best choice for security. Check out the firewall FAQ at http://www.v-one.com/newpages/faq.htm—that should get you started.

> **TIP**
>
> If your Web server happens to be on the other side of the firewall from your Visual InterDev workstation, you can still develop Web sites using Visual InterDev. You do this by communicating with the Web server via a Web Project Proxy. Search the Visual InterDev help system using the word *firewall* or *proxy* for more information.

Packet-Filtering Routers

Networks function by sending information from machine to machine in small entities called *packets*. These vary in size and content based on the network protocol being used. Here I'll assume an IP network is being used, because that is what the Internet is.

A *router* is a hardware device that connects different networks by routing packets between them. Packets have information about their destination, but it is up to the router to choose a path by which to get them there.

Because routers read a packet's information, routers can filter packets. Routers can either drop the packet or send it along its way, based on preprogrammed filtering rules. I'll show some examples of these rules later in the section. A packet can be filtered based on its address of origin or destination, and on the protocol used.

Some advantages of packet-filtering routers as they apply to Web site security are

- One router can protect an entire network if placed strategically (see Figure 26.4) and programmed properly.
- Filtering is transparent to users.
- Packet filtering is generally available. There are many commercial routers available with packet filtering. Additionally, software is available to use a computer to do routing with packet filtering.

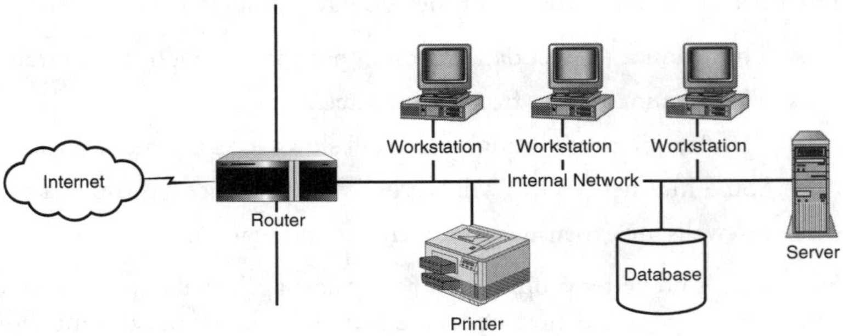

Figure 26.4.

Strategic router placement for protection of the entire network.

Some disadvantages are

■ Not all protocols are routable, so filtering through a router is not possible for every
protocol.

■ Programming routers can be difficult, and testing programmed rules also tends to
be so.

■ The information available in packets limits the kinds of rules you can enforce. For
example, you cannot limit the access of a certain user, because packets contain no
information about users.

Configuring a packet-filtering router involves writing rules and sending them to the router.
These rules tell the router which packets to allow or disallow. Your security plan might state
something like the following:

> *"Allow incoming SMTP mail from a particular machine and outgoing SMTP mail from
> any machine to a specific machine. Allow incoming and outgoing HTTP from any
> machine to any machine. Allow nothing else."*

Table 26.1 shows the router rules for this statement. It's always a good idea to write a default
rule. The router attempts to apply each rule in turn on each packet; if no rule applies, the router
generally drops the packet. To be sure, write the last rule similar to what you see here: This
ensures that the router will drop packets not covered by previous rules.

Table 26.1. Rules for programming a packet-filtering router.

Rule	Direction	Source	Destination	Protocol	Destination Port	Action
A	In	External	Any	TCP	25	Accept
B	Out	Any	External	TCP	>1023	Accept
C	In	Any	External	TCP	25	Accept
D	Out	External	Any	TCP	>1023	Accept
E	In	Any	Any	TCP	80	Accept
F	Out	Any	Any	TCP	>1023	Accept
G	In	Any	Any	TCP	80	Accept
H	Out	Any	Any	TCP	>1023	Accept
I	Either	Any	Any	Any	Any	Drop

> **NOTE**
>
> Clients for both mail and Web services generally use a random port number above 1023, SMTP servers use port 25, and HTTP servers generally use port 80 (but not always). The source and destination addresses should be translated to the specific IP addresses intended. *Internal* here implies a machine on your internal network, and *external* implies an address outside of your network.
>
> I can't give the specifics of programming every type of router here, so I've shown the rules in a generic form. You should use a form like this to capture and save the filtering rules for your router. The advantage of a generic form will prove itself when you need to move to another manufacturer's router.

This is an example of filtering by service, which is generally more useful than filtering by address. Filtering by address alone can leave you open to attacks involving forged addresses.

Consider carefully which services you allow. Some services are known to be riskier than others. As a general rule, allow only those services that are required and no others. Be sure to set up rules that restrict the local port numbers as much as possible and put only trustworthy servers on that port. That way, it doesn't matter if the client is using an untrustworthy application because it will not be able to do anything against the trusted server. Consult your router's documentation for more tips on securing ports.

Proxies

A *proxy server* sits between users of the Internet and external hosts. It allows users the illusion of being connected directly to the Net without allowing data to pass directly from the Net to the user's machine (and vice versa). Proxies are usually set up as dual-homed machines; that is, they are machines with two Network Interface Cards (NICs). One NIC is attached to the external Net, the other to the internal network. Data is passed back and forth through the proxy software, which can filter and log the transactions (see Figure 26.5).

FIGURE 26.5.

The proxy communicates between the two NICs.

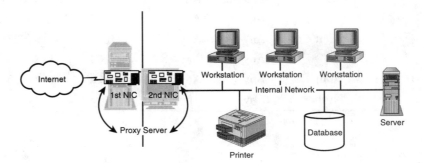

Proxies that are set up correctly can provide a good level of security for most sites. They are particularly effective for Web access, because HTTP is designed to work with proxies. However, HTTP allows downloading of applets, such as those written in Java or as ActiveX controls. A proxy will not know if this code is malicious. Furthermore, surfing through a proxy can be significantly slower than surfing directly.

MICROSOFT PROXY SERVER

Microsoft offers Proxy Server as part of its BackOffice suite. Proxy Server provides a high degree of security along with ease of use and maintenance. It also integrates extremely well with NT Server and the other BackOffice components. Proxy Server features document caching for improved performance.

On a dual-homed system, Proxy Server provides a high degree of security. Combined with a packet-filtering router, this security is equivalent to some firewalls. Microsoft claims that Proxy Server has been tested by an independent testing agency and has been shown to be resistant to spoofing, SATAN, and other common attacks.

Proxy Server comes with both Web Proxy (for HTTP, FTP, Gopher, and SSL) and WinSock Proxy (for a myriad of other protocols including VDOLive and RealAudio or any protocol written to the WinSock 1.1 API). See Figure 26.6 for a look at Proxy Server's interface.

For more information about Proxy Server try this site:

```
http://www.microsoft.com/proxy/
```

FIGURE 26.6.

The Microsoft Proxy Server interface.

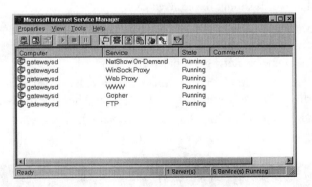

Software Security

In this section I'll talk about some generic security methods that are software based. These may be included in other components of your system (for example, passwords are managed by NT). I'll discuss each as it applies to a general site security plan.

Passwords

When a user thinks about security, passwords are usually the first topic that comes to mind. Passwords can be a powerful tool in the security arsenal, but only if applied appropriately and managed continuously. A firm policy on passwords must be written into your security plan, it must be enforced, and it must be periodically reviewed. Here is a list of potential problems with passwords:

- Simple passwords can be guessed by an intruder. Readily available tools such as Crackerjack and Crack can be used to automate the guessing and are remarkably effective. The earliest versions of Crackerjack actually sent the cracked passwords back to an individual: He collected a huge database of compromised systems!

- Users sometimes share their passwords.

- Passwords can be intercepted as they are sent across the Net. An unencrypted password is easily compromised this way.

Here are some preventative guidelines to keep in mind when you are formulating your password policy:

- Passwords should be at least 8 characters in length.

- Passwords should not be based on common information known about a user such as birthdays, the name of a pet dog, and so on.

- Passwords should have numbers and symbols, as well as letters. However, you should avoid passwords that are a word with a concatenated number.

- Passwords should have mixed case.

- Passwords should not be common words in any language.

- Passwords should not be related to popular themes such as *Star Trek* or *Star Wars*. "Wookie" is not a good password!

- Passwords should have a finite expiration date, the shorter the better. Users don't like this policy, so you might need to educate them on the issue.

- Users should be encouraged not to share their passwords.

- Do not send passwords out to the Net in clear text. Always encrypt!

TIP

Here are a few strategies for good passwords you could suggest to your users:

- Passwords can be words separated by symbols, such as drum-vine. The words should not be related.

- You could use the first letters of a phrase, such as tblpomam (the best laid plans of mice and men).

These rules should form the basis for a solid password scheme. Again, it is a good idea to review your password policy periodically and monitor compliance. As new employees come on board and veterans become complacent, passwords can become a security risk again. An administrator never rests!

Encryption

The use of encryption on your system enables confidentiality, integrity, and irrefutability for your data. In the next chapter I discuss Digital Certificates and authentication; data integrity and irrefutability are covered then. Confidentiality is the main concern here.

Encryption modifies a plain text message in some way to make it unreadable. Decryption unscrambles the coded message, rendering it into the original plain text. There are many types of encryption, but only key-based systems are covered here because they are the most widely applicable here. The two types of key encryption systems are symmetric and non-symmetric, or public key.

Symmetric systems such as DES (Data Encryption Standard) and RSA's RC2 use a single key to encrypt and decrypt a coded message. These systems are fast and can actually be implemented in hardware. However, you must distribute the key to whomever you want to read your message. This is cumbersome and potentially dangerous: The more copies of a key that are available, the higher the risk of theft or cracking.

Public key systems employ two keys: a public key used by the author of a message for encoding, and a complementary private key used by the recipient for decoding. A public key will work to decode only those messages encoded by its private key pair, and vice versa. Private keys are guarded as secret. Here's how it would work: I would use your public key to encode a message to you. You would receive the message and use your private key to decode it. If you needed to respond, you would encode your response with my public key, and I would decode it with my private key. With this system, it doesn't matter how many copies of the public key are floating around, because it can't decode anything (except messages encoded with the sister private key, something that wouldn't ordinarily happen). PGP (Pretty Good Privacy) is an example implementation of a public key system that is readily available on the Net.

CAUTION

Key encryption systems depend for their level of security on the length in bits of the key. Forty-bit systems are widely used but have been recently hacked. They are no longer considered secure. A 128-bit key is less likely to be hacked, but cannot be exported from the United States.

Also, the algorithm is only as good as its implementation. In September 1995, two students from Berkeley reverse-engineered the process by which Netscape's Navigator generates random numbers. They were able to use this information to crack the 128-bit version in 25 seconds! Netscape has changed the way these numbers are generated and has been secure since.

S-HTTP

S-HTTP, or Secure HTTP, is an extension of the HTTP protocol that provides secure transfers using encryption. Clients and servers negotiate security methodologies on connection. These methodologies can be any combination of algorithms, key management, certificates, and policies. S-HTTP's flexibility makes it possible to implement public key certificates without requiring individual users to acquire public keys. This means that a user can be sure that he is sending information to a trusted system; however, the server cannot be sure the user is who the user claims to be, because client authentication is not required. S-HTTP can be set up to require client authentication, and you'll be seeing a lot of this in the future as commerce on the Net becomes more common.

SSL

About the same time that S-HTTP was introduced, Netscape introduced its Secure Sockets Layer (SSL). Unlike S-HTTP, which works with HTTP only, SSL can secure other TCP/IP protocols.

SSL consists of two parts: the handshake protocol that establishes by negotiation the security services to be used, and the record protocol that is used to transmit data. Server authentication is provided in all implementations of SSL, but client authentication is implemented only in some.

PCT

PCT, or Private Communications Technology, is Microsoft's version of SSL. For the most part, PCT is similar to SSL, except that it has stronger client authentication. PCT is available currently only with Visual InterDev.

I will show you how to set up your system to use SLL/PCT1 in the next chapter.

NT Security

Windows NT was designed and built to provide a high degree of security. Using NT, you can build a system in which the servers, workstations, and network are all secure. Furthermore, NT provides an unmatched ease of administration for security-related tasks. These tasks are centrally administered using GUI interfaces. Users can manage access to those resources they own. NT conforms to the government's C2-level guidelines, as explained shortly.

I strongly recommend NTFS (NT File System) over FAT as the file system for your server. By using NTFS on the server, you can restrict access to folders and files based on rules set out in your security plan. With FAT, you cannot. This discussion will assume you are using NTFS.

NTFS file permissions and user and group profiles form the basis for security on NT Server. These are also the foundation for your Web site's security.

> **CAUTION**
>
> As secure as NTFS is, you should be aware that some redirector utilities allow DOS or Windows systems booted from a floppy to read files protected using NTFS security. The lesson here is that you should restrict physical access to machines with sensitive data. Physical security should be a part of your security plan.

What Is C2-Level Security?

The U.S. government has described a standard for secure computer systems. One level of this standard is C2. Some important parts of C2-level security for an operating system are

- User identification and authentication. Users must be identified uniquely. Furthermore, the system must guarantee user authenticity.

- Resource access control. The owner of a resource must be able to control its access.

- Protected memory. No resource stored in memory should be available to outside processes.

- Auditability. Security events must leave an audit trail for later perusal by an administrator.

Microsoft went to the National Computer Security Council (NCSC), a division of the National Security Agency, for verification that NT has met C2 security requirements. Windows NT (version 3.5) passed all requirements as outlined in the NSA's Orange Book.

The following sections discuss two aspects of NT security in further detail: user identification and authentication, and resource access control.

User Identification and Authentication

A user must log onto NT with a valid username and password before using any resources. A valid login will generate an access token for the user that is used in all subsequent attempts to use resources. Based on this token, a user is either allowed or denied access to a particular resource.

Users are added to an NT system using the User Manager for Domains program (see Figure 26.7). You can use this program to administer the following for each user:

- User information including username, password, and full name.

- User account restrictions such as password expiration date, restricted login times, and restricted login workstations.

- User environment profile including a home directory and a login script.

- User account type, which can be one of the built-in types such as Administrator and Guest, or an implementation-unique type such as WebUser.

- User group membership, which is discussed later.

FIGURE 26.7.

The User Manager for Domains program.

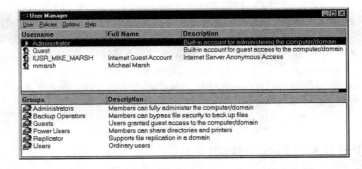

The user type, along with the user's group memberships, determines what the user can do on the system. For example, an Administrator can create new users, but a Guest cannot.

If you have a sizable number of users on your system, it is a good idea to create groups. This will allow you to apply the various grants and restrictions to a group as whole, without having to set these for each user individually.

There are three types of groups:

- Local groups apply to one machine only.
- Global groups apply on machines across the entire domain and into other trusted domains.
- Special groups are a predefined set of groups that are used by NT internally.

There are several built-in groups, just as there are for users. These groups are for users who need to perform similar tasks, such as backup and replication.

Resource Access Control

The NT resource security model protects resources by controlling their access. Access is controlled by associating a particular user with a particular resource. If a user is not associated with a resource, the user is not allowed access.

The ACL, or Access Control List, is the mechanism that NT uses to associate users and resources. The list not only permits or denies access, but also controls the level of permitted access. For example, if the resource is a file, the ACL will determine if the user has permission to write to the file.

You use the Explorer to set folder and file permissions, and thus permissions to make an entry into the ACL, on NTFS partitions (see Figure 26.8). You must have Full Control access to the folder or file, have Change Permission, and be the owner. Again, it is often most expedient to assign permissions to groups rather than to individuals.

FIGURE 26.8.

Using Explorer to set folder and file permissions.

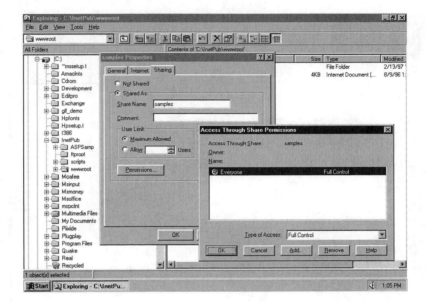

IIS Security

The Internet Information Server builds on the native NT security model by providing additional security features. This section describes NT security as it applies to IIS and native IIS security features.

Figure 26.9 shows the process that IIS uses to grant or deny an access request from a client. This graphic is based on a diagram in the online documentation for IIS. I show it here because you can clearly see the process and understand the steps that IIS takes when determining whether to grant access.

FIGURE 26.9.
How IIS determines
whether to grant or
deny an access request
from a client.

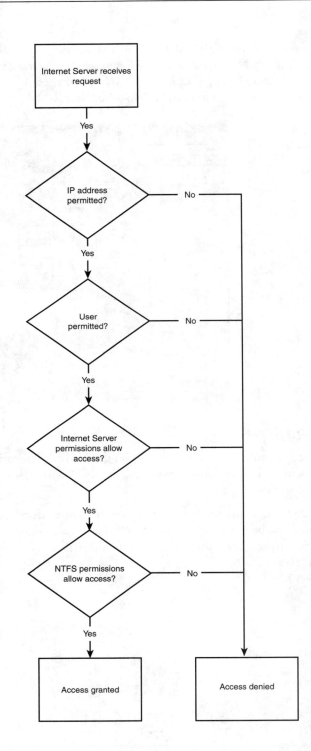

User Authentication

IIS uses authentication to grant or deny access to a client request. IIS can use NT groups and users to accomplish this, as well as its own mechanisms. IIS supports three types of user authentication:

- Windows NT Challenge/Response
- Basic authentication
- Anonymous login

You use the Internet Service Manager program to set up your authentication scheme, as shown in Figure 26.10.

FIGURE 26.10.

Setting up user authentication methods using Internet Service Manager.

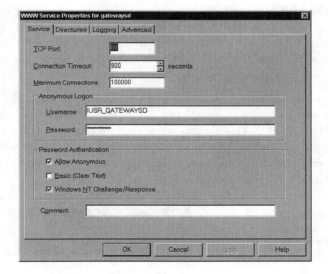

Windows NT Challenge/Response requires the client to pass user account information to the server. This information must match a valid NT user account; if it does not, the access is denied. An important part of this authentication scheme is that the account information is encrypted, making it very safe when put on the Net. However, NT Challenge/Response is available in only a limited number of clients. It is perhaps best used when you can control which browser your users will run.

Basic authentication passes unencrypted user account information between browser and server. The user must again have a valid NT account. This is the least-safe method because plain text user account information can be intercepted easily. Therefore, I strongly recommend avoiding this method.

Anonymous login uses the `IUSR_computername` account generated automatically when you install IIS. This account is permitted to log on locally to only the IIS server machine. If you are careful about setting the permissions on your site's files properly, this anonymous account can be secure.

If you have a mix of information on your site, some of which you don't want the entire public to see, you should set up a combination of anonymous login and authenticated login, preferably NT Challenge/Response, to control access. Create a group for users who can see the private material and give the desired permissions to the group for these folders and fields. This will deny access to these resources by an anonymous user, as long as the `IUSR_computername` account does not also have these privileges.

Access Control

You will want to carefully consider the permissions you grant to the folders and files that make up your Web site. As a general rule, grant Read access to content folders, Read and Execute access to program files, and Read and Write access to database folders and files. Again, you would set these permissions using the Explorer application.

When you create a project with Visual InterDev, it automatically generates virtual directories for you on the server machine. You can see these directories in the Internet Service Manager (see Figure 26.11). You can also use this app to change the two special IIS permissions: Read and Execute. These apply only to virtual directories. Clients will only be able to read from directories with the IIS Read permission, and will only be able to run programs from directories with the IIS Execute permission.

FIGURE 26.11.

Virtual directories in the Internet Service Manager.

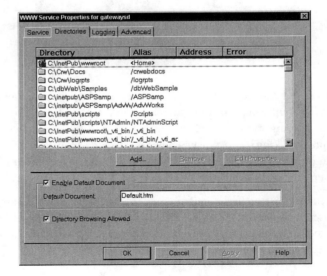

Logging

It is prudent to check for unauthorized access, or attempted access, to your site's folders from time to time. You can use the User Manager for Domains application to enable auditing for File and Object Access, as in Figure 26.12. You then use Explorer to specify particular resources to audit. The Event Viewer application shows you the audit entries (see Figure 26.13).

FIGURE 26.12.

User Manager for Domains is used to enable auditing for File and Object Access.

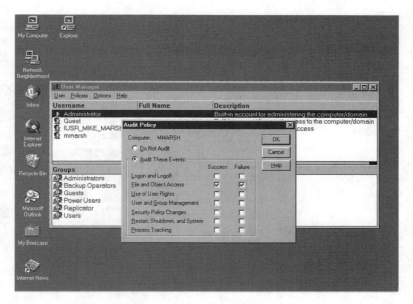

FIGURE 26.13.

Using Event Viewer to audit for unauthorized access.

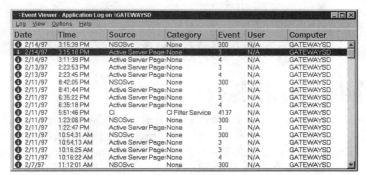

Using Visual InterDev to Grant Web Permissions

When you create a new web in Visual InterDev, it inherits the same permissions as the root web. You can change these permissions within the Visual InterDev IDE by selecting the Web

Permissions command on the Projects menu (see Figure 26.14). Here are the things you can do using this dialog:

- Set unique permissions for a Web
- Add users to a Web
- Add groups of users to a Web
- Change permissions for a user
- Change permissions for a group
- Delete users or groups on a Web

FIGURE 26.14.

The Web Permissions dialog from the Visual InterDev IDE.

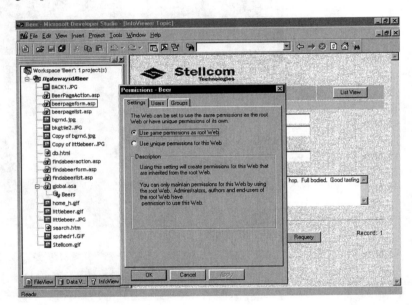

The Security Plan

A security plan for your site should be written, authorized, and implemented before you expose your site to the public. Without a coherent and shared vision for security, your site will be more vulnerable to attack. For example, without the guidance of a formal policy, naïve users could rely on crackable passwords, exposing your site to infiltration.

In the ideal world, you could adhere to that last paragraph. Alas, the real world will probably have you scrambling to create pages for Marketing's Latest Great Idea in a quarter of the time necessary. Security considerations may get pushed down on your stack. We've all been there, but you need to remember the security plan and come back to it as soon as possible. Get management to buy into the importance of the plan and you'll have an ally the next time you're getting yanked.

Getting a security plan authorized is not an easy task. You probably have strong ideas about what should be protected and how. These might not entirely agree with management's ideas, so you should be prepared to defend your reasoning, but probably compromise. You should recognize that security policy decisions, because they affect access and ease of use, will be considered in the context of your company's entire business.

The Importance of a Company-Wide Security Plan

Your site is probably only a part of your company's overall network. Your security plan should therefore be a subset of a company-wide security policy. If you have a strict security plan for your site, but your internal network is unsecured, then your site is unsecured as well. Conversely, if your internal network has a strict security policy but your site security is lax, you put the internal network at risk. Consider your site security plan carefully because it affects your general network.

Considerations When Designing a Plan

As with any plan, you should build using guiding principles. This will help resolve any conflicts and keeps things coherent. Here are some guiding principles to keep in mind:

- Cost. You probably will have a budget within which to operate. This will dictate what kinds and quantities of hardware and software you can use. It could also limit your development time.

- Ease of use. Security measures are necessarily a balance against ease of access. If users are continually stymied by your security, your business will suffer. Users might even rebel by ignoring security altogether, thus defeating the central purpose of the plan.

- Ease of administration. Make sure that you can easily accomplish the tasks associated with maintaining your site's security. If these tasks are too difficult, they will probably not be done consistently.

- Legal issues. Consider your company's special legal issues, if any. These include items such as copyrights, electronic funds, special security laws, and so on.

- Enforcement. What will the consequences of a violation of security policy be? Will a user lose privileges? Will there be warnings? How will enforcement affect day-to-day business?

Elements of a Security Plan

What elements should you include in the plan? This varies from site to site, but you should minimally include the following:

- Specific security issues. Your site may have specific concerns such as dial-in access or the protection of a particular machine. List these specifically in the plan.

- Methods for dealing with identified issues. For all of the specific issues listed previously, provide a detailed method for dealing with each.

- Physical security. No site is safe if an intruder can walk up to a workstation that is already logged on and access information. Similarly, if your servers are not physically secure, they are vulnerable.

- Identification of responsibilities. Are you responsible for security of your site or of the entire network? How do you prove that you are living up to those responsibilities? What is your manager's responsibility? How are users responsible for security?

- Methods of enforcement. Write down the specific consequences for violations of security policy. Make sure all users are aware of these consequences. Get management approval for this section particularly. There will inevitably be violations, some mild, others gross. You will have to deal with these, so documentation will be very helpful.

- Implementation details. In this section, describe exactly and technically how you will implement each part of the plan. This section is similar to a design document for a software project.

- Administration strategy. Here you identify the specific administrative tasks associated with the security plan, and how these will be accomplished.

- User education. The security plan is necessarily a technical document. You should make it available to all users, but there must also be a version written for non-technical users. This smaller document should include sections on the reasons for the security policy, tips for using the system securely, user responsibilities, and a description of the consequences of violating the security policy. Other forms of user education should be considered: perhaps a "Lunchtime Learning" lecture on famous security breaches and their consequences, or a demonstration of tips for using the system securely.

The written security plan is a crucial element in your site's overall security. It should be considered and written with the same care as any technical document. It is not an easy task and, depending on the size of your installation, could take weeks to accomplish. However, writing a security plan is considerably less onerous than dealing with the consequences of a security breach!

Current Security Issues

As I write this chapter, several security issues with Internet Explorer, IIS and Active Server Pages, and NT itself have come to light. Microsoft has resolved most of these issues. I will include links to fixes for each problem, if available. For continuing information about security issues relating to Microsoft products, check out http://www.microsoft.com/security/.

Hyperlinking to .LNK or .URL Files

A link may point to an .LNK or a .URL file that is in turn linked to an executable. This means that a page may have a link to a program that can cause harm when run. The programmer of the page would have to know the exact location of the file on a user's machine. A variation of this problem has been reported for other file types (.ISP, for example) by MIT. This problem is fixed in IE version 3.02 (downloadable for free at http://www.microsoft.com/ie/).

Unauthorized Downloads

Using versions of IE before 3.02, a user could click on a link that initiated a download before the user decided if the download was acceptable. IE would initiate the download in the background while displaying the dialog box to Open or Save the file. Small files could be downloaded in their entirety and run from the cache at a later date. This problem is fixed in IE version 3.02.

University of Maryland Security Problem

A hacker can add an icon that links to an executable on your machine. When you double-click on this icon, the program is launched without first asking. This problem is fixed in IE version 3.02.

Office 97 and Internet Mail and News Hyperlink Problem

All Office 97 products and the Internet Mail and News Reader applications that ship with versions of IE other than 3.02 can run a file associated with a URL embedded in a document. This problem is fixed in IE version 3.02.

Java/Cache Issue

For machines that are network servers and download code from Web pages, a Java applet running in the cache can access non–password-protected network resources. This problem is fixed in IE version 3.02.

Adding a Period to `.ASP` URLs

When you type the URL for a page that has the `.ASP` extension and you type one or more periods at the end of the URL, the `.ASP` file itself will be displayed instead of the HTML. If there is sensitive information in the `.ASP` file, such as database usernames and passwords, they will be viewed in the file. For a fix, link to `ftp://ftp.microsoft.com/bussys/winnt/winnt-public/fixes/usa/nt40/hotfixes-postsp2/iis-fix`. This fix requires either NT Service Pack 1a or 2.

Telnet to Port 135 Causes 100 Percent CPU Usage

This bug can be used to initiate a denial of service attack. A client that connects to port 135 through Telnet to an NT 3.51 or 4.0 server machine, and then types 10 or more random characters, will cause the server's CPU usage to go to 100%. Other services will be CPU starved until the machine is rebooted. Fixes are at the following sites:

```
ftp://ftp.microsoft.com/bussys/winnt/winnt-public/fixes/usa/nt40/
hotfixes-postsp2/rpc-fix
```

and

```
ftp://ftp.microsoft.com/bussys/winnt/winnt-public/fixes/usa/nt351/
hotfixes-postsp5/rpc-fix
```

See article Q162567 of the Knowledge Base for more information.

Telnet to Port 53 Crashes DNS Service

Another denial of service attack can be initiated by Telnetting to port 53 of an NT 4.0 server and typing a few characters. The fix is at

```
ftp://ftp.microsoft.com/bussys/winnt/winnt-public/fixes/usa/nt40/
hotfixes-postsp2/dns-fix.
```

See article Q162927 of the Knowledge Base for more information.

Syncing UNIX and NT Password Databases Opens Security Hole on NT

An enhancement to Windows NT Server 4.0 to allow NT and UNIX to sync password files can be exploited by a trojan horse that can steal usernames and passwords as they are changed in the database. At the time of this writing, I could not verify that there was a fix for this hole.

Summary

You've put your site on the Internet precisely to allow the public to access specific information about your company. But being on the Net also exposes your company to substantial risk. An attack on your site can compromise your data through theft or vandalism. Your reputation can be harmed, your business damaged, and revenue lost. I have discussed some actual incidents in this chapter to illustrate just how real the threat is. Your site must be adequately protected.

You can use hardware security measures such as firewalls, filtering routers, and proxies to physically separate your internal network from the Internet. NT Server and Internet Information Server provide a secure software infrastructure to control access to your resources. Visual InterDev provides some tools for implementing access control from within the IDE.

Finally, a security plan for your site should be written, authorized, and implemented before your site goes live. If this is not immediately possible, and in the real world it is often not, keep trying. A coherent security plan is vital to your site's health!

Digital Certificates and Authentication

by Michael Marsh

IN THIS CHAPTER

CHAPTER 27

One of the interesting properties of the Internet is that it enables us to communicate with each other even though we are not necessarily at the same location. I can have a long conversation with my friend in Germany or my editor in Indiana without hopping on a plane, boat, or bus, and without having to pay heavy long-distance phone bills! For casual conversations, these advantages outweigh the possible dangers.

Dangers? Yes, indeed. The fact that we are not face-to-face with the person or entity we are communicating with poses serious problems of proof of identity. Consider these examples:

- You are shopping in an electronic mall on the Internet. You come across a store that is selling an item that you've been wanting to buy for some time, but haven't been able to afford. The price is incredible, so you decide that now is the time. How can you be sure that this is not a bogus storefront set up to rip you off?

- Conversely, you have set up shop on the Internet. How can you be sure your customers are who they claim to be?

- You need to communicate sensitive information to a colleague who is at another facility. How can you reassure your colleague that the information in the message hasn't been tampered with and that it was in fact you who the sent the message?

- You need to send commercial transaction information over the Net. How can you assure authorities that all parties properly authorized the transaction?

- You are surfing the Web. You come to a site that wants to download some executable software to your machine and run it from there. How can you be assured that the code is not malicious?

All of these problems and more can be addressed using authentication through *Digital Certificates*. I will show you how in the rest of this chapter.

What Is a Digital Certificate?

A Digital Certificate, or Digital ID, is the electronic equivalent of a passport, driver's license, or other form of identification. It is offered as electronic proof of identity.

Digital Certificates associate your identity with a pair of encryption keys: one public and one private. A recipient entity can verify that the credentials are authentic through the *Certification Authority*.

A Certification Authority (CA) issues Digital Certificates and is trusted as a reputable entity by the recipient.

Key Pairs

The Digital Certificate creates an encryption key pair when it is installed on your machine. One key is public and is used to decrypt messages created with the second, or private key. A recipient can be assured that the message was encrypted using your private key if the recipient used your public key to do the decoding. This, in turn, gives reasonable assurance that it was in fact you who wrote the message. Public-key encryption also provides assurance that the message contents were not tampered with. See Figure 27.1.

FIGURE 27.1.
How encryption key pairs validate message provenance and contents.

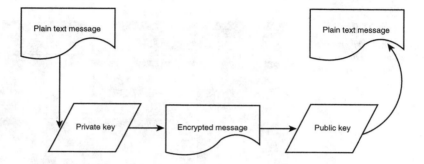

Obviously, you need to keep your private key secret. Because the private key lives on the machine where it was generated, you need to take steps to make it secure. Both Netscape Navigator and Microsoft Internet Explorer use passwords to protect your private key. When choosing a password for the key, follow all the guidelines for good passwords from Chapter 26, "Securing the Web." Also, take reasonable steps to safeguard your machine physically. Never transmit your private key over a network. Remember, your private key is like your signature: It can be used to impersonate you and cause you harm.

If you believe that your private key has been compromised, notify the issuing Certification Authority immediately. They will revoke your current Digital Certificate and give you a new one. Your old public key will no longer work, so the new one will have to be redistributed. This may be painful, but certainly much less so than repairing the damage caused by an impersonation.

If you lose or forget your private key password, you will need to get a new Digital Certificate. Again, though this may seem unfriendly, it is necessary in order to protect your all-important private key.

Typical Digital Certificate Contents

A typical Digital Certificate contains the following items:

- Your name
- Your public key
- The expiration date of the public key
- The Digital Certificate's serial number

- The Certification Authority's information
- The Certification Authority's Digital ID

Figure 27.2 shows how Internet Explorer displays a certificate's information.

FIGURE 27.2.

Internet Explorer can display a Digital Certificate's contents.

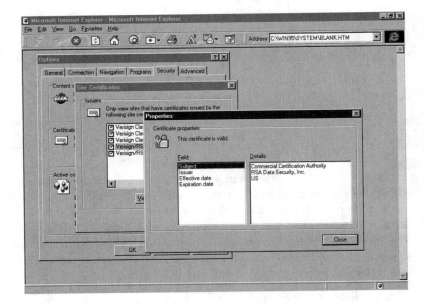

CCITT X.509 Standard

The format most widely used for Digital Certificate contents is described by the CCITT 1988 Recommendation X.509, "The Directory—Authentication Framework." This standard was created to resolve the issue of compatibility among secure software applications.

Does this mean that you can have a single Digital ID across applications? Unfortunately, not yet. You cannot use your Microsoft Internet Explorer certificate with Netscape Navigator, for example, because these applications store certificates in different ways. Certification Authorities and providers of secure applications are working on this issue now.

How Digital Certificates Work

Digital Certificates work by associating a user's information with a public-key encryption key pair. The issuing Certification Authority *digitally signs* the Digital Certificate. If you have a Digital Certificate installed in your browser, it will serve as digital identification for sites that require it. A Digital Certificate has a finite expiration date and must be renewed periodically.

Public Key Encryption

As explained in Chapter 26, public-key encryption is a method of encoding plain text using two keys: a public key and a private key. You use your private key to encode a message, and your message's recipient uses your public key to decode it. Private keys are kept secret, whereas public keys are made generally available.

Username and Other Identification

Depending on the level of authentication required for acquiring your public key, you may have to provide several forms of identification to the Certification Authority. Some require that you appear in person with a photo ID and a copy of your birth certificate. Others require fingerprints and a background check. For casual browsing on the Web, most Certification Authorities require only your e-mail address and your name.

Digital Signatures

A digital signature is an encrypted *message digest* that is unforgettable and irrefutable. A message digest is the result of running the text of the message through a special hashing algorithm that produces a unique sequence of characters for the text. A particular text will produce only one digest; no other text will produce the same digest, and it is impossible to reproduce the text itself from the digest. After you create the digest for your message, you encrypt it using your private key. The encrypted digest is the digital signature for your message. Your Digital Certificate contains such a digital signature from the issuing Certification Authority.

Digital Certificate Expiration and Time-Stamping Agencies

A Digital Certificate has a finite valid life. You should not accept a Digital Certificate that has expired. You will periodically renew your Digital Certificate just as you would a driver's license or credit card.

Some digitally signed documents must be kept for long periods of time, perhaps long past the expiration date of the certificate used. These documents can remain legal if they were registered with a time stamping service at the time they were signed. It would work this way: You create a message and its digest, then send the digest to the time stamping agency. The agency time-stamps the digest by creating a new digital signature consisting of the original digest, the date and time that the digest was received, and the time-stamping agency's digital signature. You include both the message digest and the digital time stamp with your message (see Figure 27.3).

FIGURE 27.3.

Digital time stamps.

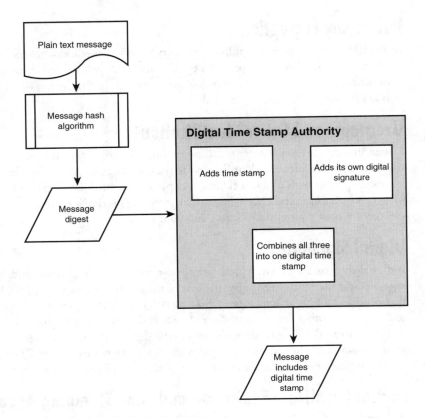

Applications of Digital Certificates

Digital Certificates can be applied in any case where the verification of authenticity is required. Some important examples include e-mail, groupware applications, and electronic commerce.

E-Mail

Suppose you want to send me a message that contains confidential information. You can use your Digital Certificate's private key to encode the message and send it encrypted to me. I would use your public key to decrypt the message and read the plain text. Because only your public key can decrypt the message, I can be assured that you wrote it. Figure 27.1 illustrates this process.

Unfortunately, anybody who has your public key can also read the message. This may not be what you intended. You could encrypt your message with your private key, ensuring provenance, and then encrypt it again using my public key. Now I can decode the message with my private key, then decode again with your public key. I can then read the plain text. Because only I can do the first decryption, only I will be able to read the message, thus ensuring privacy (see Figure 27.4).

FIGURE 27.4.

Encrypting twice for better privacy.

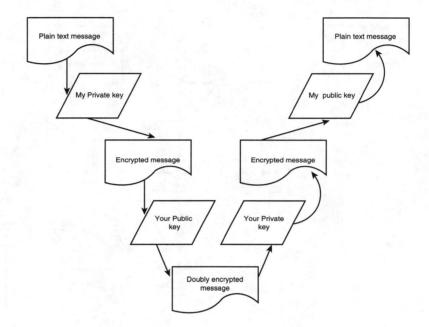

Though somewhat cumbersome, this method does indeed work. The problem is that encrypting more than a few paragraphs with a public-key encryption can take a long time, even on today's computers.

Enter the message digest, or message hash as it is sometimes called. Recall that a message digest is computed by an algorithm that creates a short set of characters that uniquely applies to the plain text. Only one hash will result from a plain text, and it is impractical to recreate the plain text from the hash. In essence, the message digest is a unique signature for the plain text. If you combine public key encryption methods with a message digest and symmetric key encryption for speed, you can create communications that are confidential, with guaranteed integrity and guaranteed provenance.

Here's how it would work: I would create a plain text message and then create its message digest. I encrypt the message text itself with a symmetric session key of my choice. I then encrypt the message digest with my private key and the session key with your public key and send everything to you. When you receive all three items, you first decrypt the session key with your private key, then decrypt the message itself with the session key. You can then also decrypt the message digest with my public key, and compare it to the message digest that you produce from the message. Figure 27.5 should make this clear.

FIGURE 27.5.

Use a message digest, symmetric key encryption, and public key encryption for the optimum in privacy and integrity for your message.

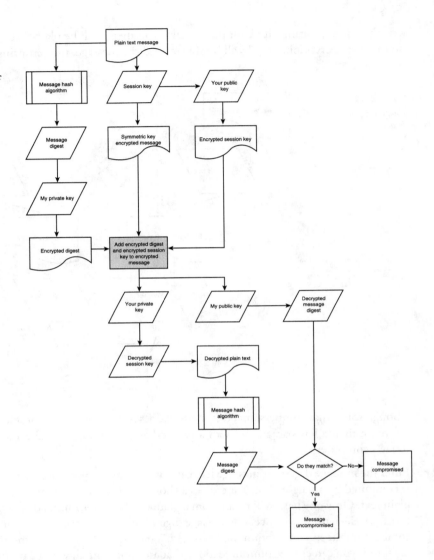

If all I want to do is sign my message, I create the message digest and encrypt it with my private key. When you receive the message, you decrypt the message digest with my public key and compare it to the message digest you generate from the text. If they match, you can be guaranteed that I wrote the message and that the message contents have not been altered. See Figure 27.6.

FIGURE 27.6.

Signing a message using a message digest and public key encryption.

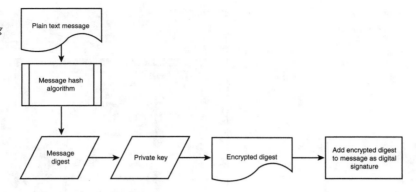

Electronic Commerce

When buying a product or service on the Net, you obviously would not want to transfer your credit card information to a site that is not secure. As a provider of products or services on the Net, how do you assure your customers that their information is private and secure? For sites using Visual InterDev, the answer is *SSL* and *PCT*.

As described in the previous chapter, SSL and PCT negotiate between client and server, deciding on an encryption algorithm and creating a symmetric session key for the duration of the communication. During this initial handshake phase, client and server may authenticate each other using Digital Certificates. When the agreements are in place, communication is secured using encryption via the negotiated session key.

Internet Information Server fully supports SSL 3.0 and PCT 1.0. It is compatible with any browser that implements these standards. You can use Visual InterDev to set up a site to use SSL and PCT. The following sections detail how to set up IIS and how to use Visual InterDev to enable SSL and PCT.

Setting Up IIS to Use SSL and PCT

The first step in enabling SSL and PCT for your Web is to set up IIS. Here are the main steps:

1. Generate the Public Key Encryption key pairs for your server and a certificate request file. You use the Key Manager application to do this, as shown in Figure 27.7.

2. Obtain a server Digital Certificate from a Certification Authority by sending the certificate request file. The generated key pair will not be valid until a Certification Authority has issued a certificate for it.

3. Install the new certificate on your server using Key Manager (see Figure 27.8).

4. Enable SSL and PCT on the virtual folders that require secure access. Use the Internet Service Manager application, as shown in Figure 27.9, to do this.

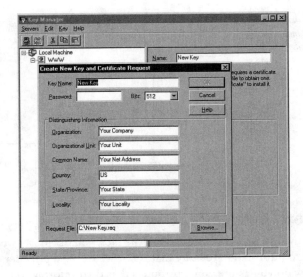

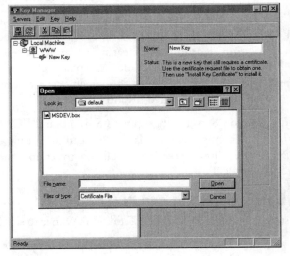

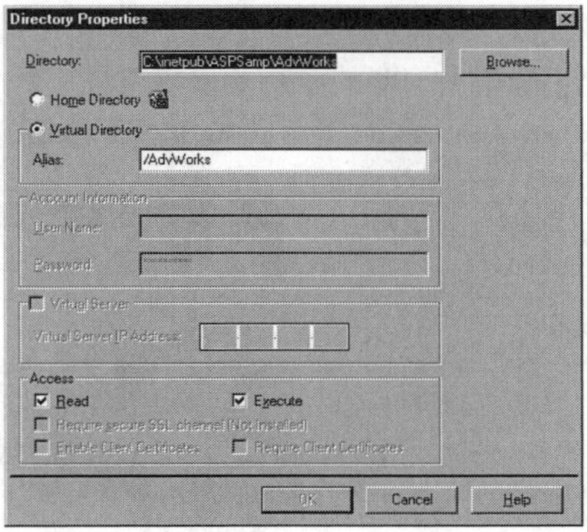

FIGURE **27.9.**

Using Internet Service Manager to enable SSL and PCT on your site's folders.

Here are a few more points to consider when enabling SSL and PCT on your Web:

5. For best performance, enable SSL and PCT only on those directories that require security.

6. Once you enable SSL and PCT on a Web, a client certificate is required for any client to gain access.

7. Keep your secure content in separate directories from your public content.

8. Use Key Manager to make a backup of your key pair. Don't forget your password! If you do, you will have to get a new certificate.

9. To point to documents on an SSL- and PCT-enabled folder, use `https://`. `http://` will not work on secured folders.

10. Once you are set up for SSL and PCT, remove the keys from the server machine and put them onto a floppy disk. Use the floppy whenever you need the key. Obviously, guard this floppy disk jealously!

Enabling SSL and PCT Using Visual InterDev

Once IIS has been set up to use SSL and PCT, enabling them for your Web is easy with Visual InterDev.

■ Use the Web Project Wizard to generate a new Web or connect to an existing Web.

■ In Step 1 of the wizard, be sure to check the Connect using SSL checkbox, as in Figure 27.10.

- Continue entering information with the wizard as usual.
- Click the Finish button.

Your Web will now be enabled for SSL and PCT secure communications.

FIGURE 27.10.

The Web Project Wizard of Visual InterDev can be used to enable SSL and PCT for your Web.

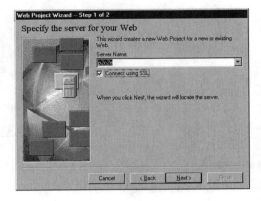

Authenticated Application Providence

When you navigate to a Web site, chances are that the site will want to download some executable code to your machine. How can you be sure that the code is not malicious?

One way is to require authenticity and accountability from the code's authors. This can be achieved by requiring that the code you allow onto your machine be digitally certified by a reputable agency; in other words, the code should be associated with a Digital Certificate issued by a known and trusted Certification Authority. If your browser supports Digital Certificates, it can notify you that code is being downloaded, and present you with the code's certificate. You can then accept or reject the download based on your trust of that certificate.

Microsoft has created its Authenticode technology to support legitimate developers in creating ActiveX controls for the Web. This set of code-signing tools is available in the ActiveX SDK. If you are going to write ActiveX controls for distribution, this technology is a must-have.

CAUTION

Code signing is not necessarily a bulletproof solution, however. Recently, a developer created an ActiveX control that would reset your machine after download. The developer actually obtained a certificate from a well-known authority. The authority revoked the certificate quickly, but the developer had already made his point. Caveat downloader!

The other major technology for downloaded code is Java. Java's inability to access the local machine's resources makes it somewhat safer in this respect. Java code can also be signed using Authenticode. The trade-off is in what a Java applet cannot do, as compared to an ActiveX control. Another issue when comparing ActiveX and Java is that not all browsers support ActiveX, while many browsers on different platforms do support Java.

Groupware Applications

In a setting where there is collaboration on a task, authentication can play an important role. Take the example of an electronic time card: These are usually signed by both the person reporting hours and by that person's supervisor. A digital signature from each applied to the electronic form would satisfy these requirements.

An issue that arises here is that signed documents often have to be kept for long periods of time. Because Digital Certificates have an associated expiration date, some mechanism must be available to keep these digitally signed documents after the expiration of the certificate. Registering the document with a digital time-stamping service will allow a certificate to be validated after it expires. A time-stamping service associates a time stamp with the document at the point that it was signed by combining the message digest with a time stamp, as described previously. If there is a dispute at some later time, the digital time stamp can be used to prove that the document was signed at the time stated.

Obtaining Digital Certificates

There are several types of certificates: personal, code, and server. Each might have different levels of protection. For example, VeriSign offers a Class 1 Personal Digital ID that assures a unique e-mail address and name, and a Class 2 ID that verifies identity against an online consumer database. Class 2 IDs are more expensive. Both are for use in browsers. VeriSign also offers personal IDs for S/MIME applications, IDs for signing code, and server certificates. The requirements for each differ, as does the process for acquiring them. There are several other authorities; here is a list of some of them:

- VeriSign Certification Authority (VeriSign, Inc.) `http://www.verisign.com/`
- Entrust (Northern Telecommunications, Inc.) `http://www.entrust.com/`
- CyberTrust (GTE, Inc.) `http://www.cybertrust.com/`
- Caviar (ISODE Consortium) `http://www.isode.com/x509Certification Authority.htm`
- BSafe/BCert (RSA Data Security, Inc.) `http://www.rsa.com/`
- Intelligent Security Agent (Zoomit International, Inc.) `http://www.zoomit.com/`

> **TIP**
>
> Microsoft is set to release its Certificate Server sometime in the second half of 1997. This software will administer the issuing, renewing, and revoking of certificates for Web sites using SSL and PCT. It can also be used for S/MIME, secure payments (SET), and Authenticode.
>
> Certificate Server works by accepting standard requests for certificates and issuing standard certificates. Because the product allows customizable policy, your organization can assume control of the certificate process, becoming a Certification Authority. This would be valuable when connecting remote users to your private intranet, when doing subscription-based business on the Net, and for secure communications with vendors and suppliers.

Programming with Digital Certificates

Most of the secure communication technology that you need to run your site is built into IIS and Internet Explorer. For those times when you need to do something beyond what is provided, Visual InterDev provides the programming support. In this section, I'll look at the CryptoAPI and Authenticode technologies, and then show you how to access client certificates using Visual InterDev.

The CryptoAPI

The CryptoAPI is the fundamental framework on which the Digital Certificate technology in IIS and Internet Explorer is built. It is part of the Win32 SDK and is, therefore, a set of C APIs in DLLs. It can be used with any language that can access C DLLs. The CryptoAPI includes support for symmetric- and public-key encryption, key generation and management, encryption and decryption, message digests, and creating and verifying digital signatures. CryptoAPI 2.0, in beta as of this writing, further includes support for certificates. The CryptoAPI is approved for export.

CryptoAPI 2.0 provides COM interfaces for access; this means that you can use VBScript within your Web pages to add crypto functionality to your site.

Microsoft Authenticode Technology

Built into Internet Explorer is the ability to authenticate a supplier of a software component: Authenticode. This technology is built on top of the CryptoAPI. It verifies to the user that the code about to be downloaded has not been tampered with and is in fact from a reputable supplier.

If you are creating ActiveX controls for distribution on the Web, you will want to sign your controls using Authenticode. Authenticode is available in the ActiveX SDK, which can be downloaded from `http://www.microsoft.com/intdev/sdk/`.

Once you have created your control, you'll need to follow these steps to get it signed:

■ Make sure you have Internet Explorer version 3.0 or above and the latest version of the ActiveX SDK.

■ Get your credentials from a Certification Authority. You can apply either as an individual or as a company. Each authority will have different procedures for certification. See the list of authorities in the previous section.

■ For a `.cab` file, add this entry in its corresponding `.ddf` file:

`.Set ReservePerCabinetSize=6144.`

For any other file type (`.exe`, `.ocx`, `.dll`, and so on), you don't need to do anything special.

■ Sign your files with the `signcode` program.

■ Check your signature with the `chktrust` program.

You have now signed your code. When a user downloads the file with Internet Explorer from a Web site, your certificate will be displayed. The user can accept or reject running your file based on this certificate. If the code has been tampered with, the browser will inform the user.

The Request Object and the `ClientCertificate` Collection

Visual InterDev provides you with easy access to client certificates through the `ClientCertificate` collection of the `Request` object. The syntax is

`Request.ClientCertificate(Key[subfield])`

where the key can be the following:

■ `Subject`: This is a string made up of subfields (see the following). If a subfield is not included, a comma-delimited string of all sub fields is returned in the form `C=US, O=Msft, ....`

■ `Issuer`: Also a string of subfields, with rules applying as with the `Subject` key.

■ `ValidFrom`: A VBScript-formatted date that specifies when the certificate becomes valid.

■ `ValidUntil`: A VBScript-formatted date that specifies when the certificate becomes invalid.

■ `SerialNumber`: A string representing the serial number of the certificate as hexadecimal bytes separated by hyphens as in `FF-FF-FF-FF`.

- ▪ `Certificate`: This string contains the entire certificate contents encoded as an ASN.1 format binary stream.
- ▪ `Flags`: Provides additional certificate information—ceCertPresent and ceUnrecognizedIssuer.

The subfields for Subject and Issuer are as follows:

- ▪ `C`: Country of origin
- ▪ `O`: Organization name
- ▪ `OU`: Organizational Unit name
- ▪ `CN`: Common Name of the user
- ▪ `L`: Locality
- ▪ `S`: State or province
- ▪ `T`: Title (of person or organization)
- ▪ `GN`: Given Name
- ▪ `I`: Initials

Listing 27.1 illustrates how to report on information about the client certificates currently in the collection. To test this code, make sure you have set up a Web that expects client certificates, and you access that Web using a client certificate. Otherwise, you'll just get a message saying that no certificates are available. Also, the include file `cervbs.inc` is needed to use the `Flags` key.

Listing 27.1. The Certificate Info Web page.

```
<%@ LANGUAGE= "VBSCRIPT" %>
<HTML>
<HEAD>
<META NAME= "GENERATOR" Content="Microsoft Visual InterDev 1.0 ">
<META HTTP-EQUIV= "Content-Type" content= "text/html; charset=iso-8859-1 ">
<TITLE>Certificate Info</TITLE>
</HEAD>
<BODY>

<!--#include file= "cervbs.inc "-->
You have the following Client Certificates in the Response object
➥collection: <BR>

<%
If Len(Request.ClientCertificate( "Subject ")) = 0 Then
    Response.Write( "None.<BR> ")
Else
    For Each key In Request.ClientCertificate
        Response.Write(key & ": " & Request.ClientCertificate(key) & "<BR> ")
    Next
End If
%>
</BODY>
</HTML>
```

Summary

The Internet affords us great new opportunities for fast communication with people regardless of their physical location. This also presents real problems of identification. How do you know that the people you are communicating with are who they say they are? How do they know who you really are?

Digital Certificates provide a means for servers and clients to authenticate themselves. They use technologies such as symmetric- and public-key encryption, message digests, and digital signing to accomplish this. Certification Authorities issue certificates and administer them.

Microsoft provides technology to support secure and authenticated Internet communication. These are based fundamentally on the CryptoAPI. Authenticode technology allows developers to sign their executables, giving users some assurance that the code is not malicious. IIS can be set up to use secure communication with SSL and PCT. Finally, Visual InterDev provides facilities for accessing Digital Certificates through the Response object's `ClientCertificate` collection.

27

**DIGITAL CERTIFI-
CATES AND
AUTHENTICATION**

Implementing a Security Architecture for Your Site with Visual InterDev

by Michael Marsh

IN THIS CHAPTER

Imagine this scenario: Your company's Web site allows your customers to browse a catalog of products for purchase. You want all your customers to be able to access the product catalog and order form pages. You want customers to be able to access their personal information pages, but not those of other customers. You need your employees to be able to update the catalog, process orders, and manage the customer information database, so employees will need full access to all pages.

Figure 28.1 illustrates a security architecture for this site. The architecture is based on two groups, Customer and Administrator. The Customer group allows a member to access the catalog and order form pages, and nothing else. The Administrator group allows a member to access all pages. Furthermore, a customer can access his information page, and his only, by login name and password. You can use a security architecture diagram such as this to plan the security of your site.

FIGURE 28.1.

A security architecture for a commercial Web site.

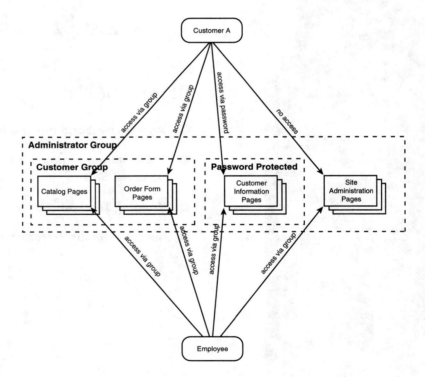

In this chapter I'll show you how to use the features of Visual InterDev and its runtime environment to implement a security architecture for your site.

Access Level and Navigation

People have come to like the Web because it is easy to navigate. A click on a hot spot here, a click on the back-arrow there, and that's all you really need to know to get around. This might be a slight exaggeration, but you get the idea: The Web is easy to navigate, and that is a big part of its charm.

When you need to limit a user's ability to access portions of your site, you have to be careful not to interfere with ease of navigation. Users probably shouldn't even be aware that there are parts of your site that are unreachable. The exception comes when a password is required; in this case, your users might even feel more comfortable because you are protecting their interests as well as your own.

To make your site secure and still provide easy access where necessary takes some planning. You need to decide which pages are going to be available to which users. You then need to look at the resulting structure and discern any natural groupings. You can use these groupings to help administer controlled access to your site. It is much easier to create a group, set permissions for that group, and then add individuals as members than it is to set permissions for each individual.

Once you have established your groups, you can get on with the nitty-gritty of managing navigation based on access privilege. I will discuss this in some detail shortly.

Defining Access Rights for Groups

Groups can be created at a number of levels: at the operating-system level, the database level, and the application level. Each level has pros and cons, as you will see. It is often advantageous to coordinate groups from different levels, although even more careful planning is required in this case.

NT Groups

For our purposes, *groups* at the operating-system level mean NT groups. NT uses groups for two purposes: to give rights to users to perform certain system tasks, such as backup, and to give users rights to access resources. We're interested in the latter.

NT has three types of groups:

■ Local: Implemented on the local machine's account database, these groups apply only to that machine. One interesting aspect of local groups is that they can contain other groups. No other NT group type can do this. Use local groups to grant access to resources of the local server machine, for example, in a workgroup installation.

28

IMPLEMENTING A
SECURITY
ARCHITECTURE

- Global: These are stored in the account database of the Primary Domain Controller (PDC) server machine of a domain. The permissions apply across the entire domain and into other trusted domains. Only user accounts from the domain, and not from other trusted domains, are allowed in the group. You would use global groups at sites with more than one server machine to allow access to other server machines in the domain. For example, your Web server may be on a different machine from your database server (see the following Tip for more information about setting up accounts to access a database on a separate server).

- Special: These are groups used internally by NT to accomplish automated system tasks. You cannot add users to these special groups, and it is generally best to leave them alone.

TIP

In order for your Visual InterDev application to see a database that is on a physically separate machine from your Web server, you must do the following:

1. IIS sets up the anonymous user account IUSR_*computername*. Add a password to this account.

2. In the User Manager program, add this user account and password to the global accounts database.

3. On the machine that is running SQL Server (or other database engine), add this user account and password to the local accounts database also.

4. Finally, you will need to grant permissions in your database for the IUSR_*computername* account name.

You use the programs User Manager and User Manager for Domains to create groups and add user members. Figure 28.2 shows the User Manager main screen.

To create a group, Choose User from the main menu, and then choose New Local Group, as shown in Figure 28.3. Fill in the information for the new group; then set the rights and permissions as appropriate.

FIGURE 28.2.

The User Manager program.

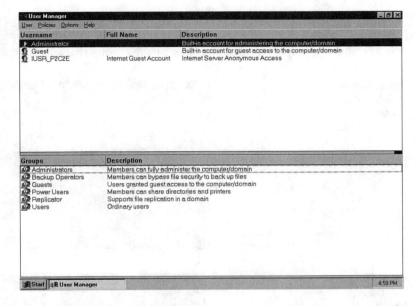

FIGURE 28.3.

Creating a new group using the User Manager program.

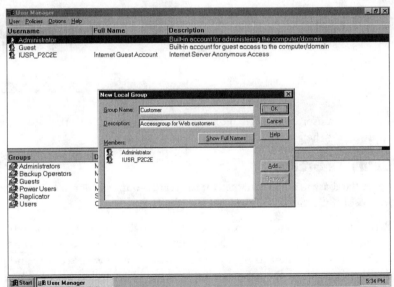

28

IMPLEMENTING A
SECURITY
ARCHITECTURE

To add a user to a group, double-click the username in User Manager. This brings up the User Properties dialog (see Figure 28.4). Click the Groups button to bring up the Groups dialog, which is shown in Figure 28.5. Assign a user to any group that appears here.

FIGURE 28.4.

The User Properties dialog from the User Manager program.

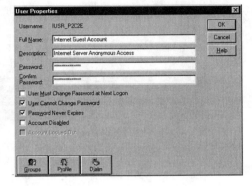

FIGURE 28.5.

The Groups dialog from the User Manager program.

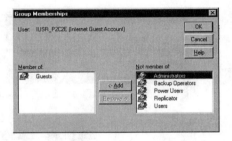

If you add a user to more than one group, the user will have the lowest set of permissions that apply across the groups.

Database Groups

Some database products enable you to create groups similar in function to NT groups. I'll use Microsoft SQL Server 6.5 in my examples here.

Permissions in a database apply to access for database objects such as tables, stored procedures, and views. With SQL Server, you can actually apply permissions down to the column level in a table. It is important to plan your database schema with security and groups in mind. The decisions you make about how to apply permissions and at what level can affect performance.

To create a group in SQL Server 6.5, you use either the SQL Security Manager or the SQL Enterprise Manager application. (See Figures 28.6 and 28.7.)

FIGURE 28.6.

The SQL Security Manager program.

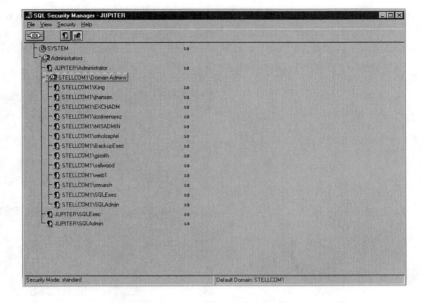

FIGURE 28.7.

The SQL Enterprise Manager program.

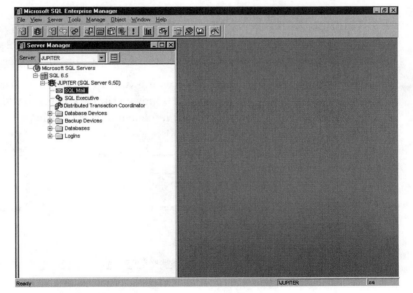

28

IMPLEMENTING A
SECURITY
ARCHITECTURE

Using SQL Enterprise Manager, choose Manage | Groups from the main menu after selecting a server and database from the Server Manager list view. This brings up the Manage Groups dialog (see Figure 28.8). To add a group and users to that group, fill in the information in the dialog, as shown in Figure 28.9.

FIGURE 28.8.

The Manage Groups dialog from the SQL Enterprise Manager program.

FIGURE 28.9.

Using the Manage Groups dialog to add groups to the database.

Application-Defined Groups

You can keep track of users and groups at the application level. This may afford you a finer control of how a user can access your site, but it obviously puts the burden on you to develop.

One method of tracking users and groups within your application is to use the database as the store for account information. Figure 28.10 shows a simple schema for doing this, while Listing 28.1 gives you a SQL Server script for implementing the schema.

FIGURE 28.10.

A schema for implementing application-administered users and groups.

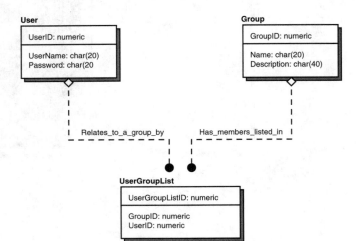

Listing 28.1. A SQL Server 6.5 script for implementing the schema in Figure 28.10.

```
CREATE TABLE Group (
        GroupID                 numeric IDENTITY,
        Name                    char(20) NULL,
        Description             char(40) NULL
)
go
ALTER TABLE Group
        ADD PRIMARY KEY (GroupID)
go
exec sp_primarykey Group,
        GroupID
go
CREATE TABLE User (
        UserID                  numeric IDENTITY,
        UserName                char(20) NULL,
        Password                char(20 NULL
)
go
ALTER TABLE User
        ADD PRIMARY KEY (UserID)
go
exec sp_primarykey User,
        UserID
go
CREATE TABLE UserGroupList (
        UserGroupListID         numeric IDENTITY,
        GroupID                 numeric NULL,
        UserID                  numeric NULL
)
go
ALTER TABLE UserGroupList
        ADD PRIMARY KEY (UserGroupListID)
go
exec sp_primarykey UserGroupList,
        UserGroupListID
go
ALTER TABLE UserGroupList
        ADD FOREIGN KEY (GroupID)
                                REFERENCES Group
go
ALTER TABLE UserGroupList
        ADD FOREIGN KEY (UserID)
                                REFERENCES User
go
exec sp_foreignkey UserGroupList, Group,
        GroupID
go
exec sp_foreignkey UserGroupList, User,
        UserID
go
```

28

IMPLEMENTING A
SECURITY
ARCHITECTURE

The idea is to add users to the User table and groups to Group table, then create group membership lists by associating a user with a group in the UserGroupList table. You can create screens to update the User and Group tables with Visual InterDev's Data Form Wizard. Figure 28.11

shows an example of the Group Administration screen. You could also use this wizard to re-turn the group that a user belongs to using a SQL query or stored procedure. Another approach is to code this query by hand. Listing 28.2 is a code fragment that shows you how to do this. The wizard is cool, but it does churn out a ton of code! Sometimes the simplicity of hand-coding a simple routine is the most flexible approach.

FIGURE 28.11.

The Group Adminis-tration screen.

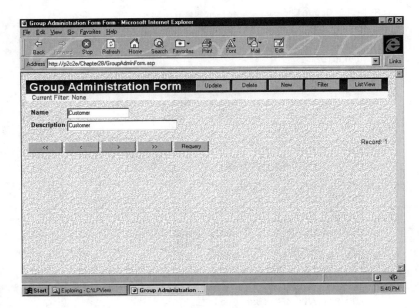

Listing 28.2. Querying for group membership.

```
<%
    strSQL = "SELECT UserGroupList.GroupID FROM `Group`, UserGroupList, `User`"
    strSQL = strSQL & " WHERE `Group`.GroupID = UserGroupList.GroupID AND "
    strSQL = strSQL & "UserGroupList.UserID = `User`.UserID AND "
    strSQL = strSQL & "`User`.UserName = '" & Request.Form("UserName") & "'"
    ' execute the query
    Set rstUser = dbUser.Execute(strSQL)
    ' report the GroupID
    Response.Write(rstUser("GroupID"))
    ' close the connection
    dbUser.Close
%>
```

Planning Ahead

When planning an architecture for your site, think about security. This is the time to identify areas of your site that must be restricted, and for recognizing the natural groupings of users based on their access privileges. A diagram like the one you saw in Figure 28.1 will help you visualize this architecture and identify all aspects of security, as they relate to page access.

You can combine the three types of groups in your site for added protection. NT privileges provide restricted access to your system's resources; you can allow Web users access only to those folders that you want to make available, and nothing else. Add to this groups within your database and you'll have the ability to restrict which database objects a user can see. Finally, at the application level you can use groups of your own creation to further refine access to your site.

> **CAUTION**
>
> Remember that as you add levels of security, your administrative burden goes up as well. Some of the most frustrating problems to resolve involve access issues, so be forewarned!

Navigation Based on Group Membership

Once you have the group membership information for a user, you can dynamically create a page with navigation to pages allowed for that group. Listings 28.3 and 28.4 show a simple example of this using the application-level groups discussed previously.

Listing 28.3 shows code for a simple .ASP page that requests a username and password (see Figure 28.12). When the user clicks the Submit button, the code brings up the page in Listing 28.4.

FIGURE 28.12.

The login screen.

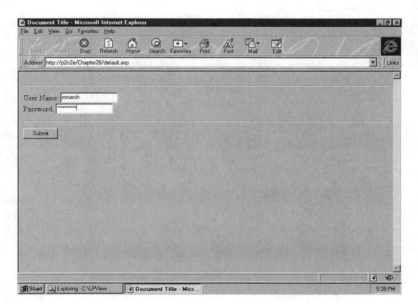

Listing 28.3. DEFAULT.ASP, which requests a username and password.

```
<%@ LANGUAGE="VBSCRIPT" %>
<HTML>
<HEAD>
<META NAME="GENERATOR" Content="Microsoft Visual InterDev 1.0">
<META HTTP-EQUIV="Content-Type" content="text/html; charset=iso-8859-1">
<TITLE>Login Page</TITLE>
</HEAD>
<BODY>
<FORM ACTION="Navigation.asp" METHOD=POST>
<HR>
User Name: <INPUT NAME="UserName" SIZE=20><BR>
Password: <INPUT NAME="Password" SIZE=20><BR>
<HR>
<INPUT NAME="Submit" TYPE="SUBMIT"><BR>
</FORM>
</BODY>
</HTML>
```

Listing 28.4. Building a page based on membership in a group.

```
<%@ LANGUAGE="VBSCRIPT" %>

<HTML>
<HEAD>
<META NAME="GENERATOR" Content="Microsoft Visual InterDev 1.0">
<META HTTP-EQUIV="Content-Type" content="text/html; charset=iso-8859-1">
<TITLE>Navigation Page</TITLE>
</HEAD>
<BODY>

<%
    ' create and open the Connection object
    Set dbUser = Server.CreateObject("ADODB.Connection")
    dbUser.Open Session("Chapter28_ConnectionString"),
➥Session("Chapter28_RuntimeUserName"), Session("Chapter28_RuntimePassword")

    ' build our SQL query
    strSQL = "SELECT UserGroupList.GroupID FROM `Group`, UserGroupList, `User`"
    strSQL = strSQL & " WHERE `Group`.GroupID = UserGroupList.GroupID AND "
    strSQL = strSQL & "UserGroupList.UserID = `User`.UserID AND "
    strSQL = strSQL & "`User`.UserName = '" & Request.Form("UserName") & "'"

    ' execute the query
    Set rstUser = dbUser.Execute(strSQL)

    ' build page based on Group membership
    If rstUser("GroupID") = 1 Then %>
        Customer: <% Response.Write(Request.Form("UserName")) %><BR>
        <HR>
        <A HREF="Catalog.asp">Catalog</A>
<%  Elseif rstUser("GroupID") = 2 Then %>
        Administrator: <% Response.Write(Request.Form("UserName")) %><BR>
```

```
        <HR>
        <A HREF="GroupAdminForm.asp">Administer Groups</A>
        <A HREF="UserAdminForm.asp">Administer Users</A>
<%  Else %>
        Not a valid User!<BR>
<%  End If

    ' close the connection
    dbUser.Close
%>
</BODY>
</HTML>
```

This page queries the database for the GroupID of the member, and then uses that ID to build itself, as shown in Figure 28.13. The page will display navigation links to pages that this user has access to, based on the user's group membership. This example is extremely simple for clarity; in reality you would want to do error trapping and decent formatting. Oh, and by the way, you might want to verify the user's password, too!

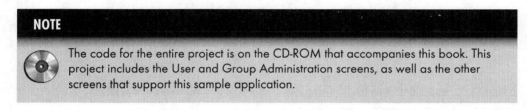

NOTE

The code for the entire project is on the CD-ROM that accompanies this book. This project includes the User and Group Administration screens, as well as the other screens that support this sample application.

FIGURE 28.13.
The Navigation screen.

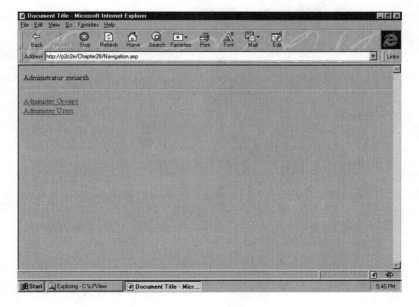

Preventing a Jump over the Login Screen

Users are smart. Even if you put your login screen as the first page of your site, they might find a way to jump over that screen and gain access to the other pages without logging in. Can you prevent this? Yes, in a couple ways.

First, if you take a look at the code in Listing 28.4, you'll see that the database query will fail if a user jumps directly here because the `Request.Form("UserName")` variable is not set. The page will build with the message `Not a valid user!`.

But what if the user jumps to one of the Admin screens? There is no check in the code for these screens to verify that the user is logged in, so if a user does jump here, access will be granted. You could add code to verify that the user has logged in, say with an application-wide Boolean variable, but you would have to add this code to every page in your site that needs protection. On a large site, this could be burdensome.

Fortunately, there is a better way: Use the `Redirect` method of the `Response` object in `GLOBAL.ASA` to send users to your login page no matter where they land in your site. To be polite, we'll check to make sure that a user has not logged in before we do the redirect. Listing 28.5 shows the `GLOBAL.ASA` file for our project where the redirect is implemented. The code is in the `OnStart` subroutine that is called at the beginning of a session.

Listing 28.5. The GLOBAL.ASA file, showing how to redirect a user who has not logged in.

```
<SCRIPT LANGUAGE=VBScript RUNAT=Server>
Sub Session_OnStart

    '==Visual InterDev Generated - DataConnection startspan==
    '--Project Data Connection
    Session("Chapter28_ConnectionString") = "DBQ=D:\WORK\Books\Visual
➥InterDev Unleashed\Chapter28\Code\ch28.mdb;DefaultDir=D:\WORK\Books\Visual
➥InterDev Unleashed\Chapter 28\Code;Driver={Microsoft Access Driver (*.mdb)};
➥DriverId=25;FIL=MS Access;ImplicitCommitSync=Yes;MaxBufferSize=512;
➥MaxScanRows=8;PageTimeout=5;SafeTransactions=0;Threads=3;UID=admin;
➥UserCommitSync=Yes;"
    Session("Chapter28_ConnectionTimeout") = 15
    Session("Chapter28_CommandTimeout") = 30
    Session("Chapter28_RuntimeUserName") = "admin"
    Session("Chapter28_RuntimePassword") = ""
    '==Visual InterDev Generated - DataConnection endspan==

    ' create a Session variable to track if the user has logged in
    Session("LoggedIn") = False

    ' make sure that if users haven't logged in that they get
    ' redirected to the login screen
    If Session("LoggedIn") = False then
        Response.Redirect("default.asp")
    End If

End Sub
</SCRIPT>
```

We also need to add some code to set the `Session` variable `LoggedIn` to `True` when the user has successfully logged in. Listing 28.6 shows a code fragment from the `NAVIGATION.ASP` file, which is where a user gets validated and logged in.

Listing 28.6. The modified `NAVIGATION.ASP` file, showing the management of the `LoggedIn` Session variable.

```
    ' build page based on Group membership
    If rstUser("GroupID") = 1 Then
        Session("LoggedIn") = True %>
        Customer: <% Response.Write(Request.Form("UserName")) %><BR>
        <HR>
        <A HREF="Catalog.asp">Catalog</A>
<%   Elseif rstUser("GroupID") = 2 Then
        Session("LoggedIn") = True %>
        Administrator: <% Response.Write(Request.Form("UserName")) %><BR>
        <HR>
        <A HREF="GroupAdminForm.asp">Administer Groups</A><BR>
        <A HREF="UserAdminForm.asp">Administer Users</A><BR>
<%   Else %>
        Not a valid User!<BR>
<%   End If
```

This is quite an elegant solution, but it will only work if all your pages have the `.ASP` extension. That's because only Active Server Pages can use the objects in `GLOBAL.ASA`. There is a very small performance penalty in making all the protected pages in your site go through Active Server parsing, but the payoff in ease of implementation more than compensates. If you need to have pages that anybody can access alongside secure pages, just make these public pages `.HTM(L)` files. They will not be redirected.

Keeping Track of a User

To keep track of users as they move from page to page, simply add `Session` variables to `GLOBAL.ASA`, as we did for the `LoggedIn` flag. You can access the variables anywhere in your code. The code fragment in Listing 28.7 shows the addition of the variables `UserName` and `Password` to `GLOBAL.ASA`. Listing 28.8 shows additions to `NAVIGATION.ASP` where the variables are set. Finally, Listing 28.9 shows how to use the variables to display the username in the `CATALOG.ASP` page. Figure 28.14 shows the Catalog page with the username displayed.

Listing 28.7. Adding the `UserName` and `Password` variables to `OnStart` in `GLOBAL.ASA`.

```
' create a Session variable to track if the user has logged in
    Session("LoggedIn") = False
    ' create a Session variables to track user name and password
    Session("UserName") = ""
    Session("Password") = ""
    ' make sure that if users haven't logged in that they get
```

continues

Listing 28.7. continued

```
' redirected to the login screen
If Session("LoggedIn") = False then
    Response.Redirect("default.asp")
End If
```

Listing 28.8. Setting the UserName and Password Session variables in NAVIGATION.ASP.

```
' Set the UserName and Password Session variables
Session("UserName") = Request.Form("UserName")
Session("Password") = Request.Form("Password")
```

Listing 28.9. Displaying the username in CATALOG.ASP.

```
<%@ LANGUAGE="VBSCRIPT" %>
<HTML>
<HEAD>
<META NAME="GENERATOR" Content="Microsoft Visual InterDev 1.0">
<META HTTP-EQUIV="Content-Type" content="text/html; charset=iso-8859-1">
<TITLE>Document Title</TITLE>
</HEAD>
<BODY>
Product Catalog.
<HR>
Customer: <% Response.Write(Session("UserName")) %>
</BODY>
</HTML>
```

FIGURE 28.14.

The Catalog page with the username displayed.

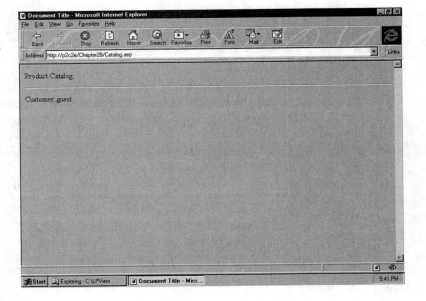

Security Versus Performance

Whenever you add a layer to your code, you are going to slow things down. By how much depends on what kind of layer you apply. You've already seen that security is a trade-off with access, and performance is a part of this equation. The good news is that the techniques used here will not affect performance to any great degree. If your users complain that your site is unresponsive, it won't be because of these techniques. The peace of mind that you will gain makes the balance tip in security's favor this time!

Summary

The time to consider security for your site is at the planning stage. Use a security architecture diagram to identify pages that require restricted visibility. You can then identify groups of users with varying degrees of access to these pages.

Groups are important because they facilitate security administration. Groups operate at three levels: the operating system, the database, and the application. Each has particular strengths and weaknesses, and each can be implemented in combination with the others.

You can use application groups for a finer level of control, but you have to do a little programming. You can also prevent a user from jumping over your login screen by using the Redirect method of the Response object. If you need to have unrestricted access to some pages alongside some secure pages, use a combination of .HTM(L) and .ASP files.

The techniques presented in this chapter will give you a flexible security system with a limited impact on site performance.

28

IMPLEMENTING A
SECURITY
ARCHITECTURE

Putting It All Together—Creating a Secure Application

by Michael Marsh

IN THIS CHAPTER

CHAPTER

29

In this final chapter on security, I'll tie things together by describing an application that encompasses many of the issues discussed previously. The application is an Electronic Time Card for a small, fictitious engineering consulting firm, Armadillo Engineering. I'll discuss the program in some detail, point out some interesting alternatives to what I've written, and suggest some other features that could be added.

This chapter is presented as a narrative from the point of view of the CEO of Armadillo Engineering, the author of the software. I will show how the CEO built the system, with a focus on security issues. I will also point out some mistakes in his thinking regarding security and their possible consequences, along with some solutions.

Vision and Scope

Armadillo Engineering is a small consulting firm with two employees who are field engineers. These field engineers work at the client site and are rarely in the Armadillo office. Their time cards are due weekly. In order to avoid a trip to the office, the field engineers have been delivering time cards by fax. There have been occasions of lost or garbled faxes that have affected Accounting's ability to bill in a timely manner. Furthermore, there have also been errors in transcribing the faxes into the accounting system's database.

The CEO, also an engineer, designed a system for inputting time card information by engineers from the field over the Web, and for having these approved by the clients, again over the Web. The information goes directly into the database, thus avoiding transcription errors.

Armadillo Engineering's biggest client is a UNIX shop; the other two clients run Microsoft Windows. One of the Windows shops uses Windows for Workgroups 3.11; the other uses Windows 95 for client machines and NT 3.51 for servers. In designing the system, the CEO had to consider the variety of browsers/clients that would be accessing the Electronic Time Card app.

To make the system as easy to use as possible, the CEO wanted login information to route the user to an appropriate page automatically, rather than forcing the user himself to do the navigation. Security was an issue here: The CEO needed to make sure that clients could not view each other's data and that field engineers could not access the database directly, because this would allow them to change their time cards after authorization.

Accounting's complaints had been growing increasingly strident, so the CEO needed a quick first solution to implement right away. The result of his effort is Armadillo Engineering's Electronic Time Card, a page of which is shown in Figure 29.1.

The Client Side

The Time Card application appears somewhat differently to each type of user after the initial common login page (see Figure 29.2). There are three types of users, each with a particular set of privileges:

- Administrators are allowed full access to the system. There are pages for maintaining the database that are available only to members of this group. Furthermore, a link to the Database Maintenance menu (Figure 29.12) appears on the Time Card page if the user is logged in as Administrator (see Figure 29.3).

FIGURE 29.1.

A page from Armadillo Engineering's Electronic Time Card application.

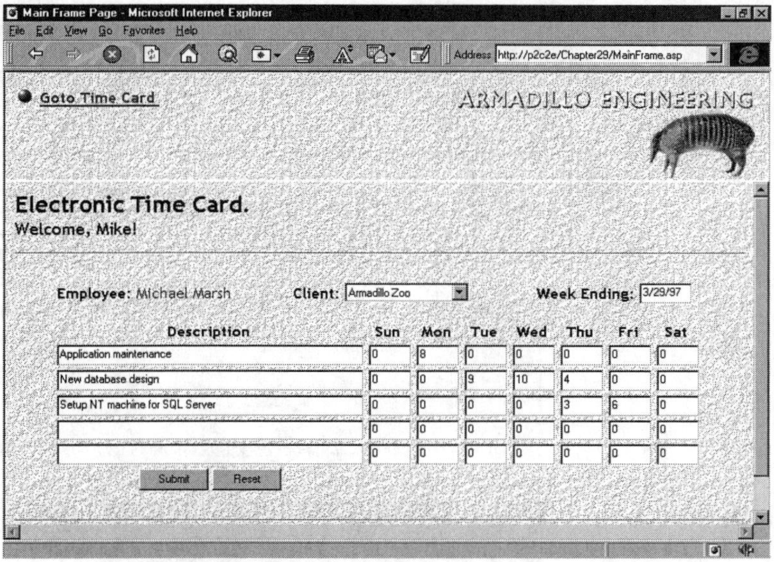

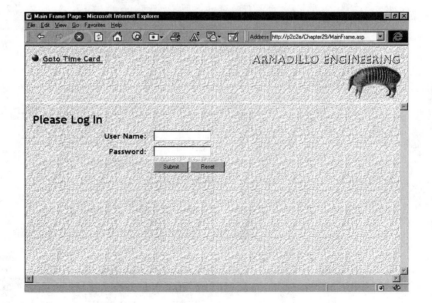

FIGURE 29.2.

The Login page.

■ Employees can see the Time Card Input page (see Figure 29.4) and the Time Card Verification page (see Figure 29.5).

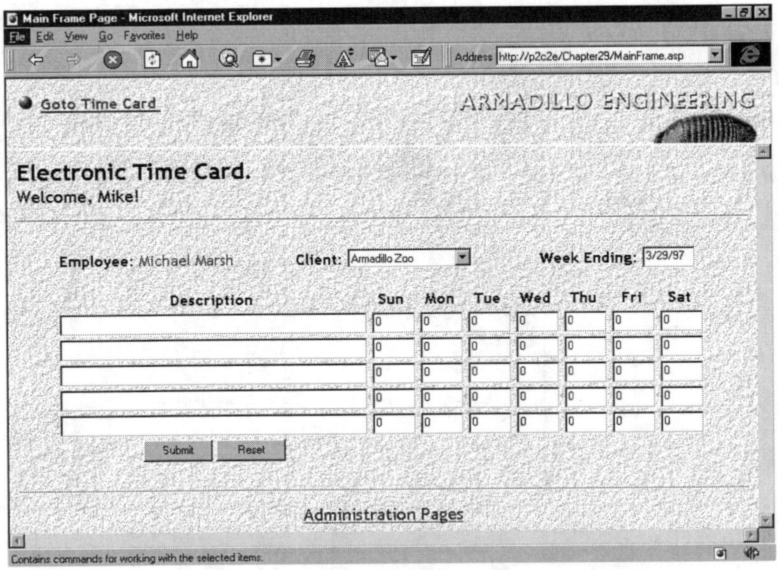

FIGURE 29.3.

The Time Card Input page with link to the Admin menu.

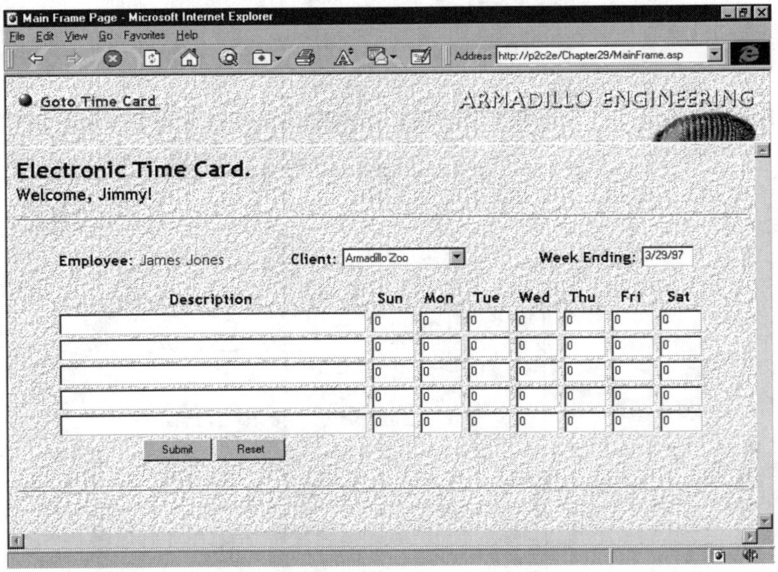

FIGURE 29.4.

The Time Card Input page as seen by a member of the Employee group.

■ Clients can search for pending time cards by employee (see Figure 28.6), see the resulting Pending Time Card Authorization page (see Figure 29.7), and then see the Time Card Authorization Verification page (see Figure 29.8). Only records for this particular client are displayed.

FIGURE 29.5.

The Time Card Verification page.

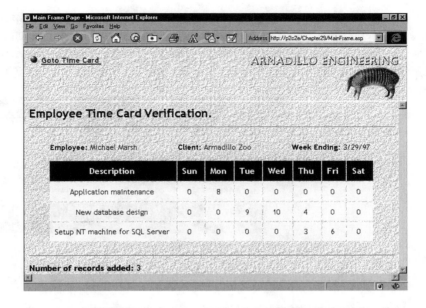

FIGURE 29.5.

The Time Card Verification page.

FIGURE 29.6.

The Client Time Card page.

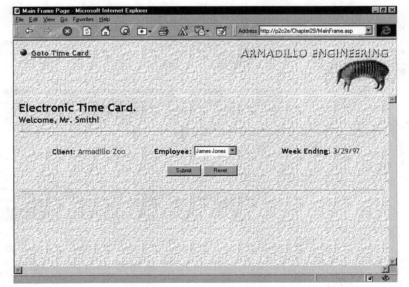

FIGURE 29.6.

The Client Time Card page.

To ActiveX or Not to ActiveX

One of the CEO's main concerns when implementing this solution was to ensure that the client code would run on a variety of browsers. Initially, the CEO wanted to implement some of the features of the app using ActiveX. In particular, he wanted to use an ActiveX spreadsheet control for presenting the Time Card data. This would have offered a substantial number of features for a lot less coding, and was therefore a very attractive solution. Unfortunately, one of his clients, the biggest one in fact, did not have a browser that could use ActiveX. Reluctantly, the CEO abandoned ActiveX in favor of a pure HTML solution for the client side.

FIGURE 29.7.

The Pending Time Card Authorization page.

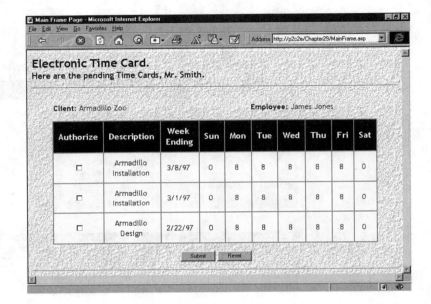

FIGURE 29.8.

The Time Card Authorization Verification page.

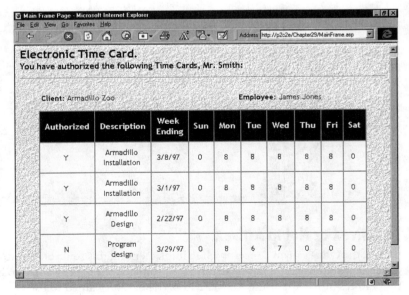

The Server Side

Armadillo Engineering is a Microsoft shop internally, with Windows 95 and Windows NT 4.0 Workstation on the clients and several server machines running Windows NT 4.0 Server. The dynamic nature of the client code made the choice of server software obvious: IIS with Active Server Pages. This in turn suggested the appropriate development tool, Visual InterDev.

After some thought, the CEO decided to use Access 97 as the database for the Time Card app. The Accounting database runs under SQL Server 6.5 on its own machine. Using Access as a "way station" for the data, with an automated import procedure for inserting data into the appropriate Accounting database tables, seemed the safest method for a quick implementation. The CEO plans to revisit this issue if and when there are scalability problems with the implementation.

Figure 29.9 shows a general architectural diagram of the system.

FIGURE 29.9.

The architecture of the Electronic Time Card application.

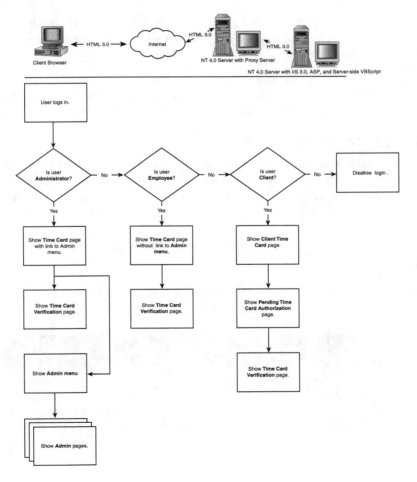

29

CREATING A
SECURE
APPLICATION

The Code

The three main components of the project are described here: the database, the client code, and the server-side code. First, though, I'll touch on how the CEO set up for the project.

Setting Up for the Project

The CEO set up his IIS server on a new machine running NT 4.0 Server. He put Proxy Server on another new machine with the same configuration. The Proxy Server machine has two NICs: one connected to his company's T1 line to the Internet, and one connected to his internal network. He set up the Web Proxy to allow HTML and SSL in and out. He disallowed FTP and Telnet, because at the moment, he has no use for either. For the WinSock Proxy, he allowed RealAudio for himself, because he likes to get his news from a radio station that broadcasts using this protocol over the Net. He figures (correctly!) that he will have to revisit this set up and tune it as time goes on.

The CEO then installed the server-side extensions on the IIS machine necessary to support Visual InterDev. He tested his installation with one of the sample sites provided by Visual InterDev.

Finally, the CEO set up his workstation with NT 4.0 Workstation and the Visual InterDev development environment. He installed Access on this workstation as well. He was now ready to move forward with the first step in his project: the database.

The Database

Armadillo Engineering's accounting database is relatively straightforward. Simply supplying the name of the client, the field engineer's name, and the hours worked for that week would be sufficient time card information for Accounting's purposes. However, the CEO would like to give his clients a little more information: exactly what the engineer was working on for those hours reported. The CEO also has an idea that he would like to use this database to track basic client and employee information.

The Schema

Figure 29.10 shows the schema for the database that the CEO designed. Tables 29.1 through 29.5 detail the physical schema for the tables.

NOTE

 The entire project, including the database with sample data, is on the CD-ROM that accompanies this book. The username and password for the administrator are `mmarsh` and `hsramm`, respectively. An employee name and password are `jjones` and `senojj`, and a client name and password are `ssmith` and `nutbrownale`.

FIGURE 29.10.

The logical schema for the database.

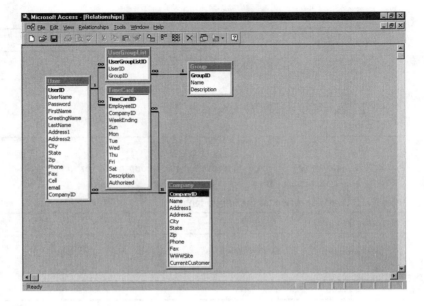

Table 29.1 shows how the user information is stored. The UserID is an AutoNumber field, which increments the value used as an ID automatically, guaranteeing uniqueness. The CompanyID field ties this user to a particular company.

Table 29.1. Physical schema for the User table.

Column Name	Data Type
UserID	AutoNumber
UserName	Text(20)
Password	Text(20)
UserName	Text(20)
FirstName	Text(30)
GreetingName	Text(50)
LastName	Text(30)
Address1	Text(50)
Address2	Text(50)
City	Text(50)
State	Text(2)
Zip	Text(10)

29

CREATING A
SECURE
APPLICATION

continues

Table 29.1. continued

Column Name	Data Type
Phone	Text(20)
Fax	Text(20)
email	Text(255)
CompanyID	LongInteger

Table 29.2 shows the physical schema for the Group table for keeping track of groups.

Table 29.2. Physical schema for the Group table.

Column Name	Data Type
GroupID	AutoNumber
Name	Text(20)
Description	Text(40)

To tie a particular user to a particular group, the join table UserGroupList is used. This table is described in Table 29.3. Note that by using a join table like this, a user may belong to more than one group. If you refer to the logical schema shown in Figure 29.10, you can see how this table ties together elements of the Group and User tables.

Table 29.3. Physical schema for the UserGroupList table.

Column Name	Data Type
UserGroupListID	AutoNumber
UserID	LongInteger
GroupID	LongInteger

The Company table stores information about companies, as shown in Table 29.4.

Table 29.4. Physical schema for the Company table.

Column Name	Data Type
CompanyID	AutoNumber
Name	Text(50)
Address1	Text(50)

Column Name	Data Type
Address2	Text(50)
City	Text(50)
State	Text(2)
Zip	Text(10)
Phone	Text(20)
Fax	Text(20)
WWWSite	Text(255)
CurrentCustomer	Text(1)

The `TimeCard` table stores the hours worked by one employee for one company over a one-week period. Each separate job that the employee lists for a single customer for a particular week goes into the database as a separate record, but is recorded on one page. If an employee works for more than one company, the employee must submit a separate time card for each. The `Authorized` field is how the application keeps track of open time cards that need a client's authorization. The `EmployeeID` and `CompanyID` fields are foreign keys relating this table to the `User` table and `Company` table, respectively.

Table 29.5. Physical schema for the `TimeCard` table.

Column Name	Data Type
TimeCardID	AutoNumber
EmployeeID	LongInteger
CompanyID	LongInteger
WeekEnding	Date/Time
Sun	LongInteger
Mon	LongInteger
Tue	LongInteger
Wed	LongInteger
Thu	LongInteger
Fri	LongInteger
Sat	LongInteger
Description	Text(255)
Authorized	Text(1)

Relationships

Figure 29.10 shows the logical schema for the database along with the relationships set up among tables. Table 29.6 shows these relationships in more detail.

Table 29.6. Relationships defined for the database.

Parent Table	Related Table	Relationship Type	Join Type
User	UserGroupList	One-To-Many	Inner
Group	UserGroupList	One-To-Many	Inner
Company	User	One-To-Many	Inner
Company	TimeCard	One-To-Many	Inner
User	TimeCard	One-To-Many	Inner

Access Versus SQL Server

As mentioned before, the CEO gave some consideration to the question of which database to use. He could have used the SQL Server machine that Accounting uses for its work, but he didn't want to rock that particular boat. He could have set up yet another machine as a database server, but for his small operation, that seemed like overkill. For now, he has decided to use Access 97, but will revisit the issue if necessary.

The Client Side

The client for this application is obviously a browser, though which particular browser is unknown. Because the code generated for client display and interaction will be pure HTML, the question of which browser will be used is moot anyway. For example, the code that the client sees for the Login page is shown in Listing 29.1. This listing shows that the code is nothing more than HTML and can be run on almost any browser.

Listing 29.1. The HTML code the client browser sees for the Login page.

```
<HTML>
<HEAD>
<META NAME="GENERATOR" Content="Microsoft Visual InterDev 1.0">
<META HTTP-EQUIV="Content-Type" content="text/html; charset=iso-8859-1">
<TITLE>Main Frame Page</TITLE>
</HEAD>

<BODY BGCOLOR = "#FFFFFF" LEFTMARGIN = 10 TOPMARGIN = 5 >

<FRAMESET ROWS = "180, *">
    <FRAME NAME = "Header" SCROLLING = NO  SRC = "Header.asp">
    <FRAME NAME = "Login"  SCROLLING = YES SRC = "Login.asp">
</FRAMESET>

</BODY>
</HTML>
```

Look and Feel

The CEO wanted Electronic Time Card to have the look and feel of a Web application. He also wanted to prominently display the company logo based on their mascot, the armadillo. Using frames would enable him to display this information everywhere but not have to code it into every page.

TIP

If you use frames in your pages, be careful of one thing. Currently with ASP, if the first page that a user comes to contains frames, you will get a `Session` object for each frame on that page. This can make keeping track of `Session` variables and the like difficult at best. Fortunately there is a workaround: Have a `default.htm` page without frames that does nothing but redirect the browser to your main framed page. The following code shows how the CEO did this for the Electronic Time Card sample.

```
<HTML>
<HEAD>
<META NAME="GENERATOR" Content="Microsoft Developer Studio">
<META HTTP-EQUIV="Content-Type" content="text/html; charset=iso-8859-1">
<META HTTP-EQUIV="Refresh" CONTENT="1; URL=MainFrame.asp">
<TITLE>Default Page</TITLE>
</HEAD>
<BODY>

<!-- Don't do anything here -->

</BODY>
</HTML>
```

User Interface

Because the CEO was limited to using HTML on the client, this pretty much dictated what kinds of controls he could use. Fortunately, the user interface is not complicated. All users will log in using the page shown in Figure 29.2. Employees will fill in their time cards using text boxes and input buttons as in Figure 29.4. Clients will use checkboxes to authorize time cards as shown in Figure 29.7. Finally, the administrator will navigate via standard HTML page links to various admin pages, and use text boxes and buttons to accomplish any tasks. Figure 29.11 shows a sample admin page.

Navigation

There is very little in the way of complex links on this site, so navigation is handled in a simple way. The main element is the Goto Time Card link on the logo frame. This enables the user to navigate back to the Time Card page regardless of where the user is on the site. Otherwise, navigation is handled by the browser's Forward and Back buttons, and by standard HTML links, such as those implemented in the Database Maintenance menu (see Figure 29.12).

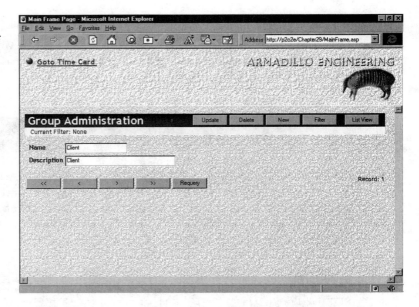

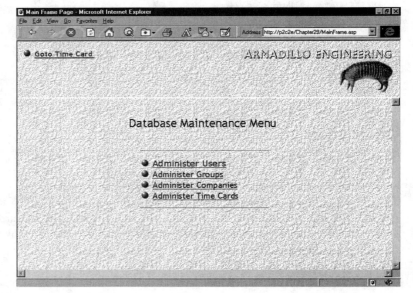

The Server Side

The server side is where most of the action is happening. The .ASP source files all have server-side scripting in them that create the client-side HTML dynamically. For example, Listing 29.2 shows the .ASP file for the Employee Time Card Input Verification page, while Listing 29.3

shows the client-side HTML that the server-side code created. Figure 29.13 shows how this page is displayed.

Listing 29.2. The .ASP code for the Time Card Input Verification page.

```asp
<%@ LANGUAGE="VBSCRIPT" %>

<HTML>
<HEAD>
<META NAME="GENERATOR" Content="Microsoft Visual InterDev 1.0">
<META HTTP-EQUIV="Content-Type" content="text/html; charset=iso-8859-1">
<TITLE>Employee Time Card Verification Page</TITLE>
</HEAD>
<BODY>

<BODY BACKGROUND = "images/Backgrnd.gif" BGCOLOR = "#FFFFFF" LEFTMARGIN =
➥"10" TOPMARGIN = "10">

    <FONT SIZE="5" FACE="Trebuchet MS, Verdana, Arial, Helvetica">
        <B>Employee Time Card Verification.</B>
    </FONT>

    <HR>

<%
    ' keep track of records added
    nRecords = 0

    ' open database connection
    Set dbChapter29 = Server.CreateObject("ADODB.Connection")
    dbChapter29.Open Session("Chapter29_ConnectionString")

    nHours = CInt(Request("Sun1")) + CInt(Request("Mon1"))
    nHours = nHours + CInt(Request("Tue1")) + CInt(Request("Wed1"))
    nHours = nHours + CInt(Request("Thu1")) + CInt(Request("Fri1"))
    nHours = nHours + CInt(Request("Sat1"))

    If nHours > 0 Then

        ' create the SQL string
        strSQL = "INSERT INTO TimeCard(EmployeeID, CompanyID, WeekEnding,
                    Description, "
        strSQL = strSQL & "Sun, Mon, Tue, Wed, Thu, Fri, Sat, Authorized) "
        strSQL = strSQL & "Values(" & Session("UserID") & ", " &
                    Request("CompanyID") & ", '"
        strSQL = strSQL & Request("WeekEnding") & "', '" &
                    Request("Description1") & "', "
        strSQL = strSQL & Request("Sun1") & ", " & Request("Mon1") & ", "
        strSQL = strSQL & Request("Tue1") & ", " & Request("Wed1") & ", "
        strSQL = strSQL & Request("Thu1") & ", " & Request("Fri1") & ", "
        strSQL = strSQL & Request("Sat1") & ", 'N')"

        ' execute the SQL command
        Set rsResults = dbChapter29.Execute(strSQL)

        nRecords = nRecords + 1
```

29

CREATING A
SECURE
APPLICATION

continues

Listing 29.2. continued

```
End If

nHours = CInt(Request("Sun2")) + CInt(Request("Mon2"))
nHours = nHours + CInt(Request("Tue2")) + CInt(Request("Wed2"))
nHours = nHours + CInt(Request("Thu2")) + CInt(Request("Fri2"))
nHours = nHours + CInt(Request("Sat2"))

If nHours > 0 Then

    ' create the SQL string
    strSQL = "INSERT INTO TimeCard(EmployeeID, CompanyID, WeekEnding,
            Description, "
    strSQL = strSQL & "Sun, Mon, Tue, Wed, Thu, Fri, Sat, Authorized) "
    strSQL = strSQL & "Values(" & Session("UserID") & ", " &
            Request("CompanyID") & ", '"
    strSQL = strSQL & Request("WeekEnding") & "', '" &
            Request("Description2") & "', "
    strSQL = strSQL & Request("Sun2") & ", " & Request("Mon2") & ", "
    strSQL = strSQL & Request("Tue2") & ", " & Request("Wed2") & ", "
    strSQL = strSQL & Request("Thu2") & ", " & Request("Fri2") & ", "
    strSQL = strSQL & Request("Sat2") & ", 'N')"

    ' execute the SQL command
    Set rsResults = dbChapter29.Execute(strSQL)

    nRecords = nRecords + 1

End If

nHours = CInt(Request("Sun3")) + CInt(Request("Mon3"))
nHours = nHours + CInt(Request("Tue3")) + CInt(Request("Wed3"))
nHours = nHours + CInt(Request("Thu3")) + CInt(Request("Fri3"))
nHours = nHours + CInt(Request("Sat3"))

If nHours > 0 Then

    ' create the SQL string
    strSQL = "INSERT INTO TimeCard(EmployeeID, CompanyID, WeekEnding,
            Description, "
    strSQL = strSQL & "Sun, Mon, Tue, Wed, Thu, Fri, Sat, Authorized) "
    strSQL = strSQL & "Values(" & Session("UserID") & ", " &
            Request("CompanyID") & ", '"
    strSQL = strSQL & Request("WeekEnding") & "', '" &
            Request("Description3") & "', "
    strSQL = strSQL & Request("Sun3") & ", " & Request("Mon3") & ", "
    strSQL = strSQL & Request("Tue3") & ", " & Request("Wed3") & ", "
    strSQL = strSQL & Request("Thu3") & ", " & Request("Fri3") & ", "
    strSQL = strSQL & Request("Sat3") & ", 'N')"

    ' execute the SQL command
    Set rsResults = dbChapter29.Execute(strSQL)

    nRecords = nRecords + 1

End If
```

```
nHours = CInt(Request("Sun4")) + CInt(Request("Mon4"))
nHours = nHours + CInt(Request("Tue4")) + CInt(Request("Wed4"))
nHours = nHours + CInt(Request("Thu4")) + CInt(Request("Fri4"))
nHours = nHours + CInt(Request("Sat4"))

If nHours > 0 Then

    ' create the SQL string
    strSQL = "INSERT INTO TimeCard(EmployeeID, CompanyID, WeekEnding,
             Description, "
    strSQL = strSQL & "Sun, Mon, Tue, Wed, Thu, Fri, Sat, Authorized) "
    strSQL = strSQL & "Values(" & Session("UserID") & ", " &
             Request("CompanyID") & ", '"
    strSQL = strSQL & Request("WeekEnding") & "', '" &
             Request("Description4") & "', "
    strSQL = strSQL & Request("Sun4") & ", " & Request("Mon4") & ", "
    strSQL = strSQL & Request("Tue4") & ", " & Request("Wed4") & ", "
    strSQL = strSQL & Request("Thu4") & ", " & Request("Fri4") & ", "
    strSQL = strSQL & Request("Sat4") & ", 'N')"

    ' execute the SQL command
    Set rsResults = dbChapter29.Execute(strSQL)

    nRecords = nRecords + 1

End If

nHours = CInt(Request("Sun5")) + CInt(Request("Mon5"))
nHours = nHours + CInt(Request("Tue5")) + CInt(Request("Wed5"))
nHours = nHours + CInt(Request("Thu5")) + CInt(Request("Fri5"))
nHours = nHours + CInt(Request("Sat5"))

If nHours > 0 Then

    ' create the SQL string
    strSQL = "INSERT INTO TimeCard(EmployeeID, CompanyID, WeekEnding,
             Description, "
    strSQL = strSQL & "Sun, Mon, Tue, Wed, Thu, Fri, Sat, Authorized) "
    strSQL = strSQL & "Values(" & Session("UserID") & ", " &
             Request("CompanyID") & ", '"
    strSQL = strSQL & Request("WeekEnding") & "', '" &
             Request("Description5") & "', "
    strSQL = strSQL & Request("Sun5") & ", " & Request("Mon5") & ", "
    strSQL = strSQL & Request("Tue5") & ", " & Request("Wed5") & ", "
    strSQL = strSQL & Request("Thu5") & ", " & Request("Fri5") & ", "
    strSQL = strSQL & Request("Sat5") & ", 'N')"

    ' execute the SQL command
    Set rsResults = dbChapter29.Execute(strSQL)

    nRecords = nRecords + 1

End If
%>

    <CENTER>
```

29

CREATING A
SECURE
APPLICATION

continues

Listing 29.2. continued

```
    <P>
    <TABLE ALIGN = CENTER WIDTH = 90%>
        <TR>
<%
            ' create the SQL string
            strSQL = "SELECT FirstName, LastName FROM User WHERE UserID = "
                    & Session("UserID")

            ' execute the SQL command
            Set rsResults = dbChapter29.Execute(strSQL)
%>
            <FONT SIZE = "4" FACE="Trebuchet MS, Verdana, Arial, Helvetica">

            <TD ALIGN = LEFT>
                <B>Employee: </B><% = rsResults("FirstName") %> 
                            <% = rsResults("LastName") %>
            </TD>

<%
            ' create the SQL string
            strSQL = "SELECT Name FROM Company WHERE CompanyID = "
                    & Request("CompanyID")

            ' execute the SQL command
            Set rsResults = dbChapter29.Execute(strSQL)
%>
            <TD ALIGN = CENTER>
                <B>Client: </B> <% = rsResults("Name") %>
            </TD>

            <TD ALIGN = RIGHT>
<%              strDate = DateAdd("w", -WeekDay(Now), Now)
                strWeekEnding = Left(strDate, InStr(strDate, " "))
%>
                <B>Week Ending: </B><% = strWeekEnding %>
            </TD>

            </FONT>
        </TR>

    </TABLE>
    </P>

    <P>
    <TABLE ALIGN = CENTER WIDTH = 90% CELLPADDING=10 CELLSPACING=2>
        <TR BGCOLOR="#000000">
            <TH>
                <FONT SIZE = "4" FACE = "Trebuchet MS, Verdana, Arial,
                Helvetica" COLOR="#FFFFFF">
                    Description
                </FONT>
            </TH>
            <TH>
                <FONT SIZE = "4" FACE = "Trebuchet MS, Verdana, Arial,
                Helvetica" COLOR="#FFFFFF">
                    Sun
                </FONT>
```

```
        </TH>
        <TH>
            <FONT SIZE = "4" FACE = "Trebuchet MS, Verdana, Arial,
            Helvetica" COLOR="#FFFFFF">
                Mon
            </FONT>
        </TH>
        <TH>
            <FONT SIZE = "4" FACE = "Trebuchet MS, Verdana, Arial,
            Helvetica" COLOR="#FFFFFF">
                Tue
            </FONT>
        </TH>
        <TH>
            <FONT SIZE = "4" FACE = "Trebuchet MS, Verdana, Arial,
            Helvetica" COLOR="#FFFFFF">
                Wed
            </FONT>
        </TH>
        <TH>
            <FONT SIZE = "4" FACE = "Trebuchet MS, Verdana, Arial,
            Helvetica" COLOR="#FFFFFF">
                Thu
            </FONT>
        </TH>
        <TH>
            <FONT SIZE = "4" FACE = "Trebuchet MS, Verdana, Arial,
            Helvetica" COLOR="#FFFFFF">
                Fri
            </FONT>
        </TH>
        <TH>
            <FONT SIZE = "4" FACE = "Trebuchet MS, Verdana, Arial,
            Helvetica" COLOR="#FFFFFF">
                Sat
            </FONT>
        </TH>
    </TR>
<%  For x = 1 To nRecords %>
    <TR>
        <TD ALIGN = CENTER BGCOLOR="#FFFFB3">
            <FONT SIZE = "3" FACE = "Trebuchet MS, Verdana, Arial,
            Helvetica" COLOR = "#000000">
<%
            strTarget = "Description" & x
            Response.Write(Request(strTarget))
%>
            </FONT>
        </TD>

        <TD ALIGN = CENTER BGCOLOR="#FFFFB3">
            <FONT SIZE = "3" FACE = "Trebuchet MS, Verdana, Arial,
            Helvetica" COLOR = "#000000">
<%
            strTarget = "Sun" & x
            Response.Write(Request(strTarget))
%>
```

29

CREATING A
SECURE
APPLICATION

continues

Listing 29.2. continued

```
        </TD>

        <TD ALIGN = CENTER BGCOLOR="#FFFFB3">
            <FONT SIZE = "3" FACE = "Trebuchet MS, Verdana, Arial,
            Helvetica" COLOR = "#000000">
<%

            strTarget = "Mon" & x
            Response.Write(Request(strTarget))
%>
        </TD>

        <TD ALIGN = CENTER BGCOLOR="#FFFFB3">
            <FONT SIZE = "3" FACE = "Trebuchet MS, Verdana, Arial,
            Helvetica" COLOR = "#000000">
<%

            strTarget = "Tue" & x
            Response.Write(Request(strTarget))
%>
        </TD>

        <TD ALIGN = CENTER BGCOLOR="#FFFFB3">
            <FONT SIZE = "3" FACE = "Trebuchet MS, Verdana, Arial,
            Helvetica" COLOR = "#000000">
<%

            strTarget = "Wed" & x
            Response.Write(Request(strTarget))
%>
        </TD>

        <TD ALIGN = CENTER BGCOLOR="#FFFFB3">
            <FONT SIZE = "3" FACE = "Trebuchet MS, Verdana, Arial,
            Helvetica" COLOR = "#000000">
<%

            strTarget = "Thu" & x
            Response.Write(Request(strTarget))
%>
        </TD>

        <TD ALIGN = CENTER BGCOLOR="#FFFFB3">
            <FONT SIZE = "3" FACE = "Trebuchet MS, Verdana, Arial,
            Helvetica" COLOR = "#000000">
<%

            strTarget = "Fri" & x
            Response.Write(Request(strTarget))
%>
        </TD>

        <TD ALIGN = CENTER BGCOLOR="#FFFFB3">
            <FONT SIZE = "3" FACE = "Trebuchet MS, Verdana, Arial,
            Helvetica" COLOR = "#000000">
<%

            strTarget = "Sat" & x
            Response.Write(Request(strTarget))
%>
        </TD>
    </TR>
<%      Next %>
```

```
        </TABLE>
        </P>

        </CENTER>

        <HR>

        <FONT SIZE="4" FACE="Trebuchet MS, Verdana, Arial, Helvetica">
            <B>Number of records added: </B> <% = nRecords %>
        </font>

<%
    ' close the connection
    dbChapter29.Close
%>

</BODY>
</HTML>
```

Listing 29.3. The HTML code produced by the code in Listing 29.2 for the Employee Time Card Verification page.

```
<HTML>
<HEAD>
<META NAME="GENERATOR" Content="Microsoft Visual InterDev 1.0">
<META HTTP-EQUIV="Content-Type" content="text/html; charset=iso-8859-1">
<TITLE>Employee Time Card Verification Page</TITLE>
</HEAD>
<BODY>

<BODY BACKGROUND="images/Backgrnd.gif" BGCOLOR="#FFFFFF" LEFTMARGIN="10"
TOPMARGIN = "10">

    <FONT SIZE="5" FACE="Trebuchet MS, Verdana, Arial, Helvetica">
        <B>
            Employee Time Card Verification.
        </B>
    </FONT>

    <HR>


    <CENTER>

    <P>
    <TABLE ALIGN = CENTER WIDTH = 90%>
        <TR>

            <FONT SIZE = "4" FACE="Trebuchet MS, Verdana, Arial, Helvetica">

            <TD ALIGN = LEFT>
                <B>Employee: </B>Michael Marsh
            </TD>


            <TD ALIGN = CENTER>
                <B>Client: </B> Armadillo Zoo
```

continues

29

CREATING A
SECURE
APPLICATION

Listing 29.3. continued

```
              </TD>

          <TD ALIGN = RIGHT>

              <B>Week Ending: </B>3/22/97
          </TD>

          </FONT>
      </TR>

  </TABLE>
  </P>

  <P>
  <TABLE ALIGN = CENTER WIDTH = 90% CELLPADDING=10 CELLSPACING=2>
      <TR BGCOLOR="#000000">
          <TH>
              <FONT SIZE = "4" FACE = "Trebuchet MS, Verdana, Arial,
              Helvetica" COLOR="#FFFFFF">
                  Description
              </FONT>
          </TH>
          <TH>
              <FONT SIZE = "4" FACE = "Trebuchet MS, Verdana, Arial,'
              Helvetica" COLOR="#FFFFFF">
                  Sun
              </FONT>
          </TH>
          <TH>
              <FONT SIZE = "4" FACE = "Trebuchet MS, Verdana, Arial,
              Helvetica" COLOR="#FFFFFF">
                  Mon
              </FONT>
          </TH>
          <TH>
              <FONT SIZE = "4" FACE = "Trebuchet MS, Verdana, Arial,
              Helvetica" COLOR="#FFFFFF">
                  Tue
              </FONT>
          </TH>
          <TH>
              <FONT SIZE = "4" FACE = "Trebuchet MS, Verdana, Arial,
              Helvetica" COLOR="#FFFFFF">
                  Wed
              </FONT>
          </TH>
          <TH>
              <FONT SIZE = "4" FACE = "Trebuchet MS, Verdana, Arial,
              Helvetica" COLOR="#FFFFFF">
                  Thu
              </FONT>
          </TH>
          <TH>
              <FONT SIZE = "4" FACE = "Trebuchet MS, Verdana, Arial,
              Helvetica" COLOR="#FFFFFF">
                  Fri
              </FONT>
```

```
            </TH>
            <TH>
                <FONT SIZE = "4" FACE = "Trebuchet MS, Verdana, Arial,
                Helvetica"COLOR="#FFFFFF">
                    Sat
                </FONT>
            </TH>
    </TR>

    <TR>
        <TD ALIGN = CENTER BGCOLOR="#FFFFB3">
            <FONT SIZE = "3" FACE = "Trebuchet MS, Verdana, Arial,
            Helvetica" COLOR = "#000000">
                Program maintenance
            </FONT>
        </TD>

        <TD ALIGN = CENTER BGCOLOR="#FFFFB3">
            <FONT SIZE = "3" FACE = "Trebuchet MS, Verdana, Arial,
            Helvetica" COLOR = "#000000">
                0
        </TD>

        <TD ALIGN = CENTER BGCOLOR="#FFFFB3">
            <FONT SIZE = "3" FACE = "Trebuchet MS, Verdana, Arial,
            Helvetica" COLOR = "#000000">
                4
        </TD>

        <TD ALIGN = CENTER BGCOLOR="#FFFFB3">
            <FONT SIZE = "3" FACE = "Trebuchet MS, Verdana, Arial,
            Helvetica" COLOR = "#000000">
                0
        </TD>

        <TD ALIGN = CENTER BGCOLOR="#FFFFB3">
            <FONT SIZE = "3" FACE = "Trebuchet MS, Verdana, Arial,
            Helvetica" COLOR = "#000000">
                4
        </TD>

        <TD ALIGN = CENTER BGCOLOR="#FFFFB3">
            <FONT SIZE = "3" FACE = "Trebuchet MS, Verdana, Arial,
            Helvetica" COLOR = "#000000">
                0
        </TD>

        <TD ALIGN = CENTER BGCOLOR="#FFFFB3">
            <FONT SIZE = "3" FACE = "Trebuchet MS, Verdana, Arial,
            Helvetica" COLOR = "#000000">
                4
        </TD>

        <TD ALIGN = CENTER BGCOLOR="#FFFFB3">
            <FONT SIZE = "3" FACE = "Trebuchet MS, Verdana, Arial,
            Helvetica" COLOR = "#000000">
                0
        </TD>
```

29

CREATING A SECURE APPLICATION

continues

Listing 29.3. continued

```
            </TR>


        </TABLE>
        </P>

        </CENTER>

        <HR>

        <FONT SIZE="4" FACE="Trebuchet MS, Verdana, Arial, Helvetica">
            <B>Number of records added: </B> 1
        </FONT>

    </BODY>
    </HTML>
```

FIGURE 29.13.

The Employee Time Card Verification page displayed from the code in Listing 29.3.

The Database Connection

The Electronic Time Card application uses a file DSN to communicate with the Access database. Figure 29.14 shows the ODBC applet displaying this DSN, called TimeCard.

Listing 29.4 shows the GLOBAL.ASA that was modified by Visual InterDev when the CEO added the data connection.

FIGURE 29.14.

The ODBC Control Panel applet displaying the database's file DSN.

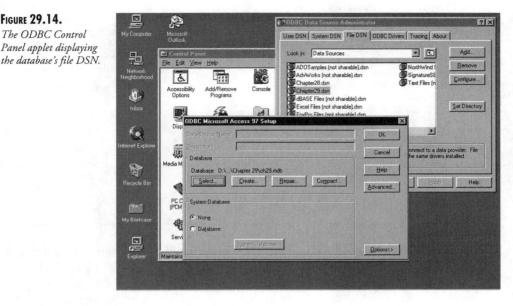

Listing 29.4. GLOBAL.ASA for the Electronic Time Card application.

```
<SCRIPT LANGUAGE="VBScript" RUNAT="Server">

'Session_OnStart       Runs the first time a user runs any page in your application
'Session_OnEnd         Runs when a user's session times out or quits your application
'Application_OnStart   Runs once when the first page of your application
'                      is run for the first time by any user
'Application_OnEnd     Runs once when the web server shuts down

</SCRIPT>

<SCRIPT LANGUAGE=VBScript RUNAT=Server>

Sub Session_OnStart

'==Visual InterDev Generated - DataConnection startspan==

    '--Project Data Connection
    Session("Chapter29_ConnectionString") = "DBQ=D:\WORK\Books\Visual
    InterDev Unleashed\Chapter 29\ch29.mdb;
    DefaultDir=D:\WORK\Books\Visual InterDev Unleashed\Chapter 29;
    Driver={Microsoft Access Driver (*.mdb)};DriverId=25;
    FIL=MS Access;ImplicitCommitSync=Yes;MaxBufferSize=512;
    MaxScanRows=8;PageTimeout=5;SafeTransactions=0;Threads=3;
    UID=admin;UserCommitSync=Yes;"

    Session("Chapter29_ConnectionTimeout") = 15
    Session("Chapter29_CommandTimeout") = 30
    Session("Chapter29_RuntimeUserName") = "admin"
    Session("Chapter29_RuntimePassword") = ""
```

continues

29

CREATING A
SECURE
APPLICATION

Listing 29.4. continued

```
'==Visual InterDev Generated - DataConnection endspan==

    ' Session wide variables to keep track of the user
    Session("UserName") = ""
    Session("UserGreetingName") = ""
    Session("UserID") = -1
    Session("Admin") = False

    ' Prevent a jump into the site w/o logging in
    if UserName = "" then
        Response.Redirect("MainFrame.asp")
    end if

End Sub

</SCRIPT>
```

Often it is much easier to hand code certain pieces of a Visual InterDev app, particularly if the wizards provided just don't create the things that you need. This was the case for the CEO in several places in the application. He needed to be able to access the database without having the luxury of a wizard to write the code for him. Listing 29.5 shows an example of how he accomplishes database access by hand.

> **TIP**
>
> Notice that in Listing 29.5, all of the script code happens before the <HTML> tag. This is so that the redirection to the appropriate pages will work. Remember that you can redirect only before you've written anything to the header of the page.

Listing 29.5. An example of accessing the database by hand coding: the LOGINVERIFICATION.ASP file.

```
<%@ LANGUAGE="VBSCRIPT" %>

<SCRIPT RUNAT=Server LANGUAGE="VBScript">

' this function cleans up spaces and NULLs in a string
Function ConvertNull(varTemp)
    If IsNull(varTemp) Then
        ConvertNull = ""
    Else
        ConvertNull = Trim(varTemp)
    End If
End Function

</SCRIPT>

<%
' open database connection
Set dbChapter29 = Server.CreateObject("ADODB.Connection")
dbChapter29.Open Session("Chapter29_ConnectionString")
```

```
' create the SQL string
strSQL = "SELECT UserID, UserName, GreetingName FROM User "
strSQL = strSQL & "WHERE UserName = '" &
                   ConvertNull(Request.Form("UserName"))
strSQL = strSQL & "' AND Password = '" &
                   ConvertNull(Request.Form("Password")) & "'"

' execute the SQL command
Set rsResults = dbChapter29.Execute(strSQL)

' see if there are any records returned
nCount = 0
While rsResults.EOF = False
    nCount = nCount + 1
    rsResults.MoveNext
Wend

If nCount = 0 Then
    Response.Redirect("Login.asp?Result=Failed")
Else
    rsResults.MoveFirst
    Session("UserName") = Request.Form("UserName")
    Session("UserGreetingName") = rsResults("GreetingName")
    Session("UserID") = rsResults("UserID")
    Response.Redirect("TimeCard.asp")
End If

dbChapter29.Close
%>

<HTML>
<HEAD>
<META NAME="GENERATOR" Content="Microsoft Visual InterDev 1.0">
<META HTTP-EQUIV="Content-Type" content="text/html; charset=iso-8859-1">
<TITLE>Login Verification Page</TITLE>
</HEAD>
<BODY>

</BODY>
</HTML>
```

Preventing Jumps Around the Login Page

A closer look at Listing 29.4, the GLOBAL.ASA file, shows that the CEO used a technique outlined in an earlier chapter to prevent a user from jumping past the Login page. The little bit of code toward the end of the file checks to see whether the user has logged on, and if not, redirects the user to the Login page. Again, this works because all the pages in this site are .ASP, with the exception of the do-nothing DEFAULT.HTM page.

Keeping Track of the User

The GLOBAL.ASA file also declares Session variables to keep track of the user. In the file LOGINVERIFICATION.ASP (refer to Listing 29.5), the user information Session variables are set upon successful login. The variables are used in other places as well, for example, to greet the user with a friendly name in the Time Card Input page.

Applying Security

Much of the application's security is handled within the application itself. The application prevents a user from accessing the system without logging in, and once logged in, prevents that user from accessing anything other than what membership in the user's group allows. This, coupled with the physical setup of the system, as described previously, gave the CEO a sufficient comfort level with security while providing the necessary ease of access for the system's users.

> **CAUTION**
>
> The CEO's comfort level with this security may have had more to do with the fact that Accounting had been pressuring him for a solution, rather than his thinking through the security implications. Though it is convenient to think that your application is limiting access to sensitive data, the fact is that you are distributing the code for your client on the Internet. It can be intercepted and used by an attacker to gain access. But as we'll see later on, there is an even more serious breach of security with this system.

Logging In

When users first enter the system, they are presented with the Login page (refer to Figure 29.2.) Users type in their username and password and then click the Submit button. The code, shown in Listing 29.6, uses the `<FORM>` tag to transfer control to the Login Verification page (Listing 29.5). The Login Verification page code uses the `Request` object to retrieve the values from the `UserName` and `Password` variables, and then uses these to query the database for a valid user.

Listing 29.6. The LOGIN.ASP file.

```
<%@ LANGUAGE="VBSCRIPT" %>

<HTML>
<HEAD>
<META NAME="GENERATOR" Content="Microsoft Visual InterDev 1.0">
<META HTTP-EQUIV="Content-Type" content="text/html; charset=iso-8859-1">
<TITLE>Login Page</TITLE>
</HEAD>
<BODY>

<BODY background="images/backgrnd.gif" bgcolor="#FFFFFF">

<% If Request.QueryString("Result") = "Failed" then %>
    <FONT SIZE="4" FACE="Trebuchet MS, Verdana, Arial,
                        Helvetica" color="#FF0000">
        <BR> 
        <B>Incorrect user name or password.  Please try again.</B>
    </FONT>
<% End If %>
```

```
<FORM ACTION="LoginVerification.asp" METHOD=POST>

<TABLE BORDER=0 CELLPADDING=5 CELLSPACING=0 WIDTH=500>

    <TR WIDTH = 500>

        <TD>
            <P ALIGN="LEFT">
                <FONT SIZE="5" FACE="Trebuchet MS, Verdana, Arial,
                                      Helvetica">
                    <B>Please Log In</B>
                </FONT>
            </P>
        </TD>

    </TR>

    <TR>
        <FONT SIZE = "4" FACE="Trebuchet MS, Verdana, Arial, Helvetica">
            <TD ALIGN = RIGHT>
                <B> User Name: </B>
            </TD>
            <TD ALIGN = LEFT>
                <INPUT NAME="UserName" SIZE=20>
            </TD>
        </FONT>
    </TR>

    <TR>
        <FONT SIZE = "4" FACE="Trebuchet MS, Verdana, Arial, Helvetica">
            <TD ALIGN = "RIGHT">
                <B> Password: </B>
            </TD>
            <TD ALIGN = "LEFT">
                <INPUT NAME="Password" SIZE="20" TYPE="PASSWORD">
            </TD>
        </FONT>
    </TR>

    <TR>
        <FONT SIZE = "4" FACE="Trebuchet MS, Verdana, Arial, Helvetica">
            <TD ALIGN = "RIGHT">
            </TD>
            <TD ALIGN = "LEFT">
                <INPUT NAME="Submit" TYPE="SUBMIT">
                <INPUT NAME="Reset" TYPE="RESET">
            </TD>
        </FONT>
    </TR>

</TABLE>

</FORM>

</BODY>
</HTML>
```

29

CREATING A
SECURE
APPLICATION

If the login data is not in the database, the login is invalid, and the user is redirected back to the Login page with the QueryString variable set to "Result=Failed". The Login page is redisplayed, this time with a message in red indicating that the login failed.

If the login data does exist in the database, the login is valid, and the user information Session variables are updated and the user is redirected to the TIMECARD.ASP page.

Listing 29.7 is a part of TIMECARD.ASP that shows how the CEO redirects a user to a page based on the user's group membership.

Listing 29.7. Portions of the TIMECARD.ASP file.

```
<%
    ' open database connection
    Set dbChapter29 = Server.CreateObject("ADODB.Connection")
    dbChapter29.Open Session("Chapter29_ConnectionString")

    ' create the SQL string
    strSQL = "SELECT `Group`.Name FROM UserGroupList, `User`, `Group` "
    strSQL = strSQL & "WHERE UserGroupList.UserID = `User`.UserID "
    strSQL = strSQL & "AND UserGroupList.GroupID = `Group`.GroupID AND "
    strSQL = strSQL & "`User`.UserID = " & Session("UserID")

    ' execute the SQL command
    Set rsResults = dbChapter29.Execute(strSQL)

    ' store the result
    strUserType = rsResults("Name")

    ' close the connection
    dbChapter29.Close

    ' set up the rest of the page depending on group membership
    Select Case strUserType
        Case "Administrator"
            Session("Admin") = True
%>
<!-- #INCLUDE FILE="EmployeeTimeCard.asp" -->
<%      Case "Client"
            Session("Admin") = False
%>
<!-- #INCLUDE FILE="ClientTimeCard.asp" -->
<%      Case "Employee"
            Session("Admin") = False
%>
<!-- #INCLUDE FILE="EmployeeTimeCard.asp" -->
<%      Case Else
            Session("Admin") = False
%>
            Error<BR>
<% End Select %>

<HR>

<%    if Session("Admin") = True Then %>
    <!-- #INCLUDE FILE="AdminNavigation.asp" -->
<%    End If %>
```

Why Not Let NT Do It?

The CEO initially toyed with the idea to use NT Challenge/Response in addition to the application-level users and groups. The idea was to match the application users and groups with identical ones added using the User Manager for Domains program. That way he could let NT itself handle the login chores, and he would simply query the system for the user information needed for his database queries. Because NT Challenge/Response uses a token to communicate with the client, the username and password never go out on the Net. This would provide very good security indeed. The trouble was that only one of his three customers had browsers that would work with NT Challenge/Response, so he scrapped the idea.

This circumstance is unhappy, because the CEO knows that user login information, including passwords, are going out unencrypted over the Net. He is concerned about this, but not overly so, because his system is small and nobody would be that interested in his data. Still, the CEO plans to obtain a Digital Server Certificate and implement SSL for his site. This would solve the encryption problem, but would entail a rewrite of some of the code. He would need to check if the SSL handshake failed, and in that case revert to the old system, so as not to lock any users out. He could easily parse the client certificate for the user information needed to verify the login. This is the next feature that the CEO is going to implement.

> ### CAUTION
>
> This is the most serious breach of security with this system. The fact that user information, including passwords, is going out on the Net is an invitation to a site hack. The CEO recognizes this, but for expediency, ignores the issue for now. SSL will solve the CEO's major security problem, but his thinking about reverting to the 'old system' is flawed: At a minimum, he should use some sort of encryption on the password. One solution would be to use the CryptoAPI for encryption algorithms. Alternatively, he could insist that any client trying to access his system must indeed use SSL. Most modern clients can do this, so it would not be a great burden on his users.
>
> Thinking that his site is small and unadvertised, and therefore uninteresting, is a curious Net fallacy. While it could be true (but not necessarily!) that professional spies and criminal hackers might bypass his site for something more interesting, it is certainly not true that his site might not be attractive to vandals. If it is easy to hack, they will hack it! There is no anonymity for sites on the Web: Remember, it is a public network!

Database Security

Access 97 implements users and groups, but the CEO thought this might be overkill for his first implementation. He could also have changed the `RuntimeUserName` in `GLOBAL.ASA` with an Access user having the appropriate restrictions, but he then decided that this would complicate the code in the case of the Administrator. He decided to let all users have Admin rights to the database and to protect his data within his application instead.

CAUTION

Again, in the name of expediency, the CEO has exposed himself to some risk. Access 97's users and groups are indeed as powerful as he surmised. There would have been no complication in the code had he added users and groups to his database that matched those in his application. At a minimum, he should have used a different `RuntimeUserName`. Giving everyone Admin access to the database gives everyone the power to do anything to the data. If an attacker gains access to his system, his data is left extremely vulnerable.

Summary

The Electronic Time Card application demonstrates some of the security features and techniques available using Visual InterDev. In particular, the system makes heavy use of application-level users and groups to control access to data. The physical setup of this site shows how a small to medium Web might be configured using Microsoft Proxy Server, or a similar product.

This sample application and accompanying scenario also points out some common mistakes made when installing a site on the (very public) Internet. I presented some solutions to these mistakes, such as using SSL when sending sensitive data across the Net, and using the built-in security provided by the database engine.

Finally, this chapter presented some of the realities of securing a site while still allowing access to your targeted group of users. Other pressures come to bear when making design decisions about security.

VII
PART

Complementary Tools for Visual InterDev

Graphics with Microsoft Image Composer and GIF Animator

by Michael Morrison

IN THIS CHAPTER

Although the technical underpinnings of a Web site are ultimately what give it power, graphical flair is often what gives it the polish necessary to wow users. This chapter takes a look at a couple of graphics tools that can be used to add significant punch to the appearance of a Web site. These tools are Microsoft Image Composer and GIF Animator, both of which are shipped standard with Visual InterDev. Image Composer is an image editing tool that is geared toward creating graphics for the Web. GIF Animator, on the other hand, is an animation tool centered around the creation of animations for the Web. Image Composer and GIF Animator are individual tools, but they can easily be used together, as you learn toward the end of this chapter.

This chapter begins with an introduction to both graphics tools, explaining the purpose of each tool and the types of scenarios where they can be used. The chapter then shifts into a tutorial style where each tool is put through its paces to create some interesting graphics for the Web. To be honest, one chapter can hardly do these tools justice, but you will learn enough in this chapter to hit the ground running with your own Web graphics. I strongly encourage you to spend some time with both of these tools after reading the chapter, because they are best learned through experimentation.

Image Composer Basics

No one can argue the fact that the Web has changed the face of computing forever. As a result, few people in the software development or publishing communities can fully predict what their role will be as the Web continues to mature. There was a time when technical people familiar with the inner workings of the Web were the ones building Web sites. However, the insurgence of graphic artists into the Web development arena has changed things significantly. Technical folks like myself are quickly learning that we can't single-handedly build compelling Web sites without the assistance of professional graphics of some sort. Those of us fortunate enough to work with graphic artists on a regular basis can relax to some degree, but the rest of us have to contend with the frustrations of trying to create professional-quality graphics with no training and few affordable graphics tools.

Microsoft, being a company largely comprised of technical people, saw a need for a graphics tool that could be used by the non-professional graphic artist to create Web graphics. Microsoft's answer to this need is Image Composer, which is an easy-to-use, Web-oriented graphics tool. Unlike the vast majority of graphics tools, Image Composer is geared toward creating graphics *compositions*, which are groups of images arranged and overlaid together. Image Composer is unique in this regard because most graphics tools focus on the editing and manipulation of a single image. With Image Composer, you can combine multiple images in many different ways to achieve a desired result. Additionally, you can manipulate images on an individual basis within a composition. Not surprisingly, the composition approach taken by Image Composer is particularly well suited for Web graphics, where text is often overlaid on an image or group of images for visual appeal.

Although the function of Image Composer ultimately boils down to image manipulation, Image Composer doesn't directly operate on images in a traditional sense. Instead, Image Composer uses *sprites*, which are images capable of having an irregular shape. The irregular shape of a sprite results from transparent areas in the sprite image. Sprites are still rectangular in area, as are all images, but their shape doesn't have to be. The concept of an image with irregular shape might seem a little strange at first, but when you think about it, many images fall under this description. For example, any image consisting solely of text has an irregular shape (transparent areas); the areas surrounding the text are transparent. In reality, most images except those that are scanned from photographs have transparency. And even some scanned images are more useful with transparency. Figure 30.1 illustrates how an image containing text has transparent areas surrounding the text, which results in an irregular shape.

FIGURE 30.1.

An irregularly shaped image containing text.

Opaque Area

Transparent Areas

The idea behind Image Composer using sprites is that images on the Web are often created as a combination of a variety of different images, along with text of some sort. Combining multiple images with text can sometimes be a difficult task in all but the most advanced graphics tools. The main problem with lower end tools is that few of them enable you to interact with multiple images independently. The advanced tools that do support combining multiple images are expensive and relatively complicated to learn and use. Graphic artists skilled with these higher end graphics tools can work with multiple overlaid images with relative ease, but not all of us have the benefit of years of schooling and practice in graphic arts. So, where does that leave us? Well, prior to Image Composer we had to tough it out with tools that weren't particularly suited to creating Web graphics. Image Composer enters the picture as a tool for the rest of us that can be used to create a wide range of Web graphics, complete with a bunch of interesting filters and image manipulation tools.

The Beauty of Sprites

The fundamental unit of interest in Image Composer is the sprite, which is an image with transparent areas that give it an irregular shape. Before you start thinking that a sprite is some type of mysterious object, understand that a sprite is nothing more than an image, with transparent areas, that can be arranged with other sprites. Sprites appear in Image Composer just as images appear in other graphics tools, with the exception that the transparent areas in a sprite are shown as transparent in Image Composer. Because of their transparent areas, sprites can be overlaid and visibly seen through the transparent parts of each other. Figure 30.2 shows a group of overlaid sprites.

FIGURE 30.2.
Overlaid fruit sprites.

Notice in the figure how the sprites are overlaid; you can see that parts of the sprites are visible through the transparent parts of other sprites above them. This figure illustrates a very important point about sprites: Each sprite in an Image Composer composition has a depth, or position, associated with it, which determines where it is positioned in relation to other sprites. In other words, the depth of a sprite impacts whether it lies above or below other sprites. You can visualize sprite depth by thinking of sprites as being stacked on top of each other on the screen. Sprites with a lower depth are displayed behind sprites with a higher depth, and therefore are lower in the "stack" of sprites.

Image Composer enables you to manipulate sprites individually or in conjunction with other sprites, depending on the operation. For example, you can rotate a sprite or alter its colors without impacting any other sprites. On the other hand, you can alter the transparency of a sprite, which indirectly impacts sprites behind the sprite because they appear through transparent portions of it. As you may be thinking, this ability to openly manipulate sprites provides a great deal of freedom in creating interesting graphics compositions.

There are two different ways to group sprites in Image Composer: through selection sets or permanent groups. A *selection set* is a temporary collection of selected sprites, to which graphical effects can be applied. A selection set goes away as soon as you click an individual sprite. A *group*, on the other hand, is a collection of sprites grouped together that is interacted with as a single entity until the sprites are explicitly ungrouped. You work with a group just as if it was an individual sprite.

Sprites can also be *flattened*, which means that they are permanently merged together into a single sprite. Unlike groups, flattened sprites are permanently merged together and cannot be ungrouped. In other words, flattened sprites permanently lose their individuality and depth, and are considered a single sprite.

Compositions

In Image Composer, a composition consists of all the sprites you are working on at any given time. Similar to a musical composition, an Image composer composition consists of a group of sprites acting in concert with one another to create a visual result greater than the sprites by themselves. The most powerful aspect of compositions is how they enable you to work with sprites on an individual basis; you can drag sprites around freely with the mouse and change their depth with ease. You can also apply filters and special effects to individual sprites, to a selection of sprites, or to an entire composition.

Although compositions are useful during the development phase of a Web graphics project, they aren't very practical when it comes to delivering graphics in final form. In other words, you wouldn't want to deliver Web graphics in composition form because you don't really care about sprites when it comes to displaying a final image. For this reason, compositions are always converted to normal images when it comes time to use them in actual Web sites. Image Composer supports a wide range of image formats including GIF 89A, TIF, and Windows BMP to name a few.

Even though compositions are converted to normal images for use in a Web site, you will still typically keep them around in composition form in case you need to make changes at a later date. It is important to keep a copy of your original compositions because a composition loses all sprite information when it is converted to a normal image. A good approach to keeping things straight is to think of a composition as being your working source information, and the resulting images as being the output of Image Composer in final form. This is analogous to source code files and executables in software development; source code is used to create final executables, and even though executables are what you distribute, you always keep source code because it represents the source you work from. Besides, you can always rebuild executables from source code. The same thing goes for Image Composer compositions; you can always convert them to normal images with little effort.

Because Web graphics are often stored in graphics formats with a limited set of colors, it is important to be able to see how a composition will look in the target format. Rather than requiring you to convert a composition to an image of a given type, Image Composer enables you to adjust the view of a composition to a particular color model. For example, for image manipulation purposes it is smarter to work with images in a high-resolution color model, such as TrueColor (24-bit). However, using 24-bit images in a Web site would be disastrous in most cases because of the enormous transfer times their large sizes would incur. The solution is to work with high-quality images in Image Composer, and then view them in 256 colors before converting them to a final image form. You can also view images with respect to a specific color palette. For instance, Image Composer ships standard with color palettes for both Internet Explorer and Netscape Navigator, which are very useful in assessing how graphics will look in a Web environment.

> **NOTE**
>
> Image Composer supports Adobe Photoshop–compatible plug-in filters, which provides you with lots of options in terms of using third-party image-enhancement tools.

The Image Composer Interface

The Image Composer interface is designed to make creating compositions as easy and intuitive as possible. Although it looks fairly complex at first, you'll find the interface easy to learn as you spend time working in Image Composer. Figure 30.3 shows Image Composer with an empty composition.

FIGURE 30.3.

Image Composer with an empty composition.

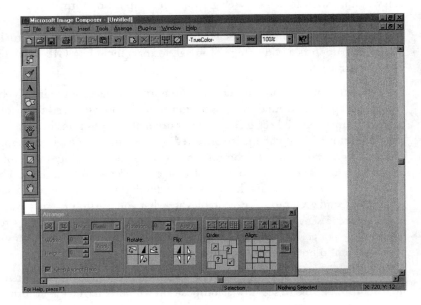

The Image Composer interface includes the following components:

- A toolbox
- A design space
- A composition guide
- A toolbar
- Menus
- A tool palette
- A status bar

The toolbox, which is located along the left side of the application window, is the heart of the Image Composer interface because it provides quick access to tools such as filtering and special effects. The toolbox also includes the Color Picker, which displays and enables you to select the current color. The current color is used in many different graphics functions throughout Image Composer. There are 10 different types of tools listed in the toolbox, some of which contain lots of individual features and options. The 10 tools are Arrange, Paint, Text, Shapes,

Patterns and Fills, Warps and Filters, Art Effects, Color Tuning, Zoom, and Pan. You learn how to use some of these tools a little later in this chapter when you create a composition.

The bulk of Image Composer's application window consists of the workspace, which is where you actually create and modify compositions. It's important to note that the workspace itself extends far beyond the window where it is displayed; you can scroll around to see all of the workspace using the scrollbars. Within the workspace is the composition guide, which is a white rectangular region that determines which part of a composition will be included in an image when the composition is flattened. The composition guide acts somewhat like a snapshot of the final image you are creating. The default color of the composition guide is white, but it can be set to any color. The point of having a workspace and a composition guide is to give you plenty of room to work with sprites, independent of the area in which the final composition is being assembled.

The toolbar in Image Composer appears just below the menus, which are a standard part of all Windows 95 applications. The toolbar provides quick access to commonly used menu commands such as commands for opening files, saving files, and so on. The toolbar also includes drop-down lists containing the color model under which the composition is displayed, as well as the zoom level at which it is being viewed.

Depending on which tool is currently selected, Image Composer displays a tool palette near the bottom of the screen. There are eight different tool palettes, each of which contains specific information regarding a particular tool. Tool palettes are responsible for the details surrounding how a tool operates. The tool palette visible in Figure 30.3 belongs to the Arrange tool.

The last element of the Image Composer interface is the status bar, which appears at the bottom of the application window. The status bar displays information regarding the composition as you work with it. For example, while resizing a sprite, the status bar displays the width and height of the sprite.

Composing Images with Image Composer

Image Composer is the type of tool that is best learned through experience. For this reason, I want to shift gears and show you how to use Image Composer to create some real Web graphics. It would be impossible to touch on every feature of Image Composer in this section, but I do want to show you some of the more important features and how they can be used through a practical example. After working through this example, you'll have the basic skills necessary to start creating and experimenting with your own compositions in Image Composer. If you choose not to work through this example in Image Composer as you read along, you can still follow the figures to see how the composition evolves.

In this example, you create title Web graphics for a hypothetical Web site called Vernie's Fruit Stand. The Web site belongs to an old friend named Vernie who is starting a high-tech fruit stand. Vernie plans to sell all kinds of fruit through the Web, and consequently needs a flashy title graphic for her Web site. Being such a devoted and talented friend, you've offered to create the title image using Image Composer.

The first step in creating any composition is to start with a clean workspace. Image Composer initially loads with a clean workspace. Alternatively, you can explicitly clear the workspace by selecting New from the File menu, which creates a new composition. There is also a toolbar button that yields the same effect. Throughout this example, you will encounter situations in which you can either select a menu item or click a toolbar button; it's entirely up to you how you prefer to work.

The composition you are creating consists of different fruit images arranged together. The CD-ROM accompanying the book includes the fruit sprites required for this example, which have been installed to your hard drive if you've installed the book's source code from the CD-ROM. If you haven't installed the source code yet, please do so now so that you can access the fruit sprites.

Inserting the Fruit Sprites

Sprites are added to Image Composer using the Insert menu, which has two pull-down menus, From File and From PhotoCD. You are interested in inserting Image Composer sprites, so select the From File command to insert the sprites. Image Composer presents you with a file selection dialog box where you choose the files you want to add to the composition. Notice that the dialog box supports the insertion of files of a variety of different types. All of the files you are inserting are Image Composer sprites, so make sure Microsoft Image Composer (`*.mic`) is selected as the file type.

You now need to locate the fruit sprites on your hard drive. Browse to the `Source\Chap30` directory beneath the directory where you installed the book's source code. You should see a list of fruit sprites in the dialog box. Select the following sprites to be inserted into the composition:

- `apple.mic`
- `banana.mic`
- `grapes.mic`
- `lime.mic`
- `orange.mic`
- `strawber.mic`

You select multiple files in the dialog box by holding down the Control key while clicking each file. After selecting the sprites, click the OK button to actually insert them into the composition. Figure 30.4 shows the workspace after inserting the sprites.

FIGURE 30.4.

The fruit sprites added to the Image Composer workspace.

Resizing the Fruit Sprites

As you can see, the sprites are all pretty large; they definitely need to be resized for use in the composition. Image Composer makes it very easy to resize sprites in a variety of different ways. Probably the most straightforward way to resize sprites is through a specific percentage, which yields very predictable results. You can also resize sprites by entering a width and/or height, depending on whether you want it to retain the same aspect ratio. Image Composer also enables you to interactively resize sprites by clicking and dragging one of the arrows at the corners of a sprite's bounding box.

> **NOTE**
>
> The aspect ratio of a sprite is the ratio between its width and height. For a sprite to have the same appearance when it is resized, the aspect ratio must remain constant. Otherwise, the sprite will appear wider or taller than the original, depending on the specifics of how it was resized.

Let's try resizing the currently selected sprite to a specific percentage. Select the Arrange tool from the toolbox, after which you see the Arrange tool palette near the bottom of the screen.

30

GRAPHICS WITH
IMAGE COMPOSER
AND GIF ANIMATOR

The Arrange tool palette contains a drop-down list called Units where you can specify how a sprite is to be resized. Select Percent in the Units drop-down to resize the sprite to a percentage. Then type 50 in the Width text box to indicate the new width is to be 50 percent of the original width. By default, the Keep Aspect Ratio checkbox is checked, meaning that the Height text box automatically changes to 50 after entering the width (as shown in Figure 30.5). Click the Apply button next to the Width and Height text boxes to resize the sprite.

FIGURE 30.5.

The Arrange tool palette set to resize the width and height of a sprite to 50 percent of its original values.

All of the fruit sprites need to be resized for this example. You might want to move the sprites around so you can select them more easily. To select a sprite, simply click anywhere on it. This is sometimes easier said than done, however, because the sprites in this example were automatically inserted on top of each other. In situations like this, it is easier to select sprites by cycling through the stack of sprites. You do this by pressing the Tab key. To move sprites around in the workspace, just click and drag them where you want them to go. Now move the fruit sprites so you can select them more easily.

Using the same approach of resizing to a percentage, resize all of the remaining sprites to 50 percent of their original size, except for the strawberry and banana. Then resize the banana to 75 percent, which makes it a little larger in proportion to the other sprites. Finally, try interactively resizing the strawberry sprite by clicking and dragging one of the arrows along the bounding box of the sprite. To keep the same aspect ratio, use one of the arrows at the corner of the bounding box and hold down the Shift key while dragging. This causes both the width and height to change in consistent amounts to keep a constant aspect ratio. Resize the strawberry sprite so that the width is 93 and the height is 110; you can check the width and height as you are resizing the sprite by looking at the right side of the status bar.

After resizing all the sprites, your composition should look similar to the one shown in Figure 30.6.

Notice how it was necessary to move some of the sprites so that they extend beyond the composition guide. This should serve as a little reminder that you can lay out and manipulate sprites anywhere within the Image Composer workspace.

FIGURE 30.6.

The composition with all the fruit sprites resized appropriately.

Flipping and Colorizing the Grapes Sprite

The next step in the example is to duplicate the grapes sprite. There are two ways to duplicate a sprite: Select the sprite and use the Duplicate command in the Edit menu, or hold down the Control key and move the sprite. Use one of these approaches and duplicate the grapes sprite. Move one of the grapes sprites to left side of the composition guide, and the other to the right side. You can align the sprites to each side of the guide by using the Align tool within the Arrange tool palette. The Align tool consists of a divided rectangle with different options for how a sprite is to be aligned. Use the Right Sides and Left Sides boxes to align the grapes sprites (as shown in Figure 30.7). After clicking one of the alignment boxes, a message box appears informing you that you must select the sprite with which you are aligning the grapes sprite. In this case, you are aligning the sprite with the composition guide, so click the OK button to exit the message box, and then click on the composition guide away from any sprites.

FIGURE 30.7.

The Left Sides and Right Sides boxes within the Align tool.

Left Sides 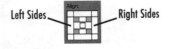 Right Sides

30

GRAPHICS WITH IMAGE COMPOSER AND GIF ANIMATOR

You now need to flip one of the grapes sprites to give the composition a little more balance. First select the grapes sprite you aligned with the left side of the composition guide, and then select the Arrange tool again. Toward the middle of the Arrange tool palette you'll see a rectangle used for flipping sprites. Within the Flip rectangle, the current position of the sprite is shown in gray, while the possible ways to flip the sprite are shown in white. To flip the sprite horizontally, click the white box located beside the gray box. Figure 30.8 shows what the grapes sprite looks like after being flipped horizontally.

NOTE

You can try the other boxes in the Flip rectangle to see how they affect the sprite. Keep in mind that you can always undo an operation in Image Composer by using the Undo command in the Edit menu.

FIGURE 30.8.

The grapes sprite after being flipped horizontally.

Although the composition looks nice and symmetrical with the grapes sprites arranged on each side, the sprites look too much alike. With Image Composer's Colorize tool, you can easily change one of the grapes sprites to look like green grapes instead of red grapes. The first step in doing this is selecting a bright green color using the Color Picker. To do this, click the Color Picker at the bottom of the toolbox and set the RGB values to 0, 255, 0, respectively. You can also drag the pointer around in the Color Picker window to arrive at a similar color if you want to take a more interactive approach. Figure 30.9 shows the Color Picker with a pure green color selected.

FIGURE 30.9.

The Color Picker with a pure green color selected.

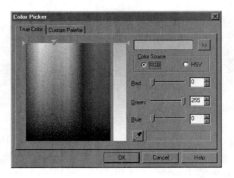

You now have the current color set to bright green, and you are ready to colorize one of the grapes sprites. Select the Warps and Filters tool on the toolbox and choose Color Enhancement from the drop-down list in the tool palette. Then select Colorize from the listbox, making sure that the color opacity is set to 50. Now select the left grapes sprite and click the Apply button in the tool palette to color the sprite green. Figure 30.10 shows the resulting sprite colored green by the Colorize tool.

FIGURE 30.10.
The left grapes sprite colored green with the Colorize tool.

Rotating the Strawberry Sprites

That finishes up the grapes sprites. The next step in creating this sample composition is to duplicate and rotate the strawberry sprite. Before duplicating the sprite, you can rotate it a little to make it look like it's lying down. Select the Arrange tool, set the Rotation text box to 30 degrees, and then click the Apply button. This rotates the sprite by 30 degrees in the clockwise direction (as shown in Figure 30.11). Optionally, you can click and drag the upper-right corner of the sprite to rotate it interactively.

FIGURE 30.11.
The strawberry sprite after being rotated by 30 degrees.

Now you're ready to create another strawberry sprite and give it a different rotation. Duplicate the sprite just as you duplicated the grapes sprite earlier, and then place it near the left side of the composition window. It's not important to align the strawberry sprites because you don't really want them along the edge of the composition window. After moving the duplicated sprite, try interactively rotating it so that it looks a little different than the first sprite.

Adjusting the Apple Sprite's Hue

Moving right along, the next step is to try the Color Tuning tool on the apple. You are going to adjust the hue of the apple so that is looks green instead of red. Select the Color Tuning tool from the toolbox and then choose Color Shifting in the tool palette. Enter 75 in the Hue textbox to set the hue, and then click the Apply button. Figure 30.12 shows what the Color Tuning tool palette looks like with these settings.

This effect transforms the red apple into a bright green Granny Smith apple. You probably didn't realize you could use Image Composer to make apples more sour! Figure 30.13 shows the apple after its hue is adjusted.

FIGURE 30.12.

The Color Tuning tool palette with the hue set to 75.

FIGURE 30.13.

The apple sprite after its hue is adjusted.

Artsy Fruit

That wraps up all the individual effects on the fruit sprites. Now it's time to apply an effect to all the sprites as a whole. At this stage of the example, the fruit sprites have a photographic look, which is fine for some situations. However, it would be neat for the title of the Web site to stand out with some artistic flair, so let's try using an art effect on the fruit. You first need to select all the sprites using the Select All command from the Edit menu. With all the sprites selected, you can apply an effect to them as a single unit. Select the Art Effects tool and choose Sketch from the dropdown list. Then select Rough Pastels from the listbox and click the Apply button to apply the effect to the sprites. Figure 30.14 shows what the composition looks like after applying the Rough Pastels effect.

FIGURE 30.14.

The fruit composition after applying the Rough Pastels art effect.

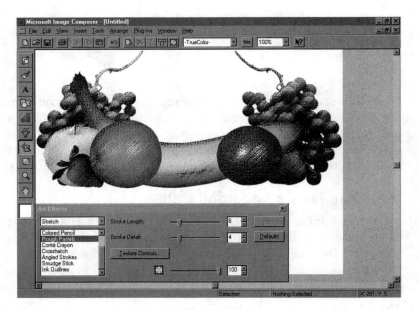

Adding Text

We're getting somewhere now! The last major step of this example is to add some text to re-flect the name of the Web site. To do this, select the Text tool and type `Vernie's` into the text-box in the tool palette. You need a larger font to really make an impression, so click the Set Font button to change the font. Set the font to bold, 48 point, Times New Roman and click the OK button. Before clicking the Apply button in the Text tool palette, make sure the cur-rent color is set to black (0, 0, 0). If it isn't, click the Color Picker and change the color. Then click the Apply button to add the text to the composition as a sprite.

You need to repeat this process two more times to add the words `Fruit` and `Stand` to the com-position. Figure 30.15 shows what the composition looks like with all the text sprites added and positioned.

FIGURE 30.15.

The fruit composition with newly added text sprites.

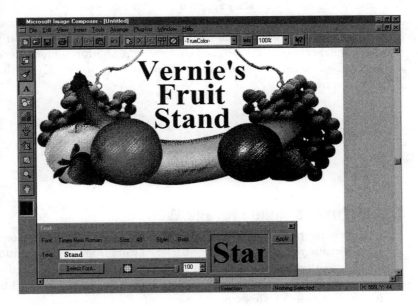

Jazzing Up the Text

Although the text is tolerable as is, it really would look a lot better if you could spice it up. Fortunately, Image Composer makes it easy to alter text in some really interesting ways. You're going to map the pixels of another sprite onto the text in the composition to make it blend better with the fruit. The sprite you're going to map pixels from is a silk tree sprite, which can be found along with the fruit sprites under the name `silktree.mic`. Insert this sprite using the From File command under the Insert menu.

The silk tree sprite is large enough to cover all the text sprites, which is necessary for the pixel transfer to work correctly. So, move the silk tree sprite so that its leaves cover up the text sprites completely. Then press the Tab key to select one of the text sprites. Select the Patterns and Fills tool and choose Sprite to Sprite from the listbox in the tool palette. Then select Transfer Full from the drop-down list and click the Apply button. You are presented with a message box notifying you that you must select the source sprite for the transfer. Click the OK button and then click the silk tree sprite.

At this point, the pixels from the silk tree sprite have been transferred to the text sprite, but you can't tell because the text sprite is still concealed. Before moving the silk tree out of the way, repeat this procedure on the two remaining text sprites. After doing this, you can delete the silk tree sprite from the composition by selecting it and pressing the Delete key.

The text sprites now have a leafy appearance instead of being solid black. The only problem is that the leafy look makes the text a little harder to read. To help alleviate this problem, select the Warps and Filters tool and choose Outlines from the drop-down list in the tool palette. Then select Relief from the listbox and click the Apply button. This effect adds a small shadow to the text. Use the Relief effect on the two remaining text sprites. Figure 30.16 shows the completed text sprites.

FIGURE 30.16.

The completed text sprites.

Generating an Image for the Web

Congratulations, the composition is just about ready to be used to create the final image for the Web. Because you might want to go back and work from the composition in the future, be sure to save it. After the composition is saved, flatten the sprites by selecting the Arrange tool and then clicking the Flatten button in the tool palette. This flattens all the sprites into one sprite, which is easier to work with. However, after the sprites are flattened you can't go back and work with them individually again.

The next step is to make sure the bounding box fits the sprites tightly by clicking the Fit Bounding Box button on the Arrange tool palette. At this point, you might be thinking the composition looks awfully large to be used in a real Web site. You are correct! The image needs to be resized smaller by adjusting its width and height in the Arrange tool palette. Using the percentage approach from earlier in the chapter, resize the composition to 40 percent of its original size.

The last step in readying the composition for prime time is to adjust the composition guide to match the size of the actual composition. Use the width and height of the flattened sprite to set the width and height of the composition guide. For example, the width and height of my composition ended up being 255 by 118. Therefore, I set the composition guide's width and height to be 255 by 118. You do this by right-clicking on the workspace and selecting Properties from the pop-up menu. Then just type in the width and height for the composition guide and click the OK button.

With the composition guide sized properly, you need to drag the sprite so that it fits perfectly into the composition window. Before generating an image from the composition, it's worth checking out one more feature of Image Composer that can come in handy while creating Web graphics: multiple composition views. Multiple views on a composition enable you to see what the composition looks like under different color models. You can easily load custom palettes and see what your composition looks like under them.

To view, edit, and load color palettes for use in Image Composer, select the Custom Palette tab from the Color Picker dialog box. Figure 30.17 shows what this tabbed dialog box looks like.

FIGURE 30.17.
The Custom Palette tab in the Color Picker dialog box.

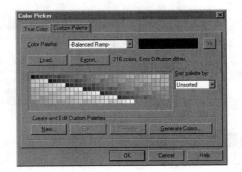

When you have a palette in mind for testing your composition, click OK to exit the dialog box. Then select New Window from the Window menu, and select Tile from the same menu. This results in two different views on the same composition, as shown in Figure 30.18.

You can now try changing the color model used for the compositions in each window; the color model is easily changed from the main application toolbar. Keep in mind that the two windows are viewing the same composition; if you're having trouble believing this, try dragging the sprite around and see how it moves in both windows. When you're satisfied with how the composition looks, you're ready to convert it to an image that can be used in a Web site. This is accomplished by selecting Save As from the File menu and then choosing the desired output file type. In most cases, you will probably want to use either the GIF or JPEG file formats. Figure 30.19 shows the final GIF image, `Vernie.gif`, of the composition you just created.

FIGURE 30.18.

Multiple views on the fruit composition.

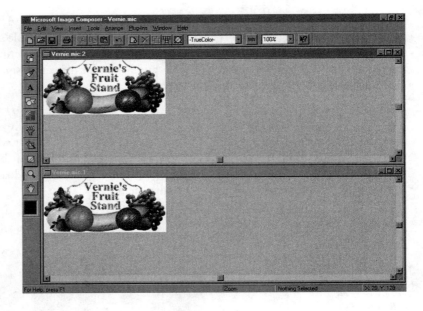

FIGURE 30.19.

The resulting GIF image of the fruit composition.

GIF Animator Basics

As you've seen, Image Composer is a very powerful tool for creating images for the Web. However, all you've seen in Image Composer is the capability to create static images. What about all those Web sites that use fancy animated images? You might have wondered how to create animated graphics of your own. The companion tool to Image Composer, GIF Animator, is a graphics tool geared toward the creation of animated GIF images. Unlike Image Composer, which supports lots of different image formats, GIF Animator is designed solely around the GIF 89A image format. This isn't really a weakness, because this image format is the most popular image format on the Web.

Before getting into some of the specifics of GIF Animator, it's important that you understand exactly what animated GIF images are and how they work. An animated GIF image is not different from a normal GIF image in terms of how an image is represented. However, animated GIFs consist of multiple images, or animation frames. In this way, an animated GIF is really just a group of GIF images grouped together. Animations are a result of Web browsers iterating through the animation frames of an animated GIF, much like a movie animates by a projector iterating through frames on film. Each frame in an animated GIF has a duration associated with it, which can be used to vary the timing of the animation.

GIF Animator enables you to create and manipulate animations by working with animation frames. Using GIF Animator, you can easily edit and arrange the individual frames of an animation, and then test the entire animation to see how it looks. When you're satisfied with an animation, you save it directly to an animated GIF file. Unlike Image Composer, which relies on intermediate compositions, you use the same GIF file in GIF Animator for both the creation and publishing of final animations.

The GIF Animator interface is very simplistic and easy to use. You'll find it much easier than Image Composer to get acquainted with simply because there aren't as many options or features. Figure 30.20 shows GIF Animator with an empty animation.

FIGURE 30.20.

GIF Animator with an empty animation.

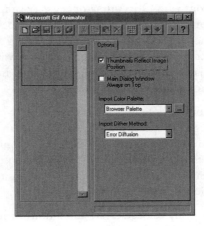

The GIF Animator interface includes the following components:

- A toolbar
- An animation display
- A tabbed set of control windows

The toolbar, which is located across the top of the application window, is the primary interface for working with common commands such as opening and saving files. The toolbar also includes editing commands, as well as animation frame navigation buttons and a preview button.

The animation display is the primary interface between you and the animation frames. The display consists of a vertically scrolling list of all the frames in the current animation. Each frame is shown in the animation display as a thumbnail of the frame image. Using the movie analogy from earlier, you can think of the animation display conceptually as a roll of movie film. The animation display is an integral part of the GIF Animator interface because you can insert and delete frames directly to and from the animation display.

30

GRAPHICS WITH
IMAGE COMPOSER
AND GIF ANIMATOR

The specific properties of an animation are controlled through a set of tabbed control windows. The following tab control windows appear in GIF Animator: Options, Animation, and Image. The Options control window enables you to specify which palette GIF Animator uses to represent the images within the animation, and how colors are represented in the saved image, along with a couple of other options. The Animation control window enables you to set the size, duration, and transparency attributes of the animation. Finally, the Image tab lets you adjust the characteristics of individual image frames within the animation.

Building Animations with GIF Animator

Building animations with GIF Animator is a very simple process if you have images for each frame of animation. Unfortunately, GIF Animator does nothing to help you create the graphics for an animation. It is designed solely for creating animations out of existing images. For this reason, it is often useful to pair Image Composer with GIF Animator to create GIF animations; you use Image Composer to create the actual images, and then use GIF Animator to build them into animations.

GIF Animator supports drag-and-drop movements, which makes creating animations in conjunction with Image Composer much easier. For instance, you can drag and drop a sprite from Image Composer into the animation display of GIF Animator to add it as an animation frame. With this approach, you can often use Image Composer with GIF Animator to build animations without even using any of the advanced composition features of Image Composer. This can make animation creation a very rapid process.

To show you how easily you can create animations with these two tools, let's work through an example. Continuing with the hypothetical fruit stand Web site from earlier in the chapter, it might be neat to have an animated strawberry getting bigger and smaller. It could be used as an animated bullet on the Web site. As you might already be guessing, the animation can be quickly created by resizing the strawberry sprite in Image Composer and then dragging it to an animation frame in GIF Animator. Let's see specifically how this is done.

Adding the First Animation Frame

To begin, start Image Composer and insert the strawberry sprite, which is located in the file strawber.mic. The sprite is inserted into Image Composer at a very large size relative to what you are using it for, so the first step is to resize it smaller. Using the Arrange tool, resize the sprite to 5 percent of its original size. Then start GIF Animator and drag the strawberry sprite to the animation display. Drop the sprite on the animation display and it will be added as the first frame of the animation (as shown in Figure 30.21).

Fleshing Out the Animation

To make the strawberry animate, you need to incrementally resize the sprite larger in Image
Composer, while adding each newly sized image as a frame to the animation in GIF Animator.
So jump back to Image Composer and resize the strawberry to 110 percent of its size, resulting
in a slightly larger sprite. Then drag the sprite onto the empty frame in the animation display
of GIF Animator, just below the first frame. This adds the slightly larger strawberry image as
the second frame of animation. Repeat this process of enlarging and inserting the strawberry
image two more times, resulting in four total animation frames. Figure 30.22 shows what GIF
Animator looks like with the four frames in place.

At this point you can try out the animation by clicking the Preview button on the toolbar; it's the next-to-last button on the right. This displays one sequence of the animation. To see the animation repeat over and over, click the Animation tab and check the Looping checkbox. Then check the Repeat Forever checkbox to make the animation loop forever. Now preview the animation again to see how it looks.

Fine-Tuning the Animation

Aside from the choppiness when the animation starts over, you probably noticed that the larger strawberry images appear from behind the smaller ones when it seems like they should be erased. This problem can be fixed by going to the Image tab and changing the way in which the images are cleaned up. Select Restore Background from the Undraw Method drop-down list to cause the background to be drawn in between the display of each animation frame. You must make this change for each of the four animation frames.

The only remaining problem with the animation is the abruptness that occurs when the animation starts over. This is due to the fact that the last frame jumps straight to the first frame, which means the largest strawberry is being displayed just before the smallest. The solution is to add two more frames at the end of the animation that show the strawberry getting small again. This is easily accomplished by dragging the third frame image to the end frame, which makes a copy of the image and places it in the last frame. Then repeat the process with the second frame image. Preview the animation again and you'll see how much smoother it now looks.

There is one more potential issue to be raised in regard to this animation: its speed. Right now the animation has no timing associated with it, meaning that the frames are drawn as fast as possible. Not only does this result in an animation that is too fast, but it can also mean that the animation speed varies according to the speed of the system it is being viewed on. You can alleviate this problem by slowing down the frame rate. This is accomplished by assigning each frame a duration, which is the amount of time the frame is displayed before moving to the next frame.

The duration for each animation frame is set in the Image tab. Enter 10 in the Duration text box for all the frames except the first frame, and then enter 30 for it. This number is in hundredths of a second, so a value of 10 gives the frames a tenth of a second duration. Likewise, a value of 30 results in roughly a third of a second duration. The point of using different values is to make the animation pause for a moment at the first frame.

Now try the animation and notice how the duration of each frame affects the way the animation looks. If you're happy with the animation, click the Save button on the toolbar and save the GIF. You can then open the GIF in Internet Explorer or Netscape Navigator, because they both support animated GIFs.

That's it for using GIF Animator! As you learned, GIF Animator is a very easy tool to use. Although you didn't learn about every little feature in this example, you covered the most important ones. Now it's your turn to experiment and have fun with these tools on your own.

Summary

Along with spurring a great deal of software development efforts, the popularity of the Web has created an enormous need for custom graphical content. Increasingly, both businesses and individuals are attempting to create their own Web site graphics with little or no artistic background. Microsoft, ever quick to seize an opportunity, realized the need for a powerful, easy-to-use tool centered on the creation of Web graphics. From this realization emerged Image Composer, a powerful, sprite-based graphics tool for creating Web graphics. Microsoft also developed a graphics tool called GIF Animator that facilitates the creation of animated GIF images, which are becoming increasingly popular on the Web.

Image Composer and GIF Animator represent an irreplaceable pair of graphics tools for those of us who aren't blessed with deep artistic talent or deep pockets. Even for those people who are, these tools, especially Image Composer, have some innovative features that are worth looking into. Additionally, you can easily use the tools together, which is a nice benefit.

30

GRAPHICS WITH
IMAGE COMPOSER
AND GIF ANIMATOR

Using Music Producer and Media Manager

by Michael Morrison

CHAPTER 31

In the early days of the Web, which was only a few short years ago, the idea of injecting different types of media into Web pages was relatively lofty. The transfer overhead associated with graphic images in Web pages seemed to be enough to deter any serious thought about other types of media such as video and sound. Well, times have clearly changed, and the Web we now know has become a vast sea of multimedia content. Granted, we're just beginning to see serious utilization of quality video and sound in the online world, but as bandwidth continues to grow, it's safe to assume that advanced media will become commonplace.

Having said that, let me introduce the topic of this chapter: multimedia! More specifically, this chapter explores two interesting tools that help facilitate the usage of multimedia on the Web: Microsoft Music Producer and Media Manager. Music Producer is a music composition tool that generates original musical compositions based on user-defined settings. In this chapter, you learn how to use Music Producer to create your own musical compositions that can be included in your Web pages. Unlike Music Producer, Media Manager doesn't directly involve the creation of media content. Rather, it is a tool for organizing and managing media content within the familiar interface of Windows Explorer.

Music Producer Basics

The concept of using sound in a Web page is fairly new, primarily because few Web developers have the ability to create music. Most Web developers, myself included, are faced with the dilemma of either paying for the rights to use copyrighted music or attempting to become a musician overnight. Because few people have the time or aptitude to become a proficient enough musician for the sole purpose of creating music for a Web site, they either pay for music or settle on not having any music at all. Most of us fall in the latter camp...until now.

Music Producer is a tool designed to give non-musicians the ability to create their own music. Music Producer defines a group of user-modifiable settings that are used to generate original musical compositions on the fly. Before you start questioning my credibility, understand that I was extremely skeptical about this concept at first. I mean, as far as artificial intelligence has come, isn't it still just a little unrealistic to think that a computer can step in and be creative in a musical sense? If a computer can honestly generate original music, could it not just as easily write this book? I don't have the answer to that question, but I'm hoping it's "no" because Music Producer does a surprisingly good job at creating original music!

Music Producer is not just a novelty; you really can create complex, textured musical compositions with a very minimal knowledge of music. The magic of Music Producer is its Interactive Music Engine, which generates music based on a group of settings that define musical attributes such as tempo, key, style, and personality, to name a few. You adjust and control these settings through the Music Producer interface, which is completely graphical and very easy to use. Before getting into the Music Producer interface and how it works, however, it's important that you understand the fundamental concepts upon which Music Producer is based.

Sound Hardware and MIDI

Music Producer works in conjunction with the sound hardware in your computer to produce music. More specifically, Music Producer uses a synthesizer in the sound hardware to produce (synthesize) sounds. The sound hardware for most PCs is actually a sound card. Most PC sound cards have synthesizers of some sort, with higher-end sound cards having high-quality synthesizers that sound a lot like real musical instruments. Music Producer generates and plays music through a sound device, which is the part of a sound card used to play musical notes. Some sound cards support multiple sound devices, although only one device can typically be used at a time. You can specify in Music Producer which sound device you want to use with it.

The compositions generated by Music Producer are output as MIDI files. MIDI, which stands for Musical Instrument Digital Interface, is a standard and very popular music protocol that defines the exchange of musical information between computers and musical instruments. MIDI files are very different from sampled audio (wave) files because MIDI files store musical instructions, as opposed to raw sampled data. This difference allows MIDI files to be much smaller than wave files, because it takes much less space to store musical instructions than sampled sound. However, the quality of a MIDI file is dependent on the synthesizer (sound device) it is being played through, where a wave file's quality is determined by information in the wave file itself.

Defining Music

The ability to create music in Music Producer revolves around musical settings. Musical settings are used by the Interactive Music Engine to generate original musical compositions. Music Producer relies on five different musical settings to determine how to compose a particular piece of music. Table 31.1 lists these settings and what aspect of the composition they control.

Table 31.1. Musical settings used to define a composition.

Musical Setting	What It Controls
Style	Musical genre and melodic arrangement
Personality	Musical mood and emotion
Band	Instruments used to play the music
Tempo	Musical speed
Key	Musical pitch

The most important setting used in Music Producer is the style setting, which determines the rhythmic and melodic style of a composition. By far, style has the greatest impact on a composition. Music Producer comes standard with more than 100 musical styles, each of which conveys a unique rhythmic feel and melodic arrangement. The style of a composition also impacts the other musical settings because each style has a default group of settings.

The personality setting impacts a composition in a much more subtle way, resulting in slight chord shifts that give the composition a different feel. Each style has an associated group of personalities that can be used to change the overall tone of the composition. Personality settings have meaningful names such as romantic, upbeat, and whimsical, which make it easier to understand what effect the personality setting will have on the composition.

The band setting is used to select the instruments that play a composition. You can think of the band setting literally as a band of people with their own musical instruments. Each Music Producer band contains exactly six members, or instruments. Music Producer automatically determines the music played by each member of a band, although you can adjust the volume and speaker balance for each instrument independently.

The tempo setting determines the speed at which a composition plays. This speed is measured in beats per minute, which is a standard musical measurement. The tempo setting impacts compositions a great deal because it alters the speed at which a composition plays, which is very noticeable.

The last setting that impacts how compositions are generated is the key setting, which specifies the musical pitch of a composition. More practically speaking, the key determines the range of notes used to play a composition. All compositions are played at a certain pitch, as determined by the key setting. By default, the key of Music Producer compositions is C, which is what most Western music is based on.

The Music Producer Interface

I mentioned earlier how easy it is to use the Music Producer interface to create compositions; let's find out why. Figure 31.1 shows the Music Producer interface.

FIGURE 31.1.

The Music Producer interface.

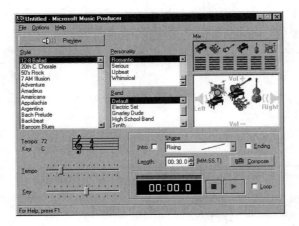

The Music Producer interface includes the following components:

- Menu
- Preview button
- Style list
- Personality list
- Band list
- Mix area
- Tempo slider
- Key slider
- Compose area
- Status bar

The menu is the interface for working with files and setting up the MIDI sound device used by Music Producer. To change the sound device, just select Setup Sound Device from the Options menu. Figure 31.2 shows the Setup Sound Device dialog box that allows you to select a sound device.

FIGURE 31.2.

The Setup Sound Device dialog box used to select sound devices.

The Preview button is used to preview the current musical settings. When you click the Preview button, Music Producer begins generating and playing music based on the current settings. The Preview button is very useful because you can change settings while the music is being played, and hear the results instantly. For example, you can change the personality of a composition being previewed to get an idea of how the different personality settings impact the composition. This is particularly useful for the personality setting, because the personality setting typically impacts a composition in a subtle way.

The Style list is used to select the style of music for the current composition. Likewise, the Personality and Band lists allow you to select the personality and band for the current composition. It's important to note that not all personalities and bands are available for each musical style; each style has its own unique set of personalities and bands.

The mix area is where you view and fine-tune the instruments in the current band by adjusting their volume and speaker balance (see Figure 31.3). The top of the mix area, the meters pane, displays each instrument in the band and whether it is currently being played. The meter below each instrument indicates the relative volume level for the instrument by displaying red rectangles that bounce up and down in response to fluctuations in volume.

FIGURE 31.3.

The mix area used to view and adjust the volume and speaker balance for band instruments.

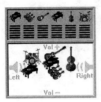

The lower part of the mix area, the mixing pane, is where you actually adjust the volume and speaker balance for the instruments. The neat thing about the mixing pane is that it is completely graphical, meaning that you click and drag instruments around in the pane to make adjustments. Moving an instrument in a vertical direction changes its volume, whereas horizontal movement changes its speaker balance. You can make these changes while a composition is being played, which allows you to see immediately how the mix adjustments affect the music. The mix area also provides information about the instruments being used. If you hold the mouse pointer above an instrument, a pop-up window will appear giving the name of the instrument.

The Tempo and Key sliders allow you to adjust the tempo and key of the composition, respectively. The current values of the tempo and key are displayed just above the sliders. The key is also displayed graphically in the form of a staff containing the clef, key signature, and time signature for the current composition. Figure 31.4 shows the staff used to graphically display the key signature of a composition.

FIGURE 31.4.

The staff used to graphically display the key signature for a composition.

The compose area of Music Producer is where you set the specifics regarding the composition being produced. Perhaps the most important composition setting is the shape of the composition, which determines the overall level of instrumental activity. Although the differences between shapes can at times be subtle, the majority of the time you can hear the differences easily. Following are the available shapes:

- Rising
- Falling
- Peaking
- Level
- Loudness

- ■ Quiet
- ■ Song
- ■ Loopable
- ■ Random

NOTE

Although the Loopable shape is specifically provided for use with looped compositions, most of the other shapes also sound fine when looped.

The Intro and Ending checkboxes, located just before and after the Shape drop-down list, allow you to add a distinctive beginning or ending to a composition. Speaking of the ending of a composition, the Length edit box is located just below the Shape drop-down list, and allows you to set the length of the composition. Composition length is specified as a length of time, meaning that you enter minutes and seconds in the Length edit box.

Just to the right of the Length edit box is the Compose button, which creates a new composition each time it is pressed. Because each composition generated by Music Producer is unique, all you must do is press the Compose button to generate new compositions. Below the Compose button are the playback controls, which allow you to stop, start, or pause the playback of the composition. Finally, the last member of the compose area is the Loop checkbox, which is used during playback to loop the composition repeatedly.

Creating Music with Music Producer

Once you understand how the interface works for Music Producer, creating musical compositions is almost trivial. All you really do to create a composition is decide on the musical and composition settings, and then click the Compose button. Admittedly, coming up with settings you are happy with can be a time-consuming process, but it can also be a lot of fun. This is primarily due to the experimental nature of the Music Producer interface, which allows you to preview musical settings as you change them.

In this section, you create a composition for the hypothetical Web site, Vernie's Fruit Stand, mentioned in the previous chapter. Unlike graphics, music isn't always as easy to nail down in terms of fitting a composition to the style of a Web site. Fortunately, Music Producer has plenty of settings to play around with, which can help you create music based solely on what you think sounds good. The "sounds good" approach is the one I highly suggest when creating your own compositions in Music Producer.

For the purposes of creating music for the hypothetical online fruit stand Web site, you should take into account the style of the site. However, because we're speaking in hypothetical terms, you have no way of knowing what the site actually looks like. Even so, you have seen some of the graphics in the site, because you created them in the previous chapter. If you recall, there was a fruit-filled title image and an animated pulsating strawberry image. Both images conveyed a degree of lightheartedness, which should be carried over to the music for the site. Also, you know the Web site is an online fruit stand, which could convey the feel of a busy street vendor selling fruit to passers-by. This information is really all you need to begin experimenting with Music Producer.

Because music is an intensely personal form of artistic expression, I'm not about to discuss the sample composition in terms of what is right or wrong. Rather, I want to show you how to create the composition I thought might go well with the Web site. After hearing my approach, you may have your own idea about music that might go better with the site. I encourage you to experiment until you find a group of settings that you are happy with. You'll get to test out your music in a real Web page for the online fruit stand in the next chapter.

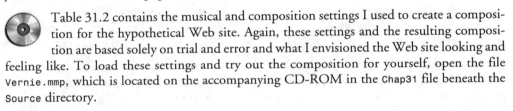 Table 31.2 contains the musical and composition settings I used to create a composition for the hypothetical Web site. Again, these settings and the resulting composition are based solely on trial and error and what I envisioned the Web site looking and feeling like. To load these settings and try out the composition for yourself, open the file `Vernie.mmp`, which is located on the accompanying CD-ROM in the `Chap31` file beneath the `Source` directory.

Table 31.2. Musical settings for the sample composition.

Setting	Set To
Style	Eastern Europe
Personality	Honest
Band	Sax City
Tempo	128
Key	C
Shape	Loopable
Length	45 seconds

NOTE

Because Music Producer creates different compositions each time the Compose button is pressed, it's impossible to generate my exact composition. However, you can listen to it by playing the MIDI file I created, `Vernie.mid`, which is located in `Chap31` under the `Source` directory on the accompanying CD-ROM.

Whether you decide to create your own composition or use mine, you need to save any work you've done in Music Producer. You do this by selecting Save from the File menu, which saves the composition in an `.mmp` file. This file format is specific to Music Producer, and contains information about the composition and its different settings. To use a composition on the Web, it needs to be in the MIDI file format (`.mid`). You save a composition as a MIDI file by selecting Save As MIDI from the File menu. That's really all there is to creating your own compositions using Music Producer.

> **NOTE**
>
> You can include a MIDI composition as the sound for a Web page when the page is loaded by specifying the composition as the background sound for the page in the FrontPage editor that ships with Visual InterDev. You learn how to do this in the next chapter, "Designing Web Pages with FrontPage 97 and Extensions."

All About Media Manager

Microsoft Media Manager is an organizer and management system for multimedia content. Its purpose is to help simplify the way developers of multimedia content store and locate their media files. Unlike other multimedia tools that ship with Visual InterDev, Media Manager is not a standalone application. Rather, it is an add-on to Windows Explorer, which means it operates within the context of the Windows Explorer interface. For example, Media Manager enhances the view options in Windows Explorer by adding thumbnail viewing capabilities for images, as well as the playback of video and audio.

To use Media Manager, you must create a root Media Manager folder somewhere on your hard drive. This folder is significant because all folders created beneath it are automatically made Media Manager folders. To create a root Media Manager folder, highlight its new parent in Windows Explorer, select New from the File menu, and then click Media Manager Folder. With a Media Manager folder created, you are ready to start moving multimedia files into or under the folder.

When you add or move a file into a Media Manager folder, Media Manager automatically extracts type-specific properties for the file if its type is supported. Media Manager also indexes the properties and contents of the file for faster, more efficient searching. When Media Manager is finished with these tasks, you are free to add your own annotations to the file, which helps provide more discrete search criteria.

At this point, you still may not see the big picture surrounding Media Manager. To get a better idea as to what Media Manager has to offer in the way of media management, consider the following benefits it provides:

■ Media Manager extracts type-specific properties from many different types of files, including information about a file, its format, or its content, which is then indexed and used by the search engine.

■ Media Manager supports user-defined annotations, which help you organize and catalog data.

■ Media Manager supports a thumbnail view of images, as well as the ability to play video and audio files in Windows Explorer.

■ Media Manager indexes all the files that you store in Media Manager folders, which greatly improves the efficiency of file searches.

Microsoft Media Manager folders are easily distinguished from normal Windows Explorer folders by their metallic briefcase icons. Figure 31.5 shows a Media Manager folder hierarchy. Although Media Manager folders look different from Windows folders, you work with them in a very similar way. When you store files in Media Manager folders instead of Windows folders, Media Manager does the following:

■ Indexes the files for searching, making sure to keep track of their names and locations.

■ Extracts type-specific file properties and allows you to add annotations to both folders and files, which can then be used as search criteria for performing more efficient searches.

■ Allows you to create and view thumbnails for image media files in Windows Explorer and from many Open and Save dialog boxes by selecting Thumbnail on the View menu.

■ Allows you to play video and audio media files in place directly in Windows Explorer.

As you might have guessed from the discussion thus far, searching is a very important process in Media Manager. Because of this, Media Manager indexes all the files it is managing to build a more efficient means of searching for information in a large group of files. The search facilities in Media Manager can be used to find a file based on the contents, attributes, or annotations in the file.

Media Manager builds indexes and performs searches using both type-specific properties and user-defined annotations for folders and files that support them. For example, you can search for all image files that have 24-bit color or are a certain width and height. The ability to search based on type-specific information is very powerful. You can also search based on annotations, which are completely user-defined. Usually, an annotation describes a property that is not intrinsic to the file or folder it belongs to. For example, the names of people in a series of photographs could be associated with the photograph images as annotations. Annotations can be text, integers, real numbers, yes/no values, or dates.

FIGURE 31.5.
A Media Manager folder hierarchy as viewed in Windows Explorer.

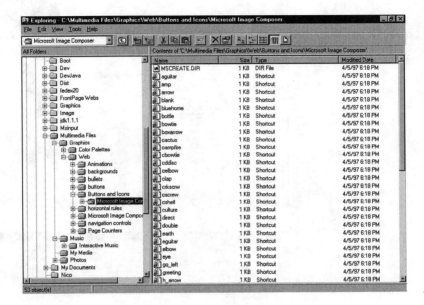

Thumbnail View

As you learned a little earlier, Media Manager supports a thumbnail view for certain media file types. This view is added to the four standard Windows Explorer views in the Windows Explorer interface, and is accessible by selecting Thumbnail from the View menu. Thumbnail viewing is a nice feature because it eliminates the need to launch an application to quickly view or play a file or group of files. Figure 31.6 shows the thumbnail view of a Media Manager folder containing images.

When thumbnail view is used with video or audio files, a small circle with an arrow is displayed at the lower-left corner of the icon representing the file. Clicking this circle displays a playback control, which can then be used to play the video or audio file in place in Windows Explorer. Figure 31.7 shows a MIDI file being played in place using the playback control in thumbnail view.

FIGURE 31.6.

The thumbnail view of a Media Manager folder containing images.

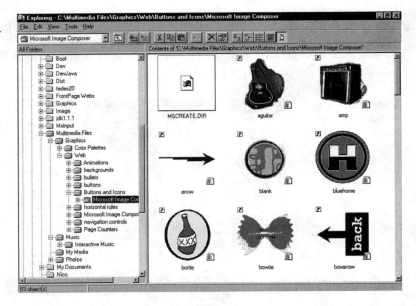

FIGURE 31.7.

The thumbnail view of a Media Manager folder containing a MIDI file.

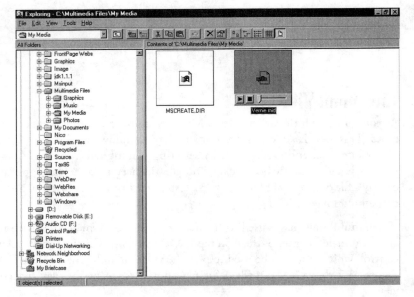

Searching Files

Media Manager indexes all the files that you store in Media Manager folders to help facilitate speedy searches based on file details. The index created and managed by Media Manager includes information describing all the properties of your Media Manager folders and files. When you issue a search on a Media Manager file or folder, Media Manager uses the index to perform the search rather than the actual folders and files. This approach to searching is akin to a database query, where elements in a database are indexed according to certain criteria.

You probably get the idea now that Media Manager provides extensive support for searching media files, but you still might not understand exactly what types of searching are supported. Following are the types of searches supported by Media Manager:

- Filename, type, and location searches
- Full text searches
- Date searches
- Property and annotation searches

To search for information in a Media Manager folder or file, select Find from the Windows Explorer Tools menu and click Files or Folders in Media Manager. You will be presented with the dialog box shown in Figure 31.8, which allows you to perform any of the aforementioned searches on your media files and folders.

FIGURE 31.8.

The Media Manager Find dialog box used to search through media files.

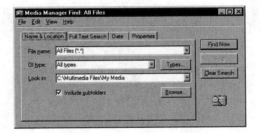

Summary

The need for powerful multimedia tools has increased rapidly due to the desire for more multimedia Web content. The Web is quickly evolving to a state where sites with multimedia content eclipse their more static brethren. It is the job of the Web developer to embrace this evolution and figure out ways to integrate media with Web sites in innovative ways. The only problem with this idea is that it requires powerful and easy-to-use multimedia tools so that Web developers can be creative without a huge learning curve.

This chapter introduced you to two very powerful and interesting tools geared toward creating and managing multimedia content. The first tool, Microsoft Music Producer, is used to create original musical compositions based on a group of user-defined settings. The second tool, Media Manager, acts as an efficient organizer and manager for media content. These tools, although both media oriented, are very different in functionality. Nevertheless, together they form a powerful pair of complementary tools for Visual InterDev.

Designing Web Pages with FrontPage 97 and Extensions

by Michael Morrison

IN THIS CHAPTER

32

CHAPTER

Microsoft FrontPage 97, or FrontPage for short, is a Web authoring and management tool designed to make it easy to design and lay out Web pages using a purely visual interface. With FrontPage, you can create Web pages without knowing the first thing about HTML, the markup language that dictates the look of Web pages. Although you can still use HTML code directly if you so desire, FrontPage is specifically designed to put a graphical spin on the creation of Web pages.

Visual InterDev provides facilities for creating and editing HTML files at the code level, but none for graphically working with HTML. Because of this, FrontPage makes a logical companion tool to Visual InterDev. Coupling FrontPage with Visual InterDev allows you to leverage the Web page design benefits of FrontPage with the power and flexibility of Visual InterDev. Realizing the usefulness of FrontPage paired with Visual InterDev, Microsoft decided to bundle the editor portion of FrontPage with Visual InterDev.

This chapter takes a look at FrontPage and how it can be used to design and create Web pages. You won't learn about every detail of FrontPage, because there are entire books devoted to that. Rather, you learn how to graphically layout Web pages using the FrontPage Editor, which is the primary benefit of using FrontPage with Visual InterDev.

FrontPage and Visual InterDev

FrontPage is a powerful tool that includes many features for building fully functioning Web sites with interactive content. Even so, FrontPage is geared toward developing Web sites with little to no database integration, which just happens to be one of the key benefits of Visual InterDev. Knowing this, it's fairly clear that Visual InterDev is a tool designed to construct Web sites a little more involved than what FrontPage can handle alone. However, FrontPage can play a vital role in building a Web site in conjunction with Visual InterDev, because it makes creating individual Web pages very simple and straightforward.

The full FrontPage product includes the FrontPage Explorer and the FrontPage Editor, which are complementary tools used to manage and develop Web sites. The FrontPage Explorer is a graphical application that functions similarly to Windows Explorer within the context of a Web site. The FrontPage Explorer is used to create, view, maintain, and publish FrontPage webs on a local computer, a Local Area Network (LAN), or the Internet. The FrontPage Explorer is the management part of FrontPage, including support for viewing all of a web's files and folders, importing and exporting files, testing and repairing hyperlinks, and automatically launching the FrontPage Editor and other applications to edit the different types of content.

The FrontPage Editor is a graphical application similar in function to a word processor that is used to create, edit, and test individual Web pages. The FrontPage Editor requires no knowledge of HTML, because it creates all the HTML code for you behind the scenes. A special version of the FrontPage Editor is bundled with Visual InterDev as a tool for editing Web pages. Although Visual InterDev supports the creation and editing of Web pages through straight

HTML coding, the FrontPage Editor provides a graphical and more intuitive alternative. Microsoft could have bundled the entire FrontPage product with Visual InterDev, but probably figured that most Web developers using Visual InterDev would prefer using only the FrontPage Editor, and not the Web site organization and management part of FrontPage (FrontPage Explorer). Besides, the complete FrontPage product is a comprehensive Web development tool in its own right that overlaps some of the functionality of Visual InterDev.

Because this book is about Visual InterDev, we're really only interested in how FrontPage impacts the development of Web sites with Visual InterDev. For this reason, the rest of this chapter focuses solely on the FrontPage Editor. The FrontPage Explorer is an important tool in its own right and can certainly be used alongside Visual InterDev if you are developing a complete Web site in FrontPage. However, most Visual InterDev projects only make use of the FrontPage Editor that ships with Visual InterDev. The rest of the chapter focuses on the FrontPage editor and how it is used to create and develop Web pages.

FrontPage Editor Basics

The FrontPage Editor is a graphical tool designed to make the design and development of Web pages a more intuitive and straightforward process. With a style much like a word processor, the FrontPage Editor is very easy to learn and use. It fully supports the HTML language, providing a means to add HTML elements in a purely graphical manner. You can easily add text, images, and tables without ever seeing any HTML code. Web pages appear in the FrontPage Editor very similarly to how they would appear in a Web browser. As you might already be thinking, the FrontPage Editor is a welcome sight in the world of Visual InterDev, where most tasks require at least some degree of coding.

Along with creating new HTML files, the FrontPage Editor can be used to edit existing HTML files; any unknown tags in an existing HTML file are preserved. The FrontPage Editor supports text in all HTML styles, and allows you to change the size, color, and formatting of text. You can add images in a variety of different formats, and the FrontPage Editor will automatically convert them into either GIF or JPEG images, which are standard for the Web. You can also create imagemaps by defining hotspots in an image, which are areas of an image that contain hyperlinks. The FrontPage Editor makes it very easy to use tables by displaying them very similarly to how they would appear in a Web browser.

In addition to supporting standard HTML elements, the FrontPage Editor also allows you to integrate more advanced features like forms and components. Using forms, you can add and manipulate text fields, checkboxes, radio buttons, drop-down lists, and pushbuttons. Components, on the other hand, bring interactivity to a whole new level by allowing you to incorporate Java applets, ActiveX controls, and FrontPage WebBots. WebBots are components designed specifically for FrontPage that provide features such as automated searching capabilities. The FrontPage Editor also supports scripting, meaning you can edit and insert JavaScript or VBScript scripts.

The FrontPage Editor includes a familiar interface that is consistent with the feel of most Windows 95/NT applications. Because the interface is the heart of FrontPage, let's take a look at it and see what it has to offer. Figure 32.1 shows what the FrontPage Editor's main application window looks like.

FIGURE 32.1.

The FrontPage Editor's main application window.

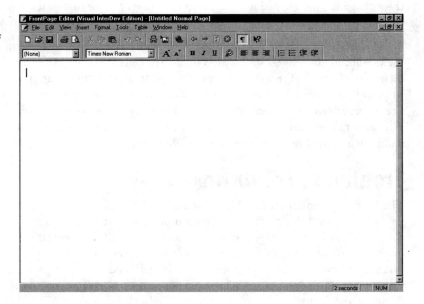

The FrontPage Editor interface includes a menu, a toolbar, and a workspace. The menu serves as a comprehensive interface to all of the commands supported by the FrontPage Editor, while the toolbar provides a more accessible interface to some of the more frequently used commands. The workspace takes up the bulk of the FrontPage Editor's application window, and is where you actually view and edit Web pages.

The FrontPage Editor's toolbar is actually divided into two separate toolbars, which are displayed on two different rows below the menu by default. You can rearrange and even undock the toolbars individually by clicking and dragging them around. The toolbar just below the menu is the standard toolbar for the FrontPage Editor, and includes buttons for performing common commands such as opening and saving files (see Figure 32.2).

The toolbar below the standard toolbar is the text-formatting toolbar (see Figure 32.3). Not surprisingly, this toolbar includes buttons for formatting text in a variety of ways. If you are accustomed to using a toolbar in a word processor, these buttons will feel familiar. They are very handy because you can quickly format text without having to sift through menus or dialog boxes.

FIGURE 32.2.
The FrontPage Editor's standard toolbar.

FIGURE 32.3.
The FrontPage Editor's text-formatting toolbar.

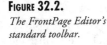

Using the FrontPage Editor

Although it's fun talking about the FrontPage Editor, you can't fully realize its value without trying it out. For this reason, the rest of the chapter is devoted to using the FrontPage Editor to create Web pages. I strongly encourage you to work along in the FrontPage Editor as you read through the remainder of this chapter. If you don't want to, however, you can still follow what's going on by looking at the figures.

Creating a New Web Page

As you've already learned, the FrontPage Editor is designed to work with HTML files, which are the official standard for Web pages. There are other document formats that are used for Web pages, but HTML reigns supreme. The FrontPage Editor allows you to either create new HTML documents or open existing HTML documents. Existing HTML documents can be opened and edited even if they weren't originally created with the FrontPage Editor.

> **NOTE**
>
> When new files are created in the FrontPage Editor, they are not automatically added to your Visual InterDev Web project; you must manually insert them into the project.

Although you can open and edit existing Web pages, you're going to create a new page now as the basis for an example of how to use the FrontPage Editor. The example uses the graphics you created with Microsoft Image Composer and GIF Animator in Chapter 30, "Graphics with Microsoft Image Composer and GIF Animator." If you recall, the graphics in Chapter 30 were designed for a hypothetical Web site called Vernie's Fruit Stand. You are now going to create the main Web page for Vernie's Web site, which will use the graphics created in Chapter 30, along with some other interesting things.

You need to launch the FrontPage Editor, which is located in the isfp\bin directory beneath the Visual InterDev installation directory. If you accepted a default installation directory when installing Visual InterDev, the full path for this directory is `\Program Files\DevStudio\VintDev\isfp\bin`. If you didn't, you need to look beneath the installation directory you specified for the `isfp\bin` directory. When you get the directory sorted out, launch the FrontPage Editor by executing the `Isfp.exe` executable.

> **NOTE**
>
> If you happen to already use FrontPage 97, you might want to use the editor included with it rather than the editor that ships with Visual InterDev. These editors provide essentially the same function, so you don't need the FrontPage editor provided with Visual InterDev if you already have the full FrontPage 97 product installed.

The FrontPage Editor application window will appear just as you saw it in Figure 32.1. By default, the FrontPage Editor starts with a blank Web page created, which is the only thing you need to get started with this example. You can also explicitly create a new page by clicking the New button on the toolbar or by selecting New from the File menu.

Adding Text

You may notice that the FrontPage Editor's workspace has a flashing cursor, much like you would see in a word processor. Creating text for a Web page is as simple as typing in the workspace. Go ahead and try typing something and see how it looks. Figure 32.4 shows some text typed directly into the FrontPage Editor workspace.

FIGURE 32.4.

Text typed directly into the FrontPage Editor workspace.

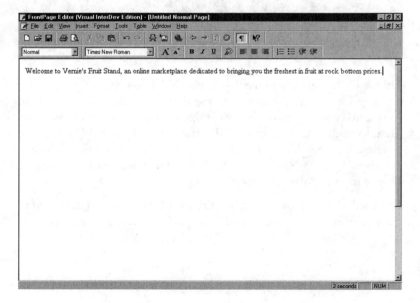

If you insert your cursor below the text, you may notice that the FrontPage Editor automatically terminates the text as a paragraph and starts a new one. Paragraphs, which are delimited by carriage returns, are significant in FrontPage just as they are in HTML, because they are often used as the basis for altering text properties and applying styles such as bold and italic. Try altering the style of the paragraph text you just typed by highlighting the text and clicking the Increase Text Size button on the toolbar. This button is located on the text-formatting toolbar immediately to the right of the Change Font edit box. Also try italicizing the text by clicking the Italic button, which is located a few buttons down from the Increase Text Size button.

Sometimes it is necessary to alter the indentation of text in a Web page. This is easily accomplished with the Decrease Indent and Increase Indent buttons, which are located on the far-right end of the text-formatting toolbar. The text you've entered thus far defaulted to having no indentation. Try increasing its indentation by clicking the Increase Indent button twice. Figure 32.5 shows the Web page with the formatted text.

FIGURE 32.5.

The formatted text in the FrontPage Editor workspace.

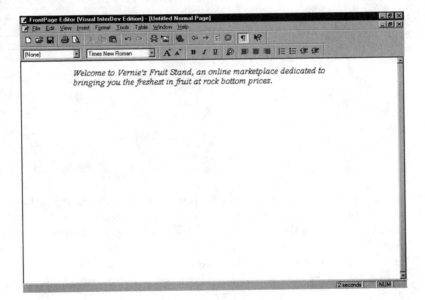

Setting Page Properties

You've learned how the toolbars in the FrontPage Editor can make the editing of text in Web pages very easy and intuitive. The toolbars are nice, but they don't tell the whole story in terms of the FrontPage interface. Another way to really speed productivity in the FrontPage Editor is to use the right mouse button. When you click the right mouse button in the FrontPage Editor, it displays a pop-up menu containing commands based on what part of the Web page the mouse pointer happens to be over. Try clicking the right mouse button while the mouse pointer is anywhere on the Web page.

One of the commands you see is the Page Properties command, which allows you to edit the properties of the current Web page. These properties include the page's title, background image or color, background sound, and margin information, among other things. The page's title is especially important because it is displayed in the title bar of a browser when the page is viewed. Go ahead and select the Page Properties command to view the properties for your page. Figure 32.6 shows the Page Properties dialog box that is displayed after selecting the Page Properties command.

NOTE

You can also access the Page Properties dialog box by selecting the Page Properties command under the File menu.

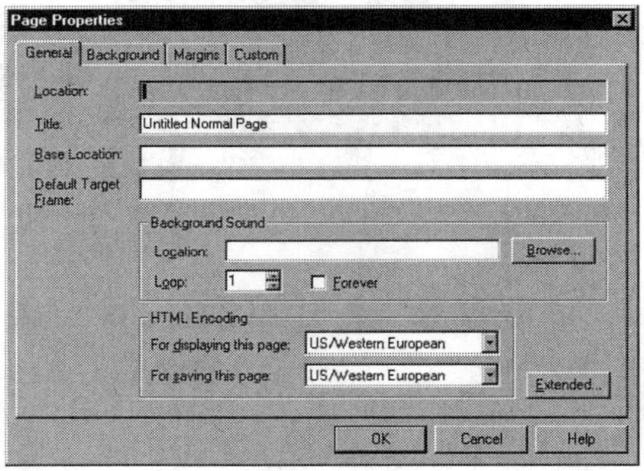

Figure 32.6.

The Page Properties dialog box is used to edit a page's properties.

Notice that the Page Properties dialog box is actually a tabbed dialog box containing different sections of page properties. The first tab, General, is used to enter general information about the page, including the title of the page and any background sound for the page, among other things. Go ahead and change the title of the page to `Vernie's Fruit Stand`, which is the text that will appear in the title bar of browsers when the page is viewed. Now click the Browse button next to the Background Sound edit box to set the background sound for the page. The background sound for a page is played whenever the page is viewed in a Web browser. You can specify how many times the sound is to be played, or that the sound should be looped indefinitely.

If you recall, a MIDI composition called `Vernie.mid` was created in Chapter 31, "Using Music Producer and Media Manager," for use in Vernie's Web site. You now need to locate this file using the Background Sound dialog box (see Figure 32.7), which is displayed after you click the Browse button. A copy of the file is located in the `Chap32` directory beneath the `Source` directory where the book's source code is installed.

FIGURE 32.7.

The Background Sound dialog box is used to specify the background sound for a page.

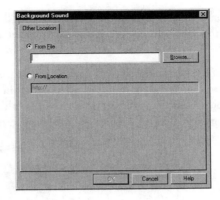

Once you've selected the `Vernie.mid` file as the background sound, you can check out some of the other tabs in the Page Properties dialog box. Go ahead and click the Background tab to set the background for the page. You have the option of setting the background to either an image or a solid color. By default, new pages are created with a white background, as you have no doubt noticed. Click the Background Image checkbox to indicate that you want to use a background image. This enables an edit box and a Browse button, which is used to locate and specify a background image. Click the Browse button to locate a background image for the page, which results in the display of the Select Background Image dialog box (see Figure 32.8). Then select the `Ivy.gif` image from the `Chap32` source directory.

FIGURE 32.8.

The Select Background Image dialog box is used to specify the background image for a page.

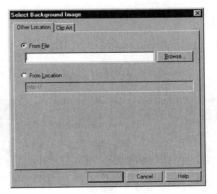

NOTE

You may have noticed in the Select Background Image dialog box that there was a Clip Art tab. This tab is used to locate and specify clip art images that come with the Microsoft Office suite of productivity tools, as well as the bonus pack that ships with FrontPage 97. Incidentally, the full FrontPage product is considered part of Microsoft Office.

You can also change the foreground text color in the Background tab of the Page Properties dialog box. For this example, just leave the text color set to white so the text contrasts well with the background. You can also set the colors of hyperlink text in this tab.

There are two other tabs in the Page Properties dialog box, Margins and Custom. The Margins tab is used to adjust the margins for the page, while the Custom tab is used to enter custom page variables. Neither of these tabs is useful for this example, so click the OK button to exit the Page Properties dialog box with the new page settings. Figure 32.9 shows the page with the new page settings.

FIGURE 32.9.

The sample Web page after editing its properties.

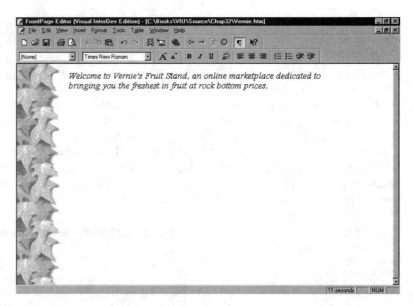

NOTE

You should save the sample Web page at some point, especially if you aren't planning on working through this chapter all at once. To save the page, just click the Save button on the toolbar or select Save from the File menu.

Adding Images and Imagemaps

I mentioned earlier in the chapter that you would use graphics that were developed in Chapter 30 using Image Composer and GIF Animator. If you recall, a title image was created in the chapter, along with a strawberry animation. You're now going to add both of these images to the Web page using the Insert Image button on the toolbar.

Let's start with the title image, `Vernie.gif`. The title image should appear at the top of the page above the text you entered earlier. So, place the cursor at the beginning of the paragraph of text and then click the Insert Image button on the toolbar. You are presented with a dialog box very similar to the one you saw when specifying the background image for the page. Browse to the `Chap32` directory under the `Source` directory and select the `Vernie.gif` image. The image is added right next to the text, which is not what you want. Simply hit the Enter key to add a carriage return after the image and separate it from the text paragraph. Then select the image by clicking it, and click the Center button on the toolbar, which centers the image on the page. Figure 32.10 shows the page with the title image added and aligned properly.

FIGURE 32.10.

The sample Web page after adding and aligning the title image.

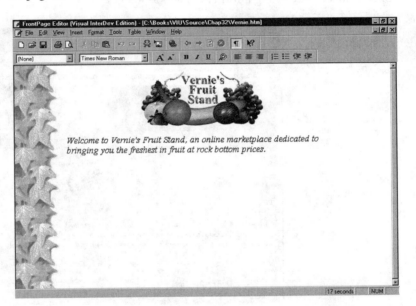

When you selected the image, you may have noticed a toolbar appear over the workspace. This is the Image toolbar, which provides quick access to the most common image manipulation commands. Because you can't actually edit images in the FrontPage Editor, "image manipulation" consists of adding and editing hotspots, as well as defining a transparent color in an image. Figure 32.11 shows the image-manipulation toolbar.

Before moving on to the strawberry image, let's add some hotspots to the title image and turn it into an imagemap. The image-manipulation toolbar makes this task painlessly easy. You're going to add hotspots for the orange and lime appearing in the title image. These hotspots will act as hyperlinks to pages on the World Wide Web providing more information about oranges and limes. Let's start with the orange; because it is circular in shape, you can use the Circle Hotspot button on the image-manipulation toolbar to create a hotspot for it. Click the Circle Hotspot button and you will notice the mouse pointer change to a pencil when you drag over the image. Draw a circle around the orange using the mouse.

FIGURE 32.11.

The FrontPage Editor's image-manipulation toolbar.

When you finish drawing the circle, a Create Hyperlink dialog box automatically appears so you can specify the page the hotspot links to. Click on the World Wide Web tab if it isn't already selected, and then type `http://www.dole5aday.com/about/citrus/citrus2.html` into the URL text box. Figure 32.12 is a Web page maintained by the Dole Food Company that contains lots of interesting information about oranges.

FIGURE 32.12.

The Dole Food Company's All About Citrus Web page.

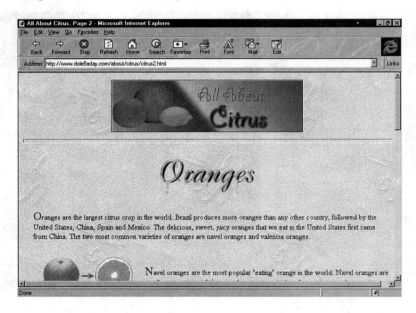

Once you've drawn the circle hotspot on the title image, you may want to position and resize it to match the orange more closely. You can position the circle by clicking and dragging it around the image. You can also resize the circle by clicking on its bounding box and dragging.

You now need to add another hotspot for the lime shown in the title image. All you have to do is follow the exact same steps you just used to add the orange hyperlink, except this time enter `http://www.dole5aday.com/about/citrus/citrusx.html` as the URL for the Web page linked to the lime hotspot. Congratulations—you just created an imagemap! Wasn't that easy?

The FrontPage Editor also supports rectangular and polygonal hotspots, and they work just like circle hotspots. Before moving on, it's worth pointing out a neat feature provided in the FrontPage Editor that deals with hotspots. I'm referring to the ability to highlight hotspots, which is very useful when you have an image that makes it difficult to see the different hotspots.

You highlight hotspots by clicking the Highlight Hotspots button on the image-manipulation toolbar. Figure 32.13 shows the example Web page with its hotspots highlighted.

FIGURE 32.13.

The sample Web page with the title image's hotspots highlighted.

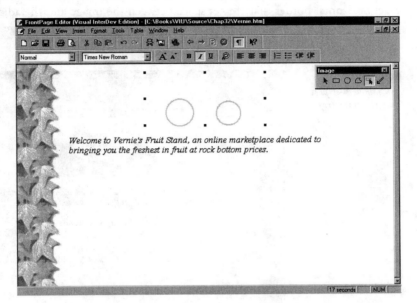

You're now ready to add the strawberry image to the page. The page is actually going to contain two copies of the strawberry image, one on each side of a text heading for the daily special. The daily special text heading is a very important heading for sales purposes and needs to catch the eye of Web users, which is why the animated strawberry image is being placed on each side of it.

To insert a strawberry image, move the cursor below the text paragraph you've already entered and click the Insert Image button on the toolbar. The strawberry image is added to the page and placed on the far-left side on top of the background image; don't worry, you'll move the strawberry over in a moment. Now type the text Today's Specials, and enlarge the font for the text twice using the Increase Text Size button on the toolbar. Then add one more strawberry image at the cursor location so that it appears to the right of the text. You can add the second strawberry image by copying and pasting the first image. You do this by selecting the first image, right-clicking the mouse, and selecting Copy from the pop-up menu. Then right-click the mouse just to the right of the heading text and select Paste from the pop-up menu.

Now align the strawberry images and heading text by selecting them all and clicking the Center button on the toolbar. At this point the strawberry images are jammed right next to the heading text, which doesn't look very good. This can easily be fixed by editing the properties for the images. To edit the image properties for one of the strawberry images, right-click on the image and select Image Properties from the pop-up menu. Then select the Appearance tab and set the Horizontal Spacing setting to 10 instead of 0. This gives the image an invisible, 10-pixel horizontal border that creates space between the image and the adjoining text. Repeat this process for the other strawberry image. Figure 32.14 shows the page after inserting and editing the strawberry images.

Figure 32.14.

The sample Web page with the strawberry images in place.

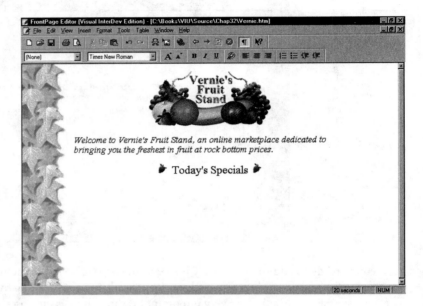

Adding a Table

Tables are popular elements in Web page development for displaying tabular information, as well as helping to coordinate the layout of other elements. You're going to add a table to the sample Web page containing a list of the daily specials and their prices. To insert a new table, position the cursor just after the heading text and strawberry images, and select Insert Table from the Table menu. The Insert Table dialog box then appears, which is shown in Figure 32.15.

This dialog box allows you to configure the table you are adding. You specify information such as the number of rows and columns in the table, along with its alignment, border size, cell spacing, and overall width. Go ahead and set the number of rows to 5 and the number of columns to 3. Then set the alignment of the table to Center, the border size to 1, the cell padding to 8, and the cell spacing to 1. Clicking the OK button creates the table and inserts it just below the heading text.

FIGURE 32.15.

The Insert Table dialog box is used to add a table to a page.

With the basic table created, you are ready to fill it with information. The first row of the table is going to be a heading for the rest of the table, which is a list of fruits and how much they cost. Enter the word `Fruit` in the upper-left cell of the table, followed by `Price per unit` and `Unit` in the next two cells in the row. Select the entire row by placing the mouse pointer just to the left of the upper-left cell in the table; the mouse pointer will turn into a horizontal arrow, which allows you to click and select the entire row of cells. Now click the Increase Text Size button in the toolbar to enlarge the cell text for the first row.

With the table heading finished, you are ready to enter information about the specific fruits on sale along with their associated prices. Figure 32.16 shows what the table should look like after entering the fruit, which gives you an idea of what you need to enter.

FIGURE 32.16.

The sample Web page with the table completed.

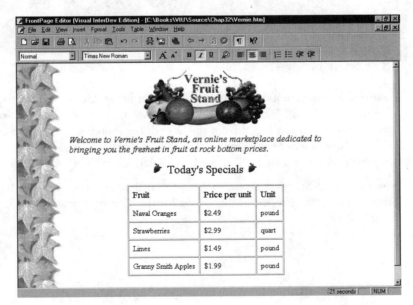

That's really all there is to creating tables. This is a pretty simple table, however; keep in mind that tables are extremely versatile. You can place anything in a table that you can place on a page, including images, imagemaps, and even other tables, to name a few things.

Using Components with the FrontPage Editor

Most really innovative Web technologies come in the form of components, which are reusable pieces of executable software that can be integrated into Web pages. The FrontPage Editor fully supports components, including Java applets, ActiveX controls, and WebBots, which are components specifically designed for use with FrontPage. In the next couple of sections, you learn how to integrate components into the example Web page using the FrontPage Editor.

WebBot Components

WebBot components are special components designed to automate common tasks required of Web sites. The FrontPage Editor comes standard with an Include component, a Search component, and a TimeStamp component. The Include component is used to include the contents of another Web page. The Search component is used to search for information on the entire Web containing the page. The TimeStamp component displays the date and time when the Web page was last modified. For this example, you're going to add a TimeStamp component so users can see when the page was last modified.

> **WARNING**
>
> WebBot components only work on Web servers that support FrontPage server extensions, so make sure your Web server supports these extensions before attempting to use WebBot components.

Before adding the component, insert your cursor below the table in the page and type the text `Last Modified on` . Make sure to include a space after the word on, because it is necessary to space the text you just typed from the WebBot component text. Then add the TimeStamp WebBot component by clicking the Insert WebBot Component button on the toolbar. You are presented with the Insert WebBot Component dialog box, which is shown in Figure 13.17.

Select the TimeStamp component from the listbox and click the OK button. You are then presented with the Properties dialog box for the TimeStamp component, which is shown in Figure 32.18.

FIGURE 32.17.

The Insert WebBot Component dialog box used to add WebBot components.

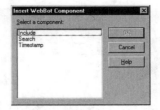

FIGURE 32.18.

The Properties dialog box for the TimeStamp WebBot component.

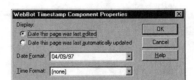

This dialog box allows you to tweak the TimeStamp component so it works just like you want it to. Practically all components have properties associated with them, which allow you to customize the components to suit your specific needs. For the purposes of this example, the default settings are fine for the TimeStamp component except for the date format, which needs to be more descriptive. Select the second date format in the drop-down list, which includes names for the day and month of the date when the page was last modified. Notice that the time format is set to none, indicating that the time isn't to be displayed. Click the OK button to accept these settings and add the component to the page.

The current date is displayed just after the text you entered so that the page's modification date reads like a complete sentence. Type a period just after the TimeStamp component to finish off the sentence effect. Because the modification date of a Web page is a minor piece of information, you want it to be relatively inconspicuous. So, select the entire line containing the text and TimeStamp component, and decrease the size twice using the Decrease Text Size button on the toolbar. Then align the entire line to the right edge of the page by clicking the Align Right button on the toolbar. Figure 32.19 shows what the page looks like after performing these steps.

The neat thing about the TimeStamp WebBot component is that it blends perfectly well with the existing text in the page; users viewing the page have no way of knowing that the date text is coming from a component. From the development side, you have the luxury of never needing to update the modification date of the page because it is automatically handled by the TimeStamp component. I would try to sell you more on the benefits of using components, but the fact that you are reading this book is a sign that you have a clue about the power of using components to add power to Web pages.

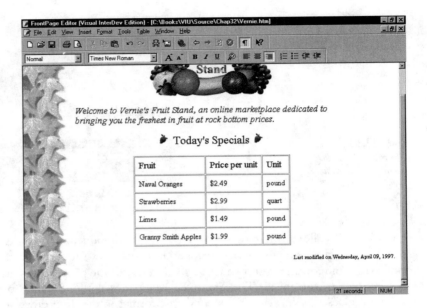

Other Components

WebBots aren't the only components you can add to Web pages using the FrontPage Editor; you can also add Java applets, ActiveX controls, plug-in components, Microsoft PowerPoint animations, Marquee components, and scripts. In this section, you add a Marquee component to the sample Web page to spice it up a little. More specifically, you use a Marquee component to scroll text across the page and catch the attention of the person viewing the page. You are actually going to insert the Marquee component in place of the text you first entered in the example. The Marquee component will automatically use the text you are inserting it over. Let's get started!

The first step in adding the Marquee component is to highlight the text you entered earlier in the example that now appears just below the title image. With the text highlighted, select Marquee from the Insert menu. This command displays the Properties dialog box for the Marquee component, which contains the text you just highlighted as the Marquee text (see Figure 32.20).

You can see that the Marquee component has quite a few properties that can be modified to make the component behave differently; you can adjust the direction the text moves, the speed of movement, and the type of movement, among other things. For the purposes of this example, you can accept the default values by clicking the OK button. This adds a Marquee component containing the text you highlighted earlier. The only problem is that the component is a little too wide and takes up too much space horizontally on the page. You need to resize the component by clicking on the right edge of its bounding box and dragging to the left.

FIGURE 32.20.

The Properties dialog box for the Marquee component.

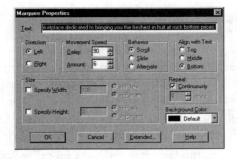

With the Marquee component added and positioned correctly, you're probably ready to see it in action. Because the FrontPage Editor is a design-time tool, you can't see (or hear) exactly how a page will look (and sound) until you view it in a real Web browser. Fortunately, the Marquee component marks the last step in this example, so you can go ahead and save the page for viewing in a browser. Just select Save from the File menu and everything will be ready to go.

All you do now is launch your favorite Web browser and open the page in it to enjoy your hard work. Figure 32.21 shows what the final page looks like in Microsoft Internet Explorer.

FIGURE 32.21.

The sample Web page being viewed in Microsoft Internet Explorer.

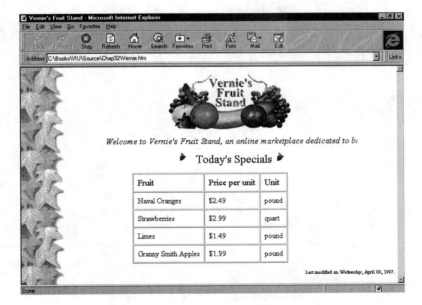

Summary

This chapter introduced you to FrontPage 97, Microsoft's graphical easy-to-use Web publishing tool. More specifically, you learned about the FrontPage Editor that comes standard with Visual InterDev. Using the FrontPage Editor, you can graphically create and edit HTML Web pages without knowing anything about HTML. The FrontPage Editor fully supports the HTML standard through its graphical interface, and also includes support for adding components such as ActiveX controls, Java applets, and WebBot components.

After covering some fundamentals about the FrontPage Editor and what it can do, this chapter moved into the development of a complete Web page that exhibits much of the functionality of the FrontPage Editor. The sample Web page you developed included formatted text, images, an imagemap, a table, a WebBot component, and a Marquee control. You also learned how to modify the properties of the page so that a background image could be displayed, along with a background MIDI sound track. Most importantly, you gained a hands-on perspective as to why the FrontPage Editor is an important companion tool to Visual InterDev.

Serving with Personal Web Server and Internet Information Server

by Glenn Fincher

IN THIS CHAPTER

CHAPTER

33

Visual InterDev provides the ability to manage Web content on any Web server from just about any vendor through its built-in FrontPage extensions. In addition to the capability of managing an existing Web site, Visual InterDev includes updated versions of Microsoft's Internet Information Server (IIS) to provide each user of Visual InterDev both the latest version of IIS and the ability to build a complete Web development environment. Whether your developers are working on Windows NT Server (NTS), Windows NT Workstation (NTW), or even Windows 95, there is an available version of IIS. Using the version appropriate for the preferred platform, a Web team can build its pieces of an intranet or Internet site on its own machine, and, only when everything is working as needed, transfer that information to the main Web server. It is also possible to use any combination of these servers to build an intranet.

NOTE

Throughout this chapter, I will use the shortcut references to Windows NT Workstation and NT Server—NTW and NTS, respectively.

IIS was first released in early 1996, and was initially only available as an add-on to NTS. Soon thereafter, Microsoft released a slimmed-down version for NTW, and finally late in 1996 released a version for Windows 95. The various flavors share most features and can be delineated primarily by excluded features. But instead of using the IIS name for all the products, Microsoft has instead decided to name each of them differently. IIS remains the name of the product for NTS, Peer Web Services is the name of the NTW product, and Personal Web Server is the Windows 95 variation. All of the servers include both Web and FTP servers, and IIS and Peer Web Service also include a Gopher service. The next release of IIS is currently referred to by its code name, "K2," and is scheduled for release in the latter part of 1997. Like its predecessors, K2 will add significant features, one of which will be integrating pieces that are available only as add-ons today such as Index Server, and Microsoft Transaction Server. K2 will support HTTP 1.1, and K2 will be an integral part of the next releases of Windows NT and Windows 95.

NOTE

To stay up-to-date on Internet Information Server (see Figure 33.1), I recommend frequent visits to this site:

`http://www.microsoft.com/iis/`

FIGURE 33.1.

The most recent details on Internet Information Server are always online.

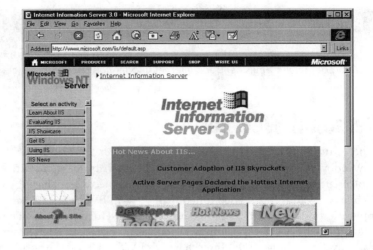

In this chapter I discuss the different flavors of available servers and their individual features and uses. Because the Windows 95 Personal Web Server (PWS) has the fewest features, I will start there and work up from this base. You may be surprised to learn that the PWS for Windows 95 is very capable of serving as a development machine, and even, if needed, as a node in a corporate intranet. The only IIS features that aren't currently supported on Windows 95 are the Index Server and the ability to assign more than one TCP/IP address to support virtual hosts as well as advanced authentication through the NTFS file system. Of course, IIS has those capabilities and more, and as expected, will run admirably as your main Internet Web server. In fact, because of its general "robustness" IIS is quickly becoming the server behind many large commercial sites on the Web. According to Netcraft, as of April 1997, Microsoft IIS became the most widely used commercial Web server, superseded only by the free Apache server for UNIX. Whether you're using PWS or IIS, you'll find a capable server to suit your purposes.

NOTE

For the latest nonbiased comparison of Web server usage, point your browser to this site:

`http://www.netcraft.com/survey/`

This chapter presents the features, installation, and configuration of each of these three servers, and their usage with Visual InterDev. Topics covered in this chapter are

- Personal Web Server
- Peer Web Services
- Internet Information Server

33

SERVING WITH PWS AND IIS

> **NOTE**
>
> Although I'll cover the most important details of IIS in this chapter, for comprehensive coverage get the Sams.net book *Internet Information Server Unleashed*.

Personal Web Server

When Microsoft released the Personal Web Server for Windows 95 in late 1996, all users of Windows 32-bit systems finally had Web servers from Microsoft. Windows 95 has a well-implemented peer network functionality that only needs web sharing to make it complete. Peer Web Services adds this needed functionality. With PWS, you can easily test most of your ASP applications without the need for a big server. A useful development environment can actually be maintained on a laptop computer, making changes to a Web site feasible even when on the road traveling. Using Visual InterDev with PWS is identical to using it with NTS. Let's look at the features of PWS to see how Microsoft has implemented this server.

> **NOTE**
>
> All examples detailed in this section use the original release of Windows 95 along with Service Pack One. Some of the details may be slightly different if you are using a later version of Windows 95, such as the release referred to as OSR2.

Features

The basic features of PWS are as you may expect. They include a complete Web Server for HTTP access, as well as an FTP server. A Gopher server is not included, which reflects the relative obscurity of Gopher services in the late 1990s. The Web server can handle the load of a typical intranet node, or as a development server in a typical Web team. The server can be configured to start automatically with the Windows 95 startup so that it is always available, or as a stand-alone server that you only start up when needed. Most administration of the server is handled exclusively through the Internet Services Administrator Web interface (see Figure 33.2), which I detail a little later in the section about the configuration of PWS. As you can see in Figure 33.2, you can configure each major section of PWS using the Web access.

> **TIP**
>
> You can access the Internet Services Administrator either from the PWS icon on the Windows 95 taskbar or from the Administration tab of the Personal Web Server applet in the Control Panel.

FIGURE 33.2.

Configuration of the Personal Web Server for Windows 95 is handled using the Internet Services Administrator.

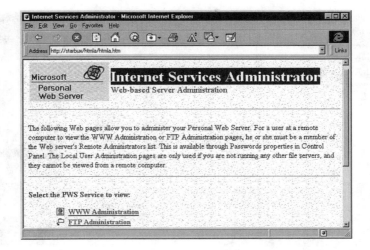

The FTP server that is part of PWS lets you create an FTP site to enable you to share files with people that aren't able to connect through the Peer Web features of Windows 95. Users of your FTP site will be able to send and receive files from your FTP service in the same way that you may already do from sites like `ftp.microsoft.com`. The FTP server is managed using the same Web interface as the Web server.

Another feature of adding PWS to a Windows 95 system is that PWS extends the Peer Networking functions in a significant manner. One of the key features of Windows 95 is the ease with which you can share resources on your machine over the net with other users of your workgroup or even the entire Internet if you wanted to do that! Sharing a folder is as easy as right clicking on the folder you want to share and selecting Sharing… from the Context menu (see Figure 33.3). After you install PWS, the resulting dialog looks like that in Figure 33.4; adding the Web Sharing… selection to the existing dialog.

> **TIP**
>
> Remember that the dialogs in your version of Windows 95 won't look like these examples until you install Peer Web Services.

An interesting fact is that when Microsoft introduced PWS for Windows NT, it didn't add the same Web Sharing button to the Properties dialog. Perhaps it will do so in a future version for Windows NT.

FIGURE 33.3.
When you want to share a folder with other computers, it's as easy as accessing the context menu of the folder.

FIGURE 33.4.
Peer Web Services adds a Web Sharing... button to the folder Properties dialog.

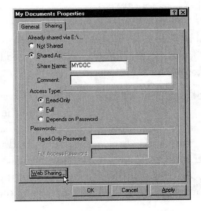

Installation

To fully enable Visual InterDev, each piece should be installed in a certain order. This order is the same whether you are using Windows 95, NTW, or NTS, and will assure that everything works correctly, as each piece depends on the previous section being loaded. The recommended load order is as follows:

1. Install Web Server
2. Install Active Server Pages
3. Install FrontPage Extensions
4. Install Visual InterDev Client

Because loading Active Server Pages and the FrontPage extensions is virtually identical on all of the servers, I won't go into great detail about the installation. The respective setup programs are well implemented and self-explanatory. Instead, I will only mention differences you may notice when you install these components. Also, we won't go through installing Visual InterDev either because you probably did that before you reached this section of the book.

Following our previous list, let's look now at installing the Web server for Windows 95. As you see in Figure 33.5, loading Personal Web Server for Windows 95 is the first option under server components on the Visual InterDev setup dialog. When you select this option, the Web Server executable files will be installed into the `\Program Files\Webserver` folder—the default location. The installation will also create your default Web server root folder in `\Webshare\wwwroot` and the FTP server root at `\Webshare\ftproot`. At the conclusion of the installation, you will be prompted to restart Windows (see Figure 33.6).

FIGURE 33.5.

Load Personal Web Server for Windows 95 from the Visual InterDev setup dialog.

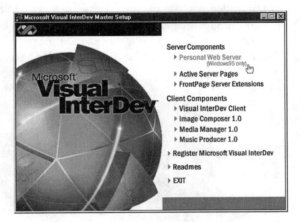

33

SERVING WITH PWS AND IIS

TIP

When installing any component of Visual InterDev, when it is suggested that a reboot is required to continue, do as suggested. Many times the installation needs to change or configure an existing setting in the system Registry, and it cannot be completed without rebooting. You may save yourself a great deal of trouble later by following this simple tip!

FIGURE 33.6.
After installing PWS,
you are prompted to
reboot to complete
installation.

If you want to configure any default portion of the installation, you should do so before you load ASP files, but I'll use the default settings for the sake of this discussion. And except for prompts reflecting the different platforms you are loading on, ASP setup is identical for all of the servers from Microsoft. The setup program includes generic files for each operating system, and automatically loads the appropriate set.

You can use the Visual InterDev setup program to load ASP, as you might have noticed in Figure 33.5. You could also load the files without having to use the dialog by running the x:\Server\Asf\setup.exe file directly (where x: represents the drive letter of your CD-ROM drive). Either way, when you run the setup program you will first see a dialog asking whether you accept the license agreement, and then a dialog similar to the one in Figure 33.7. Choosing OK will allow you to select which options you want to install (see Figure 33.8). I suggest you install all the files so that you will have sample ASP files available within Visual InterDev later.

FIGURE 33.7.
Installing ASP is the
next step on our quest
for a Visual InterDev
development machine.

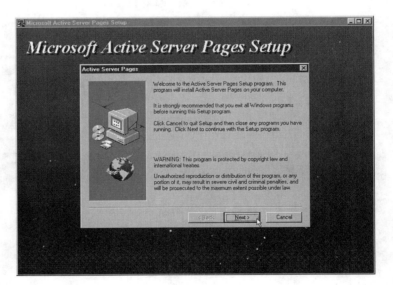

FIGURE 33.8.
Choose the option(s) you want to install and click Next.

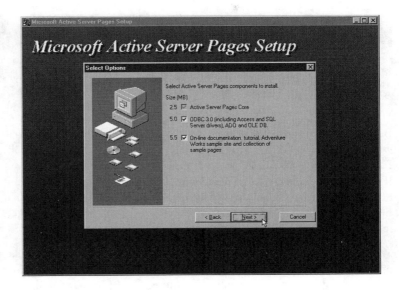

When setup is complete, you are reminded that a shortcut to the ASP Roadmap was placed in your Start menu for easy access (see Figure 33.9). On Windows 95, this ASP shortcut and an Uninstall option will be the only items in this menu, while on NTW and NTS, these are additions to the other icons.

FIGURE 33.9.
A shortcut to the ASP Roadmap is added to your Start menu.

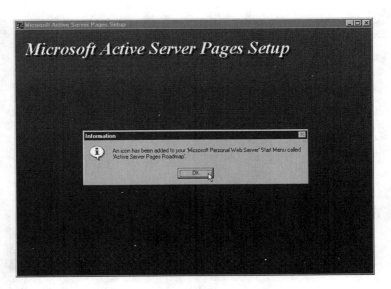

33

SERVING WITH
PWS AND IIS

> **TIP**
>
> Although installing ASP doesn't require rebooting the computer, I've found that on some Windows 95 machines the Personal Web Server won't reload automatically after the installation. Rebooting the computer restores the server and enables ASP.

Because you've already seen how to load Visual InterDev itself, the final component that you will need to install is the FrontPage server extensions. You can install this from the Visual InterDev setup or, like ASP, directly from the CD-ROM by running x:\Server\Fp\setup.exe. If you already have the full FrontPage 97 product installed, you should still load the server extensions, as the version that ships with Visual InterDev is newer than those shipped with FrontPage 97. You should also install these if you have an older version of either FrontPage or just the extensions.

When you begin to load the server extensions, you'll see a dialog similar to the one in Figure 33.10. If your server is running, setup will have to stop it before proceeding; at the end of setup it will be restarted. You will be prompted for the installation directory as in Figure 33.11. Setup of the extensions is identical on each platform with the only real difference being that setup will list only the appropriate server for the platform (see Figure 33.12). As you can see in this example, setup located the Personal Web Server; on NTW it would be Peer Web Services, and on NTS it would read Internet Information Server.

FIGURE 33.10.

Starting to load the FrontPage extensions.

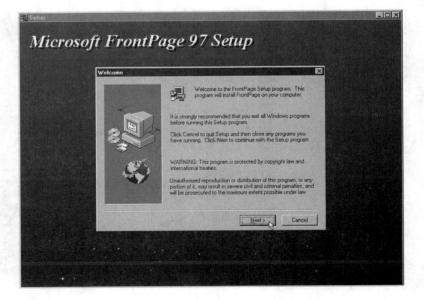

FIGURE 33.11.
This dialog details the location of the extensions.

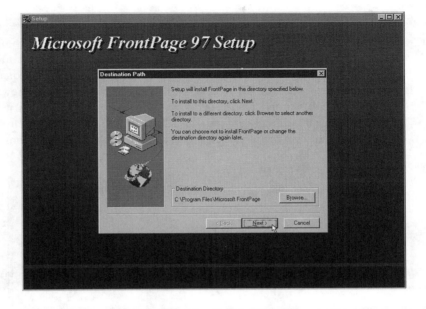

FIGURE 33.12.
Setup will detect the currently running Web server.

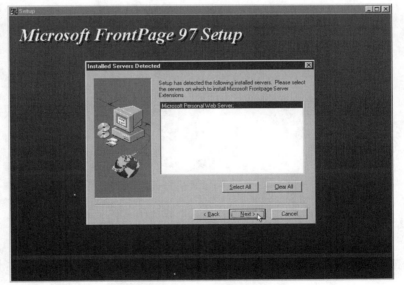

33

SERVING WITH
PWS AND IIS

After the installation, once again, reboot the computer for best results. Once you've done this, you're ready to load Visual InterDev itself. I won't cover that here because you've very likely already done it.

Configuration

If you want to change the locations of the root directories for the Web or FTP servers, the default document, or most other properties of the PWS, you'll use the Internet Services Administrator you saw earlier in Figure 33.2. Double-clicking on the Personal Web Server icon in Control Panel opens the Personal Web Server Properties dialog, as shown in Figure 33.13. The More Details button loads the included online documentation for PWS. Each of the tabs in this dialog exposes more configurations. Note that on the Startup tab (see Figure 33.14) you can start and stop the service as well as determine two startup options. Both of these options are enabled by default.

FIGURE 33.13.

The Personal Web Server Properties dialog is used to configure the services.

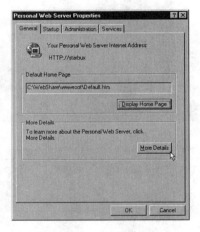

FIGURE 33.14.

Use the Startup tab of the Pesonal Web Server Properties dialog to change startup parameters.

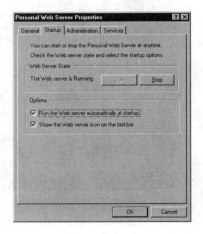

The Administration tab (see Figure 33.15) runs the Web-based administration tool—the Internet Services Administrator. And the Services tab allows you to change some of the default properties of the two services (see Figure 33.16). When you select either of the Change... buttons on the Service Properties dialog, the Internet Services Administrator will be located on the correct page to change either the default root Web folder or the default document. For example, if you have decided to use an ASP file for your default document, you would change the default document to `default.asp`.

FIGURE 33.15.

The Administration tab is used to invoke the Internet Services Administrator.

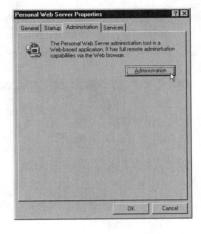

FIGURE 33.16.

The Services tab enables you to change additional properties of the Web and FTP services.

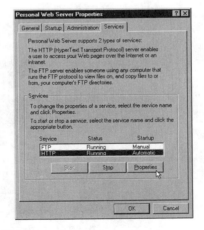

As you can see, basic configuration of PWS is straightforward and simple. Whether you need to add a directory for sharing, or change the logging frequency, it is all done using the Internet Services Administrator. Also remember that because you can administer your server from any Web browser, remote administration is a breeze! On the road and need to make a few changes? Just log in to your ISP, connect to your site via the Web, and make any necessary changes.

Access Control

Because Windows 95 only supports the FAT file system, it doesn't inherit any significant security features from the file system like NTW and NTS do. Access control is straightforward, and is implemented using the Local User Administration section of the Internet Services Administrator (see Figure 33.17). Note that in this example, we already have one user listed—the user SAMS. Clicking the New User… button allows you to add new users (see Figure 33.18). Note that each user must be added separately. You can also define groups; you use the Groups tab (see Figure 33.19) to add a group (see Figure 33.20).

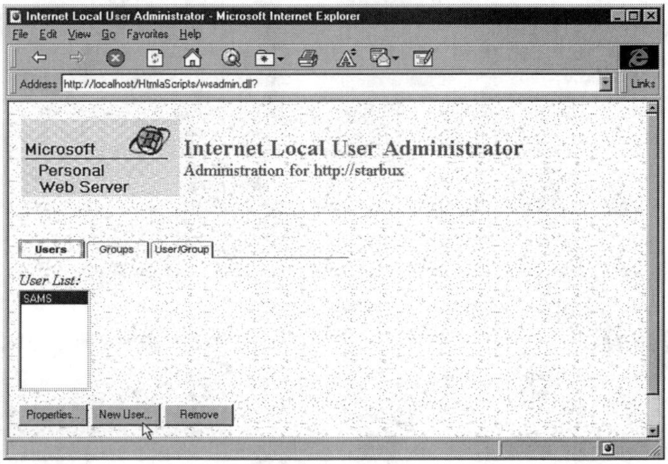

FIGURE 33.17.

Basic authentication is configured using the Local User Administration section of the Internet Services Administrator.

FIGURE 33.18.

Adding users is done with the New User page.

FIGURE 33.19.

You can also create groups of users.

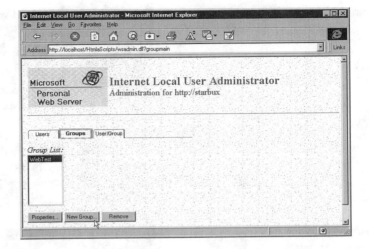

FIGURE 33.20.

Creating a new group is as easy as typing in a name and clicking Add.

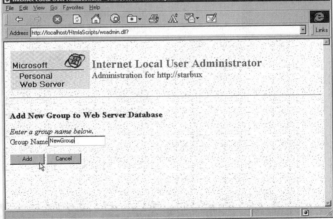

Once you have users defined, you can restrict access to individual shares using the Properties dialog for the folder you want to protect (see Figure 33.21). Adding authorized users is as easy as clicking Add… and then choosing which users or group you want to give access to (see Figure 33.22).

Figure 33.21.

To add authentication to a shared folder you use the Properties dialog.

Figure 33.22.

Choose which users you want to add to the access list for the folder.

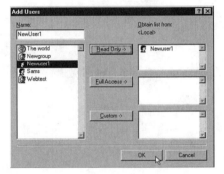

Figure 33.23 shows a new user added to the access list for the share. When users attempt to connect to a protected share, they are required to enter a login and password (see Figure 33.24) before being allowed to enter the folder.

TIP

If the Windows 95 machine is part of an NT domain, you will be able to assign domain accounts for access. This is much more secure than the simple basic authentication using local user access. In addition, you leverage the existing user list instead of being required to manage separate users.

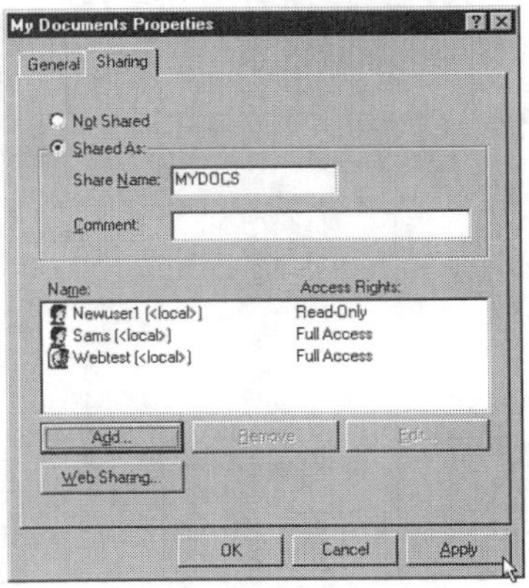

FIGURE 33.23.
The folder Properties dialog shows the current access list for the shared folder.

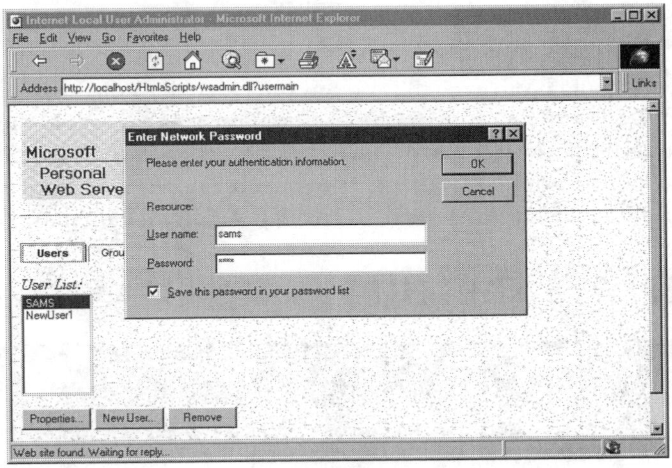

FIGURE 33.24.
A folder protected through basic authentication will require a login and password to access.

Logging

Simple logging is available for PWS through the Logging tab in the Internet Services Administrator (see Figure 33.25). You can determine the frequency that new logs are created or the maximum size for each log file. PWS's logging uses the standard NCSA format, which lists the requesting IP address, current date and time, access method, and resource requested in a straight ASCII text file. By default, this log file will be located in the \Windows folder and will be named Inxxxxx.log, where xxxxxx is the current date based on whether logging is enabled for daily, weekly, or monthly. Thus, a monthly log created on the first day of April 1997 would be named IN9704.LOG. If you want to track access statistics, you'll have to use one of the statistics packages available on the Web. Microsoft includes statistics-generating packages with IIS, but not with PWS. Look at the list in the WWW FAQ at http://www.boutell.com/faq/ for a start.

FIGURE 33.25.

You can configure your log preferences within the Internet Services Administrator.

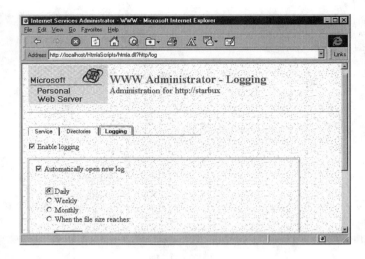

As you should be able to tell from this brief foray into the Personal Web Server for Windows 95, PWS is actually quite capable. You can use it as you would the version for Windows NT, and except for the fact that Microsoft didn't design it to run on the Internet, it would do fine for a lightly used site. We didn't discuss setting up the FTP service, but it is straightforward as well, and should present no real problems. Instead, let's look at the Peer Web Services for NTW.

Peer Web Services

> **NOTE**
>
> To differentiate between the Personal Web Server (PWS) and Peer Web Services for NT, I will use *PWS-NT* to refer to the services for NTW.

Peer Web Services for NTW (PWS-NT) were released to fill the gap created by the availability of IIS for NTS. Users of NTW needed a Web server as well, and though there were (and are) good NT-based servers from O'Reilly, Netscape, Process Software, and others, Microsoft wanted to be the provider for this important feature. Microsoft had actually already delivered an NT-based Web server as part of the NT Resource Kit for NT 3.51. This server, HTTPS, was a freeware server created by the European Microsoft Windows Academic Consortium (EMWAC) as part of the Internet Toolchest, at `http://emwac.ed.ac.uk/html/toolchst.htm`. In fact, a commercial version of HTTPS was the foundation for the successful Purveyor server from Process Software. HTTPS in itself is a basic but robust Web server.

Microsoft intends that you use PWS-NT as a development server or as a node in a small intranet even though it is very capable for more than that. As part of the End User License Agreement for Windows NT Workstation, Microsoft states that if you intend to use any features of the software as a server, you must limit inbound connections to a total of 10 simultaneous connections. This means that it is not legally acceptable to use Peer Web Services as an intranet server unless you can guarantee that the license won't be violated. Because Microsoft does not provide any metering or quota tools, it is virtually impossible to assure that you are obeying this license. Thus, it is our recommendation that you use Peer Web Services only as a development machine for use with Visual InterDev, unless you are part of a very small workgroup and therefore wouldn't break your agreement. Those comments aside, let's look at this otherwise very capable server.

> **NOTE**
>
> The examples detailed in this and the final section assume that you are using Windows NT Workstation 4.0 or Windows NT Server 4.0. When a Service Pack is mentioned as required, understand that either that service pack or one greater is sufficient to meet the requirement.

Features

PWS-NT provides most of the features you'd expect from a server product for Windows NT. It includes a Web server, an FTP server, and a Gopher server. Though Gopher is a quickly disappearing service, there may still be sites using Gopher services that could easily move the information already in Gopher to NT with little problem. With the 3.0 release of PWS-NT, Microsoft added ASP and Index Server 1.1. Any and all tools developed for IIS will run without change on PWS-NT, making it the ideal development environment for an IIS intranet or Internet site. Coupled with Visual InterDev, PWS-NT is an excellent choice for your development needs. Because of the robust NT operating system and support of the advanced NTFS file system, it is probably the best choice for development for all of your team.

Installation

Installation of PWS-NT follows the paradigm Microsoft set up for installing any network-related service or utility. In fact, installation is identical for IIS on NTS as well. To install the service, double click the Network icon in the Control Panel, as shown in Figure 33.26, to open the Network properties dialog. Click on the Services tab to access the dialog shown in Figure 33.27. All the currently installed services are shown in this dialog.

FIGURE 33.26.

Double-click the Network icon in the Control Panel to bring up the Network dialog.

FIGURE 33.27.

The Services tab of the Network properties dialog lists all the currently installed services.

To add services, click on the Add… button and select Microsoft Peer Web Services from the Select Network Service dialog, as shown in Figure 33.28. When you select the service and click OK, you will be shown the list in Figure 33.29 so you can choose the components you want to install. As you can see, I've chosen not to install the Gopher service for this example.

After you make your choices, you will be shown a dialog to allow you to change the location of the default Publishing directories. These directories will be the root directory of each of the services that you will be running (see Figure 33.30), so if you need to change the location, now is the time to do so. The services you selected will be installed according to your choices, and when complete, you will see a dialog similar to the one in Figure 33.31. After installation, clicking OK on the Network properties dialog will complete the installation of the service and prompt you to restart NT. After the reboot, you will be able to configure each of the services, as you need.

FIGURE 33.28.

Select the service you want to use from the Select Network Services dialog.

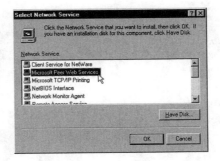

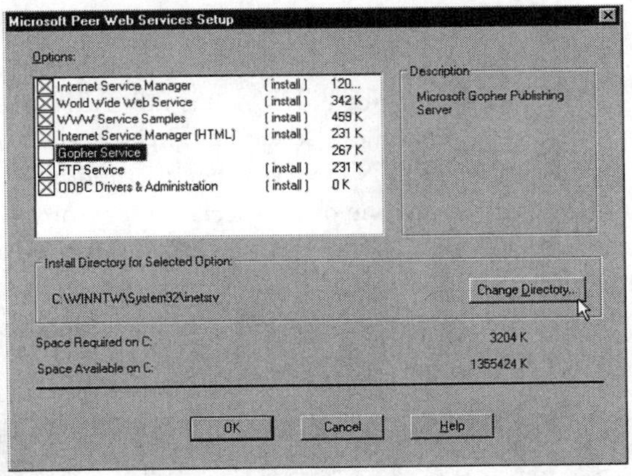

FIGURE 33.29.

Choose the components that you want to load from the Services dialog.

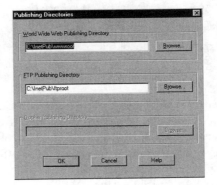

FIGURE 33.30.

You can choose the default directory for each service you install.

33

SERVING WITH
PWS AND IIS

FIGURE 33.31.

When the service installation is complete, you will see this dialog.

Although you now have PWS-NT installed, you aren't finished with the installation. The version of PWS-NT that ships with NTW 4.0 is 2.0. ASP requires 3.0 to run, so you will first need to load the newer version of the server. This is easily accomplished by installing Service Pack Two for Windows NT. NT Service Packs contain bug fixes and enhancements to the product, and are available online or by special order from Microsoft. You also may receive a new computer with a Service Pack already installed. Service Packs are inclusive and include the components of any previous Service Pack. Sometimes Service Packs themselves have bugs, and Microsoft releases "Post-SP" fixes for these specific bugs as they are discovered. These files are available online as well.

TIP

You'll always find the most recent Service Pack (for all supported languages) at

`http://ftp.microsoft.com/bussys/winnt/winnt-public/fixes/`

You can also contact your local Microsoft office to order the currently available Service Pack on CD-ROM.

If you are fortunate enough to get the Service Pack on CD-ROM, you can load any single component from the Web interface as seen in the example from Service Pack Two shown in Figure 33.32. As you can see from the figure, the 3.0 version of IIS is a prominent feature of this service release. You will be able to load the update to 3.0, ASP, and the 1.1 version of Index Server. If you were installing on NTS, you could also load the complete version of FrontPage 97 to update FrontPage 1.1 that shipped with NTS 4.0.

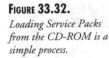

FIGURE 33.32.
Loading Service Packs from the CD-ROM is a simple process.

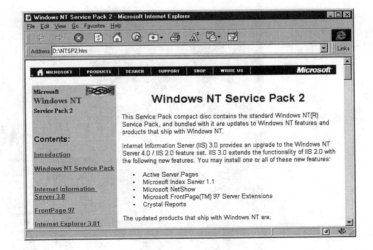

After installing a Service Pack, the system will reboot, and in addition to the bug fixes, your PWS-NT will be updated to the 3.0 version. As you did with PWS for Windows 95, you will also want to install ASP and the FrontPage server extensions. It is a good idea to install the version of these components that are on the Visual InterDev CD-ROM to assure that you are using the same version that others in your group use, as well as those tested with Visual InterDev. If a later version of these components is released as part of an NT Service Pack or an updated version of Visual InterDev, you can load that update at that time. Because I already showed you how to install ASP and FrontPage server extensions, I won't detail that here. Instead, let's look at the configuration options available to you in PWS-NT.

Configuration

Configuring PWS-NT (or IIS for that matter) is done using the Internet Service Manager accessible from the Start Menu | Programs | Peer Web Services menu (see Figure 33.33). Of course, this selection will be slightly different on NTS—the selection will be in the Internet Information Server menu instead. Unlike PWS, PWS-NT and IIS's administration tools also enable you to connect to and administer any server that it locates and for which you have administration rights. This loads the Internet Service Manager, as shown in Figure 33.34. If you select Properties | Find all Servers, the Service Manager will attempt to locate all running servers, which may surprise you if it generates a list like that in Figure 33.35. This is the dialog you will use to configure all server functions.

33

SERVING WITH PWS AND IIS

FIGURE 33.33.

Selecting the Internet Service Manager from the Start menu.

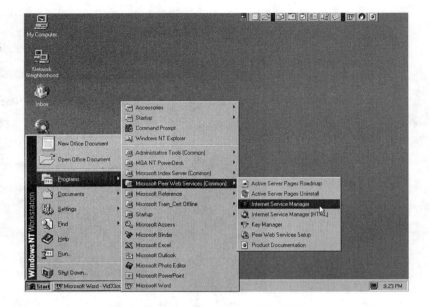

FIGURE 33.34.

The Internet Service Manager is the center for any configuration needs.

FIGURE 33.35.

You can locate all currently running servers with the Internet Service Manager.

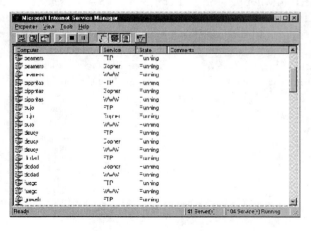

To view or change the properties for any of the services, you simply right-click with the mouse to open the Service Properties dialog for the service (see Figure 33.36). The Service tab allows you to change base features for your server such as the port number the service runs under (the default HTTP port is 80) and the kind of authentication you want to allow. The Directory tab allows you to view, change, or add new directories for Web access (see Figures 33.37 and 33.38).

FIGURE 33.36.

The WWW Service Properties dialog allows you to configure any section of your Web site.

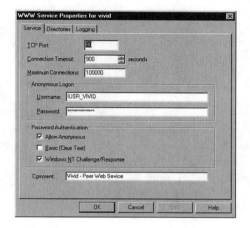

You might notice that a section of this dialog is grayed out. The section for defining a Virtual server is available only on NTS. This is one of the main differentiating features between PWS-NT and IIS, and it allows you to create any number of servers running off the same NTS machine. NT allows you to assign up to 255 dedicated IP addresses to a single Network Interface Card, and IIS allows you to assign unique content to any of those addresses. This is how some of the large ISPs offer virtual server space on their sites. Finally, the Logging tab (see Figure 33.39) allows you to change logging parameters, choose the format of the ASCII logs, or choose to store the logs in a dedicated SQL database.

FIGURE 33.37.

The Directories tab lists all currently defined directory resources.

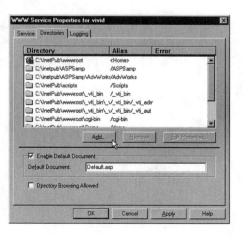

Figure 33.38.
Add a new directory for access using the Directory Properties dialog.

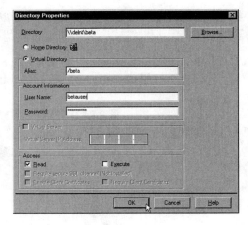

Another feature that you might notice in Figure 33.38 is that PWS-NT and IIS have the capability to share any valid UNC shared resource as a Web resource as long as you enter a valid user's credentials to the resource. So, if you want to provide access to a central file share through the Web, you simply enter the login information for the share in the Directory Properties dialog along with the name and alias for the Web.

Figure 33.39.
The Logging dialog is used for all logging configurations.

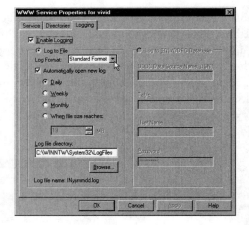

> **TIP**
>
> If you are running on an NT Domain, you will need to use a correct domain user login in the User Name field in the form:
>
> ```
> User Name: <domain name>\<user name>
> Password: <Password for user name>
> ```

Access Control

Access control with PWS-NT and IIS is detailed thoroughly in Chapter 26, "Securing the Web," so I won't go into as much detail here. Access control with these servers leverages the already existing NT access control. You manage Web users in the same manner as you manage any other user—using the NT User Manager or User Manager for Domains on NTS. Figure 33.40 shows the User Manager with a special WebUser added for secure access. Because NT provides the NTFS file system, any security that you can apply to the file system can be used for Web authentication. Once you have users and/or groups assigned in User Manager, you can control access to files and folders by either setting access permissions in the Windows NT File System (NTFS) or using access permissions in the Internet Service Manager.

FIGURE 33.40.

The User Manager with a special WebUser *added for secure access.*

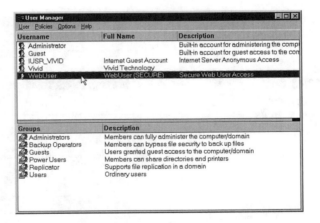

Accessing the property dialog (see Figure 33.41) of a share that you want to restrict, you assign access just as you would any other resource. Figures 33.42–33.44 step you through the process. Note that if you define access to a specific user or set of users, users will be required to enter the correct username and password to access the information as you saw earlier in Figure 33.24.

FIGURE 33.41.

Assigning access Permissions is done using the Properties dialog of any shared resource.

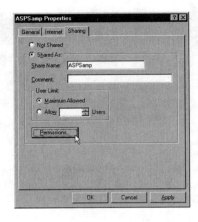

FIGURE 33.42.

Add a user or users through the Access Through Share Permissions dialog.

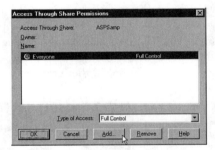

FIGURE 33.43.

After adding a user, click OK to register the change.

FIGURE 33.44.

The user's access information is now added to require authentication.

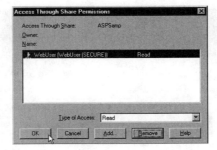

All the same configuration settings are available through the Web interface as well. This makes it even easier to manage a Web site. You can connect with any browser to service the Web site. Figure 33.45 shows the Web version of the Internet Service Manager.

FIGURE 33.45.

The Web version of the Internet Service Manager allows you to configure the server through any Web browser.

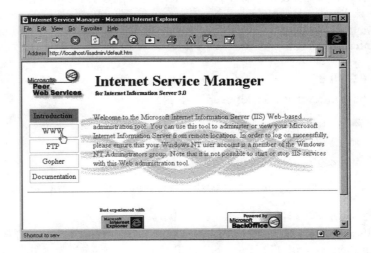

Logging

The final section I will mention is access logging. As you might expect, logging is identical to that offered for PWS. You have your choice of either NCSA's or Microsoft's standard format. Only IIS allows logging to a SQL database.

TIP

To decipher the contents of your logs, look at the online documentation:

`http://localhost/iisadmin/htmldocs/07_iis.htm#2h1`

Internet Information Server

There's not a whole lot more to say about using IIS as your Web server. IIS provides only three significant additional features over PWS-NT. Although I've mentioned two of these earlier, I'll go into a little more detail in this final section. Installation and configuration is identical to loading PWS-NT, except that you can also load FrontPage 97 if you want to use it instead of the version that comes with Visual InterDev. The only reason that you might want this version is that it comes complete with templates and wizards to assist you in creating pages and if you want to manage the Web site using the FrontPage Explorer instead of the tool within Visual InterDev.

Features

The features that IIS adds over PWS-NT are

- Virtual servers
- IP address authentication
- Logging through a SQL database

Each of these is significant, but the first two are probably the most important.

Virtual Servers

IIS will support any number of virtual servers, and allow you to assign unique root directories for their content. Like any other TCP/IP service, you will have to have dedicated IP addresses assigned to each virtual address you want to serve. Then you use the same directory services dialog that you saw in Figure 33.38. With IIS, the same dialog now allows you to enter information for a virtual server (see Figure 33.46). Each unique IP address and host name that you wish to use as a virtual server needs to have its own default root directory assigned through this dialog. Once you assign this information, connections can be made to all virtual servers you've configured such as www.company1.com or www.company2.com.

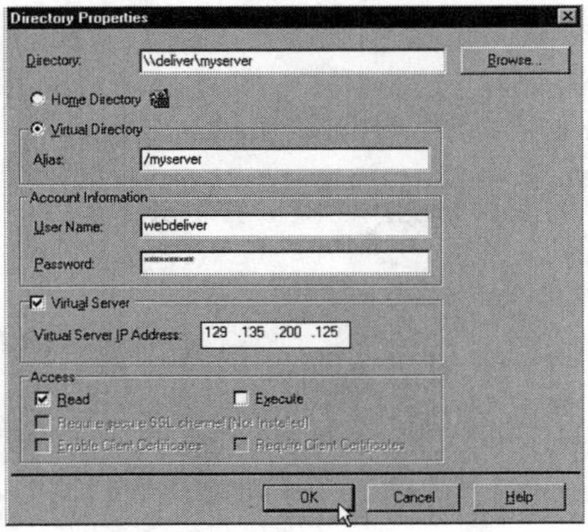

FIGURE 33.46.

IIS supports the creation of virtual servers, each with unique IP addresses.

Access Control

Additional access authentication is another feature that is added to IIS. With IIS, you can restrict access by IP addresses in addition to usernames. Using the Advanced dialog of the Internet Services Manager, you can deny access either to individual computers or to groups of computers. Figure 33.47 shows that access has been denied for a whole group of computers and for a single computer. This access restriction is applied to the entire Web, not to specific directories. If you want to only assign per-directory access restrictions, you will have to use user and group access.

FIGURE 33.47.

You can deny access to single computers or groups of users.

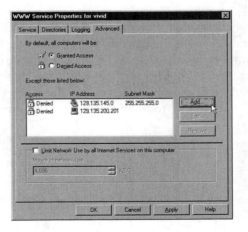

Logging

The final feature that IIS adds to PWS-NT is the ability to use a SQL database for your log files. If you use a database instead of the flat text files used with PWS and PWS-NT, you can use any valid SQL statement to query that data for detailed analysis. You could even provide live access to the data through a page generated in Visual InterDev. Figure 33.48 shows an example of setting up SQL database access logging.

FIGURE 33.48.

Access logs can be saved as SQL databases instead of flat text files.

Summary

In this chapter I have detailed the installation, configuration, and use of each of the Web server products for Microsoft operating systems. You looked at the main features and possible applications of each, as well as how to use them with Visual InterDev. Whether your Web development environment is Windows NT Server, Windows NT Workstation, or even Windows 95, you will be able to develop your site and use Visual InterDev to deploy it easily. In the next chapter you'll learn how to build database access into your site using SQL Server and Access 97.

CHAPTER 34

Web Databases with Access 97 and SQL Server

by David Silverlight

IN THIS CHAPTER

This chapter focuses on taking what you already know about database development and applying it to a web-application scenario. Not only does this chapter explain how you can apply your existing Access 97 and/or SQL Server development skill set to Visual InterDev; it also shows you how to publish your web application to the Internet.

This concept of applying preexisting database knowledge is of great importance to the many developers out there who have spent those long, lonely nights honing their database-development skills in Access, SQL Server, and other environments. It is comforting to know that you can take the skill set you so painstakingly developed and apply it to the latest tools—namely, Visual InterDev. As you might have noticed with the more recent software-development tools, the trend has been to incorporate existing skills rather than to have to throw them away and start from scratch. Visual InterDev is no exception!

Regardless of how remarkable your web application turns out to be, it does you little good if you cannot publish it to a location where it can be accessed by the world. In this chapter I will show you, step by step, how to get your web application from your local machine out to the real world.

Comparing Visual InterDev's Database-Development Tools with Access and SQL Server

Because our emphasis is on Web database development, the focal point of this comparison is on the database-centric features of Access and SQL Server, such as creating tables, queries, and stored procedures. The purpose of this comparison is to answer this burning question: "Can Visual InterDev be used in place of Access or SQL Server as my primary database-development tool?"

Visual InterDev has some capabilities that are virtually identical to those of Access and SQL Server. In fact, if your intent is to use only that subset of capabilities, you may never need to leave the Visual InterDev environment. For example, if you want to take an existing database and add a set of queries to access your data, you can accomplish that in Visual InterDev just as easily as you could in Access. On the other hand, if you are planning to create a lot of tables in an Access MDB, you will need to do that from within Access.

To see a summary of the capabilities of SQL Server and Access data sources from within Visual InterDev, see Table 34.1. The information in this table summarizes the database-development capabilities that VID offers you—the capabilities that you will have correspond to your data source type. As the table indicates, if your data source is SQL Server 6.5, you will be able to create tables and database diagrams, whereas Access data sources enable you to create only query objects. Similar restrictions apply to Oracle. To see a more detailed table, you can refer to the Visual InterDev help under the section "Inserting database items."

Table 34.1. Environment-dependent database-development capabilities.

Database Item	SQL Server 6.5	Access 97
Table	Available	Not Available
Database Diagram	Available	Not Available
Query	Project Dependent	Project Dependent
Stored Procedure	Available	Not Available

Creating Access and SQL Server Database Objects in VID: Similarities

The hands-down, best similarity between the database objects created for SQL Server and Access is the query builder. VID's query builder can create the full range of ODBC 3.0–compliant queries. The best thing about this is that you now have a single IDE that will create your queries rather that having to use the respective products. This should really simplify your life, because you no longer need to learn the peculiarities of each program to create your queries. You can now use the same IDE for all your query-building chores. To see a complete description of the query-building capabilities, please refer to Chapter 12, "Database Management with the Visual Data Tools."

Creating Access and SQL Server Database Objects in VID: Differences

If you are using SQL Server 6.5 as your data source, you will quickly notice the point at which the database object capabilities pull ahead of Access. Not only can you build queries in SQL Server, but you can also create your own tables, database diagrams, and stored procedures. You have virtually the same control over data object creation as you do in the SQL Server Enterprise Manager! If you look at Figures 34.1 and 34.2, you will see that you can insert a much more robust selection of objects into your project in SQL Server 6.5 than in Access 97.

FIGURE 34.1.
Available SQL Server database objects.

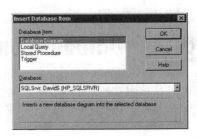

FIGURE 34.2.
Available Access database objects.

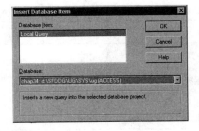

SQL Server and Access also differ in the types of queries that can be created. SQL Server and Visual InterDev will generate ODBC 3.0–compliant code, whereas Access can incorporate its own Access-specific functions.

What Is the Payoff in Using Visual InterDev?

Visual InterDev is the first development tool that enables you to do all of the following in one environment:

- Design Web pages
- Design and control webs
- Utilize easy-to-use database connectivity tools
- Create and edit database designs, including tables and queries

As noted in the prior comparison, Visual InterDev can handle various types of data object creation. Whether it can be used in place of your favorite database development tool will depend on two things. First and foremost, it depends on which database development tool you are using. Second, it depends on the types of objects that you will be creating for your web application.

Probably the best payoff is in knowing that Visual InterDev has incorporated such a robust set of database-development tools in its initial release. Because of this, we can expect that any database objects that aren't currently supported might be in the near future.

Visual InterDev has incorporated some unprecedented features under one roof to create a single developing environment for developing your web sites. Now let's look at what is involved in publishing your site on the Internet.

Publishing Your Database on the Web

If you think about the number of hours that you will invest into creating a web database application, you want to be assured that you are able to get your database published. After all, the finished product doesn't do you a whole world of good if it can only live on your local PC.

True as it is that there have been many tools for creating web pages and utilities for copying files to the Internet, only recently have there been tools designed specifically to make it easy for you to publish your finished work to the Web.

Because Visual InterDev is designed as a Web database-development tool, an integral part of its design is to enable you to relocate your site to the Web in the most elegant manner possible. You can look at this process in one of two ways, both of which are discussed in this chapter. The first way can be only described as the "If the world were a perfect place" scenario. In this scenario, everything works perfectly and, if you follow the steps outlined here, you will have your site published in minutes—easily and effortlessly. The second way is what happens when Murphy's Law kicks in at full force. We will tackle problems that you will encounter and discuss ways to avoid them.

If the World Were a Perfect Place...

In this section you are going to create a web database application from the ground up, step by step, and then publish it to the Internet. This translates to four main steps. As the section title implies, if the world were a perfect place, you could follow these steps to generate a web application:

- Step 1: Create a new local web project
- Step 2: Add database connectivity to your project
- Step 3: Add Web functionality to your project
- Step 4: Make your database accessible on the Web

> **NOTE**
>
> If you already have experience in creating a local-web database application and want to just learn how to publish to the Web, please jump ahead to step 4.

Step 1: Creating a New Web Project

In this step, you will be using the Web Project Wizard (see Figure 34.3) to create a new web project. Make sure to set the following information:

- Project Name: AdvWorks
- Location: `c:\Program Files\DevStudio\MyProjects\AdvWorks`

Now select the Create new workspace radio button and click OK.

FIGURE 34.3.

Starting off by selecting the Web Project Wizard.

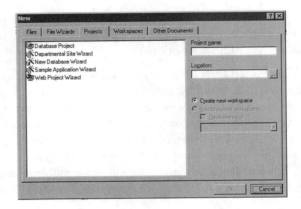

In this step, you are going to specify a web server (see Figure 34.4) for your database. At this point in the game, select the name of your virtual root web (for this example, `http://YourMachineName`) as your web server so that you can use your local machine as your server.

FIGURE 34.4.

Specifying the local web server.

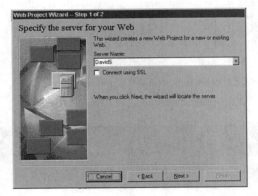

NOTE

If you are using Microsoft's Personal Web Server, the name of your virtual root web corresponds to your machine name. For example, if your computer is identified as `DavidS`, your root web will be referred to as `http://DavidS`.

This virtual root translates out to a physical directory that will house your files. By default, the directory that will correspond to your root web will be `c:\webshare\wwwroot`. The name that you specify as your new web (see Figure 34.5) will be stored in that directory.

FIGURE 34.5.

Creating the new web project.

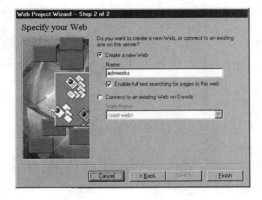

Believe it or not, your first major requirement has just been satisfied! You have a skeleton web application (see Figure 34.6), complete with a skeleton `Global.asa` file, a search page, and a subdirectory structure for your graphics.

FIGURE 34.6.

Your skeleton web application.

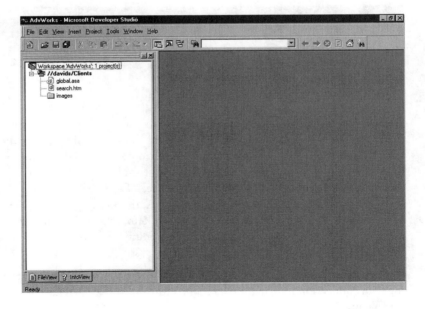

34

WEB DATABASES
WITH ACCESS 97
AND SQL SERVER

Step 2: Adding Database Connectivity to Your Project

To add a data connection to the project, click the project name (as shown in Figure 34.7) and select Add Data Connection from the menu.

FIGURE 34.7.

Selecting Add Data Connection from the menu.

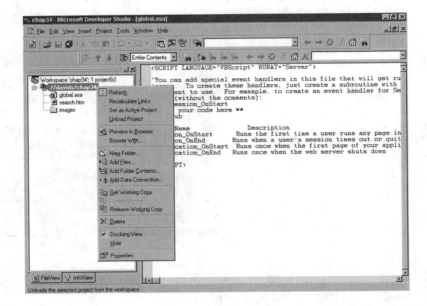

> **NOTE**
>
> For this database example, you will be using the AdvWorks sample that is included in the Active Server Pages Roadmap. If you have not yet installed Active Server Pages, you should do so now.

Because you are adding database connectivity to your workspace, you will need to indicate to Visual InterDev the name of your database and all other related information. Because Visual InterDev uses ODBC, this information needs to be contained within a DSN file. The next information it will ask you for is the Data Source Name, or DSN. To find a more detailed description of creating and distinguishing between DSNs, see the section later in this chapter, titled "DSN:What's in a Data Source Name?." At this point, your workspace consists of a Web project with database connectivity. These two items are the bare minimum that you will require for a Web database application. At this point, your workspace will appear as shown in Figure 34.8.

After you have added your database connection, you will see a confirmation screen indicating the data connection information contained in your DSN file. This file should look as you see it in Figure 34.9.

FIGURE 34.8.
Your skeleton data-enabled web application.

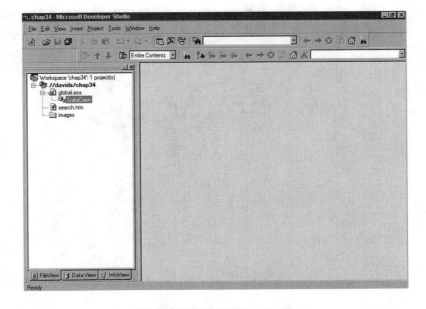

FIGURE 34.9.
Properties of your data connection.

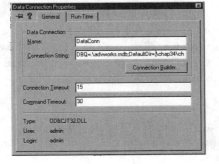

Step 3: Adding Web Functionality to Your Project

Although you have the bare-minimum requirements for a database application in your workspace, you don't have any files that will do any database processing. In this step you will change this by adding an Active Server Page to enable you to view your data.

To add files to your project, you will need to first click the FileView tab. Next, you will add the following file from your chapter subdirectory by right-clicking your web project, as shown in Figure 34.10 and adding the following Active Server Page:

```
DataDisp.asp
```

The file, DataDisp.asp, will display all the results of a query in an HTML table format.

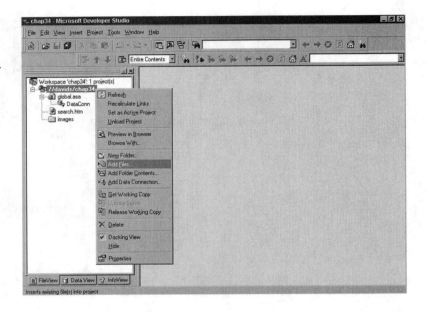

Step 4: Making Your Database Accessible on the Web

This step describes what is involved in making a data source so that it can be accessed and/or updated over the Internet. There are differences, however, depending on the type of DSN that you are using. I will cover the steps involved in using file DSNs and machine DSNs, as well as the reasons for their usage.

Using File DSNs

The advantage to using file DSNs is that you do not need to have your ISP set up a DSN entry on the server. This enables you to publish your Web database apps without the intervention of your ISP.

The disadvantage is that you must know the physical location of your database. For Access 97, you will need to know the file pathname, and for SQL Server, you will need to know the server and database name. For example, for the AdvWorks sample you would need to know that the path of the database is `C:\WebShare\wwwroot\AdvWorks\Advwork.mdb`.

> **TIP**
>
> When using file DSNs, it can simplify your testing if you have the same data directory structure as the server to which you are publishing. If you do so, you will not have to change the pathname when you publish.

Using Machine DSNs

The advantages to using machine DSNs are as follows: Once the DSN is created, you need to refer to it only by the DSN in your applications; therefore, you do not need to include any database-specific information. You can also use the same DSN in different web applications, which can simplify the coding in your VID applications. Last but not least, if anything about the database changes, such as the pathname, user ID, or password, you do not need to change your VID code; you just need to modify the DSN.

The disadvantage to using them is that you will need to set up a DSN on the server. This will usually require the intervention and cooperation of your service provider.

> **NOTE**
>
> If you are a Web developer working through an ISP, this step will show what the ISP does whenever you request that a database be published to your Web site. If you are a Webmaster, however, you will need to perform these steps in order to publish your databases.

As you will see, there is more involved here than just copying the database file to the Internet. Because this example involves the AdvWorks.mdb database, all my instructions will reference this file. I break this step down into the following substeps:

- Step 4a: Adding the database to your project
- Step 4b: Copying the database to your Web site
- Step 4c: Allowing user access to your data directory
- Step 4d: Creating the DSN for your database

If you remove the mysterious shroud of the Internet, you will find that this process is not much different than copying a database to a network for a multiuser version of your software. The two main differences are as follows:

- Because you are allowing your database to be accessed by virtually everyone, you must give permission for people to access your data without a password. Don't worry; data access can and should be maintained from within your .asp scripts.
- Because this process uses ODBC, a DSN must be used to store the information about your database.

Step 4a: Adding the Database to Your Project

This first step is not absolutely required, but it makes the process of publishing much easier. By including the database in your project, you will be able to copy the database to the Web when you publish your Web site. This can save you time by eliminating the extra step of separately copying your database using FTP or an equivalent.

Step 4b: Copying the Database to Your Web site

This step involves physically copying the database from your local server to your Web site. Fortunately, this process has been automated by the Web Copy function of VID, as shown in Figure 34.11.

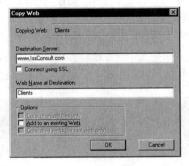

This screen will default with your local server name. You will need to supply the name of the destination server, along with the username and password, and click OK to begin the file-copy process.

As noted previosuly, when you created the sample project you selected your local virtual root, called http://DavidS, as the Web server. Following the Copy Web step, you have moved your web from your local server to your Internet server.

Step 4c: Allowing User Access to Your Data Directory

This step must be performed because in order for users to access your database, they must have the rights to access the directory that houses your database. Omitting this step is often a cause for many errors that people run into the first time they try to make a database Web accessible. Access to the database is dependent on whether your DSN points to a file-based database or a client/server database. In more detail, I can say the following:

- File-based databases: If your DSN points to a file-based database such as Access, you must ensure that the directory where the file is stored is set up as shared to any user or group that includes the IUSR_ServerName user. This is done through Windows Explorer.

- Client/Server databases: If your DSN points to a client/server database such as SQL Server or Oracle, make sure that the database specifically allows access by the user IUSR_ServerName with no password. Usually you can go ahead and give full access because your Active Server Pages will control access to your data.

As you have seen, you are making your database accessible to anyone in the world. This does not mean that you will want to give complete data access to any user who logs onto your site, however. Therefore, you will need to enforce secure access to your data through your Active Server Pages scripts.

Step 4d: Creating the DSN for Your Database

You must now create your machine DSN on the server. Using ODBC, you will be storing all the information about your data source in a DSN file. This file is set up through the ODBC icon in the Control Panel. You will need to supply all the information about the DSN in this file. You can often supply minimal information, such as the file location, user ID, and password.

Because DSNs are such an integral part of Web database applications, it is vital to have a thorough understanding of all the flavors of DSNs. Only with this knowledge can you know which one is appropriate and how to set it up properly.

DSN: What's in a Data Source Name?

Setting up a DSN is not nearly as difficult as you might think. If you know a few basic concepts, you'll find that creating DSNs is a simple process. Although there are three different flavors of DSNs with ODBC 3.0, they vary only slightly in the steps involved in creating them—primarily in how they are used. In the following sections, I define the three types of DSNs and describe the scenarios in which they should be used.

When selecting/creating a machine data source, you have the option of creating either a system data source name or a user data source name. The difference between the two is based on the rights allotted to the user who logs in to access your database.

System DSN

A *system data source name* contains information about data sources that are accessible by anyone who connects to your machine. This is appropriate for most Web sites that you will create, because you will want virtually everybody to have access to your Web site without having to enter a username/password for your server. The permissions that are set for system DSN directories are the same as those for anonymous logins.

User DSN

A *user data source name*, as the name implies, is accessible only by the user who created the data source on the server. Typically, you would create a user DSN for intranet sites where access would be limited only to privileged users. For example, let's say that you have a web database application where users may execute searches on your data. You will most likely have a maintenance site where a system administrator may insert/modify/delete records in your database. By using a user DSN, you could limit access to this maintenance site strictly to the user with a system administrator's username and password so that only the system administrator can modify your data.

File DSN

A *file data source name* works a little bit differently than either of the machine DSNs. Although it contains the same information about the data source, the contents of the file are used rather than the name of the DSN. It is sometimes referred to as a *DSN-less connection* because when you select a file DSN, the name of the DSN is not stored. Instead, all the information about the data source is stored in a Session variable named ConnectionString, where it can be accessed from anywhere within your Web application. This makes file DSNs much more portable than system or user DSNs. If anything changes about your data source, you only need to change it in the connection string instead of in a DSN on the server. File DSNs are most useful when you want to have database access, but you don't want to create a DSN on the server.

More on DSN-Less Connections

There are many arguments in favor of using DSN-less connections when defining your data connection. First, you will not need the intervention of your ISP to create your DSN on the server. This means that you can publish your Web database without requiring the assistance of your ISP. Secondly, it is more portable for you in the event that you need to relocate your Web site or database. Let say, for example, that you need to move some of your sites to a new server. If you are using machine DSNs, you will need to re-create all the DSNs as part of setting up your site. With file DSNs, you need only change the file path in your ConnectionString variable. If you maintain the same directory structure, the second step may even be avoided altogether.

Because all the information in the ConnectionString variable is obtained originally from the file DSN, it might be useful to understand the following comparison. Here, I am demonstrating what information in Advworks.mdb would be referenced if it were accessed as a file DSN.

This is the Global.Asa file:

```
On_Start subroutine
<SCRIPT LANGUAGE=VBScript RUNAT=Server>
   Sub Session_OnStart
      Session("DataConn_ConnectionString") =
         DBQ=D:\inetpub\wwwroot\sfddg\test1\ug.mdb;
         Default Dir=D:\inetpub\wwwroot\sfddg\test1;Driver=
         {Microsoft Session("ConnectionString") =
         DBQ=C:\WEBSHARE\ASPSamp\AdvWorks\AdvWorks.mdb;
         Driver={Microsoft Access Driver (*.mdb)};DriverId=25;FIL=MS
      Session("ConnectionTimeout") = 15
      Session("CommandTimeout") = 30
      Session("RuntimeUserName") = "admin"
      Session("RuntimePassword") = ""
      Session("DataConn_RuntimePassword") = ""
   End Sub
</SCRIPT>
```

This is the Advworks.DSN file:

```
Microsoft Access Driver (*.mdb)
UID=admin
UserCommitSync=Yes
Threads=3
SafeTransactions=0
PageTimeout=5
MaxScanRows=8
MaxBufferSize=512
ImplicitCommitSync=Yes
FIL=MS Access
DriverId=25
DefaultDir=C:\WEBSHARE\ASPSamp\AdvWorks
DBQ=C:\WEBSHARE\ASPSamp\AdvWorks\AdvWorks.mdb
```

When Murphy's Law Kicks In

Although you might follow the instructions in this chapter to flawless perfection, things may still go wrong. Granted, although Web developers make fewer mistakes than the rest of the human race, mistakes still occur. As Murphy's law dictates, whatever can possibly go wrong will go wrong. All that said and done, let's examine some case studies in which things should have worked, but they didn't. You will see the problems, causes, and solutions, as well as the ways that these problems could have been avoided. By examining the mistakes made by others, you can help reduce the chances of making mistakes yourself. Please note—The names have been changed to protect the ignorant.

Problem Case Studies

Here are some case studies:

Scenario 1: Acme Construction Company database-access dilemma

Problem:	In this Web database application, the Acme Construction Company has a Web site that accesses two separate data sources. The database of the first data source can be accessed without any errors. The database of the second data source, however, will generate the following error when trying to execute any queries on it: `Microsoft OLE DB Provider for ODBC Drivers error '80004005'`.
Cause:	The permissions of the database had not been set prior to copying the database to the net.
Solution:	The permissions for this second database need to allow all users to log in without a password. Using Windows Explorer, the Webmaster can set the access to the directory of the database so that it is shared by everyone and all users can access it.

How this problem could have been avoided:	It cannot be stressed enough that the directory that houses your database must allow access by all users without any password restrictions. By setting the privileges ahead of time, the Webmaster could have avoided this problem.

Scenario 2: Web server failure to locate the database specified by the ODBC DSN user for the database connection

Problem:	In this scenario, the Web application is using a file DSN. Although the database can be accessed when used on the local machine, the previously mentioned error message is generated when the database is accessed over the Internet.
Cause:	The pathname of the database on the server is different than the path of the database on the local machine.
Solution:	Instead of using hard-coded pathnames, you should use the UNC naming convention whenever referencing directories in File DSNs. This is an excellent way to assure that both machines reference the directory by the same name.
How this problem could have been avoided:	There are two methods to that can be used. First, you could use the same pathname for your local data sources as the one used by your server. Second, you could use the UNC, or Universal Naming Convention, when you reference the filename. This way, if the file location ever changes on the server, your database application will continue to work.

Bringing Your Databases Together

Up to now we have explored ways you can use either Access or SQL Server for your Web database development. In the following sections, you will learn about some of the theory behind combining the databases into a single Web database application.

When/Why to Combine Databases

In much the same way that Visual Studio enables you to work with multiple programming languages, you can incorporate multiple data sources into the same Web application. In fact, this capability has been an aspect of database development since the advent of ODBC. Because VID generates ODBC-compliant code, you can be assured that you have virtually all the capabilities afforded you by ODBC.

Although this methodology has been in use for some time, we as developers are now being forced to take advantage of it for two reasons. First and foremost, this new Web development environment is really the ideal scenario for it. If you develop serious applications on the Web, you are most likely linking separate components together under one umbrella that is transparent to the end user. Currently, you might be linking different pages, sites, discussion groups, graphics, files, and so forth together from different locations and/or different servers. Why not extend this to your data sources? Due to the nature of the Internet, you might want to also incorporate data from physically unrelated sources without having to learn the development quirks of those data sources.

Second, because technology changes so quickly, we want to take advantage of what is available today. This is especially true when it comes to accessing our data. ODBC gives us the mechanism to access existing data directly without having to first convert it. If you think back to the days prior to ODBC, you will recall that whenever you had to write an application that used existing data, you had to pray that the data was easy to convert. Even if it was, you still had to go through the painful process of writing a data conversion from the existing data to one with which you were familiar. God help you if you were off by one byte here or there; it would come back and haunt you.

Pitfalls and Limitations

Perhaps the most limiting aspect of combining different data sources is that there is no way to span data sources in the same view. As you have seen previously, you can easily create queries in which all tables originate from the same data source, but you are restricted from creating queries in which the tables exist in separate data sources.

Another way in which this limitation rears its ugly head is that you cannot access tables that were attached to an Access MDB. For example, from within Access you can attach tables from a SQL Server database and run queries that span both Access and SQL Server. When you attempt to bring this table into VID, you will no longer have access to the attached tables.

Summary

In this chapter you learned that Visual InterDev has some powerful built-in data-development tools. For basic database development, you may be able to accomplish it in VID entirely. However, there are scenarios in which you will still need to work in the Access or SQL Server IDE.

You also learned how to publish your finished web database application to the Internet, what types of DSN to use, how to create the appropriate DSN for your app, and how to publish DSN-less Web applications.

Last, but not least, you learned some of the pitfalls and finer areas to be wary of when implementing Web database access.

Understanding and Implementing the Index Server

by Keith Leavitt

As developers, we are normally concerned (and sometimes obsessed) with the technical details of the systems on which we are working. Communications protocols, network bandwidth, instruction pipelining, language syntax, caching strategies, and algorithmic efficiency all play together in a symphony of information processing, appreciable only to the developers behind the systems. It represents a world in which obscure acronyms abound, and attention to detail becomes crucial. In contrast to this world, however, the users of our products usually don't care about these minute details. In general, when it comes to information systems, users care about two things:

- Content—The information produced by the system must be relevant, accurate, and up-to-date.
- Accessibility—The information must be reasonably easy for the user to find.

From the user's standpoint, all other information becomes commentary, much to the developer's chagrin. Regarding the first point, the information produced by any system is highly dependent on the information entered in the first place (the infamous GIGO principle), and technology is very limited in its capability to circumvent this inevitability. The second point represents the area where the vast majority of recent advancements in information technologies have been applied most effectively. Paradoxically, the sheer number of these technologies (file formats, storage platforms, database management systems, and so on) has complicated the quest for a centralized repository for enterprise-wide data accessibility. This issue occurs because the most successful (a.k.a. "used") information tools are usually highly focused on accomplishing a specific set of tasks, often at the expense of standardization among systems. As a result, the information contents of a given system usually provide the daily user with high utility, but are rarely easily accessed as a component of a broader enterprise. It is this niche in the Microsoft corporate desktop/enterprise strategy that Index Server is designed to fill.

Among the BackOffice suite of servers, Index Server is probably the least promoted, which is surprising, given the utility factor of this tool. Spiders, indexing engines, and other search tools directly address one of the two factors users care about: the ability to easily access relevant information. It is no coincidence that search engine sites rank consistently among the most popular on the Web. By my own completely *un*scientific estimate, the average WWW surfer has memorized about 10 URLs, and two or three of those are search sites. Registration with the most popular search sites usually represents a first order of business for any commercial enterprise in its first venture onto the WWW.

The utility of Index Server is matched by its relative simplicity. "Zero maintenance" and "7/24 reliability" are factors touted in the Index Server white paper. From my own implementation of Index Server, I can attest to the truth of this, though most active Webmasters will want to test the server and tweak the functionality to meet their own unique requirements. Most Index Server functionality is implemented using script pages, which makes it very responsive to this sort of customization. Both the white paper and the hyperlinked Index Server guide are excellent sources of implementation data; they are posted on the Microsoft Web site at `http://www.microsoft.com/ntserver/search/docs/`.

Installation and Setup

Setting up Index Server on an existing IIS installation can be accomplished in a matter of minutes, and does not even require a reboot. Try that with SQL Server 6.5! During installation, you must specify the location for the query pages, query scripts, and the indexes themselves. First, note that all files should be installed on an NTFS formatted volume. The primary advantage of NTFS over FAT is the level of control the administrator has over the security of these files. Making content easier to find is a double-edged sword. Like any other technology, it makes life easier for the bad guys as well as the good guys. Accordingly, you will want to restrict access to any tools that provide broad access to your data.

The second issue regarding volume selection is space. As discussed in the following section, the indices will vary in size and consume a substantial percentage of your overall storage space. Note that running a query immediately following the installation of Index Server may not result in many hits because indexing is a "lazy" process initiated by the first query and accomplished in the background. It is usually out-prioritized by most other server functions. Depending on the size of the corpus (indexed documents in the web space), the filtering function may take a few hours or more to index the entire site and load the data into the master index.

> **TIP**
>
> You may have to wait a while after installation before your queries will return many hits. Loading content into the indices is a low-priority process that runs in the background; it may take a few hours to filter the whole site.

System Requirements

Depending on whose statistics you believe, the indices take up anywhere from 10 to 40 percent of the total size of the corpus. Documentation on Microsoft Technet specifies that although "...the average usage is less than 30 percent of the corpus, the peak usage of disk space can be 40 percent." Because actual storage space used will be a function of many variables (corpus size, number of documents indexed, query rate, and so on), I would stay with the conservative estimate of 40 percent. Index Server 1.1 functions on either IIS or Peer Web Services. Peer Web Services is the NT Workstation 4.0–equivalent Web service. For an NT Server 4.0 installation, you must run IIS 2.0 or better. Although the Index Server documentation specifies a minimum of 16 megabytes of RAM, those with experience running these two operating systems will tell you 24–32MB is far more realistic. In fact, the Technet documentation recommends 256MB or more for sites indexing over 500,000 documents. Query response time is a function of the number of documents being indexed and processor speed, which is, in turn, partially a function of RAM. Consequently, save yourself from learning this lesson the hard way by starting out on the conservative end, and don't scrimp on the RAM.

> **WARNING**
>
> The indices may consume up to 40% of your storage space, so include this in your functions when you are calculating how much hard drive space to order for your server!

How Does It Work?

Index Server represents a classic example of a well-designed client/server application in that most of the work goes on behind the scenes. This design shields the user, and even the web administrator, from unnecessary complexity in use and maintenance. Two basic processes are involved in the implementation and use of the Index Server: content indexing (the complex part) and content querying (the relatively simple part). The first process is performed by the server automatically and continuously after installation. It results in the formatted content index against which all queries are run. Users perform the querying process to find documents within the server corpus that conform to a broad array of user-definable parameters.

The Indexing Process

In most commercial search engines, indexing is performed continuously by a spider or crawler. This small process, or daemon, wanders the corpus (in some cases, the entire WWW) and indexes every site that will allow its entrance. Because spiders must check in before indexing a site, Webmasters can limit or even preclude this snooping with a few well-placed lines of script in their cgi-bin directories, or as meta-tags in individual HTML files on their site. The Index Server indexing process is carried out by a daemon, which implements three stages: filtering, word-breaking, and content normalization. Filtering represents the process of extracting the textual contents and attributes of each of the files in the server space. Word-breaking represents the process of formatting the continuous stream of text produced by the filtering process into discrete words, phrases, and sentences in the appropriate language. Normalizing is the final clean-up and noise word removal of the extracted data before it is stored in the content index.

The CiDaemon Process

Because Index Server runs concurrently with the IIS/PWS Web service, no method exists for an administrator to explicitly start or stop the indexing service alone. Indexing starts when, upon the first query request after installation, Index Server spawns a child content indexing process called CiDaemon. The Index Server engine gives CiDaemon a list of documents to index, which it accomplishes by identifying the appropriate dynamic link libraries to filter and parse for each file type on the list. CiDaemon consults the registration database, under the \HKEY_LOCAL_MACHINE\Software\Classes tree, for the filter DLL of each file. When the appropriate filter DLL is identified, it is applied to each document to extract text through the IFilter interface.

Once initiated, the CiDaemon process runs continually in the background, updating the index file with the textual contents and other filtering information from new and modified files in the corpus. Once the index is developed, the content indexing daemon updates it only when changes are made in the corpus. Because the daemon runs continually, its default priority is set to idle so that it does not interfere with other foreground server processes. On a busy server, a CiDaemon with idle priority may never run, resulting in stagnant (or nonexistent) content indices. Consequently, you may need to adjust the priority of CiDaemon, which is controlled by two settings: ThreadClassFilter and ThreadPriorityFilter. ThreadClassFilter specifies the priority class of the filter daemon and may be set to idle, normal, high, and real time. ThreadPriorityFilter specifies the filtering priority within each class. Bumping ThreadClassFilter from idle to normal may overcome this problem. Increasing it further to high or real time almost certainly will solve this problem, but might create other issues as the filtering portion of the indexing process starts to out-prioritize other, more basic system functions.

Filtering: The IFilter Interface

Although Index Server ships with the capability to index HTML and MS Office documents, any file format conforming to the Information Filtering or IFilter API (Application Programming Interface) standard can also be indexed within a server corpus by CiDaemon. The IFilter interface was developed for two purposes: to enable document browsing by format-independent viewers, and to permit full text searching of multiple document formats by spiders such as CiDaemon. The Index Server filtering process exploits the IFilter interface by polling documents and other files for unformatted contents, including Unicode text and properties or attributes. Textual contents are returned in *chunks*, sequential text characters with the same attribute and location within a file. This filtering process also determines the language corresponding to each chunk, and then tags it for the future application of an appropriate word-breaking dynamic link library. Examples of separate chunks in the same file include multilingual sentences, separate text boxes on a form, or separate cells in a spreadsheet.

In the process of extracting text and attributes from documents in the server corpus, the indexing process invokes four IFilter methods: IFilter::Init, IFilter::GetChunk, IFilter::GetText, and IFilter::GetValue. IFilter::Init is called to initialize a filtering session by establishing the interface to the file contents. IFilter::GetChunk positions the filter at the beginning of the next block of textual and attribute data to be extracted, and then returns a description of that chunk. IFilter::GetText retrieves text from the current chunk, and is usually called multiple times to retrieve a single chunk. IFilter::GetValue retrieves non-textual attributes from the current chunk, and it needs to be called only once per chunk.

A recent trend in information systems (at least in the area of Redmond, Washington...) has seen a move away from application-centric information and toward document-centric information. Rather than relying on a single application to manipulate proprietary file formats, Microsoft has exploited its component object model to implement more open file formats that can be viewed and edited by a variety of programs. This trend has resulted in a proliferation of compound documents, or documents that contain objects created in applications other than the container document application. One significant feature of the Index Server's filtering process is the capability to recognize and filter objects embedded in compound documents. During the chunk-extraction process, once `CiDaemon` encounters a chunk from a foreign file format, it queries the registration database for the appropriate filter `.dll`; then it parses the object with the rest of the contents of the container document. Thus, Index Server searches will return formatted text from objects linked or embedded in other file formats.

Because the `IFilter` API is an open standard, people creating original file formats can implement the `IFilter` interface standard to enable their location by the Index Server. For those who want to implement the `IFilter` interface in proprietary file formats, Microsoft has posted a complete set of `IFilter` references, including the `IFilter` SDK, at `http://www.microsoft.com/ntserver/info/indexdeveloping.htm`.

Word-Breaking

Because the filtering DLLs return an unbroken string of Unicode text characters, `CiDaemon` also has to do some text formatting to complete the indexing job on each document. Breaking strings of text into words in a particular natural language represents one of many tasks that is easy for wetware, but poses a real challenge for software. Subtle syntax and contextual variations in groups of characters constituting words occur in English and most other languages. Grammatical rules for one language do not necessarily apply in others, and multilingual documents further complicate the parsing task. Because structure and syntax vary between languages, Index Server ships with word-breaking dynamic link libraries for seven major Western languages, including English, French, German, Spanish, Italian, Dutch, and Swedish.

Normalization

To complete the indexing process, Index Server cleans up the parsed text in a process called *normalizing*. Here, *noise words*, or stop words like *a, the,* and *of,* are removed to reduce the size of the index. About half of all English text consists of approximately 100 noise words, so a relatively small list can significantly reduce the size of the index. The noise word list for each supported language may reside in the system root/system32 directory in a file named noise.enu. You can modify the noise word list to include or exclude any word you want, but I recommend not reducing it by much. Doubling the size of indices that may already consume up to 40 percent of your disk space may become hazardous to your server's health. If you still want to play with the list, each language is linked to a specific noise word list in the Registry along the following path:

```
HKEY_LOCAL_MACHINE\SYSTEM\SYSTEM\CurrentControlSet\Control\
➥ContentIndex\Language\<language>\NoiseFile
```

> **TIP**
>
> Although you can modify the content of the noise word list, think twice about reducing it by much. Excluding 100 common English words brings the size of the indices down to a mere 40% of your hard drive space!

The Indices

The final products of the CiDaemon spider are the indices. In total, three indices exist, one virtual and two persistent (stored to the hard drive). The first two are used strictly for processing purposes, and therefore are invisible to the user, who sees only the contents of the master index.

The first index is a set of *word lists*, and never is stored to the hard disk. The word lists contain data for a small number of documents. Once the word lists exceed either a predetermined size or number, they merge into a persistent *shadow index*. This step represents an intermediate step used to clear out the memory. All shadow indices are ultimately merged into the final master index, where the data is highly compressed.

In addition to a normal shadow merge, a special type of shadow merge exists called an *annealing merge*. If the system has been idle for a predetermined period of time and the number of shadow indices exceeds a predetermined number, an annealing merge is performed to consolidate all shadow indices into one. The administrator may run a master merge to merge all temporary indices into the master index. This operation becomes quite resource intensive, but speeds up subsequent queries because all the data becomes centrally located. Although merges may be performed manually, the process of creating and merging indices occurs continuously and automatically to keep the master index up to date on the latest content in the corpus.

Querying the Indices

One key distinction between natural and computer languages is objectivity versus subjectivity. Compile and run a single program on 10 different operating systems with the same input, and you will likely get the same result 10 times. Offer 10 different people the same article to read in a common language, and you'll likely get several substantially different interpretations. As effective as they are at conveying meaning between people, natural languages all have implied or interpreted elements that introduce subjectivity. This element may be wonderful (or disastrous!) for interpersonal communication, but it causes confusion for conventional computer algorithms. To address this gap between the actual and virtual worlds, Index Server supports a range of querying capabilities—from simple, single-word searches to fuzzy queries that interpret your meaning in a query.

35

UNDERSTANDING THE INDEX SERVER

The Querying Front End

The basic, context-sensitive querying capability of Index Server is as intuitive as any interface ever designed. Just type the word or phrase you want to find into the search text box, and you are off. Queries are case sensitive, and they will return hits on any files in the master index. Note, however, that punctuation marks and words contained in the noise word list (discussed previously) are ignored, and will not return any hits. If you happen to be looking for contents including standard Boolean operators (And, Or, Not) or other reserved characters (&, ¦, ^, #, @, $, (,),), you must enclose your query in quotes. More advanced querying capabilities are also available, but they require a basic familiarity with standard Boolean logical operators, and the syntax for each type of query. Index Server query syntax functions like a simplified implementation of Structured Query Language.

Figure 35.1 depicts the default screen provided for a simple content query. Three other simple query types are also available via links from this screen. Simple queries tend to either hit or miss, depending on whether the word searched for appears in a document. More advanced queries return a ranking for each hit as a function of how well the document contents matched the query. For example, Index Server query language implements a near operator, similar to the Boolean and. The near operator, however, assigns a ranking to hits of two words on the same page. The rank is proportional to the distance (in words) between the two query criteria words, with any distance greater than 50 words returning zero. Administrators can remove proximity data from the system to reduce the size of the index, but this action will eliminate the utility of the proximity operator. The syntax for this type of query is the two words separated by the word near or a tilde (~). In general, And, Or, Not, and near can be replaced by &, ¦, !, and ~, respectively.

Figure 35.1.

The user interface screen for a simple content query. The domain name has been changed to protect the innocent.

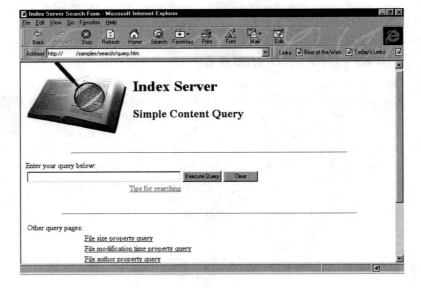

Fuzzy Queries and Linguistic Stemming

In an attempt to bridge the aforementioned gap between natural and computer languages, Index Server query language supports several *fuzzy* query techniques. The intent here is to move from rigorously objective search criteria to more forgiving subjective queries.

With fuzzy searching, Index Server queries support wildcard operators such as * and ? for searching for all instances of phrases with a particular prefix. You can also perform free-text queries by prefixing your criteria with $contents. Index Server will then locate and return documents in the corpus that have contents matching the meaning, though not necessarily the exact wording, of the query. Vector space queries provide a means of searching a list of words, and providing a weight for each word or phrase to assign its rank in the returning set of hits. The query runner, [50], marathon[60], "marathon runner"[200] will return documents with either the words or the phrase, but strongly prefers the phrase.

Index Server also interprets meaning in your queries through the implementation of a technique called linguistic stemming. This process associates query criteria words with all possible tenses or participles. For example, if you are interested in *running*, your query on this word may return hits on *run*, *ran*, or *runs*. The process of expanding the basic word to these other forms is called inflection; the reverse process (reducing an inflected word to its root) is called stemming. In general, the more highly inflected or stemmed an indexed word is from the directed query, the lower its rank will appear in the resultant list.

The Querying Back End

The precursors to Visual InterDev ActiveX Data Objects were the less full-featured, yet still effective, Internet Database Connector .idc and .htx files. These files were, and still are, used to run queries against ODBC database tables and return HTML files with the results, usually formatted in tables. The main drawbacks include considerable syntax complexity and a scarcity of tools that ease the pain of their development. With Index Server, the middle layer of the querying process is made up of a file system closely related to these forerunners called .idq and .htx files. The back end (the master index) consists of a proprietary database file format.

Internet Database Query (.idq) Files and HTML Extension (.htx) Files

The indices created by CiDaemon are stored in a proprietary database format. Just as .idc files defined queries to run against back-end databases, Internet Database Query (.idq) files are used to perform the first half of the querying process against the indices. Variables are input to the .idq file using HTML forms, as displayed in the following example:

```
<FORM ACTION="/scripts/ samples/search/query.idq" METHOD="GET">
➥  <INPUT TYPE="TEXT" NAME="Restriction" SIZE="60"
➥ MAXLENGTH="100" VALUE=""><INPUT TYPE="SUBMIT" VALUE="Execute Query"></FORM>
```

The .idq files consist of two sections: a names section and a query section. The Names section contains all nonstandard properties that can be referred to in a query. Examples include MS Office summary and custom properties such as document subject, page count, word count, edit time, and title. The Query section of the .idq file picks up the parameters from the .html form that will be used in the query. Minimally, the .idq file must specify the scope (CiScope), columns to search (CiColumns), word or phrase to query on (CiRestriction), and template file to return the results (CiTemplate). This section may look similar to the following example:

```
[Query]
CiScope=/
CiColumns=FileName
CiRestriction=%Restriction%
CiTemplate=/scripts/ samples/search/results.htx
```

HTML extension files may include many formatting variables including the number of records returned per page, confirmation of parameters submitted, query time, and others. The main section of the file is dedicated to displaying the results of the query, and is delimited with the tags <%begindetail%> and <%enddetail%>. A simple .htx results section containing the record number, link to the hit file, 250 words extracted by the filter, file size, and write time may look as follows:

```
<%CiCurrentRecordNumber%>.
<b><a href="<%EscapeURL%><%path%>"><%filename%></a></b>
<dd>
<b><i>Abscract: </i></b><%characterization%><br>
 <font size=-1>--size <%size%> bytes--<%write%> GMT</font>
```

Administration

The basic functions of Index Server will run after installation with no further effort from the administrator. These functions include automatic indexing of all HTML (3.0 or lower), Word, Excel, PowerPoint, text, and binary format files in all virtual directories of the Web site. If you selected all the default options during installation, your site search pages are located in the samples/search subdirectories of wwwroot on your server. Querying capabilities on these default search pages include simple content query (refer to Figure 35.1), query by file size, file modification time, or file author. Hits will return a link to the document, its path from the root directory, and the first 250 characters filtered out of the file by the Index Server. Figure 35.2 shows part of the list of hits returning from a query on the word information. Data returned includes the filtered text (abstract), document size, and file date and time. Hits include hyperlinks from the document title and the path to the document from the server root directory. The administrator can change virtually every aspect of this format using the .htx file.

The Administration Page

As your site grows, your requirements for search customization will likely grow with it. Although most required administrative activities are performed automatically and continuously in the background, you may want to explicitly execute some administration functions to improve search performance. Index Server offers an administration page to perform several of these functions. Script files similar to the .idq files, called .ida files, carry out the administration commands. Figure 35.3 shows the default administration page from which most standard admin functions are run.

FIGURE 35.2.

The return page from a simple query for the word information. *Note how the string* &!#vpath *_* was concatenated to the query criteria to prevent hits on FrontPage server extension directory contents.*

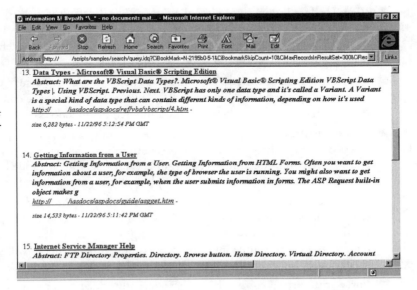

FIGURE 35.3.

The Index Server administration page provides a quick method of performing a few common maintenance and monitoring functions.

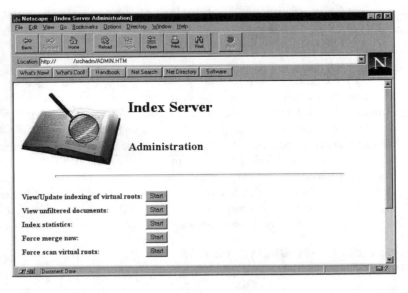

Although the administration page is available to any browser, running most of its functions requires that the user log in as an administrator. Following is a short description of each of the administration functions invoked from this page.

- **View/Update indexing of virtual roots**—Several default virtual roots exist outside the space of the Web server (wwwRoot and subdirectories). Unless you want these included in your indices, I recommend removing them from the default list, which decreases both index size and query response time.

- **View unfiltered documents**—Some documents in the corpus may not be filtered due to corruption or no valid filtering .dll. This function issues the command @Unfiltered=true to produce a list of unfiltered documents.

- **Index statistics**—21 separate statistics are available using .ida script commands. These options include cached queries (the number pending, rejected, missed, total, and so on); corpus documents (the number indexed, filtered, added, modified, total, and so on); merge status (number complete and in progress), and others.

- **Force merge now**—As previously discussed, a single master index represents the most efficient database against which to query. Forcing a merge will eliminate all pending word lists and shadow indices, thus bringing the master index up-to-date. Because this represents a very resource-intensive process, subsequent queries will run slow until the master index merge finishes.

- **Force scan virtual roots**—If you have recently added documents to the corpus that are not yet returning hits, it is likely due to the lazy indexing and filtering processes of CiDaemon. Forcing a scan of the virtual root containing these documents will solve this problem by adding their contents to the word lists.

Controlling the Scope of Indexing and Querying

The scope of the indexing process for CiDaemon can be limited or expanded by the default options available under the View/Update Indexing of Virtual Roots section of the administration page. You can expand this capability to index any virtual root off the server by specifying CiAdminOperation=UpdateRoots in the .ida script file. Two variables, combined with the HTTP GET command, control indexing of any virtual root. PROOT_virtual root specifies the mapping from a virtual root to a physical path. Including the INDEX_virtual root toggle causes the specified virtual root to get indexed, but excluding this operator will disable indexing for that root. At the individual file level, you may exclude any HTML file from indexing using any spider, such as CiDaemon, by inserting the `<meta name="robots" content="noindex">` tag into that file.

FrontPage Web-Querying Issues

The .idq files specifying each query contain a scope variable that specifies the path of the query scope from the root of the web. The default CiScope=/ specifies the entire set of subdirectories under the root. In some instances, you may have individual webs with one or more directories under the root web. FrontPage webs are organized in this way. Although the FrontPage extensions offer a nifty drag-and-drop search engine for the scope of each individual web, it is nowhere near as functional or extensible as Index Server. You can limit an Index Server query to an individual FrontPage web simply by specifying the `.idq` file scope variable as `CiScope=/<web name>`.

Webmasters running the FrontPage server extensions on their sites will have several directories in each web that implement the functions of the FrontPage Web bots. Usually, you will not want Index Server queries returning hits on content in these directories. The administration utilities offer the capability of excluding indexing of virtual roots, but this option may become inconvenient as webs are added and deleted from a server. A better method of eliminating these directories from query results is to modify the query criteria to not return hits from these directories.

A default installation will place the main query `.idq` files in the `/scripts/samples/search` directory. Each of these files assigns the query criteria from the user to a variable called `CiRestriction`. Because the FrontPage server extension directories all start with _vti, simply add the `&! #vpath "*\_vti*"` string onto the end of `CiRestriction`; then no hits from extension directories will be returned. FrontPage also installs a _private directory for the storage of forms using the Save Results bot. You can also exclude hits on contents in this directory by generalizing the preclusion string to `CiRestriction &! #vpath *\_*`, as depicted in Figure 35.2.

Index Server and Dynamic Data

Wait a minute… The whole point of Active Server Pages is *dynamic* HTML generation. These pages are temporary, and will not exist in the corpus for `CiDaemon` to filter in the first place. The static `.asp` pages that generate them are mostly code, and are therefore of little interest to most browsers. This occurrence limits the utility of document-centric search mechanisms, such as the current version of Index Server, and virtually all other popular Web crawlers.

As a way of addressing this limitation, Microsoft is expanding its indexing capabilities to some of the same sources that `.asp` pages may turn to for their content. Currently, Index Server can index Web-based, textual data in tables formatted with the Microsoft SQL Server version 6.5 relational database management system. By using a SQL Server stored procedure, Index Server can convert database records to HTML files for indexing. Additionally, an administrator may define NetWare server directories as virtual directories within the IIS Web space. To index NetWare server directories, administrators must install the Gateway Services for NetWare (GSNW) service on their Web servers. Index Server 1.1 also enables users to search Internet newsgroup (NNTP) articles stored on Microsoft Internet News Server.

In addition to these capabilities, Microsoft is also exploring the possibility of expanding future indexing capabilities to other extra-Web-server content sources, such as Exchange E-Mail Server. In case any decision makers in the Microsoft Index Server development group are listening, documenting the interface to the master index, and exposing a few key properties and methods of `CiDaemon`, would go a long way toward helping developers leverage the functionality of Index Server. In fact, I have a specific application in mind…

A Persistent Indexing Utility

With all its functionality, Index Server still returns only transient links to content currently in the corpus. These pages represent a snapshot of the indices at a point in time. Often, Webmasters are required to provide continuous indexes to all files on their Web sites, and keep these files up-to-date. As content and file structure change, this support can become a daunting task, and a real resource drain on the content maintainers.

The FrontPage Table of Contents bot provides a hyperlinked site outline, but returns only filenames, and no content, for contextual analysis. It seems the filtering utility of Index Server could be put to good use automating this task. If scheduled to run regularly, this utility could create an `index.html` file in each directory on a Web site. The file would have links to, and contextual data from, each file in a directory, and the `index.html` file in every subdirectory. This option would provide a comprehensive, updated system of `.html` files, indexing an entire site.

I have written a small utility that performs a similar indexing function. Designed as a method of indexing Web graphic files, it creates an `index.html` file providing thumbnail previews of, and hyperlinks to, all `.gif` and `.jpg` files in a directory. The indexing function also has a directory tree mode, where it will also index all subdirectories under the designated starting directory. In tree mode, it will produce links to all subdirectories by title. In addition to indexing Web graphics, the function can help to create a system of HTML navigation files for a digitized photo album. All links produced are relative, so no Web server is required for the file system to work.

Figure 35.4 depicts the user interface for the Graphic File Indexer utility, which is about as simple as it gets. The drive, directory, and file list controls are linked in classic form to indicate the user's selected starting directory. The most interesting challenge in developing this tool was programming the Visual Basic `Dir()` command to index a directory structure of unknown scope and depth. The `Dir` function cannot be called recursively, but you can circumvent this limitation by loading the results (in this case, the paths to all immediate subdirectories) of the primary call into a dynamic array. The secondary `Dir()` call can then be made in a loop through the array, further adding to it until each branch is covered. Not exactly the picture of efficiency, but on a Pentium Pro machine, it indexed the entire 1,500 directories on my `c:\` drive in about 15 seconds. And that beats writing HTML in Visual Notepad by a few orders of magnitude.

FIGURE 35.4.

The UI for the Graphic File Indexer. Visual Notepad...on steroids.

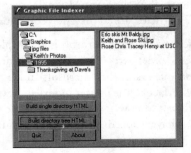

Figure 35.5 depicts the resulting `index.html` files generated by running the indexer in tree mode on a directory containing three graphic files, and one subdirectory with three more. Of course, the thumbnail sketch linked preview is only effective for graphic files; however, the code can easily be modified to include other file formats, graphic or not. Because the preview graphic has a fixed dimension, thumbnails may appear distorted depending on their original aspect ratio. Combining this persistent indexing capability with contextual data from the Index Server master index would alleviate much of the mundane maintenance burden experienced by many Webmasters. This utility was developed in VB5 and compiled to native code, so the application will run standalone, and may be scheduled as an NT service. All source code is included on the CD-ROM accompanying this book, which will facilitate translating the functionality to VB or JavaScript for implementation as an ASP file.

FIGURE 35.5.

The files created by the Graphic File Indexer utility in two directories. Clicking on the thumbnail brings up the full graphic.

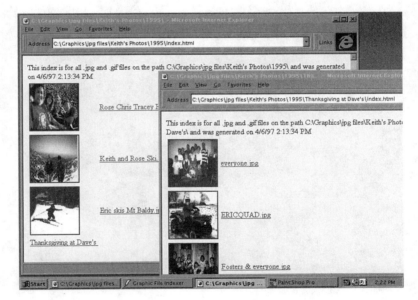

Summary

Visual InterDev 1.0 integrates the capabilities of some substantially powerful software tools such as scripting languages, DCOM, relational databases, HTML editors, Web servers, ADO, and others. As you have before, you will spend some time and effort coming up to speed on this tool set. In contrast, you can implement Index Server, a free tool, in about 15 minutes, from initiating the download to running the first query on your site. From there, you can customize its simple component structure to meet your unique requirements, or you can walk away and never think about maintaining it again. Considering both simplicity and utility, you probably won't encounter any other tool that delivers more bang for the buck than this quiet little spider.

35

UNDERSTANDING THE INDEX SERVER

IN THIS PART

Advanced Visual InterDev Topics

VIII

PART

DCOM and the Internet

by Scot Johnson

IN THIS CHAPTER

As we stand on the edge of a fundamental shift in the computing paradigm that centers on deploying applications to a thin client, we have to investigate the different components driving the trend. The fact that the Web enables traditional client/server applications is a result of a successful marriage or synergy between two separate objects, such as a new development in hardware and advancements in software. Hardware that is low in both communication and processing costs, coupled with the advent of Web-based integrated development environments (IDEs) such as Visual InterDev and Active Server Pages, has led to a revolution in Web-enabling traditional client/server applications. However, there is another fundamental shift that is often overlooked in discussions about the benefits associated with Web-enabling your client/server applications. Web-enabling a client/server application means more than putting an HTML user interface onto an existing client/server application; it also requires careful thought and discipline in creating and optimizing the architecture supporting the Internet-based system.

This chapter explains the core functionality that is essential for Web-enabling your applications. I discuss why distributed component architecture is critical to deploying your existing applications on the Internet infrastructure, Microsoft's implementation of component architecture through DCOM, and the various tools needed to develop and manage components. Furthermore, this chapter demonstrates how to use DCOM to implement component architecture to successfully create and deploy enterprise software solutions.

Why Create a Component Architecture or Distributed Application?

The concept of component architecture gradually has crept its way from the ancient needs of automation into today's Information Services (IS) departments around the world. As we approach the turn of the century, the fundamental ideals that fueled mass-market industrialization are also driving the software industry into component-based architecture. Component architecture focuses on separating large, complex software applications into smaller, more manageable modules or components. This separation or dissection of applications provides an increased programming efficiency while reducing software development, deployment, and maintenance costs.

In the component-based programming world, the time required to create an application is now directly proportional to the amount of time needed to assemble software components from existing applications or libraries. The development and deployment costs are also reduced because cross-vendor components can communicate with each other based on a standard interface or object model. The standardization of the communication model eliminates the need to invest in time and resources to create, develop, and customize components. Maintenance costs are also reduced by supplying an effective mechanism to change an application by varying a middle component without having to modify, reconfigure, or redeploy the entire client application.

To transfer component theory into an effective component implementation, two requirements must be met. First, component architecture must rely on an industry-supported standard for components to interact or communicate with each other. Second, limited component inter-action must not be limited to existing network protocols and operating systems. Microsoft's component object model (COM) and distributed component object model (DCOM) provide effective mechanisms to meet these requirements, enabling businesses to extend and leverage their existing software, hardware, and knowledge investments by enjoying the flexibility of dis-tributed applications.

How Does Component Architecture Extend the Current Business Environment?

Most business applications today are based on the traditional client/server architecture. Over time, the advantages and disadvantages of the two-tier application architecture helped evolve the formation of component architecture. Component architecture extended the two-tier model by providing benefits such as shared network resources, rapid code reuse, and flexibility in delivering and implementing applications. Further implementation benefits can be exploited by the separation of large, cumbersome business rules into logical tiers or subsections to sup-port the application logic, business services, and data-retrieval mechanisms. When the client/server model is integrated with component architecture, the software development and deploy-ment cycle is optimized to maximize the desktop development and deployment flexibility.

But component architecture forces a new mindset that is fundamentally different from devel-oping in the client/server world. The primary difference between the two environments is that distributed processing forces the transition from a client-centric viewpoint to a server-centric viewpoint. The shift reduces the emphasis of the processing power at the user level, particu-larly with a thin client approach, to requiring scaleability, robustness, and reliability at the server level. Furthermore, the implementation of multiple tiers also requires an increased develop-ment effort that focuses on managing failure, not just within the client application, but within the multitude or series of distributed components across the enterprise.

How Does Component Architecture Extend Applications on the Internet?

The advantages of developing a component-based environment are clearly centered around the advantages of expanding the desktop-based flexibility to which we have grown accustomed. With component architecture, one component can be written and accessed from a variety of sources. For example, a Win32 client application written in Delphi or Visual Basic, or a Web browser such as Internet Explorer or Netscape Navigator, can request that a static report or a dynamically generated report communicate directly with a database-retrieval component.

But the advantages of distributed computing can quickly become overshadowed without the implementation of a component manager that handles issues such as managing and distributing components across multiple servers, object instances, resource management, security, and database connectivity. With the integration of Microsoft Transaction Server (MTS) and DCOM, the expansion of your client/server systems and existing in-house COM systems can become a reality without requiring the large investments associated with managing distributed processing.

Writing a Distributed Application with DCOM

Distributed computing is founded on the philosophy that has been driving object-oriented programming (OOP): the development of self-contained modules that can be easily replaced, modified, and reused. Applying this object-oriented approach to delivering business solutions results in an increased development and deployment flexibility mechanism, increased quality control of systems, and a reduction in the number of resources required to create, implement, and maintain the systems. Although OOP itself has not achieved all its promised benefits for a variety of reasons, the concepts behind OOP technology have provided a mental foundation for developing and deploying component-based software solutions.

In their rapidly changing world, businesses were forced to realize that one logical set of business rules doomed a company to economic failure. In the face of this reality, the business community had to separate the once-sacred grouping of rules into smaller, more flexible, highly optimizable logical tiers. At the same time, advances in the physical tier, particularly in distributed computing, promoted applications to communicate across machine boundaries onto a network. The same two-phased technology shift that drove the explosive growth of the Internet can be applied toward implementing component architecture. The component architecture model can be summarized by the union of two parts or tiers: the logic tier and the physical tier. Each tier has developed significant advances over the past several years and reached a similar synergy as the Internet revolution.

How Do I Architect a Component Architecture?

Distributed systems must be carefully architected from the creation of the application, or significant time and resources will later be required to make that transition. The key is to establish a sound foundation that will provide a mechanism for extensive code reuse, easy application updates, and straightforward deployment.

Identifing the Logical Tier

The first stage in developing your component-based system is to separate your model or application into the logical and physical tiers, with greater importance and effort given to the logical tier. In traditional client/server architecture, most applications consisted of two tiers, the client and the server. The client component was responsible for establishing an interface to the user, providing a reasonable amount of processing power for client-side workloads, and managing user workflow through an application. The server component was most often responsible for housing the data store, providing data integrity in a multiuser system, and encapsulating a few business rules and a little logic in the form of stored procedures and triggers.

But as distribution and deployment issues grew exponentially, changes to the software became necessary, and the two-tier model began to segregate to keep up with rapidly changing business needs. Eventually, the segregated model formed into three general areas: user services, business services, and data services. These succinct services are the foundation of the logical tier of component architecture.

Data Services

The *data services* tier represents the same area of responsibility as the server tier in the traditional two-tier model. Data services are responsible for storing and maintaining the integrity of the data, focusing on data persistence and recovery. But data services in the component world are not involved with the business-specific rules that have been traditionally stored as functions of the database. The business-specific rules are the responsibility of the business services tier.

Business Services

The *business services* tier provides a logical layer responsible for managing the business rules for the application. The business services directly interact with the data services and the user services to provide business functionality that can be changed without requiring additional changes to the other services. The business services are usually nonvisual, isolated components that can be easily modified to meet business's changing needs. Most often, these business components focus on workflow issues and calculations, or act as a gateway to external data stores.

User Services

The *user services* tier represents the visual collaboration of the business services and the data services. These visual services are responsible for presenting information to the user, providing client-side processing of data, and accessing the business services.

Identify the Physical Tier

The specifics of the physical tier can also be further separated and related into components. These components can be encapsulated in a compiled binary form to be shared across different applications. The term *component*, in the Windows environment, traditionally refers to object linking and embedding (OLE)—the set of OLE Automation interfaces that are accessible to any OLE Automation client. These binary components can physically reside in three different locations in respect to the client: in process, out of process, or distributed on a remote system.

In-Process Components

In-process automation components are dynamic link libraries (DLLs) that offer the highest performance of all components. The terms *in process* and *out of process* refer to the location of the thread execution in memory. In-process components offer the fastest communication rate because the client and server components share the same address and process space. In-process components can also spawn multiple threads to handle concurrent connections.

Out-of-Process Components

Out-of-process components are executables that run in a separate process and address space, but still exist on the same machine. The out-of-process components suffer from slower performance than in-process servers because out-of-process servers are slower to instantiate and have to transfer data across address spaces. Out-of-process servers are often used for components that can also be implemented as standalone applications.

On a Remote System

Remote components are executables that run solely on a different machine than the client application, using the remote system's resources as needed. The client system distributes processing power from the client's machine to more powerful application servers. Remote components are the slowest of the three options because not only is the creation of a separate out-of-process server slow, but the data transfer and call rates between objects are consequently slower.

One of the keys to implementing an effective distributed system is based not on performance numbers, such as statistics from load balancing, network traffic, or CPU utilization, but on user perception, in terms of the speed and functionality of the system. To effectively implement distributed systems, take advantage of the freed processing power from the client machine to allow the user to seamlessly continue workflow in the application while a distributed task runs in the background until it finishes processing. After the background processing is complete, notify the user the task is complete.

What Is COM?

Now that you have learned about the high-level overview and planning phases required for component architecture, let's discuss the technology behind the implementation model. COM is a binary standard that enables cross-vendor components to communicate in a defined standards-based model. This interoperability of components is the core technology behind OLE and ActiveX technology. A more specific definition of a COM component is any object that supports the *Iunknown* interface. An interface provides channels of communication between objects; the Iunknown interface specifically provides a way to determine which methods are available in other components and provides a means to control its own scope or lifetime. When an object is referenced from another object, pointers are created to the exposed methods. The management of these pointers provides components with the capability to allow dynamic loading and unloading, use shared memory management, and provide communication within and across process boundaries.

Although the COM standard has existed for years, COM suffered from some drawbacks that made implementing COM objects difficult. The largest problems had to do with the communication layer between objects, specifically the low-level packet or protocol coding needed to implement Winsock and DDE. Soon NetDDE or Network OLE provided component communication across machine boundaries and onto the network, which led to the integration of remote automation into rapid application development (RAD) tools such as Visual Basic.

Then What Is DCOM?

With the rollout of NT 4.0, distributed COM (DCOM) represents Microsoft's distributed object system, formally referred to as Network OLE. DCOM is a simple extension of the COM model that allows COM objects to communicate across machine boundaries. DCOM provides remote automation and network independence between objects without the objects' needing to differentiate their relative locations. The network transparency of DCOM is based on a standards-based remote procedure call (RPC). The RPC standard is based on and is compatible with the Open Software Foundation's Distributed Computing Environment (DCE) RPC. The DCE RPC defines a standard for converting in-memory data structures and parameters into network packets.

The advantages of DCOM are a direct result of the COM interface standard and its network transparency. DCOM provides cross-platform, multitier applications based on OLE/ActiveX technology. DCOM works natively with Internet technologies such as TCP/IP, Java, and HTTP. What this means is that DCOM now provides distributed applications focused on reusable components, applications that work across different environments without modification of the client application, and a heterogeneous client base based on a standard object protocol.

What Are the Differences Among COM, OLE, DCOM, and ActiveX?

A common question about Microsoft ActiveX technology is "What are the differences among COM, OLE, DCOM, and ActiveX controls?" This question can best be answered by looking at the aforementioned terms as an evolutionary development standard. As a precursor to the OLE development standard, Microsoft had an object standard known as the *component object model* (COM). COM formalized a communication standard among objects based on the Windows operating system; it now represents a nested *object resource broker* (ORB) integrated into the operating system.

The COM standard prompted various tool vendors, such as Microsoft, Borland, and Powersoft, to push OLE Automation as a Windows development standard. OLE Automation is the capability of a COM object to expose its properties, methods, and events to other objects. OLE Automation servers existed in the COM world, but had no way of utilizing the benefits of distributing applications across machine boundaries. Without DCOM, OLE Automation servers existed in only two formats, as either in-process or out-of-process automation servers. ActiveX controls have stemmed from the in-process automation servers that run as DLLs directly in the memory space of the application to simulate component architecture using OLE as the communication medium. Out-of-process automation servers run as executables and use a combination of OLE and remote procedure calls (RPC) for communication purposes.

Simply put, an ActiveX control is an OLE control. OLE controls were renamed ActiveX controls in the continuation of the COM evolution. There are some differences between the two. OLE controls were traditionally deployed on the desktop environment, and OLE containers often contained extra interfaces and unnecessary information. Because ActiveX controls are deployed over the Internet, size and download times become critical to deploying the Web-based application. Therefore, most ActiveX controls are optimized to provide only the minimum interfaces needed for functionality to reduce code size and download times. COM also enables ActiveX controls not only to provide functionality within the Web browser, but to be used and deployed in Win32 desktop applications. This is possible because ActiveX technology is still based on fundamental COM and OLE logic.

> **NOTE**
>
> An ActiveX control is an OLE control that can be used in the Web browser *and* in Win32 client applications.

Building a COM Object

Most software vendors—including Microsoft, Borland, Powersoft/Sybase, Oracle, IBM, and Micro Focus—produce development tools that create COM controls (ActiveX or COM-enabled OLE Automation servers). After a COM object is created, it is deployed as an in-process or out-of-process object on a remote system. The tools and specific steps to create a COM object differ from vendor to vendor, but are often expedited by wizards to decrease development time and risk of insanity. However, most in-process and distributed COM objects require two stages. The first stage in creating a COM DLL is to write and compile the source code as a DLL, and the second stage requires the COM DLL to be registered on the host system. Out-of-process COM objects are compiled and run as separate executables, but they don't have to be registered on the host system. The difference between the in-process and out-of-process servers centers around system registration and security issues. For in-process COM DLLs, the Registry is used to store execution permissions, whereas execution writes for the out-of process EXEs are stored at the file level.

What Platforms and Network Protocols Support DCOM?

DCOM is designed to run on 32-bit Windows-based operating systems, including Windows 95 and Windows NT. Recent developments and demonstrations by Microsoft have extended DCOM's reach to the Macintosh and multiple UNIX-based systems. Software AG has also released a beta version of DCOM running on Solaris.

DCOM itself is a transport-neutral network protocol based on remote procedure calls. DCOM can use any transport protocol, including TCP/IP, UDP, IPX/SPX, and NetBIOS. Not only does DCOM eliminate the need for network-specific applications, but it also provides a security framework on all these protocols.

DCOM and Java

One of DCOM's major design objectives was to support various Internet technologies and standards—in particular, Java. DCOM is a specification that allows interaction between COM components across individual workstations. Java, on the hand, is a programming language that allows applications to run across various platforms. Currently, DCOM is supported only in the Windows environment, with DCOM for Solaris still in beta. Therefore, you are limited to implementing the DCOM/Java integration model in situations when you need to connect Java objects to Visual Basic, Visual J++, or Visual C++ COM objects or applications that expose themselves as COM objects. The COM interaction with Java is actually the responsibility of the Java Virtual Machine (VM). The Java VM resides in Microsoft Internet Explorer to interpret and run Java applets and standalone Java programs.

Visual J++ provides an integrated development tool to easily connect COM components to Java components. This Java-to-COM connection mechanism is based on storing type libraries that contain class, interface, entity, and other component information. The exposed type libraries are then available to any Java-based program. Visual J++ provides an OLE Object View utility and wizards to help display and access the type libraries or resources within a component.

The security of Java applets is handled by the VM in the same manner as COM security services. Java applets are usually run in a defined execution environment to help prevent malicious intent. The VM classifies Java applets as either trusted or untrusted based on the location from which the Java class files are loaded. An applet is considered *trusted* if the class files were loaded from the class path or have been safely extracted from a cabinet (.CAB) file with a digital signature, whereas *untrusted* applets are applets that were not loaded from the class path. Trusted Java applets and Java applications do not run in the restricted executions environment, often referred to as a *sandbox*. Trusted Java classes can access any COM service and provide read/write file functionality, while untrusted applets must run within the sandbox and do not have access to local file input/output or COM services.

What Are ORB, CORBA, and IIOP?

As the World Wide Web pushes component-based technology into the forefront, other distributed computing architectures have existed for some time. In 1989, the Object Management Group (OMG) was formed by technology vendors such as Sun Microsystems, Inc.; IBM Corp.; and Apple Computer, Inc. to create and adopt a distributed object standard. The most basic unit of distributed computing standard is the *Object Request Broker* (ORB). The ORB uses a formalized interface to provide communications between objects. This binary standard allows objects to invoke other objects' methods across different networks and platforms. The result of the OMG alliance was the first Common Object Request Broker Architecture (CORBA) standard. But the initial CORBA standard suffered from lack of the detail needed for objects from different vendors to work together. Because of the cross-vendor compliance's shortcoming, the OMG released CORBA 2.0. That release benefited from the previous CORBA version's mistake and specified a syntax for a network protocol, defining TCP/IP as the Inter-ORB backbone.

As the evolution of component architecture continues, various tool vendors such as Netscape, Borland, and Visigenic are promoting the shift of the standard HTTP to the CORBA 2.0 specific *Internet Inter-ORB Protocol* (IIOP). IIOP is the communication protocol for CORBA and is essentially a superset of TCP/IP with some CORBA-defined extensions that serve as a common backbone protocol. As a result, IIOP provides a standard means for Inter-ORB communication to any other CORBA-compliant object. Microsoft plans to counter IIOP's offering by linking ActiveX controls using a DCE-RPC–enabled protocol over a DCOM-based network protocol.

The primary difference between DCOM and CORBA is that DCOM is directly integrated into the Windows operating system and is not managed by an ORB; therefore, implementing a DCOM-based system is limited to the currently supported operating systems. But a DCOM-based system will expose you to a wide variety of development tools that are not available in the CORBA marketplace.

Installing, Administering, and Deploying DCOM Components

Assuming that you have successfully created and locally tested your component, the next step is to install or register it on the host machine. Because DCOM is currently supported on a limited number of operating systems, this discussion assumes you are limited to an NT 4.0 deployment environment.

Registering Your Component

The first step to deploying your distributed application on a remote system is to register the object on the remote or hosting machine (see Figure 36.1). The remote machine will be responsible for managing the resources needed by the component. Registering the component on the host machine is required by DCOM because DCOM uses the system Registry to determine the execute permissions and security levels of the component. To register the component from the command line, run the `RegSrv32` option. `RegSrv32` uses the following syntax:

```
RegSrv32 [/u] [/s] [/c] dllname
where:
/u  - Unregistar server
/s - Silent mode, display no message box
/c - Console output
```

Remember to specify the full path, including the machine name and DLL name. Registering the component on the remote machine doesn't automatically give it execution rights. The execution of the remote component is dependent on the remote machine's security setting for the component.

FIGURE 36.1.

Registering a component with the hosting system.

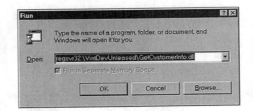

Configuring Your Component (DCOMCNFG)

To configure component permissions within NT, use the DCOMCNFG utility. You can also use REGEDIT or OLEVIEW to determine how a component is launched, but DCOMCNFG was specially tailored for DCOM configurations. After you start DCOMCNFG, the Distributed COM Configuration Properties dialog presents three tabs for Applications, Default Properties, and Default Security configuration. The Applications tab is illustrated in Figure 36.2. This tab allows you to select the COM objects that are registered on the machine and set the properties of the specific component.

Enabling DCOM

Even through DCOM comes distributed with NT 4.0, it isn't automatically implemented. You can control whether remote clients can connect to registered objects on the server by selecting the Enable Distributed COM on this computer checkbox on the Default Properties page, as shown in Figure 36.3.

Setting DCOM Security

DCOM is tightly integrated with, and based on, the NT security schema. You have the ability to regulate who can launch components, who can administer the component classes, and who can access the component, as illustrated in Figure 36.4. Further administration is available if users don't supply their own settings by using an access control list, as depicted in Figure 36.5. For example, if the payroll department uses various components to perform accounting functions on a server, you might want to allow only the payroll group to launch and access the DCOM on that machine.

FIGURE 36.2.

Using the DCOMCNFG *utility to configure DCOM.*

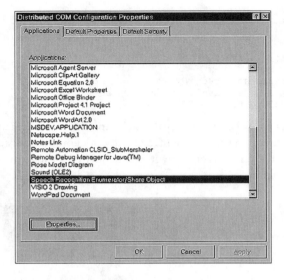

FIGURE 36.3.

Enabling DCOM on the host machine.

FIGURE 36.4.
Configuring DCOM security for access, launch, and configuration permissions.

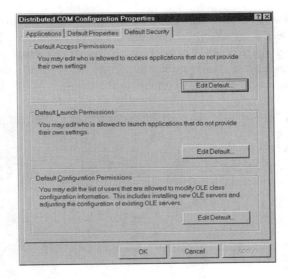

FIGURE 36.5.
Setting DCOM administration properties via an access-control list.

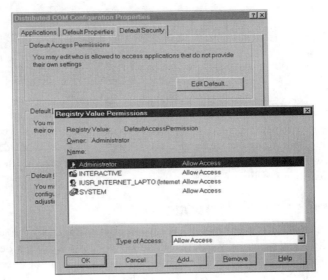

Setting Component Security

After the DCOM environment has been configured, DCOMCNFG enables you to manage and set permissions for the individual COM objects. After selecting the desired component from the Applications tab, click the Properties button to open the Object dialog window, which helps to manage the specific rights of the installed COM server. The General tab displays information about the specific control, such as the application name and type, and where the COM object is installed on the machine. The Location tab designates the location to run the server (see Figure 36.6). The Security tab provides default access, launch permissions, and administrator permissions for the component. The Identity tab specifies the user account level needed to run the component on the host machine.

FIGURE 36.6.

Selecting the location where a component will run.

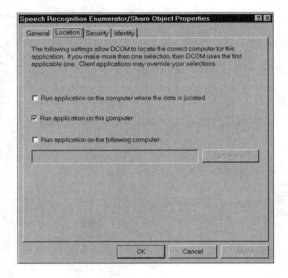

Component security is often overlooked, but should be considered while architecting your component schematic. For example, on our secure payroll server, a component is used that transfers money among customer accounts. If we provide DCOM access to this machine, it might be wise to allow only the payroll users or even specific users to use this component, as shown in Figure 36.7 and Figure 36.8.

How Is DCOM Performance?

Because DCOM is a network-level protocol, it is limited by the same factors that affect typical applications, specifically bandwidth and latency issues. When designing your distributed application, you must focus specifically on the combination of server and network optimization. The time the server takes to process a call is directly proportional to the amount of data being passed to that server and the delay required for the packets to travel from source to destination.

How Do You Load Balance Components?

DCOM itself does not provide an internal mechanism for dynamically load-balancing components, but relies on Microsoft Transaction Server (MTS) for this responsibility. (MTS is discussed later in this chapter.) If the MTS option is not available, you can manually perform mock-load balancing by allowing only a specific set of users access to a given component, creating multiple components with a select user group.

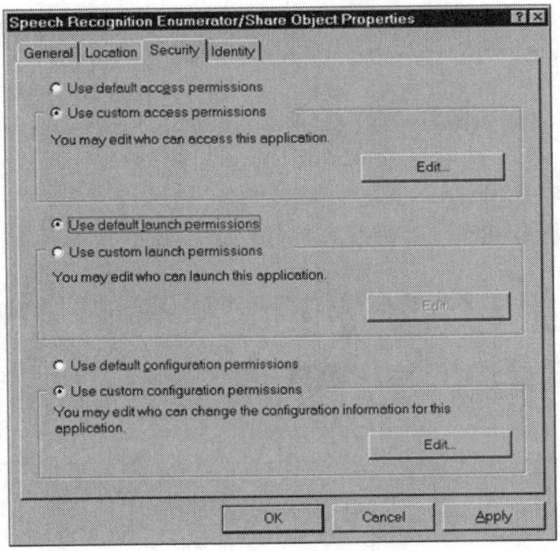

FIGURE 36.7.

*Setting the individual
DCOM component
security levels.*

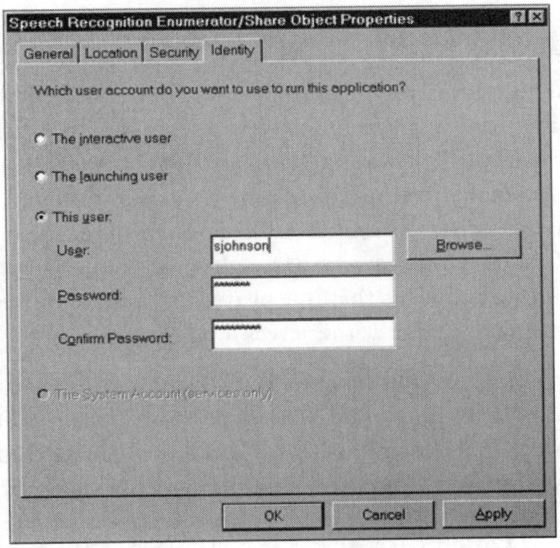

FIGURE 36.8.

*Enabling user-level
security settings on
components.*

Can You Use DCOM to Access Mainframe Data?

By this point, you are well aware that DCOM provides a network-independent connection to other ActiveX components using the distributed component architecture. But to extend the DCOM architecture a step further, DCOM objects can also be created on a variety of platforms. For example, you can create and compile a DCOM object on the NT platform at design time and then port it to UNIX for runtime. This portability provides various development platforms, such as NT, UNIX, or the mainframe, with the capability to use existing programming knowledge, hardware infrastructure, and software-development tools without significant costs.

Cedar provides the distributed transaction capability to coordinate transactions running on the mainframe with transactions running on NT or UNIX platforms. This distributed transaction ability is made possible by the CICS implementation of a protocol called *distributed program link*, which is supported from the NT environment. Cedar acts as a transitional director that integrates one programming model into another programming model. In Cedar's case, the conversion is based on transforming the DCOM object model into the CICS link and subroutine objects model.

Managing Components with Microsoft Transaction Server

In the development and deployment of mission-critical systems, transaction integrity at the data and messaging levels is essential in guaranteeing the success and future growth of your operation. The Microsoft Transaction Server (MTS) provides the transparent integrating of component resource management techniques and scaleability issues into one administrative interface based on DCOM.

Why Use the Transaction Server?

As business-rule components become easier to create and connect over a network, the emphasis now shifts from distribution across the network to efficiently managing and coordinating the interactions of the components. Particularly in larger, more complicated applications, an individual business event might require a series of different components to all successfully interact with each other. This series of component interactions and events bundled for a defined purpose is called a *transaction*. Managing transactions is critical not only to maintain data integrity and workflow at the user or desktop level, but because it can drastically affect your entire business enterprise at the server level.

Architecting business solutions not only encompasses runtime operations, but also should include planning for failure of mission-critical components. To help manage distributed component architecture, Microsoft has introduced the Transaction Server, formerly known as Viper. The Transaction Server provides one interface, as shown in Figure 36.9, to help manage the growing component infrastructure. The Transaction Server is able to manage these components because MTS itself is based entirely on DCOM. MTS provides a CORBA-compliant interface to manage, develop, and deploy components; it also reduces development costs by eliminating additional application source code development of concurrency, security, thread, and process issues while increasing the reliability of the business enterprise by hedging against component failure.

Many advantages exist to using MTS to manage your component-based system as you transition from the desktop solution; however, for purposes of this chapter, I will only highlight a few that directly benefit Web-enabling your client/server applications.

The first advantage that extends the functionality of the Transaction Server supports any component written in ActiveX. The combination of ActiveX support with DCOM now provides an extended network capable of extending your application from a non-platform, non–browser-specific interface—over the Internet Information Server—through an ActiveX component managed by the Transaction Server to another DCOM component running on the mainframe, written in Microfocus COBOL. Furthermore, the Transaction Server exposes its services to ActiveX components written in Java.

The second benefit of using the Transaction Server is the Database Connection Pool. One of the most challenging aspects of a created, database-driven Web application was managing and scaling connections to your database to potentially thousands of users. Moreover, not only did a high overhead exist with establishing and closing multiple database connections, but careful consideration and forethought were necessary to manage concurrency and lock-detection issues.

Finally, the Transaction Server is tightly integrated with the Microsoft Internet Information Server (IIS). IIS 3.0 incorporates Active Server Pages, which provide server-side execution logic when a page is requested. The server-side script can be written in VBScript, JavaScript, or any other script-compliant language. The Active Server Pages provide the HTML-based delivery of information regardless of the data source by executing ActiveX components managed by the Transaction Server. Furthermore, all ActiveX Server Components that ship with the Microsoft Internet Information Server are COM objects.

FIGURE 36.9.

Microsoft's Transaction Server.

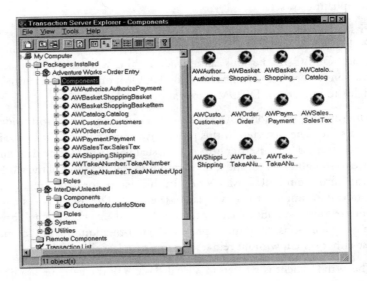

Where Does MTS Apply?

MTS relies on DCOM for the communication method among components across the network. Not only does MTS utilize DCOM for component-to-component communication, but MTS also manages the component object's instances. In the COM world, clients who invoke services of other components would control the object's lifetime as long as the reference was held. But MTS reduces development time and frustration by using a method called *just-in-time activation* to maintain the state of the object. The state of an object can either be activated or deactivated. With MTS managing the activation state of the object, a multitude of different requesting objects can reference a server object without wasting precious resources on unnecessary instantiated objects.

MTS is an excellent transaction monitor that lays the foundation for Microsoft's advances into true component architecture. For more information on the Transaction Server, visit Microsoft's Web site at `http://www.microsoft.com/transaction/`.

Putting It All Together

You can see that in order to properly architect and implement your enterprise solutions, whether on a local area network or deployed to tens of thousands of people on the Internet, you must make a significant planning effort to maximize your investment in software, hardware, and resources. Now that you have a basic understanding of the various aspects of component architecture, this section presents a simple example that highlights a few of today's development tools. The goal of this example is to transfer a client/server application, a two-tier model, into a distributed N-tier architecture using components (COM and Microsoft Transaction Server) that can be accessed either by any Win32 client or by any HTML 2.0, non–platform-specific, compliant browser.

First, the code walkthrough requires that you have an NT4.0 Server running with Service Pack 2, Active Server Pages, Visual Basic 5.0, Microsoft Transaction Server with Service Pack 1, and ODBC 3.0. For this example, everything will run on one machine to simplify the process, but can easily be deployed, using DCOM, onto other machines, assuming you have the rights to implement DCOM onto various machines.

This simple application provides a lookup feature of qualified worldwide sales leads from a central data store. The first step in this process is to break the traditional client/server tiers into the data, business, and user services tiers. Usually, separating the data and user or front-end services is straightforward, and it often results in shifting most of the work and development planning onto the middle business tier. In this demo, for deployment, we rely on an Access 7.0 database to simulate the server database engine. The user services consist of two separate sections because we want to deploy this on the local area network and over an extranet. However, in both situations, we want to present the information in a similar manner so users can easily use either system without reinvesting in a new learning pattern.

The Win32 client is written in Visual Basic 5.0; the extranet application is based on Active Server Pages, written with Visual InterDev, and implements HTML 2.0 standards. The business services are written in Visual Basic 5.0 to act as the liaison between the Web-based and Win32 clients and database services. For this application, I have created a two-form client front end using a business component that fetches the data from the database and displays the results, as pictured in Figures 36.10 and 36.11.

FIGURE 36.10.

A Win32 client making a request to a third-tier business rules component.

FIGURE 36.11.

A Win32 client displaying results from a third-tier business rules component.

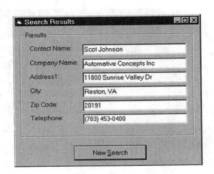

Creating the Business and User Services with Visual Basic

This example uses Visual Basic to create the graphical user interface to navigate through the application and build the COM objects to house the business rules. One of the great features of Visual Basic 5.0 is that you can build and test both the client front end and the data services inside one instance of Visual Basic 5.0, as shown in Figure 36.12. This is extremely convenient because it allows one integrated development environment to house multiple tiers of an application and provide remote debugging of remote services, eliminating often cumbersome object registration and configuration issues. (See Figure 36.14.) Here, I cover only the general concepts needed to implement this particular solution. Remember, there are many tools you can use to implement this solution, so it isn't necessary to understand the specific syntax of the displayed topic.

Open the Visual Basic DCOM project. The Project Explorer should contain two folders or groups, one containing the Visual Basic client forms and the other containing the class modules needed for the business server. The creation of the client forms is straightforward, but it is noteworthy to point out that Visual Basic uses the `CreateObject` syntax to make a connection to a registered COM object between or within the same tier or service. We use the `CreateObject` syntax to create a connection between the user service and business service that will instantiate an exposed method to the business service to retrieve data from the database. In Visual Basic, you create methods that can be accessed by other objects by creating functions with *classes,* as shown in Figure 36.11.

Even though Visual Basic 5.0 gives you the ability to maintain multiple projects within one IDE, keep in mind that the subprojects still maintain their own individual object's references. For example, the COM object that will act as the business server in our example will need to reference or include more than Visual Basic's standard object libraries because the business component needs to interface with many other objects besides the user services. The business object needs to access a database, connect to the Transaction Server, and interface with the Internet Information Server. Visual Basic includes these libraries when you select the Remote Data Object, the Transaction Server Type Libraries, and the Active Server Libraries, as shown in Figure 36.13.

FIGURE 36.12.

Visual Basic 5.0 provides an IDE for managing single and multiple components for your application.

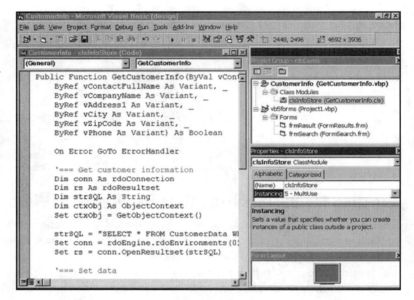

FIGURE 36.13.

Business services typically need more external object references.

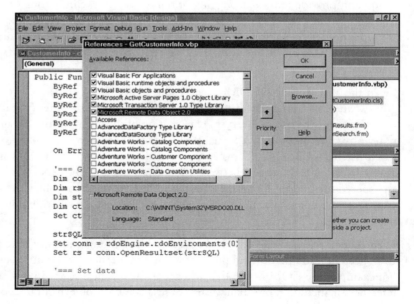

FIGURE 36.14.

User services typically need to rely on fewer external object references.

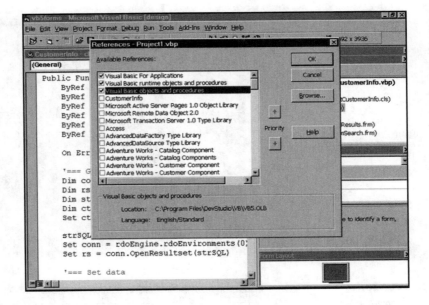

Install Component in MTS

After the business component DLL is created, you can use the Transaction Server to manage the component for scaleability, resource management, and transaction monitoring. MTS Explorer provides a hierarchical view to help manage the installed components and packages. A *package* in MTS is a set of components that run in the same server process. To install your new COM DLL, you must first create a new package. Select the Packages Installed item from Explorer tree view and select File|New from the menu bar to create a new package. With MTS, you can install prebuilt packages or create a new, empty package. After you create and name a new package, MTS must set its security rights, as shown in Figure 36.15. This enables your components to run as services with specific rights and privileges.

After the new package is installed, the component can be registered or installed by either dragging and dropping the DLL into the components folder or by again selecting File|New from the menu bar. At this point, you can either install a new component or add existing components. After you select the location of your COM DLL, MTS will install the component and provide a visual representation of the component in the Detail View of the MTS Explorer, as shown in Figure 36.16.

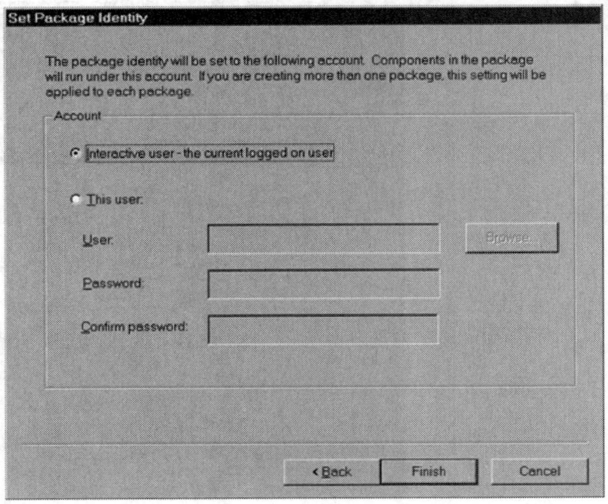

FIGURE 36.15.

The Transaction Server builds off DCOM component-level security.

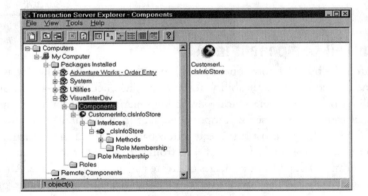

FIGURE 36.16.

Transaction Server provides a visual interface for managing components.

TIP

Using RegSrv32 is the command-line equivalent to registering your DLL with the Transaction Server Explorer.

Right-click on a specific component to gain easy access to the component's properties, such as general information, transaction support, activation environment, and security level. (See Figure 36.17.) Because MTS is based on DCOM, the attributes are similar to the variables discussed in the earlier section about DCOM component configuration.

FIGURE 36.17.

Specifying the Transaction Server environment for a component.

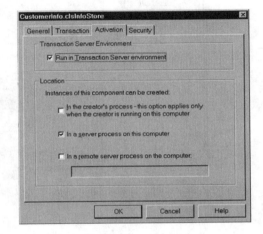

Create an ASP File in InterDev

Now that the business rule component is safely registered in MTS, the next step is to provide access to that business rule object from a Web browser interface. To do this, we will use Active Server Pages on the Internet Information Server to connect to our middle-tier business service. After you import `contactinfo.asp` into a new Visual InterDev project, notice two things about the highlighted Active Server code. (See Figure 36.18.) The first is that this page actually generates two HTML pages from the same source code. The generation of two different HTML pages is based on checking a value on a form and executing an `If...Then` loop to create the search-request and search-results forms. Second, notice the use of the `CreateObject` syntax, similar to that used in the Visual Basic client forms. The Internet Information Server will act as client, similar to the Visual Basic front-end application, to the middle-tier business server.

> **TIP**
>
> Use FrontPage 97 to generate tedious HTML code and then edit the HTML code in Visual InterDev to expand the dynamic functionality of Active Server Pages.

FIGURE 36.18.

Visual InterDev provides an IDE to access your custom-created COM server.

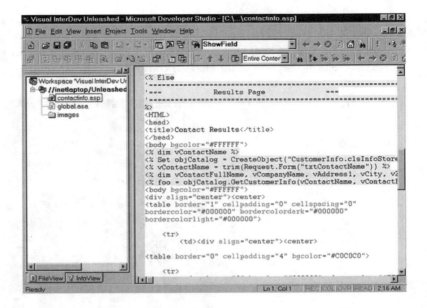

Now that you can connect to the same business rules server that the Visual Basic client application was able to connect to, you can provide the information to the user using any Web browser. Keep in mind that you can connect to any object that exposes its objects as COM objects; this includes not only your existing business object, but objects such as Lotus Notes or Microsoft Exchange objects.

For example, Figure 36.19 demonstrates the ability to enter information into a query form that connects to the COM business objects. (As you might notice by the figure, you can access this information from any browser.) After the query is submitted, the COM object returns the query result in HTML format, as shown in Figure 36.20.

> **NOTE**
>
> If you are recompiling and writing a COM DLL that is already registered and is in use by another service, you will get permission errors. Most often a client is accessing the DLL via the WWW service. To correct this problem, stop the WWW service, recompile or register the DLL, and restart the WWW service.

The beauty of this demonstration is the tight integration of COM object support across the operating system into applications such as the Win32 client applications, Transaction Server, Internet Information Server, and even your own tailored OLE Automation server.

FIGURE 36.19.

You can enter information into a query form that connects to the COM business objects.

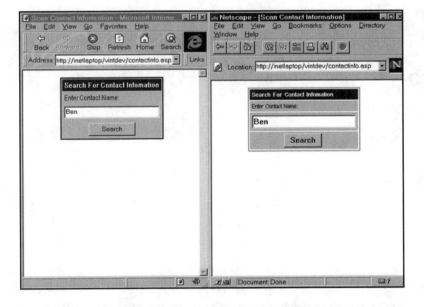

FIGURE 36.20.

Active Server Pages mimic Win32 application functionality by delivering HTML-only format.

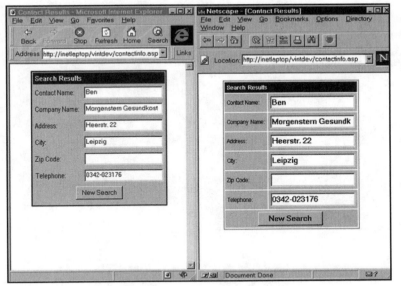

Summary

DCOM brings a scaleable, approachable, and manageable implementation of distributed applications over the Internet. These distributed systems are a culmination of proper service and tier planning and architecture; the growing vendor support needed to develop and extend components; and the continual technological evolution of hardware, software, and open-based standards.

Creating ActiveX Server Components for Active Server Pages

by Marc Gusmano

IN THIS CHAPTER

As other chapters in this book have shown, Active Server Pages and its scripting environment provide a powerful capability for creating Internet applications. By using the scripting environment of ASP and accessing the properties and methods of the ASP built-in objects, the script writer can build true, dynamically generated HTML applications. At times, however, the capabilities of the built-in objects along with the scripting capabilities do not go far enough; consequently, this represents one reason that Microsoft built the five ActiveX Server Components that come with ASP. They include Browser Capabilities, Content Linking, Ad Rotator, File Access, and the ActiveX Data Object.

Even with the components supplied by Microsoft, you will still have times when you need the ability to build your own custom components. This chapter explores the reasons why you might need to build your own components, and will give you the knowledge you need to create custom ActiveX Server Components for Active Server Pages using Visual Basic. By the time you finish this chapter, you should be able to

- Make decisions about when the building of custom ActiveX Server Components makes sense.
- Understand the mechanics of how to construct ActiveX Server Components (the technology formally known as OLE Automation) using Visual Basic 5.0.
- Add specifics to an ActiveX Server Component built in Visual Basic 5.0 that will enable the component to access the built-in objects of the Active Server Pages environment.

What Is a Custom ActiveX Server Component?

If you have worked with Active Server Pages and used the Browser Capabilities component, the ActiveX Data Object, or any of the other components that are shipped with ASP, you are already familiar with the concept of an ActiveX Server Component. Each of those components is built using the same principles and techniques described in this chapter. Based on seeing what Microsoft has provided with these components, you may already have an idea or two about an ActiveX Server Component you might want to write.

Microsoft has also released a set of component examples that you can use as a starting point for your own component development (see http://www.microsoft.com/iis for details). Because any development tool capable of building OLE Automation Server DLLs can build these components, you have many choices as far as tools are concerned, both Microsoft and third-party tools. Some of the better-known tools, such as Powersoft PowerBuilder, Borland Delphi, and others, currently support the creation of OLE Automation Server DLLs. In the Microsoft world, those tools include Visual FoxPro, Visual J++, Visual C++, and Visual Basic.

All components are instantiated in the ASP environment through the use of the `CreateObject` method of the built-in `Server` object. Once created, all properties and methods of the component can be accessed from within the ASP scripting environment. An example of the syntax necessary for creating and accessing the Browser Capabilities component appears in Listing 37.1.

Listing 37.1. Creating and accessing an ActiveX Server Component from VBScript.

```
<%
Set bc = Server.CreateObject("MSWC.BrowserType")
Response.Write "The Browser Type is " + bc.Browser
%>
```

When Should I Build My Own ActiveX Server Components?

You might have difficulty determining when to create a custom ActiveX Server Component for use in your ASP application. Several reasons exist that you may consider as valid motivation for doing so. The points in the following sections outline some of those reasons.

Managing Common Routines

If you find that you have to continually use the same script routines in every Active Server Page, you could certainly create an include file that has those routines; then it would include the routines in every ASP file that needed those routines. Another approach may be to create a custom ActiveX Server Component to contain these common routines.

Accomplishing Tasks That Cannot Be Scripted in ASP

Certainly, tasks exist that you might want to achieve within ASP that you cannot accomplish through scripting. Calling functions within DLLs represents a good example. You can use custom ActiveX Server Components to act as wrappers to this functionality.

Easing Development of Complex Routines

At times, the routines that you have scripted may become so complex that they become hard to manage or debug within the Active Server Page environment. In these cases, it may make sense to bundle these routines as multiple methods of a custom ActiveX Server Component.

Hiding Logic from a Script Writer

Any routines you create in ASP script, by definition, become available as source code to any other script writer who may need to use the routine. By compiling your routine as a custom ActiveX Server Component, you can provide a compiled solution without having to provide any source code to the script writer.

Reducing Excessive ASP Script

As a rule of thumb, if your ASP files contain more than 50% script, for the purposes of management, control, and debugging, these routines may be candidates for custom ActiveX Server Component methods.

Simplifying Object Sharing

In many cases, compiled custom ActiveX Server Components are easier to share as code components between multiple developers than, for example, many include files of common script-based procedures or other code-sharing techniques within ASPs. In these cases, use custom ActiveX Server Components to ease code sharing.

Supporting Transactions Through Microsoft Transaction Server

As of this writing, any script written within Active Server Pages does not participate in a Microsoft Transaction Server transaction, although the next version of Internet Information Server, IIS 4, will have this capability. For script that accesses database functionality—where rollback, commit, and unit of work functionality between a script and components or between components is important—a custom ActiveX Server Component may offer the only answer to providing this capability.

Allowing for Debugging

Also, as of this writing, the only line-by-line debugging capability that exists for Active Server Pages is through moving script logic to custom ActiveX Server Components. The scripting environment of Active Server Pages does not contain any line-oriented, step-through debugging capabilities, although this limitation should change as developer tools for Active Server scripting mature.

An Example of a Custom ActiveX Server Component

As an example of where a custom ActiveX Server Component can be used, Figure 37.1 presents an interface to a custom ActiveX component that communicates with a commercial credit card verification system. The credit card verification software provides a standard Visual Basic interface to its functionality that the custom ActiveX component utilizes.

FIGURE 37.1.

Credit Card Verification Custom ActiveX Server Component.

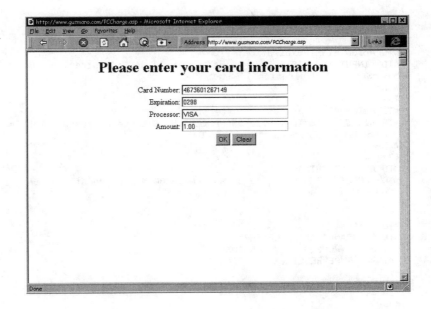

37

CREATING
ACTIVEX SERVER
COMPONENTS

The script to call the Credit Card Custom ActiveX Server Component appears in Listing 37.2.

Listing 37.2. ASP for credit card verification.

```
<%
if Request.Form("CardNumber") = "" and Request.Form("Expiration") = "" _
and Request.Form("Processor") = "" and Request.Form("Amount") = "" then
message = "Please enter your card information"
else
set o = Server.CreateObject("PCCharge.Charge")
  o.Processor = Trim(cmbProcessor)
  lblStatus = "Processing..."
 rc = o.Sale(Request.Form("CardNumber"), Request.Form("Expiration"),
➥ Request.Form("Amount"), _
               RESULT, AUTH, REFERENCE)
  Session("RESULT") = RESULT
  Session("AUTH") = AUTH
  Session("REFERENCE") = REFERENCE
  Response.Redirect ("PCChargeResult.ASP")
end if
%>
<HTML><BODY BGCOLOR="#ffffff">
<CENTER>
<H1><% = message %></H1>
<FORM METHOD=POST ACTION="<%=Request.ServerVariables("PATH_INFO")%>">
<TABLE BORDER=0>
 <TR>
  <TD ALIGN=RIGHT>Card Number:</TD>
  <TD><INPUT TYPE=TEXT SIZE=30 MAXLENGTH=30 NAME="CardNumber" VALUE=
➥"<% =Session("CardNumber") %>"></TD>
 </TR>
```

continues

Listing 37.2. continued

```
<TR>
 <TD ALIGN=RIGHT>Expiration:</TD>
 <TD><INPUT TYPE=TEXT SIZE=30 MAXLENGTH=30 NAME="Expiration" VALUE=
➥"<% =Session("Expiration") %>"></TD>
</TR>
<TR>
 <TD ALIGN=RIGHT>Processor:</TD>
 <TD><INPUT TYPE=TEXT SIZE=30 MAXLENGTH=30 NAME="Processor" VALUE=
➥"<% =Session("Processor") %>"></TD>
</TR>
<TR>
 <TD ALIGN=RIGHT>Amount:</TD>
 <TD><INPUT TYPE=TEXT SIZE=30 MAXLENGTH=30 NAME="Amount" VALUE=
➥"<% =Session("Amount") %>"></TD>
</TR>
<TR>
 <TD></TD>
 <TD COLSPAN=2 ALIGN=CENTER>
  <INPUT TYPE=SUBMIT VALUE="OK">
  <INPUT TYPE=RESET VALUE="Clear">
 </TD>
</TR>
</TABLE>
</FORM>
</CENTER>
</BODY><HTML>
```

Steps for Creating a Visual Basic ActiveX Server Component

This section outlines, step by step, the process for creating a custom ActiveX Server Component within Visual Basic 5.0.

Step 1: Create an ActiveX DLL Project

The first step to creating a custom ActiveX Server Component in Visual Basic is to create a standard ActiveX DLL. The creation of an ActiveX DLL in Visual Basic requires version 4.0 or higher. All the examples in this chapter use Visual Basic 5.0 Enterprise Edition. (You can also use Visual Basic 5.0 Control Creation Edition.) Follow these steps:

1. Create a subdirectory named [*drive*]:\Bismarck where [*drive*] represents an available hard drive.

2. Start Visual Basic from the Start menu, or select New Project from the VB File menu. Select ActiveX DLL from the Visual Basic New Project dialog box.

3. From the Tools menu, select Components to bring up the Components dialog box. Click the Selected Items Only checkbox. In the list box on the left, deselect any selected items. Click the OK button when you finish.

4. From the Project menu, select References to bring up the References dialog box. You should have only the following items selected: Visual Basic For Applications, Visual Basic Runtime Objects and Procedures, Visual Basic Objects and Procedures, and OLE Automation. Click the OK button when you finish.

5. Select the `Class1` class module by double-clicking it in the project window. The Properties—Class1 window should also be visible. Change the `Name` property to `Utility`.

6. From the Tools menu, select Add Procedure. The Add Procedure dialog box will appear. Type `TestMe` in the Name field, change the Type to `Function`, and then click the OK button. You should now be in the `TestMe` function in the Utility code window. Type the following code: `TestMe = "In TestMe"` (see Figure 37.2). Now, close the Utility code window using the Close box in the upper-right corner of the window.

FIGURE 37.2.

The `TestMe` *function in* `Utility.cls`.

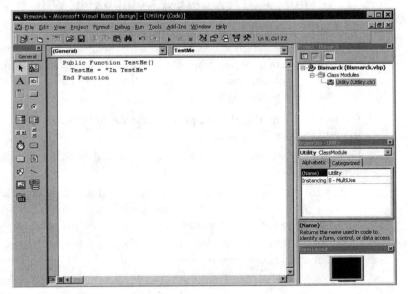

7. From the Project menu, select Project1 Properties. The Project1—Project Properties dialog box appears. Change the project name to `Bismarck`. Figure 37.3 demonstrates the completed dialog box. Click the OK button when you finish.

8. From the File menu, choose Save Project. The File Save As dialog box appears. Navigate to the `[drive]:\Bismarck` directory; then click Save for `Utility.cls` and again for `Bismarck.vbp`.

FIGURE 37.3.

The Visual Basic Project Properties dialog box.

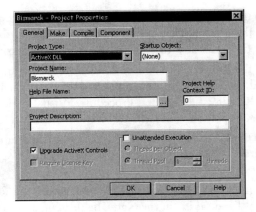

9. From the File menu, select Make Bismarck.DLL. Keep the name as `Bismarck.dll`, and click OK. You have successfully created an ActiveX Server Component!

Step 2: Test the ActiveX Server Component with a Visual Basic Client

To test that you have indeed successfully created a working ActiveX component, creating a simple Visual Basic client application that uses this component is useful. The following process walks through the steps necessary to create this simple Visual Basic client, which calls the object created in the preceding section:

1. From the current Visual Basic project, select Add Project. Select Standard EXE from the Add Project dialog box.

2. From the View menu, select Toolbox. The Visual Basic Toolbox window should appear.

3. Make sure that you can see the Form1 form. If it is not visible, select Project Explorer from the View menu. The Project Group—Group1 window should appear. Double-click Form1 in the Project window list box. The Form1 window should appear.

4. Click Project1 from the Project Group—Group1 window. Right-click this entry, and select Set as Start Up from the context menu.

5. Add a command button from the Visual Basic toolbox to the default form (Form1). You can accomplish this by double-clicking the CommandButton button in the toolbox or by dragging and dropping a command button onto Form1.

6. Double-click the created command button to bring up the code window for the `Command1_Click` event.

7. Enter the following code to the `Command1_Click` event:

```
Dim o As Object
Set o = CreateObject("Bismarck.Utility")
MsgBox o.TestMe
```

8. Save the project by selecting Save from the File menu. Navigate to the [drive]:\Bismarck directory; then click Save for form1.frm, for project1.vbp, and again for Group1.vbg.

9. From the Run menu, choose Start. A form should appear, with a button labeled Command1. Click the button. A message box containing the text In TestMe should appear.

Step 3: Test the ActiveX Server Component Within an Active Server Page

Now you can test the custom ActiveX Server Component from within an Active Server Page. The next set of steps walks through the process of creating an Active Server Page that calls the new component:

1. Create a file named TestMe.ASP in a Web server virtual directory. Make sure the Web server virtual directory has execute permission.

2. Enter the following code in the TestMe.ASP file:

```
<HTML><BODY BGCOLOR="#ffffff">
<CENTER>
<% Set r = Server.CreateObject("Bismarck.Utility") %>
<H1>The Bismarck Utility Component</H1>
<H3><% =r.TestMe %></H3>
</CENTER>
</BODY></HTML>
```

3. Request the TestMe.ASP file from a Web browser. Make sure that you request the file from its Web server virtual directory and that the directory has execute permission. You should see a page similar to Figure 37.4.

FIGURE 37.4.

Calling TestMe *from ASP.*

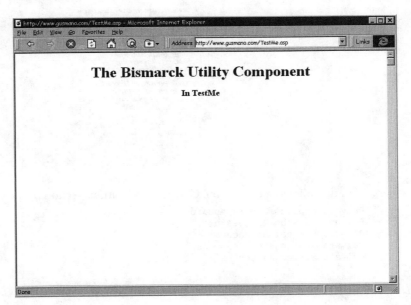

Step 4: Add ASP Specifics to the Project

Thus far, our ActiveX Server Component has no differences from any component you might build that a non-ASP application would use. You can create ASP-specific ActiveX Server Components designed to enable full use of the ASP built-in objects from anywhere within the server. To accomplish this task, create two special public methods of the ActiveX Server: OnStartPage and, optionally, OnEndPage. If they exist, ASP calls these two methods, and they enable the component builder to write code that will be run as the component is being instantiated.

The OnStartPage method includes one parameter that, in essence, serves as a *pointer* to all of the ASP built-in objects. The OnStartPage method typically uses this pointer to create references to the built-in objects within Visual Basic. The following process walks through the steps necessary to enable the referencing of these objects:

1. Open the Visual Basic project Bismarck.vbp created in the [drive]:\Bismarck directory (the ActiveX DLL project created earlier).

2. From the Project menu, select References to bring up the References dialog box. From the Available References list, select the Microsoft Active Server Pages 1.0 Object Library item, as shown in Figure 37.5. If this item does not exist in the list, click the Browse button to search for the ASP.DLL file. This file should be located wherever you installed Active Server Pages because it is the main DLL for the ASP application. Once you find the file, select it. The file now appears in the Available References list. Click OK to close the References dialog box.

FIGURE 37.5.

The References dialog box.

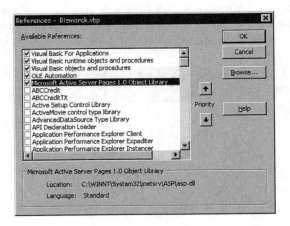

3. Add the following lines to the General Declarations section of the Utility.cls file:

```
Private Application As Application
Private Session As Session
Private Request As Request
Private Response As Response
Private Server As Server
```

4. Create a public function procedure in `Utility.cls` called `OnStartPage`. This function accepts one parameter with a type of `ScriptingContext` that we will call `myScriptingContext`. This type gets defined by the Active Server Pages reference `TypeLib` that was added earlier as a reference in Visual Basic. This function will set the five built-in object reference variables defined in the General Declarations section. You set the five variables using the following statements:

```
Set Application = myScriptingContext.Application
Set Session = myScriptingContext.Session
Set Request = myScriptingContext.Request
Set Response = myScriptingContext.Response
Set Server = myScriptingContext.Server
```

You also add a line of code that uses the Response object to write a line of HTML back to ASP, which indicates that `OnStartPage` has been called. This use of the `Response` object functions identically to its use with ASP scripting. Figure 37.6 presents the finished `OnStartPage` function.

FIGURE 37.6.

The `OnStartPage` *function.*

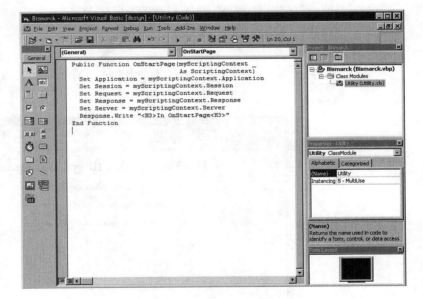

5. Add a function procedure to `Utility.cls` as follows:

```
Function TestMeASP(s As Variant)
    Response.Write "<CENTER><H3>Inside component - " _
                   + s + "</H3></CENTER>"
    Response.Write "<CENTER><H3>'Name' Session variable - " _
                   + Session("Name") + "</H3></CENTER>"
End Function
```

6. From the File menu, select Save Project. Save all files in the `[drive]:\Bismarck`.

7. From the File menu, select Make `Bismarck.DLL`. Rename the file to be created to `Bismarck02.dll`, and click OK. You have successfully created an ActiveX Server Component that can access the ASP built-in objects!

Step 5: Test the ActiveX Server Component with Active Server Pages

The following steps show you how to test the ActiveX Server Component with Active Server Pages:

1. Create a file named `TestMeASP.ASP` in a Web server virtual directory with execute permission.

2. Enter the following code in the `TestMeASP.ASP` file:

```
<HTML><BODY BGCOLOR="#ffffff">
<CENTER>
<H1>The Bismarck Utility Component</H1>
<% Set r = Server.CreateObject("Bismarck.Utility")
 Session("Name") = "Marc"
 r.TestMeASP("Happy Birthday") %>
</CENTER>
</BODY></HTML>
```

3. Request the `TestMeASP.ASP` file from a Web browser. You should see a page similar to Figure 37.7.

FIGURE 37.7.

Calling `TestMeASP` *from ASP.*

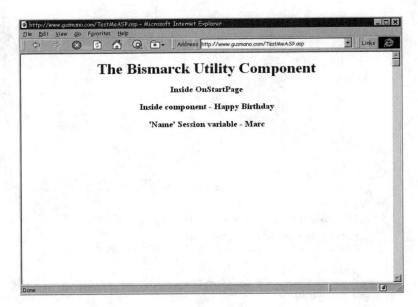

Creating a Useful ActiveX Server Component— The ActiveX Registration Component

In the examples created in this chapter so far, all you had to do to create a working ActiveX Server Component was to compile the DLL from within the Visual Basic development environment. By compiling, not only was a DLL created, but as an OLE Automation Server, the DLL was registered; consequently, needed information was written to the Windows NT or Windows 95 Registry. If the development and the deployment of this DLL occurred on the same machine, everything works fine.

What if you want to deploy this component on a Web server? The common way to register an ActiveX Server Component on the server is to run the REGSVR32.EXE command-line utility. Consider what happens if you are not physically at that Web server, and you have just FTPed the component to that machine? How do you remotely register that component? As you may have already guessed, one way is to create an ActiveX Server Component that registers other ActiveX Server Components. With an ActiveX Registration Component, remote registration becomes as easy as invoking a Web page.

This section focuses on building a useful ActiveX component for the purpose of registering other ActiveX components. You might start thinking ahead, asking yourself how the Registration Component itself will get registered remotely without having a Registration Component (a catch-22 if I ever heard one). Well, the answer is surprisingly easy—this initial registration has to occur while you are physically at the server!

The First Question: How Do You Register a Component Within VB?

The first question you have to answer before this ActiveX Registration Component can be built is how to programmatically register a component from within Visual Basic. One of the tools used to perform this task is the setup tool that comes with Visual Basic. Interestingly enough, Microsoft ships the Visual Basic source code to enable modifications to your generated setup applet. Because the setup performs the registration process, doesn't component-registration code have to exist in the sample?

Obviously, the answer to this question is yes, or we wouldn't be heading down this path. By opening the setup1.vbp project that exists in the \setupkit\setup1\ directory of your Visual Basic installation, you can begin to determine how registration occurs; then you can reuse that technique in the ActiveX Registration Component.

By searching for the RegisterFiles function in the setup1.bas file in the setup1.vbp project, you get a great starting point for figuring out the registration process. In particular, this function eventually makes a call to something called DLLSelfRegister, with a filename as a parameter. Doing a search on DLLSelfRegister shows that the call is actually a call to a function in an

37

CREATING
ACTIVEX SERVER
COMPONENTS

external DLL named VB5STKIT.DLL. No reason exists to prevent our ActiveX Registration Component from doing the same thing.

Preparing to Build the ActiveX Registration Component

Now that you have figured out how to provide the ActiveX registration functionality within the component, you need to prepare to construct the component. We can use the component created in the previous sections (Bismarck.vbp) and simply add one new property and one new method:

Property: FileName

Method: RegisterComponent

To make this component as flexible as possible, and also to illustrate several techniques for component development, you will create the RegisterComponent method to be invoked in any of three ways:

- Creating a Session variable named FileName and calling the RegisterComponent method
- Setting the FileName property of the component and calling the RegisterComponent method
- Calling the RegisterComponent method with a pFileName parameter

Creating the FileName Property and the RegisterComponent Method

Now that you understand how the ActiveX Registration Component will programmatically register other components and about the new property and method that need to be added, the work can begin. First, you create the FileName property and the RegisterComponent method. One easy way to accomplish this task is to take advantage of one of the add-ins shipped with VB 5.0—the Class Builder (see Figure 37.8).

The Class Builder is invoked from the Visual Basic Add-Ins menu. If your Add-Ins menu does not contain the Class Builder Utility… menu option, you must activate it from the Add-In Manager… menu option. Selecting this menu option opens the Add-In Manager dialog box, which shows a list of available Add-Ins. Simply check the VB Class Builder Utility checkbox and click the OK button. Now, when the Add-Ins menu is selected, the Class Builder Utility… menu option appears.

FIGURE 37.8.

The Visual Basic Class Builder.

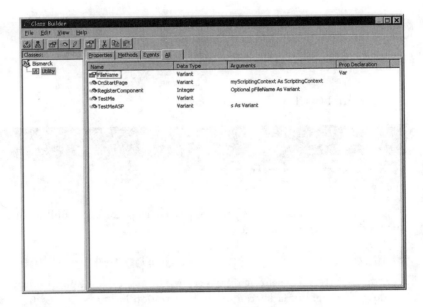

When the Class Builder utility is initially selected, a dialog box appears, indicating that your class was not initially created by Class Builder. Click the OK button, and the Class Builder utility appears. To add the FileName property, select the Utility class in the left pane, and then click the Add New Property to Current Class button (the third button from the left) from the toolbar. This action brings up the Property Builder dialog box. Fill in the Properties tab on this dialog box with the following information:

Name:	FileName
Data Type:	Variant
Declaration:	Public Property
Default Property?	Checked

When you have entered all the information, click OK. This new entry now appears in the right pane of the Class Builder utility.

Creating the RegisterComponent method works similarly to creating the FileName property. To add the RegisterComponent method, select the Utility class in the left pane, and then select the Add New Method to Current Class button from the toolbar (the fourth button from the left). This action brings up the Method Builder dialog box. Fill in the Properties tab on this dialog box with the following information:

Name:	`RegisterComponent`
Arguments:	`pFileName` as Variant
Return Data Type:	Integer

> **NOTE**
>
> Do not select Declare as Friend? or Default Method?.

When you have completed the preceding steps, close the Class Builder utility and click Yes to update the project with changes.

Adding Code to the `RegisterComponent` Method

After the `RegisterComponent` method is created from the Class Builder utility, all the code needed to allow for programmatic component registration has to be copied from the Setup application sample project (`setup1.vbp`) to this project. Because the component calls an external DLL, the declaration of that DLL is also copied into a Visual Basic standard module in the `Bismarck.vbp` project.

To make this component specifically usable with Active Server Pages as well as with other environments capable of using components (for example, Visual Basic), a Boolean variable named `ASPComponent` gets defined and initialized to `False` in the `Class_Initialize` event of `Utility.cls`. If this component is called from an Active Server Page, the `OnStartPage` method will be called and `ASPComponent` will be set to `True`. This value is used in the `RegisterComponent` method to determine if the component should expect to see a `Session` variable named `FileName`.

Also remember that in the design of this method, it was determined that the `pFileName` parameter would be an optionally passed parameter. To make the `pFileName` an optional parameter, add the keyword `optional` to the `pFilename` parameter declaration in the `RegisterComponent` function definition. In the `RegisterComponent` method, the `IsMissing` function can help detect whether this parameter was supplied. This `IsMissing` function provides a way to determine where the `FileName` information comes from. If the `pFileName` is passed as a parameter, the parameter is used. If the parameter is missing, the code will check to see if the `FileName` property is set, and if so, will use that value. If that property is not set, a check is made to see if a `Session` variable named `FileName` is set, and if so, it will use that. If none of these options was used, the `RegisterComponent` returns an error.

> **NOTE**
>
> Remember to copy the VB5STKIT.DLL file from the Setup Kit folder (\setupkit\kitfil32\) to your path so that the Registration Component can find the file when it calls the DLLSelfRegister routine.

By completing all of these tasks, the RegisterComponent method will look similar to the code in Listing 37.3.

Listing 37.3. The RegisterComponent method.

```
Public Function RegisterComponent _
(Optional pFileName As Variant) As Integer
  On Error GoTo RegisterComponentErr
  Dim sFileName As String
  If IsMissing(pFileName) Then
    If "" = mvarFileName Then
      If ASPComponent = True Then
        If "" = Session("FileName") Then
          sFileName = Session("FileName")
        Else
          RegisterComponent = 100 'No file name supplied
          Exit Function
        End If
      Else
        RegisterComponent = 100 'No file name supplied
        Exit Function
      End If
    Else
      sFileName = mvarFileName
    End If
  Else
    sFileName = pFileName
  End If
  RegisterComponent = DLLSelfRegister(sFileName)
  Exit Function
RegisterComponentErr:
  RegisterComponent = Err.Number
End Function
```

Invoking RegisterComponent from a Visual Basic Client

One way to utilize this component is with a Visual Basic form-based application. Figure 37.9 represents a simple Visual Basic form that enables you to enter and submit the path of a DLL to the RegisterComponent method.

FIGURE 37.9.

*A Visual Basic
application to invoke
the* RegisterComponent
method.

Listing 37.4 is the code behind the Submit button. This code creates an instance of the ActiveX Registration Component and then invokes the RegisterComponent method. Once the method returns, the return code gets evaluated against a set of error constants to give feedback as to the success or failure of the call.

Listing 37.4. Invoking the ActiveX Registration Component from Visual Basic.

```
Private Sub cmdSubmit_Click()
  'error constants
  Const FAIL_OLE = 2
  Const FAIL_LOAD = 3
  Const FAIL_ENTRY = 4
  Const FAIL_REG = 5
  Const FILE_NOT_FOUND = 53
  Const NO_FILE_SPECIFIED = 100
  Dim o As Object
  Set o = CreateObject("Bismarck.Utility")
  Dim rc As Integer
  rc = o.RegisterComponent(txtFileName)
  Select Case rc
    Case 0
      MsgBox "Registered successfully"
    Case FAIL_OLE
      MsgBox "OLE Failure"
    Case FAIL_LOAD
      MsgBox "Fail on file loading"
    Case FAIL_ENTRY
      MsgBox "Cannot Register - no OLE entry point in DLL"
    Case FAIL_REG
      MsgBox "Failure on registration"
    Case FILE_NOT_FOUND
      MsgBox "File not found - may be VB5STKIT.DLL"
    Case NO_FILE_SPECIFIED
      MsgBox "Failure - no file specified"
    Case Else
      MsgBox "Unknown Failure"
  End Select
End Sub
```

Invoking RegisterComponent from an Active Server Page

Another way to utilize this component is by creating an Active Server Page and scripting to the ActiveX Registration Component. Figure 37.10 represents an ASP page that can invoke the ActiveX Registration Component on the Web server. An HTML form is created to enable the path of a DLL to be entered and submitted to the RegisterComponent method.

FIGURE 37.10.

An active Web page to invoke the `RegisterComponent` *method.*

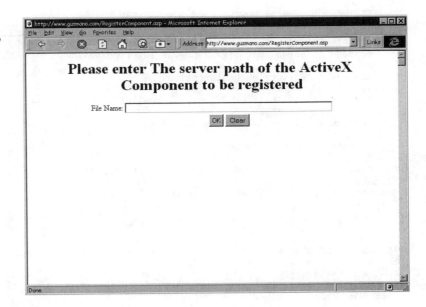

37

CREATING
ACTIVEX SERVER
COMPONENTS

Listing 37.5 shows the Active Server Page HTML and VBScript. The script creates an instance of the ActiveX Registration Component and then invokes the `RegisterComponent` method. Like the Visual Basic implementation, once the method returns, the return code gets evaluated against a set of error constants to give feedback as to the success or failure of the call.

Listing 37.5. Invoking the ActiveX Registration Component from an Active Server Page.

```
<%
if Request.Form("FileName") = "" then
  message = "Please enter The server path of the ActiveX
➡Component to be registered"
else
  'error constants
  Const FAIL_OLE = 2
  Const FAIL_LOAD = 3
  Const FAIL_ENTRY = 4
  Const FAIL_REG = 5
  Const FILE_NOT_FOUND = 53
  Const NO_FILE_SPECIFIED = 100
  Set o = Server.CreateObject("Bismarck.Utility")
  rc = o.RegisterComponent(Request.Form("FileName"))
  Select Case rc
    Case 0
      message = "Registered successfully"
    Case FAIL_OLE
      message = "OLE Failure"
    Case FAIL_LOAD
      message = "Fail on file loading"
```

continues

Listing 37.5. continued

```
    Case FAIL_ENTRY
      message = "Cannot Register - no OLE entry point in DLL"
    Case FAIL_REG
      message = "Failure on registration"
    Case FILE_NOT_FOUND
      message = "File not found - may be VB5STKIT.DLL"
    Case NO_FILE_SPECIFIED
      message = "Failure - no file specified"
    Case Else
      message = "Unknown Failure"
  End Select
  Response.Write "<HTML><BODY BGCOLOR=""#ffffff""<CENTER>"
  Response.Write message
  Response.Write "</CENTER></BODY></HTML>"
  Response.End
end if
%>

<HTML><BODY BGCOLOR="#ffffff">
<CENTER>
<H1><% = message %></H1>
<FORM METHOD=POST ACTION="<%=Request.ServerVariables("PATH_INFO")%>">
<TABLE BORDER=0>
 <TR>
  <TD ALIGN=RIGHT>File Name:</TD>
  <TD><INPUT TYPE=TEXT SIZE=60 MAXLENGTH=60 NAME="FileName" VALUE=
➥"<% =Session("FileName") %>"></TD>
 </TR>
  <TD></TD>
  <TD COLSPAN=2 ALIGN=CENTER>
   <INPUT TYPE=SUBMIT VALUE="OK">
   <INPUT TYPE=RESET VALUE="Clear">
  </TD>
 </TR>
</TABLE>
</FORM>
</CENTER>
</BODY></HTML>
```

Things That Could Be Added to the ActiveX Registration Component

The following are several other additions/enhancements that are provided as exercises to the user:

■ Generation of error events from the component back to the client

■ Validation that the FileName variable is really an existing file

■ Programmatic uploading of the file that needs to be registered (so you could do the upload and registration in one step)

Summary

If you are involved in Active Server Page development, you will probably run up against some situation that does not work with script or cannot be developed within script. In these cases, you may need to extend the ASP environment by developing your own custom ActiveX Server Components.

Custom ActiveX Server Components serve as nothing more that what users have known as OLE Automation Servers. You can create server components to be used specifically with ASP, which can utilize the built-in objects that are part of the ASP environment.

37

CREATING
ACTIVEX SERVER
COMPONENTS

Creating Design-Time Controls for Visual InterDev

by Armando Flores

IN THIS CHAPTER

CHAPTER

38

In Chapter 5, "Connecting and Using Databases," you learned how to use the Data Command control to generate the active server scripting code required to access data stored in a relational database. This process was accomplished by inserting an ActiveX design-time control into your file and typing information in the property page for the control (control ID, data connection, command type, and so on).

In this chapter, you learn why and how to build your own design-time controls. You will use the Microsoft design-time control Software Development Toolkit (SDK) to create a simple design-time control that inserts a multiple-choice question into an HTML form.

You build two versions of the multiple-choice design-time control, one using Microsoft Visual Basic 5.0 and a second version of the same control using Microsoft Visual C++ 5.0. These versions will enable you to compare the level of effort and benefits of using each tool for creating design-time controls.

> **NOTE**
>
> You can create design-time controls with any development tool used to build ActiveX controls (for example, Symantec C++, Borland Delphi, or C++) and that enables you to implement the `IActiveDesigner` interface.

What Is a Design-Time Control?

A *design-time control* is a type of ActiveX component intended for use during the development of an application. These controls can be activated in the Visual InterDev development environment to generate and modify text that can be typed in an HTML or ASP file.

You can think of a design-time control as a sort of mini-wizard that gives the Web developer a simple graphical mechanism to create and modify what would otherwise be considered a cryptic chunk of HTML or active server scripting code. Design-time controls can function as *wrappers* to just about anything that you can include in an HTML or ASP file. You can use design-time controls to generate

- Sections of a Web page that contain HTML tags constantly repeated in the file with some variations, such as in the case of multiple-choice questions in a survey.
- Web page elements that are common to multiple files, but that require some customization for each department or area. (For example, a navigation bar with links to other general interest pages, different stores in an electronic mall, and so on.)
- Front ends for HTML extensions (see the Marquee control in the SDK MFC samples).
- Front ends for Java applets (see the Billboard control in the SDK VB samples).
- Sections of a page containing VBScript or JavaScript subroutines (server and/or client side).

> **TIP**
>
> The output generated by a design-time control is not restricted to HTML or ASP statements. If your Web server or browser supports other scripting languages, such as Perl, REXX, and so on, a design-time control can help create your Web files.
>
> In other words, if you can enter it into an HTML file, a design-time control can help you create it!

Why Create Design-Time Controls?

Design-time controls enable you to extend the benefits of software component reuse to the process of Web page development. You, as a Web component developer, could create design-time controls to be used by Web application developers in other parts of your organization (intranet), or you could distribute these components to your company's business partners (extranet).

In addition, design-time controls can take advantage of a predefined set of host services to obtain information about other features of the system. For example, the Data Command control uses the Host Services of Visual InterDev to obtain database information (data connections, tables, column names, and so on) when building a database query. You learn about Host Services in a later section, but for now the main idea is that design-time controls can tap into other resources as well as their own property page to generate text.

A Closer Look at a Design-Time Control

Let's start by creating a simple HTML file and inserting an instance of the `Include` design-time control shipped with Visual InterDev. This control inserts an HTML `#INCLUDE FILE` directive into the current HTML or ASP file.

As you probably know, the `#INCLUDE FILE` directive represents an HTML extension used to insert a file into a Web page before the page is processed by a Web server. For further information about this directive, see the Visual InterDev online documentation.

To insert a design-time control into a Web page

1. Move the cursor to the line where you want to insert the control.
2. Open the editor's shortcut menu by right-clicking the mouse button.
3. Click the Insert ActiveX Control... menu option.
4. Select the Design-time tab.
5. Double-click Include Control. (See Figure 38.1.)

6. For now, ignore the URL Builder button and just enter `MyFile.htm` in the Source Input field.

7. Close the Property page and the Design Layout page by clicking on the corresponding Close button.

FIGURE 38.1.

Using the Include design-time control.

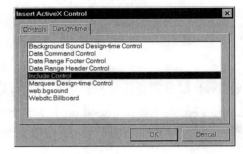

Listing 38.1 shows the output created by the Include design-time control. The output consists of two parts enclosed between the METADATA statements (lines 1 and 12). The first part of the output (lines 2 to 9) contains information used by Visual InterDev to store and recall the properties of the control the next time you edit the control.

The second part of the text created by the control (just line 11 in this case) is known as the *runtime text*. The runtime text can consist of one or multiple lines of code, as you will see in the sample programs.

Listing 38.1. Output produced by the Include design-time control.

```
Line #
 1: <!--METADATA TYPE="DesignerControl" startspan
 2:         <OBJECT ID="Include1" WIDTH=151 HEIGHT=24
 3:          CLASSID="CLSID:F602E725-A281-11CF-A5B7-0080C73AAC7E">
 4:             <PARAM NAME="_Version" VALUE="65536">
 5:             <PARAM NAME="_ExtentX" VALUE="3969">
 6:             <PARAM NAME="_ExtentY" VALUE="635">
 7:             <PARAM NAME="_StockProps" VALUE="0">
 8:             <PARAM NAME="Source" VALUE="MyFile.htm">
 9:         </OBJECT>
10: -->
11: <!--#INCLUDE FILE="MyFile.htm"-->
12: <!--METADATA TYPE="DesignerControl" endspan-->
```

Once you have inserted the control, you can change its attributes and re-create the runtime text by selecting the Edit Design-time Control... option from the shortcut menu (right-click the mouse button) while the cursor appears anywhere on the control's text (lines 1 to 12, inclusive).

You can also insert multiple instances of the same control in a Web page, and Visual InterDev can differentiate their attributes by scanning the parameters of their <OBJECT> statement.

TIP

Keep the following points in mind if you ever need to edit a file containing design-time controls with an editor that does not support this feature (Notepad, for example):

- Make sure that you do not delete or change the two `<!--METADATA...  -->` lines. If you do, you will not be able to edit the control again.
- The text contained between the `<OBJECT>...</OBJECT>` tags are not part of the HTML text to be processed by the Web server or the browser and therefore there is no need to alter it in any way.
- If necessary, you can edit the run-time text, but all changes get discarded the next time you run the design-time control. In some cases, you may be able to preserve the changes made to the run-time text by also making identical changes in the corresponding `PARM NAME=` tag.

NOTE

The information stored in the `PARAM` tag of the `<OBJECT>...</OBJECT>` statement preserves what is known as the persistency information of the control; this information helps reconstruct the control later.

Microsoft Internet Information Server (IIS) removes the persistency information before sending the Web page to a Web browser.

Design Considerations

An old expression says that if the only tool you have is a hammer, all problems look like nails. The question developers face is how do you know when to use a design-time control versus a server-side script or a plain include file?

Suppose that you need to build an Employee Satisfaction survey that requires several questions. The questions can appear in a multiple-choice fashion with three options, such as Agree, Disagree, or Don't Care; or Yes, No, or Maybe.

You can tackle the problem in several different ways:

- You could use a tool like Microsoft FrontPage97 to paint the radio buttons and go through each of the prompts to enter information about every field.

  This approach works much better than using a plain text editor to enter HTML statements, but if you have to enter many questions, you may tire of entering data in different prompts.

■ You could create a database and use a script to generate the radio buttons with Active Server Pages. This approach functions well if you also have access to the database so that you can change the questions and answers as needed. Also, you may have to run your pages on a Web server that does not offer an easy way to create HTML pages on the fly.

■ You could create a design-time control with a custom build property page, distribute this control to the organization in charge of the survey, and have the group build its own questionnaire. Remember, this approach requires you to distribute the design-time control when it changes.

Suppose that you have determined that you want to create a design-time control to generate multiple-choice questions. Let's say that you want to test your control with a simple question, such as the one shown in Figure 38.2.

FIGURE 38.2.

Sample HTML page using the MltChoiceVB *control.*

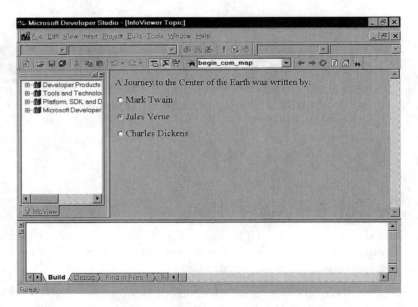

The next step requires designing the HTML code that you want to generate (see Listing 38.2) and the parts of the control that change on a case-by-case basis (see Table 38.1).

Table 38.1. Attribute names and descriptions for the MltChoiceVB **and** MltChoiceVC **controls.**

Attribute	Description
QID	Name of HTML variable for this question (Q101, for example)
Qtext	Question text (*A Journey to the Center of the Earth* was written by:)

Attribute	Description
OptionA	Text for Option A (Mark Twain)
OptionB	Text for Option B (Jules Verne)
OptionC	Text for Option C (Charles Dickens)

Listing 38.2. Runtime text created by the `MltChoiceVB` and `MltChoiceVC` controls.

```
Line #
1: <!--***Q101***-->
2:     <p>A Journey to the Center of the Earth was written by:</p>
3:     <p><input type="radio" name="Q101"value="A">Mark Twain</p>
4:     <p><input type="radio" name="Q101"value="B">Jules Verne</p>
5:     <p><input type="radio" name="Q101"value="C">Charles Dickens</p>
```

Now that you have a clear idea of the task at hand, you can get to the meat and potatoes of design-time control programming.

The Design-Time Control SDK

Before you build your first control, you must install the design-time control SDK. To install the SDK, run the `dtcsdk.exe` program in the `3RDPARTY\DTCSDK` subdirectory of the companion CD-ROM. You may also download it from Microsoft at the following URL:

`www.microsoft.com/workshop/prog/sdk/dtctrl`

If you use the default installation options, the SDK installation program will create the `Program Files\Design-time Control SDK` subdirectory, which contains the following:

- SDK documentation files
- Additional samples in Visual Basic and Visual C++
- Tools to assist you in the creation of design-time controls

> **TIP**
>
> You may find it useful to copy the `Program Files\Design-time Control SDK\Tools\regsvrdc.exe` program to a directory in your path such as `WINDOWS` (for Windows95) or `WINNT` (for Windows NT). This program will be used to register your component as a design-time control.
>
> If you are developing design-time controls in Visual Basic, you need to reference the `webdc.tlb` type library in the `Samples\VB\Common` subdirectory of the SDK. The VB sample in this chapter has instructions on how to complete this task.
>
> *continues*

> *continued*
>
> If you plan to develop design-time controls in Visual C++, you need to include some of the header files in the `Samples\Mfc\include` subdirectory. You can accomplish this process by either copying the files to your project's subdirectory, or by using the `/I` compile directive to add the `Samples\Mfc\include` subdirectory to the `include` path at compile time.
>
> In addition to the SDK, you may want to install the design-time ActiveX Control Pad program (`setupdcp.exe` on the CD-ROM). This file provides a special version for developers that enables you to test the samples in the SDK, as well as your own controls.

Creating Design-Time Controls in Visual Basic 5.0

The Visual Basic version of the multiple-choice control (`MltChoiceVB`) was designed to have a minimal user interface. Figure 38.3 shows the `Qtext` property, and you must use the All tab of the control's Properties page to enter the `Qtext`, `QID`, `OptionA`, `OptionB` and `OptionC` attributes.

FIGURE 38.3.

`MltChoiceVB` *user interface.*

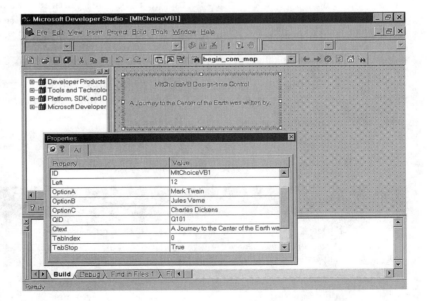

The following list summarizes the steps required to create a design-time control using Visual Basic 5.0:

- Create the `MltChoiceVB` control.
- Add support for the `IActiveDesigner` interface.
- Register the control as `WebDesigntimeControl`.

> **NOTE**
>
> Remember that you must install the SDK before you create your control.

Step 1: Create the `MltChoiceVB` Control

Here's how you create the `MltChoiceVB` control:

1. Start VB5.0, and select File | New Project from the menu bar.
2. Add two labels to the control: one for the control's title, `MltChoiceVB Design-time Control`, and one for the question text. Set the name of the second label to `lblQuestion` and its Caption to `Question?`.
3. Set the name of the project to `VID_Design-time Control` and the name of the control to `MltChoiceVB` (see Figure 38.4).

FIGURE 38.4.

Creating the MltChoiceVB *control.*

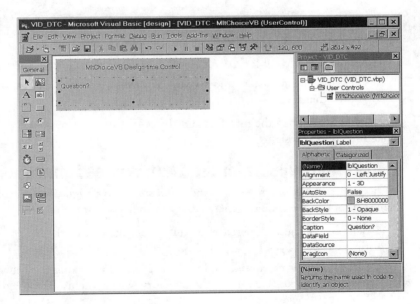

4. Save the project and control in a directory of your choice.

5. Launch the ActiveX Control Interface Wizard from the Add-ins menu bar. (Use the Add-In Manager... menu bar option to install it, if necessary.)

6. Use the Back and Next buttons in the Wizard dialog box as needed.

7. Remove all properties, methods, and events from the Selected names list box.

8. Add your QID, Qtext, OptionA, OptionB, and OptionC properties to the control.

9. Map the Qtext property to the Caption member of the lblQuestion control (see Figure 38.5).

FIGURE 38.5.

Mapping program variables to user-interface controls.

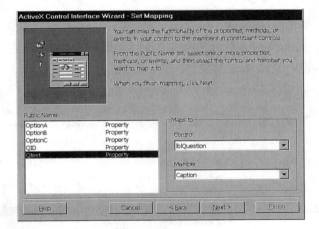

10. Set the data type of the QID, OptionA, OptionB, and OptionC properties to String.

11. Click the Finish button, and save the Wizard Summary Report in the same directory as the other files.

So far, you have coded the interface and the properties. The next step adds the features that make this control design-time enabled.

Step 2: Add Support for the IActiveDesigner Interface

In this step, you add a reference to the Microsoft Web design-time control type library, and then incorporate the code to generate the run-time text for the control.

1. Select the Project | References menu option; then check the Microsoft Web Design-time Control Type Library option.

   If the option is not found, add it to the project by clicking the Browse button; then look for the webdc.tlb file in the directory where you installed the design-time control SDK (C:\Program Files\Design-time Control SDK\Samples\VB\Common is the default location). Do not forget to put a checkmark next to the reference after you add the type library.

2. Add the following two lines of code to the top of the (General)(Declarations) section of the MltChoiceVB control:

```
'   IActiveDesigner
Implements IProvideRuntimeText
```

3. Enter the following code in the GetRuntimeText() procedure of the IProvideRuntimeText object:

```
Private Function IProvideRuntimeText_GetRuntimeText() As String
Dim strText As String
Dim strQuote As String
strQuote = Chr$(34)
strRadio = "        <p><input type=" & strQuote & "radio" & strQuote & " name="
strRadio = strRadio & strQuote & m_QID & strQuote & " value=" & strQuote
strText = "<!--***" & m_QID & "***-->" & vbCr
strText = strText & "        <p>" & lblQuestion.Caption & "</p>" & vbCr
strText = strText & strRadio & "A" & strQuote & ">" & m_OptionA & "</p>" &
➡vbCr
strText = strText & strRadio & "B" & strQuote & ">" & m_OptionB & "</p>" &
➡vbCr
strText = strText & strRadio & "C" & strQuote & ">" & m_OptionC & "</p>" &
➡vbCr
IProvideRuntimeText_GetRuntimeText = strText
End Function
```

4. Choose the File | Make VID_DTC.ocx menu option to compile your control. Save your control in the same subdirectory as the others.

Step 3: Register the Control as `WebDesigntimeControl`

By now you probably want to test your first design-time control. Before you do that, you must tell Windows that your control can be used as a design-time component.

To accomplish this task, run the REGSVRDC.EXE program using either the CLSID or ProgID from your control.

Open a DOS prompt, and set the current directory to C:\Program Files\Design-time Control SDK\Tools; then enter the following command:

```
REGSVRDC VID_DTC.MltChoiceVB
```

In this command, VID_DTC.MltChoiceVB is the ProgID of your control.

The preceding command registers your design-time control in the Windows Registry and enables Visual InterDev to use it when you select the Edit Design-time Control option from the shortcut menu. This command must be executed every time you want to test a newly compiled control. REGSVRDC is a C program distributed in the SDK, in executable and source format. Please refer to the SDK documentation for more information.

> **TIP**
>
> When you develop an ActiveX component, Visual Basic generates new CLSIDs and IIDs (the 32-byte identifier for classes and interfaces) every time you compile your project. This action can become a problem if you need to recompile a design-time control already included in your Web pages. The problem is that the CLASSID parameter in the OBJECT will not match the corresponding value in the System Registry; consequently, Visual InterDev will not be able to activate the control for editing, even if the control's name appears as a Insert ActiveX Control shortcut menu option.
>
> To avoid this problem, you need to set your project's Version compatibility to Binary Compatibility in the Component tab of the Project | Properties menu option.

To test the control, open the TestDTC.htm file, or create a new HTML page and follow these directions:

1. Move the cursor to the line where you want to insert the control.
2. Open the editor's shortcut menu by right-clicking the mouse button.
3. Click the Insert ActiveX Control menu option.
4. Select the Design-time tab.
5. Double-click VID_DTC.MltChoiceVB.
6. Enter values for QID, Qtext, OptionA, OptionB, and OptionC properties.
7. Close the property and design layout pages; save the HTML file.
8. Open the shortcut menu (right-click the mouse), and select the Preview option.

Distributing Visual Basic Design-Time Controls

As with any other ActiveX control created using Visual Basic, design-time controls require a runtime DLL. Depending on what other features and functions you have included in your control, you may need to distribute additional support files. You should use the Application Setup Wizard to ensure that you distribute the necessary support files.

Creating Design-Time Controls in Visual C++ 5.0

In this section, you build a C++ version of the multiple-choice control described earlier. This control is developed in Visual C++ version 5.0, and in particular, you use the ActiveX Template Library (ATL) feature of Visual C++ version 5.0.

You need to become very familiar with previous versions of Visual C++. This text will guide you through the steps that are unique to version 5.0.

The basic steps to create an ATL based design-time control appear in the following list. Further explanation of each step follows the list.

1. Create the `MltChoiceVC` control.
2. Add a property page to the control.
3. Add support for the `IActiveDesigner` interface.
4. Register the control as `WebDesigntimeControl`.

Step 1: Create the `MltChoiceVC` Control

1. Launch Visual C++, and choose File | New. Using the ATL COM AppWizard, click on the Projects tab to create a new project; then enter `MltChoiceATL` as the project name. Click the OK button to continue. Select the Dynamic Link Library (DLL) radio button on the Server Type Wizard dialog box, and click the Finish button to generate the ATL project. Finally, click OK to complete the generation of your new skeleton project.

2. Open the shortcut menu (right-click the mouse) of the `MltChoiceATL` classes in the ClassView, and select the New ATL Object option (see Figure 38.6).

3. You should see the ATL Object Wizard dialog box, shown in Figure 38.7. Click Controls on the left side of the dialog box and Full Control on the right side. Now, click the Next button.

FIGURE 38.6.

Adding a new ATL object to the `MltChoiceATL` *project.*

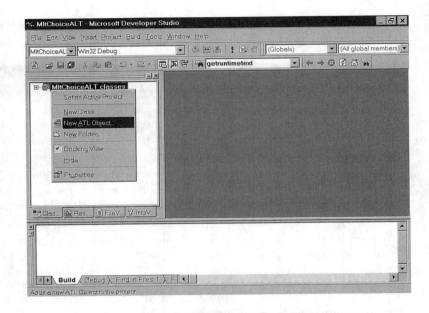

FIGURE 38.7.

Selecting a full control in the ATL Object Wizard dialog box.

4. Complete the information in the Names tab of the ATL Object Wizard Properties dialog box, as indicated in Figure 38.8. Notice that as you enter text in the Short Name field, the system will echo what you enter into the other fields.

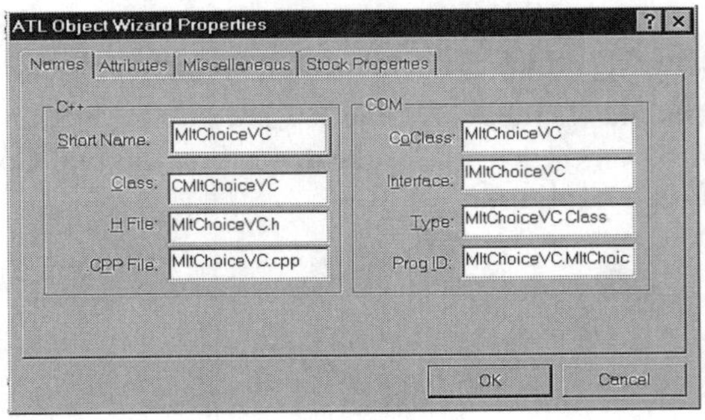

FIGURE 38.8.

Entering C++ and COM names in the ATL Object Wizard Properties dialog.

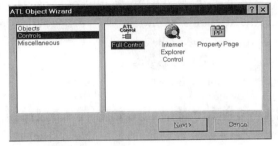

5. Expand the `MltChoiceATL` classes node in the ClassView. Open the shortcut menu (right-click the mouse) of the `IMltChoiceVC` interface, and select the Add Property option (see Figure 38.9).

FIGURE 38.9.

Shortcut menu for ATL interfaces.

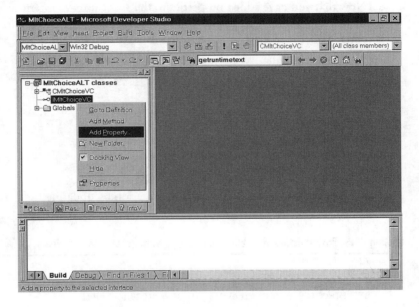

6. Select BSTR from the drop-down list of property types. Enter `QID` as the property name. Make sure that the Get Function, Put Function, and PropPut options appear checked as indicated in Figure 38.10.

FIGURE 38.10.

The Add Property to Interface dialog box.

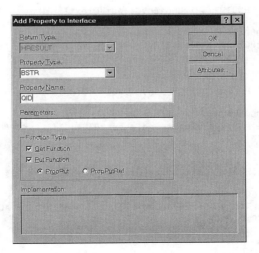

7. Repeat the preceding steps to add the Qtext, OptionA, OptionB, and OptionC properties to the IMltChoiceVC interface. Keep in mind that these names are case sensitive and must be typed as indicated.

8. Now that you have added properties to the IMltChoiceVC interface, you need to add the corresponding member variables to the CMltChoice control so that the information entered via the interface will be stored in the control itself.

   To add the member variables to the control, enter the following text at the bottom of the MltChoiceVC.h file, on the line after the HRESULT OnDraw(ATL_DRAWINFO& di); member function declaration:

```
private:
    // Member variables
    CComBSTR m_bstrQID;
    CComBSTR m_bstrQtext;
    CComBSTR m_bstrOptionA;
    CComBSTR m_bstrOptionB;
    CComBSTR m_bstrOptionC;
```

9. Add the get and put functions implementation by updating the MltChoiceVC.cpp file (see Listing 38.3).

Listing 38.3. Partial listing of MltChoiceVC.cpp with get and put functions.

```
//
// top lines omitted
//
STDMETHODIMP CMltChoiceVC::get_Qtext(BSTR * pVal)
{
// TODO: Add your implementation code here
*pVal = ::SysAllocString(m_bstrQtext); //   <<****LINE ADDED
return S_OK;
}

STDMETHODIMP CMltChoiceVC::put_Qtext(BSTR newVal)
{
// TODO: Add your implementation code here
m_bstrQtext = CComBSTR(newVal);   //   <<****LINE ADDED
return S_OK;
}

STDMETHODIMP CMltChoiceVC::get_QID(BSTR * pVal)
{
// TODO: Add your implementation code here
*pVal = ::SysAllocString(m_bstrQID); //   <<****LINE ADDED
return S_OK;
}

STDMETHODIMP CMltChoiceVC::put_QID(BSTR newVal)
{
// TODO: Add your implementation code here
m_bstrQID = CComBSTR(newVal); //   <<****LINE ADDED
return S_OK;
}
```

```
STDMETHODIMP CMltChoiceVC::get_OptionA(BSTR * pVal)
{
// TODO: Add your implementation code here
*pVal = ::SysAllocString(m_bstrOptionA); //    <<****LINE ADDED
return S_OK;
}

STDMETHODIMP CMltChoiceVC::put_OptionA(BSTR newVal)
{
// TODO: Add your implementation code here
m_bstrOptionA = CComBSTR(newVal); //    <<****LINE ADDED
return S_OK;
}
STDMETHODIMP CMltChoiceVC::get_OptionB(BSTR * pVal)
{
// TODO: Add your implementation code here
*pVal = ::SysAllocString(m_bstrOptionB); //    <<****LINE ADDED
return S_OK;
}

STDMETHODIMP CMltChoiceVC::put_OptionB(BSTR newVal)
{
// TODO: Add your implementation code here
m_bstrOptionB = CComBSTR(newVal); //    <<****LINE ADDED
return S_OK;
}

STDMETHODIMP CMltChoiceVC::get_OptionC(BSTR * pVal)
{
// TODO: Add your implementation code here
*pVal = ::SysAllocString(m_bstrOptionC); //    <<****LINE ADDED
return S_OK;
}

STDMETHODIMP CMltChoiceVC::put_OptionC(BSTR newVal)
{
// TODO: Add your implementation code here
m_bstrOptionC = CComBSTR(newVal); //    <<****LINE ADDED
return S_OK;
}
```

38

CREATING DESIGN-
TIME CONTROLS

10. Change the HRESULT CMltChoiceVC::OnDraw(ATL_DRAWINFO& di) member function at the beginning of the file MltChoiceVC.cpp as indicated.

Replace:

```
DrawText(di.hdcDraw, _T("ATL 2.0"), -1 ...
```

with:

```
DrawText(di.hdcDraw, _T("Multiple-choice DTC"), -1 ...
```

11. At this point, your program should build without any errors. You can start building it by selecting Build | Build MltChoiceATL.dll from the menu bar. If you know how to use the ActiveX Control Test Container tool, test the get and put methods of your control. Look for MltChoiceVC Class in the Insert OLE Control dialog box of the tool.

Step 2: Add a Property Page to the `MltChoiceVC` Control

The property page is the user interface of the control. It enables you to enter the information that will be inserted in the HTML code. In ActiveX programming, the property page can be an object of its own and therefore must be designed so it can be used by multiple applications.

To add the property page, proceed as follows:

1. Open the shortcut menu of the `MltChoiceATL` classes entry located at the beginning of the ClassView, and select the New ATL Object option (see Figure 38.11).

FIGURE 38.11.

Adding a new ATL object to the `MltChoiceATL` *project.*

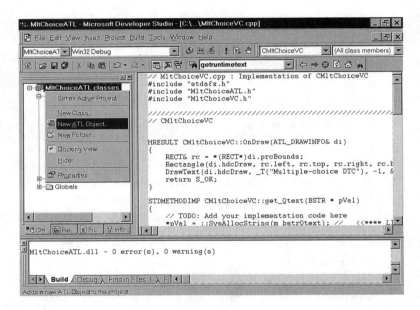

2. Select Controls on the left side and Property Page on the right side of the ATL Object Wizard dialog box; then click the Next button.

3. Enter `MltProp` in the Short Name field of the ATL Object Wizard dialog box.

4. Click the Strings tab, and then set the title of the property page to Question. Delete the entry in the Helpfile field. Click OK to generate the files required for the property page.

5. Switch to the Resource view. Edit the `IDD_MLTPROP` dialog box as indicated in Figure 38.12.

FIGURE 38.12.

Adding fields to the IDD_MLTPROP *dialog box.*

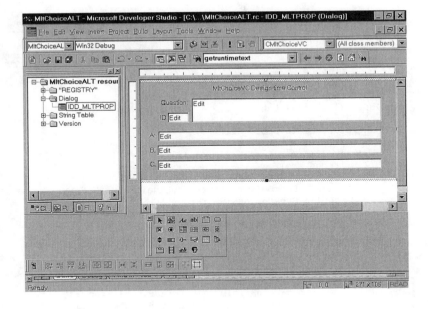

6. Set the ID of these fields as indicated in Table 38.2.

Table 38.2. ID for Edit fields in IDD_MLTPROP dialog box.

Label	Edit Field ID
Question	IDC_QTEXT
ID	IDC_QID
A	IDC_OPTIONA
B	IDC_OPTIONB
C	IDC_OPTIONC

7. You now need to enable the CMltProp class to set the properties of your control. This task will be accomplished in two steps: adding the code to move input from the property page to the control and connecting the property page to the control. You need to change MltProp.h to add an #include statement for the MltChoiceATL file, add five entries to the BEGIN_MSG_MAP, replace the Apply function, and add the OnPgChg function. The resulting file appears in Listing 38.4.

Listing 38.4. `MltProp.h` file after enabling the property page.

```
// MltProp.h : Declaration of the CMltProp

#ifndef __MLTPROP_H_
#define __MLTPROP_H_

#include "resource.h"        // main symbols
#include "MltChoiceATL.h"

EXTERN_C const CLSID CLSID_MltProp;

/////////////////////////////////////////////////////////////////////////////
// CMltProp
class ATL_NO_VTABLE CMltProp :
      public CComObjectRootEx<CComSingleThreadModel>,
      public CComCoClass<CMltProp, &CLSID_MltProp>,
      public IPropertyPageImpl<CMltProp>,
      public CDialogImpl<CMltProp>
{
public:
      CMltProp()
      {
            m_dwTitleID = IDS_TITLEMltProp;
            m_dwHelpFileID = IDS_HELPFILEMltProp;
            m_dwDocStringID = IDS_DOCSTRINGMltProp;
      }

      enum {IDD = IDD_MLTPROP};

   DECLARE_REGISTRY_RESOURCEID(IDR_MLTPROP)

   BEGIN_COM_MAP(CMltProp)
         COM_INTERFACE_ENTRY_IMPL(IPropertyPage)
   END_COM_MAP()

   BEGIN_MSG_MAP(CMltProp)
         COMMAND_HANDLER(IDC_QID, EN_CHANGE, OnPgChg)
         COMMAND_HANDLER(IDC_QTEXT, EN_CHANGE, OnPgChg)
         COMMAND_HANDLER(IDC_OPTIONA, EN_CHANGE, OnPgChg)
         COMMAND_HANDLER(IDC_OPTIONB, EN_CHANGE, OnPgChg)
         COMMAND_HANDLER(IDC_OPTIONC, EN_CHANGE, OnPgChg)
         CHAIN_MSG_MAP(IPropertyPageImpl<CMltProp>)
   END_MSG_MAP()

         STDMETHOD(Apply)(void)
         {
               USES_CONVERSION;
               ATLTRACE(_T("CMltProp::Apply\n"));
               for (UINT i = 0; i < m_nObjects; i++)
               {

                   CComQIPtr<IMltChoiceVC, &IID_IMltChoiceVC> pMlt(m_ppUnk[i]);

                   BSTR bstrDlg;

                   GetDlgItemText(IDC_QID, bstrDlg);
                         pMlt->put_QID(bstrDlg);
```

```
                GetDlgItemText(IDC_QTEXT, bstrDlg);
                        pMlt->put_Qtext(bstrDlg);

                GetDlgItemText(IDC_OPTIONA, bstrDlg);
                        pMlt->put_OptionA(bstrDlg);

                GetDlgItemText(IDC_OPTIONB, bstrDlg);
                        pMlt->put_OptionB(bstrDlg);

                GetDlgItemText(IDC_OPTIONC, bstrDlg);
                        pMlt->put_OptionC(bstrDlg);

                ::SysFreeString (bstrDlg);
            }
            m_bDirty = FALSE;
            return S_OK;
        }

        LRESULT OnPgChg(WORD wNotify, WORD wID, HWND hWnd, BOOL& bHandled)
        {
            SetDirty(TRUE);
            return 0;
        }
};

#endif //__MLTPROP_H_
```

8. Now, you need to add the property page to the control; you also need to add a few lines to the message map in MltChoiceVC.h. Open this file and add the following lines to the property map. The resulting map should look like the code that follows:

```
BEGIN_PROPERTY_MAP(CMltChoiceVC)
    // Example entries
    // PROP_ENTRY("Property Description", dispid, clsid)
    PROP_ENTRY("QID", 1, CLSID_MltProp)
    PROP_ENTRY("Qtext", 2, CLSID_MltProp)
    PROP_ENTRY("OptionA", 3, CLSID_MltProp)
    PROP_ENTRY("OptionB", 4, CLSID_MltProp)
    PROP_ENTRY("OptionC", 5, CLSID_MltProp)
END_PROPERTY_MAP()
```

9. Before proceeding to the next step, build the project to make sure that no typos or other problems exist.

Step 3: Add Support for the IActiveDesigner Interface

Now, you need to make the next set of changes to the code to convert it from a regular control to a design-time control. First, add the interface definitions, then add the GetRuntimeText to generate the HTML code with the <INPUT> tags.

1. To add support for the interface, copy the IActiveDesigner.h file from the CD-ROM, and the designer.h and webdc.h files from the Samples\Mfc\include SDK subdirectory to your project's directory.

2. Include the `IActiveDesigner.h` file at the beginning of `MltChoiceVC.h`. The first few lines of the file should now look like this code:

```
// MltChoiceVC.h : Declaration of the CMltChoiceVC
#ifndef __MLTCHOICEVC_H_
#define __MLTCHOICEVC_H_
#include "resource.h"        // main symbols
#include "IActiveDesigner.h"
```

3. Scroll to the end of `MltChoiceVC.h`; add the declaration of the `GetRuntimeText` function after the `OnDraw` function. That part of the file should now look like the following code:

```
HRESULT OnDraw(ATL_DRAWINFO& di);
HRESULT GetRuntimeText(BSTR& bstrRtt);
```

4. Add the interface to the inheritance list of the control. The last two lines of the inheritance list (near the top of the `MltChoiceVC.h` file) should look as follows:

```
public ISpecifyPropertyPagesImpl<CMltChoiceVC>, // <- Add a comma here
public IActiveDesignerImpl<CMltChoiceVC>
```

5. Now, add the interface control's COM interface map, and the last lines of the map (also in `MltChoiceVC.h`) should appear as follows:

```
        COM_INTERFACE_ENTRY(IProvideClassInfo)
        COM_INTERFACE_ENTRY(IProvideClassInfo2)
        COM_INTERFACE_ENTRY_IMPL(IActiveDesigner)
END_COM_MAP()
```

6. In the last step, add the implementation of the `GetRuntimeText` member function at the end of `MltChoiceVC.cpp` (see Listing 38.5).

Listing 38.5. The `GetRuntimeText` member function in `MltChoiceVC.cpp`.

```
HRESULT CMltChoiceVC::GetRuntimeText (BSTR& bstrRtt)
{
    CComBSTR rttx("<!--***");

    // common code for all buttons
    CComBSTR radioBtn("      <p><input type=\"radio\" name=\"");
    radioBtn += m_bstrQID;
    radioBtn.Append("\" value=\"");

    // build header
    rttx += m_bstrQID;
    rttx.Append("***-->\n");

    // build question text
    rttx.Append("      <p>");
    rttx += m_bstrQtext;
    rttx.Append("</p>\n");

    // Option A
    rttx += radioBtn;
    rttx.Append("A\">");
    rttx += m_bstrOptionA;
    rttx.Append("</p>\n");
```

```
        // Option B
        rttx += radioBtn;
        rttx.Append("B\">");
        rttx += m_bstrOptionB;
        rttx.Append("</p>\n");

        // Option C
        rttx += radioBtn;
        rttx.Append("C\">");
        rttx += m_bstrOptionC;
        rttx.Append("</p>\n");

        bstrRtt = (BSTR)rttx;

        return S_OK;
    }
```

Step 4: Register the Control as `WebDesigntimeControl`

You may have noticed that the build process registers your control every time you build it; however, you still need to add an entry in the Windows Registry to indicate that your control can be used as a design-time control.

To register your design-time control, open a DOS prompt and execute the following command:

`RERSVRDC MltChoiceVC.MltChoiceVC.1`

where `MltChoiceVC.MltChoiceVC.1` is the `ProgID` of your control.

To test the control, open the `TestDTC.htm` file, or create a new HTML page and follow these directions:

1. Move the cursor to the line where you want to insert the control.
2. Open the editor's shortcut menu by right-clicking the mouse button.
3. Click the Insert ActiveX Control menu option.
4. Select the Design-time tab.
5. Double-click `MltChoiceVC Class`.
6. Enter values for the `QID`, `Qtext`, `OptionA`, `OptionB`, and `OptionC` properties.
7. Close the property and design layout pages; then save the HTML file.
8. Open the shortcut menu (right-click the mouse), and select the Preview option.

The `IActiveDesigner` Interface

This section offers you some insight into how a design-time control works internally. You may skip it if you are not interested in learning the ins and outs of ActiveX controls.

As you probably know, the core concept behind ActiveX development is that of an interface. Think of an interface as a generic contract between your component and its potential users. The component agrees to follow (or implement) a particular set of rules (properties and methods in object-oriented terminology). Figure 38.13 demonstrates how this works for a design-time control.

FIGURE 38.13.

IActiveDesigner *and* *Visual InterDev.*

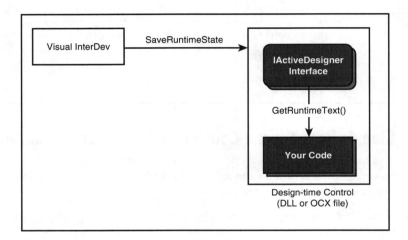

When you close the property page of your control (after you entered the QID, question text, and so on), Visual InterDev requests the SaveRuntimeState property of your control. Eventually, this process translates to generating the HTML code for your radio button and the corresponding design-time control header in the form of the <OBJECT> tag.

Your control responds to that request not because you coded the SaveRuntimeState function, but because you implemented the IActiveDesigner interface, which in turn calls your GetRuntimeText().

The IActiveDesigner interface defines the following methods and properties. Please refer to the SDK for a detailed description.

The GetRuntimeClassID Method

This method returns the CLSID of the runtime object. Because design-time controls do not have a runtime object, this method returns CLSID_NULL.

The GetRuntimeMiscStatusFlags Method

This method returns the runtime miscellaneous status flags. Because design-time controls do not have a runtime object, this method returns NULL.

The `QueryPersistenceInterface` Method

This method is used to check that a control can save enough information to be reconstructed (persistency) and that the information can be stored using a particular fashion (using a given interface).

The `SaveRuntimeText` Property

This property returns the HTML text to be inserted into the file.

The `GetExtensibilityObject` Property

This property returns the OLE Automation interface of a control. OLE Automation provides a mechanism that enables one program to control another by means of a scripting language, such as VBScript.

Design-Time Control Hosting Considerations

This chapter would not be complete without a brief description of the mechanism that enables a design-time control to access some of the features implemented in the Visual InterDev environment. Examples of these features, or services, include the URLPicker—used by the Include design-time control described earlier in this chapter—and the Query Builder—used by the Data Command design-time control described in Chapter 22, "Integrating ActiveX Database Components."

Figure 38.14 illustrates the basic components of the Host Services architecture. The site is a class implemented by the container (Visual InterDev in our case). When the control is invoked at design time, the container calls `IOleObject::SetClientSite` to give the design-time control a pointer to the site.

FIGURE 38.14.
Design-time control Host Services architecture.

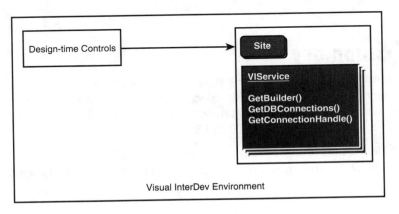

Using the site, the control can then use the QueryService to determine if the container supports one or many services. A service (VIService in our example) groups a number of related interfaces. The VIService object makes available the functions listed in Table 38.3.

Table 38.3. VIService object methods.

Method Name	Description
GetBuilder	Retrieves the builder object associated with a given GUID.
GetDBConnections	Retrieves a list of data connections currently available in your Visual InterDev session.
GetConnectionHandle	Retrieves an ODBC handle for a data connection.
ReleaseConnectionHandle	Releases the ODBC handle for a given data connection.
CallSQLBuilder	Invokes the SQL Query Builder, which enables you to visually create an SQL statement.

NOTE

A builder serves as a single modal dialog that helps to edit a property or value. The URLPicker represents an example of a builder.

You can access the VIService from Visual Basic programs, so you do not have to write C++ code to explore this capability. For more information, please refer to the Host Services document in the design-time control SDK; in particular, focus on the Data Grid sample control included in the SDK.

Summary

Design-time controls enable you to simplify the creation and maintenance of blocks of commonly used sections of HTML code, as in the case of individual questions in a multiple choice exam. Design-time controls can be developed using languages that support ActiveX development such as Visual Basic 5.0 and Visual C++.

Design-time controls can take advantage of special purpose dialogs and services of the Visual InterDev environment that can increase your productivity when developing Web applications.

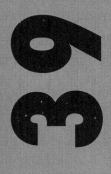

Using Java Applets with Visual InterDev

by Jerry Ablan

IN THIS CHAPTER

As you've no doubt learned by reading this far, Visual InterDev is a powerful application development and management tool. It can be used to build anything from a simple, one-page site to the most sophisticated Web site imaginable. Add Microsoft's Visual J++ product, and you can place stunning Java applets in your pages with incredible ease.

This chapter demonstrates how to use Java applets in your Visual InterDev projects. You will create a sample Web project using the Web Project Wizard and add an HTML page to hold a Java applet. You will then create a Java applet with the Java Applet Wizard and place it into the sample Web. I hope you learn a few tips and tricks along the way.

Creating a Sample Project

Before digging into the Java portion of this chapter, you need a project to hold your Web site and Java applet. To accomplish this, you'll use the Web Project Wizard. As you learned in Chapter 6, "Developing the Application and Content," the Web Project Wizard is the utility used to create an Internet World Wide Web project. In addition, the wizard creates a new workspace. The workspace is nothing more than a container for other projects. This container can then hold any type of subproject. So the wizard will place your Web site project into the container, and you'll add a Java applet project later.

First, create a new Internet World Wide Web project with the Web Project Wizard. Select New from the File menu. The tabbed New dialog box is displayed.

Click the Projects tab to see all of the project types available. Select Web Project Wizard and then type in a project name in the space provided. (I used AppletWeb.) Figure 39.1 shows what you should see.

FIGURE 39.1.

On the Projects tab, the Web Project Wizard is selected.

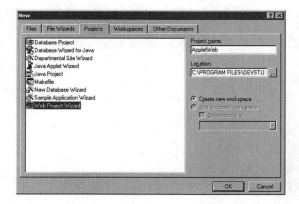

CAUTION

If you have another workspace open when you open this dialog box, you will be able to add this Web project to your current workspace. For the purposes of this chapter, please create a new workspace. It will keep sample data out of your work in progress, and it will match all the examples shown in this chapter.

After you've typed in a name and selected the Web Project Wizard, the OK button is enabled. Click it to start up the wizard.

The Web Project Wizard is a two-step wizard. The first step entails entering the name of your Web server. This server is where the Web site will be, or currently is, stored. If you are developing locally, you can specify your own machine. But you might be using a Web server that is located on another machine, or even offsite. In any case, this server must have the FrontPage 97 server extensions installed. These extensions allow Visual InterDev (and FrontPage 97) to manipulate the Web sites stored on the Web server.

Figure 39.2 shows the first of the two steps required to set up a Web project with this wizard. Enter either your computer's TCP/IP hostname (if you know what it is) or simply `localhost`.

FIGURE 39.2.

Enter the name of the server where your new Web will reside.

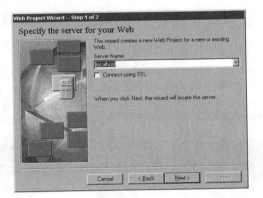

NOTE

`localhost` is a special hostname that refers to the IP address `127.0.0.1`. This IP address is, as you've probably guessed, special as well. Commonly referred to as the "loopback" address, it is a special address that programs can utilize for networking applications. It is almost always guaranteed to be on machines with TCP/IP and is like having a built-in network card.

I created our Web project on the `localhost` because that is where the Web server and the FrontPage 97 server extensions are installed. You can connect using SSL from this wizard prompt as well. Using SSL will guarantee a secure connection from your machine to the Web server. This is useful if you don't want anyone snooping in on what you're doing.

The second, and final, step the wizard asks you to perform is to select the name of your new Web. You might think you already entered the Web name, but you haven't, really. What you entered earlier is the name of the new workspace. Although it generally is the same as the Web name, the Web name is more important. Figure 39.3 shows the final step.

FIGURE 39.3.

The final step in creating a Web project with the wizard.

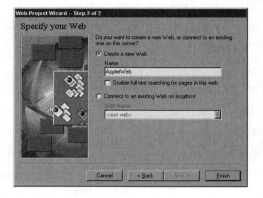

The name that you give to the Web site is the name that people will use to access it. If your Web server is `http://www.somedomain.com/` and you create a Web project called AppletWeb (as in this example), it will be available at `http://www.somedomain.com/AppletWeb`. But you might have called your workspace JavaWeb, or Beaner, or something else. They are two separate names. Just remember that this Web name is important because it becomes part of your Web's URL.

> **TIP**
>
> You might notice that under the Create a new Web selector, there is an option labeled Connect to an existing Web on <*server name*> (<*server name*> will be the server you chose in Step 1). This feature enables you to create a project based on a Web site that already exists. If you have previously created sites with FrontPage, you can use this option to import your Web site into Visual InterDev.

Click the Finish button and let the wizard do its work.

When the wizard is finished creating the new Web site, InterDev will display the site in the familiar File View. Figure 39.4 shows this screen.

FIGURE 39.4.
The File View of the new Web site is shown.

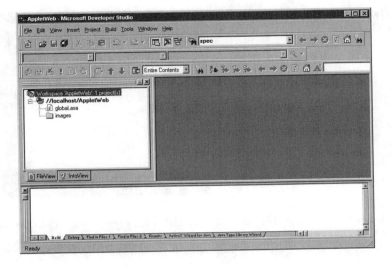

You'll notice that the wizard created an `images` directory for storing images. In addition, the wizard took the liberty of creating a `global.asa` file. This file, as you learned in Chapter 12, "Database Management with the Visual Data Tools," is where application initialization information is stored. If you choose to add Active Server scripting or database access to this Web project at a later time, the `global.asa` file will be used to facilitate these.

To complete the setup of the sample Web site, you must create a Web page to hold your Java applet. To do this, select New under the File menu. (See Figure 39.5.)

FIGURE 39.5.
The New option.

The New dialog is shown again. This time, you want to click on the Files tab to display all the available file types that can be created. The dialog, shown in Figure 39.6, lists the file types available when Visual InterDev and Visual J++ are installed on the same machine. Note that your list might vary.

FIGURE 39.6.

The Files tab.

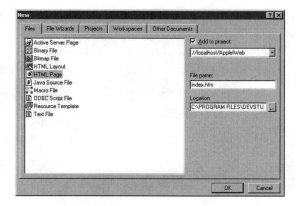

Select HTML Page from the list of available file types. Next, fill in the name for the new page. This should be your main page, so name this page index.htm. After you click the OK button, the new page, index.htm, is created and placed into your project. (See Figure 39.7.)

FIGURE 39.7.

The new HTML file inserted into the Web project.

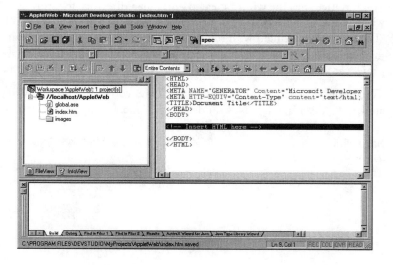

With the sample project created, and an empty Web page to hold a Java applet, you are ready to build a sample Java applet.

Creating a Sample Applet

Now that you've created a project to hold your Web site, you need to create a new project to hold your Java applet. You'll create this project using Visual J++'s Applet Wizard.

The Applet Wizard is a handy little tool that is used to create a Java applet and the hooks necessary for Visual J++ to build the applet when you add functionality.

To create a new Java applet with the Java Applet Wizard, right-click on the workspace line in the File View window. A pop-up menu will be displayed, as shown in Figure 39.8.

FIGURE 39.8.

When you right-click on the workspace line, this menu pops up.

Choose the Add New Project to Workspace... option. This option brings up the New dialog displayed in Figure 39.9. Switch to the Projects tab if it is not selected and select Java Applet Wizard from the list of available projects. Type in a name for your Java applet. For simplicity, I use the name Sample throughout the chapter. Finally, make sure you click on the Add to current workspace button. This ensures that the Java applet is added to your current project. To start the Applet Wizard, click OK.

FIGURE 39.9.

The infamous New dialog is displayed.

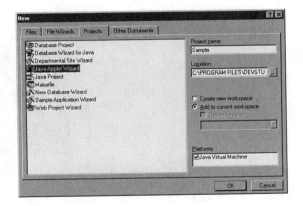

I could spend an entire chapter going over the various options available using the Applet Wizard. However, this book's focus is on Visual InterDev. So to make a long story short, simply click the Finish button when the first step of the Applet Wizard is shown. (See Figure 39.10.)

FIGURE 39.10.

Step 1 of 5 for the Java Applet Wizard.

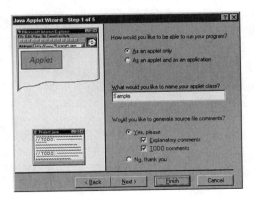

The Java Applet Wizard did a little magic of its own. First of all, it added a project to your workspace called Sample (or whatever you named yours). Second, the following were added to the project:

- A Java source file called `Sample.java`
- An HTML file, `Sample.html`, to hold the Java applet
- A resource folder that contains 18 images

Finally, this new project, Sample, was made the active project.

Building and Testing the Applet

Now that the applet has been created and added to your workspace, let's take it for a test drive. Before you can run your new applet, you must build it. This can be done one of several ways. The easiest, most hassle-free way is with the right-click pop-up menu. Right-click on the project name (Sample), and the Java project menu appears. Choose the first option, Build, to compile your Java applet. (See Figure 39.11.)

Figure 39.11.

The Java project pop-up menu is displayed.

The applet should compile with no errors or warnings; if it does, you'll see a message reflecting this fact in the output window. Your applet is now built and, if you've followed these instructions, will actually do something kind of interesting.

To run and test your new applet, select Execute Sample from the Build pull-down menu. This is the menu item with the big red exclamation mark (!) before it. This will launch your default Web browser and load the `Sample.html` file automatically. Remember, this HTML page has the information necessary to load and run your applet. If all goes well, you should see a spinning globe in your browser window. It should look like Figure 39.12.

FIGURE 39.12.
The sample Java applet running.

Adding the Sample Applet to Your Web Project

Now you've got your Java applet working. It is part of your workspace along with your Web project. You are probably curious about how to get the two separate entities to play nice. Well, here is where it is all explained.

Visual InterDev and Visual J++, while sharing a common user interface, do not share information about each other. Sure the workspace is generic and can hold projects from various tools, but you can't link projects together. So moving your Java applet into your Web project requires a bit of manual labor. But you only need to do it once.

> **TIP**
>
> This is a neat little trick you can use to get Visual InterDev to manage your Java classes for you. If you create a folder in your Web project that has the same name as your Java project, they will occupy the same space. The only catch is that the Web project won't manage any files until they are "added" to the Web project. So by simply adding your Java classes and support files to your Web project, any and all changes made to them will automatically be moved to your Web server.
>
> Beware, however, that if you release the working copies of these files, you must retrieve them or get a fresh working copy before you compile or edit them. If you don't, you'll find that your files are not there!

Getting Visual InterDev to Manage Your Applet Files

To get Visual InterDev to manage your Java files, you need to create a folder to house your applet and all your applet's classes. You should give this folder the same name as your applet's folder.

Before you create the new folder, however, be sure that the Web project (our AppletWeb example) is the active project. If the AppletWeb display line is not in boldface, it is not the active project. To activate it, right-click and select Set as Active Project from the pop-up menu. The AppletWeb line will then become boldface.

To create the new folder, right-click again and select New Folder... from the pop-up menu. The New Folder dialog is shown in Figure 39.13. Type in the name of the new folder. I've chosen the unique (and interesting!) name of Sample for the new folder.

FIGURE 39.13.

The New Folder dialog box needs a name to proceed.

Your new folder will appear in the list of items within your Web project. If you've followed the examples in this chapter, it will appear right below the Images folder.

This new folder, Sample, will hold the Java files needed to run your Java applet. To get them into this folder, use the Add Files... option available on the pop-up menu for the new folder. This option is also available under the Project menu. Choose Project | Add To Project | Files....

A dialog box is displayed asking which files to add. Below the list of files is a selection of file types. For a Java applet, you want to move all the Java class files. These are the files that have a `.class` extension. Scroll through the list and select the Java Class (`.class`) selection.

You most likely won't see anything in the list. That is because the Add Files... option opens up at the project's top level. You need to go down into the sample project's level. Double-click on the folder named Sample. There you will see one class file, `Sample.class`, as shown in Figure 39.14.

FIGURE 39.14.

The Insert Files into Project dialog box awaits your command.

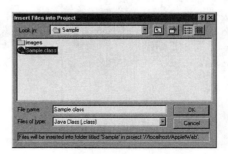

Double-click on the `Sample.class` file to add it to the Sample folder of your AppletWeb project. Congratulations, you've added a Java applet to your Web project! Now you just need to finish copying the support files. These are 18 image files that make up the spinning globe that is drawn when this applet runs.

These files need to reside in a subdirectory called `images`. Right-click on the Web's `images` subdirectory and select Add Files… from the pop-up menu.

This time, however, the file list starts in the Sample project's directory. You will see a folder in there called images. Open up the images folder, making sure to select Image Files as the file type filter. You will see the 18 GIF files waiting to be copied. Select them all and click OK. They will be copied to your images folder.

Now the applet is completely added to your Web project. Because they share a common directory, any changes made to the source code, and therefore the classes, will automatically be pushed out to your Web site. You can use this method of adding files to add other Java classes, or even third-party Java classes, to your Web projects.

> **TIP**
>
> For an excellent source of Java classes and applets, check out Gamelan at `http://www.gamelan.com/`.

Putting a Java Applet on Your Web Page

So far in this chapter you have created a new Web project, added a Java applet project to the workspace, compiled and tested the applet, and added the files to the Web project so that Visual InterDev could manage them. But just because the files are out in your Web project doesn't mean you can use them. You need to add an `<APPLET>` tag to your HTML page.

The `<APPLET>` Tag

The `<APPLET>` tag is the HTML placeholder for Java applets. The syntax of the `<APPLET>` tag is as follows:

```
<APPLET [options]>
[parameters]
</APPLET>
```

The options that can be inside the `<APPLET>` tag are shown in Table 39.1.

Table 39.1. The <APPLET> tag options.

Option	Legal Value(s)	Description
ALIGN	LEFT, CENTER, or RIGHT	Aligns the applet on the page
ALT	Text	Alternative text to display if browser does not support Java
CODE	Class name	The name of the Java applet class to run
CODEBASE	URL	The URL where the Java classes are stored
HEIGHT	Pixels	The number of pixels high this applet should be
HSPACE	Pixels	The number of pixels to space horizontally
NAME	Text	The name of the applet to other applets in this HTML page
VSPACE	Pixels	The number of pixels to space vertically
WIDTH	Pixels	The number of pixels wide this applet should be

The <PARAM> Tag

You can specify optional parameters that are passed to your applet as well. These are in the form of <PARAM> tags. These tags go between the <APPLET> and </APPLET> tags. The syntax for the <PARAM> tag is as follows:

```
<PARAM NAME="name" VALUE="value" >
```

where "`name`" is the name of the parameter, and "`value`" is the value of the parameter. For example, if you wanted to pass a configuration option to your applet, such as a debugging flag, you could use the following:

```
<PARAM NAME="debugging_flag" VALUE="1">
```

The entire applet tag with parameters could look something like this:

```
<APPLET NAME="MyApplet" CODE="MyApplet.class" WIDTH=300 HEIGHT=300>
<PARAM NAME="debugging_flag" VALUE="1">
</APPLET>
```

You can imagine the possibilities. However, let's not focus on a programming-specific issue. This overview is meant to show you the mechanics of adding your applet to your Web page. With this information, you can now edit your HTML page and place the sample applet on the page and run it.

Placing the Applet on the Web Page

There are two ways to place a Java applet on your Web page. One way is tedious; the other way is easy. The following sections cover both ways just so you know what is actually happening behind the scenes.

Using the HTML Editor

The first, or tedious, method of adding a Java applet to your Web page is by hand. This involves typing the <APPLET> tag by yourself. Just to keep you honest, let's give it a try.

Focusing back on your Web project, you have a single HTML page called `index.htm`. This is the main page. If you double-click on it, Visual InterDev will open it up in the HTML editor. Figure 39.15 shows what the HTML editor looks like with your sample page.

FIGURE 39.15.

The HTML editor is for masochists.

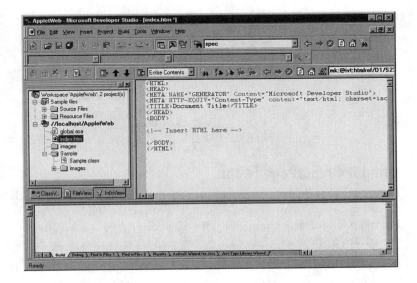

To add your Java applet on this page, simply add the following <APPLET> tag:

```
<APPLET NAME="Sample" CODE="Sample.class" CODEBASE="Sample" WIDTH=320 HEIGHT=240>
</APPLET>
```

There are no parameters, so there is no need for any <PARAM> tags. Save your work and then browse your newly enhanced `index.htm`. You'll find a Java applet on your new page. (See Figure 39.16.)

39

USING JAVA APPLETS WITH VISUAL INTERDEV

> **TIP**
>
> Even the tedious work can be made easy. You can have the Java Applet Wizard create a sample HTML page for you. It does this by default. You can just cut and paste the <APPLET> tag from that sample into any HTML page you want.

FIGURE 39.16.

The sample Java applet in action in the Visual InterDev previewer.

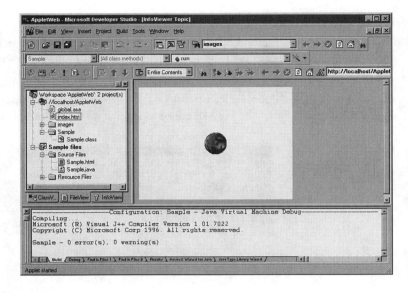

Using the FrontPage Editor

Remember that there are two ways to add a Java applet to your HTML page. One is the tedious way, which involves hand-coding HTML script. The second is an easier way, using the FrontPage editor that comes with Visual InterDev. You learned all about this editor in Chapter 6. But you probably didn't know you could use it to add a Java applet.

If you right-click on the `index.htm` file in the File View, you'll see an option Open With.... (See Figure 39.17.) Select this option to activate a dialog box that will allow you to select a different editor for your HTML pages. You can even add your own editors to the list.

FIGURE 39.17.

The Open With... option.

If you select the Microsoft FrontPage editor, it will open up with your HTML page loaded. From here you can edit your Web page in WYSIWYG format.

Because you already added the <APPLET> tag by hand, you see that it is represented by a dotted outline on the FrontPage editor display. This is actually how much space your applet will take up. To change any of the parameters, just double-click somewhere inside the applet container. The Java Applet Properties dialog will be displayed, as shown in Figure 39.18.

FIGURE 39.18.

The Java Applet Properties dialog box allows you to adjust the options in the <APPLET> tag without programming.

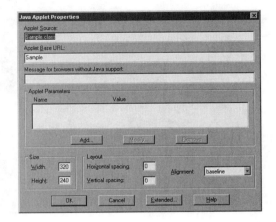

As you can see, all the options from the <APPLET> tag are represented in the dialog box. It allows you to visually change the parameters without the need for tedious HTML coding. See, it really is easier!

To insert a new or another Java applet into this Web page, simply select Insert|Other Components|Java Applet from the menu. This first brings up the Java Applet Properties dialog and then shows you the space it will take up. All in all, the FrontPage editor is the way to go for placing Java applets on your HTML pages. No fuss, no mess.

Summary

This chapter has covered a lot of territory. You created a sample Web project with the Web Project Wizard, then created a sample Java applet with the Java Applet Wizard, and finally merged the two together to get the Java applet to display on the Web page of your Web project. This was all done using Visual InterDev along with Visual J++. Using the two tools together can really leverage your development efforts.

Understanding Middleware

by Neil Jenkins

IN THIS CHAPTER

CHAPTER 40

During the development of client/server systems, there is a need to hide the complexities of interaction between the client machine and the server machine. This need has led to the development of a suite of products that provide this functionality. These products have been named *middleware*. Middleware has become a catch-all term for a range of different software technologies designed to provide connectivity in mixed computer environments. Unfortunately, due to the many different ways in which client/server systems can be built, middleware is now used to describe everything from a basic structured query language (SQL) connection used in the database environment for linking PCs to a host database to a full-blown transaction processing system like IBM's CICS.

This chapter uses the following definition of middleware: off-the-shelf connectivity software that supports distributed processing at runtime and is used by developers to build distributed software. This software provides high-level communications protocols to allow either whole applications or processes within applications to span a network.

With the advent of local area networks and interconnected PCs, more and more companies focused on interconnecting their databases and host systems. In the early days, this interconnection was handled by simple gateways. Yet these gateways could not provide the interaction that was and still is required at the client level. Companies realized that software was required to sit between these PCs and host systems—to sit in the middle, so to speak. Middleware was born. This software needed to contain the features and functionality that would make it as secure and as robust as the host systems of the time. This area is still the major development focus for middleware today. Although client software (particularly middleware) has not been noted, so far, for its distributed excellence, this fact is changing. Client software's strength has always been ease of use and installation. As a result, middleware has become a major requirement in successful client/server systems providing working distributed processing.

As the information systems world increases in complexity, the need for generic middleware solutions to enable interoperability of systems and portability of applications becomes increasingly more important. Information systems are evolving from the world in which simplicity in the connection services was sufficient to one in which transparency of connection, ease of management, portability of business function and logic, and rapid development and rapid deployment of distributed function to enable modular applications are the requirements to support the business.

In addition, this chapter provides you with an insight into the leading middleware products and introduces Microsoft's new product MSMQ, previously known as "Falcon."

The Database Connectivity Challenge

The first challenge of client/server systems is database connectivity. Database connectivity involves the capability to access multiple, heterogeneous data sources from within a single application running on the client. A second challenge is flexibility; the application should be able to directly access data from a variety of data sources without modification to the application. For example, an application could access data from Visual FoxPro in a standalone, small office environment and from SQL Server or Oracle in a larger, networked environment. These challenges are day-to-day occurrences for programmers of off-the-shelf applications and for corporate developers attempting to provide solutions to end users or to migrate data to new platforms. These challenges grow exponentially for developers and support staff as the number of data sources grows and the complexity of the completed applications increases.

Data Source Differences

Database problems become apparent in the differences among the programming interfaces, database management system (DBMS) protocols, DBMS languages, and network protocols of unrelated data sources. Even when data sources are restricted to relational DBMSs that use SQL, significant differences in SQL syntax and semantics must be resolved.

The primary differences in the implementation of each of these components are the following:

- **Programming interface.** Each DBMS supplier provides its own proprietary programming interface. The method of accessing a relational DBMS may be through embedded SQL or an API.
- **DBMS protocol.** Each DBMS supplier uses proprietary data formats and methods of communication between the application and the DBMS. For example, there are many different ways to delineate the end of one row of data and the beginning of the next.
- **DBMS language.** SQL has become the language of choice for relational DBMSs, but many differences still exist among SQL implementations. For example, one difference is the use of DECODE in Oracle.
- **Networking protocols.** Many diverse LAN and WAN protocols exist in networks today. DBMSs and applications must coexist in these diverse environments. For example, SQL Server may use DECnet on a VAX, TCP/IP on UNIX, and NetBEUI or IPX/SPX on a PC.

To access various database environments, an application developer would have to learn to use each DBMS supplier's programming interface, employ each DBMS supplier's SQL, and ensure that the proper programming interface, network, and DBMS software were installed on the client system. This complexity makes broad database connectivity unfeasible for most developers and users today. If the number of supported DBMSs increases, the complexity increases severely.

Approaches to Database Connectivity

DBMS suppliers and third-party companies have attempted to address the problem of database connectivity in a number of ways. The main approaches have included using gateways, a common programming interface, and a common protocol.

The Gateway Approach

In the gateway approach, application programmers use one supplier's programming interface, SQL grammar, and DBMS protocol. A gateway causes a target DBMS to appear to the application as a copy of the selected DBMS. The gateway translates and forwards requests to the target DBMS and receives results from it. For example, applications that access SQL Server can also access DB2 data through the Micro Decisionware DB2 Gateway. This product allows a DB2 DBMS to appear to a Windows-based application as a SQL Server DBMS. Any application using a gateway would need a different gateway for each type of DBMS it needs to access, such as DEC Rdb, Informix, Ingres, and Oracle.

The gateway approach is limited by structural and architectural differences among DBMSs, such as differences in catalogs and SQL implementations and the usual need for one gateway for each target DBMS. Gateways are a valid approach to database connectivity and are essential in certain environments, but they are typically not a broad, long-term solution.

The Common Interface Approach

In the common interface approach, a single programming interface is provided to the programmer. It is possible to provide some standardization in a database application development environment or user interface even when the underlying interfaces are different for each DBMS. This standardization is the result of creating a standard API, macro language, or set of user tools for accessing data and translating requests for, and results from, each target DBMS. A common interface is usually implemented by writing a driver for each target DBMS. Microsoft's ODBC follows this approach. Figure 40.1 shows how this interface fits architecturally within the client system.

FIGURE 40.1.

The common interface approach.

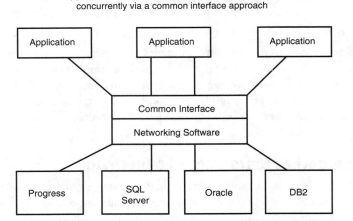

Applications accessing heterogeneous data sources concurrently via a common interface approach

The Common Protocol Approach

The DBMS protocol, SQL grammar, and networking protocols are common to all DBMSs, so the application can use the same protocol and SQL grammar to communicate with all DBMSs. Examples are remote data access (RDA) and distributed relational database architecture (DRDA). RDA is an emerging standard from SAG, but it is not available today. DRDA is IBM's alternative DBMS protocol. Common protocols can ultimately work very effectively in conjunction with a common interface.

Common interfaces, protocols, and gateways may be combined. A common protocol and interface provide a standard API for developers as well as a single protocol for communication with all databases. A common gateway and interface provide a standard API for developers and allow the gateway to provide functionality, such as translation and connectivity to wide area networks, that would otherwise need to be implemented on each client station. However, a common gateway or protocol still requires a common interface to hide complexities from developers.

A Basic View of Middleware

Figure 40.2 shows the basic view of how a client workstation interacts with a database server through a network.

FIGURE 40.2.

A simplistic view of a client/server system.

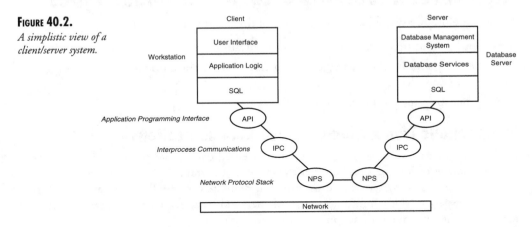

When an application at the client end requires data from the server, a transaction is sent from the application logic via SQL to the network. This transaction is passed to the server through an application programming interface, an interprocess communications protocol, and a network protocol stack. The application programming interface and the interprocess communications portions of the process can be made up of middleware.

Figure 40.3 shows where middleware sits in a client/server system. On the left side of the diagram, a business application is communicating to middleware that is then communicating to a business server on the right side of the diagram. These systems are physically separate and may be located anywhere.

40

UNDERSTANDING
MIDDLEWARE

FIGURE 40.3.
*The position of
middleware in a client/
server system.*

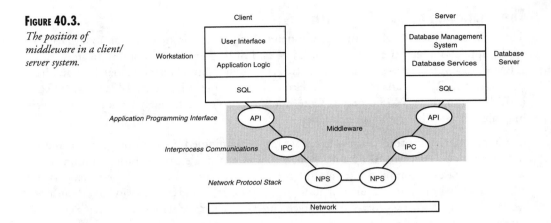

In some cases, the middleware can also provide the database language vocabulary as well. Examples of this type of middleware include Rumba Database Access and ODBC products from Microsoft.

High-Level Middleware Communications Types

Middleware products, at a high level, use one of three communications types:

- Synchronous transaction-oriented communications
- Asynchronous batch-oriented communications or message-oriented middleware (MOM)
- Application-to-server communications

Synchronous Transaction-Oriented Communications

Middleware that uses synchronous transaction-oriented communications involves back-and-forth exchanges of information between two or more programs. For example, a PC running ODBC retrieves host system–based information requested by the PC application. The synchronized aspect of this communications style demands that every program perform its task correctly; otherwise, the transaction will not be completed.

Products of this type include the following:

- Products that provide APIs that allow PC programs to communicate with an AS/400 using APPC fit in this type because APPC is synchronous transaction-oriented.
- Products that support TCP/IP sockets so that PC programs can communicate with other sockets-based systems are synchronous transaction-oriented as well. This approach is similar to the APPC approach for the AS/400. Applications that support Winsocks for Microsoft Windows work in this way.

- Products that provide APIs, high-level language APIs (HLLAPIs), or extended HLLAPIs (EHLLAPIs) that let PC programs communicate with mainframe and midrange programs through an intermediate terminal emulation program are included in the synchronous transaction-oriented group. This kind of product is the origin of the "screen scrape" programs. By using this technology, your application program communicates with a terminal emulation program package through APIs to sign on to the host computer, and then interact with the host application as if the PC program were a display session user. Examples of these packages include Rumba Office from Walldata, products from Netsoft such as Netsoft Elite, and the Attachmate series.

- Microsoft Windows–oriented communications products that support the Windows Dynamic Data Exchange (DDE) or Object Linking and Embedding (OLE) facilities to create links between host-based information (typically again accessed through Windows-based terminal emulation sessions) and native Windows programs are also synchronous transaction-oriented products. With DDE and OLE, you can create a hotlink between information on a host application screen (through terminal emulation software) and a spreadsheet handled by a native Windows application (such as Excel or Lotus 1-2-3). Note that both applications involved in DDE or OLE conversation must support the DDE or OLE formats. Both Rumba and Netsoft support these formats for the AS/400.

Asynchronous Batch-Oriented Communications

In the asynchronous batch-oriented communications type, messages are sent either one at a time or in batches with no expectation of an immediate response (or sometimes of any response at all). For example, a server database update program uses a data queue facility to send subsets of updated records to PC programs that then update the local client-based database. Or a PC program uses a file transfer API to send sales order records to an AS/400 program as they're entered. This method is commonly called *message-oriented middleware* and is covered in more detail in a later section of this chapter.

Application-to-Server Communications

Middleware can also link a business application with a generalized server program that typically resides on another system. A database server, an image server, a video server, and other general-purpose servers can communicate with an application program through a middleware solution.

Products in the server-oriented middleware range include the following:

- Products that conform to the Windows-based ODBC specification are server-oriented middleware. Under this specification, a vendor provides an ODBC driver that, on one side, provides a consistent set of SQL-oriented access routines for use by Windows programs and, on the other side, manages access to the vendor's remote database. ODBC is covered in more detail in a later section of this chapter.

40

UNDERSTANDING
MIDDLEWARE

■ Vendor-specific remote access products and a handful of generic SQL-based remote access solutions, which offer alternatives to remote database access through ODBC, are also categorized as server-oriented middleware. Oracle's Oracle Transparent Gateway range is a example of a SQL-based remote access product.

■ On the edge of the server-oriented middleware market is the transaction-processing workhorse CICS. CICS is available for OS/2, mainframes, and AS/400.

The Main Types of Middleware

Several main types of middleware can be used to build client/server systems. The following sections cover these well-known types:

DCE (distributed computing environment)

MOM (message-oriented middleware)

Transaction Processing Monitors

ODBC

DCE

The facilities outlined in this section as part of DCE have become available in many other products in some shape or form. DCE is a combined, integrated set of services that supports the development of distributed applications, including client/server. DCE is operating system– and network-independent, providing compatibility with users' existing environments. Figure 40.4 shows DCE's layered approach.

FIGURE 40.4.

The distributed computing environment.

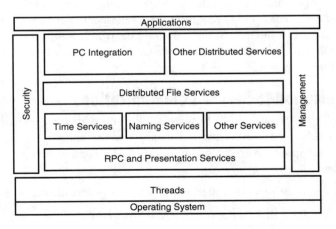

The architecture of DCE is a layered model that integrates a set of technologies, which are described in more detail in the following sections. The architecture is layered bottom-up from the operating system to the highest-level applications. Security and management are essential to all layers of the environment. To applications, the environment appears as a single logical system rather than a collection of different services. Distributed services provide tools for software developers to create the end-user services needed for distributed computing. These distributed services include the following:

- Remote procedure call and presentation services
- Naming or directory services
- Time service
- Threads service
- Security service
- Distributed file services
- PC integration service
- Management service

Remote Procedure Call

The Remote Procedure Call (RPC) capability is based on a simple premise: Make individual procedures in an application run on a computer somewhere else within the network. A distributed application, running as a process on one computer, makes procedure calls that execute on another computer. Within the application, such program calls appear to be standard local procedure calls, but these calls activate subprocedures that interact with an RPC runtime library to carry out the necessary steps to execute the call on the remote computer. RPC manages the network communications needed to support these calls, even the details such as network protocols. This means that distributed applications need little or no network-specific code, making development of such applications relatively easy. In this way, RPC distributes application execution. RPC extends a local procedure call by supporting direct calls to procedures on remote systems, enabling programmers to develop distributed applications as easily as traditional, single-system programs. RPC presentation services mask the differences between data representations on different machines, allowing programs to work across multiple, mixed systems.

RPC is used to allow applications to be processed in part on other servers, which leaves the client workstation free to do other tasks. RPC allows clients to interact with multiple servers and allows servers to handle multiple clients simultaneously. RPC allows clients to identify and locate servers by name. RPC applications, integrated with the directory services, are insulated from the details of the service. This characteristic will allow them to take advantage of future enhancements.

Naming Services

The distributed directory service provides a single naming model throughout DCE. This model enables users to identify by name resources such as servers, files, disks, and print queues and to gain access to these resources without needing to know where they are located on a network. As a result, users can continue referring to a resource by one name even when a characteristic of the resource, such as its network address, changes.

The distributed directory service seamlessly integrates the X.500 naming system with a replicated local naming system. Developers can move transparently from environments supporting full ISO functionality to those supporting only the local naming service component. The service allows the transparent integration of other services, such as distributed file services, into the directory service. The global portion of the directory service offers full X.500 functionality through the X/Open Directory Service API and through a standard management interface.

The directory service allows users or administrators to create multiple copies of critical data, assuring availability in spite of communication and hardware failures. It also provides a sophisticated update mechanism that ensures consistency. Changes to names or their attributes are automatically propagated to all replicas. In addition, replication allows names to be replicated near the people who use them, providing better performance.

The directory service is fully integrated with the security service, which provides secure communications. Sophisticated access control provides protection for entries. The directory service can accommodate large networks as easily as small ones. The capability to easily add servers, directories, and directory levels makes painless growth possible.

Time Service

A time service synchronizes all system clocks of a distributed environment so that executing applications can depend on equivalent clocking among processes. Consider that many machines operating in many time zones may provide processes as part of a single application solution. It's essential that they all agree on the time in order to manage scheduled events and time-sequenced events.

The distributed time service is a software-based service that synchronizes each computer to a widely recognized time standard. This service provides precise, fault-tolerant clock synchronization for systems in both local area networks and wide area networks. Time service software is integrated with the RPC, directory, and security services. DCE uses a modified version of DEC's Time Synchronization Service.

Threads Service

Developers want to exploit the computing power that is available throughout the distributed environment. The threads service provides portable facilities that support concurrent programming, which allows an application to perform many actions simultaneously. While one thread executes a remote procedure call, another thread can process user input. The threads service includes operations to create and control multiple threads of execution in a single process and to synchronize access to global data within an application. Because a server process using threads can handle many clients at the same time, the threads service is well-suited to dealing with multiple clients in client/server-based applications. A number of DCE components, including RPC, security, directory, and time services, use the threads service.

Security Service

In most conventional timesharing systems, the operating system authenticates the identity of users and authorizes access to resources. In a distributed computing environment in which activities span multiple hosts with multiple operating systems, however, authentication and authorization require an independent security service that can be trusted by many hosts. DCE provides such a service. The DCE security service component is well-integrated within the fundamental distributed service and data-sharing components. It provides the network with three conventional services: authentication, authorization, and user account management. These facilities are made available through a secure means of communication that ensures both integrity and privacy. The security service incorporates an authentication service based on the Kerberos system from MIT's Project Athena. Kerberos is a trusted service that prevents fraudulent requests by validating the identity of a user or service.

After users are authenticated, they receive authorization to use resources such as files. The authorization facility gives applications the tools they need to determine whether a user should have access to resources. It also provides a simple and consistent way to manage access control information.

Every computer system requires a mechanism for managing user account information. The User Registry solves the traditional problems of user account control in distributed, multivendor networks by providing a single, scalable system for consolidating and managing user information. The User Registry ensures the use of unique usernames and passwords across the distributed network of systems and services, ensures the accuracy and consistency of this information at all sites, and provides security for updates and changes. It maintains a single, logical database of user account information, including user and group naming information, login account information, and general system properties and policies. It is well-integrated with Kerberos to provide an integrated, secure, reliable user account management system.

MOM

MOM is a class of middleware that operates on the principles of message passing and/or message queuing. A peer-to-peer distributed computing model supporting both synchronous and asynchronous interactions between distributed computing processes characterizes MOM. MOM generally provides high-level services, multiprotocol support, and other systems management services. These services create an infrastructure to support highly reliable, scaleable, and performance-oriented client/server systems in mixed environments.

MOM is perhaps the most visible and currently the clearest example of middleware. One of the key attributes of middleware is that it should provide seamless integration between different environments. MOM uses the concept of a message to separate processes so that they can operate independently and often simultaneously. For example, a workstation can send a request for data, which requires collection and collation from multiple sources, while continuing with other processing.

This form of so-called asynchronous processing allows MOM to provide a rich level of connectivity in many types of business systems. MOM can handle everything from a simple message to download some data from a database server to an advanced client/server system with built-in workflow. In general terms, MOM works by defining, storing, and forwarding the messages. When a client issues a request for a service such as a database search, it does not talk directly to that service; it talks to the middleware. Talking to the middleware usually involves placing the message on a queue where it will be picked up by the appropriate service when the service is available. Some MOM products use a polling method to pick up messages instead, but the principle is the same; the messaging middleware acts as a buffer between the client and the server. More strictly speaking, middleware is the requester on the client and the service on the server; as with MOM itself, there can be many instances of both requesters and services on a single client or server. MOM insulates both the client and server applications from the complexities of network communications.

MOM ensures that messages get to their destinations and receive responses. The queuing mechanism can be very flexible, offering either a first-in, first-out scheme or one that allows priorities to be assigned to messages. The use of queues means that MOM software can be very flexible. Like other forms of middleware, it can accommodate straightforward one-to-one communications and many-to-one communications. Message passing and message queuing have been around for many years as the basis for Online Transaction Processing (OLTP) systems. The MOM software can also include system management functions such as network integrity and disaster recovery.

You can think of MOM as being similar to electronic mail systems such as Lotus cc:Mail. Although MOM uses similar mechanisms and can indeed provide the foundation for electronic mail, a key difference exists between MOM and electronic mail systems. Electronic mail passes messages from one person to another, whereas MOM passes messages back and forth between software processes.

MOM differs from database middleware in that database middleware vendors' expertise and products focus on providing their customers with the integration of data residing in multiple databases throughout the customers' enterprises. Their solutions normally require a communications component for managing and supporting sessions between the front-end client and one or more back-end database servers. Their designs are normally specific to accommodate the distribution and integration of their own DBMS on multiple platforms. Products from MOM companies that specialize in this environment provide users with a general-purpose solution that can be more readily used for any-to-any environments, including SQL to SQL and SQL to non-SQL (IMS, for example), and for non-DBMS data files. MOM products provide direct process-to-process communications and are not just restricted to accessing data.

The Advantages of Using MOM

In many modern client/server applications, there are clear advantages to using MOM. It provides a relatively simple application programming interface (API), making it easy for programmers to develop the necessary skills. The API is portable, so MOM programs can be moved to new platforms easily without changing the application code. The flexibility of the API also extends to legacy applications so that distributed computing can be introduced gradually without incurring a massive reprogramming exercise. MOM is a good tool to use as you begin your initial client/server development.

MOM is also a valid middleware technology on a system that uses object-oriented technology. Objects, by their very definition, interact with one another by using messages. Message passing and message queuing allow objects to exchange data and even pass objects without sharing control. Therefore, message-oriented middleware can be a natural technology to complement and support object technology.

Problems with MOM

The main problem with MOM is that its function is restricted to message passing. In other words, it does not include facilities to convert data formats. If, as in many systems, data is to be transferred from mainframes to PCs, the data conversion from EBCDIC to ASCII formats must be handled elsewhere. The MOM software only provides the transport and delivery mechanisms for messages; it is not concerned with the content. As a result, the application must take responsibility for creating and decoding messages. This additional responsibility increases the application's complexity.

MOM's simplicity also can slow performance because messages are usually processed from a queue one at a time. The problem can be solved by running multiple versions of the message-processing software, although this approach is not ideal. This particular problem means that MOM is not usually suitable for applications that require real-time communications within applications.

Another major problem with MOM is that there is little in the way of standardization. In 1993, a group of suppliers formed the MOM Association (MOMA) to promote common interests. Key members include IBM, Digital, Novell, Peer Logic, and Software AG. MOMA is not a standards-making body, which means MOM products are essentially proprietary in nature. MOMA does lobby standards bodies with an interest in middleware. It has ties to the Open Software Foundation (OSF) and the Object Management Group (OMG) in its work on object-oriented computing. MOM suppliers argue with some justification that the simplicity of MOM calls means that rigid standards are unnecessary. There are some individual initiatives aimed at promoting interworking both between different MOM products and with non-MOM middleware such as OSF's DCE remote procedure call (RPC) technology, which was discussed earlier in the chapter. Many third-party products also provide links to IBM's CICS to ease the migration path from legacy systems to client/server.

As MOM expands to resolve these problems, it will inevitably become more complex and start to resemble other approaches to middleware, such as transaction processing and RPC. Finally, like many other solutions to the middleware problem, tools that help create application systems around MOM and subsequently manage them are needed. Momentum Software offers one of the most promising solutions with its modeling and simulation software that sits on top of Message Express.

Available MOM Products

Microsoft has recently entered the MOM market with Microsoft Message Queue Server (hereafter referred to as "MSMQ"). This product was originally codenamed "Falcon." MSMQ enables applications running at different times to communicate across networks and systems that may be temporarily offline. Applications can use MSMQ to send messages, and MSMQ uses intermediate storage to ensure that the messages eventually reach the destination queue. MSMQ provides guaranteed message delivery, efficient routing, security, and priority-based messaging. The MSMQ product provides the following:

- **Asynchronous messaging.** With MSMQ asynchronous messaging, an application can send a message to another application and continue to operate independently in parallel.

- **Guaranteed message delivery.** When an application sends a message through MSMQ, it is guaranteed delivery of the message to the destination even though the destination application may not be running at the same time, or the networks and systems are offline.

- **Local and end-to-end transactions.** When an application sends or receives a message in transacted mode, it is guaranteed that updates to a local database and sending or receiving of the message form an atomic unit. Either all of them succeed or none of them do. The sending application can also verify that the transaction has committed on the receiving side. Transacted messages are guaranteed to arrive in order to the destination not more than once.

- **Routing and dynamic configuration.** MSMQ provides flexible routing over heterogeneous networks. The configuration of such networks can be changed dynamically without any major changes to systems and networks themselves.

- **Connectionless messaging.** Applications using MSMQ do not need to set up direct sessions with target applications. Applications using MSMQ may actually be offline when sending messages.

- **Security.** MSMQ provides secure communication based on Windows NT security and the Crypto API for encryption and digital signatures.

- **Prioritized messaging.** MSMQ transfers messages across networks based on priority so that critical applications can communicate faster at the expense of less important applications.

MSMQ consists of the following:

- A runtime kit that must be present on any system that uses MSMQ.

- A Software Developer's Kit (SDK) for developing applications that use MSMQ, including MSMQ ActiveX components, callable from Visual Basic, Internet Information Server Active Server Pages, and any other ActiveX container.

■ MSMQ servers that provide the routing service and host the MQIS, the dynamic information store that holds configuration data.

■ A Message Queue Explorer to manage the MSMQ communications.

MSMQ can pass messages over heterogeneous networks that use TCP/IP and/or IPX/SPX protocols. Applications that use MSMQ do not need to be aware of the types of networks over which their messages are sent. Apart from providing MSMQ on the Windows family of operating systems, Microsoft is working with third parties to provide interoperability with other platforms. One such gateway product, the MSMQ Gateway, is being developed by Level8 Systems. Following is a description of the Level8 MSMQ Gateway functionality.

The Level8 Systems MSMQ Gateway supports bridging the world of MSMQ on the Windows family with other platforms in three different ways:

■ **MSMQ API on legacy platforms.** The Level8 MSMQ Gateway supports the Falcon application programming interface (API) library on legacy platforms via a direct RPC-based connection from the legacy platform to the MSMQ Gateway machine, where the MSMQ call is actually being executed on behalf of the calling application. Current plans for the Level8 MSMQ Gateway are to support IBM mainframes (MVS/CICS), UNIX platforms (Sun-Solaris, HP-UNIX, and AIX), OS/2, VMS, and AS/400.

■ **MSMQ to IBM MQSeries Queue to Queue Gateway.** The Level8 MSMQ Gateway supports the mapping of native IBM MQSeries API (MQI) calls to the MSMQ API to provide IBM MQSeries applications seamless access to and from a Falcon network. The platforms supported for the MQSeries connectivity include all the MQSeries 2.0 platforms: MVS/CICS, AS/400, AIX, AT&T GIS, VMS, OS/2, and so on.

■ **MSMQ to CICS Transient Data Queue Gateway.** The Level8 MSMQ Gateway supports mapping of native CICS Transient Data application APIs to Falcon APIs, giving native CICS Transient Data applications access to Falcon networks and Falcon applications access to CICS Transient Data resources.

With gateway products such as the Level8 MSMQ Gateway, companies can use MSMQ to integrate their heterogeneous systems; the availability of the MSMQ API on a variety of platforms allows developers to write to a single API.

Companies can now move forward with innovative PC-based technologies while still maintaining existing investments in legacy systems. Moving business logic away from mainframe systems down to Windows platforms can be done gradually: New MSMQ applications on Windows can talk to legacy applications on other platforms via the gateway. For those applications running on non-Windows platforms, the company has a choice to either move the application to use the MSMQ API available on these platforms or leave the application unchanged—for example, calling the MQSeries API and letting the gateway map those calls to MSMQ.

Extensive information is available on MSMQ from the Microsoft Web site at `http://www.microsoft.com`.

Other leading MOM products come from the established systems suppliers, with IBM and Digital having the highest profile. IBM's MQSeries, originally developed for IBM's main platforms (mainframe MVS, AS/400, AIX, and IBM's UNIX), now supports a wide range of non-IBM hardware platforms such as Sun Solaris, Tandem, and AT&T GIS. MQSeries is a group of products that use IBM's Message Queue Interface (MQI) to provide communications between mixed computer platforms. IBM has begun to spread MQSeries to a wide range of platforms and environments, giving it the most comprehensive coverage for any MOM product. In addition to supporting all of IBM's key platforms, MQSeries accommodates all of the major computer languages (COBOL, C, Visual Basic) and network protocols (SNA, TCP/IP, DECnet, and IPX). Front-end client support covers Microsoft Windows, MS-DOS, and OS/2. MQSeries goes much further than many MOM products in providing support for transactional messaging and all of its associated benefits. This support includes features such as two-phase commit, security, and restart and recovery, which would normally be found in transaction management software.

Digital's DECmessageQ also supports a wide range of other vendors' operating systems. In addition to the proprietary DEC VAX VMS and Alpha platforms, DECmessageQ covers the leading UNIX implementations (IBM, Sun, H-P, SCO) and Microsoft Windows environments. Languages supported include COBOL, C, FORTRAN, Ada, Visual Basic, and C. Digital includes a wide range of queue processing features designed to help systems management. In the future, DECmessageQ will support multiple APIs and standards for formal message queuing as they emerge from standards bodies.

Among the third-party suppliers, Peer Logic's Pipes is one of the leading contenders. It supports the main platforms of DEC, IBM, and Hewlett-Packard. Again, most of the major languages and network protocols are supported. Peer Logic's position as an independent has let it build relationships with other major vendors, particularly IBM. The two companies are working to integrate the Pipes software into IBM's Distributed System Object Model (DSOM) and to provide bridges between Pipes and MQSeries. Momentum Software's Message Express and X-IPC products are also widely used.

Transaction Processing Monitors

Before client/server had developed as a concept, the concept of middleware was very much in place within transaction processing systems. Transaction Processing (TP) monitors were first built to cope with batched transactions. Transactions were accumulated during the day and then passed against the company's data files overnight. Originally, TP monitor meant teleprocessing monitor—a program that multiplexed many terminals to a single central computer. Over time, TP monitors took on more than just multiplexing and routing functions, and TP came to mean transaction processing.

By the 1970s, TP monitors were handling online transactions, which gave rise to the term Online Transaction Processing that then became a part of the majority of legacy business systems in place today. Transaction Processing systems pass messages between programs; they operate, store, and forward queues; and they send acknowledgments. They have advanced error trapping procedures and restart and recovery features in the event of a breakdown that have evolved over the past 30 years from the requirements of mainframe integrity. IBM has defined a *transaction* as an atomic unit of work that possesses four properties: atomicity, consistency, isolation, and durability. These properties are often referred to as *ACID properties.*

Atomicity effectively provides the transaction recovery needs. A transaction must be completed as a whole, or the transaction is not completed at all. Therefore, the system must have full restart and recovery capabilities, so that any transaction that goes bad can be automatically reversed. Consistency means that the results of a particular transaction must be reproducible and predictable. The transaction obviously must always produce the same results under the same conditions. Isolation means that no transaction must interfere with any concurrently operating transaction. Finally, durability means that the results of the transaction must be permanent.

As you can see from these definitions, the software required to achieve these properties is essential for robust client/server systems, yet also it is inevitably complex. The robustness of TP systems, as discussed earlier, has evolved over many years as companies have demanded strong, secure mainframe systems. Client/server still has a long way to go to match this robustness.

IBM has been in the forefront of moving TP from its mainframe roots to client/server. IBM's CICS is perhaps one of the best examples of a transaction processing system. CICS began in the late 1960s as the Customer Information Control System (not Covered In Chocolate Sauce as was initially rumored!), a robust and reliable piece of software with a great range of OLTP functionality. It has traditionally been used on mainframes, yet recently it has also been ported to OS/2 as CICS OS/2 and to RS/6000 UNIX machines as CICS/6000.

The CICS OS/2 product brings the traditional terminal emulation product and a new External Call Interface (ECI) together at the client for processing across a network to a TP server. IBM uses a technique called *function shipping* that enables TP tasks to be moved around a network. The ECI technology is the crux of the system because it provides a high level of communication between the client and server components of the TP application that is required to support function shipping. Function shipping works in a similar fashion to RPC, as outlined in the DCE section in this chapter. The benefit for CICS users is that the CICS API is the same across all the platforms, so, in theory, a mainframe CICS application could run on either CICS OS/2 or CICS RS/6000.

IBM and other TP suppliers have recognized that their products have an enormous role to play in the new era of client/server computing. Their experience in the TP world, coupled with the maturity of the product, can teach the client/server world significant lessons as development goes forward. As a result, TP products such as CICS from IBM, Tuxedo from Novell, and

Top End from NCR are beginning to meet the demands of client/server developers who need the robust, secure, and controllable features available in these products. Without a doubt, the biggest reason for not moving to client/server is that developers fear (sometimes correctly) that the systems do not have the integrity of the 30-year-old legacy systems. In comparison to these legacy systems, client/server is a newborn babe. Yet now more than ever, client/server systems based on workgroups and LANs are considerably more viable than the traditional centralized mainframe processor operating dumb terminals.

The main drawbacks of a TP system for client/server are that it is still considerably more expensive than other forms of middleware and that TP suffers from a lack of standards, similar to MOM. As companies diversify their client/server systems and move from their legacy systems to client/server, they will benefit from using TP.

Queued, Conversational, and Workflow Models

Most TP monitors have migrated from a client/server basis to a three-system model in which the client performs data capture and local data processing and then sends a request to a middle-man called a request router. The router brokers the client request to one or more server processes. Each server in turn executes the request and responds. This design has evolved in three major directions: queued requests, conversational transactions, and workflow.

Queued TP is convenient for applications in which some clients produce data and others process or consume it. E-mail, job dispatching, EDI (Electronic Data Interchange), print spooling, and batch report generation are typical examples of queued TP. TP monitors include a subsystem that manages transactional queues. The router inserts a client's request into a queue for later processing by other applications. The TP monitor may manage a pool of applications servers to process the queue. Conversely, the TP monitor may attach a queue to each client and inform the client when messages appear in its queue. Messaging applications are examples of queued transactions.

Simple transactions are one-message-in, one-message-out client/server interactions, much like a simple RPC. Conversational transactions require the client and server to exchange several messages as a single ACID unit. These relationships are sometimes not a simple request and response, but rather small requests answered by a sequence of responses (for example, a large database selection) or a large request (such as sending a file to a server). The router acts as an intermediary between the client and server for conversational transactions. Conversational transactions often invoke multiple servers and maintain client context between interactions. Menu and forms-processing systems are so common that TP systems have scripting tools to quickly define menus and forms and the flows among them. The current menu state is part of the client context. Application designers can attach server invocations and procedural logic to each menu or form. In these cases, the TP monitor (router) manages the client context and controls the conversation with a workflow language.

Workflow is the natural combination of conversational and queued transactions. In its simplest form, a workflow is a sequence of ACID transactions following a workflow script. For example, the script for a person-to-person e-mail message is compose-deliver-receive. Typical business scripts are quite complex. Workflow systems capture and manage individual flows. A client may advance a particular workflow by performing a next step in the script. A developer defines workflow scripts as part of the application design. Administrative tools report and administer the current work-in-process.

Advanced TP

Modern database systems can maintain multiple replicas of a database. When one replica is updated, the updates are cross-posted to the other replicas. TP monitors can complement database replication in two ways. First, they can submit transactions to multiple sites so that update transactions are applied to each replica, thus avoiding the need to cross-post database updates.

Second, TP systems use database replicas in a fallback scheme, leaving the data replication to the underlying database system. If a primary database site fails, the router sends the transactions to the fallback replica of the database. Server failures are thus hidden from clients, who are given the illusion of an instant switchover. Because the router uses ACID transactions to cover both messages and database updates, each transaction will be processed once. The main TP monitors available today are CICS, IMS, ACMS, Pathway, Tuxedo, Encina, and Top End.

ODBC

Open database connectivity (ODBC) is Microsoft's strategic interface for accessing data in a distributed environment made up of relational and nonrelational DBMS. Based on the Call Level Interface specification of the SQL Access Group, ODBC provides an open, supposedly vendor-neutral way of accessing data stored in a variety of proprietary personal computer, minicomputer, and mainframe databases. ODBC alleviates the need for independent software vendors and corporate developers to learn multiple application programming interfaces. ODBC now provides a universal data access interface. With ODBC, application developers can allow an application to concurrently access, view, and modify data from multiple, diverse databases. ODBC is a core component of Microsoft Windows Open Services Architecture (WOSA). ODBC has emerged as the industry standard for data access for both Windows-based and Macintosh-based applications.

The key salient points with respect to ODBC in the client/server development environment are as follows:

- ODBC is vendor neutral, allowing access to DBMSs from multiple vendors.

- ODBC is open. Working with ANSI standards, the SQL Access Group (SAG), X/Open, and numerous independent software vendors, Microsoft has gained a very broad consensus on ODBC's implementation, and it is now the dominant standard.

- ODBC is powerful; it offers capabilities critical to client/server online transaction processing (OLTP) and decision support systems (DSS) applications, including system table transparency, full transaction support, scrollable cursors, asynchronous calling, array fetch and update, a flexible connection model, and stored procedures for static SQL performance.

40

UNDERSTANDING
MIDDLEWARE

The key benefits of ODBC are the following:

- It allows users to access data in more than one data storage location (for example, more than one server) from within a single application.

- It allows users to access data in more than one type of DBMS (such as DB2, Oracle, Microsoft SQL Server, DEC Rdb, and Progress) from within a single application.

- It simplifies application development. It is now easier for developers to provide access to data in multiple, concurrent DBMSs.

- It is a portable application programming interface (API), enabling the same interface and access technology to be a cross-platform tool.

- It insulates applications from changes to underlying network and DBMS versions. Modifications to networking transports, servers, and DBMSs will not affect current ODBC applications.

- It promotes the use of SQL, the standard language for DBMSs, as defined in the ANSI 1989 standard. It is an open, vendor-neutral specification based on the SAG Call Level Interface (CLI).

- It allows corporations to protect their investments in existing DBMSs and protect developers' acquired DBMS skills. ODBC allows corporations to continue to use existing diverse DBMSs while moving to client/server-based systems.

The ODBC Solution

ODBC addresses the database connectivity problem by using the common interface approach outlined earlier. Application developers can use one API to access all data sources. ODBC is based on a CLI specification, which was developed by a consortium of over 40 companies (members of the SQL Access Group and others) and has broad support from application and database suppliers. The result is a single API that provides all the functionality that application developers need and an architecture that database developers require to ensure interoperability. As a result, a very large selection of applications use ODBC.

How ODBC Works

ODBC defines an API. Each application uses the same code, as defined by the API specification, to talk to many types of data sources through DBMS-specific drivers. A driver manager sits between the applications and the drivers. In Windows, the driver manager and the drivers are implemented as dynamic link libraries (DLLs). Figure 40.5 shows how the ODBC driver for Windows 3.1 and Windows for Workgroups works. Windows 95 and Windows NT work in a similar fashion, but because they both are 32-bit operating systems, they can use a 32-bit version of ODBC.

FIGURE 40.5.
The ODBC architecture.

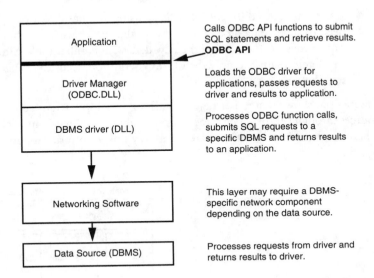

ODBC Architecture

Application — Calls ODBC API functions to submit SQL statements and retrieve results.
ODBC API

Driver Manager (ODBC.DLL) — Loads the ODBC driver for applications, passes requests to driver and results to application.

DBMS driver (DLL) — Processes ODBC function calls, submits SQL requests to a specific DBMS and returns results to an application.

Networking Software — This layer may require a DBMS-specific network component depending on the data source.

Data Source (DBMS) — Processes requests from driver and returns results to driver.

The application calls ODBC functions to connect to a data source either locally or remotely, send and receive data, and disconnect. The driver manager provides information to an application such as a list of available data sources, loads drivers dynamically as they are needed, and provides argument and state transition checking. The driver, developed separately from the application, sits between the application and the network. The driver processes ODBC function calls, manages all exchanges between an application and a specific DBMS, and may translate the standard SQL syntax into the native SQL of the target data source. All SQL translations are the responsibility of the driver developer.

Applications are not limited to communicating through one driver. A single application can make multiple connections, each through a different driver, or multiple connections to similar sources through a single driver. To access a new DBMS, a user or an administrator installs a driver for the DBMS. The user does not need a different version of the application to access the new DBMS. This is a tremendous benefit for end users and provides significant savings for IS organizations in support and development costs.

How ODBC Benefits the End User

End users do not work directly with the ODBC API; its configuration and setup are handled during installation. Users benefit in several ways when they use applications written with ODBC:

■ Users can select a data source from a list of data source names or supply the name of a data source in a consistent way across applications.

■ Users can submit data access requests in industry-standard SQL grammar regardless of the target DBMS. This capability makes ODBC ideal for what-if analysis.

■ Users can access different DBMSs by using familiar desktop applications. When users need to access data on a new platform, they will have a common level of functional capabilities while accessing the new data with familiar tools. Similarly, if data moves to a different platform, only the ODBC definition needs to change; the application can stay the same.

Figure 40.6 shows that a user may be running two applications accessing three different data sources through ODBC. The three sources might be on three completely different systems elsewhere on the network, yet they are seamlessly linked into the applications on the desktop of the client.

FIGURE 40.6.

A possible ODBC setup.

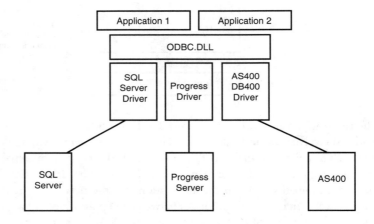

What ODBC Means to Application Developers

ODBC was designed to allow application developers to decide between using the least common denominator of functionality across DBMSs and exploiting the individual capabilities of specific DBMSs. ODBC defines a standard SQL grammar and set of function calls that are called the *core grammar* and *core functions*, respectively. If an application developer chooses only to use the core functions, he doesn't need to write any additional code to check for specific capabilities of a driver.

Using the core functions, an application can do the following:

■ Establish a connection with a data source, execute SQL statements, and retrieve results

■ Receive standard error messages

- Provide a standard logon interface to the end user for access to the data source
- Use a standard set of data types defined by ODBC
- Use a standard SQL grammar defined by ODBC

ODBC also defines an extended SQL grammar and set of extended functions to provide application developers with a standard way to exploit advanced capabilities of a DBMS. In addition to the preceding features, ODBC has extensions that provide enhanced performance and increased power through the following:

- Data types such as date, time, timestamp, and binary
- Scrollable cursors
- A standard SQL grammar for scalar functions, outer joins, and procedures
- Asynchronous execution
- A standard way for application developers to find out what capabilities a driver and data source provide

Finally, ODBC supports the use of DBMS-specific SQL grammar, allowing applications to exploit the capabilities of a particular DBMS. ODBC has a vast number of supported databases available, including IBM DB2/6000, IBM DB2/400, SQL Server, dBASE, Interbase, DEC Rdb, Microsoft Access, IBM DB2, and Progress.

ODBC is a powerful tool for providing end-user access to data stored in a wide variety of databases without requiring SQL or custom programming. It provides an excellent interface for creating client/server applications that are portable across multiple databases and even across multiple client platforms. The widespread industry (practically every database vendor has an ODBC driver for their product) acceptance of ODBC has resulted in many drivers, programs, and tools offering an outstanding array of features and capabilities.

Summary

Providing seamless access from your client machines to your distributed servers is a very complex process that is prone to difficulty. Each of the middleware types discussed in this chapter have taken a major share of the market. As time goes on, other products and techniques will emerge. Because the requirements for client/server vary considerably from company to company, it is not easy to choose one overall best technique or type. The main considerations when choosing your middleware types have to be ease of integration, ease of use, integrity to your needs, and the ease of development use. It is, after all, of no value to choose a product that you cannot develop your business applications on top of!

If, however, you think (*wish* might be more accurate) that a perfect middleware solution will become available, I am afraid that you are in for a long wait. It is perhaps best to take advantage of the existing products outlined in this chapter, develop your initial systems, build your experience, and then revisit your middleware requirements, changing products if you need to.

40

UNDERSTANDING
MIDDLEWARE

IN THIS PART

- Query Designer Primer   869

- HTTP 1.1 Specification   903

- HTML 3.2 Reference   929

- VBScript Reference   957

- Active Server Pages Scripting Reference   989

- SQL Reference   999

- Visual InterDev Design-Time ActiveX Control Reference   1005

- COM Reference   1019

- What's On the CD-ROM   1027

Appendixes

Query Designer Primer

by David Silverlight

IN THIS APPENDIX

APPENDIX A

This appendix focuses on perhaps the most important aspect of Web application development: the design of the database. If you have little or no experience in building databases, fear not. Visual InterDev contains some very powerful tools that give you what you need to create the queries and tables you require.

As Confucius would say, "He who builds Web application with weak database, creates weak Web application."

As the old cliché goes, you can't build a solid house without a strong foundation. To apply this to Web applications, you can't build an industrial-strength Web application without having a solid database design to support it. Considering the number of hours you will dedicate to creating that eye-catching Web site that will be hit by thousands and maybe millions of people, you are asking for trouble if you back it up with a poorly designed database. You will also virtually eliminate any repeat visitors by developing a database that is slow and tedious. God help you if you are developing a site for a client who is depending on the site for his livelihood. You can kiss that client good-bye.

Unfortunately, until Visual InterDev came along, there were really no decent tools that would enable you to develop queries and tables in the same development environment that you used to build your Web site. Visual InterDev incorporates some powerful tools to allow for a complete database design. You can develop any tables, queries, indexes, stored procedures, and triggers you might need in a Web application. Interestingly enough, only a small percentage of Web developers use the Visual Database tools to their fullest capacity.

This appendix should act as a reference for all the queries you will be using in your database development. Each type of query is followed by a working example, a description of the syntax, and how it could be used.

Query Designer Overview

The Query Designer, as the name implies, enables you to create a wide variety of queries to be used in the accessing of your data. The queries generated by the Query Designer follow the ODBC 3.0 specifications and are therefore usable in SQL Server, Oracle, and any other database that has an ODBC driver. Fortunately, there are ODBC drivers for virtually any data source. What this means to you is that you can begin by generating a collection of queries for your favorite data source. These queries can then be used across virtually any database your Web application might evolve into.

Action Queries

Just about any database application needs to perform the basics: adding, modifying, and deleting records. Fortunately, these functions can be accomplished in a variety of ways with action queries. *Action queries* perform an action of some type on a database, such as adding a record, modifying a field, or deleting a series of records.

The following examples demonstrate three kinds of action queries: update, delete, and insert.

Update Queries

An *update query* updates a field or fields in one or more records.

Scenario

One of our shipping contacts, Wendy Haro, found Mr. Right and married him. Oh, great! We need to update our database to change all instances of the old name, `'Wendy Haro'`, to the new name, `'Wendy Right'`:

Update Query Syntax:	Our Scenario:
`UPDATE Tablename`	`UPDATE Orders`
`SET`	`SET`
`FieldnameA = New Value,`	`ShipContactFirstName = 'Wendy',`
`FieldnameB = New Value`	`ShipContactLastName = 'Right'`
`WHERE (Search Criteria)`	`WHERE (ShipContactFirstName = 'Wendy'`
	`➡AND ShipContactLastName = 'Haro')`

To update the field in Query Designer, drag the tables included in your update query from the Data View tab to the diagram pane. This makes their fields accessible. Select the fields that you want to update. In our scenario, we are updating `'ShipContactFirstName'` and `'ShipContactLastName'`, so we check them off. The table will look something like Figure A.1.

Figure A.1.

Modifying your update query.

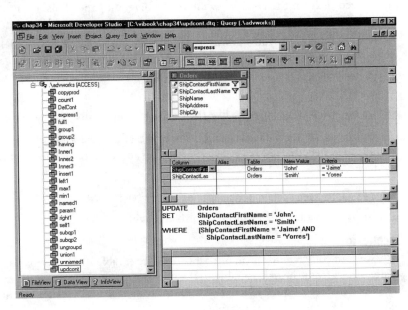

For each field, type the new value into the corresponding New Value box. As you enter the values to be set, you will notice that the SET section of the query is updated accordingly.

For each field, type in the selection criteria in the Criteria box of the Table grid. As you enter the new values, you will notice that the WHERE clause of the query is updated accordingly.

Delete Queries

A *delete query* is a type of action query that will delete one or more records in a database.

Scenario

Our newly married shipping contact, Wendy Right, suddenly decided to resign her position as shipping contact. We now need to delete her from our database. In this scenario, we want to delete all instances where the contact name equals `'Wendy Right'`:

Delete Query Syntax:	Our Scenario:
`DELETE FROM TableName`	`DELETE FROM Orders`
`WHERE (Search Criteria)`	`WHERE (ShipContactFirstName = 'Wendy') AND`
	`➥(ShipContactLastName = 'Right')`

Follow these steps to update the field in Query Designer:

1. Click the Create Delete Query button. Drag the table from which you want to delete records from the Data View tab to the diagram pane. This makes the records accessible for deletion. Note that you may select only one table in delete queries.

2. Select the fields you want to use in the selection criteria of your delete query. In our scenario, we are deleting the records in which `'ShipContactFirstName'` equals Wendy and `'ShipContactLastName'` equals Right, so we check them off and enter the criteria values.

The table will look something like the one shown in Figure A.2.

As soon as you enter the selection criteria for each field, the WHERE clause of the SQL statement changes to reflect the new selection criteria. These criteria are used in determining which records to delete.

Insert Queries

An *insert query* adds one or more records to a table.

Scenario

We want to copy records from one table to another table. In this scenario, we want to copy the daily orders from the Orders table to the OrderHistory table so that we can maintain an audit trail or a history of our orders. To accomplish this, we will need a executable query that will copy records from the Orders table into the OrderHistory table.

FIGURE A.2.
Modifying your delete query.

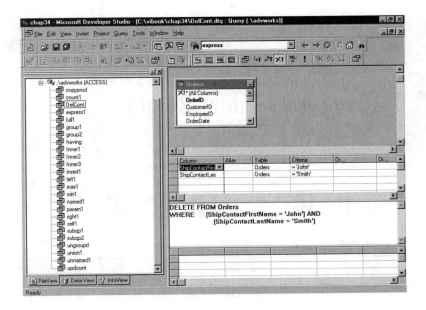

Insert Query Syntax:	Our Scenario:
`INSERT INTO TableName (Field(s))`	`INSERT INTO Orders (OrderID)`
`SELECT FieldA, FieldB, ...`	`SELECT OrderID`
`FROM TableName`	`FROM Order_Details`
`WHERE (Selection Criteria)`	`WHERE (OrderID = 1)`

To copy the orders from the `Orders` table to the `OrderHistory` table in Query Designer, follow these steps:

1. In Insert Query mode, select the table into which you want to insert data. Interestingly enough, in the first step you select tables via the dialog box shown in Figure A.3 instead of dragging the table from the Data View tab. For our scenario, select the `OrderHistory` table.

2. From this point, the steps are the same as those for a select query. Select input tables by dragging the tables from the Data View tab into the diagram pane. In this scenario, we will drag the `Orders` table into the diagram pane. If you look at the following SQL statement, you will notice that it changed to accommodate this new table. Specifically, the `Orders` table affects the `FROM` section of the SQL statement. Select the fields from the `Orders` table that you want to copy. In this scenario, we are copying all the fields, so we select the `*(All Columns)` choice. Notice that the `SELECT` section of the SQL statement changes to accommodate the selected fields.

FIGURE A.3.
Creating your insert query.

Defining How Tables Relate

When you work with multiple tables, it is essential that you understand the concepts controlling table relationships and how tables are joined. If you couple an in-depth knowledge of table relationships with a solid database design, you can retrieve virtually any set of data needed for your Web application. This section examines the three methods for joining tables (inner, outer, and self) and how they can be used to generate some essential types of queries. Table A.1 presents an overview of the various types of joins, with a brief explanation of how each type works.

Table A.1. Types of joins.

Join Type	Join Result
Inner join	Only the records with common data values on the joined field will be selected.
Left outer join	All records from the left table will be selected, but only the records in the right table with common data values in the joined field will be selected. For records in the right table that have no common data on the joined field, blanks will be used instead of data values. This relationship is effectively the inverse of the right outer join.
Right outer join	All records from the right table will be selected, but only the records in the left table with common data values in the joined field will be selected. For records in the left table that have no common data on the joined field, blanks will be used instead of data values. This relationship is effectively the inverse of the left outer join.
Full outer join	All records from both the right and left tables will be selected. For records in the left table that have no common data in the joined field, blanks will be used instead of data values. For records in the right table that have no common data in the joined field, blanks will be used instead of data values.
Self join	Records from within the same table are joined to each other based on common data for the joined field. This type of join is used for queries that show records that have data in common.

Inner Joins

An *inner join* is a relationship defined between two tables in which only the records with common data values in the joined field will be selected. In the following examples, I demonstrate how you can use inner joins to associate data between two tables.

Scenario 1

Task:

We need to see a listing of the daily orders along with their shipping methods so that we can analyze what type of shipping methods are used most often, so our query should display the OrderID from the Orders table as well as the associated shipping method from the ShippingMethods table.

Problem:

The shipping method exists in the ShippingMethods table, whereas the OrderID exists in the Orders table. Because we need fields from two different tables, we need a way to define a relationship between these tables—that is, we need a way to join these tables.

Solution:

We can join the ShippingMethods table to the Orders table using the OrderID, which is a field they have in common. If we use an inner join on OrderID, we will get only exact matches between the two tables with the data properly associated (see Figure A.4).

SQL Statement:

```
SELECT Orders.OrderID, Shipping_Methods.ShippingMethod
FROM Orders, Shipping_Methods
WHERE Orders.ShippingMethodID = Shipping_Methods.ShippingMethodID
```

 You can find the Inner1 query (Inner1.dtq) on the accompanying CD-ROM.

Scenario 2

Task:

We need to see a listing of our orders along with the names of the customers who placed them so that we can print out our daily customer report, so our query should display the OrderID from the Orders table as well as the associated customer's name from the Customers table.

Problem:

The customer's name exists in the Customers table, whereas the OrderID exists in the Orders table. We need a way to join these tables.

Solution:

We can join the Customers table to the Orders table using CustomerID, a field that they have in common. If we use an inner join on CustomerID, we will get only exact matches between the two tables with the data properly associated (see Figure A.5).

SQL Statement:

```
SELECT Orders.OrderID, Orders.CustomerID, Customers.ContactFirstName,
➥Customers.ContactLastName
FROM Orders, Customers
WHERE Orders.CustomerID = Customers.CustomerID
```

FIGURE A.4.

The output of our Inner1 *query.*

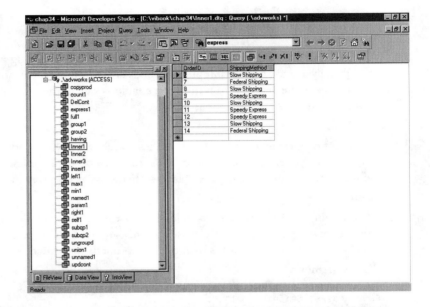

FIGURE A.5.

The output of our Inner2 *query.*

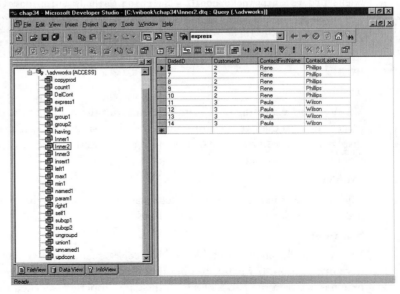

You can find the Inner2 query (Inner2.dtq) on the accompanying CD-ROM.

Scenario 3

Task:

We need to see a listing of our orders along with the names of the products purchased in each order so that we can analyze which products are sold. Therefore, our query should display the OrderID from the Orders table as well as the associated product description from the Products table.

Problem:

The product information exists in the Products table, whereas the OrderID exists in the Orders table. We need a way to join these tables.

Solution:

We can join the Products table to the Orders table using ProductID, a field they have in common. If we use an inner join on ProductID, we will get only exact matches between the two tables with the data properly associated (see Figure A.6).

SQL Statement:

```
SELECT Order_Details.OrderID, Order_Details.ProductID,
Products.ProductDescription
FROM Order_Details, Products
WHERE Order_Details.ProductID = Products.ProductID
```

FIGURE A.6.

The output of our Inner3 query.

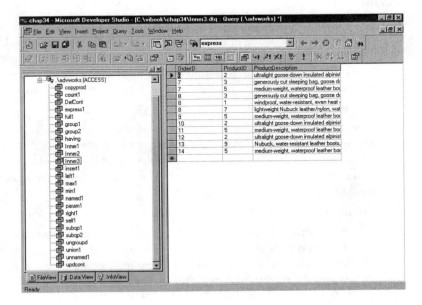

 You can find the Inner3 query (Inner3.dtq) on the accompanying CD-ROM.

> **TIP**
>
> Because null values do not match anything, inner joins on them will not return any matching rows.

Outer Joins

An *outer join* defines a relationship in which you can select all records from a primary table and only a select number of records from the secondary table. Although there are three kinds of outer joins, the primary difference between them is in the way the data is handled when the record is not found in the secondary table. In general, the query pads the unmatched record in the secondary table with blanks. The following sections explore the three kinds of outer joins: left outer joins, right outer joins, and full outer joins.

Left Outer Joins

A *left outer join* is a relationship between two tables in which all records from the left table will be selected, but only the records in the right table with common data values in the joined field will be selected. For records in the right table that have no common data on the joined field, blanks will be used instead of data values. This relationship is effectively the inverse of the right outer join.

Scenario

Task:

We want to see a listing of the products that each employee has sold. In addition, we need to see the employee name even if he has not sold anything (so that we can fire him). Therefore, our query should display all employee names from the Employees table and the related product information from the Products table.

Problem:

The employee name exists in the Employees table, and the order information exists in the Orders table. Because we need fields from two different tables, we will need a way to define a relationship between these tables—that is, we need a way to join these tables. In addition, we need a way to include the employee names even if there are no joining records in the Orders table.

Solution:

We can join the Employees table to the Orders table using EmployeeID, which is a field they have in common. If we use a left outer join on EmployeeID, we will get all employee names for employees with corresponding product records. For employees with no products, we will have blanks in place of product information (see Figure A.7).

SQL Statement:

```
SELECT Employees.EmployeeID, Employees.FirstName, - Employees.LastName,
➥Orders.OrderID,Orders.OrderDate
FROM { oj Employees LEFT OUTER JOIN Orders ON
➥Employees.EmployeeID = Orders.EmployeeID }
```

FIGURE A.7.

The output of our
left1 *query.*

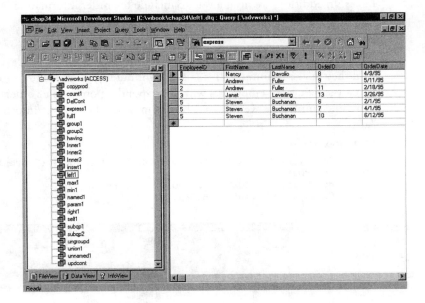

 You can find the left1 query (left1.dtq) on the accompanying CD-ROM.

Right Outer Joins

A *right outer join* is a relationship between two tables in which all records from the secondary table will be selected, but only the records in the primary table with common data values in the joined field will be selected. For records in the secondary table that have no common data in the joined field, blanks will be used instead of data values. This relationship is effectively the inverse of the left outer join.

Scenario

Task:

We want to see a listing of the orders that have been placed along with the corresponding employee's name. In addition, we need to see either the employee name or a blank if the employee is not in our database (this would indicate a corruption in the Employees table, a condition we need to track). Therefore, our query should display all orders from the Orders table and the related employee name from the Employees table.

Problem:

The order information exists in the Orders table, and the employee names exist in the Employees table. Because we need fields from two different tables, we will need a way to define a relationship between these tables—that is, we need a way to join these tables. In addition, we need a way to include the order information even if there are no joining records in the Employees table.

Solution:

We can join the Orders table to the Employees table using the EmployeeID, which is a field they have in common. If we use a right outer join on EmployeeID, we will get all employee names for employees with corresponding orders. For orders with non-matching employees, we will have blanks in place of employee information (see Figure A.8).

SQL Statement:

```
SELECT Employees.FirstName, Employees.LastName, - Orders.OrderID,
Orders.OrderDate
FROM { oj Employees RIGHT OUTER JOIN - Orders ON
Orders.EmployeeID = Employees.EmployeeID }
```

FIGURE A.8.

The output of our right1 *query.*

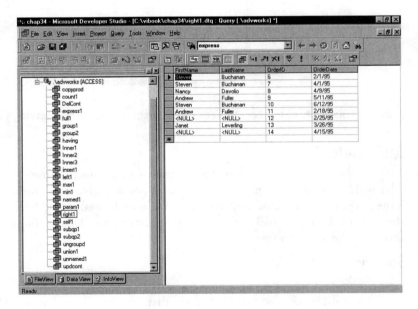

 You can find the right1 query (right1.dtq) on the accompanying CD-ROM.

Full Outer Joins

A *full outer join* is a relationship between two tables in which all records from both the primary and secondary tables will be selected. For records in the primary table that have no common data in the joined field, blanks will be used instead of data values. For records in the secondary table that have no common data in the joined field, blanks will be used instead of data values.

Self Joins

A *self join* is a way to associate records that exist in one table with other records from the same table. This type of join is useful in generating queries in which records are related to other records from the same table.

Scenario 1

Task:

An environmentalist in our company has determined that we can help save the planet if our employees start carpooling. To organize this, we will need to use our `Employees` table to generate a list of records of employees who have the same ZIP code as other employees. Therefore, our query should display all records from the `Employees` table in which employee records have the same ZIP code as other employee records (in the same `Employees` table).

Problem:

The first problem is that we are joining records in the same table, but joins require that we relate two tables.

The second problem is that we will be using ZIP code values from the `Employees` table as our selection criterion. This will require a bit of creativity because our queries are usually based from static search criteria. (Where there's a will, there's a way.)

Solution:

The solution to the first problem is simply a matter of selecting the `Employees` table twice. As you select the `Employees` table the second time, it will be referred to as `Employees1`. This naming convention allows you to relate the table to itself, yet gives a unique name to the second copy of the table for clear reference in the SQL statement:

```
(Employees.EmployeeID <> Employees1.EmployeeID)
```

The solution to the second problem is an offshoot of the first solution. Now that we have two names referencing the same table, we can use those unique names to define a relationship between fields within the same table. For example:

```
(Employees.HomeZip = Employees1.HomeZip)
```

By applying these two solutions, we can associate records in the `Employees` table to other records. This will return to us all records that are related to each other via ZIP code (see Figure A.9).

> **NOTE**
>
> In the following SQL statement, I have added an additional select query for the purpose of excluding duplicates. Because we are dealing with the same table, every record is related to itself at least once. To eliminate these records, I included
>
> ```
> (Employees.EmployeeID <> Employees1.EmployeeID)
> ```

SQL Statement:

```
SELECT Employees.EmployeeID, Employees.HomeZip,
➥Employees.FirstName, - Employees.LastName
FROM Employees, Employees Employees1
WHERE ((Employees.EmployeeID <> Employees1.EmployeeID)
➥AND (Employees.HomeZip = Employees1.HomeZip))
```

FIGURE A.9.

The output of our
self1 *query.*

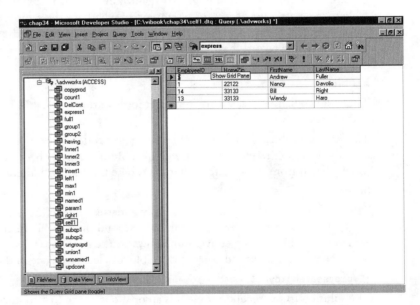

 You can find the self1 query (self1.dtq) on the accompanying CD-ROM.

Parameterized Queries

A *parameterized query* allows you to specify one or more elements of the query at runtime. This can enable you to create generic queries in which the user specifies the unknown portions on the fly. The great thing about parameterized queries is that they allow you to create a single, generic query in place of a large number of custom-written queries. In the following example,

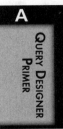

we are working with a query that will return a list of products that match a certain type. Using a parameterized query, we prompt the user to specify the product type at runtime. The output of the query is, of course, based on what the user typed in.

When should they be used? Using parameterized queries has its advantages and disadvantages. The advantage, as in the following example, is that you don't have to generate a query for every single product in your inventory. This can be quite a time-saver. In addition, you would have to generate a new query every time another product line was added to the inventory. This would be a very difficult task.

The disadvantages are that, first, the user may be taken aback at the parameter screen that he is posed with. Also, you cannot truly prevent the user from typing in an invalid parameter value. Last but not least, the user might always be running the query for the same product type (Product='Tent', for example), and might get annoyed by typing the same product each time the query is run. A key thing to remember from all this is that you must consider the environment in which the query is to be used when deciding whether to use parameterized queries.

Named Versus Unnamed Parameterized Queries

There are two flavors of parameterized queries, named and unnamed. Depending on the circumstances, you might want to use one over the other. In this section, I will show you when to use named and unnamed queries.

Unnamed Parameterized Queries

Scenario:

We want to display a listing of all the products in our Products table for a given product type. The product type will be entered by the user at runtime. In our example, the user enters Tent when prompted for a parameter (see Figures A.10 and A.11).

SQL Statement:
```
SELECT ProductID, ProductType, ProductCode, ProductName
FROM Products
WHERE (ProductType = ?)
```

 You can find the unnamed1.dtq query (unnamed1.dtq) on the accompanying CD-ROM.

Named Parameterized Queries

Following is a summary of the preceding query, but this time with a named query. There are a few minor differences that are worth noting. First, you must specify the parameter-marking characters, as shown in Figure A.12. These characters are used to indicate the beginning and ending of a named parameter. In our example, we are surrounding the characters by square brackets, [and]. This results in a parameter that looks like this: [Type].

FIGURE A.10.

The output of our unnamed1 *query.*

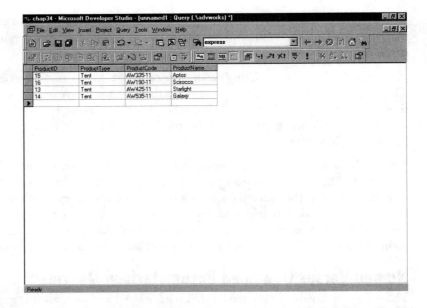

FIGURE A.11.

What you see when the query runs.

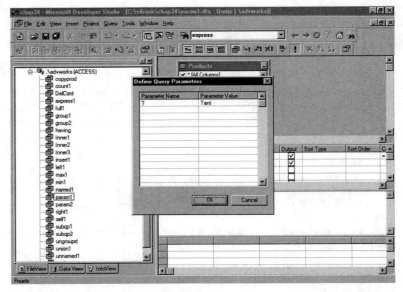

Scenario:

We want to display a listing of all the products in our Products table for a given product type. The product type will be entered by the user at runtime. In our

example, the user enters Tent when prompted for a parameter (see Figure A.13). Also, in this example we want to prompt the user with the parameter by name (see Figure A.14).

FIGURE A.12.
The named parameter screen.

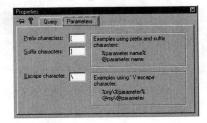

SQL Statement:
```
SELECT ProductType, ProductID, ProductCode, ProductName
FROM Products
WHERE (ProductType = [type])
```

FIGURE A.13.
The output of our
Named1 *query.*

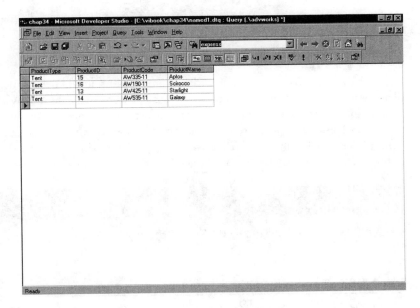

 You can find the named1.dtq query (named1.dtq) on the accompanying CD-ROM.

FIGURE A.14.

The named parameter execution screen.

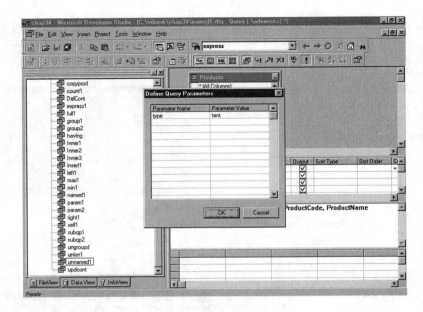

Grouping Related Data

Typically, when you create a listing of data from a table, you will need to perform some degree of analysis and/or summarization on it, such as I've done in Table A.2. Whether it is simply a subtotaling of data or a count of the number of records, the need is usually there. Fortunately, the Query Designer exposes some simple, yet very powerful, functions that you can exploit in your queries. These functions are known as *aggregate functions*, which are functions that return only a single value, such as the sum or average for a column in your query.

TIP

To enable grouping, you must right-click on the Query pane.

Table A.2. Data to be used in the grouping examples.

OrderDetailID	OrderID	ProductID	Quantity	UnitPrice	Discount
18	6	2	1	310	0
19	7	3	2	200	0
20	7	5	1	98	0
21	8	3	1	200	0
22	8	1	2	390	0

OrderDetailID	OrderID	ProductID	Quantity	UnitPrice	Discount
23	8	7	1	78	0
24	9	5	1	98	0
26	10	2	1	310	0
28	11	5	1	98	0
30	12	2	2	310	0
32	13	9	1	87	0
33	14	5	2	98	0

 You can find this query (`ungroupd.dtq`) on the accompanying CD-ROM.

GROUP BY

When you add a GROUP BY clause to a query, you will return a result set in which only unique values for that field are contained. If the GROUP BY clause contains more than one field, the query returns one row for each combination of fields that is unique.

Scenario 1:

We are trying to generate a unique listing of OrderIDs from our Order_Details table (see Figure A.15).

SQL Statement:

```
SELECT OrderID
FROM Order_Details
GROUP BY: OrderID
```

 You can find this query (`group1.dtq`) on the accompanying CD-ROM.

Scenario 2:

We are trying to generate a listing of orders in our Order_Details table. In this listing we also want to see the total sales per order and the total quantity of items per order (see Figure A.16).

SQL Statement:

```
SELECT OrderID, SUM(UnitPrice) AS TotalSales, SUM(Quantity) AS TotalQuantity
FROM Order_Details
GROUP BY: OrderID
```

 You can find this query (`group2.dtq`) on the accompanying CD-ROM.

FIGURE A.15.

The output of our group1 *query.*

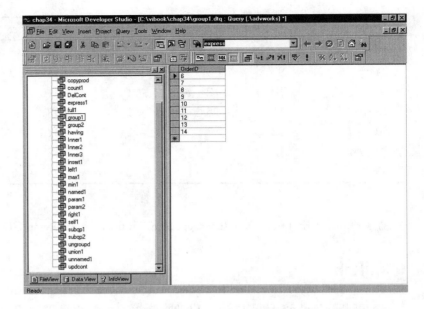

FIGURE A.16.

The output of our group2 *query.*

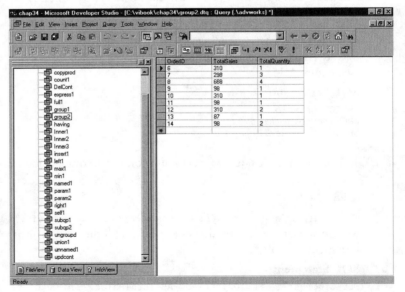

MIN

MIN is an aggregate function that will return the smallest value for all rows within the group of a column.

Scenario:

We are trying to generate a listing of orders in our `Order_Details` table. In this listing we also want to see the cheapest items sold per order (see Figure A.17).

SQL Statement:

```
SELECT OrderID, MIN(UnitPrice) AS LeastExpensive
FROM Order_Details
GROUP BY: OrderID
```

FIGURE A.17.

The output of our min1 *query.*

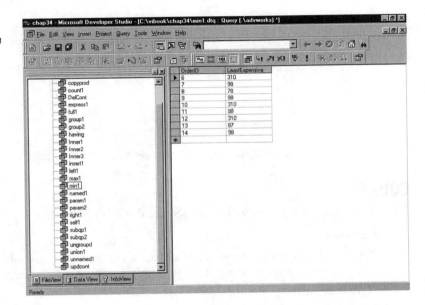

 You can find this query (`min1.dtq`) on the accompanying CD-ROM.

MAX

The MAX aggregate function returns the largest value for all rows within the group of a column.

Scenario:

We are trying to generate a listing of orders in our `Order_Details` table. In this listing we also want to see the most expensive items sold per order (see Figure A.18).

SQL Statement:

```
SELECT OrderID, MAX(UnitPrice) AS MostExpensive
FROM Order_Details
GROUP BY: OrderID
```

 You can find the max1.dtq query (`max1.dtq`) on the accompanying CD-ROM.

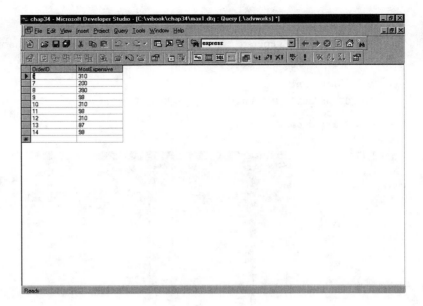

FIGURE A.18.

The output of our max1 *query.*

COUNT

The COUNT aggregate function will return the number of rows within the group of a column.

Scenario:

We are trying to generate a listing of orders in our Order_Details table. In this listing we also want to see how many items were sold per order (see Figure A.19).

SQL Statement:

```
SELECT OrderID, COUNT(OrderID) AS ItemsPerOrder
FROM Order_Details
GROUP BY: OrderID
```

 You can find the count1.dtq query (count1.dtq) on the accompanying CD-ROM.

Expression

The Expression function enables you to custom-define formulas based on the results of aggregate functions. It should be noted that only aggregate functions may be used to generate these expressions.

Scenario:

We are trying to generate a listing of orders in our Order_Details table. In this listing we also want to see the value of each order before and after tax has been added (see Figure A.20).

FIGURE A.19.
The output of our
count1 *query.*

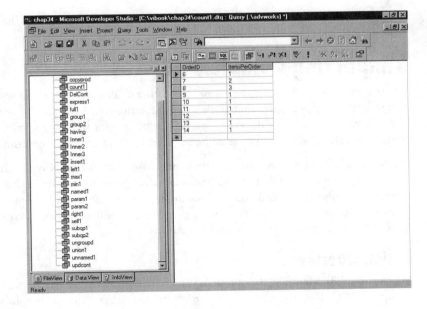

SQL Statement:
```
SELECT OrderID, SUM(UnitPrice) AS RegPrice, RegPrice * 1.06 AS TaxPrice
FROM Order_Details
GROUP BY: OrderID
```

FIGURE A.20.
The output of our
express1 *query.*

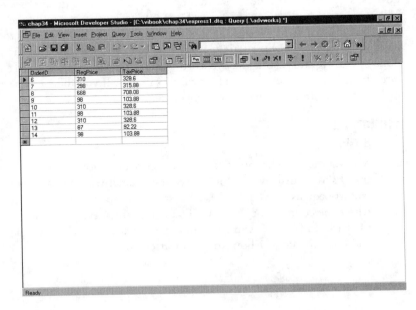

You can find this query (express1.dtq) on the accompanying CD-ROM.

Simplifying Complex Queries

At least once, everyone has come across the mother of all queries—you know, the query that is just so horrifyingly complex that you end up throwing your hands in the air and deciding that the only way to return the data that you need is by custom-writing a small application. Don't worry; it's OK to admit it. We've all been there. Queries can be tough sometimes.

As luck would have it, there are a few types of queries that can simplify the chore of developing truly complex queries. The two mechanisms we are going to explore in this section are union queries and subqueries. You will see how union queries allow you to combine two practically separate queries into one result set and how subqueries will allow you to break down one complex selection criterion into two smaller sections.

Union Queries

A *union query* is essentially the concatenation of the output of two separate queries into a single result set. VID does not offer any way to create entire union queries graphically. Therefore, it is imperative that you understand the mechanics of union queries at the SQL level.

First, because union queries concatenate two separate queries, both queries must contain the same number of fields. Second, the output of the queries is a union of the output of the two queries, so you should expect that the result set will return a distinct set of data (that is, you will not see any duplicate records). Last but not least, you cannot build the union query graphically, but you can build the two subqueries graphically. What this means to you is that you will want to build the two subqueries graphically, but the final union of the two queries will be done by cutting and pasting the two existing SQL statements into a third SQL statement separated by the word UNION (see the following example). If you follow these guidelines, you will maintain your sanity for that much longer.

Scenario 1

Task:

We want to see a listing of all our contacts who reside in the United States, so our query should display the shipping contact names from the Orders table where the country equals 'USA' as well as all customer contact names from the Customers table where the country equals 'USA'. To the untrained eye, this would sound like a walk in the park. In fact, we estimate to our client that it will take about 15 minutes (but we pad the estimate to 1 hour to cover ourselves).

Problem:

Some of our contact names are in the Orders table, and the rest of them are in the Customers table. We will need customer contacts followed by shipping contacts. Unfortunately, there is no way to join the tables so that we can concatenate the two listings. There is no join that can save us now! Although we could easily generate either set of names by itself, it is no small task to generate the combination.

Solution:

We can concatenate the two listings by generating the union of the two separate listings (see Figure A.21). This works nicely even if the queries use different tables and different selection criteria. The general format is

```
"CustomerContactSQL"
UNION
"ShippingContactSQL"
```

SQL Statement:

```
SELECT ContactFirstName, ContactLastName
FROM Customers
WHERE Country = 'USA'
UNION
SELECT ShipContactFirstName, ShipContactLastName
FROM Orders
WHERE ShipCountry = 'USA'
```

FIGURE A.21.
The output of our
union1 *query.*

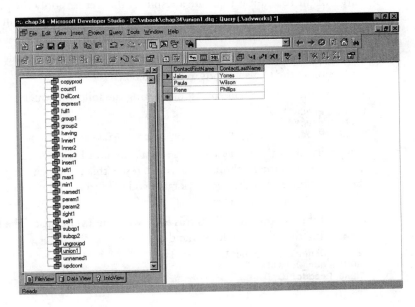

 You can find this query (union1.dtq) on the accompanying CD-ROM.

Using Subqueries

Subqueries enable you to use the results of one query as the selection query for a second query. Sound abstract? Well, it could be if you try to grasp it as one single step, but it can become much simpler if you think of it as a two-step process. Remember, the trick is in breaking it into two steps. Thankfully, there is a payoff for this abstraction, the payoff being that you can create queries with pretty complex selection criteria in a very simplified format. Let's examine a scenario in which we can apply subqueries.

Scenario

Task:

We want to see a listing of orders related to products whose size is either "S-XXL" or "XS-XL." Also, we expect that this criteria will become increasingly more complicated as more sizes come into stock.

Problem:

We realize that we could accomplish this task with a semi-complicated set of joins and selection criteria, but we would like to simplify these criteria so that they can be changed easily by us or by somebody less experienced.

Solution:

Part 1 of the solution is to create a result set that returns only the product IDs that match the sizes specified. This is a rather simple task, and the results can be changed fairly easily.

Part 2 of the solution is to create a query that uses Part 1 as the selection criteria.

Let's explore the two solutions in more detail.

Part 1 of the solution will consist of creating the following query:

```
SELECT ProductID
FROM Products
WHERE (ProductSize = 'S-XXL') OR (ProductSize = 'XS-XL')
```

The query in Part 1 will generate the data shown in Figure A.22. This result set will be used as input in the final query. As you can see, this is a much simpler way to visualize the contribution that the Products table will lend to the final output than would be joining with selection criteria.

Part 2 of the solution combines this SQL with the IN() clause. The final query, prior to inserting the SQL, will look like this:

```
SELECT OrderID, ProductID, Quantity
FROM Order_Details
WHERE ProductID IN()
```

The preceding SQL expects that what is contained inside of the IN() clause will consist of a query that produces a list of Product IDs. Hence, if the order's Product ID is in the Product IDs list, it will be included in the final result set (see Figure A.23).

SQL Statement:

```
SELECT OrderID, ProductID, Quantity
FROM Order_Details
WHERE ProductID IN
(SELECT ProductID
FROM Products
WHERE (ProductSize = 'S-XXL')
OR
(ProductSize = 'XS-XL'))
```

FIGURE A.22.

The output of our first subquery section.

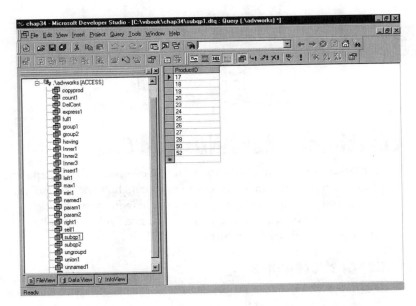

Notice that all the Product IDs in the preceding result set are also in the result set of the query from Part 1.

 You can find this query (subqp2.dtq) on the accompanying CD-ROM.

FIGURE A.23.

The output of our
subqp2 *query.*

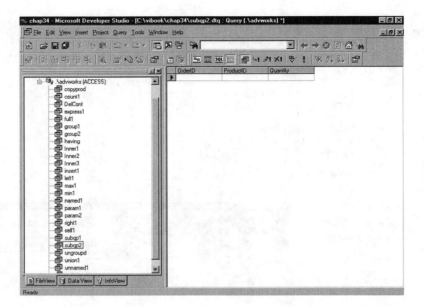

Combining Your ANDs and ORs

You can develop queries of almost every level of complexity by incorporating combinations of AND and OR operators. But first, you must understand how the operators are interpreted. When you get beyond that understanding, you will need to know how these operators work together when they are used in conjunction with one another. Only then will you be able to know what data to expect your queries to return.

Order of Precedence

The AND has precedence over the OR; therefore, when both the AND and OR are used in the same query, the AND is interpreted first, followed by the OR. This precedence can be changed by the use of parentheses in the same manner that any arithmetic precedence can be changed.

Understanding the way queries are represented when operators are combined should be learned first at the SQL pane level and then at the grid pane level.

How Precedence Is Represented in the SQL Pane

At the SQL level, conditions are interpreted in a mathematical fashion. This interpretation is based on logical precedence, usage of parentheses, and the distributive law. Let's examine some sample combinations of operators. In our examples, we will be using these three conditions:

ConditionA:	Quantity > 1
ConditionB:	Size <> 'small'
ConditionC:	Size <> 'medium'

Scenario 1: A or B and C

Breakdown1	A or (B and C)	Reason: The AND has precedence over the OR.
Breakdown2	(A or B) and (A or C)	Reason: Distributive law of mathematics.

Figure A.24 shows how this is displayed in both panes.

FIGURE A.24.

How the andor1 *query is displayed in the SQL pane and the grid pane.*

Grid pane —

SQL pane —

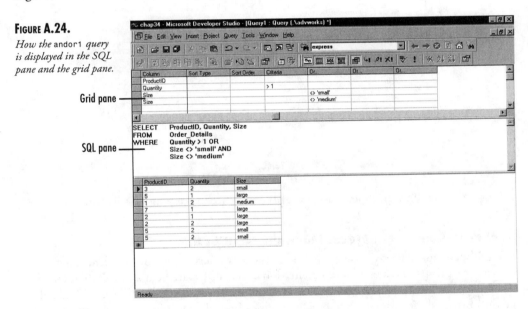

 You can find this query (andor1.dtq) on the accompanying CD-ROM.

Scenario 2: A and (B or C)

| Breakdown1 | A and (B or C) | Reason: The parentheses force the OR to be evaluated first. |
| Breakdown2 | (A and B) or (A and C) | Reason: Distributive law of mathematics. |

How this appears in both panes is shown in Figure A.25.

FIGURE A.25.
The SQL pane display of our andor2 *query.*

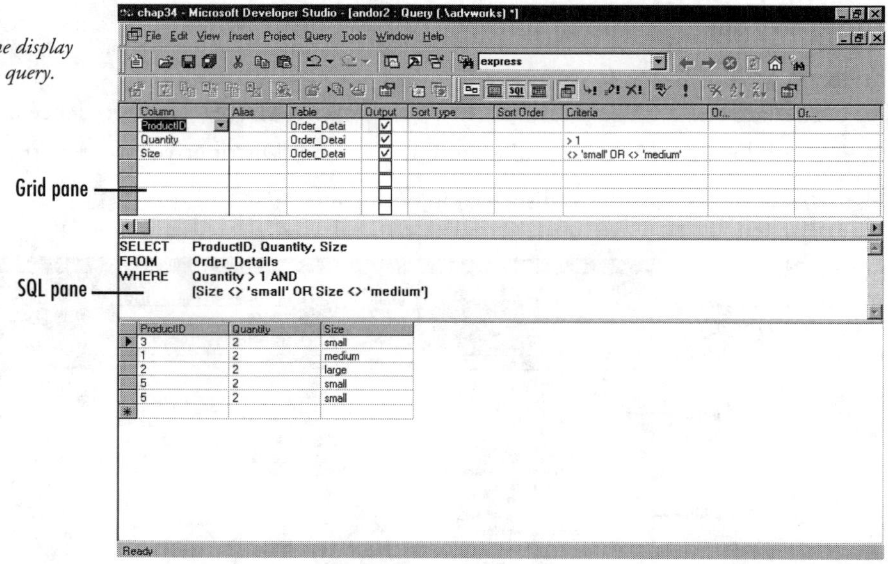

You can find this query (andor2.dtq) on the accompanying CD-ROM.

How Precedence Is Represented in the Query Pane

The grid pane in Figure A.26 corresponds to the first query in our most recent example. As you can see, this pane is a tabular representation of the SQL statement and will therefore need to represent the entire query, regardless of how complex, in a single tabular format. And it does. To the untrained eye, this table can be a little misleading when it comes to representing queries that contain a great deal of AND/OR operators. Fortunately, once you understand the format that is used, this becomes a very elegant way of compactly representing queries of any level of complexity.

FIGURE A.26.

The grid pane representation of our andor1 query.

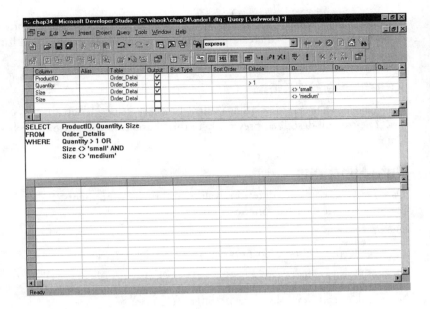

Following are some guidelines for working with the grid pane:

- When evaluating the grid pane, read it in a column-wise fashion. Each column contains a series of conditions that will be ANDed with the other conditions within that column. The results of each column will be ORed with the other columns in the query.

- If your SQL contains a condition that is ANDed or ORed with a combination of conditions that are within parentheses, you will notice that the grid pane will repeat that condition for each element in the parentheses. This is the way the grid pane applies the distributive law.

- Sometimes it is easier to create or change the SQL in the SQL pane and then select Verify SQL Syntax to update the corresponding SQL statement in the grid pane. This is most useful in cases where you are using parentheses to change the precedence.

Using Expressions in Your Queries

An *expression* is a combination of functions, column values, constants, and literals that will generate a single value. Because they generate a single value, they can be used in the same way that any column can be used in a query. They are, in a sense, virtual columns because they generate values dynamically as the query is executed. Because expressions can include functions, they can be used to create powerful queries. In this section, I will list and demonstrate some of the built-in functions that are supported by ODBC 3.0.

Aggregate Functions

Aggregate functions are those that return summary values. They are Avg, Count, Min, Max, and Sum. They are all described previously in this chapter, in the section titled "Grouping Related Data."

Date Functions

Date functions compute date/time values and their components. Following is an example of the SQL for the Curdate function:

```
SELECT OrderID
FROM Orders
WHERE OrderDate < { fn CURDATE () }
```

This will return a listing of all orders prior to today.

Now look at this example of the DateDiff function:

```
SELECT OrderID
FROM Orders
WHERE { fn DateDiff ('ww', OrderDate, { fn CURDATE()}) } > 4
```

This will return a listing of all orders older than 4 weeks.

Other date functions are DateAdd, DateName, and DatePart.

String Functions

String functions perform operations on binary data, character strings, and expressions. Substring returns a section of a string, and Right returns the rightmost *x* character(s) from a string. The other string functions are +, Ltrim, Soundex, Ascii, patindex, space, char, replicate, str, charindex, reverse, stuff, difference, lower, rtrim, and upper.

Mathematical Functions

Mathematical functions perform operations on numeric data. abs returns the absolute value of a given value. The other mathematical functions are Rand, acos, asin, atan, atn2, ceiling, cos, cot, degrees, exp, floor, log, log10, pi, power, radians, round, sign, sin, sqrt, and tan.

Niladic Functions

Niladic functions allow a system-supplied value to be inserted into a table when no value is specified. They are Current_TimeStamp, Current_User, Session_User, System_User, and User.

System Functions

System functions return system-defined information from the database. The are the following: Coalesce, Col_Length, Col_Name, DataLength, DB_ID, DB_Name, GetAnsiNull, Host_Name, Ident_Incr, Ident_Seed, Index_Col, IsNull, NullIf, Host_ID, Object_Name, Stats_Date, Suser_ID, Suser_Name, User_ID, User_Name, and Object_ID.

Text and Image Functions

The *text and image functions* perform operations on text and image data. They are PatIndex, TextPtr, SetTextSize, and TextValid.

Type-Conversion Functions

The *type-conversion function*, Convert, converts data from one type to another.

The preceding functions are a subset of the entire listing of built-in functions and their definitions. To see a full listing, you should read the ODBC specifications for the server you use.

HTTP 1.1 Specification

by John Jung

IN THIS APPENDIX

APPENDIX B

Everybody knows about the World Wide Web and what it can do. Also, almost everybody knows that the Web uses Hypertext Transfer Protocol (HTTP) to accomplish some of its tasks. What most people don't know about HTTP is exactly what it is, and what it specifies. Most of the time, HTTP runs quietly in the background, interacting between the Web server and your Web browser. The only time HTTP actually "tells" you anything is when there's some sort of error. This appendix covers almost everything about HTTP, from its protocol specifications to its error codes.

Overview

HTTP is a *request/response protocol*. When a Web browser sends a request to a Web server, the request is made in the form of an HTTP header, with some extra information in a MIME file. The HTTP header is probably the most important aspect of HTTP because it determines how the HTTP body will be interpreted. The Web server responds with some data pertaining to the user's request. It, too, uses the HTTP header for some general information and a MIME body for extra data. But what are the components of the HTTP header, anyway? And what are the new features in HTTP 1.1?

The Request Header

As previously mentioned, HTTP is a request/response protocol, meaning that a client sends out a request to a system, and the system processes the request and sends the appropriate information back to the client. In the case of HTTP, the client is your Web browser, and the system that does the processing is the Web server. Obviously, being processed in between are the actual Web pages, fill-out forms, and other features of the Web. The request usually takes the form of an HTTP command, followed by the argument (sometimes known as the *resource*), and finally the HTTP version the Web browser supports. The request also can contain some extra header information to be further processed by the Web server.

The Response Header

The response header is by far more complicated than the request header because it's sending information to the person's Web browser that tells it what to do with the requested information. Whereas the client simply requested some information, or passed along some predetermined information, the response holds much more. It has to tell the client the success or failure of the request header, some server information, some date information, and the MIME type for the data being returned. After the response header is sent, the response data, such as the Web page requested, must follow. Most of the information in the response header is pretty straightforward; it's discussed in detail later in this appendix.

Differences Between HTTP 1.0 and HTTP 1.1

HTTP 1.0 was the original specification for the protocol. After it was in use for a while, however, some of its shortcomings became obvious. As a result, it was revised and enhanced to become HTTP 1.1. You, as a Webmaster, have little to worry about concerning the migration to HTTP 1.1, because most Web servers have already moved there.

One of the less noticeable but more important enhancements that HTTP 1.1 brought was a tighter definition of the protocol. It was possible for two different programmers to implement HTTP 1.0 in two different forms. Further, the differences between these implementations could be quite significant—so significant, in fact, that a Web browser written based on one implementation might not work properly on a Web server based on the other implementation.

Another improvement that HTTP 1.1 has over the original protocol is to provide support for persistent connections. HTTP 1.0 opened separate network connections for each Web page, image, or object; therefore, for a large Web page with lots of images, the Web browser made multiple requests. Each request required a new network connection, both from the browser and the server. With persistent connections, you can use one network connection to get all the data for a Web page. This means that you can pass all the data for a single Web page through one network connection. This helps open up Web servers so that you can handle more users.

HTTP 1.1 is more robust. HTTP 1.0 made a number of assumptions about the environment HTTP would be running in. The revised protocol provides support for a wider array of system and network configurations. Further, it puts into place protocol constructs, making it more reliable. It's not more reliable in the sense that the Web servers won't crash as often, but in the sense that the information sent back from the Web server is more meaningful.

The HTTP Request

When a Web browser requests some data, any type of data, from the Web server, it does so by issuing a request. The request is made by sending an HTTP command, some header information, and an optional request body. The HTTP command, a single line known as the *request line*, has two arguments. After the request line comes the request header, which can be any of three different templates. Any number of these templates can be used within the same request header. The header used, and the data that goes into those headers, is determined by the client. Finally there comes a carriage return, followed by the request body.

The Request Line

The first part of any HTTP request is the request line. This is a single line of text containing the HTTP command that is being issued, the argument that the command is applied to, and finally, the HTTP version. Here's the syntax for a typical request line:

```
[command] /[object] HTTP/[major].[minor]
```

where [command] is the HTTP command issued, [object] is what the [command] will affect, [major] is the major release of HTTP that the browser supports, and [minor] is the minor version of HTTP. The last part of the request line is probably the easiest of the three parts to understand. Here, the request line is simply asking which version of HTTP the client supports. So, if the Web browser supports only HTTP 1.0, it will use HTTP/1.0. Most modern Web browsers support HTTP 1.1, and so would send out HTTP/1.1 in their request lines.

Request-Line Commands

There are seven possible commands that a client can pass on the request line. Each command causes the corresponding command-line argument, or resource, to be interpreted in different ways. As a result, it's difficult to make any general statements about their behavior.

DELETE

The DELETE request-line command asks the server to delete the specified resource. There is no guarantee that the command will actually be executed. However, if the server intends to either delete the resource, or make it inaccessible, a successful response code should be sent back.

If information pertaining to the DELETE request is included in the response body, a 200 response code is sent. If the request has been accepted, but not yet acted upon, a 202 response code is sent. Finally, if the request was valid, but no information is stored in the response body, a 204 response code is issued. Responses to the DELETE command are not cached.

GET

Probably the most commonly used request-line command, the GET command, asks the server to send the requested argument. This command can be turned into a conditional GET if any of the following fields are specified: If-Modified-Since, If-Unmodified-Since, If-Match, If-None-Match, or If-Range. The header fields that are used will be the ones that constrain the conditional GET. Also, the GET command can turn into a partial GET if the Range header field is specified. You'll learn more about the various header fields later in this appendix. Responses from GET commands can be cached.

HEAD

The HEAD command is similar to the GET command with one big difference: It doesn't return the response body containing the requested resource. The only information returned to the HEAD command is the response header—the same response header you would expect from the GET command. Everything, including the date of the requested argument, the size of the argument, and even the MIME type, must be identical to that information returned from the GET. This information is useful for getting information that is not data critical about the requested argument.

OPTIONS

The OPTIONS command queries the Web server for information about how to communicate with the requested argument. OPTIONS makes it possible to determine some characteristics about the desired argument without actually retrieving it. If the resource specified for this command is an asterisk (*), information about the server itself is returned. Any nonerror responses from the server will contain communications-related information about the requested argument. Responses to this request cannot be cached.

POST

The POST command is used to ask the Web server to accept the request body and process it using the specified argument. Thus, the POST command can be used as a method of annotation for existing data, posting a message, returning a block of data such as data from form fields, and extending a database by appending data. What is actually done to the data, and how it relates to the argument, is left entirely up to the Web server.

In turn, if the Web server successfully accepts the POST data but can't allow access to that information, it returns either a 200 or 204 response code. However, if the user can access his posted data, the response from the Web server is a 201 response code. Finally, if the data being posted has been redirected by the Web server, a 303 response code is sent.

PUT

The PUT command makes it possible for the client to create data on the Web server itself. The argument specified indicates the data that the client is requesting to be created. The request body itself contains the data that should be stored in the specified resource. If the requested resource already exists, the new data being created using the PUT command should be considered a new version of that resource. If the specified argument doesn't exist, and the client has appropriate privileges, the new resource can be created.

If an existing resource is modified, either the 200 or 204 response codes can be issued. If a new resource is created, the 201 response code will be sent. If the server wants the specified resource to be created somewhere else, it should return a 301 response code. If the specified argument could not be created or modified, an appropriate error response code should be sent. Further, any header field names beginning with Content cannot be ignored. If the server doesn't understand, or can't process, such header fields, a 501 response code must be returned. PUT responses cannot be cached.

TRACE

A type of diagnostic command, the TRACE command enables the client to see what the server is receiving from the client. The behavior of this command is controlled solely by its request headers, so no request body is needed. If successful, the response code to the TRACE command is a 200. Also, for successful requests, the response body must contain the entire request message, both the header and body. The Content-Type for the reply must be set to message/http, and cannot be cached.

Of particular importance to this command are the Max-Forwards and Via header fields. The Max-Forwards value enables you to check on the behavior of a particular proxy if you're behind a firewall. A Max-Forwards value of 0 will be processed only by the first proxy or gateway. The Via header field is used only by gateways and proxies, and specifies the hosts between the client and the server. Requests and responses to this command cannot be cached.

Request-Line Resources

After the request-line command comes a space and then the argument. The argument, some-times known as a *resource*, is technically known as the Uniform Resource Identifier (URI). In very general terms, the URI can be any string of characters that identify a resource by name, location, or any other characteristic. However, to make the situation easier to understand, you can think of a URI as basically being either a URL (Uniform Resource Locator) or an absolute file path on the remote system (URN). This is not the definitive explanation for a URI, but it's sufficient for the time being.

This isn't a perfect definition because the URI enables you to refer to any resource, on any computer, on any network. This means that you're not restricted to simply accessing files and directories. HTTP makes it possible for you to refer to database objects, messages in a discussion forum, or even hardware devices. There's no guarantee that URIs have to look like URLs; it's just that URLs are the most commonly used uniform resources.

General Header

One of the possible header templates available after the request line is the general header. This header template is applicable to both request and response messages. That means that these header fields apply only to the message being transferred, not the data it contains. Any unrecognized general header field is treated as an entity header. (See "Entity Header," later in this appendix.)

Cache-Control

The `Cache-Control` header field is one of the additions to HTTP 1.1. It enables both the client and the server to control how caches are used. All servers handling the HTTP header must follow the directives within this field. Unlike other general header fields, this field has both a request format and a response format. All commands in the `Cache-Control` field are intended to be followed only for the current message, so replies to the current message need not follow the same cache mechanism. The syntax for this field is as follows:

```
Cache-Control: request-directive | response-directive
```

That is, the `Cache-Control` field can only be a *request-directive* or a *response-directive*. It cannot, however, be both. Because there are two separate sets of acceptable commands, most of the directives apply either to the request or the response.

Common Directives

There are actually a handful of directives that can be used by both request and response messages. Table B.1 outlines the commands, the corresponding syntax, and what they do.

Table B.1. Common commands for the Cache-Control general header.

Command	Syntax	Purpose
cache-extension	*command* [="*string*" ¦ *value*]	This is a general catch-all for allowing extensions to the currently implemented caching scheme. *command* specifies whatever new cache extension is defined. You can optionally specify either a *string* or a numeric *value* as a value.
max-age	max-age=*seconds*	The *seconds* value specifies the maximum number of seconds between connections before the cached data is considered obsolete.
no-cache	no-cache [="*field-name*"]	Specifies that the message should not be cached at all. If *field-name* is specified in quotes, only that field will not be cached.
no-store	no-store	This command forces all caches between the client and server to not store the entire message or responses to it. This can be considered a much more aggressive form of no-cache. All caches between the client and server must not store the information, and must erase it from memory as soon as possible.

Request Directives for Cache-Control

Aside from the common Cache-Control directives specified earlier, request messages have their own set of directives. There are a total of three other commands that you can use in the Cache-Control header field. Table B.2 details the other possible headers for request messages.

Table B.2. Commands for the `Cache-Control` general header for request messages.

Command and Syntax	Purpose
`max-stale [ = seconds ]`	This command specifies that the client will accept responses that exceed its expiration time. If it's set equal to *seconds*, it will only accept responses that many seconds after expiration.
`min-fresh [ = seconds ]`	Tells the server that the client will accept a response that will still be fresh for at least that number of seconds.
`only-if-cached`	This command tells all servers to use cached responses, so long as they follow other constraints of the request.

Response Directives for `Cache-Control`

In contrast to the request directives for the `Cache-Control` headers, there are five possible commands for response headers. There are five possible values for the `Cache-Control` field of the general header for response messages. Table B.3 covers what they are, their parameters (if any), and what they do.

Table B.3. Commands for the `Cache-Control` general header for response messages.

Command and Syntax	Purpose
`must-revalidate`	When this command is used, it forces the cache to verify responses with the server. This is intended to be used to positively ensure the correct response for the specified request. This allows for reliable operation, through caches, only when necessary.
`no-transform`	Some proxies have been known to convert some message headers and message bodies into different formats. Typically, this is done to save space or reduce the amount of network traffic for a proxy. This command prevents anything in the message from being converted.
`private [ ="field-name" ]`	The `private` command enables the server to specify that the response is intended for a single user, and so the response shouldn't be cached. If it's made equal to *field-name*, only that field name will be private.
`proxy-revalidate`	Similar to the `must-revalidate` command, this command doesn't apply to the client's cache.
`public`	This command indicates that all aspects of the reply are `public` and can be cached by anybody.

Connection

The `Connection` field for the general header is only intended to be used by proxies. It has a single value of any text string that tells the proxy what to do. Additionally, the `Connection` field value is not to be forwarded by the proxy to any other system. The syntax of this header field is

```
Connection: string
```

where `string` is the command to be executed by the proxy. Currently, the only accepted `Connection` string is `close`, which is used to indicate nonpersistent connections.

Date

The `Date` general header field is used to specify the date. It's supposed to contain the date the message, request or response, was originated. However, the date can be specified any time during the message's creation process. Three date formats are allowed by the protocol: Mon, 10 Aug 1997 14:00:00 GMT; Monday, 10-Aug-97 14:00:00 GMT; and Mon Aug 10 14:00:00 1997. The format of the `Date` header field is

```
Date: date
```

where `date` is the date in one of the three acceptable formats.

Pragma

The `Pragma` field for the general header is used to specify options to be processed by any proxy, or gateway, handling the message. This field must always be passed along, even if the proxy or gateway doesn't need or use it. If a proxy or gateway doesn't understand the specified options, it should ignore them. The `Pragma` field has the following syntax:

```
Pragma: string[=value]
```

where `string` is the option being issued. Optionally, a `value` can be assigned to the specified `string`. Currently, the `Pragma` field is only defined to provide support for the `no-cache` string. When present, the `no-cache` string causes the entire `Pragma` header line to act as `Cache-Control: no-cache`. (Refer to "Cache-Control," earlier in this appendix.)

Transfer-Encoding

Normally, most data is sent between client and server as MIME types, which is the safest method of transport across the Internet. However, for those with 8-bit clean connections between client and server, there's a new method available. This method, which sends data in chunks, was first introduced in HTTP 1.1. The `Transfer-Encoding` header field is used to specify when the non-MIME method of sending data is being used. The `Transfer-Encoding` line takes this form:

```
Transfer-Encoding: string
```

where `string` is any defined transportation method other than MIME. Currently, the only transportation method available is the chunked method. When this method is used, the message body is no longer a MIME body, but is rather a chunked body. The chunked body is basically a set of 8-bit data separated by a single 0 and entity headers. The chunked body would be sent as follows:

```
Chunk data
0
Entity Header
```

where `Chunk data` is the actual information sent across, and `0` marks the end of the data. Next comes a complete entity header (see "Entity Header," later in this chapter), ending with a carriage return and line feed.

Upgrade

Another general header field is `Upgrade`. This field lets the client specify additional protocols that it supports and would like to use if the server supports them as well. Multiple protocols are presented as a comma-separated list. The syntax for the `Upgrade` field is

```
Upgrade: protocol/major-version.minor-version [, ...]
```

where `protocol` is the additional protocol the client supports, and `[, ...]` represents extra protocols. `major-version` and `minor-version` are the numerical version numbers for the protocol supported. When switching between protocols, the Web server must send out a `101` response code. Further, this field is only applicable for the immediate connection, so it isn't applicable to other connections.

Via

The `Via` general header field is only used by gateways and proxies. It enables them to identify themselves by the protocol they support, the version of that protocol, hostname, and an optional comment. If the protocol being used is HTTP, then the protocol name is not needed. It's used to track the intermediate servers and protocols between the server and the client. The `Via` line takes the form of

```
Via: received-protocol/protocol-version received-by [comment]
```

where `received-protocol` is the name of the protocol used to receive the request, and `protocol-version` represents the version used. The `received-by` value is specified in the form of the hostname of the server, and, optionally, the port number used by that machine. For security reasons, gateways and proxies can specify a pseudonym instead of their actual hostnames. Finally, the `[comment]` value is strictly optional and can be used to specify additional server information.

Request Header

Along with the general header, clients can also use request header templates. These have different field names and values, and obviously affect how the server will respond. Because all three header templates can be used together, there's no restriction as to which one comes first.

Accept

The `Accept` header field enables the client to specify the data types that it prefers to receive. Further, it can be used to specify the order of media types that are received. Thus, it's possible to specify primary, secondary, tertiary, and lesser preferred data types. If the specified data types are not available, the server will return a `406` response code. If this field is missing, the server assumes that all data types are acceptable. The syntax for the `Accept` header is as follows:

```
Accept: major-type/minor-type [ ; parameter ¦ ; q=value [ extension ] ... ]
```

where `major-type` and `minor-type` represent the MIME major and minor data type values. Optionally, the data types themselves can also specify a `parameter` when it's preceded with a semicolon. Further, to specify the degree of preference for a particular data type, its `value`, from 0.0 to 1.0, must be specified by the q= string. The higher the q value, the more preferred the specified parameter is. The ellipsis represents that multiple data types and preferences for them can also be specified. Data types and their preferences are separated by commas.

Accept-Charset

The `Accept-Charset` header field enables the client to indicate in which character set it prefers data to be returned. In HTTP terms, the character set is defined to be a set of symbols that represents a particular language. Acceptable character sets are defined by the IANA/ISO standards. Additionally, preferred character sets can be specified on the same line, using the same characteristic as the `Accept` field. The syntax of the `Accept-Charset` field is

```
Accept-Charset: character-set [ ; q=value ... ]
```

where `character-set` is the named IANA/ISO character set name. The value of q indicates the level of preference for that particular character set. If the server is unable to support the preferred character sets, it must return a `406` response code. Character sets and their degree of preference are separated by commas.

Accept-Encoding

This header field for requests informs the server that the client prefers the response body to be in the specified encoding. The syntax for the `Accept-Encoding` field is

```
Accept-Encoding: encoding-name
```

where `encoding-name` is the name of the preferred encoding method. This is different from the `Accept` field because it applies to the data as it's transmitted, so that it's possible to have a preferred data type but have it encoded in a different format. Typically, this field is used to indicate a preferred compression scheme to be used in the response message body.

Accept-Language

Clients can use the `Accept-Language` field to indicate to servers the preferred natural language for all data to be sent in. Further, a list of preferred languages, and their level of preference, can be specified by this header field. The preferred natural language specified must be identified by a unique string of one to eight characters. The syntax for the `Accept-Language` field is as follows:

```
Accept-Language: language-name [ ; q=value ... ]
```

where `language-name` is the unique name of the preferred language. As with the `Accept` and `Accept-Charset` values, the q indicates the level of preference for that language. Multiple languages can be separated by commas.

Authorization

`Authorization` is used to indicate that the client wants to authorize itself with the server. This field name is commonly implemented for password-protected Web pages. The syntax for this header field takes the form of

```
Authorization: credentials
```

where `credentials` is any mutually agreed upon method of authorization between the client and server. Typically, the method is to specify the domain for authorization, username for that domain, and the corresponding password.

From

This is perhaps one of the easiest header fields to understand. The `From` field is intended to store the e-mail address of the person in charge of the client. Most of the time, this is the end user; however, for some large organizations, this isn't necessarily the case. The `From` field may be used for logging purposes by the server, but there's no requirement that it be done. The field takes the following appearance:

```
From: e-mail-address
```

where `e-mail-address` is any Internet e-mail address string.

Host

The `Host` field indicates the Internet hostname for the argument on the request line. It can optionally specify the port number to access that argument on that particular host. All HTTP 1.1 messages must include this field, and any messages without this field will receive a `400` response code. This field has the following syntax:

```
Host: hostname [ :port ]
```

where `hostname` is the complete Internet hostname where the requested resource is stored. By default, the server will try to use port 80 for the resource, unless a different port number is specified. Use the colon (:) to specify port numbers.

If-Modified-Since

The `If-Modified-Since` header field enables `GET` commands to become conditional `GET`s. It is given one value, the date and time that the client wants to act as the cut-off point. That is, any resources retrieved after the specified time should be transmitted. This field has the following format:

```
If-Modified-Since: date
```

where *date* is one of the three acceptable date formats.

If-Match

The If-Match field can also turn a GET command into a conditional GET. It specifies one or more entity tags that it wants the server to compare. If there is a match, the requested command and argument from the request line are acted upon by the server. If the response to the request would result in a nonsuccess code, this field must be ignored. The If-Match field has the following syntax:

```
If-Match: * ¦ entity-tag [...]
```

where *entity-tag* is a defined Etag for the requested argument. (See "Etag," later in this appendix.) The * value is used to match all entity tags for the specified resource. Multiple entity tags can be specified by separating them with commas. If none of the entity tags match, or the * was specified and no entities were found, a 412 response code is issued.

If-None-Match

The If-None-Match field is the inverse of the If-Match field. It asks the server to compare the specified Etag, and if they don't match, the server will process the request message. Otherwise, if any of the entity tags did match, the request is rejected. The syntax for this field is as follows:

```
If-None-Match: * ¦ entity-tag [...]
```

If-Range

Another approach to converting the GET command into a conditional GET uses this header field. The If-Range field specifies either an entity tag or the date for the requested argument. The server compares the If-Range value with the resource being requested. If the comparison matches, the server will inform the client of the attributes of the resource. This enables the client to intelligently maintain a fresh copy of its cache contents. All it has to do is use the If-Range field to determine which resources have changed. The format for this field is

```
If-Range: date ¦ entity-tag
```

where *date* is one of the three accepted date formats, and *entity-tag* is a previously defined Etag.

If-Unmodified-Since

When the If-Unmodified-Since field is specified, the client is asking the server to perform a possible conditional GET. That is, it's asking the server to check the modification time for the requested resource. If it has been modified since that time, a 412 response code is sent back. Otherwise, the request header and body should be processed. The field has the following appearance:

```
If-Unmodified-Since: date
```

date specifies the last modification time, and is in one of the three accepted time formats.

Max-Forwards

The Max-Forwards field is used in conjunction with the TRACE request-line command. (See "TRACE," earlier in this appendix.) It limits the number of gateways, or proxies, the HTTP message can be sent through. As each proxy or gateway gets the message, the value is decremented. If the received value is 0, the message should not be forwarded. The Max-Forwards field looks like the following:

```
Max-Forwards: value
```

where *value* is any whole integer number.

Proxy-Authorization

The Proxy-Authorization field is similar to the Authorization field. The only difference is that this field is only applicable to proxies. Further, because of its limited scope, it is interpreted and removed by the first outbound proxy; that is, the first proxy with an immediate connection to the Internet will interpret and remove this header field. This provides a form of security for proxies behind a firewall. This field appears as follows:

```
Proxy-Authorization: credentials
```

where *credentials* is a previously agreed upon method of identifying the client.

Range

The Range field name is only meaningful when the request-line command being issued is GET. This field enables the GET, or even a conditional GET, to retrieve only a range of data. All values within the Range field refer to the number of bytes in the specified file. The Range field has the following syntax:

```
Range: value-range ¦ offset
```

where Range can be set equal to either *value-range* or *offset*. Multiple values for Range can be set if they are separated by commas. If *value-range* is specified, the value is represented as *x-y*, where *x* is the number of bytes from the beginning of the file, and *y* is the ending byte position. If *offset* is specified, the value would be *-number*, where *-number* indicates the number of bytes from the end of the file. Both acceptable values for Range enable the client to use GET to obtain a definite portion of any file it wants.

Referer

The Referer field is used by clients that want to help out the server. It stores the URI that the client used to attempt to access the requested resource. There are a number of uses for the Referer field, among them logging and link maintenance. Typically, Web servers use the Referer field to indicate invalid links. The format of the Referer field is as follows:

```
Referer: absolute-URI ¦ relative-URI
```

This field can be set to either *absolute-URI* or *relative-URI*. No URI fragments are allowed in this field. The syntax of the URI is dependent on the protocol being used. For the most part, URLs are used in the Referer field.

User-Agent

The User-Agent field is used by the client to identify itself to the server. This enables the server to do statistical analysis of which clients visit the most. Additionally, the server can quietly tailor the requested resource to suit the limitations of the browser. The format of this field is

```
User-Agent: product ¦ comment [...]
```

where *product* or *comment* is some unique string that identifies the client. The ellipsis indicates that more than one *product* and *comment* can be specified. If this is done, each entry must be separated by a comma.

Entity Header

The entity header is another template of header fields available to both request and response messages. This header identifies certain pieces of information about the entity body. If no entity body is present, the entity header will store information about the resource.

Allow

The Allow field identifies which request-line commands are available to a particular resource. Generally, this field enables servers to identify to clients which operations are valid. If a 405 response code is issued, the Allow header must be utilized to identify which commands can be used. The syntax of the Allow header is as follows:

```
Allow: command [...]
```

where *command* is a valid request-line command, and the ellipsis indicates multiple values. Multiple values must be separated by commas. Proxies handling this header field must not modify this header field value in any way, even if the proxy doesn't recognize it.

Content-Base

Another header field used by servers is the Content-Base field. This field is used to indicate the base URI that will be used for resolving relative URIs. It has the form of

```
Content-Base: absolute-URI
```

where *absolute-URI* is a string that identifies the top-level portion for URIs. If Content-Base is not defined, the server will try to figure it out. It will look at the Content-Location field and try to determine the base. Failing that, it will use the URI that was sent to initiate the request.

Content-Encoding

The Content-Encoding is similar to Accept-Encoding, except that it isn't a request. It simply states which encoding method was used to store and transmit the message body. This field is typically used to indicate a compression scheme that was applied to the body, to allow for faster transportation. The format of this field is

```
Content-Encoding: encoding-name
```

where *encoding-name* is a string that identifies the encoding method used.

Content-Language

This field, also used by servers, is similar to the Accept-Language request header field, except that it isn't a request. Content-Language tells the client in what language the message body is being transmitted. As with the Accept-Language header, the language is identified by a string that is one to eight characters in length. This header has the following syntax:

```
Accept-Language: language-name [ ... ]
```

The *language-name* indicates the language for the body. Multiple languages can be specified if they are separated by commas.

Content-Length

The Content-Length field is used to indicate the size, in bytes, of the message body. The acceptable value is any integer number greater than, or equal to, zero. The Content-Length field has the following appearance:

```
Content-Length: value
```

The *value* should be used by the application, regardless of its data type. This enables the application to reliably know when the message body has finished transmitting.

Content-Location

This field is used to indicate the URI location of the included resource. Content-Location is not a replacement for the original requested URI, but is intended for informational purposes. The Content-Location field has the form of

```
Content-Location: absolute-URI ¦ relative-URI
```

where the field can either be an *absolute-URI* or a *relative-URI* path.

Content-MD5

The Content-MD5 header field is intended to provide a means of ensuring correct data transmission of the message body. It complies with the established MD5 digest protocol and is only generated by the originating server. Proxies and gateways should not modify, or generate, the Content-MD5 header. This field has the following syntax:

Content-MD5: *base64-string*

The *base64-string* is a string of characters, using base64 encoding, of the 128-bit MD5 digest format. This allows for the detection of accidental alteration of the message body. It cannot, reliably, be used to detect any malicious attacks.

Content-Range

This entity header is sent with a partial entity body, typically in response to partial GETs, from the client. The Content-Range field indicates where the partial body should be inserted, in relation to the entire file. It has the following appearance:

Content-Range: *x-y/z*

x is the starting position in the resource for the start of the message body, and *y* represents the ending position. *z* specifies the total size of the requested argument, in terms of bytes.

Content-Type

The Content-Type entity header is used to specify the media data type that the message body is being sent in. This means that the major and minor MIME types are used in this header. This header field has the following format:

Content-Type: *major-type/minor-type [; charset=language]*

The *major-type* and *minor-type* values are those that are pulled from the MIME specifications. Optionally, this line can also be used to indicate the *language* character set, in which the body was stored.

Etag

Etag is short for "entity tag," which is used as a form of content checking. Basically, Etags assign a particular value to a specific resource. When the contents of the resource has changed, the Etags should be changed as well. Hence, it's possible to use Etags to check for modification. Etag has the following syntax:

Etag: *[w/] string*

string can be any string of characters used to uniquely identify the resource. A *w/* before the string means the Etag is a weak entity tag. A weak entity tag may be shared among two resources if they can be substituted with each other. Weak entity tags can only be compared against other weak entity tags.

Expires

For caches, the `Expires` field is useful in determining when responses should be ignored. In particular, the `Expires` field gives the time and date after which responses should be considered obsolete. It's then up to the cache to update itself to deal with the stale response. `Expires` has the following format:

```
Expires: date
```

where *date* is any of the three acceptable date formats. Servers should not send out an `Expires` date that is more than one year in advance. Such dates should be treated, by caches, as if they have no expiration dates.

Last-Modified

The `Last-Modified` field is used by servers to specify when they think the requested argument was last modified. The exact meaning of this field varies depending on the server implementation and the resource being accessed. For files, this could represent the last file modification time. For databases, it could indicate the last time the record was saved. The `Last-Modified` field has the following syntax:

```
Last-Modified: date
```

where *date* is any of the three acceptable date formats.

The HTTP Response

After the client sends a request, it's processed by the server. The processed result is sent back, from the server to the client, via the HTTP response. Like the HTTP request, the HTTP response follows a rigidly defined set of standards. The first line of the HTTP response is the status line, which is similar to the request line. Next come some message headers that describe the message body, then a carriage return, and finally, the message body itself.

The Status Line

Like the request line, the *status line* is a single line of text made up of three components. The first is the protocol identification string followed by a space, then the response code, another space, and finally a short descriptive text. The typical status line looks like this:

```
protocol/major-version.minor-version response-code response-string
```

protocol is typically HTTP, while the *major-version* and *minor-version* specify the *protocol* that the server supports. Generally, this will either be 1.0 or 1.1. The *response-code* is a number that is one of the predefined HTTP response codes. After that is the *response-string*, which is a short description of the response code. The *response-string* can actually be tailored to suit a particular site's need, but most use the default. Response codes are unique three-digit numbers that specify the status of the request. Although clients don't have to know what all the codes mean, they should at least understand the class they come from. Table B.4 lists all the standard HTTP 1.1 response codes, the classes they belong to, their default response strings, and a brief explanation of their meanings.

Table B.4. HTTP response codes.

Response Code	Class	Response String	Meaning
100	Informational	Continue	This is to inform the client that the initial request has not been rejected, and to continue with its request. If the request has been sent, the response should be ignored.
101	Informational	Switching Protocols	The server understands the requested upgrade protocol and its parameters, and can support it. It will switch to the preferred protocol when it's advantageous.
200	Successful	OK	The request was successfully completed.
201	Successful	Created	The request was completed successfully and a new resource was created. The URL for the new resource will be returned in the entity body.
202	Successful	Accepted	The request was accepted, but has not been acted upon yet. It may, or may not, be completed at some later date.
203	Successful	Non-Authoritative Information	The server cannot verify the information returned in the entity header. The information was retrieved from a local or third-party copy.
204	Successful	No Content	The request was fulfilled, but there is no new data to be returned.

continues

Table B.4. continued

Response Code	Class	Response String	Meaning
205	Successful	Reset Content	The request was successfully completed, and the client should refresh its display.
206	Successful	Partial Content	The server has successfully completed a partial GET.
300	Redirection	Multiple Choices	The requested resource resolved into multiple possible choices, each with its own location. It's up to either the client or the user to decide which one to use.
301	Redirection	Moved Permanently	The requested resource has been assigned a new, permanent URI. If possible, the client should automatically relink references to the new URI.
302	Redirection	Moved Temporarily	The requested resource can be temporarily found under a different URI.
303	Redirection	See Other	The response to the request can be found under a different URI, and should be retrieved with a new GET command.
304	Redirection	Not Modified	This informs the client that the conditional GET requested will not be fulfilled because the requested resource has not been modified.
305	Redirection	Use Proxy	The requested resource can only be accessed by a proxy. The location of the proxy will be stored in the Location header field.
400	Client Error	Bad Request	The request could not be understood by the server, due to incorrect syntax.

Response Code	Class	Response String	Meaning
401	Client Error	Unauthorized	The requested resource is password-protected and requires user authentication.
402	Client Error	Payment Required	This code is reserved for future use.
403	Client Error	Forbidden	The request was understood by the server, but the server will not act upon it. User authentication will not resolve the issue.
404	Client Error	Not Found	The server couldn't find the requested URI.
405	Client Error	Method Not Allowed	The request-line command was not compatible with the requested resource.
406	Client Error	Not Acceptable	The requested resource can only create a response, which characteristics are incompatible with the specified request headers.
407	Client Error	Proxy Authentication Required	The client must authenticate itself with the proxy before the request can be processed.
408	Client Error	Request Time-out	The client did not send a request within the time specified by the server.
409	Client Error	Conflict	The request could not be fulfilled because of a conflict with the current state of the resource.
410	Client Error	Gone	The requested resource is no longer available, and its new URI is unknown.
411	Client Error	Length Required	The request was rejected because the header didn't have a Content-Length field.

B

HTTP 1.1
SPECIFICATION

continues

Table B.4. continued

Response Code	Class	Response String	Meaning
412	Client Error	Precondition Failed	One or more of the preconditions in the request header did not evaluate successfully.
413	Client Error	Request Entity Too Large	The request was rejected because the server is unwilling, or unable, to process the request entity.
414	Client Error	Request-URI Too Large	The server is refusing to process the request because the Request-URI is larger than it's willing to interpret.
415	Client Error	Unsupported Media Type	The requested media type is not supported by the server. As a result, the request is being rejected.
500	Server Error	Internal Server Error	The server encountered an unexpected error, which prevented it from completing the request.
501	Server Error	Not Implemented	The server does not support the functionality needed to process the request.
502	Server Error	Bad Gateway	While acting as a gateway or proxy, the server encountered an invalid response when talking with the other server.
503	Server Error	Service Unavailable	The server cannot fulfill the request due to an overloading of the server, or because of server maintenance.
504	Server Error	Gateway Time-out	While acting as a gateway or proxy, the server didn't receive a reply to its request in a timely fashion.
505	Server Error	HTTP Version Not Supported	The server cannot, or will not, support the requested version of HTTP.

Response Header

After the status line of the response is sent, any number of the three different types of headers can be sent. The three headers available to all responses are the general header, the entity header, and the response header. The first two header templates have been discussed earlier in this appendix. The response header enables the server to pass additional information about the response that can't be placed on the status line. Typically, this information covers aspects of the response message body itself. There are nine possible header fields for the response header, and only those that the server needs will be used.

Age

Typically used by HTTP caches, the Age response header tells the client approximately how old the message from the server is. Cached responses are considered fresh if they don't exceed their freshness lifetime. The freshness lifetime, as well as the age, must follow a specified set of time calculations. The Age field has the following syntax:

```
Age: seconds
```

where *seconds* is, roughly, the number of seconds since the cache received a response, and when the response was actually generated. *seconds* can be any nonnegative, integer number between 0 and 2,147,483,648 (2^{31}). All HTTP 1.1 caches must return an Age header field.

Location

Sometimes, after the request message has been processed, the client needs to be told about the resource's location. For example, for 201 response messages, the Location field would specify the URI for the newly created resource. For the Redirection class of response codes, this field could be used to specify the new URI. When the field is used in this manner, the client can automatically use GET to retrieve the new URI. The Location field has the following format:

```
Location: absolute-URI
```

where *absolute-URI* refers to the new location for either the moved or created resource.

Proxy-Authenticate

For all responses that issue a 407 code, the Proxy-Authenticate header field must be used. This field issues a "challenge" to the client, which basically specifies its authentication scheme and the parameters to be used. It is up to the client to properly interpret this field and support it to fully utilize the proxy. This field is different from WWW-Authenticate because it only applies to the current connection. The format for the Proxy-Authenticate field is as follows:

```
Proxy-Authenticate: challenge
```

where *challenge* is the authentication scheme and necessary parameters to authenticate the user to the proxy.

Public

The `Public` header field is used by the server to indicate to the client which request-line commands are applicable. The applicable commands aren't what's valid for the requested resource; instead, they are information about the capabilities of the server. For acceptable commands for the requested resource, the `Accept` header field may be used instead. This field has the following syntax:

```
Public: command
```

where *command* is a valid request-line command. Multiple commands can also be specified, but they must be separated by commas. A proxy must remove the `Public` header field or replace it with one that specifies the proxy's capabilities.

Retry-After

The `Retry-After` header field is used to indicate, to the client, when the server will be able to accept connections again. This header field, generally used in conjunction with the `503` response code, has the following appearance:

```
Retry-After: date ¦ seconds
```

where the field can have either a *date* or *seconds* value. For the *date* value, it indicates a specific time and date when the server will be available again. The *date* must be in one of the three date formats that HTTP recognizes. If specified, *seconds* indicates the number of seconds until the server can receive connections again.

Server

Probably one of the easier header fields to understand, the `Server` field is similar to the `User-Agent` field in a request header. This field identifies itself to the client, enabling the client to recognize its capabilities. Further, it can also list other servers with which the current server is compatible. The `Server` field has the following format:

```
Server: product ¦ comment
```

where either the *product* name, or a *comment* about the server itself, is a string of text. It's up to the programmer of the Web server to specify the string returned in this field. Proxies should ignore this header field so that the client can accurately recognize the type of server it's talking to. Though possible, specifying the version number of the server software is not recommended. Doing so will enable others to exploit possible bugs with that version of the server.

Vary

The `Vary` header field is used to indicate to the client where the returned resource may vary from the actual resource. Typically, this is done by HTTP servers utilizing a cache to indicate, approximately, where possible discrepancies may arise. The syntax of the `Vary` header field is as follows:

```
Vary: * ¦ request-header-field-name
```

Typically, the values for the Vary header field are the field names that the client sent in its request header. Such names are represented by *request-header-field-name*, and may also be a comma-separated list of such names. A value of * indicates that all specified fields may be different from the actual resource.

Warning

Although the response code is a good mechanism for identifying the message body, it's not perfect. As a result, the Warning header field is intended to help give more concise information about the entire response. Clients should display as many warning codes and messages as possible, and within the order received. The Warning header field has the following appearance:

Warning: *warning-code warning-agent warning-text*

The *warning-code* is a two-digit number that specifies the HTTP standard set of warning codes. (See Table B.5.) The *warning-agent* is the hostname, or pseudonym, for the server that issued the warning code. Optionally, it can include the port number from which the server was accessed. Finally comes the *warning-text*, which is simply a text string that elaborates on the meaning of the warning code. Multiple warnings can be issued, but each must have its own Warning header.

Table B.5. Standard warning codes and their meanings.

Code	Meaning	When Used
10	Response Is Stale	This code is used to indicate that the data returned, typically from a cache, is not fresh. This means that the cache may be returning a potentially old, outdated response. A cache can't remove this warning code until it knows the response is fresh.
11	Revalidation Failed	Similar to the 10 warning code, except that this code is applicable to revalidation. Again, typically, this warning code would come from a cache.
12	Disconnected Operation	Whenever a cache intends to remove itself, either temporarily or permanently, it should issue this warning code.
13	Heuristic Expiration	This warning code is issued when a cache will consider a cached response valid, even if the response was more than 24 hours old.

continues

Table B.5. continued

Code	Meaning	When Used
14	Transformation Applied	Typically used by a cache or proxy when the message body has been converted. As allowed by HTTP, caches and proxies can better utilize network traffic by converting the message body to something more suited to their tastes. When this happens, the response returned must also include this warning code.
99	Miscellaneous Warning	A general catch-all warning code. Typically, the warning text is more descriptive.

WWW-Authenticate

All responses using the 401 response code must include the WWW-Authenticate header field. It specifies, to the client, the authentication scheme and parameters needed, that it's using. This field has the following syntax:

WWW-Authenticate: *challenge*

where *challenge* is a specification for the authentication scheme used and the parameters it accepts. Multiple challenges may be issued, but all must be separated by commas.

HTML 3.2 Reference

by Dick Oliver

IN THIS APPENDIX

APPENDIX **C**

This appendix is a reference to the HTML tags you can use in your documents. Unless otherwise noted, all the tags listed here are supported by both Microsoft Explorer 3.0 and Netscape Navigator 3.0. Note that some other browsers do not support all the tags listed.

The proposed HTML style sheet specification is also not covered here. Refer to the Netscape (http://home.netscape.com/) or Microsoft (http://www.microsoft.com/) Web sites for details on this and other late-breaking changes to the HTML standard.

HTML Tags

These tags are used to create a basic HTML page with text, headings, and lists. An (MS) beside the attribute indicates that it is supported only by Microsoft Internet Explorer.

Comments

`<!-- ... -->`	Creates a comment. Can also be used to hide JavaScript from browsers that do not support it.
`<COMMENT>...</COMMENT>`	The new official way of specifying comments.

Structure Tags

Tag	Attribute	Function
`<HTML>...</HTML>`		Encloses the entire HTML document.
`<HEAD>...</HEAD>`		Encloses the head of the HTML document.
`<BODY>...</BODY>`		Encloses the body (text and tags) of the HTML document.
	`BACKGROUND="..."`	The name or URL of the image to tile on the page background.
	`BGCOLOR="..."`	The color of the page's background.
	`TEXT="..."`	The color of the page's text.
	`LINK="..."`	The color of unfollowed links.
	`ALINK="..."`	The color of activated links.
	`VLINK="..."`	The color of followed links.
	`BGPROPERTIES="..."`(MS)	Properties of the background image. Currently allows only the value FIXED, which prevents the background image from scrolling.

Tag	*Attribute*	*Function*
	`TOPMARGIN="..."`(MS)	Top margin of the page, in pixels.
	`BOTTOMMARGIN="..."`(MS)	Bottom margin of the page, in pixels.
`<BASE>`		Indicates the full URL of the current document. This optional tag is used within `<HEAD>`.
	`HREF="..."`	The full URL of this document.
`<ISINDEX>`		Indicates that this document is a gateway script that allows searches.
	`PROMPT="..."`	The prompt for the search field.
	`ACTION="..."`	Gateway program to which the search string should be passed.
`<LINK>`		Indicates a link between this document and another document. Generally used only by HTML-generating tools. `<LINK>` represents a link from this entire document to another one, as opposed to `<A>`, which can create multiple links in the document. Not commonly used.
	`HREF="..."`	The URL of the document to call when the link is activated.
	`NAME="..."`	If the document is to be considered an anchor, the name of that anchor.
	`REL="..."`	The relationship between the linked-to document and the current document; for example, `"TOC"` or `"Glossary"`.
	`REV="..."`	A reverse relationship between the current document and the linked-to document.
	`URN="..."`	A uniform resource number (URN), a unique identifier different from the URL in `HREF`.

continues

C

HTML 3.2
REFERENCE

Tag	Attribute	Function
	TITLE="..."	The title of the linked-to document.
	METHODS="..."	The method with which the document is to be retrieved; for example, FTP or Gopher.
<META>		Indicates meta-information about this document (information about the document itself); for example, keywords for search engines, special HTTP headers to be used for retrieving this document, expiration dates, and so on. Meta-information is usually in the form of a key/value pair. Used in the document <HEAD>.
	HTTP-EQUIV="..."	Creates a new HTTP header field with the same name as the attribute's value; for example, HTTP-EQUIV="Expires". The value of that header is specified by the CONTENT attribute.
	NAME="..."	If meta-data is usually in the form of key/value pairs, NAME indicates the key; for example, Author or ID.
	CONTENT="..."	The content of the key/value pair (or of the HTTP header indicated by HTTP-EQUIV).
<NEXTID>		Indicates the "next" document to this one (as might be defined by a tool to manage HTML documents in series). <NEXTID> is considered obsolete.

Headings and Title

Tag	Attribute	Function
<H1>...</H1>		A first-level heading.
<H2>...</H2>		A second-level heading.
<H3>...</H3>		A third-level heading.

Tag	Attribute	Function
`<H4>...</H4>`		A fourth-level heading.
`<H5>...</H5>`		A fifth-level heading.
`<H6>...</H6>`		A sixth-level heading.
`<TITLE>...</TITLE>`		Indicates the title of the document. Used within `<HEAD>`.

All heading tags accept the following attribute:

	Attribute	Function
	`ALIGN="..."`	Possible values are CENTER, LEFT, and RIGHT.

Paragraphs and Regions

Tag	Attribute	Function
`<P>...</P>`		A plain paragraph. The closing tag (`</P>`) is optional.
	`ALIGN="..."`	Align text to CENTER, LEFT, or RIGHT.
`<DIV>...</DIV>`		A region of text to be formatted.
	`ALIGN="..."`	Align text to CENTER, LEFT, or RIGHT.

Links

Tag	Attribute	Function
`<A>...</A>`		With the HREF attribute, creates a link to another document or anchor; with the NAME attribute, creates an anchor that can be linked to.
	`HREF="..."`	The URL of the document to be called when the link is activated.
	`NAME="..."`	The name of the anchor.
	`REL="..."`	The relationship between the linked-to document and the current document; for example, `"TOC"` or `"Glossary"`. `REL="..."` is not commonly used.

continues

C

HTML 3.2
REFERENCE

Tag	*Attribute*	*Function*
	REV="..."	A reverse relationship between the current document and the linked-to document (not commonly used).
	URN="..."	A uniform resource number, a unique identifier different from the URL in HREF (not commonly used).
	TITLE="..."	The title of the linked-to document (not commonly used).
	METHODS="..."	The method with which the document is to be retrieved; for example, FTP, Gopher, and so on (not commonly used).
	TARGET="..."	The name of a frame that the linked document should appear in.

Lists

Tag	*Attribute*	*Function*
<OL>...</OL>		An ordered (numbered) list.
	TYPE="..."	The type of numerals to label the list. Possible values are A, a, I, i, and 1.
	START="..."	The value with which to start this list.
<UL>...</UL>		An unordered (bulleted) list.
	TYPE="..."	The bullet dingbat to use to mark list items. Possible values are DISC, CIRCLE (or ROUND), and SQUARE.
<MENU>...</MENU>		A menu list of items.
<DIR>...</DIR>		A directory listing; items are generally smaller than 20 characters.
<LI>		A list item for use with <OL>, <UL>, <MENU>, or <DIR>.

Tag	Attribute	Function
	TYPE="..."	The type of bullet or number to label this item with. Possible values are DISC, CIRCLE (or ROUND), SQUARE, A, a, I, i, and 1.
	VALUE="..."	The numeric value this list item should have (affects this item and all below it in <OL> lists).
<DL>...</DL>		A definition or glossary list.
	COMPACT	The COMPACT attribute specifies a formatting that takes less whitespace to present.
<DT>		A definition term, as part of a definition list.
<DD>		The corresponding definition to a definition term, as part of a definition list.

Character Formatting

Tag	Attribute	Function
<EM>...</EM>		Emphasis (usually italic).
<STRONG>...</STRONG>		Stronger emphasis (usually bold).
<CODE>...</CODE>		Code sample (usually Courier).
<KBD>...</KBD>		Text to be typed (usually Courier).
<VAR>...</VAR>		A variable or placeholder for some other value.
<SAMP>...</SAMP>		Sample text (not commonly used).
<DFN>...</DFN>		A definition of a term.
<CITE>...</CITE>		A citation.
<B>...</B>		Boldface text.
<I>...</I>		Italic text.
<TT>...</TT>		Typewriter (monospaced) font.

continues

Tag	*Attribute*	*Function*
`<PRE>...</PRE>`		Preformatted text (exact line endings and spacing will be preserved—usually rendered in a monospaced font).
`<BIG>...</BIG>`		Text is slightly larger than normal.
`<SMALL>...</SMALL>`		Text is slightly smaller than normal.
`<SUB>...</SUB>`		Subscript.
`<SUP>...</SUP>`		Superscript.
`<STRIKE>...</STRIKE>`		Puts a strikethrough line in text.

Other Elements

Tag	*Attribute*	*Function*
`<HR>`		A horizontal rule line.
	`SIZE="..."`	The thickness of the rule, in pixels.
	`WIDTH="..."`	The width of the rule, in pixels or as a percentage of the document width.
	`ALIGN="..."`	How the rule line will be aligned on the page. Possible values are LEFT, RIGHT, and CENTER.
	`NOSHADE`	Causes the rule line to be drawn as a solid line instead of a transparent bevel.
	`COLOR="..."` (MS)	Color of the horizontal rule.
` `		A line break.
	`CLEAR="..."`	Causes the text to stop flowing around any images. Possible values are RIGHT, LEFT, and ALL.
`<NOBR>...</NOBR>`		Causes the enclosed text to not wrap at the edge of the page.
`<WBR>`		Wraps the text at this point only if necessary.
`<BLOCKQUOTE>...</BLOCKQUOTE>`		Used for long quotes or citations.

Tag	Attribute	Function
`<ADDRESS>...` `</ADDRESS>`		Used for signatures or general information about a document's author.
`<CENTER>...</CENTER>`		Centers text or images.
`<BLINK>...</BLINK>`		Causes the enclosed text to blink in an irritating manner.
`<FONT>...</FONT>`		Changes the size of the font for the enclosed text.
	`SIZE="..."`	The size of the font, from 1 to 7. Default is 3. Can also be specified as a value relative to the current size; for example, +2.
	`COLOR="..."`	Changes the color of the text.
	`FACE="..."`	Name of font to use if it can be found on the user's system. Multiple font names can be separated by commas, and the first font on the list that can be found will be used.
`<BASEFONT>`		Sets the default size of the font for the current page.
	`SIZE="..."`	The default size of the font, from 1 to 7. Default is 3.

Images, Sounds, and Embedded Media

Tag	Attribute	Function
`<IMG>`		Inserts an inline image into the document.
	`ISMAP`	This image is a clickable imagemap.
	`SRC="..."`	The URL of the image.
	`ALT="..."`	A text string that will be displayed in browsers that cannot support images.

continues

Tag	*Attribute*	*Function*
	ALIGN="..."	Determines the alignment of the given image. If LEFT or RIGHT, the image is aligned to the left or right column, and all following text flows beside that image. All other values, such as TOP, MIDDLE, and BOTTOM, or the Netscape-only TEXTTOP, ABSMIDDLE, BASELINE, and ABSBOTTOM, determine the vertical alignment of this image with other items in the same line.
	VSPACE="..."	The space between the image and the text above or below it.
	HSPACE="..."	The space between the image and the text to its left or right.
	WIDTH="..."	The width, in pixels, of the image. If WIDTH is not the actual width, the image is scaled to fit.
	HEIGHT="..."	The height, in pixels, of the image. If HEIGHT is not the actual height, the image is scaled to fit.
	BORDER="..."	Draws a border of the specified value in pixels to be drawn around the image. In the case of images that are also links, BORDER changes the size of the default link border.
	LOWSRC="..."	The path or URL of an image that will be loaded first, before the image specified in SRC. The value of LOWSRC is usually a smaller or lower resolution version of the actual image.
	USEMAP="..."	The name of an imagemap specification for client-side image mapping. Used with <MAP> and <AREA>.
	DYNSRC="..." (MS)	The address of a video clip or VRML world (dynamic source).

Tag	Attribute	Function
	CONTROLS (MS)	Used with DYNSRC to display a set of playback controls for inline video.
	LOOP="..." (MS)	The number of times a video clip will loop. (-1, or INFINITE, means to loop indefinitely.)
	START="..." (MS)	When a DYNSRC video clip should start playing. Valid options are FILEOPEN (play when page is displayed) or MOUSEOVER (play when mouse cursor passes over the video clip).
<BGSOUND> (MS)		Plays a sound file as soon as the page is displayed.
	SRC="..."	The URL of the WAV, AU, or MIDI sound file to embed.
	LOOP="..." (MS)	The number of times a video clip will loop. (-1, or INFINITE, means to loop indefinitely.)
<SCRIPT>		An interpreted script program.
	LANGUAGE="..."	Currently only JAVASCRIPT is supported by Netscape. Both JAVASCRIPT and VBSCRIPT are supported by Microsoft.
	SRC="..."	Specifies the URL of a file that includes the script program.
<OBJECT>		Inserts an image, video, Java applet, or ActiveX control into a document.

continues

C

HTML 3.2
REFERENCE

NOTE

Usage of the <OBJECT> tag is not yet finalized. Check http://www.w3.org/ for the latest attributes supported by the HTML 3.2 standard.

Tag	Attribute	Function
<APPLET>		Inserts a self-running Java applet.
	CLASS="..."	The name of the applet.
	SRC="..."	The URL of the directory where the compiled applet can be found (should end in a slash [/] as in http://mysite/myapplets/). Do not include the actual applet name, which is specified with the CLASS attribute.
	ALIGN="..."	Indicates how the applet should be aligned with any text that follows it. Current values are TOP, MIDDLE, and BOTTOM.
	WIDTH="..."	The width of the applet output area, in pixels.
	HEIGHT="..."	The height of the applet output area, in pixels.
<PARAM>		Program-specific parameter. (Always occurs within <APPLET> or <OBJECT> tags.)
	NAME="..."	The type of information being given to the applet or ActiveX control.
	VALUE="..."	The actual information to be given to the applet or ActiveX control.
	REF="..."	Indicates that this <PARAM> tag includes the address or location of the object.
<EMBED>		Embeds a file to be read or (Netscape only!) displayed by a plug-in application.

NOTE

In addition to the following standard attributes, you can specify applet-specific attributes to be interpreted by the plug-in that displays the embedded object.

Tag	Attribute	Function
	`SRC="..."`	The URL of the file to embed.
	`WIDTH="..."`	The width of the embedded object in pixels.
	`HEIGHT="..."`	The height of the embedded object in pixels.
	`ALIGN="..."`	Determines the alignment of the media window. Values are the same as for the `<IMG>` tag.
	`VSPACE="..."`	The space between the media and the text above or below it.
	`HSPACE="..."`	The space between the media and the text to its left or right.
	`BORDER="..."`	Draws a border of the specified size in pixels to be placed around the media.
`<NOEMBED>...` `</NOEMBED>`		Alternative text or images to be shown to users who do not have a plug-in installed.
`<MAP>...</MAP>`		A client-side imagemap, referenced by `<IMG USEMAP="...">`. Includes one or more `<AREA>` tags.
`<AREA>`		Defines a clickable link within a client-side imagemap.
	`SHAPE="..."`	The shape of the clickable area. Currently, only RECT is supported.
	`COORDS="..."`	The left, top, right, and bottom coordinates of the clickable region within an image.
	`HREF="..."`	The URL that should be loaded when the area is clicked.
	`NOHREF`	Indicates that no action should be taken when this area of the image is clicked.

C

**HTML 3.2
REFERENCE**

Forms

Tag	*Attribute*	*Function*
`<FORM>...</FORM>`		Indicates an input form.
	`ACTION="..."`	The URL of the script to process this form input.
	`METHOD="..."`	How the form input will be sent to the gateway on the server side. Possible values are GET and POST.
	`ENCTYPE="..."`	Normally has the value `application/x-www-form-urlencoded`. For file uploads, use `multipart/form-data`.
	`NAME="..."`	A name by which JavaScript scripts can refer to the form.
`<INPUT>`		An input element for a form.
	`TYPE="..."`	The type for this input widget. Possible values are CHECKBOX, HIDDEN, RADIO, RESET, SUBMIT, TEXT, SEND FILE, or IMAGE.
	`NAME="..."`	The name of this item, as passed to the gateway script as part of a name/value pair.
	`VALUE="..."`	For a text or hidden widget, the default value; for a checkbox or radio button, the value to be submitted with the form; for Reset or Submit buttons, the label for the button itself.
	`SRC="..."`	The source file for an image.
	`CHECKED`	For checkboxes and radio buttons, indicates that the widget is checked.
	`SIZE="..."`	The size, in characters, of a text widget.
	`MAXLENGTH="..."`	The maximum number of characters that can be entered into a text widget.

Tag	Attribute	Function
	ALIGN="..."	For images in forms, determines how the text and image will align (same as with the `<IMG>` tag).
`<TEXTAREA>...` `</TEXTAREA>`		Indicates a multiline text entry form element. Default text can be included.
	NAME="..."	The name to be passed to the gateway script as part of the name/value pair.
	ROWS="..."	The number of rows this text area displays.
	COLS="..."	The number of columns (characters) this text area displays.
	WRAP="..."	Controls text wrapping. Possible values are OFF, VIRTUAL, and PHYSICAL.
`<SELECT>...</SELECT>`		Creates a menu or scrolling list of possible items.
	NAME="..."	The name that is passed to the gateway script as part of the name/value pair.
	SIZE="..."	The number of elements to display. If SIZE is indicated, the selection becomes a scrolling list. If no SIZE is given, the selection is a pop-up menu.
	MULTIPLE	Allows multiple selections from the list.
`<OPTION>`		Indicates a possible item within a `<SELECT>` element.
	SELECTED	With this attribute included, the `<OPTION>` will be selected by default in the list.
	VALUE="..."	The value to submit if this `<OPTION>` is selected when the form is submitted.

Tables

Tag	Attribute	Function
<TABLE>...</TABLE>		Creates a table that can contain a caption (<CAPTION>) and any number of rows (<TR>).
	BORDER="..."	Indicates whether the table should be drawn with or without a border. In Netscape, BORDER can also have a value indicating the width of the border.
	CELLSPACING="..."	The amount of space between the cells in the table.
	CELLPADDING="..."	The amount of space between the edges of the cell and its contents.
	WIDTH="..."	The width of the table on the page, in either exact pixel values or as a percentage of page width.
	ALIGN="..." (MS)	Alignment (works like IMG ALIGN). Values are LEFT or RIGHT.
	BGCOLOR="..."	Background color of all cells in the table that do not contain their own BACKGROUND or BGCOLOR attribute.
	BACKGROUND="..." (MS)	Background image to tile within all cells in the table that do not contain their own BACKGROUND or BGCOLOR attribute.
	BORDERCOLOR="..." (MS)	Border color (used with BORDER="...").
	BORDERCOLORLIGHT="..." (MS)	Color for light part of 3-D–look borders (used with BORDER="...").
	BORDERCOLORDARK="..." (MS)	Color for dark part of 3-D–look borders (used with BORDER="...").
	VALIGN="..." (MS)	Alignment of text within the table. Values are TOP and BOTTOM.

Tag	Attribute	Function
	FRAME="..." (MS)	Controls which external borders will appear around a table. Values are void (no frames), above (top border only), below (bottom border only), hsides (top and bottom), lhs (left side), rhs (right side), vsides (left and right sides), and box (all sides).
	RULES="..." (MS)	Controls which internal borders appear in the table. Values are none, basic (rules between THEAD, TBODY, and TFOOT only), rows (horizontal borders only), cols (vertical borders only), and all.
<CAPTION>... </CAPTION>		The caption for the table.
	ALIGN="..."	The position of the caption. Possible values are TOP and BOTTOM.
<TR>...</TR>		Defines a table row, containing headings and data (<TR> and <TH> tags).
	ALIGN="..."	The horizontal alignment of the contents of the cells within this row. Possible values are LEFT, RIGHT, and CENTER.
	VALIGN="..."	The vertical alignment of the contents of the cells within this row. Possible values are TOP, MIDDLE, BOTTOM, and BASELINE.
	BGCOLOR="..."	Background color of all cells in the row that do not contain their own BACKGROUND or BGCOLOR attributes.
	BACKGROUND="..."(MS)	Background image to tile within all cells in the row that do not contain their own BACKGROUND or BGCOLOR attributes.

C

HTML 3.2
REFERENCE

continues

Tag	*Attribute*	*Function*
	BORDERCOLOR="..."(MS)	Border color (used with BORDER="...").
	BORDERCOLORLIGHT="..."(MS)	Color for light part of 3-D–look borders (used with BORDER="...").
	BORDERCOLORDARK="..."(MS)	Color for dark part of 3-D–look borders (used with BORDER="...").
<TH>...</TH>		Defines a table heading cell.
	ALIGN="..."	The horizontal alignment of the contents of the cell. Possible values are LEFT, RIGHT, and CENTER.
	VALIGN="..."	The vertical alignment of the contents of the cell. Possible values are TOP, MIDDLE, BOTTOM, and BASELINE.
	ROWSPAN="..."	The number of rows this cell will span.
	COLSPAN="..."	The number of columns this cell will span.
	NOWRAP	Does not automatically wrap the contents of this cell.
	WIDTH="..."	The width of this column of cells, in exact pixel values or as a percentage of the table width.
	BGCOLOR="..."	Background color of the cell.
	BACKGROUND="..." (MS)	Background image to tile within the cell.
	BORDERCOLOR="..." (MS)	Border color (used with BORDER="...").
	BORDERCOLORLIGHT="..." (MS)	Color for light part of 3-D–look borders (used with BORDER="...").

Tag	*Attribute*	*Function*
	BORDERCOLORDARK="..." (MS)	Color for dark part of 3-D–look borders (used with BORDER="...").
`<TD>...</TD>`		Defines a table data cell.
	ALIGN="..."	The horizontal alignment of the contents of the cell. Possible values are LEFT, RIGHT, and CENTER.
	VALIGN="..."	The vertical alignment of the contents of the cell. Possible values are TOP, MIDDLE, BOTTOM, and BASELINE.
	ROWSPAN="..."	The number of rows this cell will span.
	COLSPAN="..."	The number of columns this cell will span.
	NOWRAP	Does not automatically wrap the contents of this cell.
	WIDTH="..."	The width of this column of cells, in exact pixel values or as a percentage of the table width.
	BGCOLOR="..."	Background color of the cell.
	BACKGROUND="..." (MS)	Background image to tile within the cell.
	BORDERCOLOR="..." (MS)	Border color (used with BORDER="...").
	BORDERCOLORLIGHT="..." (MS)	Color for light part of 3-D–look borders (used with BORDER="...").
	BORDERCOLORDARK="..." (MS)	Color for dark part of 3-D–look borders (used with BORDER="...").

C

HTML 3.2 REFERENCE

Frames

Tag	Attribute	Function
`<FRAMESET>...` `</FRAMESET>`		Divides the main window into a set of frames that can each display a separate document.
	`ROWS="..."`	Splits the window or frameset vertically into a number of rows specified by a number (such as 7), a percentage of the total window width (such as 25%), or as an asterisk (*) indicating that a frame should take up all the remaining space or divide the space evenly between frames (if multiple * frames are specified).
	`COLS="..."`	Works similar to ROWS, except that the window or frameset is split horizontally into columns.
	`BORDER="..."`	Size of frame border in pixels (0 turns off borders). This tag is Netscape-specific—Microsoft IE uses FRAMEBORDER and FRAMESPACING instead.
	`FRAMEBORDER="..."` (MS)	Specifies whether to display a border for a frame. Options are YES and NO.
	`FRAMESPACING="..."` (MS)	Space between frames, in pixels.
`<FRAME>`		Defines a single frame within a `<FRAMESET>`.
	`SRC="..."`	The URL of the document to be displayed in this frame.
	`NAME="..."`	A name to be used for targeting this frame with the TARGET attribute in `<A HREF>` links.
	`MARGINWIDTH="..."`	The amount of space to leave to the left and right sides of a document within a frame, in pixels.

Tag	Attribute	Function
	`MARGINHEIGHT="..."`	The amount of space to leave above and below a document within a frame, in pixels.
	`SCROLLING="..."`	Determines whether a frame has scrollbars. Possible values are YES, NO, and AUTO.
	`NORESIZE`	Prevents the user from resizing this frame (and possibly adjacent frames) with the mouse.
`<NOFRAME>...` `</NOFRAME>`		Provides an alternative document body in `<FRAMESET>` documents for browsers that do not support frames (usually encloses `<BODY>...</BODY>`).

Character Entities

Table C.1 contains the possible numeric and character entities for the ISO-Latin-1 (ISO8859-1) character set. Where possible, the character is shown.

> **NOTE**
>
> Not all browsers can display all characters, and some browsers might even display characters different from those that appear in the table. Newer browsers seem to have a better track record for handling character entities, but be sure to test your HTML files extensively with multiple browsers if you intend to use these entities.

Table C.1. ISO-Latin-1 character set.

Character	Numeric Entity	Character Entity (if any)	Description
	`&#00;`–`&#08;`		Unused
	`&#09;`		Horizontal tab
	`&#10;`		Line feed
	`&#11;`–`&#31;`		Unused
	`&#32;`		Space
!	`&#33;`		Exclamation point

continues

Table C.1. continued

Character	Numeric Entity	Character Entity (if any)	Description
"	&#34;	&quot;	Quotation mark
#	&#35;		Number sign
$	&#36;		Dollar sign
%	&#37;		Percent sign
&	&#38;	&amp;	Ampersand
'	&#39;		Apostrophe
(	&#40;		Left parenthesis
)	&#41;		Right parenthesis
*	&#42;		Asterisk
+	&#43;		Plus sign
,	&#44;		Comma
-	&#45;		Hyphen
.	&#46;		Period (fullstop)
/	&#47;		Solidus (slash)
0–9	0–9		Digits 0–9
:	&#58;		Colon
;	&#59;		Semicolon
<	&#60;	&lt;	Less than
=	&#61;		Equal sign
>	&#62;	&gt;	Greater than
?	&#63;		Question mark
@	&#64;		Commercial "at"
A–Z	A–Z		Letters A–Z
[	&#91;		Left square bracket
\	&#92;		Reverse solidus (backslash)
]	&#93;		Right square bracket
^	&#94;		Caret
—	&#95;		Horizontal bar
`	&#96;		Grave accent

Character	Numeric Entity	Character Entity (if any)	Description
a–z	a–z		Letters a–z
{	&#123;		Left curly brace
|	&#124		Vertical bar
}	&#125;		Right curly brace
˜	&#126;		Tilde
	&#127;–		Unused
¡	&#161;	&iexcl;	Inverted exclamation point
¢	&#162;	&cent;	Cent sign
£	&#163;	&pound;	Pound sterling
¤	&#164;	&curren;	General currency sign
¥	&#165;	&yen;	Yen sign
¦	&#166;	¦ or brkbar;	Broken vertical bar
§	&#167;	&sect;	Section sign
¨	&#168;	&uml;	Umlaut (dieresis)
©	&#169;	© (Netscape only)	Copyright
ª	&#170;	&ordf;	Feminine ordinal
‹	&#171;	&laquo;	Left angle quote, guillemot left
¬	&#172;	&not;	Not sign
	&#173;	&shy;	Soft hyphen
®	&#174;	® (Netscape only)	Registered trademark
¯	&#175;	&hibar;	Macron accent
°	&#176;	&deg;	Degree sign
±	&#177;	&plusmn;	Plus or minus
²	&#178;	&sup2;	Superscript two
³	&#179;	&sup3;	Superscript three

C

HTML 3.2 REFERENCE

continues

Table C.1. continued

Character	Numeric Entity	Character Entity (if any)	Description
´	&#180;	&acute;	Acute accent
µ	&#181;	&micro;	Micro sign
¶	&#182;	&para;	Paragraph sign
·	&#183;	&middot;	Middle dot
¸	&#184;	&cedil;	Cedilla
¹	&#185;	&sup1;	Superscript one
º	&#186;	&ordm;	Masculine ordinal
›	&#187;	&raquo;	Right angle quote, guillemot right
¼	&#188;	&frac14;	Fraction one-fourth
½	&#189;	&frac12;	Fraction one-half
¾	&#190;	&frac34;	Fraction three-fourths
¿	&#191;	&iquest;	Inverted question mark
À	&#192;	&Agrave;	Capital A, grave accent
Á	&#193;	&Aacute;	Capital A, acute accent
Â	&#194;	&Acirc;	Capital A, circumflex accent
Ã	&#195;	&Atilde;	Capital A, tilde
Ä	&#196;	&Auml;	Capital A, dieresis or umlaut mark
Å	&#197;	&Aring;	Capital A, ring
Æ	&#198;	&AElig;	Capital AE diphthong (ligature)

Character	Numeric Entity	Character Entity (if any)	Description
Ç	&#199;	&Ccedil;	Capital C, cedilla
È	&#200;	&Egrave;	Capital E, grave accent
É	&#201;	&Eacute;	Capital E, acute accent
Ê	&#202;	&Ecirc;	Capital E, circumflex accent
Ë	&#203;	&Euml;	Capital E, dieresis or umlaut mark
Ì	&#204;	&Igrave;	Capital I, grave accent
Í	&#205;	&Iacute;	Capital I, acute accent
Î	&#206;	&Icirc;	Capital I, circumflex accent
Ï	&#207;	&Iuml;	Capital I, dieresis or umlaut mark
Ð	&#208;	&ETH;	Capital Eth, Icelandic
Ñ	&#209;	&Ntilde;	Capital N, tilde
Ò	&#210;	&Ograve;	Capital O, grave accent
Ó	&#211;	&Oacute;	Capital O, acute accent
Ô	&#212;	&Ocirc;	Capital O, circumflex accent
Õ	&#213;	&Otilde;	Capital O, tilde
Ö	&#214;	&Ouml;	Capital O, dieresis or umlaut mark

C

HTML 3.2 REFERENCE

continues

Table C.1. continued

Character	*Numeric Entity*	*Character Entity (if any)*	*Description*
×	&#215;		Multiply sign
Ø	&#216;	&Oslash;	Capital O, slash
Ù	&#217;	&Ugrave;	Capital U, grave accent
Ú	&#218;	&Uacute;	Capital U, acute accent
Û	&#219;	&Ucirc;	Capital U, circumflex accent
Ü	&#220;	&Uuml;	Capital U, dieresis or umlaut mark
Ý	&#221;	&Yacute;	Capital Y, acute accent
Þ	&#222;	&THORN;	Capital THORN, Icelandic
ß	&#223;	&szlig;	Small sharp s, German (sz ligature)
à	&#224;	&agrave;	Small a, grave accent
á	&#225;	&aacute;	Small a, acute accent
â	&#226;	&acirc;	Small a, circumflex accent
ã	&#227;	&atilde;	Small a, tilde
ä	&#228;	&aauml;	Small a, dieresis or umlaut mark
å	&#229;	&aring;	Small a, ring
æ	&#230;	&aelig;	Small ae diphthong (ligature)
ç	&#231;	&ccedil;	Small c, cedilla
è	&#232;	&egrave;	Small e, grave accent

Character	Numeric Entity	Character Entity (if any)	Description
é	&#233;	&eacute;	Small e, acute accent
ê	&#234;	&ecirc;	Small e, circumflex accent
ë	&#235;	&euml;	Small e, dieresis or umlaut mark
ì	&#236;	&igrave;	Small i, grave accent
í	&#237;	&iacute;	Small i, acute accent
î	&#238;	&icirc;	Small i, circumflex accent
ï	&#239;	&iuml;	Small i, dieresis or umlaut mark
ð	&#240;	&eth;	Small eth, Icelandic
ñ	&#241;	&ntilde;	Small n, tilde
ò	&#242;	&ograve;	Small o, grave accent
ó	&#243;	&oacute;	Small o, acute accent
ô	&#244;	&ocirc;	Small o, circumflex accent
õ	&#245;	&otilde;	Small o, tilde
ö	&#246;	&ouml;	Small o, dieresis or umlaut mark
÷	&#247;		Division sign
ø	&#248;	&oslash;	Small o, slash
ù	&#249;	&ugrave;	Small u, grave accent
ú	&#250;	&uacute;	Small u, acute accent

C

*HTML 3.2
REFERENCE*

continues

Table C.1. continued

Character	Numeric Entity	Character Entity (if any)	Description
û	&#251;	&ucirc;	Small u, circumflex accent
ü	&#252;	&uuml;	Small u, dieresis or umlaut mark
ý	&#253;	&yacute;	Small y, acute accent
þ	&#254;	&thorn;	Small thorn, Icelandic
ÿ	&#255;	&yuml;	Small y, dieresis or umlaut mark

VBScript Reference

by Michael Morrison

IN THIS APPENDIX

APPENDIX **D**

As this book illustrates, Visual InterDev relies heavily on scripting through ActiveX scripting. Microsoft's scripting language of choice is VBScript, which is a Visual Basic–derived scripting language that provides a great deal of power in a relatively simple package. This appendix is devoted to the nuts and bolts of the VBScript scripting language. If you're new to VBScript, you can learn a great deal about it here, but you might want to read through an introductory book to learn the basics at a more relaxed pace. If you have some experience with VBScript, you'll find this appendix a great reference for language details such as the intrinsic functions provided by VBScript.

VBScript and HTML

The code for scripts written in VBScript is listed directly in Web pages containing the script. The <SCRIPT> tag is used to enclose VBScript scripts. The LANGUAGE parameter is used to identify the language for the script, which in the case of VBScript is "VBScript". Within the <SCRIPT> block, the code for a script is contained within a comment tag, <!>. This causes browsers that don't support VBScript to see the script code as comments. Following is the basic format of VBScript code:

```
<SCRIPT LANGUAGE="VBScript">
<!--
' The script code goes here.
-->
</SCRIPT>
```

Data Types

VBScript directly supports only one data type, *Variant*. The Variant data type is somewhat of a generic, all-purpose data type in that it can represent a variety of different information, depending on its usage. Variants are context-sensitive, meaning that the context they are used in determines how they are interpreted. So, for example, when a Variant is used in a numeric context it behaves like a number. Similarly, Variants can just as easily represent strings when used in a context where a string would be the most appropriate representation of information.

The reason VBScript uses a single data type is primarily to make typing more automatic for script writers. The main idea behind scripting languages is ease of use, and Variants directly support this idea by automatically acting like different data types as necessary. Because Variant is the only data type in VBScript, all VBScript functions return a type Variant.

You may be a little confused about how a Variant can "act" like another data type. The specific data types that can be represented by a Variant are called *subtypes*. Table D.1 shows the different subtypes supported by VBScript Variants, along with what they mean:

Table D.1. Subtypes of the Variant data type.

Subtype	Meaning
Empty	Variant is uninitialized
Null	Variant intentionally contains no valid data
Boolean	Variant is either True or False
Byte	Variant is an integer in the range 0 to 255
Integer	Variant is an integer in the range −32,768 to 32,767
Long	Variant is an integer in the range −2,147,483,648 to 2,147,483,647
Single	Variant is a single-precision, floating-point number in the range −3.402823E38 to −1.401298E-45 for negative values; 1.401298E–45 to 3.402823E38 for positive values
Double	Variant is a double-precision, floating-point number in the range −1.79769313486232E308 to −4.94065645841247E–324 for negative values; 4.94065645841247E–324 to 1.79769313486232E308 for positive values
Date/Time	Variant is a number representing a date between January 1, 100 to December 31, 9999
String	Variant is a variable-length string
Object	Variant is an object
Error	Variant is the number of a system error

As you can see, variants give you plenty of freedom in representing and storing all kinds of different data. Generally speaking, you can simply put the kind of data you want in a Variant and it will automatically behave appropriately. If you want to explicitly convert Variant data from one subtype to another, there is a rich set of standard conversion functions you can use. These are covered later in this appendix in the "Intrinsic Functions" section.

Variables

No programming language would be complete without variables, which are placeholders for memory locations where you can store data that may change while your program is running. In VBScript, variables can be used for all kinds of different tasks, but they are always of type Variant. For example, you might want to display a message in a Web page and have it change every few minutes. You would store this message in a variable so that it can easily be changed.

VBScript variables, like variables in most programming languages, are always referred to by name. This name is specified when a variable is created (declared) and is used thereafter to view or modify the value of the variable. Variables are declared using the `Dim` statement, like this:

```
Dim Length
```

You can also declare a group of variables at once by separating them with commas, like this:

```
Dim Length, Width, Height
```

The `Dim` statement approach to variable declaration is known as *explicit declaration*. You can also *implicitly declare* a variable by simply using it in a script with no formal declaration at all. Even though VBScript supports implicit declaration, as a rule it's not a good idea because you could easily misspell a variable name and get unexpected results.

Avoiding implicit declaration doesn't guarantee you won't run into the variable name misspelling problem, however. You could explicitly declare a variable and then accidentally misspell it somewhere else in the script. In this case, you would still get confusing results because the misspelled name would be used as an implicit declaration. The solution to this problem is the `Option Explicit` statement, which forces a script to require explicit declarations for all variables. The `Option Explicit` statement must be the first statement of a script.

Variables wouldn't be of much use if you couldn't assign them values. VBScript variable assignment works much like variable assignment in other programming languages. In VBScript, the variable appears on the left side of an expression and the value to be assigned to it appears on the right. For example

```
Temperature = 73
```

Arrays

Typically, VBScript variables are *scalar*, meaning that they contain a single value. However, VBScript also supports *arrays*, which are variables that contain a series of values. Array variables are declared similarly as scalar variables, except that array variable declarations use parentheses following the variable name. The parentheses are used to list the number of elements to be contained in an array. Following is an example of declaring an array containing 5 elements:

```
Dim GroceryList(4)
```

You are no doubt curious about the array containing 5 elements while the declaration used the number 4. This seemingly strange numbering has to do with the fact that all arrays in VBScript are *zero-based*. In a zero-based array, the number of array elements is always the number shown in parentheses plus one. This kind of an array is also called a *fixed-size array*.

Data is assigned to individual array elements by using an index into the array. Following is an example of assigning data to the `GroceryList` variable array:

```
GroceryList(0) = "Milk"
GroceryList(1) = "Bread"
```

```
GroceryList(2) = "Orange Juice"
GroceryList(3) = "Bananas"
GroceryList(4) = "Carrots"
```

Just as data can be assigned to an array through an index, it can also be retrieved. For example:

```
GroceryItem = GroceryList(3)
```

The GroceryList array is an example of a *single-dimension array*. VBScript also supports *multi-dimension arrays*, such as two- or three-dimensional arrays. Multi-dimension arrays are declared by separating an array's size numbers in the parentheses with commas. In a two-dimensional array, the first number specifies the number of rows while the second number specifies the number of columns. The following example shows how to declare a two-dimensional array consisting of 4 rows and 6 columns:

```
Dim Gameboard(3, 5)
```

> **NOTE**
>
> VBScript supports multi-dimension arrays with as many as 60 dimensions. However, it's difficult for most people, myself included, to comprehend more than about three or four dimensions.

The Gameboard array is a fixed-size array because its size is specified in its declaration. VBScript also supports *dynamic arrays*, which are arrays whose size can change during the execution of a script. Dynamic arrays are declared with no size or number of dimensions inside the parentheses, like this:

```
Dim AnotherGroceryList()
```

Dynamic arrays aren't usable until they are given a specific size. This is accomplished with the ReDim statement, as the following example illustrates:

```
ReDim AnotherGroceryList(9)
```

The ReDim statement in this case resizes the array to 10 elements. Because the array is dynamic, the ReDim statement could be used again to change the size of the array. Typically, the ReDim statement clears the contents of an array when it resizes the array. You can preserve the contents of an array when resizing it by using the Preserve keyword with the ReDim statement, like this:

```
ReDim Preserve AnotherGroceryList(9)
```

In the following example, ReDim sets the initial size of the dynamic array to 25 elements. A subsequent ReDim statement resizes the array to 30 elements, but uses the Preserve keyword to preserve the contents of the array as the resizing takes place.

```
ReDim OneMoreGroceryList(24)
ReDim Preserve OneMoreGroceryList(29)
```

D

You can resize an array as many times as you want. However, keep in mind that any time you make an array smaller, you lose the data in the eliminated elements regardless of whether you used the Preserve keyword.

Scope and Lifetime

Scoping is an important programming concept, and refers to the visibility of a variable with regard to different parts of a program. In VBScript, there are two different types of scope a variable can have: procedure-level and script-level. *Procedure-level* scope applies to variables declared and used in a procedure. When you declare a variable within a procedure, only code within that procedure can access or change the value of that variable. In other words, the scope of the variable doesn't extend beyond the procedure. Procedure-level variables are also sometimes called *local variables*.

Script-level variables, on the other hand, are declared at the script level and consequently have scope throughout an entire script. Variables with script-level scope are visible even inside of procedures. Script-level variables are also sometimes called *global variables*.

The length of time a variable exists is known as its *lifetime*. A script-level variable's lifetime extends from the time it is declared until the script finishes running. A procedure-level variable's lifetime begins the time it is declared (as the procedure begins), and ends when the procedure ends. Procedure-level variables are typically used as temporary storage space, because they go away when a procedure exits. Unlike script-level variables, you can have procedure-level variables of the same name in several different procedures because each is recognized only within the procedure in which it is declared.

Naming

VBScript variable names must adhere to a standard set of rules. Actually, the naming rules for variables apply to all VBScript names, including subroutine and function names. These rules follow:

- Must begin with an alphabetic character
- Must not exceed 255 characters
- Cannot contain an embedded period
- Must be unique in the scope in which it is declared

Limits on the Number of Variables

Unlike many programming languages, VBScript has practical limitations surrounding how many variables can be used in a script. Even so, I seriously doubt you would ever run into any of these limitations because they aren't very restrictive. The following two rules limit the number of variables used in a script:

- There can't be more than 127 global variables in a script.
- There can't be more than 127 local variables in a procedure.

NOTE

Just in case you're wondering, arrays count as a single variable, regardless of how many elements they contain.

Operators

VBScript supports a wide range of operators, such as arithmetic operators, comparison operators, and logical operators, to name a few. The next few sections cover each of these operators.

Addition (+)

The addition operator (+) is used to add two numbers. Its syntax follows:

```
Result = Number1 + Number2
```

You can also use the addition operator to concatenate two character strings, but it's generally not a good idea because there is a concatenation operator (&) designed specifically for concatenating strings.

And

The And operator is used to perform a logical AND operation on two expressions. Its syntax follows:

```
Result = Expression1 And Expression2
```

The And operator can also be used to perform a bitwise AND operation on two numeric expressions.

Concatenation (&)

The concatenation operator (&) is used to force a string concatenation of two expressions. Its syntax follows:

```
Result = Expression1 & Expression2
```

If either of the expressions is not a string, it is converted to a String subtype before performing the concatenation. If one of the expressions is Null, the expression is treated as a zero-length string ("") when concatenated with the other expression.

Division (/)

The division operator (/) is used to divide two numbers and return a floating-point result. Its syntax follows:

```
Result = Number1 / Number2
```

Eqv

The Eqv operator is used to perform a logical equivalence on two expressions. Its syntax follows:

```
Result = Expression1 Eqv Expression2
```

The Eqv operator can also be used to perform a bitwise comparison on two numeric expressions.

Exponentiation (^)

The exponentiation operator (^) is used to raise a number to the power of an exponent. Its syntax follows:

```
Result = Number ^ Exponent
```

Imp

The Imp operator is used to perform a logical implication on two expressions. Its syntax follows:

```
Result = Expression1 Imp Expression2
```

The Imp operator can also be used to perform a bitwise implication on two numeric expressions.

Integer Division (\)

The integer division operator (\) is used to divide two numbers and return an integer result. Its syntax follows:

```
Result = Number1 \ Number2
```

Before the division is performed, the numeric expressions are rounded to Byte, Integer, or Long subtype expressions.

Is

The Is operator is used to compare two object reference variables. Its syntax follows:

```
Result = Object1 Is Object2
```

Mod

The Mod operator is used to divide two numbers and return the remainder. Its syntax follows:

```
Result = Number1 Mod Number2
```

Multiplication (*)

The multiplication operator (*) is used to multiply two numbers. Its syntax follows:

`Result = Number1 * Number2`

Negation (-)

The negation operator (-) is used to indicate the negative value of a numeric expression. Its syntax follows:

`-Number`

Not

The Not operator is used to perform a logical negation on an expression. Its syntax follows:

`Result = Not Expression`

The Not operator can also be used to perform a bitwise inversion on a numeric expression.

Or

The Or operator is used to perform a logical OR operation on two expressions. Its syntax follows:

`Result = Expression1 Or Expression2`

The Or operator can also be used to perform a bitwise OR operation on two numeric expressions.

Subtraction (-)

The subtraction operator (-) is used to find the difference between two numbers. Its syntax follows:

`Result = Number1 - Number2`

Xor

The Xor operator is used to perform a logical XOR operation on two expressions. Its syntax follows:

`Result = Expression1 Xor Expression2`

The Xor operator can also be used to perform a bitwise XOR operation on two numeric expressions.

Operator Precedence

When several operations occur in an expression, each part of the expression is evaluated and resolved in a predetermined order based on the different operators. This order is known as *operator precedence.* Arithmetic operators are always evaluated first, comparison operators are evaluated next, and logical operators are evaluated last. Comparison operators all have equal precedence, meaning that they are evaluated in the left-to-right order in which they appear. Table D.2 shows the operator precedence for arithmetic and logical operators, with precedence decreasing as you move down the table.

Table D.2. Operator precedence for arithmetic and logical operators.

Arithmetic	*Logical*
Exponentiation (^)	Not
Negation (-)	And
Multiplication and division (*, /)	Or
Integer division (\)	Xor
Modulus arithmetic (Mod)	Eqv
Addition and subtraction (+, -)	Imp
String concatenation (&)	&

NOTE

Technically, the string concatenation operator (&) is not an arithmetic operator, but in precedence it falls after arithmetic operators and before all comparison operators.

There are times when you want an expression to be resolved in an order different than that determined by operator precedence. You can use parentheses to override the order of precedence and force parts of an expression to be evaluated before others. Operations within parentheses are always performed before those outside of the parentheses. Within parentheses, however, normal operator precedence is maintained.

Statements

VBScript includes a rich set of statements for performing a wide range of useful actions. The next few sections cover each of these statements.

Call

The Call statement transfers control to a subroutine or function. Its syntax and parts follow:

```
Call Procedure [(ArgumentList)]
```

Procedure—name of the procedure to call

ArgumentList—comma-delimited list of variables, arrays, or expressions to pass to the procedure

The Call statement is not required when calling a subroutine or function. If Call is used to call a procedure that requires arguments, *ArgumentList* must be enclosed in parentheses. If Call is used to call a function, the return value is discarded.

Dim

The Dim statement declares and allocates storage space for variables. Its syntax and parts follow:

```
Dim VarName0[([Subscripts0])][, VarName1[([Subscripts1])]]
```

VarName—name of the variable

Subscripts—dimensions the variable if it is an array

When variables are initialized using Dim, numeric variables are initialized to 0 and string variables are initialized to zero-length (" ").

Do...Loop

The Do...Loop statement repeats a block of statements while a condition is True or until a condition becomes True. Its syntax and parts follow:

```
Do [{While ¦ Until} Condition]
    [Statements]
    [Exit Do]
    [Statements]
Loop
```

Optionally, you can use this syntax:

```
Do
    [Statements]
    [Exit Do]
    [Statements]
Loop [{While ¦ Until} Condition]
```

Condition—numeric or string expression that evaluates to True or False

Statements—one or more statements that are repeated while or until *Condition* is True

The Exit Do statement is used to exit the loop prematurely, transferring control to the statement immediately following the loop.

Erase

The `Erase` statement reinitializes the elements of fixed-size arrays and frees storage space associated with dynamic arrays. Its syntax and parts follow:

```
Erase Array
```

Array—name of the array variable to be erased

Exit

The `Exit` statement exits a block of `Do...Loop`, `For...Next`, `Function`, or `Sub` code. Its syntax for each of these scenarios follows:

```
Exit Do
```

```
Exit For
```

```
Exit Function
```

```
Exit Sub
```

For Each...Next

The `For Each...Next` statement repeats a group of statements for each element in an array or collection. Its syntax and parts follow:

```
For Each Element In Group
    [Statements]
    [Exit For]
    [Statements]
Next [Element]
```

Element—variable used to iterate through the elements of the collection or array

Group—name of the object collection or array

Statements—one or more statements that are executed on each item in *Group*

The `Exit For` statement is used to exit the loop prematurely, transferring control to the statement immediately following the loop.

For...Next

The `For...Next` statement repeats a group of statements a specified number of times. Its syntax and parts follow:

```
For Counter = Start To End [Step Step]
    [Statements]
    [Exit For]
    [Statements]
Next
```

Counter—numeric variable used as a loop counter

Start—initial value of the loop counter

End—final value of the loop counter

Step—amount the loop counter is changed each time through the loop; defaults to 1 if not specified

The Exit For statement is used to exit the loop prematurely, transferring control to the statement immediately following the loop.

Function

The Function statement declares the name, arguments, and code that form the body of a function procedure. Its syntax and parts follow:

```
[Public ¦ Private] Function Name [(ArgList)]
    [Statements]
    [Name = Expression]
    [Exit Function]
    [Statements]
    [Name = Expression]
End Function
```

Name—name of the function

ArgList—list of variables representing arguments that are passed to the function when it is called

Statements—any group of statements to be executed within the body of the function

Expression—return value of the function

The Public keyword indicates that the function is accessible to all other procedures in all scripts, while the Private keyword indicates that the function is accessible only to other procedures in the script where it is declared. If Public or Private is not explicitly specified, functions default to being public.

The *ArgList* argument has the following syntax and parts:

```
[ByVal ¦ ByRef] VarName[( )]
```

VarName—name of the variable representing the argument

The ByVal keyword indicates that the argument is passed by value, while the ByRef keyword indicates that the argument is passed by reference.

The Exit Function statement is used to exit the function prematurely, transferring control to the statement immediately following the function. Similar to subroutines, functions can take arguments, perform a series of statements, and change the values of its arguments. However, unlike subroutines, functions can be used on the right side of expressions because they always return a value. Functions are called using the function name followed by the argument list in parentheses. You can also call a function using the `Call` statement.

To return a value from a function, you simply assign the value to the function name. Function name assignments can occur anywhere in a function. If no return value is assigned, functions return a default value (`0` for numeric functions or `" "` for string functions). Functions that return an object reference return `Nothing` if no return value is set.

If...Then...Else

The `If...Then...Else` statement conditionally executes a group of statements, depending on the value of an expression. Its syntax and parts follow:

```
If Condition Then Statements [Else ElseStatements ]
```

Optionally, you can use the block form syntax:

```
If Condition0 Then
    [Statements]
[ElseIf Condition1 Then
    [ElseIfStatements]]
[Else
    [ElseStatements]]
End If
```

Condition—a numeric or string expression that evaluates to `True` or `False`, or an expression of the form `TypeOf ObjectName Is ObjectType`

Statements—one or more statements to be executed if *Condition* is `True`

You can use the single-line form of `If...Then...Else` for simple tests. However, the block form provides more structure and flexibility, and is usually easier to read, maintain, and debug. The `Else` and `ElseIf` clauses are both optional; you can have as many `ElseIf` statements as you want in an `If` block, but none can appear after the `Else` clause.

On Error

The `On Error` statement enables error-handling and allows execution to continue in the face of a run-time error. Its syntax follows:

```
On Error Resume Next
```

If you don't use an `On Error Resume Next` statement, any run-time error that occurs is fatal, meaning that an error message is displayed and execution stops.

Option Explicit

The Option Explicit statement is used to force the explicit declaration of all variables. Its syntax follows:

```
Option Explicit
```

If used, the Option Explicit statement must appear in a script before any procedures.

Randomize

The Randomize statement initializes the random-number generator with a number. Its syntax follows:

```
Randomize [Number]
```

Number—a numeric expression

The Randomize statement uses *Number* to initialize the random-number generator used by the Rnd function. *Number* is used as the seed value for the random-number generator. If *Number* is omitted, the current system time is used as the seed value.

ReDim

The ReDim statement is used to declare dynamic array variables and allocate or reallocate storage space. Its syntax follows:

```
ReDim [Preserve] VarName(Subscripts) [, VarName(Subscripts)]
```

VarName—name of the array variable

Subscripts—dimensions of the array

The Preserve keyword preserves the data in an array when the array is resized. If you use the Preserve keyword, you can resize only the last array dimension, and you can't change the number of dimensions at all.

Rem

The Rem statement is used to include explanatory remarks in a program. Its syntax follows:

```
Rem Comment
```

Optionally, you can use a single quote in place of the Rem statement, like this:

```
' Comment
```

Comment—comment text; a space is required after the Rem keyword before the comment

Select Case

The `Select Case` statement executes one of several groups of statements, depending on the value of an expression. Its syntax follows:

```
Select Case TestExpression
    [Case Expression0
        [Statements0]]
    [Case Else Expression1
        [ElseStatements1]]
End Select
```

TestExpression—any numeric or string expression

Expressions—delimited list of one or more expressions used to match *TestExpression*

Statements—one or more statements executed if *TestExpression* matches an *Expression*

ElseStatements—one or more statements executed if *TestExpression* doesn't match any of the *Expressions*

Set

The `Set` statement assigns an object reference to a variable or property. Its syntax follows:

```
Set ObjectVar = {ObjectExpression ¦ Nothing}
```

ObjectVar—name of the variable or property to set

ObjectExpression—an expression evaluating to an object

The `Nothing` keyword gets rid of the association between *ObjectVar* and the object it references, releasing all system and memory resources associated with the object if it has no other variable references.

Sub

The `Sub` statement declares the name, arguments, and code that form the body of a subroutine. Its syntax follows:

```
[Public ¦ Private] Sub Name [(ArgList)]
    [Statements]
    [Exit Sub]
    [Statements]
End Sub
```

Name—name of the subroutine

ArgList—list of variables representing arguments that are passed to the subroutine when it is called

Statements—any group of statements to be executed within the body of the subroutine

The Public keyword indicates that the subroutine is accessible to all other procedures in all scripts, while the Private keyword indicates that the subroutine is accessible only to other procedures in the script where it is declared. If Public or Private is not explicitly specified, subroutine defaults to being public.

The *ArgList* argument has the following syntax and parts:

```
[ByVal ¦ ByRef] VarName[( )]
```

VarName—name of the variable representing the argument

The ByVal keyword indicates that the argument is passed by value, while the ByRef keyword indicates that the argument is passed by reference.

The Exit Sub statement is used to exit the subroutine prematurely, transferring control to the statement immediately following the subroutine. Like functions, subroutines can take arguments, perform a series of statements, and change the values of its arguments. However, unlike functions, subroutines do not return any value, which means they can't be used as part of an expression. You can also call a subroutine using the Call statement.

While...Wend

The While...Wend statement executes a series of statements as long as a given condition is True. Its syntax follows:

```
While Condition
     [Statements]
Wend
```

Condition—numeric or string expression that evaluates to True or False

Statements—one or more statements executed while *Condition* is True

Intrinsic Functions

VBScript supports a surprising amount of intrinsic functions that provide a wide range of functionality. The next few sections cover each of these functions.

Abs()

The Abs() function returns the absolute value of a number, which is the number's unsigned magnitude. The syntax for the Abs() function follows:

```
Abs(Number)
```

Number—any valid numeric expression

Asc()

The Asc() function returns the ANSI character code corresponding to the first letter in a string. Its syntax follows:

Asc(*String*)

String—any valid string expression

Atn()

The Atn() function returns the arctangent of a number. Its syntax follows:

Atn(*Number*)

Number—any valid numeric expression

CBool()

The CBool() function converts an expression to a Variant of subtype Boolean. Its syntax follows:

CBool(*Expression*)

Expression—any valid expression

CByte()

The CByte() function converts an expression to a Variant of subtype Byte. Its syntax follows:

CByte(*Expression*)

Expression—any valid expression

CDate()

The CDate() function converts an expression to a Variant of subtype Date. Its syntax follows:

CDate(*Date*)

Date—any valid date expression

CDbl()

The CDbl() function converts an expression to a Variant of subtype Double. Its syntax follows:

CDbl(*Expression*)

Expression—any valid expression

Chr()

The Chr() function returns the character associated with the specified ANSI character code. Its syntax follows:

Chr(*CharCode*)

CharCode—a number identifying a character

CInt()

The CInt() function converts an expression to a Variant of subtype Integer. Its syntax follows:

CInt(*Expression*)

Expression—any valid expression

CLng()

The CLng() function converts an expression to a Variant of subtype Long. Its syntax follows:

CLng(*Expression*)

Expression—any valid expression

Cos()

The Cos() function returns the cosine of an angle. Its syntax follows:

Cos(*Number*)

Number—any valid numeric expression that expresses an angle in radians

CSng()

The CSng() function converts an expression to a Variant of subtype Single. Its syntax follows:

CSng(*Expression*)

Expression—any valid expression

CStr()

The CStr() function converts an expression to a Variant of subtype String. Its syntax follows:

CStr(*Expression*)

Expression—any valid expression

Date()

The Date() function returns the current system date. Its syntax follows:

Date

DateSerial()

The DateSerial() function returns a Variant of subtype Date for a specified year, month, and day. Its syntax follows:

DateSerial(*Year*, *Month*, *Day*)

Year—a numeric expression that evaluates to a number in the range 100 through 9999

Month—any numeric expression

Day—any numeric expression

DateValue()

The DateValue() function returns a Variant of subtype Date. Its syntax follows:

DateValue(*Date*)

Date—any expression (usually a string) representing a date from January 1, 100 through December 31, 9999

Day()

The Day() function returns a whole number in the range 1 through 31, representing the day of the month. Its syntax follows:

Day(*Date*)

Date—any expression that can represent a date

Exp()

The Exp() function returns the base of natural logarithms, e (approximately 2.718282), raised to a power. Its syntax follows:

Exp(*Number*)

Number—any valid numeric expression

> **NOTE**
>
> The Exp function is sometimes referred to as the antilogarithm function because it complements the Log function.

Fix()

The Fix() function returns the integer portion of a number; if the number is negative, Fix() returns the first negative integer greater than or equal to the number. The syntax for the Fix()function follows:

Fix(*Number*)

Number—any valid numeric expression

Hex()

The Hex() function returns a string representing the hexadecimal value of a number. Its syntax follows:

Hex(*Number*)

Number—any valid expression

If *Number* is not already a whole number, it is rounded to the nearest whole number before being evaluated.

> **NOTE**
>
> Hexadecimal numbers can be represented directly by preceding them with &H. For example, &H3F represents decimal 63 in hexadecimal notation.

Hour()

The Hour() function returns a whole number in the range 0 through 23, representing the hour of the day. Its syntax follows:

Hour(*Time*)

Time—any expression that can represent a time

InputBox()

The InputBox() function displays a text input box in a dialog box, waits for the user to input text, and returns the contents of the text input box. Its syntax follows:

InputBox(*Prompt*[, *Title*][, *Default*][, *XPos*][, *YPos*][, *HelpFile*, *Context*])

Prompt—string expression displayed as the prompt message in the dialog box

Title—string expression displayed in the title bar of the dialog box; if no title is specified, the application name is used

Default—string expression displayed in the text input box as the default response

XPos—numeric expression that specifies, in twips, the horizontal distance of the left edge of the dialog box from the left edge of the screen; if no distance is specified, the dialog box is horizontally centered

YPos—numeric expression that specifies, in twips, the vertical distance of the top edge of the dialog box from the top edge of the screen; if no distance is specified, the dialog box is vertically centered

HelpFile—string expression that identifies the Help file used to provide context-sensitive help for the dialog box

Context—numeric expression identifying the help context number used to reference a specific help topic

InStr()

The InStr() function returns the position of the first occurrence of one string within another. Its syntax follows:

```
InStr([Start, ]StringSearched, StringSought[, Compare])
```

Start—numeric expression that sets the starting position for each search; if the starting position isn't specified, the search begins at the first character position

StringSearched—string expression being searched

StringSought—string expression sought

Compare—specifies the type of string comparison (0 or 1); 0 (default) results in a binary comparison, while 1 results in a textual, case-insensitive comparison

Int()

The Int() function returns the integer portion of a number. If the number is negative, Int() returns the first negative integer less than or equal to the number. The syntax for Int() follows:

```
Int(Number)
```

Number—any valid numeric expression

IsArray()

The IsArray() function returns a Boolean value indicating whether a variable is an array. Its syntax follows:

```
IsArray(VarName)
```

VarName—any variable

IsDate()

The IsDate() function returns a Boolean value indicating whether an expression can be converted to a date. Its syntax follows:

IsDate(*Expression*)

Expression—any date or string expression recognizable as a date or time

IsEmpty()

The IsEmpty() function returns a Boolean value indicating whether a variable has been initialized. Its syntax follows:

IsEmpty(*Expression*)

Expression—any expression; usually a variable because expressions always result in a False result

IsNull()

The IsNull() function returns a Boolean value that indicates whether an expression contains no valid data. Its syntax follows:

IsNull(*Expression*)

Expression—any expression

IsNumeric()

The IsNumeric() function returns a Boolean value indicating whether an expression can be evaluated as a number. Its syntax follows:

IsNumeric(*Expression*)

Expression—any expression

IsObject()

The IsObject() function returns a Boolean value indicating whether an expression references a valid ActiveX object. Its syntax follows:

IsObject(*Expression*)

Expression—any expression

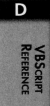

D

VBSCRIPT REFERENCE

LBound()

The LBound() function returns the lower bound for the specified dimension of an array. Its syntax follows:

LBound(*ArrayName*[, *Dimension*])

ArrayName—name of the array variable

Dimension—whole number indicating the dimension in which to find the lower bound; 1 (default) indicates the first dimension, 2 indicates the second dimension, and so on

> **NOTE**
>
> The default lower bound for a dimension is always 0.

LCase()

The LCase() function returns a string that has been converted to lowercase. Its syntax follows:

LCase(*String*)

String—any valid string expression

Left()

The Left() function returns a specified number of characters from the left side of a string. Its syntax follows:

Left(*String*, *Length*)

String—string expression from which the leftmost characters are returned

Length—numeric expression indicating how many characters to return

Len()

The Len() function returns the number of characters in a string or the number of bytes required to store a variable. Its syntax follows:

Len(*String* ¦ *VarName*)

String—any valid string expression

VarName—any valid variable name

Log()

The Log() function returns the natural logarithm of a number. Its syntax follows:

Log(*Number*)

Number—any valid numeric expression greater than zero

LTrim()

The LTrim() function returns a copy of a string with leading spaces trimmed away. Its syntax follows:

LTrim(*String*)

String—any valid string expression

Mid()

The Mid() function returns a specified number of characters from a string. Its syntax follows:

Mid(*String*, *Start*[, *Length*])

String—string expression from which characters are returned

Start—character position in the string where the characters to be returned begin

Length—number of characters to return

Minute()

The Minute() function returns a whole number in the range 0 through 59, representing the minute of the hour. Its syntax follows:

Minute(*Time*)

Time—any expression that can represent a time

Month()

The Month() function returns a whole number in the range 1 through 12, representing the month of the year. Its syntax follows:

Month(*Date*)

Date—any expression that can represent a date

MsgBox()

The MsgBox() function displays a message in a dialog box, waits for the user to press a button, and returns a value indicating which button the user pressed. Its syntax follows:

MsgBox(*Prompt*[, *Buttons*][, *Title*][, *HelpFile*, *Context*])

Prompt—string expression displayed as the message in the dialog box

Buttons—numeric expression that is the sum of values specifying the number and type of buttons to display, the icon style to use, the identity of the default button, and the modality of the dialog box; if omitted, the default value is 0

Title—string expression displayed in the title bar of the dialog box; if no title is specified, the application name is used

HelpFile—string expression that identifies the Help file used to provide context-sensitive help for the dialog box

Context—numeric expression identifying the help context number used to reference a specific help topic

Table D.3 shows the different possible constant values that can be specified in the *Buttons* argument.

Table D.3. Constant values used to specify the style of the dialog box displayed by the MsgBox() function.

Value	Description
0	Display OK button only
1	Display OK and Cancel buttons
2	Display Abort, Retry, and Ignore buttons
3	Display Yes, No, and Cancel buttons
4	Display Yes and No buttons
5	Display Retry and Cancel buttons
16	Display Critical Message icon
32	Display Warning Query icon
48	Display Warning Message icon
64	Display Information Message icon
0	First button is default
256	Second button is default
512	Third button is default
768	Fourth button is default
0	Application modal
4096	System modal

The first group of values (0–5) describes the number and type of buttons displayed in the dialog box, while the second group (16–64) describes the type of icon displayed. The third group of values (0–768) determines which button is the default, and the fourth group (0 and 4096) determines the modality of the message box. Exactly one number from each group can be used when specifying the style of the dialog box. The style is determined by simply adding the desired numbers from each group.

The `MsgBox()` function returns a value indicating the button that was pressed to exit the dialog box. Table D.4 lists these values and which buttons they represent.

Table D.4. Constant values returned by the `MsgBox()` function indicating which button was pressed.

Value	Button Pressed
1	OK
2	Cancel
3	Abort
4	Retry
5	Ignore
6	Yes
7	No

Now()

The `Now()` function returns the current date and time based on the system date and time. Its syntax follows:

`Now`

Oct()

The `Oct()` function returns a string representing the octal value of a number. Its syntax follows:

`Oct(Number)`

`Number`—any valid expression

Right()

The `Right()` function returns a specified number of characters from the right side of a string. Its syntax follows:

`Right(String, Length)`

`String`—string expression from which the rightmost characters are returned

`Length`—numeric expression indicating how many characters to return

Rnd()

The Rnd() function returns a random number greater than or equal to zero and less than one. Its syntax follows:

Rnd[(*Number*)]

Number—any valid numeric expression

The random number returned by Rnd() is generated based on the value of the *Number* argument. If *Number* is less than zero, Rnd() returns the same number every time, using *Number* as the seed. If *Number* is greater than zero or is not supplied, Rnd() returns the next random number in the sequence. Finally, if *Number* is equal to zero, Rnd() returns the most recently generated number.

RTrim()

The RTrim() function returns a copy of a string with trailing spaces trimmed away. Its syntax follows:

RTrim(*String*)

String—any valid string expression

Second()

The Second() function returns a whole number in the range 0 through 59, representing the second of the minute. Its syntax follows:

Second(*Time*)

Time—any expression that can represent a time

Sgn()

The Sgn() function returns an integer indicating the sign of a number. Its syntax follows:

Sgn(*Number*)

Number—any valid numeric expression

If *Number* is greater than zero, Sgn() returns 1. If *Number* is equal to zero, Sgn() returns 0. If *Number* is less than zero, Sgn() returns -1.

Sin()

The Sin( ) function returns the sine of an angle. Its syntax follows:

Sin(*Number*)

Number—any valid numeric expression that expresses an angle in radians

Space()

The Space() function returns a string consisting of the specified number of spaces. Its syntax follows:

Space(*Number*)

Number—the number of spaces to be included in the string

Sqr()

The Sqr() function returns the square root of a number. Its syntax follows:

Sqr(*Number*)

Number—any valid numeric expression greater than or equal to zero

StrComp()

The StrComp() function returns a value indicating the result of a string comparison. Its syntax follows:

StrComp(*String0*, *String1*[, *Compare*])

String0—any valid string expression

String1—any valid string expression

Compare—specifies the type of string comparison (0 or 1); 0 (default) results in a binary comparison, while 1 results in a textual, case-insensitive comparison

If *String0* is greater than *String1*, StrCmp() returns 1. If *String0* is equal to *String1*, StrCmp() returns 0. If *String0* is less than *String1*, StrCmp() returns -1.

String()

The String() function returns a string of the length specified containing a repeating character. Its syntax follows:

String(*Number*, *Character*)

Number—length of the string to be returned

Character—character code specifying the character or string expression whose first character is used to build the return string

Tan()

The Tan() function returns the tangent of an angle. Its syntax follows:

Tan(*Number*)

Number—any valid numeric expression that expresses an angle in radians

Time()

The `Time()` function returns a Variant of subtype `Date` indicating the current system time. Its syntax follows:

```
Time
```

TimeSerial()

The `TimeSerial()` function returns a Variant of subtype `Date` containing the time for a specific hour, minute, and second. Its syntax follows:

```
TimeSerial(Hour, Minute, Second)
```

Hour—number in the range 0 (12:00 A.M.) through 23 (11:00 P.M.), or a numeric expression

Minute—any numeric expression

Second—any numeric expression

TimeValue()

The `TimeValue()` function returns a Variant of subtype `Date` containing the time. Its syntax follows:

```
TimeValue(Time)
```

Time – any expression (usually a string) representing a time in the range 0:00:00 (12:00:00 A.M.) through 23:59:59 (11:59:59 P.M.)

Trim()

The `Trim()` function returns a copy of a string with leading and trailing spaces trimmed away. Its syntax follows:

```
Trim(String)
```

String—any valid string expression

UBound()

The `UBound()` function returns the upper bound for the specified dimension of an array. Its syntax follows:

```
UBound(ArrayName[, Dimension])
```

ArrayName—name of the array variable

Dimension—whole number indicating the dimension in which to find the upper bound; 1 (default) indicates the first dimension, 2 indicates the second dimension, and so on

UCase()

The UCase() function returns a string that has been converted to uppercase. Its syntax follows:

UCase(*String*)

String—any valid string expression

VarType()

The VarType() function returns a value indicating the subtype of a variable. Its syntax follows:

VarType(*VarName*)

VarName—any variable

Table D.5 lists the VarType() return values corresponding to the possible data subtypes.

Table D.5. Constant values returned by the VarType() function indicating data subtype of a given variable.

Value	Variable Subtype
0	Empty
1	Null
2	Integer
3	Long integer
4	Single-precision floating-point number
5	Double-precision floating-point number
6	Currency
7	Date
8	String
9	ActiveX object
10	Error
11	Boolean
12	Variant
13	Non-ActiveX object
17	Byte
8192	Array

D

VBSCRIPT REFERENCE

It is important to note that the value representing the array subtype (8192) is always returned summed with another subtype value. For example, the subtype value for an array of Booleans would be 8203 (8192 + 11).

Weekday()

The Weekday() function returns a whole number representing the day of the week. Its syntax follows:

Weekday(*Date*, [*FirstDayOfWeek*])

Date—any expression that can represent a date

FirstDayOfWeek—a value that specifies the first day of the week, where 1 indicates Sunday (default), 2 indicates Monday, and so on

Year()

The Year() function returns a whole number representing the year. Its syntax follows:

Year(*Date*)

Date—any expression that can represent a date

Active Server Pages Scripting Reference

by John West

IN THIS APPENDIX

APPENDIX

E

Active Server Pages allows components on the server to process data and create resulting HTML pages on the fly. In effect, it allows server-side applications to be run at the request of HTML clients. This appendix has been written to introduce you to the objects that come built into an Active server and provides sample scripting code on their use. It should be noted that the examples used here are in Visual Basic Scripting code, but that these objects can be used by any of the supported scripting codes of the Active Server Framework.

Object Reference

Objects are used in Active server application to perform designated functions within the application. The Active Server framework includes some very useful components which can be used to maximize the capabilities of your Active Server application.

The Active Server Pages framework provides five built-in objects:

- `Application`
- `Request`
- `Response`
- `Server`
- `Session`

The following information details the function of each of these objects and their associated methods.

The Application Object

The `Application` object is used to share information among all users of a single application. An example of a use for the `Application` object is the application that is used to show the number of people who have viewed a particular site.

Syntax:

`Application.method`

Methods:

- `Lock`—The `Lock` method basically prevents other clients from modifying the `Application` object. This is important to prevent erroneous data being entered while another user has the item open.
- `Unlock`—The Unlock method allows other clients to modify the Application object. It is usually called after the completion of a function that was modifying a locked object.

Example:

The following is an example of the `Application` object in use in an Active Server script:

```
Application.Lock
Application("NuVisits") = Application("NuVisits") + 1
Application.Unlock
 %>

This page has been visited
<%= Application("NuVisits") %> times!
```

The preceding example uses the application variable `NuVisits` to store the number of times a particular page has been accessed. The `Lock` method is called to make sure that only the current client can access or alter `NuVisits`. Calling the `Unlock` method then enables other users to access the `Application` object.

The Request Object

When clients contact an Active server via HTTP, they pass values to the server that include server and state information. The `Request` object allows an application to request that information and bring it into the application.

Syntax:

`Request[.Collection](variable)`

Where a collection can be one of the following:

- `ClientCertificate`
- `Cookies`
- `Form`
- `QueryString`
- `ServerVariables`

Collections

The details of collections and their use are explained in the sections that follow.

ClientCertificate

The `ClientCertificate` collection contains values passed to the server from the client about any of the security certificate values stored on the client.

Syntax:

`Request.ClientCertificate(Key[SubField])`

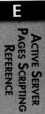

where *Key* can be one of the following values:

- `Subject`—A string that contains a list of subfield values that themselves contain information about the subject of the certificate. If this value is specified without a `SubField`, the `ClientCertificate` collection returns a comma-separated list of sub-fields. For example: `C=US`, `O=Msft`, and so on.

- `Issuer`—This is a string that contains information about the issuer of the certificate. If you do not specify a subfield, the `ClientCertificate` collection returns a comma-separated list of all available subfields.

- `ValidFrom`—This key specifies the beginning date that the certificate is valid from. For example: in the U.S.: 4/26/97 12:25:59 AM.

- `ValidUntil`—This key gives the date that the certificate expires.

- `SerialNumber`—This key contains the certificate's serial number. This number is stored in ASCII (Text) format and appears as shown in this example: 02-FE-E3-02.

- `Certificate`—This key contains the entire contents of the certificate and presents it in the ASN.1 format.

- `Flags`—A set of flags that provide additional client certificate information. The following flags may be set: `ceCertPresent`, `ceUnrecognizedIssuer`.

Example:

```
If Len(Request.ClientCertificate("Subject")) = 0 Response.Write("No client
certificate was presented")
End if
```

Cookies

The `Cookies` collection maintains any cookie information passed to the server from the client.

Syntax:

```
Request.Cookies(cookie)[(key)¦.attribute]
```

Example:

```
Here is the value of the cookie named myCookie:
<%= Request.Cookies("myCookie") %>
```

Form

The `Form` collection contains form values passed to the server from the client.

Syntax:

```
Request.Form(parameter)[(index)¦.Count]
```

parameter can equal any object that is storing a value.

index is an optional parameter that enables you to access one of the multiple values for a parameter.

Example:

Form Code:

```
<FORM ACTION = "/scripts/submit.asp" METHOD = "post">
<P>Your first name: <INPUT NAME = "firstname" SIZE = 48>
<P>What is your favorite color: <SELECT NAME = "color">
<OPTION>Orange
<OPTION>Red
<OPTION>Brown
<OPTION>Blue</SELECT>
<p><INPUT TYPE = SUBMIT>
</FORM>
```

From that form, the following is sent:

```
firstname=John&color=Blue
```

The following script can then be run to retrieve the information.

```
Welcome,  <%= Request.Form("firstname") %>.
Your favorite color is <%= Request.Form("color") %>.
```

QueryString

The `QueryString` collection returns the values of variables in the HTTP query string. This collection is useful for retrieving information that has been stored in an application and delivering that information to an Active Server Page (ASP).

Syntax:

```
Request.QueryString(variable)[(index)¦.Count]
```

Variable—The variable that contains the data you want to query.

Index—An optional parameter that is used to retrieve specific values from a multivalue variable.

Example:

The client request:

```
/scripts/directory-lookup.asp?name=John&number=26
```

results in this QUERY_STRING value:

```
name=John&number=26.
```

The `QueryString` collection would then contain two members, name and number. You could then use the following script:

```
Welcome,  <%= Request.QueryString("name") %>.
Your number is  <%= Request.QueryString("number") %>.
```

The output would be:

```
Hi, John. Your number is 26.
```

ServerVariables

The `ServerVariables` collection returns information concerning environment variables of the server.

Syntax:

`Request.ServerVariables (variable)`

Here is a description of the different variables and an explanation of their use:

- `AUTH_TYPE`—The authentication method that the server uses to validate users when they attempt to access a protected script.

- `CONTENT_LENGTH`—The length of the content as given by the client.

- `CONTENT_TYPE`—The data type of the content. Used with queries that have attached information, such as the HTTP queries `POST` and `PUT`.

- `GATEWAY_INTERFACE`—The revision of the CGI specification used by the server.

- `HTTP_<HeaderName>`—The value stored in the header *HeaderName*. Any header other than those listed in this table must be prefixed by `HTTP_` in order for the `ServerVariables` collection to retrieve its value.

- `LOGON_USER`—The Windows NT account that the user is logged into.

- `PATH_INFO`—Extra path information as given by the client. You can access scripts by using their virtual path and the `PATH_INFO` server variable. If this information comes from a URL, it is decoded by the server before it is passed to the CGI script.

- `PATH_TRANSLATED`—A translated version of `PATH_INFO` that takes the path and performs any necessary virtual-to-physical mapping.

- `QUERY_STRING`—Query information stored in the string following the question mark (?) in the HTTP request.

- `REMOTE_ADDR`—The IP address of the remote host making the request.

- `REMOTE_HOST`—The name of the host making the request. If the server does not have this information, it will set `REMOTE_ADDR` and leave this empty.

- `REQUEST_METHOD`—The method used to make the request. For HTTP, this is `GET`, `HEAD`, `POST`, and so on.

- `SCRIPT_NAME`—A virtual path to the script being executed. This is used for self-referencing URLs.

- `SERVER_NAME`—The server's host name, DNS alias, or IP address as it would appear in self-referencing URLs.

- `SERVER_PORT`—The port number to which the request was sent.

- `SERVER_PORT_SECURE`—A string that contains either 0 or 1. If the request is being handled on the secure port, then this will be 1. Otherwise, it will be 0.

- **SERVER_PROTOCOL**—The name and revision of the request information protocol. Format: protocol/revision
- **SERVER_SOFTWARE**—The name and version of the server software answering the request (and running the gateway). Format: name/version
- **URL**—Gives the base portion of the URL.

If a variable with the same name exists in more than one collection, the Request object returns the first instance that the object encounters.

Example:

The following ServerVariables collection example uses the Request object to display several server variables:

```
<HTML>
<!-- This example displays the content of several ServerVariables. -->
ALL_HTTP server variable =
<%= Request.ServerVariables("ALL_HTTP") %> <BR>
CONTENT_LENGTH server variable =
<%= Request.ServerVariables("CONTENT_LENGTH") %> <BR>
CONTENT_TYPE server variable =
<%= Request.ServerVariables("CONTENT_TYPE") %> <BR>
QUERY_STRING server variable =
<%= Request.ServerVariables("QUERY_STRING") %> <BR>
SERVER_SOFTWARE server variable =
<%= Request.ServerVariables("SERVER_SOFTWARE") %> <BR>
</HTML>
```

The next example uses the ServerVariables collection to insert the name of the server into a hyperlink.

```
<A HREF = "http://<%= Request.ServerVariables("SERVER_NAME") %>
/scripts/MyPage.asp">Link to MyPage.asp</A>
```

The Response Object

The Response object is used to send data to the client.

Syntax:

The syntax for the command is as follows:

```
Response.collection¦property¦method
```

Collection:

- **Cookies**—Specifies cookie values. Using this collection, you can set cookie values.

Properties:

- **Buffer**—Indicates whether page output is buffered.
- **ContentType**—Specifies the HTTP content type for the response.

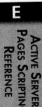

■ Expires—Specifies the length of time before a page cached on a browser expires.

■ ExpiresAbsolute—Specifies the date and time on which a page cached on a browser expires.

■ Status—The value of the status line returned by the server.

Methods:

■ AddHeader—Sets the HTML header name to value.

■ AppendToLog—Adds a string to the end of the Web server log entry for this request.

■ BinaryWrite—Writes the given information to the current HTTP output without any character-set conversion.

■ Clear—Erases any buffered HTML output.

■ End—Stops processing the .asp file and returns the current result.

■ Flush—Sends buffered output immediately.

■ Redirect—Sends a redirect message to the browser, causing it to attempt to connect to a different URL.

■ Write—Writes a variable to the current HTTP output as a string.

Example:

```
Response.Cookies("Type") = "Chocolate Chip"
Response.Cookies("Type").Expires = "July 31, 1997"
Response.Cookies("Type").Domain = "msn.com"
Response.Cookies("Type").Path = "/www/home/"
Response.Cookies("Type").Secure = FALSE
```

The Server Object

The Server object provides access to methods and properties on the server. Most of these methods and properties serve as utility functions.

Syntax:

```
Server.method
```

The following section documents the available methods.

Methods:

■ CreateObject—Creates an instance of a server component.

■ HTMLEncode—Applies HTML encoding to the specified string.

■ MapPath—Maps the specified virtual path, either the absolute path on the current server or the path relative to the current page, into a physical path.

■ URLEncode—Applies URL encoding rules, including escape characters, to the string.

Server Properties:

The Server object has the following property:

ScriptTimeout

The ScriptTimeout property specifies the maximum amount of time a script can run before it is terminated.

The time-out will not take effect while a server component is processing.

Syntax:

Server.ScriptTimeout = *NumSeconds*

Where *NumSeconds* specifies the maximum number of seconds that a script can run before the server terminates it. The default value is 90 seconds.

> **NOTE**
>
> Do not set the ScriptTimeout value to a value that is less than the value that is stored in the NT Registry. Doing so will not produce the desired effect. The values in the Registry will override your settings if they are less.

Example:

The following example causes scripts to time out if the server takes longer than 30 seconds to process them:

```
<% Server.ScriptTimeout = 30 %>
```

The following example retrieves the current value of the ScriptTimeout property and stores it in the variable TimeOut:

```
<% TimeOut = Server.ScriptTimeout %>
```

The Session Object

You can use the Session object to store information needed for a particular user-session. Variables stored in the Session object are not discarded when the user jumps between pages in the application; instead, these variables persist for the entire user-session.

The Web server automatically creates a Session object when a Web page from the application is requested by a user who does not already have a session. The server destroys the Session object when the session expires or is abandoned.

One common use for the Session object is to store user preferences set on a previous visit to the Web application, such as high, medium, or low graphics.

Note that the Session state is only maintained for browsers that support cookies.

Syntax:

Session.*property*¦*method*

Properties:

- SessionID—Returns the session identification for this user.
- Timeout—The time-out period for the Session state for this application, in minutes.

> **NOTE**
>
> You should not use the SessionID property to generate primary key values for a database application. This is because if the Web server is restarted, some SessionID values may be the same as those generated before the server was stopped. Instead, you should use an autoincrement column data type, such as IDENTITY with Microsoft SQL Server, or COUNTER with Microsoft Access.

Methods:

- The Session object has only one method: the Abandon method.
- Abandon—This method destroys a Session object and releases its resources.

Example:

```
<%
Session("name") = "MyName"
Session("year") = 96
Set Session("myObj") = Server.CreateObject("someObj")
```

Summary

You now have a good understanding of the objects included in Internet Information Server 3.0 and its active server content. The examples provided here should give you a good idea of what you can do to enhance your Active Server applications with this data. For more information on writing active server scripts, check out the Active Server Pages Resource Guide at http://aci.net/iasdocs/ASPDocs/guide/asgovr.htm.

SQL Reference

by John Jung

IN THIS APPENDIX

APPENDIX

F

SQL stands for Structured Query Language, and it is the basis for many DBMSs (Database Management Systems). It is an internationally recognized language for accessing database records. Its full and complete specifications are so detailed that they span more than 1,000 pages. Because of its size and complexity, I won't be covering all aspects of SQL. There are numerous books and computer classes that can offer a more complete picture of SQL. In addition, because of SQL's complexity, I'm not going to explain any of the terminology. Rather, you're going to learn about only the parts of SQL that pertain to this book. Specifically, this appendix is a reference for Chapter 34, "Web Databases with Access 97 and SQL Server." There are also two different, but similar, flavors of SQL: the ANSI version and the ISO version. This appendix uses the ISO version, which differs from the ANSI version only in some arguments.

Procedures

The first SQL concept that we'll talk about is the *procedure*. This concept is similar to what programmers are accustomed to using in other languages, with names such as functions, procedures, and methods. Procedures enable you to run subroutines within your main SQL code. Thus, if you run a certain set of commands regularly, you can simply make them into procedures.

Running Procedures

When a procedure call is invoked in SQL, all its activity is recorded. If there were no errors while the procedure was being called, all data it modified will be kept. However, all savepoints created during its execution will be discarded entirely. If there were any problems during the execution of the procedure, an exception is raised. When this occurs, the system tries to find its exception condition. If one exists, it will execute the condition. Otherwise, changes made to SQL data, or the schemas, are canceled. Additionally, this failure of execution for the procedure causes diagnostic information to be stored in the diagnostic area.

Syntax of Procedures

SQL procedures are created by using the following syntax:

```
AYSNC (number)SQL_executable_statement
```

where the parentheses and number are strictly optional. The string ASYNC is used to indicate that the procedure should be executed asynchronously. If the parentheses and number are used, the number specifies an asynchronous identifier. This number is used to determine the priority of asynchronous commands. Although you can mix asynchronous and synchronous procedures, the effect will be that they all are executed synchronously. Further, it's up to the DBMS to decide whether it wants to run the procedure asynchronously. If it chooses not to, it will raise an exception to the procedure. SQL_executable_statement can be an SQL schema statement, data statement, transaction statement, connection statement, session statement, or diagnostic statement.

Full SQL Compliance

Now that you know the general definition of an SQL procedure, you must know its limitations. The full SQL specifications call for a number of restrictions for SQL procedures. First is that ASYNC procedures are completely disallowed. Also, SQL schema, session, and transaction statements are restricted in their use. Only some of these statements can be used in a procedure.

Tables

SQL enables you to store your data in a wide variety of methods. The most commonly used one is that of the table. An SQL table, which can be any data type, is a collection of rows, which must be of the exact same data type. Rows are the single smallest elements that you can use with tables; you can only add individual rows or delete them. You cannot add or delete a single element within a row.

Using Tables

There are three different types of tables you can create: a set table, a multiset table, or a list table. A set table can't have any duplicate rows, whereas a list table must have some sort of ordering of the rows. The data type of the table must specify both the type of table it is and the row data type.

There are two different classifications of tables available: a base and derived. Permanent and temporary viewed tables, and a table that is not specified to be temporary, are considered base tables. A locally declared table is also a base table. On the other hand, a derived table is one that's derived from one or more other tables. An SQL query must be used in creating the derived table.

Syntax of Tables

The syntax for a table is somewhat complicated; it looks like the following:

```
table_name [ AS table_name (derived_column_list)] |
[ derived_name AS correlation_name (derived_column_list) ]
```

That is, the table_name must first be defined. Next, the table definition can be of one of three formats. The first is to have the string AS, followed by a table_name and the derived_column_list in parentheses. If you want to create a derived table, you must specify the derived_name, and then the AS and the derived_column_list in parentheses. It's also possible to create joined tables when creating tables. The syntax for that, however, is beyond the scope of this book.

Inserting Rows

After you have some tables created, you'll probably want to add elements into them. As you might recall, you can work with rows only when manipulating data in tables. As a result, you can insert only entire rows. This operation has an easy-to-understand syntax for its usage. To insert a row of data into a table, use the following example:

```
INSERT INTO { table_name ¦ CURSOR cursor_name }
➡[ (column_name) ] ¦ query ¦ default_values
```

You could specify the `table_name` string, which indicates the name of the table into which to insert the data. Or, if you've previously defined a cursor, you could specify the `cursor_name` after using the string `CURSOR`. After you've specified where you want to insert the data, you must specify *what* you want to insert. You can specify the names in a comma-separated string of names you want inserted. You can also create a new table row and specify that its contents be the values of those returned by the specified *query*. Finally, you can create a table row with a default set of values. These default values can be defined by specifying value expressions.

Deleting Rows

Obviously, you can't just keep piling up the data into your database. There'll come a time when you need to clear out that data. If you use tables to store your data, you can delete only entire rows. As a result, extreme caution must be used when deleting a row. You wouldn't want to accidentally delete some valuable data. The ability to delete a row uses the following syntax:

```
DELETE FROM table_name WHERE [ CURRENT OF cursor_name ¦ search_condition ]
```

where `table_name` is the name of the table from which you want to delete rows. You can either choose to delete rows from the specified `cursor_name` position, or you can have SQL execute the `search_condition` to find the row, or rows, to delete. If you choose to delete table rows from a `cursor_name`, you're executing a *positioned* delete. Otherwise, you're running a *searched* delete. Both are perfectly valid forms of deleting data with SQL.

Triggers

A trigger is a relatively new concept to the world of SQL. It allows commands to be executed before or after a particular table is accessed. This allows the database to perform such tasks as checking on the integrity of the data. Or, it could be used to ensure that there is no previously stored data that will be overridden.

Behavior of Triggers

Because triggers call other instructions, once they're activated, they may very well hit another trigger. Thus, multiple triggers can occur simply because one of them was accessed. Further, triggers are wholly dependent on the current cursor mode. If it's set to cascade off, the execution of the triggered commands will be deferred. They'll be deferred until the database is closed or the changes are committed. Otherwise, the trigger code will be executed dependent on the condition of the trigger.

Syntax of Triggers

The syntax of triggers is rather complex and involved, but they take this general form:

```
CREATE TRIGGER trigger_name [ BEFORE ¦ AFTER ] [ INSERT ¦ DELETE ¦ UPDATE
➥[ OF [ trigger_column_name ] ]> ON [ table name ] [ FOR EACH
➥[ ROW ¦ STATEMENT ] ] [ WHEN (search_condition) ] triggered_SQL_command
```

trigger_name is the name of the trigger you're creating. Triggers can occur before or after an INSERT, DELETE, or UPDATE of *table_name*. If an UPDATE is selected, the name of the column of the table that's being triggered can optionally be specified by *trigger_column_name*. Also, you can specify that the *triggered_SQL_command* be executed for every row or statement. Additionally, if you want to narrow the execution of a trigger, you can specify that when the *search_condition* is True, the *triggered_SQL_command* is executed. Finally, it's even possible to order, or even reference, a table for the *triggered_SQL_command* to use. Unfortunately, these topics are beyond the scope of this book.

Visual InterDev Design-Time ActiveX Control Reference

by Craig Eddy

APPENDIX G

IN THIS APPENDIX

This appendix covers the design-time controls that ship with Visual InterDev. These controls make the task of creating Active Server pages less tedious. They do so by inserting HTML and script code into your pages. The exact code that's inserted depends on how you set the various properties available for the controls. Essentially, the design-time controls are code generators. Because these controls are design-time only, they do not have methods or events like you would find in the typical ActiveX control.

The controls covered in this appendix are the Include, the Data Command, the Data Range Header, and the Data Range Footer controls. These are the controls that ship with Visual InterDev. Because Visual InterDev supports these ActiveX controls, you can develop a design-time control to be used with Visual InterDev. In the future you will more than likely be exposed to many design-time controls. Hopefully this appendix will give you the background to quickly utilize these new controls.

Using the Design-Time Controls

If you're familiar with Visual Basic, using the design-time controls is akin to using a custom control that has no runtime user interface or events associated with it. You can set the properties of these design-time controls within the Visual InterDev environment, but you cannot modify these properties using script code. To use the controls, you must have the Active Server Page on which the controls will be used open in InterDev's code editor window.

Inserting Design-Time Controls

To insert a design-time control, follow these steps:

1. If the Active Server Page that will use the control is not opened in the code editor, open it by double-clicking its name in the Workspaces pane.

2. Place the cursor at the spot in the page where the control will be inserted. The exact location varies depending on which control you're using.

3. Choose Insert | Into HTML | ActiveX Control from the menubar.

4. The Insert ActiveX Control dialog appears, as shown in Figure G.1. Click the Design-time tab.

5. Select the control you want to insert in the list of available controls. Click the OK button.

6. The control's builder window opens. Set the properties using the available properties sheets.

7. Close the builder window to return to the updated Active Server Page containing the code generated by the control.

FIGURE G.1.
The Insert ActiveX Control dialog.

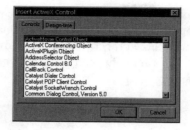

Editing Design-Time Controls

In general, you should not directly edit any of the HTML or script code inserted by a design-time control. This is the code that appears between the startspan and endspan comment tags. You should only edit the properties of the design-time control itself.

To edit the control's properties, follow these few steps:

1. If the Active Server Page that will use the control is not opened in the code editor, open it by double-clicking its name in the Workspaces pane.
2. Place the cursor anywhere between the control's startspan and endspan comment tags.
3. Right-click with the mouse and select Edit Design-time Control from the shortcut menu, or use the Edit | ActiveX Control in HTML menu from the main menubar.
4. The control's builder window opens. Edit the necessary properties using the available Properties sheets.
5. Close the builder window to return to the updated Active Server Page containing the code generated by the control.

The Include Control

The Include control is a handy way of adding #INCLUDE FILE or #INCLUDE VIRTUAL directives to the Active Server Page. Using the control, you can use a visual URL Builder dialog to easily construct the URL to be used with the #INCLUDE FILE or #INCLUDE VIRTUAL directive.

The #INCLUDE directives instruct the Web server to insert the specified file at that point in the output stream. These are also called *server-side includes*. This is useful for inserting common elements (such as copyright information) into multiple pages. Using these allows you to easily maintain these common elements since you only have to change a single file, not each file on which you've used the directives. The #INCLUDE directives are processed each time the script is requested.

The Include control has only one property, Source. When the control is inserted or edited, its Properties sheet appears as shown in Figure G.2. You can enter the URL to the file to be included directly in the Source property's text box. However, this would almost defeat the purpose of using the design-time control. Instead, click on the URL Builder button to display the Edit URL dialog shown in Figure G.3.

FIGURE G.2.

The Include control's Properties sheet.

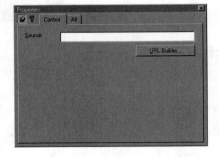

FIGURE G.3.

The Edit URL dialog.

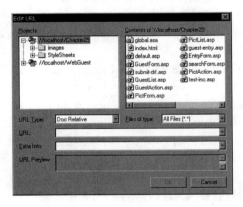

Using the Edit URL dialog, you can simply select the file you want to include from the Web of any project in the current workspace. Simply select the directory from the left pane and then the appropriate file from the right pane.

You can specify whether the #INCLUDE directive should be relative to the current script's path (select Doc Relative in the URL Type drop-down) or relative to the server's root directory (select Root Relative in the URL Type drop-down).

You can type a URL directly into the URL text box. You can append additional qualifiers to the URL using the Extra Info text box. A typical example is an HTML bookmark.

The URL Preview field at the bottom of the dialog is a read-only text box that displays the URL that will be inserted with the #INCLUDE directive.

> **NOTE**
>
> Because server-side includes are processed before the script code is processed, you cannot dynamically build the #INCLUDE directives using Active Server script.

> **WARNING**
>
> You can include another Active Server Page with the #INCLUDE directive. However, if this script page contains an #INCLUDE directive that includes the original page, an infinite loop would be created. The Active Server engine will detect such a condition, generate an error response, and halt the processing of the requested ASP file.

The Data Command Control

The Data Command control inserts script code into your Active Server Page that creates ActiveX Data Objects (ADO). The ADO objects created are a Connection object, a Command object, and a Recordset object. The properties of these objects are based on how you set the Data Command control's properties. For more information on using the Data Command control or the ADO objects, see Chapter 22, "Integrating ActiveX Database Components."

The properties sheet for the Data Command control is shown in Figure G.4. The following sections detail the properties of the Data Command control.

FIGURE G.4.

*The Data Command
control's Properties
sheet.*

The CacheSize Property

The CacheSize property determines how many records returned by the recordset are stored in the local memory versus at the provider. Setting this property can affect (positively or negatively) the performance of the recordset.

The default value is 10. This property is set on the Advanced tab of the control's properties sheet.

The CommandText Property

The CommandText property specifies the text of the command to be executed by the data connection specified by the Data Command control's DataConnection property. The CommandText property is linked to the CommandType property in that the CommandType specified determines what can reside in the CommandText property. You should always set the DataConnection and CommandType properties prior to setting the CommandText property.

Using the Data Command control's properties sheet, you can enter the text directly into the edit box. In addition, if you are using the SQL command type and have specified a data connection, you can use the SQL Builder button to launch the Query Designer discussed in Chapter 21, "Creating and Debugging Queries, Stored Procedures, and Triggers." If you have chosen View or Stored Procedure as the command type and the database referenced by the chosen data connection has such entities, the Command Text drop-down list will contain all the available stored procedures or views. You can choose from this list to specify the CommandText property.

The CommandTimeout Property

The CommandTimeout property specifies the amount of time, in seconds, that the ADO engine will give a command to complete its execution. The default is 30 seconds. Setting this property to 0 will cause the ADO engine to wait indefinitely for the command to finish processing.

Setting this property will set the CommandTimeout property of the Connection object that is created by the Data Command control. The Command object created will inherit this value from the Connection object.

The CommandType Property

The CommandType property specifies what is contained in the CommandText property. Setting this property allows the ADO engine to optimize the execution of the CommandText property and it changes the behavior of the properties sheet's Command Text edit box and SQL Builder button.

The values available are

- SQL—The CommandText property will be a SQL statement. You can enter the text of the statement directly in the edit box or you can use the SQL Builder button to invoke the Query Designer. This is the default value for this property.

- Stored Procedure—The `CommandText` property will specify a stored procedure available in the database. You can enter the name of the stored procedure directly in the edit box or you can select it from the drop-down list. If the stored procedure has a parameter list, the Parameters tab of the properties sheet is enabled. On this tab you will enter the information about the parameters.

- Table—The `CommandText` property specifies the name of a table in the database. You can enter the table name directly in the edit box or you can select it from the drop-down list.

- View—The `CommandText` property specifies the name of a view defined in the database. You can enter the table name directly in the edit box or you can select it from the drop-down list.

The CursorType Property

The `CursorType` property determines what type of cursor is created for the `Recordset` object that the Data Command control creates. The possible values for `CursorType` are

- Forward Only—Allows you to move through the recordset in the forward direction only. This type of cursor is ideal when you need to make a single pass through the records in the recordset. This is the default value for the `CursorType` property.

- Keyset—Similar to a dynamic cursor except that records added by other users are not visible to the recordset. Data changes to records in the recordset are visible, however, and records deleted by other users become inaccessible to the recordset. You can move in any direction through the recordset.

- Dynamic—Any modifications, additions, or deletions made by other users are visible in the recordset. Also, every form of record navigation is available. Bookmarks are only available if the OLE DB provider supports them. You can move in any direction through the recordset.

- Static—Produces a static copy of the recordset. No additions, deletions, or modifications are visible to the recordset. You can move in any direction through the recordset.

This property is set on the Advanced tab of the control's properties sheet.

The DataConnection Property

The `DataConnection` property specifies which of the project's available data connections will be used to execute the specified `CommandText` against. Select from the drop-down list. If nothing appears in the list, either there have been no data connections added to the project or the Active Server Page to which the Data Command control is being added has not yet been added to the project.

The ID Property

Specifies a valid, unique VBScript name for the control. The property will default to a unique value, but you can change this provided you follow the naming rules imposed by VBScript. These rules include

■ The ID must begin with a letter.

■ The ID cannot contain a period.

■ The ID must shorter than 255 characters.

■ The ID must be unique within the page on which it resides.

The LockType Property

The LockType property specifies the type of locking to be used when editing data with the Recordset object created by the Data Command control. Not all providers support all of the available lock types. The valid values are

■ Default—The lock type is determined by the ADO provider. This typically will be a read-only lock.

■ Read Only—The data returned by the Recordset object cannot be edited.

■ Pessimistic—The data provider will take drastic steps to ensure that the data is updated successfully. Typically this is done by locking the record at the data store as soon as editing begins. This could prevent other users from accessing the data.

■ Optimistic—The data provider will not lock the record until the actual update is initiated.

■ BatchOptimistic—Optimistic batch updates. This setting is required when you'll be using the batch update features of the ADO engine.

This property is set on the Advanced tab of the control's properties sheet.

The MaxRecords Property

The value for the MaxRecords property determines the maximum number of records that the data provider will return to the recordset. This is useful for providing a practical limit on the amount of data returned from the data store. The default value is 0, which specifies that all records should be returned.

This property is set on the Advanced tab of the control's properties sheet. Clear the All Records checkbox to set a value other than 0.

The Prepared Property

The Prepared property is a boolean (True/False) property that specifies whether the ADO provider should compile the query before it is executed. Not all ADO providers support this capability. The default value is False.

Visual InterDev Design-Time ActiveX Control Reference

APPENDIX G

1013

G

DESIGN-TIME
ACTIVEX CONTROL
REFERENCE

By setting the Prepared checkbox, you are setting the Prepared property to True. This will increase the amount of time it takes to execute the command the first time it is executed. However, subsequent executions will be faster since the provider will use the compiled version of the command.

This property is set on the Advanced tab of the control's properties sheet.

The Data Range Header Control

The Data Range controls insert script into your Active Server Pages that will do much of the grunt work necessary to output a recordset's data onto the Web page. There is a Data Range Header and a Data Range Footer control. The two controls work in tandem, but depending on how the data is to be displayed on the page, you can use the Data Range Header control by itself.

More information on the Data Range Header control can be found in Chapter 22.

The BarAlignment Property

The BarAlignment property determines how the navigation bar will be aligned on the HTML output page. The navigation bar only appears if record paging is being used (meaning that the PageSize property is set to a value other than 0) and a Data Range Footer control is added to the ASP file.

The navigation bar can be turned off in your script code by setting the variable fHideNavBar to True. This must be done with script code placed between the Header control's code and the Footer control's code.

The CacheRecordset Property

The CacheRecordset property is a boolean property that specifies whether or not the recordset's data is cached in a Session property. If your Web server's user load (that is, the number of concurrent users) is not an issue, enabling caching will improve the performance of the recordset. If load is an issue, you should disable caching and thus conserve server resources.

> **NOTE**
>
> Setting the CacheRecordset property to True requires that the cursor type be either Keyset or Static. If you attempt to enable caching without the proper cursor type setting, InterDev will display a message box and prevent you from enabling caching.

The CacheSize Property

The CacheSize property determines how many records returned by the recordset are stored in the local memory versus at the provider. Setting this property can affect (positively or negatively) the performance of the recordset.

The default value is 10. This property is set on the Advanced tab of the control's properties sheet.

The CommandText Property

The CommandText property specifies the text of the command to be executed by the data connection specified by the Data Range Header control's DataConnection property. The CommandText property is linked to the CommandType property in that the CommandType specified determines what can reside in the CommandText property. You should always set the DataConnection and CommandType properties prior to setting the CommandText property.

Using the Data Range Header control's properties sheet, you can enter the text directly into the edit box. In addition, if you are using the SQL command type and have specified a data connection, you can use the SQL Builder button to launch the Query Designer discussed in Chapter 21. If you have chosen View or Stored Procedure as the command type and the database referenced by the chosen data connection has such entities, the Command Text drop-down list will contain all of the available stored procedures or views. You can choose from this list to specify the CommandText property.

The CommandTimeout Property

The CommandTimeout property specifies the amount of time, in seconds, that the ADO engine will give a command to complete its execution. The default is 30 seconds. Setting this property to 0 will cause the ADO engine to wait indefinitely for the command to finish processing.

Setting this property will set the CommandTimeout property of the Connection object that is created by the Data Command control. The Command object created will inherit this value from the Connection object.

The CommandType Property

The CommandType property specifies what is contained in the CommandText property. Setting this property allows the ADO engine to optimize the execution of the CommandText property, and it changes the behavior of the properties sheet's Command Text edit box and SQL Builder button.

The values available are

■ SQL—The CommandText property will be an SQL statement. You can enter the text of the statement directly in the edit box or you can use the SQL Builder button to invoke the Query Designer. This is the default value for this property.

- Stored Procedure—The `CommandText` property will specify a stored procedure available in the database. You can enter the name of the stored procedure directly in the edit box or you can select it from the drop-down list. If the stored procedure has a parameter list, the Parameters tab of the properties sheet is enabled. On this tab you will enter the information about the parameters.

- Table—The `CommandText` property specifies the name of a table in the database. You can enter the table name directly in the edit box or you can select it from the drop-down list.

- View—The `CommandText` property specifies the name of a view defined in the database. You can enter the table name directly in the edit box or you can select it from the drop-down list.

The `CursorType` Property

The `CursorType` property determines what type of cursor is created for the `Recordset` object that the Data Command control creates. The possible values for `CursorType` are

- Forward Only—Allows you to move through the recordset in the forward direction only. This type of cursor is ideal when you need to make a single pass through the records in the recordset. This is the default value for the `CursorType` property.

- Keyset—Similar to a dynamic cursor except that records added by other users are not visible to the recordset. Data changes to records in the recordset are visible, however, and records deleted by other users become inaccessible to the recordset. You can move in any direction through the recordset.

- Dynamic—Any modifications, additions, or deletions made by other users are visible in the recordset. Also, every form of record navigation is available. Bookmarks are only available if the OLE DB provider supports them. You can move in any direction through the recordset.

- Static—Produces a static copy of the recordset. No additions, deletions, or modifications are visible to the recordset. You can move in any direction through the recordset.

This property is set on the Advanced tab of the control's properties sheet.

The `DataConnection` Property

The `DataConnection` property specifies which of the project's available data connections will be used to execute the specified `CommandText` against. Select from the drop-down list. If nothing appears in the list, either there have been no data connections added to the project or the Active Server Page to which the Data Command control is being added has not yet been added to the project.

The ID Property

The ID property specifies a valid, unique VBScript name for the control. The property will default to a unique value, but you can change this provided you follow the naming rules imposed by VBScript. These rules include

- The ID must begin with a letter.
- The ID cannot contain a period.
- The ID must be shorter than 255 characters.
- The ID must be unique within the page on which it resides.

The LockType Property

This property specifies the type of locking to be used when editing data with the Recordset object created by the Data Range Header control. Not all providers support all the available lock types. The valid values are

- Default—The lock type is determined by the ADO provider. This typically will be a read-only lock.
- Read Only—The data returned by the Recordset object cannot be edited.
- Pessimistic—The data provider will take drastic steps to ensure that the data is updated successfully. Typically this is done by locking the record at the data store as soon as editing begins. This could prevent other users from accessing the data.
- Optimistic—The data provider will not lock the record until the actual update is initiated.
- Batch Optimistic—Optimistic batch updates. This setting is required when you'll be using the batch update features of the ADO engine.

This property is set on the Advanced tab of the control's properties sheet.

The MaxRecords Property

The value for this property determines the maximum number of records that the data provider will return to the recordset. This is useful for providing a practical limit on the amount of data returned from the data store. The default value is 0, which specifies that all records should be returned.

This property is set on the Advanced tab of the control's properties sheet. Clear the All Records checkbox to set a value other than 0.

The PageSize Property

The PageSize property sets the number of records which will appear on each page of the Data Range output. If you set this property to a value other than its default of 0, you should also insert a Data Range Footer control to provide the navigation bar and the recordset scrolling and navigation code. If this property is set to 0, the navigation bar will not be displayed and all of the recordset's data will be output to a single page.

If the recordset could return a large number of records, you can improve your application's performance by using record paging. This will produce smaller pages that return to the user much faster.

To set this property, check the Record Paging checkbox and enter a value for the page size. The default page size when record paging is enabled is 10.

> **NOTE**
>
> Using record paging requires that the cursor type be either Keyset or Static. If you attempt to enable paging without the proper cursor type setting, InterDev will display a message box and prevent you from performing the action.

The Prepared Property

This is a boolean (True/False) property that specifies whether or not the ADO provider should compile the query before it is executed. Not all ADO providers support this capability. The default value is False.

By setting the Prepared checkbox, you are setting the Prepared property to True. This will increase the amount of time it takes to execute the command the first time it is executed. However, subsequent executions will be faster since the provider will use the compiled version of the command.

This property is set on the Advanced tab of the control's properties sheet.

The RangeType Property

The setting for this property affects both what the Copy Fields dialog copies to the clipboard and the code that will be output by the Data Range Footer control. The possible settings are

- Text (default)—Causes the Copy Field dialog to copy script code such as
  `<%= DataRangeHdr1("Address1") %><br>` to the clipboard.

- Form—Causes the Copy Field dialog to copy script code such as `<INPUT TYPE="Text" SIZE=25 MAXLENGTH=50 NAME=Address1 VALUE="<%= DataRangeHdr1("Address1") %>"> <br>` to the clipboard. The value used in the MAXLENGTH element is derived from the size of the field in the database.

- Table—Causes the Copy Field dialog to copy script code such as
  `<%= DataRangeHdr1("Address1") %><br>` to the clipboard. Also instructs the Data Range Footer control to output a `</TABLE>` tag to the script. This forces the navigation bar to display below the table in the output page.

The Data Range Footer Control

If you are using paging to display the records in your recordset, you must insert a Data Range Footer control into your script. The only property that's useful on the designer window for this control is the ID property. The script code generated utilizes the values of the variables created by the Data Range Header control. The Data Range Header control is where your data range's properties should be defined.

You can customize the look of the Data Range Footer control's output by changing the values of several boolean variables created by the Data Range Header control. These variables must be modified in script code that appears between the Data Range Header and the Data Range Footer controls. The variables you can modify are

- fHideRule—Determines whether or not a horizontal rule is displayed above the navigation bar's buttons.
- fHideNavBar—Determines whether or not the navigation bar is displayed.
- fHideNumber—Determines whether or not the page number is displayed on the output page.
- fHideRequery—Determines whether or not the Requery button will be displayed.

You can also change the value of the query string passed in the URL when the paging buttons are clicked. To do so, modify the value of the stQueryString variable. Be sure to include the leading ? as the value of stQueryString will simply be appended to the URL for the Active Server Page that contains the Data Range controls.

More information on the Data Range Header control can be found in Chapter 22.

COM Reference

by Michael Morrison

IN THIS APPENDIX

Practically all the technology used in Visual InterDev is dependent on COM, which stands for Component Object Model. COM was originally developed by Microsoft as a binary standard for software components, but has since been handed over to a standards body for public review. In short, COM is an object-oriented, platform-independent, distributed system for creating binary software components. More important to Visual InterDev, COM forms the foundation for Microsoft's ActiveX component technology. This appendix explores COM by taking a look at what it accomplishes, how it works, and where it fits in with other technologies.

The Origins of COM

Long before ActiveX meant anything, some insightful software engineers at Microsoft had an idea about developing a language-independent standard for distributed software objects. They called the specification COM and designed it as a binary standard for determining how software objects interact with each other and as a programming model that effectively hides an object's inner workings. They made sure that COM accomplished its goals in a language-independent manner, meaning that COM objects can be developed using a variety of different programming languages.

At first glance, COM might not seem like a big deal; it's such a low-level technology that it's hard to see the practicality of it. However, consider the effect of designing all the software objects in a system to support the COM standard. Because the objects all understand how to communicate with each other, they can easily be integrated together. This creates some very powerful opportunities. Even though object communication within a system is powerful in itself, COM goes much further; COM defines a standard for objects to communicate with each other in any environment, including distributed networks.

At the center of COM is the concept of a *software component*, which is a reusable piece of software in binary form that can be easily integrated with other components with relatively little effort. Additionally, software components can be mixed and matched with components from different vendors without worrying about whether their respective APIs will work together; if they support COM, they will work together. For example, a spell checking component from one vendor could be used with a thesaurus component made by a different vendor, both within the same word processing application. As simple and logical as this example is, it has been extremely difficult realizing this type of scenario in the realm of computer software. COM is a major step forward for ushering in a new way of developing and integrating software.

Understanding COM

To fully understand COM as a software component technology, you need to take a few steps back and understand exactly what COM aims to accomplish. Being an object model, COM is completely based on the concept of an object. There probably isn't a more overused or abused word in the programming world, so let's start by posing the question, "What is an object?" Ask a dozen people in the programming community and chances are you will get a dozen different answers. Although a concise definition of an object is sometimes elusive even to experienced programmers, for the purposes of COM it is quite clear: at the bare minimum, an object is a set of related data plus a set of functions that act on this data. In most object-oriented programming languages these functions are commonly referred to as *member functions* or *methods*. The functions are called member functions because programmers, at least conceptually, often think of them as members of the object upon which they are acting.

COM is a specification defining how objects interact with one another. It describes how member functions are laid out in memory and how they're called, along with describing a standard set of member functions that all objects support. To fully grasp COM, it is important to understand that it is not an object-oriented language or programming API, but a standard. In fulfilling its role as a component object standard, COM does nothing to specify the structure of applications reliant on COM objects. What COM does do is specify a programming model that enables COM objects to interact with other objects, including applications. The physical location of these objects is irrelevant; they can exist within a single process, in separate processes on a single machine, and even on different machines entirely. The internal structure of the objects can be completely different provided they both fully support COM. The point is that COM provides a means of creating and deploying fully reusable software objects.

The following list summarizes the primary goals, and in turn, the benefits of COM as a software component model:

- COM is an all-purpose component object model that supports reusable objects.
- COM defines the binary structure and communication protocol for component objects.
- COM is a true system object model in that it addresses the many problems inherent in object-based systems.
- COM supports distributed objects.

Take a closer look at each of these aspects of COM. First, how does COM support reusable objects? COM's formal specification of how objects are structured is primarily what allows them to be reused. In other words, COM provides programmers a means of structuring their objects in such a way so that applications can fully ascertain and make use of the functionality provided by the object. This idea is closely linked with the concept of *encapsulation*, which is an object-oriented term referring to the hiding of an object's internal implementation. By hiding the internal details of an object from its clients, the clients are forced to use the object in a uniform fashion, thereby making the object more reusable.

Unlike traditional object-oriented programming languages, COM defines a completely standardized mechanism for creating objects, as well as outlining the communication protocol between clients and objects. These standardized mechanisms are independent of the programming languages used to create the objects, not to mention the applications the objects are being used with. In defining such a mechanism, COM introduces a binary interoperability standard rather than a language-based interoperability standard on any given hardware platform.

This is critical because it alleviates the need for COM objects to be developed in a common programming language.

A true system object model is one that allows a distributed, ever evolving system to support a vast number of interrelated objects without the risk of failure. COM is a true system object model because it meets this requirement. More specifically, COM solves the many problems inherent in a complex system through a variety of different facilities, some of which follow:

■ COM uses globally unique *object identifiers* to identify object classes and the interfaces they support.

■ COM presents a single programming model for object communication regardless of whether it is being performed locally or remotely.

■ COM keeps a close watch on the lifecycle of objects.

■ COM provides a solid, extensible foundation for security at the object level.

COM supports distributed objects by allowing programmers to construct an application as a group of different component objects, each of which can be located on a different computer. Through network transparency, COM allows the various distributed application components to appear to be located on the same machine. In other words, an entire network appears to be one large computer with enormous processing power and capacity.

COM Interfaces

A COM object is wholly defined by its interface. A COM *interface* refers to a group of logically similar member functions that can act on a COM object. Unlike C++ and Java objects, which can expose both data and interface, COM objects have no facility to allow visibility to anything but an interface. In fact, it is impossible to get a pointer to a COM object, like in C++; you must always interact with a COM object through a pointer to an interface of the object. You might have noticed the mention of *an* interface rather than *the* interface. This is because COM objects can and almost always do have multiple interfaces. These interfaces are independent of each other and provide different types of access to the object, depending on how the object and interfaces are implemented.

> **NOTE**
>
> COM interfaces are actually very similar to Java interfaces, because they describe the functionality provided by an object without actually having anything to do with the specific implementation of the functionality.

After an interface is established for a COM object, it cannot be changed—ever. This is a fundamental tenet of COM that must always be observed. To add additional functionality to an existing COM object, you must always create a new interface for the object. This restriction is what provides the seamless upgradability of COM objects, since old interfaces are always preserved. In this way, you are guaranteed that applications dependent on a COM object will always work with newer versions of the object.

The COM interface takes the form of a table of virtual function pointers, a *v-table*, which is very similar to the virtual function table found in C++ objects. Also similar to a C++ object is the COM object's logical representation, shown in Figure H.1. Actually, this representation applies to practically any object-oriented programming language, including C++ and Java. The most important distinction between the COM approach and that of object-oriented programming languages is that COM only allows access to an object through its interface by way of the v-table.

FIGURE H.1.

The logical representation of a COM object.

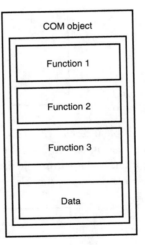

To work with a COM object, you must obtain an interface pointer, or v-table pointer, to the object. One of the extremely powerful features of COM is how it enables you to query an object regarding its functionality at runtime. An application can query a COM object at runtime to find out what capabilities it has via its available interfaces. Depending on the version of the object and the system configuration, the application may be able to engage more advanced features on different systems. The key to this feature is the interface, which you undoubtedly are starting to realize is the key to COM as a whole.

Let's look at an example of a COM object with multiple interfaces. Figure H.2 shows a COM object with three interfaces. You know these interfaces are really just tables of function pointers, so by getting a pointer to an interface, you are really just getting a pointer to a table of function pointers. This effectively gives you access to a set of functions, or methods in object-oriented terms, to act on the COM object. Different sets of methods correspond to different interfaces. When working with a COM object with multiple interfaces, you must always commit to an interface because the interface is the only communication medium you have to the COM object. After selecting an interface, you can call only methods defined in that interface. In Figure H.2, Interface B is being accessed by the object user. In this example, Interfaces A and C are unused, and the functionality they provide is unused as well.

FIGURE H.2.

Accessing a single interface of a COM object.

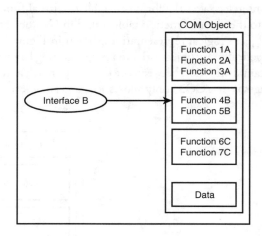

It is possible to have multiple interface pointers to the same COM object, as shown in Figure H.3. Here, the user is accessing two interfaces on the same object. The object vendor could later implement more interfaces for this object, and the user could query for their existence and access them as needed.

FIGURE H.3.

Accessing multiple interfaces of a COM object.

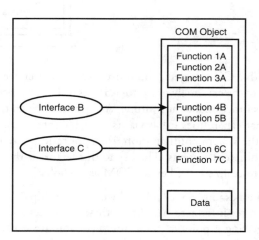

COM, OLE, and ActiveX

Although COM is a very useful technology in and of itself, its real significance in terms of Visual InterDev is how it relates to ActiveX. To understand the relationship between COM and ActiveX, you have to go back a few years to the days of OLE, the predecessor to ActiveX. OLE, which stands for Object Linking and Embedding, was originally designed to provide a more document-centric architecture for Windows. However, as the need for a more complete object model arose, OLE evolved into a rich set of object-oriented system interfaces and services forming a standard framework for building reusable, integrated software components. Sounds pretty familiar, right?

It should come as no surprise that OLE is built on top of COM; it is an open, extensible architecture built on the foundation of COM. OLE and COM are so intertwined that they were often used interchangeably when discussing component software technology. In fact, because OLE is based on the underlying object architecture of COM, it forms the basis of the strategic evolution of the Windows operating system family into fully object-based operating systems. Every feature of OLE depends on COM to provide the basic inter-object communication. In other words, COM provides the "plumbing and wiring" of OLE.

The OLE technology provides a wide range of services, including application automation, re-usable components, version management, standardized drag-and-drop, documents, object linking and embedding, and visual object editing. These services have shared great success and account for much of the power and ease of use evident in the Windows operating systems and applications.

That's all fine and well, but isn't OLE a thing of the past? The answer is yes and no. OLE as an industry buzzword is certainly a thing of the past, but OLE lives on in ActiveX. ActiveX came to be when Microsoft turned its attention to the Internet and began thinking about a software technology geared toward the needs of the online world. Because Microsoft had put so much into OLE, it was already a very stable and powerful technology with a broad range of industry support, at least on the Windows platform. Therefore, Microsoft decided to figure out a way to extend and rework OLE to better support the Internet. The new improved OLE for the Internet was named ActiveX. ActiveX builds on the success of OLE, and takes it to a new level by giving it the capability to thrive in the online world of the Internet. And COM is still at its heart just as it is in OLE.

Distributed COM

Although COM is certainly a sound technology at its core and a good basis for ActiveX, Microsoft realized that it still lacked some of the support necessary for the widely distributed type of computing presented by the Internet. Sure, COM provides the necessary extensibility for distributed computing, but it doesn't do much in the way of providing specific distributed communication mechanisms. Rather than add lots of overhead to COM itself, Microsoft opted to deal with the distributed computing issue by developing a complementary standard for COM known as DCOM (Distributed COM). DCOM picks up where COM leaves off by focusing on the communication protocols between distributed objects. Where COM fleshes out the low-level physical issues for distributed binary objects themselves, DCOM addresses the communication protocols necessary to transfer information between these objects.

Like COM, DCOM is also designed as a component of the ActiveX technology. The difference is that DCOM addresses the application-level issue of handling remote communication between objects, whereas COM specifies the handling of local communication and the binary makeup of objects. The goal of DCOM is to provide a reliable, secure, and efficient means for software components to communicate in a distributed environment such as the Internet. DCOM is implemented as a generic protocol layered on the DCE (Distributed Computing Environment) RPC (Remote Procedure Call) specification. Because of its relationship to the RPC specification, DCOM is sometimes also referred to as Object RPC, or ORPC.

What's On the CD-ROM

by Bob Correll

IN THIS APPENDIX

■ About the Software   1028

On the *Microsoft Visual InterDev Unleashed* CD-ROM you will find the sample files that have been presented in this book, along with a wealth of other applications and utilities.

Microsoft Products

- Microsoft Visual J++ 1.1, Trial Edition
- Microsoft Visual Basic, Control Creation Edition
- Microsoft Internet Information Server 3.0
- Microsoft Internet Explorer 3
- Microsoft ActiveX Control Pad and HTML Layout Control

Electronic Books

- *World Wide Web Database Developer's Guide with Visual Basic 5*
- *Laura Lemay's Web Workshop: FrontPage 97*

HTML Tools

- Hot Dog 32-bit HTML editor demo
- HoTMetaL HTML editor demo
- Spider 1.2 demo
- Web Analyzer demo

Graphics, Video, and Sound Applications

- Paint Shop Pro
- SnagIt screen-capture utility
- ThumbsPlus image viewer and browser

Utilities

- Adobe Acrobat viewer
- WinZip for Windows NT/95
- WinZip Self-Extractor

About the Software

Some of the software on this CD-ROM is shareware. Shareware is not free. Please read all documentation associated with a third-party product (usually contained with files named `readme.txt` or `license.txt`) and follow all guidelines.

I
INDEX

W

Laura Lemay's Web Workshop: Advanced FrontPage 97

—Denise Tyler

As the follow-up to the national best-selling title *Laura Lemay's Web Workshop: Microsoft FrontPage 97*, this clear, hands-on guide shows users how to create and maintain Web sites with this powerful tool and successfully use Microsoft's Image Composer.

Organized into small, task-oriented chapters with real-world examples.

CD-ROM, designed to be an interactive workshop, includes Microsoft Visual J++ 1.1 Trial Edition and Microsoft Visual Basic Control Creation, as well as other tools, software, and the author's examples from the book.

Covers Microsoft FrontPage 97.

Price: $39.99 USA/$56.95 CAN   *User Level: Accomplished—Expert*
ISBN: 1-57521-308-7   *700 pages*

Visual C++ 5 Unleashed, Second Edition

—Viktor Toth

This is the perfect book for advanced Visual C++ programmers. Its nearly 1,100 pages explore the most advanced topics, while its enclosed CD-ROM allows the user to quickly learn by working through the programs in the book. It not only covers Visual C++ 5 and its capabilities, but also teaches LAN programming, OLE, DLLs, OLE Automation, and how to update old programs to the new version of Visual C++.

Provides extensive information on such advanced topics as I/O timers, LAN programming, and Windows 95. CD-ROM contains source code and illustrative programs from the book.

Covers Visual C++ 5.

Price: $49.99 USA/$70.95 CAN   *User Level: Accomplished—Expert*
ISBN: 0-672-31013-9   *1,069 pages*

Teach Yourself ActiveX Control Programming with Visual Basic 5 in 21 Days

—Keith Brophy & Tim Koets

Visual Basic is a programming language that lets users add interactivity and multimedia to their Web sites by working with Microsoft's ActiveX technologies. This book shows users how to maximize Visual Basic to create ActiveX applications that can be used with Microsoft's Internet Explorer Web browser.

CD-ROM contains all the source code from the book, powerful utilities, and third-party software.

Covers Visual Basic and ActiveX.

Price: $39.99 USA/$56.95 CAN *User Level: Casual—Expert*
ISBN: 1-57521-245-5 *600 pages*

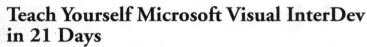

Teach Yourself Microsoft Visual InterDev in 21 Days

—L. Michael Van Hoozer

Using the familiar, day-by-day format of the best-selling *Teach Yourself* series, this easy-to-follow tutorial will provide users with a solid understanding of Visual InterDev, Microsoft's new Web application development environment. In no time, they will learn how to perform a variety of tasks, including front-end scripting, database and query design, content creation, server-side scripting, and more.

Shows how Active Desktop features such as HTML, Java, JScript, VBScript, and ActiveX enable developers to build Web applications on intranets and the Internet.

CD-ROM contains Internet Explorer 3.0, Microsoft ActiveX and HTML development tools, plus additional ready-to-use templates, graphics, scripts, Java applets, and ActiveX controls.

Covers Microsoft Visual InterDev.

Price: $39.99 USA/$56.95 CAN *Casual—Accomplished*
ISBN: 1-57521-093-2 *816 pages*

Add to Your Sams.net Library Today
with the Best Books for Internet Technologies

ISBN	Quantity	Description of Item	Unit Cost	Total Cost
1-57521-308-7		Laura Lemay's Web Workshop: Advanced FrontPage 97	$39.99	
0-672-31013-9		Visual C++ 5 Unleashed, Second Edition	$49.99	
1-57521-245-5		Teach Yourself ActiveX Control Programming with Visual Basic 5 in 21 Days	$39.99	
1-57521-093-2		Teach Yourself Visual InterDev in 21 Days	$39.99	
		Shipping and Handling: See information below.		
		TOTAL		

Shipping and Handling: $4.00 for the first book, and $1.75 for each additional book. If you need to have it NOW, we can ship product to you in 24 hours for an additional charge of approximately $18.00, and you will receive your item overnight or in two days. Overseas shipping and handling adds $2.00. Prices subject to change. Call between 9:00 a.m. and 5:00 p.m. EST for availability and pricing information on latest editions.

201 W. 103rd Street, Indianapolis, Indiana 46290

1-800-428-5331 — Orders   1-800-835-3202 — FAX   1-800-858-7674 — Customer Service

Book ISBN 1-57521-285-4

MACMILLAN COMPUTER PUBLISHING USA

A VIACOM COMPANY

Technical ---- Support:

If you need assistance with the information in this book or with a CD/Disk accompanying the book, please access the Knowledge Base on our Web site at **http://www.superlibrary.com/general/support**. Our most Frequently Asked Questions are answered there. If you do not find the answer to your questions on our Web site, you may contact Macmillan Technical Support **(317) 581-3833** or e-mail us at **support@mcp.com**.

Installing the
CD-ROM

The companion CD-ROM contains all the source code and project files developed by the authors, as well as an assortment of evaluation versions of third-party products. To install the software, please follow these steps:

Windows 95/NT 4 Installation Instructions

1. Insert the CD-ROM into your CD-ROM drive.
2. From the Windows 95/NT 4 desktop, double-click the My Computer icon.
3. Double-click the icon representing your CD-ROM drive.
4. Double-click the icon titled setup.exe, which will start the CD-ROM installation program.

Should you have any questions concerning this EULA, or if you desire to contact Microsoft for any reason, please contact the Microsoft subsidiary serving your country, or write: Microsoft Sales Information Center/One Microsoft Way/Redmond, WA 98052-6399.

LIMITED WARRANTY

NO WARRANTIES. Microsoft expressly disclaims any warranty for the SOFTWARE PRODUCT. The SOFTWARE PRODUCT and any related documentation is provided "as is" without warranty of any kind, either express or implied, including, without limitation, the implied warranties or merchantability, fitness for a particular purpose, or noninfringement. The entire risk arising out of use or performance of the SOFTWARE PRODUCT remains with you.

NO LIABILITY FOR DAMAGES. In no event shall Microsoft or its suppliers be liable for any damages whatsoever (including, without limitation, damages for loss of business profits, business interruption, loss of business information, or any other pecuniary loss) arising out of the use of or inability to use this Microsoft product, even if Microsoft has been advised of the possibility of such damages. Because some states/jurisdictions do not allow the exclusion or limitation of liability for consequential or incidental damages, the above limitation may not apply to you.

owned by Microsoft or its suppliers. The SOFTWARE PRODUCT is protected by copyright laws and international treaty provisions. Therefore, you must treat the SOFTWARE PRODUCT like any other copyrighted material except that you may install the SOFTWARE PRODUCT on a single computer provided you keep the original solely for backup or archival purposes. You may not copy the printed materials accompanying the SOFTWARE PRODUCT.

5. DUAL-MEDIA SOFTWARE. You may receive the SOFTWARE PRODUCT in more than one medium. Regardless of the type or size of medium you receive, you may use only one medium that is appropriate for your single computer. You may not use or install the other medium on another computer. You may not loan, rent, lease, or otherwise transfer the other medium to another user, except as part of the permanent transfer (as provided above) of the SOFTWARE PRODUCT.

6. U.S. GOVERNMENT RESTRICTED RIGHTS. The SOFTWARE PRODUCT and documentation are provided with RESTRICTED RIGHTS. Use, duplication, or disclosure by the Government is subject to restrictions as set forth in subparagraph (c)(1)(ii) of the Rights in Technical Data and Computer Software clause at DFARS 252.227-7013 or subparagraphs (c)(1) and (2) of the Commercial Computer Software—Restricted Rights at 48 CFR 52.227-19, as applicable. Manufacturer is Microsoft Corporation/One Microsoft Way/Redmond, WA 98052-6399.

7. EXPORT RESTRICTIONS. You agree that neither you nor your customers intend to or will, directly or indirectly, export or transmit (i) the SOFTWARE or related documentation and technical data or (ii) your software product as described in Section 1(b) of this License (or any part thereof), or process, or service that is the direct product of the SOFTWARE, to any country to which such export or transmission is restricted by any applicable U.S. regulation or statute, without the prior written consent, if required, of the Bureau of Export Administration of the U.S. Department of Commerce, or such other governmental entity as may have jurisdiction over such export or transmission.

MISCELLANEOUS

If you acquired this product in the United States, this EULA is governed by the laws of the State of Washington.

If you acquired this product in Canada, this EULA is governed by the laws of the Province of Ontario, Canada. Each of the parties hereto irrevocably attorns to the jurisdiction of the courts of the Province of Ontario and further agrees to commence any litigation which may arise hereunder in the courts located in the Judicial District of York, Province of Ontario.

If this product was acquired outside the United States, then local law may apply.

⇦ *continues*

c. **Separation of Components.** The SOFTWARE PRODUCT is licensed as a single product. Its component parts may not be separated for use by more than one user.

d. **Rental.** You may not rent, lease, or lend the SOFTWARE PRODUCT.

e. **Support Services.** Microsoft may provide you with support services related to the SOFTWARE PRODUCT ("Support Services"). Use of Support Services is governed by the Microsoft policies and programs described in the user manual, in "online" documentation, and/or in other Microsoft-provided materials. Any supplemental software code provided to you as part of the Support Services shall be considered part of the SOFTWARE PRODUCT and subject to the terms and conditions of this EULA. With respect to technical information you provide to Microsoft as part of the Support Services, Microsoft may use such information for its business purposes, including for product support and development. Microsoft will not utilize such technical information in a form that personally identifies you.

f. **Software Transfer.** You may permanently transfer all of your rights under this EULA, provided you retain no copies, you transfer all of the SOFTWARE PRODUCT (including all component parts, the media and printed materials, any upgrades, this EULA, and, if applicable, the Certificate of Authenticity), **and** the recipient agrees to the terms of this EULA. If the SOFTWARE PRODUCT is an upgrade, any transfer must include all prior versions of the SOFTWARE PRODUCT.

g. **Termination.** Without prejudice to any other rights, Microsoft may terminate this EULA if you fail to comply with the terms and conditions of this EULA. In such event, you must destroy all copies of the SOFTWARE PRODUCT and all of its component parts.

3. UPGRADES. If the SOFTWARE PRODUCT is labeled as an upgrade, you must be properly licensed to use a product identified by Microsoft as being eligible for the upgrade in order to use the SOFTWARE PRODUCT. A SOFTWARE PRODUCT labeled as an upgrade replaces and/or supplements the product that formed the basis for your eligibility for the upgrade. You may use the resulting upgraded product only in accordance with the terms of this EULA. If the SOFTWARE PRODUCT is an upgrade of a component of a package of software programs that you licensed as a single product, the SOFTWARE PRODUCT may be used and transferred only as part of that single product package and may not be separated for use on more than one computer.

4. COPYRIGHT. All title and copyrights in and to the SOFTWARE PRODUCT (including but not limited to any images, photographs, animations, video, audio, music, text, and "applets" incorporated into the SOFTWARE PRODUCT), the accompanying printed materials, and any copies of the SOFTWARE PRODUCT are

⇦ *continues*

SOFTWARE designated as "Sample Code" ("SAMPLE CODE") for the sole purposes of designing, developing, and testing your software product(s), and to reproduce and distribute the SAMPLE CODE, along with any modifications thereof, only in object code form provided that you comply with Section d(iii), below.

(ii) Redistributable Components. In addition to the rights granted in Section 1, Microsoft grants you a nonexclusive royalty-free right to reproduce and distribute the object code version of any portion of the SOFTWARE listed in the SOFTWARE file REDIST.TXT ("REDISTRIBUTABLE SOFTWARE"), provided you comply with Section d(iii), below.

(iii) Redistribution Requirements. If you redistribute the SAMPLE CODE or REDISTRIBUTABLE SOFTWARE (collectively, "REDISTRIBUTABLES"), you agree to: (A) distribute the REDISTRIBUTABLES in object code only in conjunction with and as a part of a software application product developed by you that adds significant and primary functionality to the SOFTWARE and that is developed to operate on the Windows or Windows NT environment ("Application"); (B) not use Microsoft's name, logo, or trademarks to market your software application product; (C) include a valid copyright notice on your software product; (D) indemnify, hold harmless, and defend Microsoft from and against any claims or lawsuits, including attorney's fees, that arise or result from the use or distribution of your software application product; (E) not permit further distribution of the REDISTRIBUTABLES by your end user. The following **exceptions** apply to subsection (iii)(E), above: (1) you may permit further redistribution of the REDISTRIBUTABLES by your distributors to your end-user customers if your distributors only distribute the REDISTRIBUTABLES in conjunction with, and as part of, your Application and you and your distributors comply with all other terms of this EULA; and (2) you may permit your end users to reproduce and distribute the object code version of the files designated by ".ocx" file extensions ("Controls") only in conjunction with and as a part of an Application and/or Web page that adds significant and primary functionality to the Controls, and such end user complies with all other terms of this EULA.

2. DESCRIPTION OF OTHER RIGHTS AND LIMITATIONS.

   a. Not for Resale Software. If the SOFTWARE PRODUCT is labeled "Not for Resale" or "NFR," then, notwithstanding other sections of this EULA, you may not resell, or otherwise transfer for value, the SOFTWARE PRODUCT.

   b. Limitations on Reverse Engineering, Decompilation, and Disassembly. You may not reverse engineer, decompile, or disassemble the SOFTWARE PRODUCT, except and only to the extent that such activity is expressly permitted by applicable law notwithstanding this limitation.

⇦ *continues*

END-USER LICENSE AGREEMENT FOR MICROSOFT SOFTWARE

Microsoft Visual Basic, Control Creation Edition

IMPORTANT—READ CAREFULLY: This Microsoft End-User License Agreement ("EULA") is a legal agreement between you (either an individual or a single entity) and Microsoft Corporation for the Microsoft software product identified above, which includescomputer software and may include associated media, printed materials, and "online" or electronic documentation ("SOFTWARE PRODUCT"). By installing, copying, or otherwise using the SOFTWARE PRODUCT, you agree to be bound by the terms of this EULA. If you do not agree to the terms of this EULA, do not install or use the SOFTWARE PRODUCT; you may, however, return it to your place of purchase for a full refund.

Software PRODUCT LICENSE

The SOFTWARE PRODUCT is protected by copyright laws and international copyright treaties, as well as other intellectual property laws and treaties. The SOFTWARE PRODUCT is licensed, not sold.

1. GRANT OF LICENSE. This EULA grants you the following rights:

   a. **Software Product.** Microsoft grants to you as an individual, a personal, nonexclusive license to make and use copies of the SOFTWARE for the sole purposes of designing, developing, and testing your software product(s) that are designed to operate in conjunction with any Microsoft operating system product. You may install copies of the SOFTWARE on an unlimited number of computers provided that you are the only individual using the SOFTWARE. If you are an entity, Microsoft grants you the right to designate one individual within your organization to have the right to use the SOFTWARE in the manner provided above.

   b. **Electronic Documents.** Solely with respect to electronic documents included with the SOFTWARE, you may make an unlimited number of copies (either in hardcopy or electronic form), provided that such copies shall be used only for internal purposes and are not republished or distributed to any third party.

   Redistributable Components.

   (i) **Sample Code.** In addition to the rights granted in Section 1, Microsoft grants you the right to use and modify the source code version of those portions of the

⇦ *continues*

La présente Convention est régie par les lois de la province d'Ontario, Canada. Chacune des parties à la présente reconnaît irrévocablement la compétence des tribunaux de la province d'Ontario et consent à instituer tout litige qui pourrait découler de la présente auprès des tribunaux situés dans le district judiciaire de York, province d'Ontario.

Au cas où vous auriez des questions concernant cette licence ou que vous désiriez vous mettre en rapport avec Microsoft pour quelque raison que ce soit, veuillez contacter la succursale Microsoft desservant votre pays, dont l'adresse est fournie dans ce produit, ou écrire à: Microsoft Sales Information Center, One Microsoft Way, Redmond, Washington 98052-6399.

Si vous avez acquis votre produit Microsoft au CANADA, la garantie limitée suivante vous concerne:
Garantie Limitee

GARANTIE LIMITEE—Sauf pour celles du REDISTRIBUTABLES, qui sont fournies "comme telles", sans aucune garantie quelle qu'elle soit, Microsoft garantit que (a) la performance du LOGICIEL sera substantiellement en conformité avec le(s) manuel(s) de produits qui accompagne(nt) le LOGICIEL pour une période de quatre-vingt-dix (90) jours à compter de la date de réception; et (b) tout matériel fourni par Microsoft accompagnant le LOGICIEL sera exempt de défaut de matière première ou de vice de fabrication dans des conditions normales d'utilisation et d'entretien pour une période d'un an à compter de la date de réception. Toute garantie implicite concernant le LOGICIEL et le matériel est limitée à quatre-vingt-dix (90) jours et un (1) an, respectivement.

RECOURS DU CLIENT—La seule obligation de Microsoft et votre recours exclusif seront, au choix de Microsoft, soit (a) le remboursement du prix payé ou (b) la réparation ou le remplacement du LOGICIEL ou du matériel qui n'est pas conforme à la Garantie Limitée de Microsoft et qui est retourné à Microsoft avec une copie de votre reçu. Cette Garantie Limitée est nulle si le défaut du LOGICIEL ou du matériel est causé par un accident, un traitement abusif ou une mauvaise application. Tout LOGICIEL de remplacement sera garanti pour le reste de la période de garantie initiale ou pour trente (30) jours, selon laquelle de ces deux périodes est la plus longue.

AUCUNE AUTRE GARANTIE—MICROSOFT DESAVOUE TOUTE AUTRE GARANTIE, EXPRESSE OU IMPLICITE, Y COMPRIS MAIS NE SE LIMITANT PAS AUX GARANTIES IMPLICITES DU CARACTERE ADEQUAT POUR LA COMMERCIALISATION OU UN USAGE PARTICULIER EN CE QUI CONCERNE LE LOGICIEL, LE(S) MANUEL(S) DE PRODUITS, LA DOCUMENTATION ECRITE ET TOUT MATERIEL QUI L'ACCOMPAGNENT. CETTE GARANTIE LIMITEE VOUS ACCORDE DES DROITS JURIDIQUES SPECIFIQUES.

PAS D'OBLIGATION POUR LES DOMMAGES INDIRECTS—MICROSOFT OU SES FOURNISSEURS N'AURONT D'OBLIGATION EN AUCUNE CIRCONSTANCE POUR TOUT AUTRE DOMMAGE QUEL QU'IL SOIT (Y COMPRIS, SANS LIMITATION, LES DOMMAGES ENTRAINES PAR LA PERTE DE BENEFICES, L'INTERRUPTION DES AFFAIRES, LA PERTE D'INFORMATION COMMERCIALE OU TOUTE AUTRE PERTE PECUNIAIRE) DECOULANT DE L'UTILISATION OU DE L'IMPOSSIBILITE D'UTILISATION DE CE PRODUIT MICROSOFT, ET CE, MEME SI MICROSOFT A ETE AVISE DE LA POSSIBILITE DE TELS DOMMAGES. EN TOUT CAS, LA SEULE OBLIGATION DE MICROSOFT EN VERTU DE TOUTE DISPOSITION DE CETTE CONVENTION SE LIMITERA AU MONTANT EN FAIT PAYE PAR VOUS POUR LE LOGICIEL.

⟵ *continues*

If you have a specific question regarding the licensing of redistributables, you may call the Microsoft Technical Sales Information Team at (800) 426-9400 (United States only) or send inquiries by fax to Microsoft Visual C++ Licensing Administrator, (206) 936-7329 (United States only).

LIMITED WARRANTY

LIMITED WARRANTY. **Except with respect to the REDISTRIBUTABLES, which are provided "as is," without warranty of any kind,** Microsoft warrants that (a) the SOFTWARE PRODUCT will perform substantially in accordance with the accompanying written materials for a period of ninety (90) days from the date of receipt, and (b) any hardware accompanying the SOFTWARE PRODUCT will be free from defects in materials and workmanship under normal use and service for a period of one (1) year from the date of receipt. Some states and jurisdictions do not allow limitations on duration of an implied warranty, so the above limitation may not apply to you. To the extent allowed by applicable law, implied warranties on the SOFTWARE PRODUCT and hardware, if any, are limited to ninety (90) days and one year, respectively.

CUSTOMER REMEDIES. Microsoft's and its suppliers' entire liability and your exclusive remedy shall be, at Microsoft's option, either (a) return of the price paid, or (b) repair or replacement of the SOFTWARE PRODUCT or hardware that does not meet Microsoft's Limited Warranty and that is returned to Microsoft with a copy of your receipt. This Limited Warranty is void if failure of the SOFTWARE PRODUCT or hardware has resulted from accident, abuse, or misapplication. Any replacement SOFTWARE PRODUCT or hardware will be warranted for the remainder of the original warranty period or thirty (30) days, whichever is longer. **Outside the United States, neither these remedies nor any product support services offered by Microsoft are available without proof of purchase from an authorized international source.**

NO OTHER WARRANTIES. To the maximum extent permitted by applicable law, Microsoft and its suppliers disclaim all other warranties, either express or implied, including, but not limited to, implied warranties of merchantability AND fitness for a particular purpose, with regard to the SOFTWARE PRODUCT, and any accompanying hardware. This limited warranty gives you specific legal rights. You may have others, which vary from state/jurisdiction to state/jurisdiction.

NO LIABILITY FOR CONSEQUENTIAL DAMAGES. To the maximum extent permitted by applicable law, in no event shall Microsoft or its suppliers be liable for any special, incidental, indirect, or consequential damages whatsoever (including, without limitation, damages for loss of business profits, business interruption, loss of business information, or any other pecuniary loss) arising out of the use of or inability to use thE software product, even if Microsoft has been advised of the possibility of such damages. Because some states and jurisdictions do not allow the exclusion or limitation of liability for consequential or incidental damages, the above limitation may not apply to you.

⇐ *continues*

4. U.S. GOVERNMENT RESTRICTED RIGHTS. The SOFTWARE PRODUCT and documentation are provided with RESTRICTED RIGHTS. Use, duplication, or disclosure by the Government is subject to restrictions as set forth in subparagraph (c)(1)(ii) of the Rights in Technical Data and Computer Software clause at DFARS 252.227-7013 or subparagraphs (c)(1) and (2) of the Commercial Computer Software—Restricted Rights at 48 CFR 52.227-19, as applicable. Manufacturer is Microsoft Corporation/One Microsoft Way/Redmond, WA 98052-6399.

5. EXPORT RESTRICTIONS. You agree that neither you nor your customers intend to or will, directly or indirectly, export or transmit (i) the SOFTWARE or related documentation and technical data or (ii) your software product as described in Section 1(f) of this EULA (or any part thereof), or process, or service that is the direct product of the SOFTWARE, to any country to which such export or transmission is restricted by any applicable U.S. regulation or statute, without the prior written consent, if required, of the Bureau of Export Administration of the U.S. Department of Commerce, or such other governmental entity as may have jurisdiction over such export or transmission.

6. NOTE ON JAVA SUPPORT. THE SOFTWARE PRODUCT CONTAINS SUPPORT FOR PROGRAMS WRITTEN IN JAVA. JAVA TECHNOLOGY IS NOT FAULT TOLERANT AND IS NOT DESIGNED, MANUFACTURED, OR INTENDED FOR USE OR RESALE AS ONLINE CONTROL EQUIPMENT IN HAZARDOUS ENVIRONMENTS REQUIRING FAIL-SAFE PERFORMANCE, SUCH AS IN THE OPERATION OF NUCLEAR FACILITIES, AIRCRAFT NAVIGATION OR COMMUNICATIONS SYSTEMS, AIR TRAFFIC CONTROL, DIRECT LIFE SUPPORT MACHINES, OR WEAPONS SYSTEMS, IN WHICH THE FAILURE OF JAVA TECHNOLOGY COULD LEAD DIRECTLY TO DEATH, PERSONAL INJURY, OR SEVERE PHYSICAL OR ENVIRONMENTAL DAMAGE.

MISCELLANEOUS

If you acquired this product in the United States, this EULA is governed by the laws of the State of Washington.

If you acquired this product in Canada, this EULA is governed by the laws of the Province of Ontario, Canada. Each of the parties hereto irrevocably attorns to the jurisdiction of the courts of the Province of Ontario and further agrees to commence any litigation which may arise hereunder in the courts located in the Judicial District of York, Province of Ontario.

If this product was acquired outside the United States, then local law may apply.

Should you have any questions concerning this EULA, or if you desire to contact Microsoft for any reason, please contact the Microsoft subsidiary serving your country, or write: Microsoft Sales Information Center/One Microsoft Way/Redmond, WA 98052-6399.

⇔ *continues*

c. **Limitations on Reverse Engineering, Decompilation, and Disassembly.** You may not reverse engineer, decompile, or disassemble the SOFTWARE PRODUCT, except and only to the extent that such activity is expressly permitted by applicable law notwithstanding this limitation.

d. **Separation of Components.** The SOFTWARE PRODUCT is licensed as a single product. Its component parts may not be separated for use on more than one computer.

e. **Rental.** You may not rent, lease, or lend the SOFTWARE PRODUCT.

f. **Support Services.** Microsoft may provide you with support services related to the SOFTWARE PRODUCT ("Support Services"). Use of Support Services is governed by the Microsoft policies and programs described in the user manual, in "online" documentation, and/or in other Microsoft-provided materials. Any supplemental software code provided to you as part of the Support Services shall be considered part of the SOFTWARE PRODUCT and subject to the terms and conditions of this EULA. With respect to technical information you provide to Microsoft as part of the Support Services, Microsoft may use such information for its business purposes, including for product support and development. Microsoft will not utilize such technical information in a form that personally identifies you.

g. **Software Transfer.** You may permanently transfer all of your rights under this EULA, provided you retain no copies, you transfer all of the SOFTWARE PRODUCT (including all component parts, the media and printed materials, any upgrades, this EULA, and, if applicable, the Certificate of Authenticity), **and** the recipient agrees to the terms of this EULA. If the SOFTWARE PRODUCT is an upgrade, any transfer must include all prior versions of the SOFTWARE PRODUCT.

h. **Termination.** Without prejudice to any other rights, Microsoft may terminate this EULA if you fail to comply with the terms and conditions of this EULA. In such event, you must destroy all copies of the SOFTWARE PRODUCT and all of its component parts.

3. COPYRIGHT. All title and copyrights in and to the SOFTWARE PRODUCT (including but not limited to any images, photographs, animations, video, audio, music, text, and "applets" incorporated into the SOFTWARE PRODUCT), the accompanying printed materials, and any copies of the SOFTWARE PRODUCT are owned by Microsoft or its suppliers. The SOFTWARE PRODUCT is protected by copyright laws and international treaty provisions. Therefore, you must treat the SOFTWARE PRODUCT like any other copyrighted material except that you may install the SOFTWARE PRODUCT on a single computer provided you keep the original solely for backup or archival purposes. You may not copy the printed materials accompanying the SOFTWARE PRODUCT.

⇦ *continues*

(B) *Provided that* your end user complies with all other terms of this EULA, you may permit your end users to reproduce and distribute the object code version of the files listed below, designed to be redistributed as a Component Object Model (COM) object, for use in development of another application ("COM Files"), only in conjunction with and as a part of an application and/or Web page that adds significant and primary functionality to the COM Files. **COM Files:** Msvcrt.dll, Olepro32.dll, Mfc42.dll, and Msvcirt.dll;

(C) You may permit your end users to reproduce and distribute the object code version of the REDISTRIBUTABLES for use in development of an application created by your end user ("End-User Application"), *provided that* your end user agrees to: (i) distribute the REDISTRIBUTABLES in object code only in conjunction with and as a part of a software application product developed by them that adds significant and primary functionality to the REDISTRIBUTABLES ("End-User Application"); (ii) distribute **all** of the REDISTRIBUTABLES if they choose to distribute any one or more of them in an End-User Application; (iii) not use Microsoft's name, logo, or trademarks to market the End-User Application; (iv) include a valid copyright notice on the End-User Application; (v) indemnify, hold harmless, and defend Microsoft from and against any claims or lawsuits, including attorney's fees, that arise or result from the use or distribution of the End-User Application; and (vi) not permit further distribution of the REDISTRIBUTABLES by the user of the End-User Application.

2. DESCRIPTION OF OTHER RIGHTS AND LIMITATIONS.

   a. **Academic Edition Software.** If the SOFTWARE PRODUCT is identified as "Academic Edition" or "AE," you must be a "Qualified Educational User" to use the SOFTWARE PRODUCT. To determine whether you are a Qualified Educational User, please contact the Microsoft Sales Information Center/One Microsoft Way/Redmond, WA 98052-6399 or the Microsoft subsidiary serving your country.

   If you are a Qualified Educational User, you may either (i) exercise the rights granted in Section (1), OR (ii) if you intend to use the SOFTWARE PRODUCT solely for instructional purposes in connection with a class or other educational program, you may install a single copy of the SOFTWARE on a single computer for access and use by an unlimited number of student end users at your educational institution, provided that all such end users comply with all other terms of this EULA.

   b. **Not for Resale Software.** If the SOFTWARE PRODUCT is labeled "Not for Resale" or "NFR," then, notwithstanding other sections of this EULA, you may not resell, or otherwise transfer for value, the SOFTWARE PRODUCT.

⇦ *continues*

c. Storage/Network Use. You may also store or install a copy of the SOFTWARE PRODUCT on a storage device, such as a network server, used only to install or run the SOFTWARE PRODUCT on your other computers over an internal network; however, you must acquire and dedicate a license for each separate computer on which the SOFTWARE PRODUCT is installed or run from the storage device. A license for the SOFTWARE PRODUCT may not be shared or used concurrently on different computers.

d. Sample Code. In addition to the rights granted in Section 1(a), Microsoft grants to you the right to use and modify the source code version of those portions of the SOFTWARE PRODUCT that are identified as sample code in the documentation ("SAMPLE CODE"), for the sole purposes of designing, developing, and testing your software product(s), *provided* that you comply with Section 1(f), below.

e. Redistributable Files. *Provided* that you comply with Section 1(f), in addition to the rights granted in Section 1(a), Microsoft grants to you a nonexclusive, royalty-free right to reproduce and distribute the object code version of the following portions of the SOFTWARE PRODUCT (collectively, the "REDISTRIBUTABLES"): (i) SAMPLE CODE (including any modifications you make); and (ii) the Java Support for Internet Explorer files: msjava.inf, jautoexp.dat, javaDbg.txt, javaEE.dll, javasntx.dll, setdebug.exe, regsvr32.exe, jit.dll, javaprxy.dll, jdbgmgr.exe, msjava.dll, msawt.dll, vmhelper.dll, javart.dll, jview.exe, mfc40.dll, msvcrt40.dll, classr.exe, classd.exe, javasup.vxd.

f. Redistribution Requirements. If you redistribute the REDISTRIBUTABLES, you agree to: (i) distribute the REDISTRIBUTABLES in object code only in conjunction with and as a part of a software application product developed by you that adds significant and primary functionality to the REDISTRIBUTABLES ("Licensed Product"); (ii) distribute **all** of the REDISTRIBUTABLES if you choose to distribute any one or more of them in your Licensed Product; (iii) not use Microsoft's name, logo, or trademarks to market your Licensed Product; (iv) include a valid copyright notice on your Licensed Product; (v) indemnify, hold harmless, and defend Microsoft from and against any claims or lawsuits, including attorney's fees, that arise or result from the use or distribution of your Licensed Product; (v) not permit further distribution of the REDISTRIBUTABLES by your end user.

The following **exceptions** apply to Subsection (f)(v), above:

(A) You may permit further redistribution of the REDISTRIBUTABLES by your distributors to your end-user customers if your distributors only distribute the REDISTRIBUTABLES in conjunction with, and as part of, your Licensed Product and you and your distributors comply with all other terms of this EULA;

END-USER LICENSE AGREEMENT FOR MICROSOFT SOFTWARE

Microsoft Visual J++ version 1.1, Trial Use Edition

IMPORTANT—READ CAREFULLY: This Microsoft End-User License Agreement ("EULA") is a legal agreement between you (either an individual or a single entity) and Microsoft Corporation for the Microsoft software product identified above, which includes computer software and may include associated media, printed materials, and "online" or electronic documentation ("SOFTWARE PRODUCT"). By installing, copying, or otherwise using the SOFTWARE PRODUCT, you agree to be bound by the terms of this EULA. If you do not agree to the terms of this EULA, do not install, copy, or use the SOFTWARE PRODUCT.

Software PRODUCT LICENSE

The SOFTWARE PRODUCT is protected by copyright laws and international copyright treaties, as well as other intellectual property laws and treaties. The SOFTWARE PRODUCT is licensed, not sold.

1. GRANT OF LICENSE. This EULA grants you the following rights:

   a. **Software Product.** Microsoft grants to you, as an individual, a personal, nonexclusive license to make and use copies of the SOFTWARE for the sole purposes of designing, developing, and testing your software product(s). Except as provided in Section 2(a), you may install copies of the SOFTWARE PRODUCT on an unlimited number of computers provided that you are the only individual using the SOFTWARE PRODUCT. If you are an entity, Microsoft grants to you the right to designate one individual within your organization to have the right to use the SOFTWARE PRODUCT in the manner provided above.

   b. **Electronic Documents.** Solely with respect to electronic documents included with the SOFTWARE PRODUCT, you may make an unlimited number of copies (either in hardcopy or electronic form), provided that such copies shall be used only for internal purposes and are not republished or distributed to any third party.

⇦ *continues*